THE LEGAL SYSTEM

OF

NORTHERN IRELAND

Fifth Edition

THE QUEEN'S ANNIVERSARY PRIZES

The Queen's Anniversary Prizes for Higher and Further Education recognise the contribution of universities and colleges to the social, economic, cultural and intellectual life of the nation.

In 1994, the inaugural year of the competition, The Queen's University of Belfast was awarded a prize for the work of Servicing the Legal System.

The prize citation for SLS in 1994 read:

"This is an outstanding service to overcome the special problems of distributing knowledge about new law inside a small jurisdiction. It is an international exemplar."

THE SERVICING THE LEGAL SYSTEM PROGRAMME

This programme was inaugurated in August 1980 in the Faculty of Law at Queen's University, Belfast to promote the publication of commentaries on various aspects of the law and legal system of Northern Ireland. Generous financial and other support for the programme has been provided by the Northern Ireland Court Service, the Inn of Court of Northern Ireland, the Bar Council of Northern Ireland, the Law Society of Northern Ireland and Queen's University. Details of other SLS publications may be obtained from the SLS Office, School of Law, Queen's University Belfast, Belfast BT7 1NN.

The Legal System
of
Northern Ireland

Fifth Edition

Brice Dickson

Professor of Law at the Queen's University of Belfast

SLS Legal Publications (NI)
2005

Published 2005 by SLS Legal Publications (NI),
School of Law, Queen's University, Belfast BT7 1NN.

First edition 1984
Second edition 1989
Third edition 1993
Fourth edition 2001
Reprinted 2004

ISBN 0 85389 884 7

Typeset by SLS Legal Publications (NI)
Printed by MPG Books Ltd, Cornwall

For Lia and Isaac

PREFACE

For this edition I have brought together into a new Chapter 4 the sections dealing with levels and types of crime, with anti-terrorism measures and with policing, prison and probation services. In previous editions these had been scattered among three different chapters of the book. Chapter 4 precedes a chapter which is now restricted to the procedures used in criminal courts, just as the following chapter is devoted purely to the procedures used in civil courts. I have also expanded the number of oversight bodies described in Chapter 9. Otherwise the structure of the book remains much as before, with only some of the section titles being altered and a few more sub-headings being inserted. On readers' advice I have also included an additional appendix, containing a glossary of special terms for quick reference.

As before, updated information has had to be introduced at several points on almost every page. The most notable new institutions mentioned include the Judicial Appointments Commission, the Magistrates' Courts Service Inspectorate, the Public Prosecution Service, the Northern Ireland Legal Services Commission, the Independent Monitoring Commission, the Proscribed Organisation Appeals Commission, the Assets Recovery Agency, the District Policing Partnerships, the Police Ombudsman, the Life Sentence Commissioners, the Prisoner Ombudsman, the Criminal Justice Inspectorate, the Justice Oversight Commissioner, the Commissioner for Public Appointments, the Commissioner for Children and Young People, the Electoral Commission and the Northern Ireland Law Commission. Reference is also made to the Review of Public Administration, part of the purpose of which is to reduce the number of public bodies in Northern Ireland, and to the work of auditing bodies such as the Northern Ireland Audit Office and Parliament's Public Accounts Committee.

The most significant new pieces of legislation alluded to include the Justice (NI) Acts 2002 and 2004, the Criminal Injuries Compensation (NI) Order 2002, the Criminal Justice (NI) Order 2003, the Access to Justice (NI) Order 2003, the Employment (NI) Order 2003, the Criminal Justice (NI) Order 2004, the Criminal Justice (Evidence) (NI) Order 2004, the Anti-social Behaviour (NI) Order 2004, the Employment Relations (NI) Order 2004, the Prevention of Terrorism

Act 2005, the Inquiries Act 2005 and the Constitutional Reform Act 2005.

More footnotes have been inserted, many of them containing references to websites where more detailed information can be obtained. To try to break up the text a bit more, and to provide clear statistical information, I have included more Tables (there are now 25, compared with 14 in the previous edition). Overall the book is some 25% longer than in 2001 and 200% longer than the first edition, published in 1984. It is still worth reminding readers, however, that on virtually every topic the book does not provide all the detail that is necessary for a *complete* understanding of the area described.

As far as possible I have tried to ensure that the information contained in the book is accurate as of 1 August 2005. As always I would be grateful to hear from anyone who spots mistakes.

Brice Dickson

Belfast, 31 August 2005

ACKNOWLEDGEMENTS

I am grateful to virtually all of the organisations mentioned in this book for dealing with queries that I have raised with them at one time or another. I am also grateful to David Capper and Dr Brian Jack, both of Queen's University Belfast, for their assistance with the sections on legal aid and European Union matters respectively. Thanks too to Maria Glover, a trainee solicitor with Napier & Co in Belfast, who provided research assistance for Chapter 6 and Appendix 2. Sara Gamble, at SLS Legal Publications, has been as courteous and helpful as ever in bringing the book to publication, not least through preparing the Tables of Legislation and Cases. I am extremely grateful to her for her industry, meticulousness and patience. Sincere thanks are also due to Michelle Madden, whose word processing skills contributed greatly to the book's appearance.

I could not have enjoyed working on this new edition so much without the strong support of my wife, Patricia Mallon.

Errors remaining in the text are the author's alone.

CONTENTS

TABLE OF CASES

*(Multiple case report references are given here; in the text itself only
the most authoritative reference is given for each case.)*

TABLE OF PRIMARY LEGISLATION

*(Including Orders In Council and Acts of the
Northern Ireland Parliament and Assembly)*

TABLE OF SECONDARY LEGISLATION

LIST OF TABLES

ABBREVIATIONS

ABWOR	Assistance by way of representation
AC	*Appeal Cases Reports*
All ER	*All England Law Reports*
BHRC	*Butterworths Human Rights Cases*
BNIL	*Bulletin of Northern Ireland Law*
Camb LJ	*Cambridge Law Journal*
Ch	*Chancery Reports* or Chancery Division
CLP	*Current Legal Problems*
Cm, Cmd, Cmnd	Command Paper
CMLR	*Common Market Law Reports*
Cr App R	*Criminal Appeal Reports*
Crim LR	*Criminal Law Review*
EC	European Community
ECHR	European Convention on Human Rights
EHRLR	*European Human Rights Law Review*
EHRR	*European Human Rights Reports*
EPA	Northern Ireland (Emergency Provisions) Act
EPLJ	*European Public Law Journal*
EU	European Union
EWCA Admin	Administrative Court of England and Wales
EWCA Civ	Civil Division of the Court of Appeal of England and Wales
Fam	*Family Reports* or Family Division
HL	House of Lords
HRLJ	*Human Rights Law Journal*
J	Mr Justice
LCJ	Lord Chief Justice
LGR	*Local Government Reports*
LJ	Lord Justice
LQR	*Law Quarterly Review*
MLR	*Modern Law Review*
New LJ	*New Law Journal*
NI	*Northern Ireland Law Reports*
NICA	Northern Ireland Court of Appeal
NICC	Northern Ireland Crown Court
NICty	Northern Ireland county court
NIJB	*Northern Ireland Judgments Bulletin*

NILQ	*Northern Ireland Legal Quarterly*
NIMag	Northern Ireland magistrates' court
NIO	Northern Ireland Office
NIQB	Northern Ireland Queen's Bench
OJLS	*Oxford Journal of Legal Studies*
PACE	Police and Criminal Evidence
PL	*Public Law*
PTA	Prevention of Terrorism (Temporary Provisions) Act
QB	*Queen's Bench Reports* or Queen's Bench Division
QC	Queen's Counsel
RM	Resident Magistrate
RTR	*Road Traffic Reports*
Statute LR	*Statute Law Review*
UKHL	United Kingdom, House of Lords
WLR	*Weekly Law Reports*

CHAPTER ONE

NORTHERN IRELAND'S LEGAL HISTORY

1.1 EARLY LEGAL HISTORY

The history of a legal system is inevitably linked to the political history of the territory where the legal system has operated. For that reason alone the legal history of Northern Ireland is long and complex.[1] A true appreciation of it is essential, however, if the workings of the legal system today are to be properly understood. As well as throwing light on why things are as they are, the history helps us to identify those aspects of the system which are overdue for change. The importance of an historical approach will be made particularly apparent in Chapter 2, when the sources of law in Northern Ireland are examined. The first three sections of this opening chapter provide a brief sketch of the general legal history of the area, while the subsequent two sections describe the bodies and persons who have inherited the political and professional responsibility for operating the legal system in Northern Ireland.

The Brehon law system[2]

Before the arrival of the Normans in 1169, Ireland was governed by Brehon law. This was a legal system based on traditional custom; the laws being formulated and applied by respected native jurists called Brehons. Brehon law continued to apply after 1169 in areas outside the Normans' control and even in areas within their control it continued to govern the native Irish. The Normans themselves were subject to the English "common law" system, which at that time was unifying the various local legal systems throughout England following William I's invasion and conquest in 1066: it was creating a system which was "common" to the whole of the country.

As the Normans extended their influence, English law slowly became more important in Ireland. In 1171 King Henry II is said to have held a Council near Waterford, "where the laws of England were by all freely

---

[1] See T. Hennessey, *A History of Northern Ireland 1920-1996* (1997) and J. Whyte, *Interpreting Northern Ireland* (1990).
[2] For an account of the content and procedures of Brehon law see F. Kelly, *A Guide to Early Irish Law* (1988) and L. Ginnell, *The Brehon Laws: A Legal Handbook* (1993).

received and confirmed", but it is more likely that the English laws were only gradually accepted during the course of the following century.[3] By 1300 English law applied in most of Ireland, and some 30 years later the policy of leaving the native Irish to be governed by Brehon law was reversed. By this time, however, the Irish were beginning to regroup, with the object of repelling the Norman invaders. Consequently, the influence of English law went into gradual decline. By 1500 English law extended only to the area around Dublin known as the Pale; the rest of Ireland had returned to Brehon law.

All this changed again with the Tudor re-conquest of Ireland, which culminated in the Flight of the Earls in 1607 and the Plantation of Ulster in the early years of the seventeenth century.[4] The whole of Ireland was then under English control and Brehon law completely ceased to apply. In a famous piece of litigation known as *The Case of Tanistry* (1607),[5] Brehon law was declared to be incompatible with the common law of England and therefore incapable of remaining any part of the law in Ireland. Since then the provisions of Brehon law have been referred to by judges in a few Irish cases concerning ancient fishing rights,[6] but otherwise Brehon law has played no part at all in the modern legal history of Ireland.

The common law system

The system of law which has existed throughout Ireland since the seventeenth century is called the common law system, although it is important to note that this is only one sense in which the expression "common law" can be used. We will encounter its other meanings in due course. The most fundamental feature of the common law system is the doctrine of binding precedent. According to this doctrine, which is explained more fully in Chapter 2.3, once judges have made a ruling on a particular point of law, that ruling must be applied whenever judges in lower courts are dealing with the same point in subsequent cases. The ruling is said to have become a "binding legal authority" or a "precedent". Today many more laws are created by Parliament than was the case a century or so ago (such laws are called "legislation"), so there are not so many matters which are regulated by judge-made law

---

[3] See F. Newark, "The Bringing of English Law to Ireland" (1972) 23 NILQ 3.
[4] See J. Bardon, *The History of Ulster* (1992), Chaps. 4 and 5.
[5] See F. Newark, "The Case of Tanistry" (1952) 9 NILQ 215.
[6] But no reference was made to Brehon law in a recent Northern Ireland case on fishing rights in tidal waters: *Adair* v *National Trust* [1998] NI 33.

alone, but the doctrine of precedent still operates whenever judges have to decide what the words used in legislation actually mean. For example, if an appeal court rules that the words "motorised vehicle" in a particular piece of legislation refers to "quadricycles" as well as cars then that ruling is binding on all judges in lower courts if and when they are faced with the same question with regard to the same piece of legislation.[7] The ruling would not, however, be a precedent for whether, say, an electric scooter is a motorised vehicle or even for whether a quadricycle is a vehicle for the purposes of a different piece of legislation. The doctrine of precedent does not operate in so rigid a fashion in countries such as France and Germany, where a so-called "civil law" system exists that is largely derived from concepts developed as part of the law of ancient Rome. In such countries the law is contained almost exclusively in codes and even when judges interpret these codes their decisions are not binding on judges in later cases.[8]

After the seventeenth century the law in Ireland and England developed along much the same lines until the early twentieth century. The countries were administered differently, but the actual content of the law was almost identical. Some significant differences were created during the nineteenth century in an attempt to solve the intractable land problem in Ireland, and the two jurisdictions got out of step with regards to family law and some other matters, but generally the laws remained very similar. Even since the partition of Ireland in 1921 the law throughout the two islands (with the exception of Scotland, where the legal system is more of a mixture of common law and civil law[9]) has been based on the same fundamental common law concepts. The creation of separate Parliaments, though, and the adoption of a written Constitution in Ireland, have inevitably caused some divergences.

1.2 PARLIAMENTS AND ASSEMBLIES

Just as the Parliament in England developed out of the King's Council (the "Curia Regis"), a Parliament in Ireland evolved, during the thirteenth century, out of the jurisdiction of the Justiciar, the King's

---

[7] A resident magistrate came to this decision in *Chief Constable of the PSNI* v *McClean* [2005] NIMag 2. But decisions of magistrates are not binding precedents.

[8] Art. 5 of the French Civil Code actually prohibits judges from making law.

[9] See D.M. Walker, *The Scottish Legal System: An Introduction to the Study of Scots Law* (8th ed., 2001).

official representative in Ireland. For two centuries there were Parliaments in both England and Ireland, each claiming the power to make laws for Ireland, and not until 1495 was it declared at a gathering at Drogheda that only legislation approved by the English Council could be passed by the Parliament in Ireland (this is the so-called Poynings' Law - named after Sir Edward Poynings, the Secretary for Ireland at the time). The Irish Parliament continued to exist until 1800 and it did make some unapproved laws. Between 1782 and 1800, when it was known as Grattan's Parliament, it even regained some of its former pre-eminence, because most of Poynings' Law was repealed by Yelverton's Law in 1781.

From the Act of Union in 1800, the Act which joined Great Britain (*i.e.* England, Wales and Scotland) with Ireland to form a larger "United Kingdom", and until 1921, the only legislative body with powers to make laws for Ireland was the Parliament of the United Kingdom, sitting at Westminster in London. But, while a lot of the legislation enacted for England and Wales also extended to Ireland,[10] not all of it did so: some Acts were applied to Ireland only at a later date or in an amended version,[11] some were not extended to Ireland at all[12] and some were specifically enacted for Ireland and never applied in England, Wales or Scotland.[13]

With the partitioning of Ireland in 1921, separate legal systems were established for the North and the South of the island. The North, of course, comprises six of the nine counties constituting the province of Ulster,[14] but it has come to be referred to colloquially as "the province of Northern Ireland". Each part of the island was given its own Parliament as well as its own system of courts. In the South the old law continued to apply only when it was not inconsistent with the Constitution of the new state. For many years this resulted in few alterations, although in the past 40 years or so the Irish Constitution of 1937 has played an increasingly important role in the law's

---

[10] *E.g.* the Offences Against the Person Act 1861, sections of which are still in force today in the Republic of Ireland as well as in Northern Ireland and England.

[11] *E.g.* the Supreme Court of Judicature (Ireland) Act 1877, based on the Supreme Court of Judicature Act 1873.

[12] *E.g.* the Matrimonial Causes Act 1857.

[13] *E.g.* the Landlord and Tenant Law Amendment (Ireland) Act 1860 ("Deasy's Act").

[14] Antrim, Armagh, Down, Fermanagh, Londonderry and Tyrone. Cavan, Donegal and Monaghan are counties of Ulster but lie within the Republic of Ireland.

development in the Republic.[15] It is still the case, however, that many new laws created for the United Kingdom are later imitated in some shape or form in the Republic of Ireland.[16]

The Stormont Parliament[17]

In Northern Ireland some scope for legal development distinct from that occurring in England was created by the transfer to a new local Parliament of the right to enact legislation "for the peace, order and good government" of the province.[18] This had been the phrase used when Britain had earlier devolved power to Canada, Australia and South Africa. From 1932 the Parliament of Northern Ireland was located at Stormont, near Belfast. Prior to then it sat in the Presbyterian Church's Theological College beside the Queen's University Belfast.

The matters which were "transferred" to the Northern Ireland Parliament included law and order, local government, health and social services, education, planning, internal trade, industrial development and agriculture. Certain "excepted" and "reserved" matters, though, could be dealt with only by the Parliament at Westminster. Excepted matters were those which were of imperial or national concern, for which it was felt to be undesirable to enact local variations. They included the armed forces, external trade, weights and measures and copyright law. Reserved matters were those which were to be the preserve of the proposed Council of Ireland (which in fact was never created) and included postal services, the registration of deeds, some taxes (not road tax or stamp duty) and the Supreme Court of Northern Ireland.

The Northern Ireland Parliament consisted of two chambers - the House of Commons and the Senate - but there continued to be elections for representatives to sit on behalf of Northern Ireland constituencies at

[15] The current standard works are M. Forde, *Constitutional Law* (2nd ed., 2004), G. Hogan and G. Whyte, *Kelly's The Irish Constitution* (4th ed., 2003) and J. Casey, *Constitutional Law in Ireland* (3rd ed., 2000). See too T. Murphy and P. Twomey (eds.), *Ireland's Evolving Constitution 1937-97: Collected Essays* (1998).

[16] See *e.g.* Cheques Act (UK) 1957 and Cheques Act (Ir.) 1959; Insolvency Act (UK) 1986 and Bankruptcy Act (Ir.) 1988. For an excellent introduction to the Republic's legal system see R. Byrne and P. McCutcheon, *The Irish Legal System* (4th ed., 2001).

[17] See, generally, N. Mansergh, *The Government of Northern Ireland: An Experiment in Devolution* (1937), H. Calvert, *Constitutional Law in Northern Ireland: A Study in Regional Government* (1968) and J. Oliver, *Working at Stormont* (1978).

[18] Government of Ireland Act 1920, s. 4(1).

Westminster. A person could sit in both Parliaments if elected or appointed to both.[19] The Monarch was represented in Northern Ireland by the Governor, residing at Hillsborough in County Down.[20] The general policy of the Stormont Parliament was to keep in step with legislation enacted for Great Britain, although in certain areas Northern Ireland either failed to follow changes or introduced new laws of its own devising. As the years went by, differences became particularly apparent in the laws relating to social services, education and housing.[21] The Abortion Act 1967 (which made abortion more readily available in Great Britain) and the Sexual Offences Act 1967 (which legalised homosexuality when conducted privately in Great Britain) were not extended to Northern Ireland.[22]

Northern Ireland under direct rule[23]

Devolution of powers in the North continued until March 1972, when, despite its best efforts to achieve positive change,[24] the Stormont Parliament had to be suspended by Westminster because of its inability to cope with the serious civil unrest that had developed in the province since 1968. This unrest was made the subject of a tribunal of inquiry chaired by an English High Court judge, Mr Justice Scarman,[25] while a

---

[19] When the Irish Free State became a Republic in 1949, and left the Commonwealth, members of its Parliament could no longer also be members of the Westminster Parliament. However this position was reversed by the combined effect of s. 36(5) of the Northern Ireland Act 1998 and the Disqualifications Act 2000.

[20] The successive Governors of Northern Ireland were the Duke of Abercorn (1922-45), Earl Granville (1945-52), Lord Wakehurst (1952-64), Lord Erskine (1964-68) and Lord Grey (1968-72).

[21] See D. Birrell and A. Murie, *Policy and Government in Northern Ireland: Lessons of Devolution* (1980).

[22] Abortion law in Northern Ireland is still largely governed by the Offences Against the Person Act 1861; for the current legal position see *Family Planning Association of Northern Ireland* v *The Minister for Health, Social Services and Public Safety* [2004] NICA 39. For comments on Kerr J's judgment at first instance ([2003] NIQB 48) see B. Hewson, "The Law of Abortion in Northern Ireland" [2004] PL 234. The law on homosexuality was mostly brought into line with that in Great Britain by the Homosexual Offences (NI) Order 1982. See, generally, R. Murray, "Family and Sexual Matters", Chap. 17 in B. Dickson and M. O'Brien (eds.), *Civil Liberties in Northern Ireland: The CAJ Handbook* (4th ed., 2003).

[23] An almost day-by-day chronology of events in Northern Ireland since 1968 is available on www.cain.ulst.ac.uk. For a range of social and political perspectives see D. Watt (ed.), *The Constitution of Northern Ireland: Problems and Prospects* (1981).

[24] See *A Record of Constructive Change* (Cmd. 588 (NI); 1971).

[25] Later Lord Scarman. See *Violence and Civil Disturbances in Northern Ireland in 1969* (Cmnd. 566; 1972).

commission chaired by an English Law Lord, Lord Diplock, was tasked with bringing forward proposals for how the law could better deal with the problem of terrorism.[26] Internment had been introduced by the Northern Ireland Government in August 1971 and allegations of security force brutality in that context led to a further inquiry.[27] "Direct rule" was the form of government after March 1972, with laws on transferred matters being made by the Privy Council in London in the form of Orders in Council (see Chap. 2.2) and executive powers being exercised by the Secretary of State for Northern Ireland, a member of the British Cabinet.

In September 1972 the seven political parties which had had representatives in the prorogued Northern Ireland Parliament were invited by the UK Government to take part in a conference in Darlington, England. Only three of them attended.[28] The following month the Government published a consultative document stating the criteria which firm proposals for the future of Northern Ireland would have to meet.[29] On 8 March 1973, a referendum was held on whether the border between Northern Ireland and the Republic of Ireland should be retained;[30] out of an electorate of just over one million, some 600,000 voted (many nationalists did not vote) and of these 591,820 voted to stay within the United Kingdom. Later that same month the Government published a White Paper containing further proposals for the way forward.[31] These suggested that there should be a new legislature in Northern Ireland elected by proportional representation, with the executive and other legislative committees containing representatives from both communities. The proposals were then given legislative form through the Northern Ireland Assembly Act 1973 and the Northern Ireland Constitution Act 1973. Two-thirds of the 78 people who were then elected to the Assembly, which met for the first time in July 1973, were in favour of the Government's proposals.

---

[26] See *Report of the Commission to consider legal procedures to deal with terrorist activities in Northern Ireland* (the Diplock Report) (Cmnd. 5185; 1972). See too T. Hadden and P. Hillyard, *Justice in Northern Ireland: A Study in Social Confidence* (1973).

[27] See *Report of the enquiry into allegations against the security forces of physical brutality in Northern Ireland arising out of events on the 9th August 1971 (the Compton Report)* (Cmnd. 4823; 1971).

[28] The Ulster Unionist Party, the Alliance Party and the Northern Ireland Labour Party.

[29] *The Future of Northern Ireland: A Paper for Discussion.*

[30] Under the Northern Ireland (Border Poll) Act 1972.

[31] *Northern Ireland Constitutional Proposals* (Cmnd. 5259).

After further talks, and a conference in Sunningdale in Berkshire in December 1973, agreement was reached on creating a Northern Ireland Executive and on setting up a Council of Ireland comprising seven members of the Executive and seven ministers from the Irish Government, a consultative Assembly and a secretariat. The Executive was sworn in on 1 January 1974, with the Chief Executive being Mr Biran Faulkner, leader of the Official Unionist Party. Powers to make laws (called "Measures") were vested in the one-chamber elected Assembly.

However, due to further civil unrest linked to the Ulster Workers' Council strike, this experiment in devolution collapsed in May 1974, when the Assembly was suspended and responsibility for governing Northern Ireland was again returned to the Secretary of State.[32] Yet more proposals were put forward in a government White Paper issued in July 1974[33] and these were given effect in law by the Northern Ireland Act 1974. They provided for a Constitutional Convention to be elected, again with 78 members, with the job of considering over a six-month period "what provision for the government of Northern Ireland is likely to command the most widespread acceptance among the community there". Elections were held for the Convention in May 1975 and it began work almost immediately, under the chairmanship of the then Lord Chief Justice of Northern Ireland, Sir Robert Lowry. It reported, as planned, in November 1975,[34] but as its proposals were based very largely on unionist ideas only the British Government rejected them[35] and the Convention was formally dissolved in March 1976.

In 1982 one more 78-member Northern Ireland Assembly, again with only one chamber and sitting at Stormont, was elected under the Northern Ireland Act 1982.[36] It did not have any law-making powers -

---

[32] See D. Anderson, *14 May Days* (1994). Only four Measures were made in the less than five months of that Assembly's existence.

[33] *The Northern Ireland Constitution* (Cmnd. 5675).

[34] *Report of the Northern Ireland Constitutional Convention*, HC 1 (1975-76).

[35] It made one last effort to allow the Convention to reach agreement, but this too failed: see *The Northern Ireland Constitutional Convention: Text of a letter from the Secretary of State for Northern Ireland to the Chairman of the Convention* (Cmnd. 6387; 1976).

[36] This followed three government discussion papers: *The Government of Northern Ireland: A Working Paper for a Conference* (Cmnd. 7763; 1979), *The Government of Northern Ireland: Proposals for Further Discussion* (Cmnd. 7950; 1980) and *Northern Ireland: A Framework for Devolution* (Cmnd. 8541; 1982).

only "scrutiny, consultative and deliberative powers" - but the UK Government hoped that in due course some such powers could be transferred to it under the principle of so-called "rolling", or partial, devolution. Once again the experiment proved unsuccessful and the Assembly was dissolved in 1986.[37]

The signing of the Anglo-Irish Agreement at Hillsborough, County Down, in November 1985[38] led to the establishment of the Anglo-Irish Inter-Governmental Conference, which convened periodically to allow representatives from the Government of the Irish Republic to put forward their views on the governance of the province. It also created an Anglo-Irish Parliamentary Council, which allowed 25 members from each of the British and Irish Parliaments to meet from time to time to discuss matters of mutual interest. The 1985 Agreement, however, was a treaty between two sovereign states and did not have the force of internal domestic law in either country. The reality is that from May 1974, despite intermittent efforts to bring greater democracy to Northern Ireland, direct rule applied in Northern Ireland right up until the end of 1999, the arrangements being renewed annually by Westminster as required by the Northern Ireland Act 1974. It was widely accepted that the failure to achieve devolution in Northern Ireland had produced a significant "democratic deficit" in the province.

The Belfast (Good Friday) Agreement 1998

Following various other inter-governmental initiatives, including a Downing Street Declaration in 1993, a Framework Document in 1995[39] and the publication of ground rules for substantive all-party negotiations in 1996,[40] the political parties within Northern Ireland and the British and Irish Governments eventually reached a new agreement on the way forward in Northern Ireland on Good Friday (10 April) 1998.[41] A path facilitating the agreement had been cleared by ceasefires

---

[37] C. O'Leary. S. Elliott and R. Wilford, *The Northern Ireland Assembly 1982-1986: A Constitutional Experiment* (1988).

[38] See A. Kenny, *The Road to Hillsborough: The Shaping of the Anglo-Irish Agreement* (1986); T. Hadden and K. Boyle, *The Anglo-Irish Agreement: Commentary, Text and Official Review* (1989).

[39] Cm. 2964.

[40] Cm. 3232. See also E. Mallie and D. McKittrick, *The Fight for Peace: The Secret Story of the Irish Peace Process* (1996).

[41] Cm. 3883. Available on-line at, *e.g.*, ofmdfmni.gov.uk/publications/ba.htm. For the story of the genesis of the Agreement, see M. Mansergh, "The Background to the Irish Peace Process" in M. Cox, A. Guelke and F. Stephen (eds.), *A Farewell to*

that had been declared by both loyalist paramilitaries in October 1994 and republican paramilitaries in July 1997 (an earlier IRA ceasefire in August 1994 was breached in February 1996). The Belfast (Good Friday) Agreement[42] was put to the electorates in both Northern Ireland and the Republic of Ireland on the same day in May 1998 and was approved by substantial majorities in both jurisdictions - 71% in Northern Ireland and 95% in the Republic of Ireland.

In June 1998 an election was held in Northern Ireland to choose six representatives from each of the 18 Westminster constituencies to sit as Members of a new Northern Ireland Assembly. The powers of this Assembly, and other aspects of the Belfast (Good Friday) Agreement, were then enshrined in law by a Westminster Act, the Northern Ireland Act 1998. The Assembly's powers were to become live whenever the Secretary of State determined that an Executive Committee (*i.e.* a Cabinet) could be formed, and seats on this Executive Committee were to be allocated in accordance with the "d'Hondt" system, thereby giving proportional ministerial representation to the four largest parties in the Assembly. The First Minister designate was to be David Trimble MP, the leader of the Ulster Unionist Party, and the Deputy First Minister designate was to be Seamus Mallon MP, the deputy leader of the Social Democratic and Labour Party.

Considerable difficulties were encountered in securing agreement for the formation of the full Executive Committee. The largest unionist party, the Ulster Unionist Party, would not agree to share power with the second largest nationalist party, Sinn Féin, unless there were greater guarantees concerning the decommissioning of Irish Republican Army weapons. Eventually, in November 1999, a deal was hammered out and on 2 December 1999 powers were finally devolved to the new administration in Belfast. This was several months after different forms of devolution had already commenced in Scotland and Wales.[43]

On 11 February 2000 the Secretary of State for Northern Ireland suspended the Assembly[44] because the Ulster Unionist Party was on the

---

Arms? From "long war" to long peace in Northern Ireland (2nd ed., 2005, forthcoming), Chap. 1. For their part in producing the Agreement David Trimble and John Hume, the leader of the SDLP, were awarded the Nobel Peace Prize in 1998.

[42] See generally A. Morgan, *The Belfast Agreement: A practical legal analysis* (2000) and T. Hennessey, *The Northern Ireland Peace Process: End of the Troubles?* (2000).

[43] Under, respectively, the Scotland Act 1998 and the Government of Wales Act 1998.

[44] By the Northern Ireland Act 2000 (Commencement) Order 2000.

verge of withdrawing from it due to the fact that no republican weaponry had yet been decommissioned. After a few more weeks of negotiations a deal was again struck and the Assembly was reinstated on 30 May 2000.[45] When there was further stalling on decommissioning, however, David Trimble resigned as First Minister on 30 June 2001 and the Assembly was dissolved for single days in both August and September 2001 to allow further six-week periods to elapse so that new elections for a First and Deputy First Minister could take place. Meanwhile the British and Irish Governments agreed at Weston Park in Shropshire on how best to proceed on a range of issues if the Assembly were restored.[46] An act of decommissioning by republicans took place on 23 October 2001[47] and David Trimble and Mark Durkan (the new leader of the SDLP) were finally elected on 6 November 2001[48] but on 14 October 2002 the Secretary of State again suspended the Assembly[49] because of allegations of "spying" by republicans.

The 2002 suspension was still in place at the time of writing, despite a Declaration by the British and Irish Governments in April 2003[50] and new elections to the Assembly in November 2003. An agreement between the two parties which performed best in those elections, the Democratic Unionist Party (DUP) and Sinn Féin,[51] was almost reached in December 2004 (after preliminary talks at Leeds Castle in Kent in September 2004), but negotiations broke down at the last minute, supposedly over the unwillingness of Sinn Féin to allow the

---

[45] By the Northern Ireland Act 2000 (Restoration of Devolved Government) Order 2000.

[46] www.nio.gov.uk/proposals0108.pdf.

[47] Two further such acts took place on 8 April 2002 and 21 October 2003, but on none of these occasions were details made public of exactly what arms were destroyed.

[48] Their election was challenged by Peter Robinson MP as being unauthorised under the Northern Ireland Act 1998. He eventually lost in the House of Lords (by 3 to 2): [2002] NI 390. See M. Lynch, *"Robinson v Secretary of State for Northern Ireland*: Interpreting Constitutional Legislation" [2003] PL 640.

[49] By the Northern Ireland Act 2000 (Suspension of Devolved Government) Order 2002. During suspension, for a period of 6 months, para. 1 of the Sch. to the Northern Ireland Act 2000 allows legislation to be made by Order in Council for any matter for which the Assembly may have legislated; the 6 month period may be, and has been, extended, most recently by the Northern Ireland Act 2000 (Modification) Order 2005 until 14 October 2005.

[50] See www.foreignaffairs.gov.ie/angloirish and www.nio.gov.uk.

[51] The DUP won 30 seats in the Assembly, the Ulster Unionist Party 27, Sinn Féin 24, the SDLP 18, the Alliance Party 6 and three smaller parties 1 each.

decommissioning of weapons to be photographed. The British and Irish Governments went ahead and published their proposals for the basis for an agreement[52] but it soon became clear[53] that there was no prospect of a further settlement being reached until well after the UK general election due in May 2005. In that election the DUP and Sinn Féin increased their mandates even further. [54]

During the period of direct rule between 1974 and 1999, and again since 2002 until the time of writing, the process of assimilation between the content of the law in Northern Ireland and that in England and Wales has, if anything, been fortified. In addition, harmonisation continues to be fostered through the United Kingdom's obligations as a member state of the European Union and the Council of Europe (see Chap. 2.5).

Northern Ireland under the 1998 model of devolution

Although the Northern Ireland Assembly (when it is sitting) is still not permitted to pass laws on "excepted" or "reserved" matters,[55] categories which are now defined differently from the way in which they were defined during previous periods of devolution, all other matters are deemed to be "transferred" and are therefore within what is called "the legislative competence" of the Assembly.[56] Northern Ireland is similar to Scotland in that, while remaining a part of the United Kingdom, it has a devolved Parliament with limited powers. However it is different from Scotland in the important respect that, by section 1 of the Northern Ireland Act 1998, Northern Ireland is to remain a part of the United Kingdom only if a majority of the electorate in Northern Ireland want that to be the case.[57]

---

[52] See note 45 above.

[53] Especially after a massive bank robbery in Belfast on 20 December 2004, attributed to the IRA, and the murder of Robert McCartney in Belfast on 30 January 2005, again allegedly committed by members of the IRA.

[54] In those elections the DUP won 9 of the 18 seats, the UUP 1, Sinn Féin 5 and the SDLP 3. In 2001 the seats won, respectively, had been 6, 5, 4 and 3. Sinn Féin MPs do not actually take their seats at Westminster, nor (because of their refusal to declare allegiance to the state) do they qualify for certain grants available to political parties: see *In re Sinn Féin's Application* [2004] NICA 4 (an appeal to the House of Lords was withdrawn).

[55] Schs. 2 and 3, respectively, to the Northern Ireland Act 1998.

[56] www.ni-assembly.gov.uk/index.htm.

[57] See generally B. O'Leary, "The Nature of the Agreement" (1999) 22 Fordham International Law Journal 1628; C. Harvey, "The New Beginning: Reconstructing Constitutional Law and Democracy in Northern Ireland" in C. Harvey (ed.), *Human*

The powers of the Northern Ireland Assembly and of the Scottish Parliament are not, moreover, exactly the same. Far fewer powers have been initially transferred to the Northern Ireland Assembly because the UK Government wishes first to ensure that the new arrangements work properly. If they do, it is envisaged that several matters which are now "reserved" (a category unknown in Scotland) will become "transferred". Among the matters which are currently reserved to the Secretary of State for Northern Ireland are policing, security policy, prisons, criminal justice and the regulation of telecommunications and broadcasting. If a new agreement is reached between the local political parties and the two Governments in 2005 or 2006 it is expected that many of these matters will indeed be "transferred" to the Northern Ireland Assembly in due course.

Until such further transfer of powers occurs, Northern Ireland will continue to have laws passed for it not just by the Northern Ireland Assembly but also by the Privy Council (in the form of Orders in Council) and by Parliament at Westminster (in the form of Acts and statutory instruments). The UK Government will continue to play an important role in administering the area through the Northern Ireland Office, a department headed by the Secretary of State for Northern Ireland (see 1.4 below). Even after full devolution of powers, Northern Ireland constituencies will carry on electing 18 MPs to the Parliament at Westminster, the Northern Ireland Affairs Committee of the House of Commons will still have power to consider whatever matters affecting the province it wishes to consider,[58] and there will probably remain in existence a so-called Northern Ireland Grand Committee at Westminster (which has sat from time to time since 1997). The various forms which Parliamentary law can take today are more fully described in Chapter 2.1 and 2.2.

The Belfast (Good Friday) Agreement provided for a number of other institutions apart from the Northern Ireland Assembly and the

---

Rights, Equality and Democratic Renewal in Northern Ireland (2001); G. Anthony, "Public Law Litigation and the Belfast Agreement" (2002) EPLJ 401; C. Campbell, F. Ní Aoláin and C. Harvey, "The Frontiers of Legal Analysis: Reframing the Transition in Northern Ireland" (2003) 66 MLR 317.

[58] www.parliament.uk/parliamentary_committees/northern_ireland_affairs.cfm.   This Committee examines the expenditure, administration and policy of the Northern Ireland Office and associated public bodies: see further Chap. 9.1.

Executive Committee.[59] There is a North/South Ministerial Council,[60] which, like the Executive, had its first meeting in December 1999. Six new North/South implementation bodies have been established to implement the policies agreed by the Ministers at Council meetings.[61] These bodies are Waterways Ireland,[62] the Food Safety Promotion Board,[63] the Trade and Business Development Body,[64] the Special European Union Programmes Body,[65] the North-South Language Body[66] and the Foyle, Carlingford and Irish Lights Commission.[67] The British-Irish Council (also known as the "Council of the Isles") has also met: it includes representatives not just from Ireland, Northern Ireland and England, but also from Scotland, Wales, the Isle of Man, Jersey and Guernsey.[68] There is a British-Irish Inter-Governmental Conference which replaced the Anglo-Irish Inter-Governmental Conference established under the Anglo-Irish Agreement 1985.[69] There is also a Civic Forum, paid for by Northern Ireland's Department of Finance and Personnel.[70] Many of these bodies (although not the Civic Forum) have continued to operate in some shape or form during the most recent period of the Assembly's suspension.

1.3 COURTS AND TRIBUNALS

The Four Courts

The Normans did not introduce a new system of law into England after the Battle of Hastings in 1066. In fact, William the Conqueror declared

---

[59] For comments on the North-South strand in the Agreement see C. McCall, "From Barrier to Bridge: Reconfiguring the Irish Border after the Belfast Good Friday Agreement" (2002) 53 NILQ 479.

[60] Attendance from Northern Ireland is governed by s. 52 of the Northern Ireland Act 1998. In 2001 two Sinn Féin MLAs successfully sought judicial review of David Trimble's refusal to nominate them for meetings of the North-South Ministerial Council: *In re De Brun and McGuinness' Application* [2001] 8 BNIL 12 (NICA).

[61] *Ibid.* s.55.

[62] www.waterwaysireland.org.

[63] www.safefoodonline.com.

[64] www.intertradeireland.com

[65] www.northsouthministerialcouncil.org/trade.htm.

[66] www.northsouthministerialcouncil.org/language.htm.

[67] www.northsouthministerialcouncil.org/aqua.htm.

[68] See note 59 above.

[69] By s. 54(2) of the Northern Ireland Act 1998 the First and Deputy First Ministers must ensure that there is cross-community attendance by Ministers and junior Ministers at meetings of the Conference.

[70] *Ibid.* s. 56. See www.civicforumni.org.

that he did not wish to change the law at all. But in order to keep control over the whole country the Norman kings did assume responsibility for the administration of justice and they created a new system of courts based at Westminster. These courts, supported by the royal power, gradually came to deal with the most important types of legal dispute, and it was from the rules devised by judges to settle disputes in these courts that there emerged a body of law which was common to the whole kingdom. Hence the phrase "the common law".

To begin with there were three courts to handle three broad categories of case: (i) cases involving the King's interest in the maintenance of law and order were dealt with by the Court of King's Bench; (ii) taxation cases were heard in the Court of Exchequer; and (iii) disputes involving only "common" (here meaning "private") individuals went to the Court of Common Pleas. These courts met regularly at Westminster, but twice a year the justices would tour the country, on what were known as Assizes, to dispense the King's justice and reassert his authority in each of the counties. Each case was decided by one judge, usually sitting with a jury of 12 "true and honest" men.

There were many disputes which could not be dealt with in these three courts. Petitions sent to the King to settle such cases were referred by him to his Chancellor (who at that time was usually an influential cleric), for justice to be done "according to the conscience of the case". From this practice there emerged another court, the Court of Chancery. The tradition developed that the justice dispensed by the Court of Chancery was "equity", while the justice dispensed by the King's other courts was "common law".[71] Amazingly, it was not until 1875 in England (1877 in Ireland)[72] that common law and equity could be administered in one and the same court: until then the two types of law had to be kept quite separate. A person might, for instance, lose a case in a common law court but then take it to a court of equity and win. After the fusion of equity and common law in the 1870s, all courts could apply both sets of principles and in the event of a conflict the "equitable" as opposed to the "legal" principles were to prevail.[73]

---

[71] For a recent attempt to distil the essence of judge-made common law. See M. Arnheim, *Principles of the Common Law* (2004).

[72] Supreme Court of Judicature Act 1873 and Supreme Court of Judicature (Ireland) Act 1877.

[73] For further details on the history of the Court of Chancery and equity, see P. Pettit, *Equity and the Law of Trusts* (9th ed., 2001), Chap. 1.

However even today confusion still occasionally arises as a result of the co-existence of the two separate approaches to justice.[74]

When the Normans established themselves in Ireland they naturally introduced a system of courts modelled on the English system. Accordingly the Four Courts (of King's Bench, Exchequer, Common Pleas and Chancery) were set up in Dublin, in a building which still bears that name today. As in England, the judges in most of these courts went on Assizes each spring and summer throughout those parts of Ireland under Norman control. Cases were therefore ordered to be tried in Dublin, unless before (in Latin, *nisi prius*) the given date of trial the Assize judge came to the county where the litigants lived (hence the establishment of local *nisi prius* courts).

These four courts formed the heart of the legal systems in England and Ireland until late in the nineteenth century. Over time other courts were established to deal with special types of case and with appeals.[75] To the four "superior" courts in Dublin were added five more: (i) a Court of Admiralty, to deal with shipping cases, (ii) a Court of Bankruptcy and Insolvency, (iii) a Court of Probate, to deal with disputes concerning wills, (iv) a Court for Matrimonial Causes and (v) a Landed Estates Court, which was part of the effort to solve the land problem in Ireland. Two appeal courts called the Court of Exchequer Chamber and the Court of Appeal in Chancery were added. For cases involving claims to small amounts of money there was created a system of "civil bill courts" or "county courts" (see Chap. 6.4), and power to try less serious criminal cases was given to magistrates' courts (see Chap. 5.4). It can be seen that by the 1870s the court structure in Ireland had become exceedingly complicated and unmanageable.

The Court of Judicature of Northern Ireland

In 1877 a thorough reorganisation of the superior courts took place, again along English lines. The nine courts were amalgamated into one High Court, which by 1900 came to have only two divisions: (i) the Chancery Division, which took over the work of two of the old courts - the Court of Chancery and the Landed Estates Court; and (ii) the Queen's Bench Division, which took over the work of the other seven

---

[74] A. Burrows, "We Do This at Common Law but That in Equity" (2002) 22 OJLS 1.

[75] See generally F. Newark, "Notes on Irish Legal History" (1947) 7 NILQ 121, reprinted in an updated form in F. McIvor (ed.), *Elegantia Juris: Selected Writings of F. H. Newark* (1973).

courts. The appeal courts were also amalgamated into one Court of Appeal. The new High Court and the Court of Appeal together constituted the Supreme Court of Judicature - a rather misleading title, since there could always be a second appeal from the Court of Appeal in Dublin to the real "supreme" court for the whole of the United Kingdom, the Appellate Committee of the House of Lords in London.

When the Government of Ireland Act of 1920 created separate court structures for the two parts of the island, the existing court system was closely followed in the North. A Supreme Court of Judicature of Northern Ireland was set up, comprising a High Court and a Court of Appeal. A Court of Criminal Appeal was added in 1930. As can be seen from the hierarchy of courts laid out in Table 1 (see p. 19), the position remains much the same today, except that three important changes were made by the Judicature (NI) Act 1978: (i) a third division of the High Court, the Family Division, was created; (ii) the Crown Court replaced the old system of Assizes; and (iii) the Court of Criminal Appeal was merged with the Court of Appeal.

At this moment, therefore, the Supreme Court of Judicature in Northern Ireland comprises the Court of Appeal, the High Court and the Crown Court, and judges entitled to sit in those courts are referred to as judges of the Supreme Court even though a further appeal still lies on many occasions from the Court of Appeal to the House of Lords.[76] Within a few years, however, as a result of the Constitutional Reform Act 2005, the picture will change slightly. The judges in the House of Lords will be transferred into a new Supreme Court for the United Kingdom[77] and they will then be known as Justices of the Supreme Court. The Supreme Court of Judicature of Northern Ireland will become simply the Court of Judicature of Northern Ireland (equivalent to the Senior Courts of England and Wales)[78] and the judges serving in it will become simply senior judges.

The regional organisation of the courts in Northern Ireland and the precise location of the Crown Court and of the so-called inferior courts (county courts and magistrates' courts) are displayed in Table 2 (see p. 20). It can be seen that the province is divided into four circuits, seven county court divisions and 20 petty sessions districts. They are

---

[76] The judgments of the House of Lords since 1997 are available on-line at www.parliament.the-stationery-office.co.uk/pa/ld/ldjudinf.htm.

[77] Constitutional Reform Act 2005, Pt. 3, ss. 23-60.

[78] *Ibid.* s. 59.

all administered centrally by the Northern Ireland Court Service in Belfast. The county courts for Derry/Londonderry and Belfast are called Recorder's courts, but their powers do not differ from those of other county courts.

The jurisdiction of the ordinary courts is more fully described in Chapters 5 and 6 of this book, while Chapters 7 and 8 examine the jurisdiction of some other specialised courts and tribunals. It should be noted that names are often given unofficially to courts whenever they are sitting to hear particular matters. Examples would be the commercial court,[79] the companies court, the bankruptcy court, the bail court and the motions court. In fact these are all manifestations of the ordinary High Court.[80] The bail court, obviously, decides whether persons arrested and charged with criminal offences should be released on bail rather than remanded in custody (see Chap. 5.2). The motions court hears applications for interim court orders prior to a main trial.

The High Court also contains what is termed a Divisional Court, which is a special court within the Queen's Bench Division that usually comprises two judges and mainly hears applications for *habeas corpus* (see Chap. 5.2).[81] Two judges will also sometimes sit to hear applications for judicial review in criminal matters (see Chap. 6.7)[82] or contempt of court proceedings.[83] In England the Queen's Bench Divisional Court plays a much more important part in the legal system, since it also deals with appeals on pure points of law in criminal cases that have first been heard in the magistrates' courts or the Crown Court. England also has Divisional Courts within the Family and Chancery Divisions of the High Court, although these sit infrequently.

---

[79] See, *e.g.* the Queen's Bench Division (Commercial List) Practice Direction No.1/2000 [2000] 7 BNIL 64, as amended in 2002: [2002] 8 BNIL 61. See too Practice Direction No.6/2002: Expert Evidence: [2002] 8 BNIL 60.
[80] In England the High Court also has a Technology and Construction Court.
[81] See, *e.g.*, *Re Maughan's Application* [1998] NI 293.
[82] See, *e.g.*, *Re Cunningham's Application* [2004] NIQB 7.
[83] See, *e.g.*, *Re Attorney General for Northern Ireland's Application* [2004] NIJB 97, where Carswell LJ and Kerr J fined the *Sunday Life* £4,000.

TABLE 1: THE HIERARCHY OF COURTS IN THE LEGAL SYSTEM OF NORTHERN IRELAND

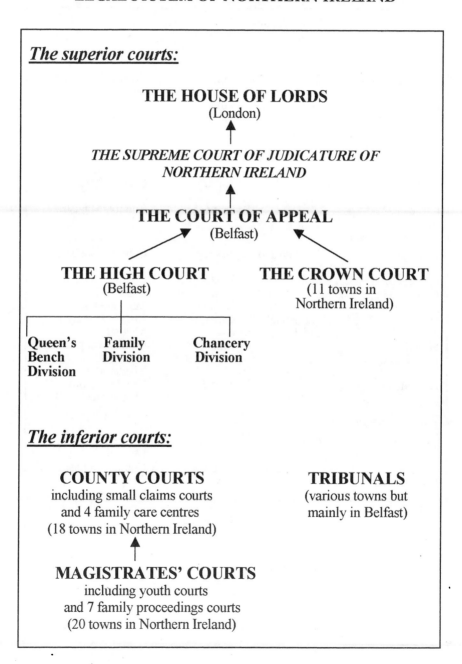

The superior courts:

THE HOUSE OF LORDS
(London)

THE SUPREME COURT OF JUDICATURE OF NORTHERN IRELAND

THE COURT OF APPEAL
(Belfast)

THE HIGH COURT
(Belfast)

THE CROWN COURT
(11 towns in Northern Ireland)

Queen's Bench Division   Family Division   Chancery Division

The inferior courts:

COUNTY COURTS
including small claims courts
and 4 family care centres
(18 towns in Northern Ireland)

TRIBUNALS
(various towns but
mainly in Belfast)

MAGISTRATES' COURTS
including youth courts
and 7 family proceedings courts
(20 towns in Northern Ireland)

TABLE 2: THE ORGANISATION AND LOCATION OF COURTS IN NORTHERN IRELAND

Town/City	County Court Division	Petty Sessions District	Courts
Northern Circuit			
Derry/Londonderry	Derry/Londonderry	Derry/Londonderry	Crown, Recorder's, Magistrates'
Limavady		Limavady	Magistrates'
Magherafelt		Magherafelt	County, Magistrates'
Coleraine	Antrim	North Antrim	Crown, County, Magistrates'
Ballymena		Ballymena	Crown, County, Magistrates'
Antrim		Antrim	Crown, County, Magistrates'
Larne		Larne	County, Magistrates'
Southern Circuit			
Armagh	Armagh and South Down	Armagh	County, Magistrates'
Banbridge		Banbridge	County, Magistrates'
Newry		Newry and Mourne	Crown, County, Magistrates'
Omagh	Fermanagh and Tyrone	Omagh	Crown, County, Magistrates'
Strabane		Strabane	County, Magistrates'
Enniskillen		Fermanagh	Crown, County, Magistrates'
Dungannon		East Tyrone	Crown, County, Magistrates'
Eastern Circuit			
Craigavon	Craigavon	Craigavon	Crown, County, Magistrates'
Lisburn		Lisburn	County, Magistrates'
Downpatrick	Ards	Down	Crown, County, Magistrates'
Newtownards		Ards and Castlereagh	County, Magistrates'
Bangor		North Down	Magistrates'
Belfast			
Belfast	Belfast	Belfast	Crown, Recorder's, Magistrates'

1.4   CENTRAL AND LOCAL GOVERNMENT

The overall shape of the legal system in Northern Ireland has been decided by Parliaments, whether in London or Belfast, but the responsibility for supervising the administration of justice on a day-to-day basis falls in particular on three members of the British Government: (i) the Lord Chancellor, (ii) the Secretary of State for Northern Ireland and (iii) the Attorney General. The actual operation of the system is the professional responsibility of officials such as the Director of Public Prosecutions, judges, magistrates and the police. A few words will be said in the next section about each of these types of officials, while the role of practising lawyers will be described in Chapter 3.2. In the present section we concentrate on the part played by the Government in the administration of the legal system.

Central and local government

As already explained in 1.2 above, although Northern Ireland has its own devolved Assembly (though currently suspended), it is still administered in part by a central UK government department, the Northern Ireland Office. This is headed by the Secretary of State for Northern Ireland, who is assisted by two (or, at times when the Assembly is suspended, four) other Ministers.[84] The Northern Ireland Office operates out of offices in both London and Belfast, with most of the staff in the former belonging to the UK civil service and those working in Belfast usually being seconded from the Northern Ireland civil service.

It is the Northern Ireland civil service which staffs the various departments of government within Northern Ireland (whether headed by Ministers in the Northern Ireland Executive or by Ministers in the Northern Ireland Office). The chief of the Northern Ireland civil service (currently Mr Nigel Hamilton) co-ordinates the work of the ten Northern Ireland departments. These departments are:

- the Department of Agriculture and Rural Development,

- the Department of Culture, Arts and Leisure,

---

[84] www.nio.gov.uk. For a history of the UK Government's attitudes towards Northern Ireland see M. Cunningham, *British Government Policy in Northern Ireland 1969-89: Its Nature and Execution* (1991).

- the Department of Education,

- the Department of Enterprise, Trade and Investment,

- the Department of the Environment,

- the Department of Finance and Personnel,

- the Department of Health, Social Services and Public Safety,

- the Department of Employment and Learning,

- the Department for Regional Development, and

- the Department for Social Development.

In addition there is the Office of the First Minister and Deputy First Minister (the OFMDFM), which retains responsibility for matters such as economic policy, equality, European affairs, the Information Service, community relations, freedom of information, victims and women's issues.[85] There are also two junior Ministers attached to the OFMDFM. Each of the government departments obviously has a wide variety of matters to administer and each will encounter legal problems on very many points. Like all other individuals and organisations, however, they are not permitted to defy the law, even though they may often be instrumental in having the law changed. In particular, the Northern Ireland Act 1998 specifically prohibits both the Assembly and the Executive from taking any action which contravenes the European Convention on Human Rights.[86]

The present system of local government in Northern Ireland dates from 1973.[87] There are 26 local authorities: two city councils (Belfast and Derry[88]), 13 borough councils and 11 district councils. The 26 councils are now subdivided into 582 wards. Every four years between five and seven councillors are elected under a single transferable vote system to represent each district electoral area. City and borough councils may call the chairperson of their council the Mayor (in Belfast, the Lord

---

[85] www.ofmdfmni.gov.uk.

[86] Ss. 6(2)(c) and 24(1)(a). For further details, see B. Dickson, "Northern Ireland", Chap. 6 in A. Lester and D. Pannick (eds.), *Human Rights Law and Practice* (2nd ed., 2004). See also Chap. 2.5 of this book.

[87] Local Government Act (NI) 1972, as amended. This followed the report of the Review Body on Local Government in Northern Ireland (the Macrory Report) (Cmd. 546 (NI); 1970).

[88] The official name of the council is Derry City Council, but the county is still officially called Londonderry.

Mayor) and may designate up to one quarter of their councillors as "aldermen"; they may also confer the freedom of the city or borough on distinguished persons. Otherwise the powers and functions of all 26 authorities are the same. These are by no means as extensive as those given to local authorities in Great Britain: housing, education, health and social services, for instance, are no part of their concern, being handled instead by, respectively, the Northern Ireland Housing Executive,[89] Education and Library Boards and Health and Personal Social Services Boards. But the councils still have responsibilities for, amongst other things, environmental health, noise, nuisances, consumer protection, litter prevention, the enforcement of building regulations and the licensing of street-trading. The Anti-social Behaviour (NI) Order 2004 allows local authorities (as well as the Northern Ireland Housing Executive and the police) to apply to magistrates' courts for anti-social behaviour orders (ASBOs) in respect of any person over the age of 10 whose actions are such that others need to be protected against them. The proposed Local Government (NI) Order 2005 will increase slightly further the powers of local authorities by, for example, allowing them to regulate businesses carrying out cosmetic piercing or sun-tanning.

Councils can now pay basic allowances to councillors, as well as their expenses.[90] Like central government departments, local authorities are not above the law: their decisions can often be challenged in a court or tribunal. This was made clear in several court cases arising out of some councillors' opposition to Sinn Féin or to the Anglo-Irish Agreement of 1985.[91]

The Review of Public Administration[92]

In June 2002, mindful that there were more than 150 public bodies in Northern Ireland for a population of less than 1.7 million, the UK Government initiated a Review of Public Administration in the province. The Review Team was supported by a Panel of Independent Experts, chaired by Mr Tom Frawley, the Northern Ireland

---

[89] www.nihe.gov.uk.
[90] Local Government (Payments to Councillors) Regs. (NI) 1999.
[91] See, *e.g.*, *Re Curran and McCann's Application* [1985] NI 261 and *In re Neeson's Application* [1986] 13 NIJB 24. For further details, see B. Hadfield, "The Northern Ireland Constitution Act 1973: Lessons for Minority Rights", in P. Cumper and S. Wheatley (eds.), *Minority Rights in the 'New' Europe* (1999), pp. 129-46.
[92] www.rpani.gov.uk.

Ombudsman (see Chap. 9.2). The Review has so far published two consultation documents and some relevant research. The most recent consultation document, issued in March 2005, suggests that the number of local councils in Northern Ireland should be reduced from the present 26 to 18, 15, 11 or perhaps just seven. Likewise, it is proposed to reduce the more than 30 bodies dealing with health and personal social services in Northern Ireland to five or seven. The bodies responsible for education will be reduced too. The aim of the rationalisation process is not just to save money but to improve services. To that end the Review has been looking at systems operating in other parts of the United Kingdom, particularly Scotland. If all goes according to plan the new local councils will be in place in time for the next elections to those bodies, due in May 2009.

The Privy Council

The Privy Council of the United Kingdom should be mentioned at this stage because, as will be further explained in Chapter 2.2, this is technically the body which made most of the important laws for Northern Ireland between 1972 and 1999 and still does so during periods when the Assembly is suspended. These laws are called Orders in Council and they constitute one type of "secondary" legislation authorised by Act of Parliament (in this case the Northern Ireland Acts 1974 or 2000[93]). There used to be a separate Privy Council for Northern Ireland, but this no longer meets and no further appointments can be made to it: its functions have been transferred to the Secretary of State for Northern Ireland.

The Privy Council consists of advisers to the Queen. Appointment to it is a recognised reward for public and political service or for attaining high political office. The total membership exceeds 400, all of them entitled to use the prefix "The Right Honourable" for the rest of their lives, but the active section at any particular time mostly comprises the current Cabinet Ministers. Meetings are organised by the Lord President of the Council, who is sometimes (but not always) also the Leader of the House of Commons, that is, the Minister in charge of organising government business in that House. Orders in Council are made when the Queen formally approves the draft Orders presented to her by the Ministers who happen to be closely involved with the matter in hand; they are signed by the Clerk of the Privy Council. They must

---

[93] Originally the Northern Ireland (Temporary Provisions) Act 1972.

then be submitted to Parliament for approval (see Chap. 2.2), although in urgent situations they may come into force even before Parliament has approved them.[94]

One part of the Privy Council is actually a court - its Judicial Committee.[95] This was set up in 1833 with the task of acting as the last court of appeal for cases originating throughout the British Empire, whether civil or criminal. Vestiges of this role remain, as the Judicial Committee still hears appeals from places such as the Channel Islands, the Falkland Islands, Gibraltar, the Isle of Man, Jamaica, Mauritius, Trinidad and Tobago and various other West Indian islands. Decisions taken by the Judicial Committee on appeals from foreign jurisdictions are not binding precedents within any part of the United Kingdom, but they can be of great persuasive influence and some of them have indeed altered the content of our common law (see Chap. 2.3).[96] Under the Northern Ireland Act 1998 the Judicial Committee became the final court of appeal on questions concerning the scope of the powers devolved to the Northern Ireland Assembly,[97] a role it also played when powers were devolved to the Northern Ireland Parliament from 1921 to 1972.[98] In addition, the Judicial Committee deals with appeals from

---

[94] *E.g.* the Northern Ireland (Emergency Provisions) Act 1996 (Amendment) Order 1999, which outlawed the Red Hand Defenders and the Orange Volunteers.

[95] Some amendments to the way in which the Judicial Committee of the Privy Council operates are contained in the Constitutional Reform Act 2005, Sch. 13.

[96] Two important examples are the decisions in *Overseas Tankship (UK) Ltd* v *Morts Dock & Engineering Co Ltd (The Wagon Mound)* [1961] AC 388 (on the test for deciding what loss is too remote to be compensated in a tort action) and *Hedley Byrne & Co Ltd* v *Heller & Partners Ltd* [1964] AC 465 (on whether liability exists for a negligent misstatement). Decisions of the Judicial Committee of the Privy Council are now available on-line at www.privy-council.org.uk/judicial-committee/index.htm.

[97] See Judicial Committee (Devolution Issues) Rules Order 1999; information notes on these rules are reproduced at [1999] 3 BNIL 86. The Judicial Committee can also deal with devolution issues arising in Scotland and Wales. See, *e.g.*, *Brown* v *Stott (Procurator Fiscal, Dunfermline)* [2003] 1 AC 681, where the Privy Council held that requiring a keeper of a vehicle to answer questions as to the identity of the driver at a certain time (under the Road Traffic Act 1988, s. 172) is not a violation of Art. 6 of the European Convention on Human Rights.

[98] Only one case was actually decided by the Judicial Committee in this context, namely *In re Section 3 of the Finance Act (NI) 1934* [1936] AC 352 (The Education Levy case). Under the Northern Ireland Constitution Act 1973, s. 18, the Secretary of State for Northern Ireland retained the power to ask the Judicial Committee to decide whether provisions in an Act of the Stormont Parliament, a Measure of the 1974 Assembly, or a "relevant subordinate instrument" were void because they discriminated on religious or political grounds. This power was never exercised.

certain professional disciplinary bodies within the United Kingdom, such as the General Medical Council and the equivalents for chiropractors, dentists, opticians, osteopaths and veterinary surgeons.

The judges who sit in the Judicial Committee are Privy Councillors who are present or former senior judges in the United Kingdom (or, sometimes, the Commonwealth). In most cases they are the same judges as those who sit as Law Lords in appeals to the House of Lords (see 1.5 below). Five judges usually sit in each case, not wearing judicial wigs or robes and using a room at 1 Downing Street in London. Their decisions take the form of "advice to Her Majesty", although dissenting opinions have been allowed since 1966.[99]

From time to time an *ad hoc* committee of Privy Councillors is set up to consider specific matters. This is the way, for instance, in which the matters leading up to the invasion of the Falkland Islands by Argentina in 1982 were investigated.[100] Another such committee was established to review the operation of the Anti-terrorism, Crime and Security Act 2001.[101]

The Lord Chancellor[102]

The Lord Chancellor currently occupies a unique position in the United Kingdom but his or her role is in the process of changing significantly. At present the post-holder is not only a senior Minister in the Government appointed by the Prime Minister, with a seat in the Cabinet as Secretary of State for Constitutional Affairs,[103] but also the Speaker of the House of Lords when it is acting in its legislative capacity as the second chamber of Parliament. Until the appointment of the current incumbent, Lord Falconer,[104] the Lord Chancellor was also the senior judge when the House of Lords was acting in its judicial

---

[99] See Judicial Committee (Dissenting Opinions) Order 1966.
[100] See the Report of the Committee chaired by Lord Franks, (Cmnd. 8787; 1983).
[101] Under s. 122 of the Act. The Committee, chaired by Lord Newton of Braintree, issued its report on 18 December 2003: *Anti-terrorism, Crime and Security Act 2001: Review*, HC 100.
[102] www.dca.gov.uk.
[103] A post created only in 2003: see the Secretary of State for Constitutional Affairs Order 2003.
[104] His immediate predecessors were Lord Irvine (1997-2003) and Lord Mackay (1987-97).

capacity (although in recent times he did not participate in many cases[105]).

Under the Constitutional Reform Act 2005 the Lord Chancellor has lost his roles as head of the judiciary and as Speaker of the House of Lords.[106] Indeed the person appointed as Lord Chancellor no longer has to be either a qualified lawyer or a member of the House of Lords.[107] In the past the post-holder was often a former Attorney General. His salary is higher than that of any other member of the Government (including the Prime Minister) or any member of the judiciary. At present two Under-Secretaries of State answer questions in the House of Commons on matters falling within the bailiwick of the Lord Chancellor.

The Constitutional Reform Act 2005 also requires the Lord Chancellor to lay annually before Parliament a report on how he or she has discharged the duty to ensure that there is an efficient and effective system to support the business of the courts in Northern Ireland.[108]

The Northern Ireland Court Service

The Lord Chancellor exercises his or her executive functions in Northern Ireland through the Northern Ireland Court Service,[109] which corresponds to part of the Department for Constitutional Affairs in England and Wales. It issues a corporate plan and an annual report and has a Director General (currently Mr David Lavery). The civil servants in this office help to arrange the business of the courts, service the judges and magistrates and advise the Lord Chancellor on legal policy issues. It is the Lord Chancellor who is responsible within the Government for the organisation of the courts, the appointment of most judges and court officials, and the general efficiency of the legal system, including the legal aid schemes (see Chap. 3.3).

---

[105] See A. Bradney, "The Judicial Role of the Lord Chancellor", Chap. 8 in B. Dickson and P. Carmichael (eds.), *The House of Lords: Its Parliamentary and Judicial Roles* (1999).

[106] Constitutional Reform Act 2005, ss. 7(1) and 18 and Sch. 6. The Lord Chief Justices of England and Wales and of Northern Ireland are to become the Heads of the Judiciary in each jurisdiction.

[107] S. 2.

[108] S. 10, inserting s. 68A into the Judicature (NI) Act 1978.

[109] www.courtsni.gov.uk.

The Secretary of State for Northern Ireland

Until the Northern Ireland Assembly began functioning in December 1999, one of the main responsibilities of the Secretary of State, who is a member of the UK Cabinet, was the actual content of the law in Northern Ireland. It was he or she who had to consider introducing into Parliament at Westminster measures of law reform (see also Chap. 9.14) or updating social and welfare policies for the province. After devolution these responsibilities are confined to the "excepted" and "reserved" matters listed in Schedules 2 and 3 to the Northern Ireland Act 1998. This means that the Secretary of State is still in charge of matters such as the criminal law and the treatment of offenders, a function performed in England by the Home Secretary. In this capacity he or she has power to release prisoners on licence or grant them special remission, and to grant pardons. He or she also has special functions under the province's anti-terrorism laws (see Chap. 4.3). The present Secretary of State for Northern Ireland is Mr Peter Hain (he is also the Secretary for Wales). He is the fifteenth person to have held the office since 1972.[110]

The Attorney General

The Attorney General is the chief law officer of the Government,[111] with responsibility for advising government departments and representing the Government's interests in important legal disputes. Like the Lord Chancellor he or she is a political appointee (although not a full member of the Cabinet) and answers questions on legal matters in Parliament. By tradition the Attorney General is meant to be non-political when giving legal advice (*e.g.* on whether the invasion of Iraq in 2003 was permitted under international law[112]) or when acting in his or her capacity as head of the barristers' profession (the Bar).

---

[110] The others have been William Whitelaw (1972-73), Francis Pym (1973-74), Merlyn Rees (1974-76), Roy Mason (1976-79), Humphrey Atkins (1979-81), Jim Prior (1981-84), Douglas Hurd (1984-85), Tom King (1985-89), Peter Brooke (1989-92), Patrick Mayhew (1992-97), Mo Mowlam (1997-99), Peter Mandelson (1999-2001), John Reid (2001-03) and Paul Murphy (2003-05).

[111] The Attorney General heads the Treasury Solicitor's Department: www.treasury-solicitor.gov.uk.

[112] After extracts from the Attorney General's initial advice on this were leaked to the press, the Government eventually put the whole document into the public domain on 28 April 2005. In this document he hedged his bets as to whether an invasion would be illegal, but 10 days later his advice was clear that it would be legal.

Before the abolition of the Stormont Parliament in 1972 there was a separate Attorney General for Northern Ireland; now (and this is so even after devolution to the new Assembly) the English Attorney General acts for Northern Ireland as well,[113] although a senior and junior barrister are appointed to be the Attorney General's counsel in most cases requiring his or her involvement in Northern Ireland. Such counsel would, for instance, act for the Government in cases brought against it under the European Convention on Human Rights (see Chap. 2.5). Service as the Attorney General's senior counsel in Northern Ireland is regarded by some as a passport to eventual appointment as a High Court judge. At the time of writing the Attorney General for England, Wales and Northern Ireland is Lord Goldsmith QC.

Under the Justice (NI) Act 2002, when responsibility for justice is eventually devolved to the Northern Ireland Assembly a separate Attorney General will be appointed for Northern Ireland by the First and Deputy First Ministers acting jointly,[114] but the Attorney General for England and Wales will continue to have responsibilities concerning the remaining "reserved" and "excepted" matters and when acting in that capacity he or she will be known as the Advocate General for Northern Ireland.[115]

The Attorney General has power to exercise some important discretions in selected matters involving the criminal law: his or her consent is required for the commencement of a wide range of prosecutions (although in most cases the consent can also be provided by the Director of Public Prosecutions: see 1.5 below) and he or she can decide that criminal proceedings which are already in progress should be terminated by entering a document called a *nolle prosequi* ("unwilling to prosecute"). Under the anti-terrorism laws in Northern Ireland the Attorney General can "de-schedule" certain offences, which means that they will not be tried in the juryless "Diplock" courts (see Chap. 4.2). He or she also takes the lead in prosecuting newspapers which may have committed contempt of court.[116]

In matters concerned with the civil law (*i.e.* disputes between private individuals) his or her approval is needed for actions taken by private citizens to protect the public interest (these are called "relator

---

[113] Northern Ireland Constitution Act 1973, s. 10.
[114] S. 22(2).
[115] S. 27 and Sch. 7.
[116] See, *e.g.*, *Re Attorney General for Northern Ireland's Application* [2004] NIJB 97.

actions"[117]) and, exceptionally, proceedings can be initiated by the Attorney General in person. Sometimes he or she, or a representative, is asked to attend court as *amicus curiae*, that is, as "a friend of the court", to give general legal advice on points at issue in a case. The Attorney General has the power to challenge legislation of the new Northern Ireland Assembly if he or she believes that the Assembly has no power to make it[118] and the Attorney General can direct the holding of an inquest even though a coroner has decided that an inquest is not necessary.[119]

The Attorney General's deputy is called the Solicitor General, although he or she too is a barrister and a political appointee; currently the office is held by Mike O'Brien MP. The Attorney General appoints Crown Solicitors for Northern Ireland, whose services are then available to any Northern Ireland executive authority or any UK government department (see the next section).[120] The role of ordinary barristers and solicitors in Northern Ireland is explained in Chapter 3.2.

1.5 LEGAL OFFICIALS AND JUDGES

The Public Prosecution Service[121]

Prior to 1972 most prosecutions in Northern Ireland were conducted by police officers, but prosecutions on behalf of government departments, as well as all prosecutions for indictable (*i.e.* serious) offences were the responsibility of Crown Solicitors and Crown Counsel. Following the recommendations of both the Hunt Report on the Royal Ulster Constabulary[122] and the MacDermott Working Party on Public Prosecutions,[123] the role of the police in prosecutions was diminished and the involvement of Crown Solicitors was abolished. To take over these responsibilities the Office of the Director of Public Prosecutions

---

[117] For further details see T. Ingman, *The English Legal Process* (10th ed., 2004), pp. 440-1.

[118] Northern Ireland Act 1998, s. 11(1) (referring Bills to the Judicial Committee of the Privy Council) and s. 71(2) (bringing proceedings concerning legislation to a court or tribunal).

[119] Coroners Act (NI) 1959, s. 14; for a case where this happened, see *In re Hemsworth's Application (No.1)* [2003] NIQB 5. For inquests in general, see Chap. 7.3.

[120] *Ibid.* s. 35.

[121] www.ppsni.gov.uk.

[122] *Report of the Advisory Committee on Police in Northern Ireland* (Cmnd. 535; 1969).

[123] *Report of the Working Party on Prosecutions* (Cmnd. 554; 1971).

(DPP) was created, by the Prosecution of Offences (NI) Order 1972. The present holder of the position of DPP (and only the second incumbent since 1972[124]) is Sir Alasdair Fraser.

The DPP is appointed by the Attorney General. He or she must exercise his or her functions under the superintendence of the Attorney General and is subject to any directions given by the Attorney General, but a failure to comply with the attorney's wishes will not affect the validity of anything done by or on behalf of the DPP.[125] The Attorney General may, however, remove the DPP from office on the grounds of inability or misbehaviour.[126] He or she must be a barrister or a solicitor who has practised in Northern Ireland for not less than 10 years. The Director is assisted by a Deputy and by professional and other staff working in the offices of the DPP in the new Bar Library building beside the Royal Courts of Justice in Belfast and in offices in some other towns. By April 2004 the number of people employed by the DPP had doubled within just two years, to almost 300.[127]

The procedures by which the office of the DPP becomes involved in conducting prosecutions are explained in more detail in Chapter 5.3. Until the changes introduced by the Justice (NI) Act 2002 come fully into effect (see below), the police will continue to have responsibility for prosecuting minor cases, which numerically amount to at least 75% of all cases. At present, therefore, the chief function of the office of the DPP is to bring prosecutions for "indictable" criminal offences, as well as for such less serious criminal offences as the DPP considers should be dealt with by the office. To date the DPP has considered it right to control the prosecution of all offences arising out of incidents of a political nature, as well as the prosecution of offences allegedly committed by police officers. If requested to do so the DPP's office will also engage barristers to conduct prosecutions on behalf of government departments in magistrates' courts and it will act for the Crown in appeals to a county court by defendants who have been convicted in a magistrates' court (see Chap. 5.4). The DPP's office also represents the Crown in all criminal cases in the Court of Appeal and the House of Lords, no matter in which court the case began. For these purposes it retains the services on a more or less permanent basis of

---

[124] The first was Sir Barry Shaw, who retired in 1989.
[125] Justice (NI) Act 2002, s. 40(2).
[126] *Ibid.* s. 40(3).
[127] *Annual Report on the Criminal Justice System of Northern Ireland.*

three senior and three junior Crown Counsel and it functions as the solicitors for these barristers.

Special cases and reform

If a proposed prosecution is a private one, or one to be brought by the police, the consent of the DPP (or of the Attorney General) is very often required before the proceedings can officially be begun and the Director can step in to take over private prosecutions if this is in the public interest. Decisions of the DPP are rarely, if ever, capable of being judicially reviewed (see Chap. 6.7).[128] In 1982 the practice emerged of using "supergrasses", or "converted terrorists", from some of whom evidence was obtained in exchange for immunity from prosecution (this is called "turning Queen's evidence").[129] In these cases the evidence was collected by the police but the immunity was granted by the DPP. A total of 223 defendants had been tried on the word of a supergrass by the end of 1986; 53 convictions remained outstanding after appeals had been heard, but in all of these cases there was evidence to corroborate the testimony of the supergrass.

In addition to actually conducting prosecutions, the DPP can require the police to investigate incidents which appear to him or her to involve an offence, or to make further investigations into matters already referred to the DPP. If someone knows of evidence relating to an alleged crime, he or she is at liberty to make it known directly to the DPP's Office rather than to the police. Whenever a defendant is applying for bail (see Chap. 5.2) the DPP's Office can make representations in such cases as the DPP thinks fit, which goes some way to ensuring that uniform standards on this issue are applied throughout Northern Ireland. Finally, if it appears to a coroner after an inquest (see Chap. 7.3) that a criminal offence may have been committed, the coroner must submit a written report on the case for consideration by the DPP.

Following some worries that the Office of the DPP was not operating with sufficient transparency and independence, its ways of working were closely examined by the Criminal Justice Review Group, a body established as a result of the Belfast (Good Friday) Agreement in 1998

---

[128] P. Osborne, "Judicial Review of Prosecutors' Discretion: The Ascent to Full Reviewability" (1992) 43 NILQ 178 and *R* v *DPP, ex parte Adams* [2001] NI 1.

[129] See S. Greer, *Supergrasses: A Study in Anti-Terrorist Law Enforcement in Northern Ireland* (1995).

(see Chap. 4.1). The Review's recommendations, published in March 2000, led to the enactment of the Justice (NI) Act 2002, which changed the Office of the DPP into the Public Prosecution Service for Northern Ireland (PPS),[130] bringing it more into line with the Crown Prosecution Service in England and Wales.[131] The new PPS was formally launched in June 2005. The aim is to transform the old service from one that handles 10,000 cases each year, with just 150 staff, to one that handles 75,000 cases each year, with nearly 600 staff. The new service will be split into four regions: Belfast, Northern, Western and Southern and Eastern, and will have six offices in all. These will not all be fully functional until the end of 2006, but the Belfast and Western and Southern regions should be operating by mid-2005.

As well as taking prosecution decisions in all cases, including those heard in county courts, magistrates' courts and youth courts, the PPS will eventually provide prosecutorial advice to the police and an enhanced service to victims and witnesses. It has issued a code of practice for prosecutors, laying down standards of conduct and practice and giving guidance on general principles to be applied when determining whether criminal proceedings should be instituted and, if so, what charges should be preferred.[132] The DPP must also issue an Annual Report.[133]

The Crown Solicitor's Office

The office of the Crown Solicitor acts as the solicitor for government departments or agencies (including the Police Service, the Policing Board and the Chief Electoral Office) whenever they are involved in court cases. Most of its work has to do with civil rather than criminal court actions because the latter are usually handled by the DPP (see above). A lot of its work is in the area of debt recovery, but it also handles civil litigation, conveyancing and probate (*i.e.* the administration of someone's property after he or she dies) and judicial review applications (see Chap. 6.7). The office provides legal staff for the Compensation Agency (see Chap. 6.5) and for the Criminal Justice

---

[130] Ss. 29-39. The relationship between the DPP and the Attorney General is regulated by ss. 40-3.

[131] Created by the Prosecution of Offences Act 1985. There is also HM Inspectorate of the Crown Prosecution Service in England and Wales (see www.hmcpsi.gov.uk), but this has no jurisdiction in Northern Ireland.

[132] Justice (NI) Act 2002, s. 37. A draft code was issued for consultation in 2004.

[133] *Ibid.* s. 39. The first such report had not appeared by the time of writing.

Division of the Northern Ireland Office. The head of the office is currently Mr Oswald Paulin. On 1 April 2003 there were 72 people employed in the Crown Solicitor's Office.[134]

The Official Solicitor

The Official Solicitor represents the interests of litigants in cases where they would not otherwise be adequately protected, such as those involving children or persons who are in custody for committing contempt of court. He or she must conduct such investigations and render such assistance as may be authorised by the Rules of the Supreme Court or required by any direction of a court for the due administration of justice. The present Official Solicitor is Ms Brenda Donnelly.[135]

Judges

Information about the present judiciary in Northern Ireland is summarised in Table 3, below. Details of the main types of case heard by the judges in each of the courts are supplied in Chapters 5 and 6.

Apart from deciding cases, judges in Northern Ireland are also involved in making Rules of Court to govern the practice and procedure for dealing with cases in each of the various courts. There are, for instance, a Supreme Court Rules Committee and a County Court Rules Committee. These Rules are a form of secondary legislation (a concept explained in Chap. 2.2) and they are amended and updated at irregular intervals. From time to time judges are also appointed to conduct important inquiries. Lord Justice Campbell, for instance, headed the group which reviewed the civil justice system from 1998 to 2000.[136] The same judge chairs the Judicial Studies Board for Northern Ireland, which arranges training sessions for all members of the judiciary, including the magistracy. Mr Justice Gillen heads the Children Order Advisory Committee (see Chap. 7.1) and Mr Justice Morgan chairs the Law Reform Advisory Committee for Northern Ireland (see Chap.9.14).

---

[134] *Digest of Information on the Northern Ireland Criminal Justice System* (4th ed., 2004), p. 131.
[135] In 2003 there were 117 patient referrals to the Official Solicitor. At the year's end she had 647 cases involving patients and 480 involving children. See Northern Ireland Judicial Statistics 2003, Tables B.40 and B.41.
[136] Civil Justice Reform Group, *Review of the Civil Justice System in Northern Ireland: Final Report* (2000).

Judges enjoy what is called "immunity from suit" when they are performing in court. This means that you cannot sue a judge for compensation even if he or she has obviously taken a wrong decision which has caused you loss or has damaged your reputation by saying something derogatory about you. The immunity is lost as regards junior judges only if he or she can be shown to have acted out of personal malice, which is *extremely* difficult to prove.

TABLE 3: THE JUDICIARY IN NORTHERN IRELAND IN 2005

Office	Number (Deputies)	Qualifications	Retire -ment	How addressed	Salary
Lay Magistrates	272	No formal qualifications	70	"Your Worship"	Expenses only
Resident Magistrates	19 (18)	7 years' practice as solicitor or barrister	70	"Your Worship"	£90,760
District Judges	4 (7)	7 years' practice as solicitor	70	"Your Honour"	£90,760
County Court Judges	15 (35)	10 years' practice as solicitor or barrister	70	"Your Honour"	£113,121
High Court Masters	8	Generally, 10 years' practice as solicitor or barrister	70	"Master"	£90,760
High Court Judges	10 (1) + LCJ	10 years' practice as barrister	70	"My Lord" or "Your Lordship"	£150,878
Court of Appeal Judges	3 + LCJ	15 years' practice as barrister or service as High Court judge	70	"My Lord" or "Your Lordship"	£170,554
House of Lords Judges	12 + LC	15 years' practice as barrister or 2 years in high judicial office	70	"My Lord" or "Your Lordship"	£179,431

Nor is there any effective way of challenging the appointment of a judge, but in line with recommendations made by the Review of the

Criminal Justice System in Northern Ireland[137] the Justice (NI) Acts 2002 and 2004 have provided for a Northern Ireland Judicial Appointments Commission, which will give more transparency to the appointments process.[138] Judges are, however, "workers" for the purposes of some employment legislation.[139] Their presence in a case can also be challenged if they have too close a personal interest in the proceedings; in such situations they can be required to stand down (this is called being "recused"). This famously happened to Lord Hoffmann, one of the Law Lords hearing the *Pinochet* case,[140] because of his links to Amnesty International, which had been allowed to "intervene" in the case.

The House of Lords [141]

The most senior judges in the United Kingdom are the Lords of Appeal in Ordinary, who hear appeals in the House of Lords whenever that body is sitting in its judicial capacity. However the Constitutional Reform Act 2005 provides that the House of Lords is to cease to serve as the highest court in the United Kingdom, probably from 2008,[142] and the Lords of Appeal will then become justices of the Supreme Court, with the senior Lord of Appeal (Lord Bingham) becoming the President of the Supreme Court. Thereafter the justices will be chosen by specially created selection commissions[143] and there is scope for appointing acting judges,[144] a supplementary panel of retired judges[145] and even specially qualified advisers.[146] There will be a Chief

---

[137] Chap. 6 (2000). See also C. Blair, *Judicial Appointments*, Research Report No. 5, prepared for the Review.
[138] See p. 47 below. Justice (NI) Act 2002, s. 3 and Sch. 2; Justice (NI) Act 2004, ss. 2 and 3 and Sch. 1. The latter ensures that the NIJAC can be appointed even if responsibility for justice is not devolved to the Northern Ireland Assembly.
[139] *Perceval-Price* v *Department of Economic Development* [2000] NI 141.
[140] *R v Bow Street Metropolitan Stipendiary Magistrate, ex parte Pinochet Ugarte (No. 2)* [2000] 1 AC 119, where the House of Lords granted a petition to set aside its earlier decision in the case. When it was re-heard a slightly different conclusion was reached: see [2000] 1 AC 147. See D. Woodhouse (ed.), *The Pinochet Case: A Legal and Constitutional Analysis* (2000).
[141] For further details see T. Ingman, *The English Legal Process* (10th ed., 2004), pp. 4-14.
[142] The new Supreme Court building will be the Middlesex Guildhall in Parliament Square in London.
[143] Constitutional Reform Act 2005, s. 26 and Sch. 8
[144] *Ibid.* s. 38.
[145] *Ibid.* s. 39.
[146] *Ibid.* s. 44.

Executive of the Supreme Court, who will prepare an annual report on the Court's activities. These reforms have not been unanimously supported by current or recently retired Lords of Appeal.[147] To avoid confusion over terminology, what was formerly known as "the Supreme Court of Judicature of Northern Ireland" is to be known instead simply as "the Court of Judicature of Northern Ireland".[148]

At present the Lords of Appeal are sometimes referred to as Law Lords and are appointed, as are all full-time senior judges, by the Queen, who by custom and practice acts on the advice of the Prime Minister (and who in turn must consult the Lord Chancellor). Law Lords must have been in possession of a "Supreme Court qualification" for at least 15 years, which means that during that period they must have had the right to speak on behalf of clients in all proceedings in the Supreme Court of England and Wales or in the top courts in Scotland. A person from Northern Ireland can be appointed only if he or she has been a Supreme Court judge for two years or a barrister for 15 years.[149] Lords of Appeal appointed after 31 March 1995 must retire at the age of 70; those appointed earlier can carry on until they reach the age of 75 if they wish.[150]

There can be 12 Lords of Appeal at any one time and they each currently earn £179,055.[151] The first woman to hold the post, Lady Hale, was appointed only in 2004. The best-known Lords of Appeal at the moment are probably Lord Hoffmann and Lord Saville.[152] As mentioned above, the former is famous for allegedly having failed to declare his interests with Amnesty International during the first hearing

---

[147] For contrasting views see Lord Steyn, "The Case for a Supreme Court" (2002) 118 LQR 382; Lord Cooke, "The Law Lords: An Endangered Heritage" (2003) 119 LQR 49; Lord Hope, "A Phoenix from the Ashes? - Accommodating a New Supreme Court" (2005) 121 LQR 253.

[148] Constitutional Reform Act 2005, s. 59. By the same section, "the Northern Ireland Supreme Court Rules Committee" is to become "the Northern Ireland Court of Judicature Rules Committee" and "the Supreme Court of England and Wales" is to become "the Senior Courts of England and Wales".

[149] Only four have ever been appointed: Lord MacDermott, Lord Lowry, Lord Hutton and Lord Carswell. There now appears to be a constitutional convention that each Lord Chief Justice of Northern Ireland will be appointed as a Law Lord in due course.

[150] Judicial Pensions and Retirement Act 1993, s. 26. Of the current Law Lords, only Lords Steyn and Hoffmann were appointed before 31 March 1995.

[151] The Senior Lord of Appeal in Ordinary (currently Lord Bingham) earns £185,705.

[152] The full list, in order of seniority, is Lords Bingham, Nicholls, Steyn, Hoffmann, Hope, Saville, Scott, Rodger, Walker, Lady Hale, Lords Carswell and Brown.

into whether ex-President Pinochet of Chile was entitled to claim "sovereign" immunity.[153] The case had to be re-heard as a result.[154] Lord Saville is well-known in Northern Ireland because he headed the second public inquiry into the events on Bloody Sunday in Derry / Londonderry in 1972.[155] Just before he retired as a Lord of Appeal, Lord Hutton, a former Lord Chief Justice of Northern Ireland, conducted a controversial inquiry into the death of Dr David Kelly, a government official who allegedly leaked information about intelligence on Iraq to a BBC journalist.[156] By tradition, two of the Law Lords at any particular time are Scottish lawyers. There is no invariable custom that one of the Lords must be from Northern Ireland, but each of the last three Lords Chief Justice of Northern Ireland, Lord Lowry, Sir Brian Hutton and Sir Robert Carswell, were indeed appointed as Law Lords. Lords of Appeal are assisted from time to time by retired Lords of Appeal who have not yet reached the age of 75.

Decisions on whether to grant permission for a case to be given a full hearing before the Appellate Committee of the House of Lords are usually taken by only three Lords of Appeal, sitting as the Appeal Committee.[157] As an Appellate Committee the House of Lords usually sits as a bench of five judges, and never with a jury. Very important cases are sometimes heard by seven judges: examples are *Pepper* v *Hart*,[158] when the Lords decided that in interpreting an Act of Parliament judges can legitimately refer to what was said by government Ministers during Parliamentary debates, and the second hearing into ex-President Pinochet's position.[159] On two recent occasions the Law Lords have sat as a bench of nine judges to deal with particularly controversial matters: once to determine whether, if a person has been charged with an offence after an unreasonable time has elapsed, contrary to Article 6(1) of the European Convention on

---

153 [2000] 1 AC 119.
154 [2000] 1 AC 147.
155 This is expected to continue until 2005 and to cost approximately £165 million.
156 See *Report of the Inquiry into the Circumstances Surrounding the Death of Dr David Kelly CMG*, HC 247 (2004).
157 For further details see B. Dickson, "The Lords of Appeal and Their Work, 1966-96", Chap. 7 in B. Dickson and P. Carmichael (eds.), *The House of Lords: Its Parliamentary and Judicial Roles* (1999). Decisions to refuse leave to appeal are noted in the Weekly Law Reports.
158 [1993] AC 593.
159 [2000] 1 AC 147.

Human Rights, the proceedings must then be dismissed (held, no)[160] and once to determine whether the detention without trial provisions in the Anti-terrorism, Crime and Security Act 2001 were compatible with the European Convention on Human Rights (again, held, no).[161]

Many legal disputes occurring in Northern Ireland may in theory proceed as far as the House of Lords. In practice, of course, very few do - only two or three a year on average.[162] For minor civil cases arising in Northern Ireland the final court to which a case can be taken is the province's own Court of Appeal. In some instances it is possible to take a case beyond the House of Lords into Europe, but the courts there are not really hearing "appeals" as such (see Chap. 2.5).

The Supreme Court of Judicature of Northern Ireland[163]

In Northern Ireland the judges of the Court of Appeal and the High Court are appointed by the Queen on the advice of the Lord Chancellor (in England the Prime Minister has a say in who should be appointed to the Court of Appeal, but not in Northern Ireland). Since the Court of Appeal, the High Court and the Crown Court together make up the Supreme Court of Judicature of Northern Ireland, these judges are sometimes referred to as Supreme Court judges, but as explained above these terms will change slightly when the Constitutional Reform Act 2005 comes into force. Since 1921 there have been 43 Supreme Court judges in Northern Ireland, all of them men. Their names and periods of service are set out in Table 4 (p. 40). Three of the judges were the sons of judges, and all were previously barristers. In days gone by judges were often former Unionist politicians,[164] but such political appointments are now unthinkable.

Only barristers who have practised for at least 10 years are eligible for appointment as Supreme Court judges in Northern Ireland, the more

---

[160] *Attorney General's Reference (No. 2 of 2001)* [2004] 2 AC 72 (the Scottish Law Lords, Lords Hope and Rodger, dissented)

[161] *A and others v Secretary of State for the Home Department* [2005] 2 AC 68; by 8 to 1 the House decided that the provisions were not compatible.

[162] In 2004 there were 3 such cases: *Re McKerr* [2004] 1 WLR 807; *Re McFarland* [2004] 1 WLR 1289; *and Kerr v Department for Social Development* [2004] 1 WLR 1372.

[163] Judicature (NI) Act 1978, ss. 1-15.

[164] According to D. McKittrick and D. McVea, in *Making Sense of the Troubles* (2000), at p. 11, between 1937 and 1968 13 sitting Unionist MPs were appointed judges (not all, of course, in the High Court).

liberal provisions in England and Wales on this point[165] not yet applying. Vacancies on the bench are now advertised, but the Lord Chancellor can still appoint someone who has not applied.[166]

TABLE 4: NORTHERN IRELAND'S SUPREME COURT JUDGES 1921-2005

Sir James Andrews	LJ	1921-37	LCJ	1937-51
Sir Anthony Babington	LJ	1937-49		
Richard Best	LJ	1925-39		
Arthur Black	Ch	1943-49	LJ	1949-64
Thomas Brown	QB	1922-44		
Sir Anthony Campbell	Ch/QB	1988-98	LJ	1998-
Sir Robert Carswell	QB	1984-93	LJ	1993-97 LCJ 1997-04
Sir Patrick Coghlin	QB	1998-		
Sir Lancelot Curran	Ch	1949-56	LJ	1956-75
Sir Donnell Deeny	QB	2004-		
Sir Maurice Gibson	Ch	1968-75	LJ	1975-87
Sir John Gillen	QB/Fam	1999-		
Sir Paul Girvan	Ch	1995-		
Sir Anthony Hart	QB	2005-		
Sir Denis Henry	LCJ	1921-25		
Sir Eoin Higgins	QB/Fam	1984-93	LJ	1993-93
Sir Malachy Higgins	QB/Fam	1993-		
Sir Brian Hutton	QB/Fam	1979-88	LCJ	1988-97
Sir Edward Jones	QB	1968-73	LJ	1973-84
Sir Basil Kelly	QB	1973-84	LJ	1984-95
Sir Brian Kerr	QB	1993-2004	LCJ	2004-
William Lowry	QB	1947-49		
Lord Lowry	Ch/QB	1964-71	LCJ	1971-88
Lord MacDermott	QB	1944-47	LCJ	1951-71
Sir John MacDermott	QB/Fam	1973-87	LJ	1987-98
Sir Liam McCollum	QB	1987-97	LJ	1997-2004
Sir Ambrose McGonigal	QB	1968-75	LJ	1975-79
Sir Richard McLaughlin	QB	1999-		
Sir Herbert McVeigh	Ch	1956-64	LJ	1964-73
Robert Megaw	Ch	1932-43		
Sir William Moore	LJ	1921-25	LCJ	1925-37
Sir Declan Morgan	QB	2004-		
Edward Murphy	LJ	1939-45		
Sir Donald Murray	QB/Ch	1975-89	LJ	1989-93
Sir Michael Nicholson	QB	1986-95	LJ	1995-
Turlough O'Donnell	QB	1971-79	LJ	1979-90
Samuel Porter	LJ	1946-56		
Sir John Pringle	QB	1993-99		
Charles Sheil	QB	1949-68		
Sir John Sheil	QB/Fam	1989-2004	LJ	2004-
Sir Ronald Weatherup	QB	2001-		
Sir Reginald Weir	Ch	2003-		
Daniel Wilson	Ch	1921-32		

---

[165] Courts and Legal Services Act 1990, s. 71.
[166] The first High Court judge to be appointed in this way was McLaughlin J. in 1999. He was also the first to be sworn in during a public ceremony.

Supreme Court judges must retire from the bench when they reach the age of 70; they can be removed from office before then if both Houses of Parliament so recommend, but this has not occurred anywhere in the United Kingdom in modern times. Opinions vary over whether the judges in Northern Ireland were too establishment-minded during Northern Ireland's troubles.[167] They certainly had to lead rather sheltered lives because they were under constant threat from republican paramilitaries.

The most important judge in Northern Ireland is the Lord Chief Justice of Northern Ireland. The office replaced that of the Lord Chancellor of Ireland in 1921. To date there have been eight holders of the post: Sir Denis Henry (1921-25), Sir William Moore (1925-38), Sir James Andrews (1938-51), Lord MacDermott (1951-71), Lord Lowry (1971-88),[168] Sir Brian Hutton (1988-97), Sir Robert Carswell (1997-2004) and Sir Brian Kerr (2004-). The salary for the post is the same as that of the Senior Law Lord, £185,705. The Lord Chief Justice is President of the Court of Appeal, the High Court and the Crown Court and in this capacity assigns work to the judges of the various courts and has a number of other administrative responsibilities. In England the Lord Chief Justice (Lord Phillips from October 2005) acts as President of the Criminal Division of the Court of Appeal, while the President of the Civil Division is the Master of the Rolls. This latter post is the one from which Lord Denning retired after 20 years' service in 1982;[169] from October 2005 the office-bearer will be Lord Justice Clarke. There is no Master of the Rolls in Northern Ireland.

The Court of Appeal of Northern Ireland consists of the Lord Chief Justice and three other judges called Lords Justices of Appeal. At present these are Nicholson LJ, Campbell LJ and Sheil LJ and there have been 19 other Lords Justices since 1921. The three currently in post each earn £170,554. In criminal cases, moreover, all judges of the High Court are eligible to sit as judges of the Court of Appeal. The Lord Chief Justice can also ask a Lord Justice of Appeal to sit in the

---

[167] See B. Dickson, "Northern Ireland's Troubles and the Judges", Chap. 9 in B. Hadfield (ed.), *Northern Ireland: Politics and the Constitution* (1992). Seven of today's 13 Supreme Court judges would be perceived as coming from the Catholic tradition and six from the Protestant. See also S. Livingstone, "And Justice for All? The Judiciary and the Legal Profession in Transition" in C. Harvey (ed.), *Human Rights, Equality and Democratic Renewal in Northern Ireland* (2001).

[168] Lord Lowry died in 1999. For fulsome tributes, see (1999) 50 NILQ 1.

[169] Lord Denning is probably the most famous British or Irish judge of the 20th century. He died in 1999 at the age of 100.

High Court, or a High Court judge to sit even in civil cases in the Court of Appeal. (For the distinction between criminal and civil cases, see Chaps. 2.6 and 6.1.) A case in the Court of Appeal will usually be heard by three judges, always sitting in Belfast, but some matters may be dealt with by a two-judge bench and some (incidental matters) by one judge sitting alone. Occasionally a retired judge will be asked to assist in the Court of Appeal.[170] A jury is never involved.

The High Court of Justice consists of the Lord Chief Justice and up to ten other judges.[171] These judges are officially called "puisne" (pronounced "puny") judges and are referred to as "Mr Justice..." Knighthoods have been automatically conferred on High Court judges only since 1988. The ten currently in post, in order of seniority, are Higgins J., Girvan J., Coghlin J., Gillen J., McLaughlin J., Weatherup J., Weir J., Deeny J., Morgan J. and Hart J. Their annual salary is £150,878. Today the High Court judges may sit in any of the Divisions of the High Court, but six are formally allocated to the Queen's Bench Division, with Girvan J. working in the Chancery Division and Gillen J. in the Family Division. Except for hearings in the Divisional Court (see the end of 1.3 above), a High Court case will involve only one judge, always sitting in Belfast. Juries (since 1962 they have consisted of just seven persons, not 12 as in England) are now used quite rarely; they are to be found mainly in libel cases. Most applications for judicial review (see Chap.6.7) will be heard by Weatherup J. To ease the burden on High Court judges, the Lord Chancellor may from time to time request a county court judge to sit as a judge of the High Court.

The inferior courts

County court judges, of whom there are now 15 (including three women), with no fewer than 40 deputies, sit throughout Northern Ireland. Again, at least 10 years' practice as a barrister is required before a person can be considered for appointment, although deputy county court judges, who may after three years be made full county court judges, can be appointed from the ranks of resident magistrates (see below) or from solicitors of 10 years' standing. The retirement age is 70 and the salary is £113,121. County court judges are referred to as "His/Her Honour Judge..." The judges who sit for Belfast and Derry /

---

[170] E.g. *Re McConnell's Application* [2000] 4 BNIL 71.
[171] The number was increased from 9 in 2004. See the Maximum Number of Judges (NI) Order 2004.

Londonderry are called "Recorders" (currently Judges Burgess and Philpott respectively).

There are also four district judges (and seven deputies), who assist the county court judges and exercise an important jurisdiction in the so-called "small claims courts" (see Chap. 6.3). They were formerly known as circuit registrars. Their current salary is £90,760.

Magistrates' courts are not staffed by judges at all but by resident magistrates, lay panellists or (rarely) justices of the peace. All of these offices are described below.

Statutory officers (Masters and clerks)

After consultations with the Lord Chief Justice of Northern Ireland, the Lord Chancellor appoints certain "statutory officers". These include the Official Solicitor (see above) and eight Masters. The Masters (and their deputies) are former legal practitioners of 10 years' standing whose job it is to deal with a variety of procedural and relatively minor substantive issues before a dispute reaches a High Court judge. In effect they exercise the jurisdiction of a judge sitting in chambers, except in respect of certain specified matters. An appeal against their decisions usually lies to such a judge. The title "Master" is used even though the post-holder may be a woman.

Of the eight Masters, two assist the Queen's Bench Division (including appeals), two assist the Chancery Division (including bankruptcy) and two assist the Family Division (dealing with probate and matrimonial work and with the care and protection of children and mental patients). In addition there is a Master who assesses lawyers' costs in certain cases (the Taxing Master) (see Chap. 3.4) and a Master responsible for the enforcement of judgments (see Chap. 6.8). There are Supreme Court Offices corresponding with each of the Master's roles, that for Queen's Bench and Appeals being called the Central Office. A Master earns £90,760 annually, the same as a district judge or a resident magistrate. Being, in effect, junior High Court judges, Masters cannot be judicially reviewed (see Chap. 6.7).[172]

The main administrators in county court divisions are called chief clerks (formerly Clerks of the Crown and Peace), while those in magistrates' courts are called clerks of petty sessions.

---

[172] *Re Rice's Application* [1998] NI 265.

Resident magistrates

One of the major differences between the legal systems of Northern Ireland and England is that in Northern Ireland the responsibility for trying less serious criminal offences lies with full-time, legally qualified magistrates called "resident magistrates" (RMs). In England much of this work is still done by part-time justices who have no formal legal qualifications, although they undergo periodic training after they are appointed. Only in larger towns and cities are there full-time magistrates in England (where they are called "stipendiary" magistrates, to indicate that they receive a stipend, or salary).

The explanation for this difference between Northern Ireland and England relates to the troubled history of Ireland: at the end of the eighteenth century there were parts of Ireland where there were not enough "proper" persons to act as ordinary part-time justices, so it was found necessary to appoint full-time magistrates (not necessarily lawyers) who were required to reside in these areas to assist the justices. This worked so well that during the nineteenth century the practice of appointing resident magistrates was extended throughout the whole of the island. Until 1935 part-time lay justices could also sit with the RMs in magistrates' courts in Northern Ireland, but in that year this power was taken away, so that only RMs can now sit in these courts, which deal mainly with minor criminal offences. The lay justices, who are now called lay magistrates, do however retain an important role in the legal system (see below).

Today only barristers and solicitors of seven years' standing are eligible for appointment as RMs. They are appointed by the Queen on the recommendation of the Lord Chancellor. There are currently 17 in office, with 19 deputies. They must retire when they reach the age of 70 and their salary is £90,760. In court they are addressed as "Your Worship". Moves are now afoot, moreover, to appoint some RMs on a part-time basis. It is also planned to rename RMs as "district judges".

In addition to trying comparatively minor criminal offences, RMs conduct committal proceedings in the more serious criminal cases (see Chap. 5.5). They also deal with some private (*i.e.* civil) law disputes, especially in matrimonial matters, and are responsible for a number of issues which might be said to be more administrative in nature than judicial, such as the renewal of licences for public houses (see Chap. 6.2). They are immune from being sued for causing loss to litigants unless they act entirely "without jurisdiction" (*i.e.* beyond their powers): see *McC* v *Mullan*, a Northern Ireland case that reached the House of Lords.[173]

Justices of the Peace and Lay Magistrates

Until recently the people who acted as lay justices in Northern Ireland were called Justices of the Peace (JPs). The office is a very ancient one, first established in Ireland (as in England) in the fourteenth century. In England and Wales JPs still act as full-scale magistrates but, as noted above, in Northern Ireland their powers have been severely limited since 1935. As a result of the Criminal Justice Review, published in 2000, JPs are now being phased out completely in Northern Ireland, to be replaced by persons officially designated as lay magistrates.[174]

Persons became JPs through appointment under the Queen's Commission of the Peace, which was issued for each county court division by the Lord Chancellor. They remained in office for life but were not normally called upon to serve as a JP after reaching the age of 70. The Lord Chancellor selected persons on the basis of recommendations made to him by local advisory committees in each county court division. The composition of these committees was secret, but the chairman was usually the Lord Lieutenant of the county (a representative of the Queen). Nominations could be submitted to the Court Service by any person or group and those appointed were invariably respected people who, over the years, had gained the trust and the admiration of the local community.

In 2004 an extensive advertising campaign took place to attract more persons to the new role of lay magistrate. More than 5,000 people applied and eventually 272 were appointed. They must reside or work in, or within 15 miles of, the county court division to which their appointment relates and they must not hold certain specified offices or occupations (*e.g.* as a solicitor).[175] Although not legally qualified they are nevertheless members of the judiciary in Northern Ireland. Of the new recruits the majority (54%) are female and 38% are Catholic. They have all been appointed for a five-year term, renewable until they reach the age of 70. As was the case for JPs, lay magistrates receive no payment for their services, only out-of-pocket expenses. On 1 April 2005 certain functions of JPs and all the functions of persons formerly

---

[173] [1985] AC 528.
[174] Justice (NI) Act 2002, ss. 9-11.
[175] Lay Magistrates (Eligibility) (NI) Order 2004.

called lay panellists (who sat in youth courts with RMs) were transferred to the new lay magistrates.

Most of the powers of lay magistrates may be exercised only within the county for which they have been appointed. Their main task is the signing of summonses, warrants and various official forms, such as forms relating to state pensions. Summonses are documents which direct people to appear in court on a certain day in order to answer a particular allegation (see Chap. 5.1). Warrants are documents authorising the police to arrest someone who is suspected of having committed a crime (see, again, Chap. 5.1) or to search premises where, for instance, stolen goods are thought to be hidden; or they may take the form of written authorisation for extending a person's detention or committing a person for trial or to prison on remand. Lay magistrates have the power to conduct committal proceedings (see Chap. 5.5) and, provided that the accused person consents, they can try summarily some minor criminal offences, such as poaching. In practice, however, these functions are now rarely exercised.

Like RMs, lay magistrates retain the somewhat controversial power to "bind over" persons to keep the peace or be of good behaviour. This power, which derives from the common law and from the Justices of the Peace Act 1361, enables magistrates to require people to forfeit a sum of money or serve a period of imprisonment if they break a promise to keep the peace or be of good behaviour during a stipulated period, which must not exceed two years. Strangely, such persons do not first have to be convicted of a criminal offence. On at least one occasion in England the power has been exercised in a way which has been held to contravene the European Convention on Human Rights (because of its vagueness),[176] so reform of the law may be imminent.

Judicial Appointments Commissioners

The Criminal Justice Review recommended that the system for appointing judges in Northern Ireland should be made more transparent.[177] Pending the creation of a statutory Judicial Appointments Commission, a non-statutory part-time Commissioner for Judicial Appointments (Mr John Simpson) took up office in January

---

[176] *Hashman and Harrap* v *UK* (1999) 30 EHRR 241; but see, by way of contrast, *Steel* v *UK* (1998) 28 EHRR 603.
[177] Recommendations 77-86.

2002[178] with the task of overseeing and monitoring the fairness of all aspects of the existing appointments system.[179]

The Commissioner audits the appointments processes for judges, Queen's Counsel and tribunal members by, for example, attending as an observer relevant assessment panel meetings and interviews and sending a report on each round of appointments to the Lord Chancellor. He also handles complaints, considers comments relating to the appointment processes and oversees the development of a strategy for broadening the pool of potential applicants for the positions in question. He does not himself have any role in making or recommending appointments but he tries to ensure that appointments are made entirely on merit.

In the past year or so the Commissioner has been particularly interested in the process by which over 250 new lay magistrates have been appointed in Northern Ireland. Following a recommendation made in his Audit Report published in August 2003,[180] research is on-going into the factors which affect the decisions of barristers and solicitors, and in particular women, regarding whether to apply for judicial appointments. Mr Simpson is also a Deputy Commissioner for Judicial Appointments in England and Wales,[181] which allows him to ensure that procedures in Northern Ireland are broadly comparable with those in that jurisdiction. The cost of running his office in Northern Ireland in 2003-04 was £220,000.

In the Justice (NI) Act 2002 provision was made[182] for the creation of a statutory body to be known as the Judicial Appointments Commission, which was to come into being after responsibility for justice had been devolved to the Northern Ireland Assembly. In view of the suspension of the Assembly since October 2002 the UK Government ensured that in the Justice (NI) Act 2004 provision was made[183] for creating such a Judicial Appointments Commission even in the absence of this aspect

---

[178] See www.courtsni.gov.uk/cjani.

[179] Except those relating to the appointment of the Lord Chief Justice of Northern Ireland.

[180] Progress on implementing the recommendations in that report is set out in App. 3 to the Commissioner's Annual Report for 2003-04.

[181] The Commission for Judicial Appointments for England and Wales is chaired by Sir Colin Campbell, Vice-Chancellor of the University of Nottingham. See www.cja.gov.uk. There is also a Judicial Appointments Board in Scotland: www.judicialappointmentsscotland.gov.uk.

[182] S. 3 and Sch. 2.

[183] Ss. 1-3.

of devolution. Its membership was announced in June 2005, the chairperson being Sir Brian Kerr, the Lord Chief Justice of Northern Ireland.[184] It mirrors the body which is planned for England and Wales under the Constitutional Reform Act 2005.[185] That Act also confirms in explicit terms that government ministers throughout the United Kingdom must uphold the independence of the judiciary;[186] the Lord Chancellor, for example, must not seek to influence particular judicial decisions through any special access to the judiciary.[187] Additional guarantees are provided exclusively for the judiciary in Northern Ireland[188] and the Lord Chief Justice of Northern Ireland has the power to lay matters relating to any aspect of the administration of justice before Parliament at Westminster or the Assembly at Stormont if they appear to be of importance.[189]

Judicial Appointments and Conduct Ombudsman

The Constitutional Reform Act 2005 provides for the appointment of a Judicial Appointments and Conduct Ombudsman for the United Kingdom[190] and a Northern Ireland Judicial Appointments Ombudsman,[191] but neither official has yet been appointed.

HM's Inspectorate of Court Administration[192]

The Criminal Justice Review, published in 2000, recommended that courts in Northern Ireland, like courts in England and Wales, should be periodically inspected to ensure that they are providing a satisfactory service to members of the public. Consequently the Magistrates' Courts Service Inspectorate was asked to extend its work to the province and in 2004 it inspected all courthouses and other Court Service facilities in

---

[184] www.nijac.org.
[185] S. 61 and Sch. 12.
[186] S. 3(1).
[187] S. 3(5)
[188] Justice (NI) Act 2002, s. 1, as amended by the Constitutional Reform Act 2005, s. 4(1).
[189] Constitutional Reform Act 2005, ss. 5 and 6.
[190] S. 62 and Sch. 13.
[191] S. 124 and Sch. 15, inserting Sch. 3A into the Justice (NI) Act 2002.
[192] www.hmica.gov.uk. From 1 April 2005, under the Courts Act 2003, this new body superseded pre-existing bodies including the Magistrates' Courts Service Inspectorate. It inspects the systems that support the Crown Court, county courts, magistrates' courts and Children and Family Court Advisory and Support Service (CAFCASS) in England and Wales, and can inspect the courts in Northern Ireland by invitation.

Northern Ireland. The conclusions of these visits are available on the Court Service's website. A fuller report is due to be published in 2005.

The Insolvency Service

Within the Department of Enterprise, Trade and Investment[193] there is a branch called the Insolvency Service which administers and investigates the affairs of individuals who become bankrupt and companies which go into compulsory liquidation. It handles the disqualification of directors in corporate insolvencies and deals with any fraudulent activity in the management of insolvent businesses. It also regulates the insolvency profession and formulates insolvency legislation and policy which are specific to Northern Ireland. The Insolvency Service does not get involved in the day-to-day handling of administrations, administrative receiverships, voluntary liquidations or the majority of "voluntary arrangements". For details on the law relating to these matters readers should consult specialist works on bankruptcy and company law.

At present the most relevant pieces of legislation are the Insolvency (NI) Order 1989 and the Company Directors Disqualification (NI) Order 2002; these seek to deal fairly with not only the creditors but also the insolvent individual or company. But, following responses to a consultation paper on modernisation of the legal framework for personal and corporate insolvency issued by the Department of Enterprise, Trade and Industry in 2003, both of these Orders will be replaced the Insolvency (NI) Order 2005 and Company Directors Disqualification (Amendment) (NI) Order 2005.

Other officials

There are several other officials whom you may encounter in Northern Ireland if you have a brush with the law. The Army, which includes the Royal Irish Regiment and the Military Police (the "red caps"), continues to assist the police in maintaining law and order in Northern Ireland and has been granted special powers to that end (see Chap. 4.3).[194] Some organisations, such as railway, airport and seaport

---

[193] www.detini.gov.uk.

[194] www.usite.army.mod.uk/HQNI/Index.htm. The army has divided Northern Ireland into 3 brigade areas, to match the three police regions. There are still about 12,000 soldiers in the province. At the height of the troubles, in 1972, there were 27,000. The Government has said that it wants to reduce troop levels to a permanent garrison of

authorities, are empowered to set up their own police services for specific purposes. Traffic wardens have all the powers of police officers as regards the control of road traffic.

Process servers and bailiffs are private individuals or firms who are engaged by both public and private bodies to deliver official documents or to enforce court orders. If you are forming a company you will have dealings with the office of the Registrar of Companies, and if you attempt to do your own conveyancing when moving house you will need to make use of the Land Registry,[195] the Statutory Charges Register or the Registry of Deeds. The Registrar General, with headquarters in Belfast and officers in every district council area, has responsibility for recording all births, deaths and marriages.[196] The Registrar General now issues a quarterly report, which is available on-line.[197]

5,000. From the IRA ceasefire in 1994, 64 of the 105 military installations occupied by the Army had been vacated by February 2005.

[195] www.lrni.gov.uk.

[196] See *82nd Annual Report of the Registrar General 2003* (2004), issued pursuant to s. 56 of the Marriages (Ireland) Act 1844, s. 16 of the Registration of Marriages (Ireland) Act 1863 and art. 3(3) of the Births and Deaths Registration (NI) Order 1976.

[197] www.nisra.gov.uk/Uploads/publications/rg_qtr4_2004.pdf.

CHAPTER TWO

SOURCES OF NORTHERN IRELAND'S LAW

In Chapter 1 we concentrated on the history of the present-day legal system and described briefly the role of various organisations and officials in administering that system. In this Chapter we will examine more closely the ways in which the legal system actually creates, applies and develops the law. Our aim here is not to investigate the nature of law or consider what exactly the law is on a certain point: we are taking for granted a conception of law as a set of socially binding rules and principles and are simply inquiring into how those rules and principles come to be fashioned. The bulk of our inquiry will concern the two main sources of law identified in Chapter 1: (i) Parliament and (ii) the courts. We will then close with a short explanation of the ways in which the various sources of law are combined to create branches of law.

2.1 PRIMARY LEGISLATION

All branches of law have at least one feature in common: the rules which they contain are derived not only from legislation, which is law created by Parliament, but also from judicial precedent, which is law created by judges (see also Chap. 1.3). Practically every legal issue is governed partly by legislation and partly by judge-made law. Two other sources of law are custom and the opinions of eminent scholars, but in practice these are resorted to infrequently; both legislation and judge-made law take priority over them. On the rare occasions when the law as laid down by Parliament is in conflict with the law as laid down by judges, it is parliamentary law which must prevail. If parliamentary law is itself at odds with earlier parliamentary law, the later in time must prevail[1] – unless the earlier law is the Human Rights Act 1998, but even then the later law will remain valid if it is itself an Act of Parliament.

Legislation consists not just of Acts of Parliament - which are called "statutes" - but also of the very numerous orders, rules, regulations and schemes which are made under the authority of an Act of Parliament.

---

[1] In nearly every case the later piece of legislation will expressly repeal the earlier piece. If it does not then the so-called doctrine of implied repeal applies.

This latter body of laws is called secondary, subordinate or delegated legislation, but to all intents and purposes it is just as binding on everyone as the primary legislation enshrined in statutes. Secondary legislation is considered in more detail in the next section.

There is actually a third type of legislation which ought to be mentioned in passing: legislation created under the Royal Prerogative. This takes the form of prerogative Orders in Council, whereby the Queen simply assents to proposals put before her by senior Ministers who have been appointed Privy Councillors (see Chap. 1.4). The matters regulated by the Royal Prerogative in this way are now limited to particular fields such as the civil service, the armed forces and coinage. In 1984, when the Prime Minister wished to ban trade unions at Government Communications Headquarters at Cheltenham (GCHQ), she issued a ruling under a power conferred on her by a Prerogative Order in Council, namely the Civil Service Order 1982. The legitimacy of the Order was the subject of considerable litigation, but it survived all challenges.[2]

Prerogative Orders with a legislative character are inserted in an appendix in the annual volumes of UK statutory instruments (explained in the next section) but they are quite different from Parliamentary Orders in Council (also explained in the next section), which are made under the authority of an Act of Parliament. Prerogative Orders are not themselves statutory instruments, whereas Parliamentary Orders are. In a sense, Prerogative Orders are subordinate legislation (because Parliament can qualify the power to make them) but not secondary legislation (because Parliament's authority is not required for the creation of any particular order). They invariably apply throughout the United Kingdom, not just to one part of it (England and Wales, Scotland or Northern Ireland).

Under the Human Rights Act 1998, strangely, Prerogative Orders in Council cannot be invalidated as incompatible with the European Convention on Human Rights,[3] but most Parliamentary Orders in Council, including those made under the Northern Ireland Acts 1974 or 2000, can be.[4]

---

[2] *Council of Civil Service Unions* v *Minister for the Civil Service* [1985] AC 374.

[3] P. Billings and B. Pontin, "Prerogative Powers and the Human Rights Act: Elevating the Status of Orders in Council" [2001] PL 21.

[4] *In re King's Application* [2002] NICA 48, although neither in that case nor in any other case has any part of an Order in Council yet been declared invalid by a court in Northern Ireland.

The primacy of statute law

In the United Kingdom, unlike in most other countries, including Ireland, it is not possible (except in one type of situation) for the courts to refuse to apply primary legislation on the grounds that it is invalid or in some way unconstitutional. The United Kingdom does not have a written Constitution which takes priority over ordinary legislation. Nor can courts in the United Kingdom attempt to alter the wording of Parliament's laws. Parliament at Westminster is supreme; whatever it enacts cannot be queried. Only a later Parliament can undo the things which a previous Parliament has done. Constitutional lawyers call this "the doctrine of parliamentary sovereignty (or supremacy)".

The only exception relates to the fact that membership of the European Union means that whenever UK domestic law, whether parliamentary or judge-made, runs counter to the law emanating from the institutions of the European Community, it is the latter which must be given priority, even by British judges. In at least two cases the British courts have already had to "disapply" a piece of primary legislation because of its inconsistency with European Community law. But some people do not see even this type of situation as an exception to the doctrine of Parliamentary sovereignty because it is itself a consequence of the Act of Parliament whereby the United Kingdom joined the European Community in the first place - the European Communities Act 1972. We return to this European dimension at the end of this Chapter (see 2.5 below).

The Human Rights Act 1998 does *not* create a further exception to the doctrine of Parliamentary sovereignty. In fact, it bolsters the doctrine. Rather than give judges the power to declare an Act of Parliament to be invalid if it is inconsistent with the European Convention on Human Rights, the 1998 Act only permits them to declare that the Act in question is "incompatible" with the Convention. This leaves the Act valid and intact, unless and until it is amended by Parliament (and the 1998 Act provides for a fast-track amendment procedure for just such occasions[5]). To date a judge in Northern Ireland has only once declared any part of an Act of Parliament to be incompatible with the European Convention.[6]

---

[5] See s. 10.
[6] *In re McR* [2002] NIQB 58, where Kerr J declared s. 62 of the Offences against the Person Act 1861 (dealing with the crime of buggery) to be incompatible with Art. 8 of the Convention (right to a private life).

As regards Northern Ireland, however, it has to be remembered that
from 1921 to 1972 the Government of Ireland Act 1920 did effectively
provide the province with a written constitution. The legislative powers
of the Belfast Parliament were deliberately restricted by that Act:
excepted and reserved matters could be dealt with only by the
Parliament at Westminster (see Chap. 1.2). If the Belfast Parliament
trespassed into these areas, courts in Northern Ireland were entitled to
declare the legislation (whether primary or secondary) to be beyond the
powers of (*ultra vires*) the Parliament. As regards primary Stormont
legislation, this almost happened in a case called *R (Lynn)* v
Gallagher.[7] The Milk and Milk Products Act (NI) 1934 required all
sellers of milk in Northern Ireland to have a licence from the Ministry
of Agriculture. Mr Gallagher was refused a licence because his dairy
farm was situated outside Northern Ireland, even though he sold milk
within the province. Upon his conviction for the crime of selling milk
without a licence Mr Gallagher, on appeal, tried to argue that the 1934
Act was beyond the power of the Stormont Parliament to make
because, by section 4(1) of the Government of Ireland Act 1920, that
Parliament could not make laws in respect of trade. He lost his case
because first the Court of Appeal of Northern Ireland and then the
House of Lords held that the 1934 Act was *not* one in respect of trade
but one in respect of the peace, order and good government of Northern
Ireland and so was valid.

The Northern Ireland Act 1998 has likewise conferred limited powers
on the Northern Ireland Assembly and if the Assembly were to attempt
to make laws which are outside its powers a challenge could again be
mounted in the courts. A new ground for challenge, one which did not
apply under the 1920 Act, is that the Assembly's law is incompatible
with the European Convention on Human Rights.[8] In addition, the
Northern Ireland Act 1998 provides various other safeguards to ensure
that the Assembly acts within its powers. For instance, a Minister in
charge of a Bill must, on or before its introduction in the Assembly,
publish a statement that in his or her view the Bill is within the
Assembly's powers, and a Bill cannot to be introduced if the Presiding
Officer decides that it is outside the Assembly's powers.[9] The question

---

[7] [1938] NI 21.
[8] Northern Ireland Act 1998, s. 6(2)(c) (for the Assembly) and s. 24(1)(a) (for the
Executive); see too the Human Rights Act 1998, s. 3.
[9] Northern Ireland Act 1998, ss. 9 and 10.

whether an Assembly Bill is within or without the Assembly's powers can also be referred to the Judicial Committee of the Privy Council.[10]

Different types of statutes

Statutes are made by being first drafted and then enacted. The precise methods of drafting and enactment differ according to the type of statute in question. For the moment we can identify two types. In the first place there are public Acts, which are statutes affecting the whole public and are by far the commonest type of primary enactment, with several dozen being created by the Westminster Parliament each year (in 2003 and 2004 there were 45 and 38 respectively) and more are now being added by the devolved Parliaments (the new Northern Ireland Assembly has so far enacted 35 Acts[11]). Then there are local, or private, Acts, which are statutes concerned only with a particular locality or company.[12] Between 1921 and 1972, during which time Northern Ireland possessed its own Parliament, no differentiation was made between the three types of Acts; Acts such as the Londonderry Corporation Act (NI) 1970 and the Allied Irish Banks Act (NI) 1971 were published as public general Acts. This will probably be the case with Acts of the Northern Ireland Assembly too.

Local and private Acts should not be confused with Private Members' Bills, which are proposals for laws introduced and piloted through Parliament by an MP who does well in a ballot at the start of the Parliamentary session.[13] Usually only one or two of these Bills eventually get passed into law each year, most of them being opposed by the Government. Famous examples of those which did get passed are the Obscene Publications Act 1959, introduced by Roy Jenkins MP, and the Abortion Act 1967, introduced by David Steel MP. It is rare for

---

[10] *Ibid.* ss. 79-83 and Sch. 10. See also Chap. 1.4.

[11] Four in 2000 (beginning with the Financial Assistance to Political Parties Act (NI) 2000, 17 in 2001 and 14 in 2002 (ending with the State Pension Credit Act (NI) 2002). The Assembly was suspended on 14 October 2002. The Scottish Parliament passed 19 Acts in 2003 and 12 in 2004.

[12] There were 5 of these in 2003 and 6 in 2004, *e.g.* the London Local Authorities Act 2004 (which confers new powers concerning abandoned vehicles, public health, the environment, licensing etc.) and the University of Manchester Act 2004 (which merged two universities in Manchester).

[13] Members of the House of Lords can also introduce Private Members' Bills, *e.g.* the Criminal Cases Review (Insanity) Act 1999, which was prompted by the decision of the Court of Appeal in Northern Ireland in *Criminal Cases Review Commission's Reference under s. 14(3) of the Criminal Appeal Act 1995* [1998] NI 275.

a Private Members' Bill at Westminster to extend directly to Northern Ireland (neither of the two just mentioned did so), although some of them later lead to equivalent legislation for the province in the shape of an Order in Council. Only two Private Members' Bills have been successfully piloted through the House of Commons by Northern Ireland MPs: Gerry Fitt MP introduced what became the Chronically Sick and Disabled Persons (NI) Act 1978 and Martin Smyth MP introduced the Disabled Persons (NI) Act 1989. Both Acts largely reflect earlier legislation already in place for England and Wales.

During the imposition of direct rule (see Chap. 1.2), the UK Parliament continues to enact both public and local Acts for Northern Ireland, although the latter are rare. Even public Acts are seldom used specifically for the province: if they are applied to Northern Ireland they usually apply to the whole of the United Kingdom. But obviously exceptions are made when Westminster needs to deal with constitutional or electoral crises in Northern Ireland.[14] The main way in which legislation confined to Northern Ireland has been enacted in the past 30 years has been by adopting the Parliamentary Order in Council procedure under the Northern Ireland Act 1974. This is an example of secondary legislation and is therefore described more fully in the following section.

Whenever the Westminster Parliament wishes to enact a law concerning an "excepted" matter (see Chap. 1.2), it has to embody it in a public general Act, such as the Northern Ireland (Emergency Provisions) Act 1996. If the subject of the proposed law is a "transferred" matter then such an Act tends to be employed only if the Government wishes to ensure a full parliamentary debate, such as with the Fair Employment (NI) Act 1989.[15] For legislation dealing with "reserved" matters, see the paragraphs dealing with Orders in Council in Chapter 2.2 below. Acts confined in operation to the province will have the words "Northern Ireland" or "Ulster" either in the main part of the title of the Act or within brackets before the word "Act". Statutes of the Stormont Parliament 1921-1972 are distinguished from English statutes with similar titles by adding the phrase "Northern Ireland" *after* the word "Act", as in the Occupiers' Liability Act (NI) 1957.

---

[14] *E.g.* the Northern Ireland Constitution Act 1973, the Northern Ireland Acts 1974, 1998 and 2000, and the Electoral Registration (NI) Act 2005.
[15] But when the Government wished to amend this Act, even quite significantly, it preferred the Order in Council procedure: Fair Employment and Treatment (NI) Order 1998.

Some statutes are passed wholly or mainly to *consolidate* previous statutes, that is, to bring into one place the various existing enactments already dealing with a particular matter. Examples are the Employment Protection (Consolidation) Act 1978 and the Social Security Contributions and Benefits (NI) Act 1992, but in recent years there have been very few such Acts.[16] Occasionally statutes are passed in order to *codify* existing statute *and* judge-made law on a topic. These statutes represent a fresh start on the topic and usually change the existing law. An example is the Theft Act (NI) 1969.

The drafting and enacting of statutes

Acts of the UK Parliament are officially made by "The Queen in Parliament". This means that they must be approved by the House of Commons, the House of Lords and the Monarch. Since 1911, however, the power of the House of Lords to curb the legislative zeal of the House of Commons has been severely restricted. Recent examples of legislation passed by the Commons alone are the War Crimes Act 1991, the European Parliamentary Elections Act 1999 and the Hunting Act 2004. The composition and functions of the House of Lords were reviewed by a Royal Commission chaired by Lord Wakeham, which reported in 2000;[17] even before then the Government had decided to abolish the right of hereditary peers to sit in the House of Lords and this was brought about by the House of Lords Act 1999. The Monarch, moreover, no longer refuses to assent to an Act of Parliament presented to her.[18] As the House of Commons is usually dominated by Members of Parliament belonging to the political party which has formed the Government, it is in practice the Government - and within that the Cabinet - which decides what legislation should be passed. The Government's intentions are made clear in the Queen's Speech at the beginning of each Parliamentary session.

The great majority of public Acts start life as proposals put to the Cabinet, either by a Cabinet committee or by a particular government department through its representative on the Cabinet.[19] Often the

---

[16] See A. Samuels, "Consolidation: A Plea" (2005) 26 Statute LR 56.
[17] Cm. 4534.
[18] There is now a constitutional convention that the Queen will not refuse the Royal Assent to a Bill passed by both Houses of Parliament, although it has been suggested that she has a personal human right to refuse to assent: R. Blackburn, "The Royal Assent to Legislation and a Monarch's Fundamental Human Rights" [2003] PL 205.
[19] See generally M. Zander, *The Law-Making Process* (6th ed., 2004), Chap. 1.

proposals will have been preceded by a government White Paper on the topic, and perhaps by a Green Paper before that. From the Cabinet the proposals are sent in the form of departmental instructions to the Office of Parliamentary Counsel, whose staff have the task of actually drafting the legislation. A similar office existed in Northern Ireland when there was a Parliament at Stormont from 1921 to 1972; from then it existed in the form of the Office of the Legislative Draftsman, which confined its attention to drafting Orders in Council issued under the Northern Ireland Act 1974 and helping with the drafting of Northern Ireland statutes to be enacted at Westminster. With the return of a devolved administration in 1999, the local experts in drafting are again working on statutes considered by the Northern Ireland Assembly.

Legislative drafting is a specialised skill. The policy instructions of the government department in question have to be translated into unambiguous legal language, with care being taken not to distort the intention behind the instructions or to leave any gaps. The Act must also be tied in with whatever legislation already exists on the topic. During the legislation's passage through Parliament the draftsperson must always be at hand to advise Ministers and prepare any necessary amendments.

Passage through Parliament, or the enactment of the legislation, is usually a long and complicated process.[20] At Westminster the standard procedure is for a Bill to be introduced into the House of Commons, where it is dealt with in five stages:

(1)   the First Reading (a formality);

(2)   the Second Reading;

(3)   the Committee Stage;

(4)   the Report Stage; and

(5)   the Third Reading.

It is at the committee and report stages that detailed amendments to the Bill are mostly considered. The Bill is then sent to the House of Lords, where similar stages must be gone through, and if any amendments are suggested these must be returned to the House of Commons to be considered further.

---

[20] *Ibid.* Chap. 2.

In nearly every case, mainly because of the Government's majority in the House of Commons and the relative powerlessness of the House of Lords, the final form of the law differs little from that put forward at the initial stages. The House of Lords can delay a Bill only by a year: thereafter the House of Commons can enact the Bill notwithstanding the opposition of the Lords.[21] A Bill which does not complete all of its stages during one Parliamentary session can be carried over to a second session (this happened with the Constitutional Reform Bill in 2004), but a Bill cannot be carried over from one Parliament to the next (when a general election is called there is usually a rush to get as many as possible of the Bills then before Parliament through all their stages before Parliament rises for the election campaign). Once the Parliamentary stages of a Bill are complete it is then accorded Royal Assent and immediately becomes an Act, although the date on which it comes into force will depend on what the Act itself says about its commencement (see below).

Legislation in the Northern Ireland Assembly may potentially go through even more stages than legislation at Westminster.[22] Standing Orders, amended in June 2000,[23] provide for:

(1)   a *First Stage*, when the Bill is formally introduced by the Clerk of the Assembly reading its title;[24]

(2)   a *Second Stage*, when there is a general debate on the Bill's general principles;

(3)   a *Committee Stage*, when, normally within 30 days, the details of the Bill are investigated and reported to the Assembly together with proposals for amendments;

(4)   a *Consideration Stage*, when the Members of the Legislative Assembly (MLAs) can vote on the details of the Bill, including proposed amendments;

---

[21] Parliament Act 1949, amending the Parliament Act 1911. The legality of the 1949 Act was confirmed in litigation brought by the Countryside Alliance in relation to the Hunting Act 2004: see *R (on the application of Jackson and others)* v *HM Attorney General* [2005] EWCA Civ 126. A separate case is pending on whether the Hunting Act 2004 is compatible with the European Convention on Human Rights.

[22] Northern Ireland Act 1998, s. 13.

[23] See in particular Standing Orders 28-40. They are readable on-line at www.ni-assembly.gov.uk/so.htm.

[24] An explanatory and financial memorandum must accompany the Bill on its introduction.

(5)   a *Further Consideration Stage*, when further such votes can take place; and

(6)   a *Final Stage*, when the Bill is either passed or rejected without further amendment.

At any point before the Final Stage, the Bill can also be referred to the Northern Ireland Human Rights Commission for advice on whether the Bill is compatible with human rights and/or to an *ad hoc* Assembly Committee on Conformity with Equality Requirements for a report on whether the Bill complies with standards on equality and human rights.[25] After the Final Stage, the Bill can be reconsidered by the Assembly if, for example, the Judicial Committee of the Privy Council decides that part of it is not within the legislative competence of the Assembly. Normally there must be an interval of five working days between each stage of a Bill; the stages can be accelerated but no Bill can pass all its stages in less than 10 days. An uncompleted Bill can be carried forward from one Assembly session to the next if the Assembly so agrees. A Bill is sent for Royal Assent once all the Assembly stages have been gone through.

The granting of Royal Assent does not automatically bring an Act into force (whether it is an Act of the Westminster Parliament or of the Northern Ireland Assembly). This will be so only if the Act contains no other indication as to when or how it is to be brought into force. Often an Act says that it is to come into force when a "Commencement Order" has been made (often by a government Minister). In some cases this is not made until years after the granting of Royal Assent. The Equal Pay Act (NI) 1970 was not brought into force until 1976; section 3(1) of the Carriage by Air and Road Act 1979 was not brought into force until 22 October 1998.[26] The Easter Act 1928 (which provided for a fixed date for Easter), the Employment of Children Act 1973 and the Smoke Detectors Act 1991 (which required all new dwellings to be fitted with smoke detectors) are examples of Acts where the mechanism for bringing them into force has *never* been activated.[27]

There is a constitutional convention (*i.e.* custom and practice) to the effect that legislation should not be retrospective in operation, but occasionally this is ignored, as when the Government needs to validate

---

[25] To date neither type of referral has occurred.

[26] Carriage by Air and Road Act 1979 (Commencement No. 3) Order 1998.

[27] *Current Law Statutes (Service File)* contains a useful loose-leaf table listing alphabetically the statutory provisions enacted since 1949 which are not yet in force.

some actions which would otherwise be illegal. An example is the Northern Ireland Act 1972, which declared that as from 1920 the law was different from that laid down by the judges in *R (Hume)* v *Londonderry Justices* (1972).[28] In a recent case a Northern Ireland judge said that if a statute was silent as to whether it was retrospective or not then a test of fairness had to be applied to see whether it should operate retrospectively.[29]

The enactment of legislation usually takes months, although at Westminster Bills which are really urgent can be dealt with in a day or two. The Northern Ireland Act 1972 obtained its second reading in the Commons and Royal Assent within the space of four-and-a-half hours. In 1974, following the Birmingham pub bombings, the Prevention of Terrorism (Temporary Provisions) Act was passed in great haste too, as was the Criminal Justice (Terrorism and Conspiracy) Act 1998 in the wake of the Omagh atrocity in August 1998.

The form of statutes

Today, statutes are set out in a traditional format, an example of which is given in Appendix 1 of this book. The Act which is partly reproduced there, the Theft Act (NI) 1969, is still largely in force today, although it has been amended from time to time, most notably by the Theft (NI) Order 1978 (also reproduced in Appendix 1) and the Theft (Amendment) (NI) Order 1997.[30] Its format displays most of the standard features. We can note 10 of these:

(1)   The Chapter number ("16"). This is the number given to the Act at the time of its publication; its purpose is simply to make identification of the Act easier when it is being looked up.

(2)   The long title. This provides a brief summary of the Act's purposes and effects; it expands upon the Act's short title, which is simply the Theft Act (NI) 1969 (see (9) below).[31]

---

[28] [1972] NI 91. See also 2.3 below.

[29] *Re Partition Acts 1868 and 1876, Ulster Bank Ltd* v *Carter* [1999] NI 93.

[30] The law on theft in Northern Ireland is identical to that in England and Wales, where the equivalent legislation is the Theft Act 1968, the Theft Act 1978 and the Theft (Amendment) Act 1996. For a fully amended version of the Theft Act (NI) 1969, see www.northernireland-legislation.hmso.gov.uk/legislation/northernireland/nisr/ni-welcome.htm.

[31] An Act's short title can be changed by a later Act. The Constitutional Reform Act 2005, Sch. 11, para. 1, changes the name of the Supreme Court Act 1981 to the Senior Courts Act 1981.

(3)   The date ("10th July 1969"). This is the date on which the Act
        was finally made, that is, the date on which the Royal Assent
        was given. In this particular Act, however, section 33(1)
        provides that the Act is not to come into force until 1 August
        1969. Had there not been any such provision, the Act would
        have come into force from the date given after the long title.

(4)   The enacting words ("Be it enacted..."). This is a standard
        formula placed at the beginning of all Northern Ireland statutes
        enacted between 1921 and 1972 simply to indicate which
        Parliament made the statute. The enacting words for UK statutes
        differ accordingly,[32] as do those for Acts made by the new
        Northern Ireland Assembly.

(5)   Sections and subsections. Each Act is divided into sections,
        which are numbered 1, 2, 3, etc. Sections are in turn divided into
        subsections, which are numbered (1), (2), (3), etc. Subsections
        can then be split into paragraphs: (a), (b), (c) etc. The next
        subdivision is called a subparagraph: (i), (ii), (iii), etc. Reference
        is made to a subparagraph by writing it as follows: s. 32(2)(b)(i)
        (pronounced as "section thirty-two, two, b, one"). While a statute
        is passing through Parliament it is called a Bill, not an Act, and
        its provisions are divided into clauses, not sections, but further
        subdivisions are still called subsections and paragraphs.

(6)   Marginal notes. The words in the margins beside each section
        summarise the effect of the section for ease of reference; strictly
        speaking they do not constitute part of the law. Whenever other
        statutes are mentioned in sections a reference is placed in the
        margin to enable the reader to find them more easily when
        looking them up in a library or on the internet.

(7)   The interpretation section. Most statutes contain a section near
        the end defining more precisely some of the expressions used
        earlier. The Theft Act (NI) 1969 makes do with defining some
        words in section 32(2); note that an exact definition of
        "enactment" is provided, whereas only partial explanations of
        "gain", "loss" and "goods" are given. This leaves it open to a
        judge to say that those terms embrace other things as well.

---

[32] A different form of words is used for those Acts passed by the House of Commons
alone.

(8)   The commencement section. The penultimate or final section of every Act usually contains a provision concerning the operation in time of the Act: see section 33(1) of the 1969 Act. In UK statutes this section will also cover the geographical extent of the Act, that is, whether it is to apply in Scotland and in Northern Ireland as well as in England and Wales; some statutes apply in only a part or parts of the United Kingdom, for example the Public Services Ombudsman (Wales) Act 2005 applies only in Wales[33] while the Congenital Disabilities (Civil Liability) Act 1976 applies throughout the United Kingdom except Scotland. Any Act with the words "Northern Ireland" in the title will, with the exception perhaps of one or two sections, apply only in Northern Ireland.

(9)   The short title etc. section. Every statute ends with a section giving the short title of the Act; when a statute is passed dealing with a topic for which legislation already exists, the Acts can be referred to together (*e.g.* the Fatal Accidents Acts 1959-1977).

(10)   Schedules. Many Acts contain one or more Schedules setting out further details of matters mentioned in the body of the Act (see Sch. 1 to the 1969 Act) or listing in tabular form the statutory provisions repealed by the Act (see Sch. 3). Sometimes a Schedule will also set out the amendments being made by the Act (see Sch. 2), but if there are not too many of these they may be catered for in the body of the Act itself. Schedules are not self-enacting: somewhere in the Act there must be a provision stating that the Schedules are to have the force of law: see sections 30(1), 31(1) and 31(2) of the 1969 Act.

An important formal feature of statutes which is not illustrated by the Theft Act (NI) 1969 is the division of longer Acts into Parts.[34] This is simply a method of ensuring that all the provisions concerned with a particular matter are bunched together in the same place within a statute. Occasionally, Parts of statutes are sub-divided into Chapters.[35]

---

[33] See generally T. Jones and J. Williams, "Wales as a Jurisdiction" [2004] PL 78.
[34] Although Sch. 3 to the 1969 Act *is* divided into two Parts, Pt. I listing "Penal enactments superseded by this Act" and Pt. II listing "Consequential and miscellaneous repeals".
[35] *E.g.* Constitutional Reform Act 2005, Pt. IV (headed "Judicial Appointments and Discipline").

To help the reader to find a particular provision, some pieces of long legislation are now published with an index.

The problems of looking for statute law

Even if you can recognise and read a statute when you find one, this will not be much help to you unless you know how to look for it in the first place. The trouble is that most Acts of Parliament are designed to operate prospectively, that is, for the future and not the past. They remain in force even after the Parliament which made them has been dissolved. When new legislation is enacted, amendments (*i.e.* changes) often have to be made to the statutes which are already in force. It can thus be very difficult to discover the current legal position on a certain matter if there are several statutes purporting to deal with it, some dating back a long time.

In Northern Ireland the problems are accentuated by the fact that - as noted in Chapter 1 - since the fourteenth century there have been many Parliaments claiming the power to legislate for the area which is now Northern Ireland. As a result, the Northern Ireland "statute book" - the complete collection of statutory provisions currently in force in the province - is very large indeed. The collection comprises the work of seven separate legislatures:

(1)   the Parliament of England, from 1226 to 1707;

(2)   the Parliament of Ireland, from 1310 to 1800;

(3)   the Parliament of Great Britain, from 1707 to 1800;

(4)   the Parliament of the United Kingdom, from 1801 to the present;

(5)   the Parliament of Northern Ireland, from 1921 to 1972;

(6)   the Northern Ireland Assembly, 1974;[36] and

(7)   the new Northern Ireland Assembly, from 2000.

Many of the statutes of these Parliaments remain in force, or partly in force, even though they are of virtually no significance in practice: about 50 statutes of the Parliament in Ireland still apply, as do about 70 statutes of the Parliaments of England and Great Britain. In more recent times statutes have included provisions to repeal earlier statutes which are being superseded and indeed sometimes whole Acts are passed purely to rid the statute book of redundant laws such as the Statute Law

---

[36] The enactments of this Assembly were called Measures, not Acts.

(Repeals) Act 2004 (which extends to Northern Ireland).[37] It can still be difficult, though, to determine precisely the current statutory position on a particular topic. Sometimes statutory provisions are repealed even before they have been brought into force,[38] and some Acts, amazingly, contain provisions repealing some of their own provisions![39] The difficulty is compounded when one realises that some statutes passed by Parliament at Westminster have not made it clear whether they are meant to apply in Northern Ireland as well as in the rest of Britain, although the rule is that, if the Act itself is silent on the matter, it is presumed to apply throughout the United Kingdom.

Were it simply a matter of knowing which statutes have been repealed and which are still in force, the problem of looking for statute law would be fairly manageable. But we have to remember that statutes can be amended as well as totally repealed. When this occurs (see, *e.g.* Sch. 2 to the Theft Act (NI) 1969), the earlier statute is not re-enacted, or even reprinted, in its new form: you have to read it in its original form and then read what the amending statute provides. Amendments can be introduced by Acts which have very little in common with the original statute, for example by a Criminal Justice (Miscellaneous Provisions) Act or an Administration of Justice Act.[40] They can even be introduced by secondary legislation, described in the next section. Occasionally the up-to-date version of a heavily amended statute is reproduced in a legal textbook. As we shall see, the internet is of help in this context too.

---

[37] Such Acts are usually the outcome of reviews carried out by the Law Commissions (see Chap. 9.14). Note too that under the Regulatory Reform Act 2001, s. 6(1), the Government is able to make Orders to amend or repeal provisions in primary legislation which are considered to impose a burden on businesses or others and which could be reduced or removed without removing any necessary protection.

[38] *E.g.* s. 44 of the Criminal Procedure and Investigations Act 1996 repealed some sections of the Criminal Justice and Public Order Act 1994 before they were commenced and reinstated some provisions which had been repealed by the 1994 Act.

[39] *E.g.* Sch. 13 to the Justice (NI) Act 2002 repeals (or "revokes") s. 9(10) and (13) of the Act itself. Presumably these reflect last minute changes to the Act.

[40] Consider this example: The Employment Rights (NI) Order 1996, art. 67, was amended by the insertion of art. 67K by the Public Interest Disclosure (NI) Order 1998, art. 3, and then again by the insertion of art. 67KA by the Police (NI) Act 2003, s. 26(1).

Printed volumes of legislation

To make the search for statute law easier, The Stationery Office publishes various auxiliary volumes. The statutes themselves are published and sold singly at the time they are enacted, as well as collectively in bound or loose-leaf volumes at the end of each calendar year. In Northern Ireland these annual volumes continued to be produced after 1972, even though they contained not primary legislation but Orders in Council made under the Northern Ireland Acts 1974 and 2000. Each pre-1972 volume contains Tables showing the UK and Northern Ireland Acts repealed or amended by Northern Ireland Acts during that year, as well as Tables showing the Northern Ireland Acts affected by UK Acts passed during the year and the full list of UK Acts passed that year which were applicable in Northern Ireland. The annual index to the statutes also lists the amendments made to Acts by secondary legislation.

Every three years or so an index is published to all the statutory provisions currently in force in Northern Ireland, arranged under distinct subject-headings. Another Table is now published in loose-leaf form listing all the statute law which affects, or has affected, Northern Ireland, this time arranged in chronological order and with amendments and repeals noted (the latest edition covers up to the end of 2003). Both these works amount to weighty tomes (in fact the index is in two volumes), but they are indispensable because they also include references to statutes passed for the whole of the United Kingdom. They permit you to tell at a glance what primary legislation exists on any matter and whether primary legislation which once existed has been amended or repealed. The position can be so complicated, however, that even in these volumes mistakes and omissions are not uncommon.

The *Statutes Revised, Northern Ireland* is a 16-volume collection of the public Acts of the Parliaments of Ireland, England, Great Britain, the United Kingdom and Northern Ireland which have affected Northern Ireland up to 1950, whether or not they deal with matters which were finally placed within the legislative competence of the Parliament of Northern Ireland. The texts are reprinted as amended, with the amending and repealing schedules therefore excluded. In 1982 the Statutory Publications Office of the Department of Finance and Personnel produced in loose-leaf form a nine-volume second edition of the *Statutes Revised*, which sets out in chronological order the text, also amended, of all the statutes affecting Northern Ireland between 1921 and 1981. Unfortunately this excludes the relevant UK statutes enacted since 1920, but a four volume series (A-D) appended to the edition reprints the amended texts of all pre-1920 legislation, from whatever parliamentary source, still in force in Northern Ireland. Cumulative supplements to *Statutes Revised* are now published annually to show what changes have occurred during the past year - these are *vital* to anyone looking up the current state of legislation in Northern Ireland.

All UK statutes, as well as being published singly and in annual collections, are indexed by the two-volume *Index to the Statutes* published every two years. Two private publishing companies also produce versions of these statutes with comments and annotations: these are the series known as *Halsbury's Statutes* and *Current Law Statutes*. The latter now include an "arrangement of sections" at the start and an index at the end of each statute as well as, for consolidating statutes, a Table of Derivations showing where provisions were previously to be found in legislation and a Table of Destinations showing where old provisions now appear in the new statute. *Statutes in Force* provides the service for England and Wales which *Statutes Revised* provides for Northern Ireland; it comprises scores of loose-leaf volumes.

Legislation on the internet

The advent of computerised information retrieval systems has immensely facilitated the search for primary (as well as secondary) legislation. All primary legislation enacted by the Westminster Parliament since 1988 is on-line,[41] as are *all* Acts issued by the new Northern Ireland Assembly,[42] the Scottish Parliament[43] and the Irish Parliament (the Oireachtas).[44] Legislation can often be accessed through commercial information systems, such as LEXIS, or from non-official websites such as that of the British and Irish Legal Information Institute.[45]

Users of Northern Ireland legislation, however, have an advantage over users of other laws in the United Kingdom in that there is a website which sets out *in amended form* all the Acts of the Stormont Parliament

---

[41] www.opsi.gov.uk/acts.htm.
[42] *Ibid.*
[43] *Ibid.*
[44] www.acts.oireachtas.ie/en.toc.decade.html (all Acts back to 1922).
[45] www.bailii.org.

or Assembly and all the Orders in Council made during periods of direct rule.[46] Updating occurs once a year and the site is currently accurate up to the end of 2003. The site does not include Acts passed at Westminster which apply in Northern Ireland. Thus, it carries up-to-date versions of laws such as the Theft Act (NI) 1969 and the Children (NI) Order 1995, but not the Judicature (NI) Act 1978 or the Northern Ireland Act 1998. It is nevertheless an extremely useful tool for all lawyers and students of law in Northern Ireland.

An on-line Statute Law Database for legislation applying in England and Wales (some of which will be relevant to Northern Ireland as well) is still under construction. When completed it will allow users to access the up-to-date text of all 3,500 or so Acts of the Westminster Parliament still in force, together with secondary legislation.

2.2 SECONDARY LEGISLATION

All pieces of secondary legislation are ultimately the offspring of a parent (or "enabling") Act of Parliament. They are used in order to lay down the law in more detail than is normally contained in primary legislation, or where it would be too time-consuming to invoke the full Parliamentary process just to make a fairly minor alteration in some existing legislative arrangements. The parent Act will give power to a law-making authority to issue detailed laws on a particular matter. The law-making authority is usually the head of a government department (*i.e.* a Secretary of State) but it can also be, for instance, the Privy Council (which makes Orders in Council), a committee of judges and lawyers (which makes Rules of Court) or a district council or public authority (which makes byelaws). The exact title of the particular piece of secondary legislation will depend on the wording of the parent Act: it may provide for an Order in Council, an order, regulations, rules, schemes or byelaws. Nothing turns on the differences in title - all varieties of secondary legislation are equally binding as laws of the land, but not all of the documents will be equally easy to find: not all of them, for example, are published as "statutory rules". Some examples of secondary legislation, together with their parent Acts and the authority empowered by the Acts to make the legislation are given in Table 5 on page 71 below.

---

[46] www.northernireland-legislation.hmso.gov.uk/legislation/northernireland/nisr/ni-welcome.htm.

Other official documents

There are various official documents which the lay person often believes have the full force of law but which in fact do not. Even though they are sometimes issued pursuant to a power conferred by an Act of Parliament, they can only influence, not dictate, the judges' views on what the law should be. Such publications include the Highway Code (published by the Department for Transport but only some of the rules it contains are actually legal requirements), the Guide to Effective Practice in Religious Equality of Opportunity in Employment (issued by the former Department of Economic Development in Northern Ireland), the Public Authority Equality Scheme Guidelines (issued by the Equality Commission for Northern Ireland[47]), the codes of practice agreed to by various trade associations (see Chap. 9.13), the standing orders issued to the Northern Ireland Prison Service by the Northern Ireland Office and the codes of practice issued by the Northern Ireland Office under the Police and Criminal Evidence (NI) Order 1989 (see Chap. 5.1). Indeed codes of practice are becoming common in all sorts of legal fields.[48] There are now also documents called codes of courtesy, for example, those on the use of Irish and Ulster Scots issued by the Northern Ireland Court Service in 2004.

Her Majesty's Revenue and Customs[49] frequently issues policy statements which are treated by the courts as having this semi-legislative status: the statements declare that the Revenue will make extra-statutory concessions, that is, not charge tax on certain specified payments. Statements of practice published by insurance companies, and circulars put out by the Home Office and other government departments on a wide range of legal matters are also in this category. Judges, Masters and registrars announce what are called "Practice Directions" in order to provide for better organisation of

---

[47] See Chap. 9.3.

[48] *E.g.* the Code of Practice for financial investigators (issued in 1998 under the Proceeds of Crime (NI) Order 1996) and the Code of Practice on picketing (issued in 1998 by the Department of Economic Development under the Industrial Relations (NI) Order 1992).

[49] From 1 April 2005 this is the new name of the now combined Inland Revenue and HM Customs and Excise: see the Commissioners for Revenue and Customs Act 2005 (which also established a Revenue and Customs Prosecution Office).

proceedings within the courts.[50] Just because a matter is catered for in some such semi-official document (which may not even be available to the general public), rather than in a piece of secondary legislation, does not mean that it is of little legal significance - it more usually means that strict legal standards are deemed inappropriate for the matter. Consequently, issues as diverse as the level of permissible noise from ice-cream vans and the strip-searching of persons in police custody are dealt with by this kind of document.

Types of secondary legislation

Although all pieces of secondary legislation have the same legal status, they nevertheless differ in form. Quite apart from the variations in their titles, mentioned above, it is helpful to distinguish between three different types of secondary legislation affecting Northern Ireland. The first two are special because they are made in England; only the third type is made within Northern Ireland itself. Because of this difference in the origins of secondary legislation it can often be quite difficult, as in the case of primary legislation, to determine exactly which law is applicable in the province. However, the difficulty is not as acute as in the case of primary legislation because secondary legislation did not become common until the nineteenth century. We shall look next at the three types of secondary legislation separately. Meanwhile Table 5, below, illustrates the varieties of means by which secondary legislation can be generated. It can be seen that each piece of secondary legislation is usually given a number to aid its identification. Statutory instruments which relate to Northern Ireland, or which specify when another piece of legislation is to commence (*i.e.* come into force), or which create rules of procedure for courts, are given not just an SI number but also a number prefixed with NI, C or L.

---

[50] These are available on the website of the Northern Ireland Court Service (under "Judicial Decisions") and are reprinted in the *Bulletin of Northern Ireland Law*. For a recent important example see Supreme Court Practice Direction No.1/2005, covering the use of skeleton arguments in the Court of Appeal and High Court and the preparation of "appeal books" in both civil and criminal appeals: [2005] 2 BNIL 72.

TABLE 5: EXAMPLES OF SECONDARY LEGISLATION

(1) The parent Act →   (2) The law-making authority →   (3) The secondary legislation
Northern Ireland Act 2000, Sch., para. 1(1) →   Her Majesty (*i.e.* the Privy Council) →   Anti-social Behaviour (NI) Order 2004 (SI 1998; NI 12), art. 1(2) →   The Secretary of State (for Northern Ireland) →   Anti-social Behaviour (2004 Order) (Commencement No.1) Order (NI) 2004 (SR 373; C. 16)
Communications Act 2003, s. 411 →   The Secretary of State (for Culture, Media and Sport) →   Communications Act 2003 (Commencement No. 3) Order 2004 (SI 3309; C.150)
Employment Relations Act 2004, s. 42 →   The Secretary of State (for Trade and Industry) →   Information and Consultation of Employees Regulations 2004 (SI 3426)
Civil Procedure Act 1997, s. 2 →   Civil Procedure Rules Committee →   Civil Procedure (Amendment) Rules 2004 (SI 1306; L.8)
Public Lending Rights Act 1979, s. 3 →   The Secretary of State (for Culture, Media and Sport) →   Public Lending Rights Scheme 1982

Statutory instruments

In England and Wales most of the secondary legislation is published in the form of consecutively numbered "statutory instruments". There were 3,452 issued in 2004 (including 297 made by the National

Assembly of Wales).[51] A common type of statutory instrument is a "commencement order", which stipulates when an Act, or a certain section of an Act, is to come into force. Commencement orders are now given a separate "C" number when published, as well as an "SI" number. There were 160 of them in 2004.

Some statutory instruments, being made under the authority of a parent Act which extends beyond England and Wales, are applicable in Northern Ireland. Thus, for example, the Trade Marks (Fees) Rules 1998 apply in Northern Ireland because the enabling Act is a statute in force throughout the United Kingdom, namely the Trade Marks Act 1994. But the Packaging and Labelling of Dangerous Substances Regulations 1978 do not apply in Northern Ireland because their enabling Act (the Consumer Protection Act 1961) does not apply outside England, Wales and Scotland. So it is not always possible to tell merely from the title of a statutory instrument whether it applies in Northern Ireland; one has to read the statutory instrument itself or look back at the enabling Act.

Contrariwise, as some Westminster statutes have an effect only within Northern Ireland, the legislative powers delegated by such Acts can themselves be effective only within Northern Ireland. Their title will contain the words "Northern Ireland" *before* the word "Rules", "Regulations", "Order", etc. An example is the Northern Ireland Act 2000 (Modification) Order 2005, made under the authority of paragraph 1(4) of the Schedule to the Northern Ireland Act 2000.[52] There are usually a dozen or so of these each year.

In 2003, for example, 30 statutory instruments were made affecting only Northern Ireland.[53] A further 517 were made affecting the United Kingdom generally[54] (out of 3,452 made altogether). A large percentage of statutory instruments are made in order to comply with the UK's obligations as a member of the European Union: section 2(2)

---

[51] A further 566 were made by the Scottish Parliament, but these are published separately from the UK Statutory Instruments.

[52] There is a section of the Northern Ireland legislation website listing Acts of the UK Parliament since 1996, and UK statutory instruments since 1997, which apply exclusively or primarily in Northern Ireland: www.opsi.gov.uk/legislation/northern ireland/ni-acts/htm.

[53] Northern Ireland Statutory Rules 2003, Pt. IV, pp. 3203-4. An example is the Terrorism Act 2000 (Code of Practice on Video Recording of Interviews) (NI) Order 2003.

[54] *Ibid.* pp. 3205-25.

of the European Communities Act 1972 is one of the most important enabling provisions in our law.

Orders in Council

Orders in Council are in fact just one species of the more general category of statutory instruments described above. They are often viewed as the most important type of secondary legislation because they are formally made by the Queen on the advice of her Privy Councillors (*i.e.* senior government Ministers of the day: see Chap. 1.4). But in general they carry no more weight than any other type of delegated legislation and in appropriate cases can be invalidated by Parliament or by the courts to just the same extent (see below).

There are a number of Acts providing for the making of Orders in Council which might apply in Northern Ireland as well as in other parts of the United Kingdom, for example the Administration of Justice Act 1985. However, the reason for listing Orders in Council here as a separate type of secondary legislation is that, since the suspension of the Northern Ireland Parliament in 1972, there have been four enabling Acts which in effect have substituted legislation in the form of Orders in Council for legislation which, had it not been suspended or abolished, the Parliament or Assembly at Stormont would have enacted. These four Acts, which succeeded one another, are the Northern Ireland (Temporary Provisions) Act 1972, the Northern Ireland Act 1974, the Northern Ireland Act 1998 and the Northern Ireland Act 2000.

For example, Orders in Council made under the Northern Ireland Act 1974 created laws for Northern Ireland on subjects which, being "transferred matters" under the Northern Ireland Constitution Act 1973, would have been legislated for by the Northern Ireland Assembly if it had survived the first few months of 1974. "Reserved" matters under the Northern Ireland Constitution Act 1973 were also dealt with by Orders in Council. Only "excepted" matters needed to be legislated for by an Act of Parliament at Westminster. "Law and order" was a reserved matter but "terrorism" was an excepted matter, which is why there were Northern Ireland (Emergency Provisions) *Acts* rather than *Orders*.

Orders in Council after the Good Friday Agreement

When powers were devolved to the Northern Ireland Assembly in 1999, the Order in Council procedure provided for in the Northern Ireland Act 1974 was abolished.[55] The position reverted, more or less, to what it was prior to the abolition of Stormont in 1972: some Acts governing Northern Ireland were made in Belfast, while others were made in London, and likewise some pieces of secondary legislation governing Northern Ireland (statutory rules) were made in Belfast while others (statutory instruments) were made in London. It is to be noted, however, that the categories of "transferred", "reserved" and "excepted" matters are not the same under the Northern Ireland Act 1998 as they were under the Northern Ireland Constitution Act 1973 or under the Government of Ireland Act 1920. However, because the range of "reserved" matters is greater in the 1998 Act than it was in the 1973 Act, the 1998 Act keeps in place the Privy Council's power to make Orders in Council for Northern Ireland.[56] More particularly, it allows Orders in Council to be made which amend existing Northern Ireland legislation on reserved matters; drafts of these Orders have to be referred to the Northern Ireland Assembly for its consideration and if the Assembly reports its views to the Secretary of State the latter must submit a copy of this report along with a draft of the Order to both Houses of Parliament at Westminster.[57] This is the procedure adopted for the Financial Investigations (NI) Order 2001, which amended the Proceeds of Crime (NI) Order 1996.

When the Northern Ireland Assembly was suspended in February 2000 (for what turned out to be about four months), the power to make Orders in Council at Westminster was revived by virtue of the Northern Ireland Act 2000.[58] The Equality (Disability, etc) (NI) Order 2000 and the Flags (NI) Order 2000 were made during this period. A Sinn Féin Assembly member challenged the Secretary of State's right to place the Flags (NI) Order (and the Flags Regulations (NI) 2000), before Parliament for its consideration, but he failed.[59] When the Assembly was again suspended at midnight on 14 October 2002, the Northern Ireland Act 2000 operated to restore the power to make Orders in

---

[55] The whole of that Act was repealed by the Northern Ireland Act 1998.
[56] Ss. 84-86.
[57] S. 85(4)-(6).
[58] Para. 1(1) of the Sch.
[59] *In re Murphy's Application* [2001] 8 BNIL 11.

Council. In 2003 there were 19 Orders in Council made under the 2002 Act and in 2004 there were 23.

Orders in Council made under the Northern Ireland Acts 1974 and 2000 are published and numbered as UK statutory instruments, a separate "NI" number being given to them for publication in annual collections of Northern Ireland Orders in Council. These collections continue the series known as Acts of the Northern Ireland Parliament, so many people would view these Orders as having, to all intents and purposes, the status of primary legislation. This is not strictly the case, because unlike primary legislation they can be challenged by the courts (see below). As we shall see, it is not unusual for Orders made under the 1974 and 2000 Acts to sub-delegate law-making powers to other authorities, even though the general rule for secondary legislation is that further delegation of powers is not possible.[60] These Orders can also amend or repeal primary legislation, which again is contrary to the normal rule for secondary legislation. Sections in Acts which allow secondary legislation to amend primary legislation are called Henry VIII clauses, because they became popular during that king's reign (1509-47).[61] There is a copy of a typical Order in Council set out in Appendix 1 of this book (the Theft (NI) Order 1978).

It should be noted that not every item of legislation given the title "Order" is in fact an Order in Council. Of the 30 statutory instruments affecting only Northern Ireland in 2003 that were not Orders in Council, 20 were entitled Orders (the rest being Regulations). An example is the Northern Ireland Act 2000 (Modification) Order 2003. Even more confusingly, the word "Order" is also used for some more ordinary pieces of secondary legislation which fall within the third type, described next.

Statutory rules

Statutory rules are made by law-making authorities in Northern Ireland under a power conferred by an Act of the UK Parliament, by an Act of the Parliament or Assembly of Northern Ireland or by an Order in Council made under the Northern Ireland Acts 1974, 1998 or 2000. They are really Northern Ireland equivalents to the statutory

---

[60] The Latin maxim is *delegatus non potest delegare*.

[61] They are becoming popular again today. See N. Barber and A. Young, "The Rise of Prospective Henry VIII Clauses and their Implications for Sovereignty" [2003] PL 112.

instruments made for the rest of the United Kingdom. Sometimes they differ from the corresponding statutory instruments in title alone, the actual content remaining virtually identical. The title will always contain the words "Northern Ireland" placed in brackets *after* the words "Rules", "Regulations", "Order", "Scheme", etc. A typical illustration of statutory rules would be the General Food Regulations (NI) 2004, which were made by the Department of Health, Social Services and Public Safety in Northern Ireland under powers conferred by the Food Safety (NI) Order 1991 and which are almost identical to the General Food Regulations 2004,[62] made under the Food Safety Act 1990 and applying only in England, Wales and Scotland. An example of statutory rules creating a "Scheme" is the Farm Nutrient Management Scheme (NI) 2005, made by the Department of Agriculture and Rural Development in exercise of powers conferred by the Agriculture and Fisheries (Financial Assistance) (NI) Order 1987.

As in the case of Orders, not all laws with the title "Rules" are in fact what they seem. They may not be statutory rules at all but statutory instruments issued just for Northern Ireland on a reserved or excepted matter; an example is the European Parliamentary Elections (NI) Regulations 2004. Such statutory instruments are recognisable from the position of the words "Northern Ireland" *before* the word "Rules". To repeat, however, the difference in title does not affect the legislation's status.

In 2004 there were 527 statutory rules made for Northern Ireland. They were issued by over a dozen rule-making bodies, particularly by the Department of Agriculture and Rural Development and the Department of the Environment, and they dealt with a huge range of subjects. As in the case of statutory instruments there are types of statutory rules which recur frequently, such as commencement orders and those setting new financial amounts to keep pace with inflation. Respective examples would be the Protection of Children and Vulnerable Adults (Commencement No.1) Order (NI) 2004[63] and the Health and Safety (Fees) Regulations (NI) 2004.

There is a copy of a typical statutory rule reproduced in Appendix 1 of this book, namely the Employer's Liability (Compulsory Insurance) (Amendment) Regulations (NI) 2004, made by the Department of

---

[62] Both sets of Regulations implement various requirements of European Community law. See further 2.5 below.
[63] There were 30 commencement orders issued as statutory rules in 2004.

Enterprise, Trade and Investment in exercise of powers conferred by the Employer's Liability (Defective Equipment and Compulsory Insurance) (NI) Order 1972. At least half of all statutory rules issued these days are ones which amend existing rules.

Many statutory rules, like statutory instruments, deal with local matters such as road traffic or railways. A recent example is the Motor Hackney Carriages (Belfast) (Amendment) Byelaws 2004, made by the Department of the Environment in exercise of powers conferred by article 65 of the Road Traffic (NI) Order 1981. It sets out how much licensed taxi drivers in Belfast can charge their customers. Byelaws, incidentally, can also be made by many other public authorities, such as the Fisheries Conservancy Board for Northern Ireland,[64] the Trustees of the Ulster Folk and Transport Museum, Northern Ireland Railways and Harbour Authorities. Byelaws made by district councils are not published as statutory rules but they have the same legal status as such rules.

The making of secondary legislation

Whatever type of secondary legislation is eventually made, and in whatever form, it is invariably drafted only after a period of consultation with interested parties. Except occasionally, the final drafting is performed by civil servants within the legal branches of the government department concerned, not, as is the case with primary legislation, by parliamentary counsel (*i.e.* experts trained in drafting).

Orders in Council issued under the Northern Ireland Act 2000 are given special treatment, as were those issued under the 1974 and 1998 Acts. Proposals for new Orders are first considered by a committee of senior civil servants and then by a committee of government Ministers. Instructions for a draft Order are then sent to the Legislative Draftsman's Office in Belfast. When a draft has been prepared and approved by the Ministers it is circulated to the public in the form of a "Proposal for a Draft Order in Council" and is accompanied by an Explanatory Memorandum. Usually about six weeks are allowed for comments. The Northern Ireland Grand Committee at the House of Commons might be consulted if the area being dealt with is a contentious one. The comments made on the proposal are then considered and the drafting expert prepares a final draft to be laid before Parliament.

---

[64] *E.g.* the Fisheries Byelaws (NI) 1997.

Parliamentary procedures

Speaking very generally, the precise method of creating secondary legislation depends on the importance of the secondary legislation in question. In all cases, however, the legislation must be affirmed or annulled by Parliament (or the Northern Ireland Assembly) in its entirety: it cannot be amended while it is being debated, although it can be withdrawn and re-laid later in a revised form. Usually the most important pieces of secondary legislation - and Orders in Council made under the 1974 and 2000 Acts fall into this category - must be laid in draft form before both Houses of Parliament, and be approved by both Houses, before being presented to the Queen for her formal assent. This process puts the onus on the Government to find time for Parliament to debate and affirm the legislation before it can finally be made: if no debate takes place then the secondary legislation cannot come into operation. Secondary legislation which is urgent, and for which no time is immediately available for a parliamentary debate, can be made without first being laid before Parliament, but it must cease to have effect if each House does not approve it within a specified period, usually 28 or 40 days. No Order in Council for Northern Ireland seems to have been made under this urgent procedure since 1987. Both of these legislative processes may be termed "affirmative" procedures because the legislation does not have effect, or ceases to have effect, unless it is affirmed. The Northern Ireland Assembly, when it is not suspended, also allows for these two kinds of process and each of them ("the affirmative resolution procedure" and "the confirmatory resolution procedure") has been used on a few occasions.

An alternative is the "negative" procedure, whereby the legislation takes effect, or continues to have effect if already made, unless a "prayer" in either House (or in the Northern Ireland Assembly) specifically annuls it within 40 days. Given the quantity of secondary legislation requiring to be made, this is the preferred method of proceeding. The negative resolution procedure is also employed for those Orders in Council which are almost identical to English legislation already enacted and for which a separate parliamentary debate is deemed unnecessary. In such cases the English Act will contain a section saying that equivalent legislation can be made for Northern Ireland under the negative resolution procedure and the preamble to the Order in Council will state that it is being made for purposes corresponding to those of the provisions of the equivalent

English Act. The Theft (Amendment) (NI) Order 1997, for example, has a preamble stating "Whereas this Order is made only for purposes corresponding to the purposes of the Theft (Amendment) Act 1996".[65] When this negative resolution procedure is used the draft Order is not preceded by a published proposal but is simply made by the Privy Council and laid before Parliament. The vast majority of today's statutory rules are put through the Northern Ireland Assembly (or the Parliament at Westminster if the Assembly is suspended) by this negative resolution procedure. There is just not enough time for full debates on every proposed statutory rule.

Less important secondary legislation may be required to be laid before Parliament but is not subject to either the affirmative or the negative procedure. Such legislation cannot be debated, but ministerial questions can be asked about it, and because it must be laid it cannot usually come into force before the date of laying. If it is essential that the statutory instrument comes into force before being laid, the Speakers of the House of Commons and the House of Lords must be notified.

The least important secondary legislation need not be laid before Parliament at all, although again questions can be asked about it if an MP or peer happens to have his or her attention drawn to it. The statutory instruments which are afforded this most cursory treatment are mostly local in nature. An unfortunate consequence of direct rule in Northern Ireland is that the secondary legislation which would have been subject to the negative resolution procedure if the Assembly had been sitting is no longer required to be laid before Parliament at all. This is due to the fact that the replacement of Assembly Acts by Westminster Orders in Council requires the whole of the legislative machinery for Northern Ireland to be, as it were, taken down a level: delegated legislation which was previously subject to the negative procedure at Stormont has therefore been rendered subject to no parliamentary scrutiny whatsoever.

It should be noted, finally, that the making of secondary legislation is not the same as the bringing of it into force. Secondary legislation which is required to be laid before Parliament - even if already made (and not just in draft form) - cannot come into force before it is laid, except very rarely. Even if the legislation does not need to be laid, or is laid in draft form and made later, it may still itself provide (and usually

---

[65] See App. 1. Sometimes the preamble to an Order refers to only part of the equivalent English Act (see, *e.g.*, the Protection from Harassment (NI) Order 1997).

does) that it is not to come into force until a certain period has elapsed after it has been made.

Parliamentary control of secondary legislation

Secondary legislation is controlled by two bodies: (i) Parliament and (ii) the judiciary. The control of the Westminster Parliament or the Belfast Assembly comes into play not only at the stage when the parent Act is being enacted – for its delegating provisions can then be debated and amended – but also at the stage when, as is often required, the secondary legislation itself is laid before the body for approval (or "affirmation"). The maximum time allowed for debates on such approval on the floor of the House of Commons is usually just 90 minutes. In addition (or more usually instead) they can be discussed for up to two-and-a-half hours by a Standing (or "Merits") Commons Committee on Delegated Legislation[66] and the debate there will obviously be influential on the way MPs vote on resolutions in the House if a debate subsequently takes place there. By constitutional convention the House of Lords does not vote down secondary legislation proposed by the Government. The Northern Ireland Act 1998 does not specify exactly what procedures are to be followed whenever a Minister of the Executive Committee wishes to issue secondary legislation,[67] but the Assembly's Standing Orders provide that they are to be scrutinised by Assembly Committees.[68]

All UK statutory instruments - except Orders in Council made under the Northern Ireland Acts 1974 and 2000 - can also be scrutinised from a technical rather than a merit point of view by a Joint Select (or "Scrutiny") Committee of the House of Commons and the House of Lords. This Committee consults the law-making authority concerned if it thinks that the instrument is technically defective, and the attention of Parliament can then be drawn to the matter.

The inspection of Northern Ireland secondary legislation to see if it is technically defective is carried out by a Statutory Committee in the Assembly (when the Assembly is not suspended) or by an official called the Examiner of Statutory Rules.[69] Either body can draw the

---

[66] The debates for the 2003-04 Parliamentary session are available at www.publications.parliament.uk/pa/cm200304/cmstand/cmdeleg.htm.
[67] See in particular ss. 22-25.
[68] Standing Order No. 41.
[69] *Ibid.*

attention of the Assembly (or of Parliament if the Assembly is suspended) to those statutory rules which are in some way questionable because, for example, they impose a charge on the public revenues, they purport to have retrospective effect without any justification, they have been unjustifiably delayed, they appear to be *ultra vires* (*i.e.* outside the powers conferred by the parent Act), they are unclear or they are defectively drafted. The Examiner of Statutory Rules generally complains if there is a gap of less than 21 days between the laying of a statutory rule and its coming into force but in practice he or she finds fault with only a tiny minority of the rules examined. Whenever the Examiner complains that a rule may be *ultra vires*, the appropriate law-making authority either lobbies to have the parent Act extended or issues a further rule repealing the offending provision.

Judicial control of secondary legislation

Control by the courts over secondary legislation is sometimes described as judicial review, which is described in more detail in Chapter 6.7. It takes the form of a decision that a piece of secondary legislation of whatever nature is *ultra vires* (*i.e.* beyond the powers conferred by the parent Act). Whether such is the case or not can often be a very controversial legal issue, as is illustrated by the conflicting speeches of the Law Lords in the Northern Ireland case of *McEldowney* v *Forde*.[70] In that case the issue arose indirectly and not in judicial review proceedings properly so called, but the difficulty of the point was nonetheless great. The question was whether the Minister of Home Affairs for Northern Ireland was acting *ultra vires* the Civil Authorities (Special Powers) Act (NI) 1922 when he added "republican clubs and any like organisation howsoever described" to the list of associations which were unlawful under that Act. The decision turned on whether the Minister's action was "for the preservation of the peace and maintenance of order" (this being how the 1922 Act limited the law-making power) and by a majority of three to two the Law Lords held that it was.

---

[70] [1971] AC 632. See H. Calvert "The 'Republican Clubs' Case" (1970) 21 NILQ 191 and (on the Court of Appeal's decision) "Special Powers Extraordinary" (1969) 20 NILQ 1; D. N. MacCormick, "Delegated Legislation and Civil Liberty" (1970) 86 LQR 171.

The scope of the powers conferred by a parent Act was also in issue (again indirectly) in *R (Hume)* v *Londonderry Justices.*[71] There the High Court decided that the granting of power to an army officer to order an assembly of persons to disperse was beyond the power of the Stormont Parliament (and its delegates) because the Government of Ireland Act 1920 said that the Parliament of Northern Ireland was not to have power to make laws "in respect of the army". In *Dunkley* v *Evans*[72] an English court held that the West Coast Herring (Prohibition of Fishing) Order 1978, which was made under the Sea Fish (Conservation) Act 1967 and prohibited herring fishing within a defined area, was partly invalid in that the defined area included an area of the sea adjacent to the coast of Northern Ireland which was expressly excluded from the scope of the 1967 Act; the order remained valid as regards the other areas mentioned.

These are all instances of secondary legislation being challenged for substantive violation of the parent Act. Procedural violations, such as failure to consult the appropriate authorities before making the statutory rule or including a provision which prevents the courts from pronouncing on the rule's validity (a so-called *ouster clause*), are also grounds for judicial review, but again the exact attitude of the courts to these problems is somewhat unpredictable.[73] If a piece of secondary legislation is ambiguous to the point of absurdity judges are able to add, omit or substitute words to correct the obvious drafting error.[74] In all cases where secondary legislation is held to be *ultra vires* it ceases to have any force in law and can be disobeyed with impunity.

---

[71] [1972] NI 91. Interestingly, the incident at issue in this case occurred before Bloody Sunday on 30 January 1972 but the decision was announced thereafter. The effect was to make some of the army's actions on that day illegal but the hastily enacted Northern Ireland Act 1972 retrospectively validated all such actions.

[72] [1981] 1 WLR 1522.

[73] For recent examples where courts in England were invited to invalidate secondary legislation, see *R* v *Secretary of State for the Environment, Transport and the Regions, ex parte Spath Holme Ltd* [2001] 2 AC 349 (where the statutory instrument was ultimately held to be valid by the House of Lords) and *R* v *Secretary of State for Health, ex parte US Tobacco International Inc* [1992] 1 QB 353 (where the regulations in question were quashed by the Divisional Court).

[74] *R (Confederation of Passenger Transport UK)* v *Humber Bridge Board* [2004] QB 310, where the Court of Appeal added words to an SI, thereby allowing tolls on the Humber Bridge to be levied even on buses carrying more than 16 passengers.

The form of secondary legislation

Pieces of secondary legislation are more numerous and often more lengthy than pieces of primary legislation. The Insolvency Rules (NI) 1991, for example, run for 948 pages (596 of which are taken up by prescribed forms). Appendix 1 reproduces a typical example of a short Order in Council made under the Northern Ireland Act 1974. It is the Theft (NI) Order 1978, which makes amendments to the Theft Act (NI) 1969 (also reproduced in Appendix 1 of this book and annotated at pp.61-3 above). The following features of a typical Order in Council may be noted:

(1)   *Its number* ("23"). Each Order in Council made under the Northern Ireland Acts 1974 or 2000 is given both a UK statutory instrument number (here it is 1251) and a Northern Ireland Order in Council number (here it is 23).

(2)   *Dates* ("29 September 1978"). The date on which an Order in Council is made is the date on which the Queen assents to her Privy Counsellors' recommendations. The date on which the Order comes into force is provided for in the body of the Order itself (see article 1 of the Theft (NI) Order); sometimes it does not come into force until a further statutory commencement order is made naming an appointed day.

(3)   *The enacting words* ("Now, therefore, Her Majesty..."). This is another example of a standard formula; the preliminary phrase beginning "Whereas a draft..." is called the preamble.

(4)   *Articles.* Each Order is divided into articles (not sections), with the further subdivisions being referred to as paragraphs and subparagraphs. The numbering and lettering systems are the same as for statutes, for example article 2(3)(b). (International treaties are also divided into Articles and paragraphs, but the custom is to capitalise the initial letter of the word "Article" in that context.)

(5)   *The first articles.* These are devoted to setting out the title of the Order, its commencement date (if known), and the meaning of expressions used in it. In statutes, by contrast, these matters are usually dealt with by sections at the end.

(6)   *Explanatory note.* This is provided at the very end of all secondary legislation in order to give a brief indication of the effects of the legislation. It is comparable to the long title of a

statute (rather than to the explanatory memorandum now accompanying some statutes) but, unlike the long title, it forms no part of the actual enactment and should not be used as an aid to interpretation of the legislation.

Appendix 1 also reproduces a short, but fairly normal, statutory rule: the Employer's Liability (Compulsory Insurance) (Amendment) Regulations (NI) 2004. There are no special features of this which require highlighting. We can see that its number in the collection of statutory rules for 2004 is 449, and the attached explanatory note is helpful in placing the rule in context. Note that, even though it is a statutory rule, its title refers to "Regulations"; this is because the Employer's Liability (Defective Equipment and Compulsory Insurance) (NI) Order 1972, the enabling legislation in this case, says that the Department of Enterprise, Trade and Investment may do certain things "by regulation". Each particular provision can therefore be termed a regulation; if the enabling legislation had authorised the issuing of Rules, or of an Order, then each particular provision would have been termed, respectively, a rule or an article.

The problems of looking for secondary legislation

As with statutes, secondary legislation is published singly as well as collectively in annual bound volumes. Orders in Council made under the Northern Ireland Acts 1974 and 2000 are published in the series which used to contain the Acts of the Stormont Parliament. Each of these annual volumes of Orders in Council, as well as reprinting the Orders themselves, includes tables showing the UK and Northern Ireland Acts (and previous Orders in Council) which have been repealed, amended or otherwise affected by Orders in Council made during the year. Further tables indicate the UK Acts passed during the year which apply in Northern Ireland and the effects of these Acts on previous Irish Acts, Northern Irish Acts and Orders in Council. The consequences for earlier Acts and Orders of the statutory instruments and statutory rules made during the year are also tabulated.

The last volume for each year of the statutory rules for Northern Ireland contains a list of that year's UK statutory instruments which affect the province (other than Orders in Council made under the 1974 and 2000 Acts) and there is an index categorising the rules on the basis of the authorities which made them. Further tables supply lists of the changes made by the year's statutory rules not just to earlier Acts and Orders (information which is also given in the annual volume of Orders in Council) but also to earlier statutory rules. A large loose-leaf index to all the statutory rules in force, arranged under subject headings, is now updated every year, but it does not give details of the amendments which later statutory rules may have made to earlier ones: the fully amended text can be gleaned only from reading all of the relevant rules together.

All of Northern Ireland's statutory rules made since 1991 are now available on-line,[75] as are Orders in Council made under the Northern Ireland Acts since 1987 (together with all other statutory instruments made since then).[76] *The Stationery Office* also sells a CD-Rom (entitled *All Law of Northern Ireland*) which contains virtually all legislation (and most case law) applicable in the province. But there is still no online service which provides access to statutory rules *as amended*. It can therefore still be difficult to pinpoint the exact up-to-date position regarding the particular subject-matter in question.

2.3 JUDGE-MADE LAW

The courts are almost as important a source of new law as Parliament. The law which they create is sometimes referred to as case law or common law, as opposed to Parliament's statute law or legislation; this is yet another sense in which the expression common law can be used. Generally speaking, new law is created by the courts in two types of situation: (i) where existing legislation has nothing at all to say about the point in issue, and (ii) where what is said in legislation is unclear. In the latter situation the role of the courts is to *interpret* the existing legislation; the techniques they adopt in doing so are examined more closely in the following section. The traditional view, by the way, is that decisions by courts do not really create new law at all - judges are simply "finding" the law and "declaring" what it is. But today there are few lawyers who still adhere to this somewhat fictional view of the judicial function. Whether we like it or not, judges do make law.[77]

---

[75] www.northernireland-legislation.hmso.gov.uk/legislation/northernireland/ni-srni.htm #2004. Draft Rules are available from 2000.

[76] www.northernireland-legislation.hmso.gov.uk/legislation/northernireland/ni-oic.htm. Draft Orders are available from 1997.

[77] See S. Hedley, "How has the Common Law Survived the 20th Century?" (1999) 50 NILQ 283.

Decisions by judges on novel points of law enter the corpus of case law by being "reported". Only a very small fraction of judicial decisions are reported, and not all of those which do get reported are significant, for they may simply confirm a point which is already fairly well settled. Reported decisions, however, are important because they are available thereafter for lawyers and judges to refer to in future cases in order to back up an argument: what has been decided in the past is often a good guide for what should be decided in the present (or, as it is sometimes put, "like cases should be decided alike").[78] Records of decisions which are unreported can still be accessed in court libraries, and lawyers will sometimes trawl through these unreported cases to see whether they do after all contain a ruling which can be taken as authoritative on a particular point. Judges, however, are wary of relying on previous unreported cases, which means that the people who decide what decisions should be reported and which should not (*i.e.* editors of series of law reports and moderators of websites) can wield considerable influence. Law reports are written records of the judges' reasons for decisions. They are not records of everything that was said during the hearing of the case, whether by the judges, lawyers or witnesses. These latter records are called "transcripts" and are based on audio recordings, the work of court stenographers or the judge's notes. Law reports of most important judgments are today freely available on the internet[79] and some of them are also sold as printed hard copies. Transcripts, on the other hand, have to be specifically requested from the court and can cost as much as £5 per page.

Printed law reports[80]

In Northern Ireland there are two main series of printed law reports: the *Northern Ireland Law Reports* and the *Northern Ireland Judgments Bulletin*. Both are now published by a commercial firm (Butterworths) under the auspices of the Incorporated Council of Law Reporting for Northern Ireland. The former is the senior series because it was begun in 1925, but all the reports, before they are published, are checked by the judges in question to make sure that an accurate account has been

---

[78] But in England judges now insist that lawyers cite only cases that are relevant and useful to the case at hand: Supreme Court Practice Direction (Citation of Authorities) [2001] 1 WLR 1001.

[79] In Northern Ireland some county court judgments have been available since January 2004: see Civil Practice Note No. 7 [2004] 2 BNIL 78.

[80] See generally I. McLeod, *Legal Method* (5th ed., 2005), pp. 107-115 and 333-336; M. Zander, *The Law Making Process* (6th ed., 2004), Chap. 6.

given of what was said in the case. The *Northern Ireland Law Reports* now appear in two parts per year and contain cases determined in the superior courts in Northern Ireland and on appeal therefrom to the House of Lords. Only occasionally are decisions by the House of Lords in cases emanating from Northern Ireland reported in the English series of law reports.

The *Judgments Bulletin*, previously called the Bluebook from the colour of its cover, has been published since 1970, and now also appears twice a year. It simply reproduces the judges' speeches in a case without including an editor's summary of the facts and the decision (in what is called a "headnote") or details of the barristers' arguments (which are occasionally given in the *Northern Ireland Law Reports*). Otherwise there is little to choose between the two series of reports and one has to wonder why they cannot be merged. Occasionally cases reported in the *Judgments Bulletin* are later reported in the *Law Reports* too, but less so today than in the past. An index to all Northern Ireland cases reported in printed series between 1921 and 1997 was published in 1998. For more recent cases the search engine on the Northern Ireland Court Service's website can be used.

Appendix 1 of this book contains a copy of a reported case from the *Northern Ireland Law Reports*: *Campbell* v *Armstrong and others*.[81] The summary at the start of the case, written by the editor of the series, is the headnote. There then follows a list of the previously reported cases (and their law report references) mentioned by the judge in this case, some of which are Northern Ireland cases and some English. If you read the report you will see a typical example of how a judge goes about deciding a dispute on the basis of existing case law and legislation. The case also illustrates the process of statutory interpretation, which is discussed in the next section.

In England there are several series of printed law reports. The "official" ones, published by the Incorporated Council of Law Reporting,[82] are the *Weekly Law Reports* (published in three volumes each year) and the *Law Reports*. The latter are sub-divided into four series, namely (i) Appeal Cases, for decisions by the House of Lords and Privy Council,

---

[81] [1981] NI 180.
[82] www.lawreports.co.uk. The Council is a charitable organisation set up in 1865 by members of the profession. All the Council's reporters are barristers or solicitors who are present in court for both the hearing and judgment in cases they report. The Council's mission is "to report any cases which change or modify the law."

(ii) Queen's Bench cases, (iii) Chancery cases and (iv) Family cases; the last three also contain Court of Appeal decisions in each category. If cases are reported in these reports as well as elsewhere, judges require references to be given to these reports.[83] The most commonly used "unofficial" (i.e. privately published[84]) series is called the *All England Law Reports*, which appears in four volumes per year and now also has separate volumes specifically devoted to European Community law cases and commercial law cases. The quality newspapers in England publish short reports of important decisions; the most respected of these series is that issued in *The Times*. All law reports are referred to by well established abbreviations, such as *All ER* for the *All England Law Reports* and *WLR* for the *Weekly Law Reports*.

In both Northern Ireland and England the decisions of inferior courts (magistrates' courts and county courts) are virtually never reported, because if a truly novel legal point arises in such courts the case will almost inevitably be appealed to a higher court, where the decision will be reported. In practice, of course, by no means every novel point is appealed, often because the litigants cannot afford the time or money involved. This means that many important points never get the full legal airing they deserve and hence, to the general public's amazement, the law on many commonplace problems can be hazy. With the advent of the internet, however, some decisions of the inferior courts are now getting a wider distribution (see p. 89).

For some areas of the law special series of law reports have been devised to help publicise lower courts' decisions as well as the decisions of higher courts which would not otherwise qualify for inclusion in one of the major series. In Northern Ireland we have special series of this sort for decisions of the Lands Tribunal, industrial tribunals and social security appeal tribunals (see Chap. 8). Decisions of courts and tribunals which might not otherwise get reported but which may nevertheless be of some legal interest are noted in the *Bulletin of Northern Ireland Law*, a publication of the Servicing the Legal System programme at Queen's University, Belfast, which attempts to list all developments of legal interest to Northern Ireland on an almost month-by-month basis.[85] In a typical year there would be no

---

[83] Practice Direction (Judgments; Form and Citation) (Supreme Court) [2001] 1 WLR 194.
[84] By LexisNexis Butterworths.
[85] The Bulletin summarises all new primary and secondary legislation applying in Northern Ireland (including commencement orders), all written judgments delivered

more than 200 new cases reported in Northern Ireland.[86] In England there could be as many as 2,500.

In the last few years a system for the "neutral" citation of case decisions has been developed throughout the United Kingdom, meaning that it is free from any indication of the publisher of the decision or of the form of publication. It shows, in square brackets, the year the decision was issued, then a unique court identifier and then the number of the decision.[87] Thus, [2004] UKHL 6 refers to the sixth decision of the United Kingdom's House of Lords issued in the year 2004. And [2005] NIQB 9 refers to the ninth decision of the Queen's Bench Division of Northern Ireland's High Court issued in 2005. A full list of such abbreviations used in this book, and what they mean, can be found at the start of the book. Cases cited in this way also have their judgments divided into numbered paragraphs and it is now customary to refer to these rather than to page numbers (which may differ depending on the form of publication).

Case law on the internet

Reports of important decisions taken in the Crown Court, High Court and Court of Appeal in Northern Ireland are now available more or less immediately on the excellent website of the Northern Ireland Court Service, and occasionally a county court decision or resident magistrate's decision will be reported there too.[88] Judgments in cases reaching the House of Lords are placed on that body's website on the day they are delivered.[89] A very good website for looking up British

---

by the Court of Appeal, High Court and county courts in Northern Ireland, selected decisions of tribunals, all personal injury awards in the High Court, notices issued by the Northern Ireland Court Service (including judicial appointments), Practice Directions, many consultation documents or proposals for legislation and some developments in EC law and in the law of England and Wales: www.sls.qub.ac.uk.

[86] In 2003 there were 30 cases reported in the *Northern Ireland Law Reports*, 45 in the *Northern Ireland Judgments Bulletin* and (in addition to these) approximately 100 on the website of the Northern Ireland Court Service.

[87] For further details see Supreme Court Practice Direction (Judgments: Form and Citation) [2001] 1 WLR 194 (summarised at [2001] 3 BNIL 64) and Supreme Court Practice Direction (Judgments: Neutral Citations) [2002] 1 WLR 346. For a summary see [2001] 3 BNIL 64.

[88] www.courtsni.gov.uk/en-GB/Judicial+Decisions.

[89] www.publications.parliament.uk/pa/ld199697/ldjudgmt/ldjudgmt.htm. This system started on 16 November 1996. Earlier decisions are not usually available on-line.

and Irish law in general, whether legislation or case law, is that of the British and Irish Legal Information Institute.[90]

The rules of the doctrine of precedent[91]

In the vast majority of court cases the dispute is really about the facts of the case - what was done, by whom, and when - rather than about the law which is applicable to those facts. Do not expect to visit a courtroom and see the lawyers and judges poring over law books. But when law reports do need to be referred to, the doctrine of "precedent" comes into play. This doctrine (already mentioned in Chap. 1.1), which is sometimes referred to by the Latin phrase *stare decisis* (meaning "stand by things that have been decided"), states that a lower court is obliged to follow a higher court's earlier decision in a similar case unless the previous decision can be "distinguished". A higher court can overrule a previous decision by a lower court, but this just means that the higher court is changing the law from that time onwards, not that the losing party in the earlier decision (which may have been taken years previously) can now have that decision reversed.

As the highest court in Northern Ireland's legal system is the House of Lords, the decisions of that court are binding on all the other courts in Northern Ireland. Strictly speaking this is true only of the House's decisions in cases originating in Northern Ireland, but in practice all of its decisions are followed. It has been accepted that an English or Scottish House of Lords decision must be preferred to a conflicting decision of the Court of Appeal in Northern Ireland. Decisions of the Judicial Committee of the Privy Council (see Chap. 1.4) are not absolutely binding on courts in either Northern Ireland or England, but their authority is nevertheless persuasive, as exemplified on page 25 above. Within the province itself, decisions of the Court of Appeal are binding on the High Court and Crown Court, and their decisions are in turn binding on the county courts and magistrates' courts.

Decisions of courts at equivalent levels

The rules are less clear when a court on one level is confronted with an earlier decision of another court on the same level. For many years the

---

[90] www.bailii.org.
[91] See M. Zander, *The Law Making Process* (6th ed., 2004), Chaps. 5 and 6 and T. Ingman, *The English Legal Process* (10th ed., 2004), Chap. 8. See too F. Newark, "Law and Precedent in Northern Ireland" (1972) 23 NILQ 100.

House of Lords adhered to the practice of holding itself bound by its own previous decisions, regardless of how much it had come to disagree with them. But by 1966 it was apparent that this practice was leading to the law becoming fossilised while the courts waited for Parliament to enact reforming legislation. It also encouraged judicial resort to spurious distinctions and tenuous refinements in order to escape injustices. In that year, accordingly, the Law Lords issued a Practice Statement stating that in future, while they would normally treat former decisions of the House as binding, they would depart from them whenever it appeared right to do so.[92] In the years since, this new power has been sparingly exercised: there are perhaps ten *clear* instances of its use but on more than one occasion the House has refused to overrule an earlier decision even though it thought that it was wrong.[93]

In England there has been considerable controversy over whether the Court of Appeal in that jurisdiction should be bound by its own previous decisions.[94] The great advocate for its not being bound was Lord Denning, who as Master of the Rolls was in charge of the Court of Appeal's Civil Division from 1962 to 1982. But as often as Lord Denning refused to follow former cases, even one in which he himself had participated, the House of Lords, on appeal, said that he was incorrect to do so. On this stricter view the Court of Appeal can refuse to follow its own earlier decisions in only three situations: (i) where there are in fact two such decisions which already conflict; (ii) where the earlier Court of Appeal decision is inconsistent with a subsequent House of Lords decision; and (iii) where the earlier decision was announced without proper consideration having been given to earlier cases or statutes pointing the other way (in legal language, *per incuriam*). There is also a practice whereby a Court of Appeal consisting of three judges is not bound by decisions taken by a Court of Appeal consisting of only two judges but, conversely, a court consisting of more than three judges is not considered to have more binding authority. In appeals in criminal cases the Court of Appeal tends to adopt a more flexible attitude to its own previous decisions in

---

[92] [1966] 1 WLR 1234.
[93] See generally I. McLeod, *Legal Method* (5th ed., 2005), Chap. 11 and B. Harris, "Final Appellate Courts Overruling their Own 'Wrong' Precedents: The Ongoing Search for Principle" (2002) 118 LQR 408.
[94] For details see I. McLeod, *Legal Method* (5th ed., 2005), Chap. 12 and M. Zander, *The Law Making Process* (6th ed., 2004), pp. 230-49.

situations where the appellant's loss of liberty would be too high a price to pay for case law uniformity. There is also flexibility in cases where a further appeal beyond the Court of Appeal is not possible.

As it operates in a different jurisdiction the Court of Appeal in Northern Ireland is, strictly speaking, not bound by decisions of the English Court of Appeal. But it still accords those decisions the greatest respect and will follow them unless there are very strong reasons for not doing so. As regards its own earlier decisions, the Court of Appeal in Northern Ireland adopts the same practice as the Court of Appeal in England. In situations where there is no possibility of a further appeal to the House of Lords - as for nearly all civil cases begun in the province's magistrates' courts or county courts (see Chap. 6.2 to 6.5) - the Court of Appeal in Northern Ireland may disregard its earlier decision if it considers that it is plainly wrong or too vague and that to follow it would be unjust or unfair. There has to be this flexibility, for otherwise the law would stagnate. In the days before the reorganisation of the courts in Ireland in the 1870s (see Chap. 1.3), it was possible for all judges of the Irish Court of Appeal to sit together as a full Court of Appeal in order to review its previous decisions, and the House of Lords would sometimes ask all the High Court judges to advise it on a certain point, but both these practices have long since been abandoned.

In England and Northern Ireland the High Court will abide by its own previous decisions unless persuaded that these are wrong. Each of these High Courts will also be deferential to earlier decisions of its counterpart, especially if in other respects the law on the matter in question is the same in both countries. One can say the same about the attitude of today's Court of Appeal and High Court in Northern Ireland to decisions of the Court of Appeal and High Court in Ireland taken before partition of the island in 1920: they are not technically binding but will be followed unless patently wrong.

In England, the Divisional Courts (see Chap. 1.3) adopt the same attitude to their own previous decisions as does the Court of Appeal. Because the Divisional Court in Northern Ireland rarely sits, it is not possible to state what practice it favours.

The *ratio decidendi* of a case[95]

Of course, whether an earlier decision is wrong or not is largely a matter of opinion, which underlines the fact that the doctrine of precedent is not always as limiting a constraint on the inventiveness of judges as might at first be imagined. It must be stressed, moreover, that the doctrine of precedent obliges lower courts to follow higher courts only if the earlier decisions are exactly in point. This makes it essential to deduce from every reported case the precise principle for which it may later be cited as an authority. This nub of the case is called, in Latin, the *ratio decidendi* or simply the *ratio*, that is to say the "reason for deciding" the case. Whatever is said by the judges which is not directly on the main point is called *obiter dictum*, literally "something said by the way". Only the *ratio* of a case is binding on later judges. The later judge can avoid applying it only if the facts of the case being dealt with can be significantly distinguished from those of the earlier case. Lawyers expend much time and expertise in attempting to find a valid distinction from an earlier case in order to avoid the rigours of the doctrine of binding precedent.

2.4 STATUTORY INTERPRETATION[96]

However elaborately it is phrased, no rule embodied in primary or secondary legislation can hope to cater for all the circumstances which may arise for consideration. It can be taken for granted that administrators and judges will need to interpret the legislation in order to decide whether or not it applies to a given fact situation.[97] For instance, if Parliament were to pass a law making glue-sniffing a criminal offence and included in the Act a list of the substances which were to be treated as glue for the purpose of this offence, a court of law might still have to decide what exactly amounted to "sniffing". The people who draft legislation obviously try to reduce the uncertainties as much as possible, but the need for judicial interpretation is ultimately inescapable: human foresight and the English language cannot avoid it. Indeed the task of statutory interpretation is one which occupies a great

---

[95] I. McLeod, *Legal Method* (5th ed., 2005), Chap. 9.
[96] See I. McLeod, *Legal Method* (5th ed., 2005), Chap. 20; M. Zander, *The Law Making Process* (6th ed., 2004), Chap. 3; T. Ingman, *The English Legal Process* (10th ed., 2004), pp. 261-312.
[97] Likewise common law may be affected by legislation: J. Beatson, "The Role of Statute in the Development of Common Law Doctrine" (2001) 117 LQR 247.

deal of our judges' time; certainly the majority of reported cases involve a point of interpretation at some juncture. An important recent example is the case of *R* v *Z*, where Girvan J. had to decide whether the term "Irish Republican Army", which was an illegal organisation for the purposes of the Terrorism Act 2000, included the Real IRA. He held that it did not, but the Court of Appeal, and then the House of Lords, reversed this decision.[98] Another illustration is provided by *Campbell* v *Armstrong and others*,[99] the sample case reproduced in Appendix 1 of this book.

The doctrine of binding precedent applies to the topic of statutory interpretation as much as to any other in the law. This means that if the Northern Ireland Court of Appeal were to pronounce on whether inhaling the vapours of glue through one's mouth qualifies as sniffing glue, then all the lower courts in Northern Ireland would have to construe the same Act in the same way. If there is a pertinent English decision on the point and if the English legislation is identical to the Northern Ireland legislation then the English court's decision will virtually always be followed in this jurisdiction.[100]

Every piece of legislation within one jurisdiction is unique and the interpretation placed on it by judges will rarely be relevant to the interpretation of other legislation even if the very same words are in issue. But there are certain approaches to the whole process of interpretation which judges tend to apply to all sorts of statutes. They range from what really amount to general philosophies concerning judicial activity to what are in practice quite specific presumptions. Over the centuries the law has fluctuated in its adherence to these various approaches, some of which conflict. Controversy still rages today,[101] so one cannot be dogmatic in asserting that a statutory provision must be interpreted with such and such an attitude in mind. All the approaches, it is readily admitted, have exceptions. With these

---

[98] [2004] NICA 23 and [2005] WLR 1286.

[99] [1981] NI 180.

[100] There is legislation concerning glue-sniffing in Scotland: the Solvent Abuse (Scotland) Act 1983 talks of "misusing a volatile substance by deliberately inhaling, other than for medical purposes, that substance's vapour". In the rest of the United Kingdom it is the supply of glue which can sometimes be a criminal offence, not the sniffing of it: see the Intoxicating Substances (Supply) Act 1985.

[101] For a recent but not entirely convincing attempt to reconcile conflicting approaches, see R. Graham, "A unified theory of statutory interpretation" (2002) 23 Statute LR 91.

qualifications in mind, we can briefly attempt to state the prevailing views on statutory interpretation in Northern Ireland today.

The rules of interpretation[102]

In the first place the court should try to ascertain the intention of Parliament when it drafted the particular provision. Until very recently the judges were obstructed in their efforts to do this by the rule that reports of proceedings in Parliament (*i.e. Hansard*) could not be looked at to see what the MPs and peers who voted for the provision thought it meant. In England Lord Denning more than once deviated from this practice but he was roundly criticised by the House of Lords for doing so. In *Pepper* v *Hart*[103] the House of Lords (by a majority of six Law Lords to one, the Lord Chancellor dissenting) finally accepted that the rule should be relaxed so as to allow reference to clear statements made by a Minister or other promoter of the legislation and to other parliamentary material which was necessary to understand these statements and their effects.

The intention of Parliament can also be deduced from the long title of the Act, the unambiguous effects of other provisions in the Act, the omissions from the Act, the state of the pre-existing law, official reports preceding the enactment of the legislation, the practical consequences of preferring one interpretation over another, and the conventional maxims of interpretation which it must be assumed the draftsman was aware of when the Act was written (see below). In recent years the Government has begun to issue Explanatory Notes at the same time as it publishes new Bills; however, these are not used by judges as a reliable guide to the intended effect of the provisions. The most important indication of Parliament's intention is the ordinary meaning of the words themselves; if one of the interpretations being contended for is at variance with that ordinary meaning, it is likely that the ordinary meaning will be preferred. To that extent a purely literal approach to interpretation is shunned. A purposive approach - one which asks the question "What was Parliament really getting at?" - is nowadays adopted.

---

[102] The leading authority in this area is F. Bennion, *Statutory Interpretation* (4th ed., 2002).

[103] [1993] AC 593. See K. Mullan, "The Impact of *Pepper* v *Hart*", Chap. 11 in B. Dickson and P. Carmichael (eds.), *The House of Lords: Its Parliamentary and Judicial Roles* (1999).

Left at that, one might conclude, to return to our hypothetical example, that inhaling glue vapours through the mouth is tantamount to "sniffing" it. Literally, sniffing is a process carried out only through the nose; colloquially, however, glue-sniffing is used to describe a variety of types of solvent abuse and the intention of Parliament would probably be frustrated if inhaling through the mouth was held not to be covered by the Act. But it is at this point that countervailing principles, presumptions and maxims concerning statutory interpretation must be brought into play. One of these is that legislation which creates a criminal offence must be interpreted as narrowly as possible so as to preserve a person's freedom of action. Another is that the express mention of one of a class of things by implication excludes other items of the same class, so that if the Act in one place refers to sniffing as meaning sniffing through the nose, inhaling through the mouth should not be taken to be covered by the same word. In some instances these principles and presumptions are so well embedded in our law that they have ceased to be merely arguments to be taken into account by the judge and have become instead obligations requiring the judge to decide the case in a certain way. An example of this is the principle that one cannot take advantage of one's own illegal act in order to claim a right under a statute[104] - for instance a murderess cannot claim a widow's pension if the person she murdered was her husband.

Some questions of interpretation recur so frequently that Parliament has provided set solutions. These are to be found in the Interpretation Act (NI) 1954 and the Interpretation Act 1978. The former covers the interpretation of Acts of the Northern Ireland Parliament as well as Orders in Council made under the Northern Ireland Acts 1974 and 2000. The latter covers Westminster legislation applying in Northern Ireland. They deal with such problems as the meaning of "month", whether "man" includes "woman" and whether the singular includes the plural. The Law Commission (see Chap. 9.14) is still seeking to persuade the Government to adopt more systematic measures for the avoidance of problems in statutory interpretation.

2.5 INTERNATIONAL SOURCES

There are many agencies in the world which promote the conclusion of international agreements. When the Government of the United

---

[104] This is sometimes put in Latin as *ex turpi causa non oritur actio*. ("no claim can arise out of a base foundation").

Kingdom signs these agreements, which may be called treaties, conventions or covenants, it does so on behalf of the people of Northern Ireland as well as those of Great Britain. But merely signing the treaty does not render it a part of UK national law, nor, usually, does it oblige the United Kingdom to comply with the treaty's provisions *vis-à-vis* other states. For the treaty to be made a part of our national law it must be "incorporated" by an Act of Parliament; sometimes the treaty will be appended to the Act in a Schedule, at other times its provisions will be reworded but with more or less the same effect. It is Parliament's prerogative to depart from the terms of the treaty to whatever extent it wishes.

For the treaty to be made a part of the international law binding the United Kingdom it is usually enough if it has been ratified by the Government and has received the stipulated number of ratifications from other countries to enter into force. Ratification in the United Kingdom is normally taken to have occurred after the treaty has been signed and laid before Parliament for 21 days (the so-called "Ponsonby" rule). Very important treaties, such as the Maastricht Treaty of European Union of 1992, are usually submitted to Parliament for its express approval. Exceptionally, as was planned for the Treaty Establishing a Constitution for Europe, signed in Rome in October 2004, the matter will be made the subject of a referendum throughout the whole country. Within the United Kingdom, unlike in most other countries, there are no precise constitutional requirements in this field. What is clear, however, is that ratified treaties that have not yet been incorporated into domestic law are not binding on our judges.[105]

Examples of domestic statutes incorporating treaties, or parts of treaties, into our national law are the Carriage of Passengers by Road Act 1974, the State Immunity Act 1978,[106] the Human Rights Act 1998 and the International Criminal Court Act 2001.[107] These Acts, in effect,

---

[105] *Maclaine Watson & Co Ltd* v *Department of Trade and Industry* [1990] 2 AC 418 (the International Tin Council case); but see the comments of Lord Steyn in *Re McKerr* [2004] 1 WLR 807, paras 48-50, where he thought the time might soon come for the orthodox approach to be altered.

[106] This was the Act in dispute during the court cases in England on whether ex-President Pinochet of Chile could be brought to justice.

[107] Technically, the Human Rights Act 1998 did not "incorporate" the 1950 European Convention on Human Rights, it merely made some of the rights set out in that Convention part of domestic UK law. In *Re McKerr* [2004] 1 WLR 807 this distinction was used to justify the non-retrospectivity of the Human Rights Act 1998.

implemented Conventions which were concluded, respectively, in 1968, 1973, 1950 and 1998, each by a different international agency. Sometimes an Act is passed to comply with an international convention but without actually incorporating the convention into domestic law: the Landmines Act 1998 marks the United Kingdom's signing in December 1997 of the Ottawa Convention on the Prohibition of the Use etc. of Anti-Personnel Mines. Occasionally, because of differences between the pre-existing law in Northern Ireland and that in England, separate legislation is required for the province when treaties are incorporated into Northern Ireland law, for example the Adoption (Hague Convention) Act (NI) 1969. A good example of a treaty which at the moment is binding upon the United Kingdom in international law but not in domestic law is the United Nations' Convention on the Rights of the Child (1989).

The only context in which the sources of Northern Ireland law are to be found outside the United Kingdom altogether is that of public international law, the area of law which concerns relations between states. This has some of its sources in international custom, in international agreements (whether binding - "hard law" - or non-binding - "soft law"), particularly in the field of human rights,[108] and in the decisions of international tribunals such as the International Court of Justice at The Hague in the Netherlands.[109] It is sometimes said that European Community (EC) law is another such context, but strictly speaking this is not so: as will be explained below, EC law has effect in Northern Ireland (and elsewhere in the United Kingdom) only because a UK statute says so. In recent years the House of Lords has begun to pay much more attention to public international law as a source of domestic national law. It did so when ruling that General Pinochet *could* be extradited to Chile[110] and that the provision for indefinite detention without trial in the Anti-terrorism, Crime and Security Act 2001 was incompatible with the European Convention on Human Rights.[111]

---

[108] For a useful compendium see P. Ghandhi, *International Human Rights Documents* (4th ed., 2004).

[109] www.icj-cij.org. See, *e.g.*, the ICJ's Advisory Opinion on the Legal Consequences of the Construction of a Wall in the Occupied Palestinian Territory, 9 July 2004.

[110] *R v Bow Street Stipendiary Magistrate, ex parte Pinochet Ugarte No. 3)* [2000] 1 AC 147.

[111] *A and others v Secretary of State for the Home Department* [2005] 2 WLR 87.

While the International Court of Justice handles disputes between states,[112] the International Criminal Court, also based at The Hague, tries *individuals* for war crimes, crimes against humanity and genocide. It can investigate crimes allegedly committed by nationals of those states which have agreed to the Court's Statute (as the United Kingdom has), or by anyone on the territory of those states, and it can also investigate crimes which are referred to it by the United Nations.[113] States can themselves try people for such crimes rather than refer them to the Court. For specific instances, notably Rwanda and the Former Republic of Yugoslavia, the United Nations has set up special War Crime Tribunals, again at The Hague.

European Community law[114]

When, on 1 January 1973, the United Kingdom joined the European Economic Community (the Common Market) as well as the European Coal and Steel Community and the European Atomic Energy Community, the treaties establishing these Communities (including the Treaty of Rome 1957) were incorporated into UK law by virtue of the European Communities Act 1972. Subsequent treaties amending the Treaty of Rome have also been incorporated.[115] According to the most commonly accepted interpretation of the 1972 Act, the rules of the common law of the three UK legal systems (England and Wales, Scotland and Northern Ireland), as well as existing and future UK legislation, have effect subject to European Community (EC) law. In 1973 EC law thereby became a new and "higher" source of law in Northern Ireland.

EC law falls into three categories: (i) the provisions of the various treaties setting up the Communities, which can be said to constitute the primary law of the EC; (ii) the Regulations, Directives, Decisions, Recommendations and Opinions[116] of the EC institutions, that is, the

---

[112] For a recent example see the case taken by several countries against Israel in relation to the building of the so-called "peace wall" in Palestine:

[113] For more details see W. Schabas, *An Introduction to the International Criminal Court* (2004).

[114] See generally J. Steiner and L. Woods, *Textbook on EC Law* (8th ed., 2003), I. McLeod, *Legal Method* (5th ed., 2005), ch.5 and M. Zander, *The Law-Making Process* (6th ed., 2004), pp.423-42.

[115] *E.g.* the European Communities (Amendment) Act 1998 incorporated the Treaty on European Union (the Treaty of Amsterdam 1997).

[116] Recommendations and Opinions are, technically, non-binding, but the European Court of Justice has held that the former can be taken into account when

Council of the European Union, the European Parliament and the European Commission, all of which can be called the secondary law of the EC; and (iii) the rulings and decisions of the Court of First Instance and Court of Justice of the European Communities, the case law of the EC.

Some of the legislative acts in the second category (namely, Regulations and most Decisions) are "directly applicable" in Member States of the EC, which means that they have the force of law without the need of any further national legislation. They are said to be "self-executing". Regulations are binding in their entirety on all Member States, while Decisions are binding only on those states, corporations or individuals to whom they are addressed.

Sometimes Regulations do require Member States to adopt national measures to implement them: Council Regulation 1257/99, for example, required Member States to introduce measures to create rural development plans. It may also be necessary to put in place administrative measures to give effect to the rights created by Regulations, but in such cases the Regulations still remain directly applicable, so if the administrative measures are not adopted in time it will still be possible for people to rely directly upon the Regulations in any legal dispute. For example, the General Food Regulations (NI) 2004, mentioned at 2.2 above in the section explaining secondary legislation, partly implement EC Regulation No.178/2002.[117]

Decisions of the EC institutions are always binding on the people or bodies to whom they are addressed without the need for any further implementation. They are designed to deal with specific situations, such as whether a Member State should be allocated structural funding for a specific project or whether a company is in breach of competition law. The addressees of such decisions have the standing to challenge the decisions before the European Court of Justice. Decisions are also used by the Council of the European Union to set out policy positions. For instance, the Sixth Environmental Action Plan set out the EC's priorities in environmental law for the period 2000 to 2010. These sorts of decisions are not addressed to anyone in particular and so cannot be challenged in the European Court of Justice.

---

interpreting national laws adopted to implement EC measures. It is therefore possible to argue that Recommendations and Opinions are persuasive authorities in Northern Ireland's courts.

[117] OJ No.L31 1.2.2002.

Directives, despite their name, are not directly applicable: they are binding only as to the result to be achieved by them and each Member State is free to decide upon the means for giving the Directives legal and administrative effect. A Directive will, however, set a time limit for the implementation of its provisions. Thus, by a Directive of October 1995 the United Kingdom had to alter its law on the protection of individuals with regard to the processing and movement of personal data; this it did by passing the Data Protection Act in July 1998. Often a Directive is implemented in Northern Ireland through the issuing of statutory rules.[118] Every now and then the Government issues a European Communities (Designation) Order[119] to indicate the authorities in the United Kingdom which, under section 2(2) of the European Communities Act 1972, are empowered to make UK regulations giving effect to EC law.

If a member State fails to implement an EC Directive by the deadline, or if it implements it incorrectly or incompletely, individuals may still be able to rely on the Directive's provisions in national proceedings against state bodies before national courts. In particular, if a Directive clearly aims to confer rights and duties on individuals, a person who suffers loss as a result of the Government's failure to change national law within the time specified may be able to sue the Government to recover compensation for losses suffered (in a so-called *Francovich* action).[120] This occurred in a case in Northern Ireland involving the Government's failure to implement the Working Time Directive.[121] Directives can also have an indirect effect in that national courts can be asked by litigants to interpret national laws in a way which complies with an unimplemented Directive.

It is now clear that courts throughout the United Kingdom can refuse to apply even an Act of Parliament if the judges are of the view that the Act conflicts with EC law. In the *Factortame* case[122] the House of Lords, following a ruling by the European Court of Justice, held that provisions in the Merchant Shipping Act 1988, and regulations made

---

[118] *E.g.* the Posting of Workers Directive (96/71/EC) was implemented by the Equal Opportunities (Employment Legislation) (Territorial Limits) Regs. (NI) 2000.

[119] *E.g.* the European Communities (Designation) (No. 6) Order 2004.

[120] *Francovich* v *Italy* [1992] IRLR 84.

[121] *Re Burns' Application* [1999] NI 175. The Working Time Directive was issued in 1993 (93/104/EC) and was supposed to have been implemented within three years. The Working Time Regs. 1998 eventually implemented the Directive two years late.

[122] *Factortame Ltd* v *Secretary of State for Transport (No. 2)* [1991] 1 AC 603.

thereunder, should be "disapplied". Much the same conclusion was reached by the House of Lords itself - without needing a prior determination by the European Court of Justice - concerning a provision in the Employment Protection (Consolidation) Act 1978: see *R* v *Secretary of State for Employment, ex parte the Equal Opportunities Commission.*[123] For a case where a court in Northern Ireland "disapplied" provisions in legislation because of their inconsistency with EC law, see *Perceval-Price* v *Department of Economic Development.*[124]

The European Court of Justice[125]

The European Court of Justice, which sits at Luxembourg, is staffed by 25 judges and eight advocates-general, all of whom are chosen by the governments of the 25 Member States of the European Union.[126] The judges are selected from the people who are eligible for appointment to the highest judicial posts in their own countries or who are jurists of recognised competence. They are appointed for six years at a time. Britain's first judge, Lord Mackenzie Stuart, was appointed in 1972 and was reappointed twice. His successor was Sir Gordon Slynn, who later became a Law Lord. He was followed by Sir David Edward and the current UK judge is Sir Francis Jacobs (formerly an advocate-general at the Court). The Irish judge is Aindrias Ó Caoimh, appointed in 2004. The judges elect their own President, for a three-year term. The incumbent (elected in October 2003) is the Greek judge, Vassilios Skouris. The Court of Justice may sit in chambers of three or five judges, as a Grand Chamber or as a full court. Most cases are heard by a chamber, but a Member State or a Community institution that is a party to proceedings can request that a case be heard by a Grand Chamber of 13 judges. Very rarely the Court sits as a full Court when it considers a case to be of exceptional importance.

Advocates-general are similar to the court advisers used in continental legal systems but unfamiliar in common law countries. One of them is

---

[123] [1994] 2 WLR 409.
[124] [2000] NI 141.
[125] www.curia.eu.int. See T. Ingman, *The English Legal Process* (10th ed., 2004), pp.91-99.
[126] These are Belgium, Cyprus, the Czech Republic, Denmark, Estonia, Finland, France, Germany, Greece, Hungary, Ireland, Italy, Latvia, Lithuania, Luxembourg, Malta, the Netherlands, Poland, Portugal, Slovakia, Slovenia, Spain, Sweden and the United Kingdom.

allocated to each case coming before the Court of Justice. In reporting
to the judges their task is threefold: (i) to suggest a solution to the case,
(ii) to relate that solution to the existing law and (iii) to set out the
likely future developments in the law. But the advocates-general do not
actually participate in the drafting of the Court's judgments, nor in the
discussions which lead to the Court's decisions. Although their
submissions are not binding on the Court, they are reported alongside
the Court's judgment (which is usually very terse and provides no
detail of any dissenting opinions) and are often followed. They
certainly serve as useful background material explicating the judgment.
Since 1973 the Court's judgments have been published in English in
the European Court Reports. Every decision (since the Court began
operating in 1953) is also available on-line.[127]

Jurisdiction and judgments

The Court of Justice has jurisdiction to hear many different types of
case involving EC law, but the most important are probably those
concerned with the validity or interpretation of acts of the Community
institutions. If such matters arise during the course of a case before any
national court or tribunal of a Member State they can be referred to the
Court of Justice under Article 234 of the Treaty of Rome.[128] The
opinion of that Court is then handed back to the local court so that it
can be applied to the facts of the particular case. Such referrals will, of
course, take months if not years to complete. Examples of referrals
made from Northern Ireland are those made by the resident magistrate
in the case of *Pigs Marketing Board (NI)* v *Redmond*,[129] by the
President of Industrial Tribunals in *Johnston* v *Chief Constable of the
RUC*[130] and by the Court of Appeal in *Gillespie* v *Northern Health and
Social Services Board*.[131] Courts and tribunals "of last instance", that is,
from which there is no further appeal, are obliged to refer such matters
to the Court of Justice unless the correct interpretation is quite clear;
the Northern Ireland Court of Appeal is a court of last instance in
several matters and so is affected by this obligation. The House of

[127] www.curia.eu.int/en/content/juris/index.htm.
[128] Prior to the renumbering of Articles in the Treaty of Rome as a result of the coming
into force of the Treaty on European Union (the Treaty of Amsterdam) in 1999, this
was Art.177.
[129] [1978] NI 73.
[130] [1987] QB 129.
[131] [1996] All ER (EC) 284 and [1997] NI 190.

Lords even more so, and from time to time it does indeed refer a case to Luxembourg.

The judgments of the European Court of Justice are binding on the national courts and authorities of all 25 EC countries - witness the compliance of the UK Government with the decision in the *Marshall* case in 1986 concerning the eligibility of women to retirement pensions.[132] If the national authorities continue to default the ECJ cannot hold national law to be void but it can impose financial penalties on the state in question.[133] This power was first used against Greece, which had failed to comply with an ECJ judgment on toxic waste.[134] In the vast majority of cases, of course, the national authorities do eventually comply with the Court's judgments.

The Court of Justice, in line with the practice followed in the civil law countries which constitute the majority of EC Member States, adopts what to British and Irish lawyers seems an unashamedly creative attitude when faced with problems of statutory interpretation. However, judges in the United Kingdom are beginning to imitate their European counterparts when EC legislation requires to be interpreted. Through time this is bound to lead to a more "purposive" approach to the interpretation of national legislation as well (see 2.4 above). British draftsmen may also take a leaf out of the European book and begin to draft legislation in more general terms. The Court of Justice is also much less committed than British courts to the notion of binding precedent in case law (it can refuse to follow its own previous decisions) and this too may gradually persuade British judges to slacken a little their adherence to that notion.

The European Court of First Instance

In 1989 a second court was established at Luxembourg to help take the burden off the Court of Justice. Called the Court of First Instance, it hears disputes between the staff of the European Community and their employers, disputes over the rules on commercial competition and cases arising from the Coal and Steel Treaty. Appeals lie to the Court of Justice on points of law or serious breaches of procedure. The Court comprises 25 members, each appointed for renewable six-year terms,

---

[132] *Marshall v Southampton and SW Hampshire Area Health Authority* [1986] QB 401.
[133] Art. 228(2) of the Treaty of Rome, as amended.
[134] *Commission v Greece*, Case C-387/97, [2004] ECRJ-5047.

but there are no separate advocates-general to assist these judges. Usually cases are dealt with by chambers of three or five judges. The UK judge is currently Mr Nicholas Forwood, appointed in 1999, and the Irish judge is Mr John Cooke, appointed in 1996.[135]

Judicial Panels

The jurisdiction of the European Court of Justice and the Court of First Instance is currently under review. The Treaty of Nice 2001 also provided for the creation of a third tier of courts - judicial panels. In November 2004 the ECJ established the first of these panels (or tribunals), to deal with civil service cases, and it is at present considering the establishment of a panel to deal with patent cases. Once the Treaty of Nice is fully implemented some preliminary references by national courts (in areas yet to be specified) will be transferred from the European Court of Justice to the Court of First Instance and this latter court will also acquire jurisdiction over some annulment actions, actions for failure to act and applications for damages against the EU.

The European Court of Auditors[136]

The function of this body, which is not a court in the usual English sense of the word, is to check that the EU's budget is being properly managed. It has the power to investigate any organisation which handles EU money, if necessary carrying out on-the-spot checks in Member States, and it will draw the attention of the Commission to any problems it uncovers. Every year it presents an overall report on the previous financial year to the European Parliament and the Council, a report which is very influential in helping the Parliament to decide whether to approve the Commission's handling of the budget. The Court of Auditors is also asked for its opinion before the EU's financial regulations are adopted. Although it can comment on other matters at any time, it does not have any legal powers of its own: it merely transmits relevant information to other EU bodies who must then decide what, if any, action to take. Approximately 550 staff work at the Court of Auditors, about half of them being qualified auditors.

---

[135] Guidance for lawyers taking cases before the Court of First Instance has recently been issued: see Practice Note [1999] All ER (EC) 641.

[136] www.europa.eu.int/institutions/court-auditors/index_en.htm.

The European Convention on Human Rights

The European Court of Justice should not be confused with the European Court of Human Rights, which sits at Strasbourg in France. The Court of Human Rights has the job of interpreting the European Convention for the Protection of Human Rights and Fundamental Freedoms, which was drawn up by the Council of Europe in 1950. The Council of Europe is an international organisation formed in 1949 and now comprises 46 European states; it is distinct from the European Community, being more active on social and cultural fronts than in economics or politics. The United Kingdom was amongst the first to ratify the Convention on Human Rights in 1951, but although the Convention entered into force internationally in 1953 the UK Government did not permit people in the United Kingdom to take cases to Strasbourg until 1966 and it did not take legislative action to incorporate Convention rights into domestic law until the Human Rights Act was enacted in 1998.[137] This Act makes the Convention enforceable in all British courts as from 2 October 2000, although the Acts which devolved powers to administrations in Edinburgh, Cardiff and Belfast in 1999 had already precluded those authorities from doing anything which contravenes the Convention. Courts in the United Kingdom have in the past occasionally looked to the Convention as an aid to the interpretation of ambiguous domestic statutes or to the establishment of the modern common law position on issues concerning human rights.

The states which are parties to the Convention may be proceeded against for an alleged violation of the Convention by other such states or, if they admit this right (as they all now do), by their own individual citizens. Only two inter-state cases have so far resulted in full judgments from the Court.[138] States are not liable for actions committed in a state which is not party to the Convention[139] and a person outside a

---

[137] The last Member State of the Council of Europe to incorporate the European Convention into its domestic law was Ireland, which did so from 1 January 2004 by virtue of the European Convention on Human Rights Act 2003.

[138] *Ireland* v *UK* (1979-80) 2 EHRR 25 (a case on interrogation practices used by security forces in Northern Ireland) and *Cyprus* v *Turkey* (2002) 35 EHRR 30 (a case on the occupation of part of Cyprus by Turkey since 1974).

[139] *Bankovic and others* v *Belgium and others*, App. 52207/99, decision of 12 December 2001, where the Court declared inadmissible a complaint by Serbs against the bombing of Yugoslavia by NATO countries in 1999. See S. Williams and S. Shah [2002] EHRLR 775.

state, generally speaking, cannot claim that that state has breached his or her Convention rights.[140]

Until November 1998 complaints to Strasbourg had first to be considered by the European Commission of Human Rights, which decided whether they were "admissible" within the terms of the Convention. In that month, however, the Commission was merged with the Court, which then became a full-time body,[141] so it is now a three-judge committee of the Court which decides the admissibility question. Complaints will not be admissible, for example, if all avenues for redress in the national courts have not yet been exhausted or if more than six months have elapsed since the date of the final decision in the national courts. If the complaints are admissible (in 2004 as many as 19,780 applications were held *not* to be admissible), the Court will carry out an inquiry and seek to bring about a friendly settlement (in 2004 there were 68 friendly settlements). If no such settlement is possible, the case will be referred to a Chamber of the Court (comprising seven judges) for a full hearing and a decision.[142] That Chamber can in turn refer the case to a Grand Chamber of 17 judges if it feels that it is particularly important (and all inter-state cases must go to the Grand Chamber).[143]

There are as many judges eligible to sit in the European Court of Human Rights as there are Member States of the Council of Europe; each Government nominates one judge. The judges are appointed for six-year terms and must now retire when they reach the age of 70. At the moment the UK judge is Sir Nicholas Bratza and the President of the Court is a Swiss, Luzius Wildhaber. Decisions of the European Court of Human Rights are binding on all the states involved in the case, although in practice states wait some time before altering their national law to bring it into line with the pronouncements of the Court. On occasions the Court may order a national government to pay compensation to an aggrieved party, but in most cases the decision that the Convention has been breached is deemed by the Court to be a sufficient remedy. The ultimate responsibility for ensuring that the

---

[140] *In re Doherty's Application* [2004] NIQB 41, where a prisoner in Ireland failed in his claim against the Northern Ireland Prison Service over its refusal to transfer him to Northern Ireland.
[141] As a result of Protocol 11 to the Convention.
[142] The Court's Registrar issues press releases on many judgments: see http://www.echr.coe.int/eng/Press/PressReleases.htm.
[143] In 2004 just 15 of the 718 Court judgments were delivered by the Grand Chamber.

Court's decisions are executed in the Member States concerned belongs to the Committee of Ministers of the Council of Europe.[144] This Committee is a political rather than a legal body and can reach a decision only if two-thirds of the delegates agree.

The Court of Human Rights is creaking under the weight of applications made to it. In 2004 it issued 718 judgments, compared with just 177 as recently as 1999.[145] It requires a large injection of extra funding from Council of Europe Member States if it is to fulfil its potential as the most important court for some 800 million Europeans. Recently a new Protocol 14 to the Convention was drawn up[146] allowing single judges, rather than committees of three judges, to declare applications to be inadmissible,[147] adding a new ground of inadmissibility (namely, that "the applicant has not suffered a significant disadvantage, unless respect for human rights as defined in the Convention and the Protocols thereto requires an examination of the application on the merits and provided that no case may be rejected on this ground which has not been duly considered by a domestic tribunal"[148]) and allowing committees of three judges to issue decisions on the merits.[149]

The Convention's effect on Northern Ireland law[150]

The European Court of Human Rights has held against the United Kingdom in scores of cases. In 2004 alone there were 23 decisions in cases brought against the United Kingdom, and 25 in 2003. Of these 48 cases, breaches of the Convention were found to exist in 39 of them; in

---

[144] A Council of Europe website is devoted to the execution of the Court's judgments: www.coe.int/T/E/Human_rights/execution.

[145] The entire jurisprudence of the Court is available on-line at www.echr. coe.int/eng/Judgments.htm. A summary of the decisions made in 2004 is also on-line at www.echr.coe.int/eng/EDocs/SUBJECTMATTER2004.pdf.

[146] S. Greer, "Protocol 14 and the Future of the European Court of Human Rights" [2005] PL 83.

[147] Arts. 4 and 6 of Protocol 14, inserting new Arts. 24(2) and 26(1) into the Convention.

[148] Art. 12 of Protocol 14, inserting a new Art. 35(3)(b) into the Convention.

[149] Art. 8 of Protocol 14, inserting a new Art. 28(1)(b) into the Convention.

[150] See also B. Dickson, "Northern Ireland and the European Convention", Chap. 5 in B. Dickson (ed.), *Human Rights and the European Convention* (1997); B. Dickson, "Northern Ireland", Chap. 6 in A. Lester and D. Pannick (eds.), *Human Rights Law and Practice* (2nd ed., 2004); S Foster, "The Protection of Human Rights in Domestic Law: Learning Lessons from the European Court of Human Rights" (2002) 53 NILQ 232.

seven cases there were friendly settlements and in only two was there a decision that no right had been violated. Over the years, as a result of decisions by the Court of Human Rights the UK Government has had to change the law on (amongst other things) contempt of court, the closed shop, courts-martial, immigration, telephone tapping, prisoners' rights, defamation law and corporal punishment in schools. In one recent case, for example, two young people in England who were sued for libel by McDonalds were held to have had their rights breached when they could not get access to legal aid to defend themselves.[151]

Several of the cases brought against the UK Government have originated in Northern Ireland. The Court has issued judgments in almost 30 of these and perhaps 50 Northern Irish cases have been declared inadmissible by the Commission or by a committee of the Court.[152] Following a partially substantiated complaint by the Irish Government in the 1970s[153] - the first of only two inter-state cases ever to have reached the Court - the instructions to security forces in Northern Ireland with regard to interrogation techniques had to be altered, and following a complaint by an individual the law on homosexual offences in Northern Ireland was reformed (*Dudgeon* v *UK*).[154] However, a challenge to the legality of the use of plastic bullets in Northern Ireland failed before the European Commission (*Stewart* v *UK*).[155]

Cases on Northern Ireland's emergency laws

In November 1988 the Court held in *Brogan* v *UK*[156] that detention for more than four days and six hours under the Prevention of Terrorism (Temporary Provisions) Act 1984 was a breach of Article 5(3) of the Convention, which requires detainees to be brought promptly before a judge. The Government then officially "derogated" from (*i.e.* opted out of) the Convention in this respect, as it claimed to be allowed to do under Article 15 of the Convention. In a subsequent challenge to this

---

[151] *Steel and Morris* v *UK*, App. 68416/01, decision of 15 February 2005.
[152] It is not possible to be exact because the Strasbourg authorities do not register applications in accordance with the part of the UK where the applicant resides.
[153] *Ireland* v *UK* (1979-80) 2 EHRR 25. The European Commission held that the techniques in question amounted to torture, but the European Court downgraded the finding to one of "inhuman or degrading treatment".
[154] (1982) 4 EHRR 149.
[155] (1985) 7 EHRR 453.
[156] (1989) 11 EHRR 117.

derogation (*Brannigan and McBride* v *UK*)[157] the Court held that it was indeed valid under Article 15 because there was "a public emergency threatening the life of the nation" and the steps taken were not more than those "strictly required by the exigencies of the situation".

In 1996 a partially successful challenge was mounted to the law in Northern Ireland which allowed inferences of guilt to be drawn from the silence of someone who had been arrested and questioned by the police under their anti-terrorist powers but who had not had the benefit of a solicitor's advice (*Murray (John)* v *UK*).[158] Two later decisions of the Court in 2000 further condemned the unavailability of legal advice in situations where inferences of guilt could be drawn (*Averill* v *UK*[159] and *Magee* v *UK*[160]). In 1998 the UK Government lost another case where it had tried to prevent two applicants from challenging the Secretary of State's decision that they had no right to claim that they had been discriminated against on religious or political grounds in the allocation of a public sector contract (*Tinnelly and McElduff* v *UK*).[161]

In May 2001 the European Court held that Article 2 of the Convention (on the right to life) had been breached in relation to 11 individuals shot by the police or army in Northern Ireland (and 1 by the UDA) because there had not been thorough, prompt and impartial investigations into the killings (*Jordan* v *UK*,[162] *Kelly and others* v *UK*,[163] *McKerr* v *UK*[164] and *Shanaghan* v *UK*[165]). As a result the Government had to make changes to the inquest and prosecution systems in Northern Ireland. Whether enough has been done to comply with these and subsequent judgments in the same vein[166] is still being considered by the Council of Europe's Committee of Ministers.[167]

The Standing Advisory Commission on Human Rights in Northern Ireland recommended as long ago as 1977 that a Bill of Rights based

---

[157] (1994) 17 EHRR 539.
[158] (1996) 22 EHRR 29.
[159] (2000) 8 BHRC 430.
[160] (2001) 31 EHRR 35.
[161] (1999) 27 EHRR 249. This decision was later applied in two further similar cases, *Devenney* v *UK* (2002) 35 EHRR 643 and *Devlin* v *UK* (2002) 34 EHRR 1029.
[162] (2003) 37 EHRR 52
[163] App. 30054/96.
[164] (2002) 34 EHRR 20.
[165] App. 37715/97.
[166] *McShane* v *UK* (2002) 35 EHRR 593 and *Finucane* v *UK* (2003) 37 EHRR 656.
[167] See the Committee's Interim Resolution at www.coe.int/T/E/Com/press/ News/ 2005/20050224_rec_cm.asp.

on the European Convention should be enacted for the whole of the United Kingdom[168] and various bodies, most notably the Northern Ireland Human Rights Commission (see Chap. 9.6), have since published proposed drafts of a Bill of Rights for Northern Ireland which draw heavily on the Convention while going substantially beyond it in several important respects. In 1978 the members of a Select Committee of the House of Lords could not agree on whether a Bill of Rights was desirable for the United Kingdom as a whole but were unanimous that, if there were to be a Bill, it should be based on the European Convention.[169] It rejected the proposal that the European Community should, as a body, become a party to the Convention, and the European Court of Justice has ruled that this is not legally possible in any event.[170] The European Union has, however, included a Charter of Fundamental Rights in the draft Constitution for the European Union and this includes not just the standards laid down in the European Convention and developed by the European Court of Human Rights but also economic and social rights which are not protected by that Convention.[171] The Constitution also makes provision for the European Union to accede to (*i.e.* become a party to) the European Convention.

2.6 BRANCHES OF LAW

Criminal and civil law

The most common way of classifying law is to distinguish between criminal and civil law. Criminal law is that part of the law which prohibits acts deemed to be contrary to public order and the interests of society as a whole. It calls these acts "offences" and prescribes a variety of punishments for any person convicted of committing them. Some offences, such as murder or rape, are extremely serious; others, such as failure to wear a seatbelt, are comparatively minor. But they are all crimes and as such are dealt with by a special set of courts applying special procedures (see Chap. 5).

Most non-lawyers tend to think that criminal law is far and away the chief branch of the law. In fact, it is only one relatively small part of it.

---

[168] Cmnd. 7009; 1977.
[169] Report of the Select Committee on a Bill of Rights, HL 106.
[170] Opinion 2/94 [1996] 2 CMLR 265.
[171] I. Rogers, "From the Human Rights Act to the Charter: Not Another Human Rights Instrument to Consider?" [2002] EHRLR 343.

Students who study for a law degree usually spend less than one-tenth of their time on criminal law. The most senior judges may spend a quarter of their time on criminal cases, although judicial involvement is not a good way of measuring the law's impact. It has to be remembered that as well as controlling public order and determining how people should be punished for disrupting it, the law must make provision for regulating practically every sphere of human behaviour. It lays down rules for enabling citizens to achieve certain objectives (such as renting a house, buying a car, running a business, making a will, getting married) and it creates principles for the settlement of private disputes - disputes which do not involve breaches of public order. All law which is not criminal law is sometimes referred to as "civil" law, although, like "common" law, that expression has a variety of meanings depending on the context.

The main feature which distinguishes crimes from civil wrongs lies not in the nature of the behaviour being questioned but in the method by which the behaviour is dealt with by the legal system. A single piece of behaviour can constitute both a crime and a civil wrong (*e.g.* damaging someone's property or stealing something), but the criminal aspects of the incident will be dealt with by criminal courts (where the accused person - the defendant - is "prosecuted", then "convicted" or "acquitted" and, if convicted, "punished") and the civil aspects by civil courts (where the defendant is "sued", then held "liable" or "not liable" and, if liable, compelled to pay "damages"). Crucially, the standard of proof required in criminal and civil cases differs dramatically. In criminal cases a defendant can be found guilty only if the prosecution produce evidence leading to this conclusion "beyond a reasonable doubt". In civil cases a defendant can be held liable provided that the evidence leads to this conclusion "on the balance of probabilities". This is why some people (*e.g.* O.J. Simpson in the USA) are held not guilty in criminal proceedings but found liable in civil proceedings. The higher standard of proof is required in criminal cases because much more is usually at stake in such cases - such as whether the defendant should be sent to prison or not.

Under legislation such as the Criminal Justice (NI) Order 1980, a criminal court can at times award compensation to the victim of a crime without the need for separate civil proceedings, but this power is rarely used in practice (see Chap. 5.4). A civil court, moreover, occasionally awards "punitive" (or "exemplary") damages and it may issue a "declaration" that certain behaviour *would* be criminal if it were to be carried out. It should also be noted that applications to be compensated by the state for loss suffered as a result of criminal activity are actually civil law claims and are dealt with accordingly (see Chap. 6.5). Applications for judicial review (see Chap. 6.7) are also classified as civil law matters, even when the review applied for relates to a decision taken in a criminal case. In such cases the distinction between criminal and civil proceedings becomes somewhat blurred.

In both criminal and civil appeals the party appealing is termed the "appellant". In civil cases the opposing party is called the "respondent" and in criminal cases the party is referred to either as the prosecutor or the defendant as the case may be.

Branches of civil law[172]

The names of the various branches of the civil law are mostly self-explanatory. They include land law, family law, contract law and company law. Each of these can in turn be subdivided and some of the subdivisions overlap with other subdivisions or with other main branches; examples are landlord and tenant law, housing law, divorce law, employment law, consumer law, banking law, partnership law and insolvency law. Of the less obviously named branches, the law of torts is for the most part concerned with the compensation of people who have been injured (or whose property has been damaged) through someone's carelessness; the law's term for such carelessness is "the tort of negligence". A subdivision of tort law is the law on libel and slander (or "defamation"). Other torts include trespass (which refers to interference with not only land but also people and goods), nuisance, false imprisonment and breach of confidence.

The expression "property law" is sometimes used to refer to those branches of the civil law which inform us about our rights and duties in relation to the things we own or rent or in which we have some other kind of interest. As the most important form of property is land (called, in law, "real property", or, in the USA, "realty") - an expression which in law embraces the buildings erected on land - the term property law is often used to mean the same as land law. Strictly speaking it should also refer to the law concerning property which is not land. There are

---

[172] For further help with the terms referred to in this section see I. McLeod, *Legal Method* (5th ed., 2005), Chap. 2; K. Smith and D. Keenan, *Smith and Keenan's English Law* (14th ed., 2004) and G. Slapper and D. Kelly, *The English Legal System* (7th ed., 2004). See also the illuminating text by F. Cownie, A. Bradney and M. Burton, *The English Legal System in Context* (3rd ed., 2003).

innumerable forms of such property (collectively known as "personalty"), ranging from the most tangible,[173] such as cars and antiques, to the most intangible,[174] such as shares in a company, premium bonds or copyright in a book. To discourage too much property becoming vested in one person, our law has devised methods for splitting up the interests which might be held in a single piece of property: someone who owns a house, for instance, might "lease" (*i.e.* rent) it to someone or give an interest in it to a building society in return for a "mortgage" (*i.e.* a loan). A specific device which both English and Irish law have developed for splitting up people's interests in property is the "trust". If a fund of money, for instance, is held on trust, the purse-strings are controlled by persons called trustees and the people who actually receive payments out of the fund are called the beneficiaries of the trust. It is in the form of trusts that most charities carry on their work.

Public and private law

Some branches of the civil law, together with the criminal law, are sometimes lumped together to form the category known as "public law" in contrast to "private law". While private law regulates relations between individuals, public law regulates relations between individuals and public bodies, including the state. Thus, the branch of public law called constitutional law tells us about the way in which we are governed and what our civil liberties are. This is a particularly important branch of Northern Ireland law.[175] Human rights law is concerned with the obligations placed on public bodies to respect the basic rights of individuals.[176] Administrative law deals mainly with controlling the powers of central and local government and other public bodies; it also allows the courts to supervise the work of administrative tribunals (see Chap. 8.1). Some of the principles developed within administrative law, such as those concerned with natural justice (*e.g.* each side to a dispute must be given a fair hearing), are beginning to infiltrate into private law subjects such as contract law and tort law. Welfare law explains the operation of the welfare state, setting out the

---

[173] A piece of tangible property is sometimes referred to as a *chose in possession.*

[174] A piece of intangible property is sometimes referred to as a *chose in action.*

[175] See B. Hadfield, *The Constitution of Northern Ireland* (1989) and B. Dickson and M. O'Brien (eds.), *Civil Liberties in Northern Ireland: The CAJ Handbook* (4th ed., 2003).

[176] The Human Rights Act 1998 applies only to public authorities, although this includes private authorities exercising public functions.

conditions which must be satisfied before people will qualify for state benefits. International law can be part of public law or private law: it is public whenever it concerns the relations between states, or between states and individuals (this is called international human rights law), but private whenever it deals with the relations between individuals from different states.[177] The distinction between public and private law is also important as regards court proceedings involving children (see Chap. 7.1).

Substantive and procedural law

All the branches of law so far mentioned can be labelled "substantive" legal subjects because they concern the actual substance or content of the law: they reveal to us our rights, our duties and our privileges. "Procedural" or "adjectival" legal subjects, on the other hand, regulate the methods by which the substance of the law is applied. The law on criminal procedure determines how crimes are to be prosecuted, how the rights of an accused person are to be protected and how punishments are to be enforced. The law on civil procedure similarly lays down the steps which must be taken whenever a civil dispute develops into a civil legal action. Chapters 5 and 6 of this book are concerned with criminal and civil procedure respectively. The law of evidence contains a mass of detailed rules to specify the sort of testimony and documents which can be used in either a civil or a criminal court to support an argument.

All of these procedural subjects are important because, if the rules of procedure are not properly complied with, substantive legal rights can sometimes be lost. For example, it is a general rule of civil procedure that a legal action claiming compensation for personal injuries must be brought within three years of the injuries coming to light; if the action is not brought within this so-called "limitation period", the right to claim compensation is lost (or "time-barred").[178]

---

[177] Private international law is also known as "the conflict of laws".
[178] The details of the law are mostly to be found in the Limitation (NI) Order 1989, as amended.

CHAPTER THREE

LEGAL SERVICES

3.1 SEEKING LEGAL HELP

Identifying a legal problem

When lay people think of law they usually connect it in their minds with bodies such as the police, the courts and judges. Chapters 1 and 2 may have reinforced this impression, but at this point it is necessary to make it clear that the legal system consists of a great deal more than just police work and court cases. In fact only a very small fraction of legal matters ever involve such steps.

Legal problems arise at very many points in our lives but in the overwhelming majority of instances they are easily solved and no further difficulty ensues. They may arise because we want to achieve some objective but we do not know what is the "proper" way of going about it: we do not know what forms to complete, whose permission to seek, what fees to pay, etc. Typical instances are when we want to make a will, buy a house, borrow money or set up a business. Alternatively, problems may arise during some quite ordinary everyday activity and we suddenly find ourselves having a dispute with another party. For example, we may buy an article in a shop only to discover when we take it home that it does not work properly; we may be in regular receipt of income support but we find that it is not meeting our needs; we may be sacked from our job; we may have an accident while driving a car; or we may be unable to produce a television licence when the detector van calls at our house. The other party in such disputes may be an individual, a firm, an official agency or a branch of government.

Before we are able to seek legal help with any of these problems we must be aware that the problem facing us is indeed a legal one. Yet the existence of a legal problem is by no means always as obvious as might be imagined. We may be in breach of legal regulations but not know this; we may be legally entitled to some benefit or award but, again, be ignorant of this right; we may be perfectly aware that we are in dispute with someone, but neither of us may think of it as a legal dispute – we may simply consider it to be an administrative or an organisational wrangle.

Once we begin to think that the law may have something to say about our predicament, we should act quickly. First of all it is sensible to tell a friend or relative about it. As often as not, just talking over the problem with someone can help us to see another way out of it. Our attention may be drawn to some aspect of the situation which enables us to clear things up. But if this is not so and we feel the need for further advice or assistance, there are many bodies who may be able to help. Before we consult them we should try to gather together all relevant documents relating to our case. If letters have already been written about it, it helps to have copies of these, or at any rate a summary of what was said in them or during relevant telephone conversations. A list giving the precise dates of the various stages in the dispute up to this time can also be most useful.

Advice agencies

There are basically two types of bodies which can give advice on legal matters. There are "private" agencies and "public" agencies. The private agencies consist of membership organisations which either run an advisory service to allow members to cope themselves with particular kinds of problems or are prepared to treat a member's problem as in effect their own problem and to act on it accordingly.

Examples of these private agencies are trades unions, employers' and traders' associations, some clubs, tenants' groups, claimants' groups and insurance companies. Members of a trade union, for instance, will often find their union more than willing to take up a grievance relating to employment. Insurance companies, too, will often offer to act for their customers, as in disputes concerning road accidents. Doctors may find that their legal costs can be paid for by the Medical Defence Union when they are sued for medical negligence.[1] Obviously the schemes which each of these private organisations operates will differ widely in the degree of assistance they provide; some will expect personal and financial commitments from their members, others will not. But the mere fact that someone else is interested enough to help a person find a way out of a predicament can be a great comfort!

---

[1] www.the-mdu.com (the UK's leading medical defence organisation, providing medico-legal advice and assistance and professional indemnity insurance).

The public agencies are those which exist for the benefit of all people in the community, whether or not they are members of a scheme. Some are general agencies: they offer advice on practically every problem brought to them, even if it is just to explain where more specialised help can be obtained. Others deal only with particular types of problems. All of them, however, are usually ready to help not just on the legal aspects of the problem but also on its other dimensions - its personal, social and financial features. They provide their services free of charge, although of course they welcome donations so that they can develop their work. To an increasing extent these "public" agencies are staffed by trained professionals, but they also have many volunteers working for them. There is a general on-line advice service for England and Wales called Community Legal Services Direct,[2] and in many instances the advice given there would be applicable in Northern Ireland too. The Legal Action Group is a UK-wide support organisation for advice agencies which publishes a very useful Bulletin every month (called *Legal Action*). We will now examine a few of the public agencies working in Northern Ireland in more detail.

Citizens' Advice Bureaux

Probably the best known agencies accessible to the general public are the Citizens' Advice Bureaux (CABx). The establishment of bureaux began in England in 1939, with the first being opened in Northern Ireland in 1964. There are currently 28 bureaux in Northern Ireland, many of them with a number of "outreach" centres: altogether advice is available from 100 outlets, including many located in community centres and health centres in rural areas. The addresses of the main bureaux can be found in Appendix 2 of this book (and in the telephone directory). Their opening hours vary. A home visiting service is offered by most of the bureaux and a National Minimum Wage Helpline has been established.[3] During the year ending 31 March 2004, CABx throughout Northern Ireland handled inquiries from an astonishing 138,269 people, more than 8% of the population. By far the largest category of inquiry was social security, which accounted for 56%. A further 14% concerned consumer matters and more than 9% related to employment issues.

---

[2] See www.clsdirect.org.uk, where you can also calculate whether you are your eligible for civil legal aid. Access to free quality-controlled legal information and advice is available by phoning 0845 3454 345.

[3] 0845 6500 207.

When a person visits a CAB (often after having been referred there by another agency), he or she is interviewed in private by one of the advisers. A written record of the case will be kept on computer so that if some other adviser has to take it over at a later stage he or she will know at a glance what has already happened. In most cases it does not take more than half-an-hour for the adviser to listen to the story and give an indication of what action is recommended. Sometimes the advice will be that the person being advised should take certain steps; at other times the adviser will be happy to write letters or make contacts on the person's behalf.

If the case is a complex one or involves a lot of money, the adviser will probably recommend that a solicitor be contacted. Every CAB in Northern Ireland has a "referral list" which gives the names of practising solicitors in the area who have agreed to receive cases passed on to them by the bureau. The adviser will usually be able to say a little about some of these solicitors so that the person being advised can decide more easily which of them might handle the case best, but usually no official recommendation is made so that the client's freedom of choice is preserved. Some of the bureaux actually have solicitors acting as advisers: they will be there on a rota basis at a set time each week, ready to be consulted about any case which requires their expertise. If it transpires that the case is one which should be dealt with by a solicitor acting in his or her office rather than as a CAB adviser, it is possible for the solicitor in the bureau to take over the case in a professional capacity. This is allowed, however, only if the solicitor has been previously granted a "waiver" by the professional body for solicitors, the Law Society of Northern Ireland (see 3.2 below); without this waiver it would be a breach of the rules restricting the advertising in which solicitors are allowed to engage.

CAB advice workers may themselves represent individuals at tribunals. Indeed in 2003 this occurred in some 1,400 tribunal cases, which makes CABx the largest single source of help for tribunal applicants in Northern Ireland. Representation greatly increases the chances of the applicant winning his or her case at the tribunal: in 2003 there were 13,638 social security and disability appeal tribunals heard in Northern Ireland, but only in 37% of these (down from 46% in 1999) was the applicant represented. In those cases where there was representation the success rate was 44%, whereas in cases where there was no representation the success rate was just 17%.

All the CABx in Northern Ireland belong to Citizens' Advice Northern Ireland,[4] which provides the local bureaux with up-to-date information about changes in the law. Advisers have access to a sophisticated on-line information database. The association also provides training for advisers. In 2003-04, out of a total income of some £802,000, the grant from the Department for Social Development for the work of Citizens' Advice was £394,000, the rest being provided from various charitable sources. The money was largely used for the salaries of the 17 staff in Citizens' Advice's headquarters. Citizens' Advice has a Board with a representative from each Bureau.[5] The parent organisation based in London, Citizens' Advice, publishes many pamphlets dealing with various aspects of the law likely to be encountered by advisers. It also runs an on-line advice and information service covering all parts of the United Kingdom.[6] Citizens' Advice also produces its own publications, such as *Fairness at Work, Accessing Social Security* and *Debt Handbook for Advisers*. These can be ordered through its website and a quarterly newsletter, *Advice*, can also be downloaded from that site.

In May 2004 a case concerning eligibility for a social fund funeral expenses payment, which was first brought to the CAB in Bangor, County Down, went all the way to the House of Lords, where it was decided in the claimant's favour.[7] This gives some indication of how significant the work of CABx can be.

Other advice centres

A second important type of generalist advice agency is the independent advice centres. Like the CABx, these exist to give advice on all sorts of matters, not just those involving legal issues. As their name implies, the centres are the result of local initiatives and are often funded, in part at least, by the local district council. Not all are open daily, since their staff are often volunteer advisers or community workers who have many other responsibilities to fulfil. A few of the advisers are qualified lawyers, but most are not. The Law Society does not grant a waiver (see above) to solicitors who do voluntary work in an advice centre, so they are not allowed to take over any of the cases privately.

---

[4] www.citizensadvice.co.uk.
[5] The Chief Executive is Mr Derek Alcorn.
[6] www.advicedirect.co.uk.
[7] *Kerr v Department for Social Development* [2004] 1 WLR 1372.

At the moment there are approximately 80 independent legal advice centres in Northern Ireland, although they may not always describe themselves by this title. During their busiest periods they may handle a total of 2,000 inquiries a month. They provide the same sort of personal attention and confidentiality as does a Citizens' Advice Bureau, but unfortunately the centres do not enjoy the relatively comprehensive back-up services which are provided to the Bureaux.

Various other advice agencies exist in Northern Ireland, most of them designed to deal with problems which are peculiar to a particular locality or kind of person. There are many community and tenant organisations, and other bodies such as Alcoholics Anonymous, Belfast Housing Aid, the Children's Law Centre, the Chinese Welfare Association, Gamblers Anonymous, Gingerbread (for one-parent families), the Housing Rights Service, the Multi-Cultural Resource Centre, the Northern Ireland Council for Ethnic Minorities, Relate (for people with relationship problems), the Samaritans, Shelter and Women's Aid. There are two Consumer Advice Centres - in Belfast and Derry/Londonderry - which deal with the wide range of consumer affairs. For further details of these agencies, apply to the addresses given in Appendix 2 of this book or look up the heading *Counselling and Advice* in the Yellow Pages.

Advice[ni] (formerly the Association of Independent Advice Centres) is a body which works to promote the activities of its member organisations, all of which are in the business of giving advice to ordinary members of the public. It seeks to develop creative community development approaches to advice-giving and to co-ordinate and support individual advice centre initiatives. The organisation is also an assessment centre for NVQ accredited training in advice and guidance and it publishes social policy briefing papers as well as a quarterly magazine called *adviceMatters*. Its members are listed county by county on its website.[8]

The Law Centre (NI)[9]

One of the disadvantages of the advice agencies so far described is that they are limited in what they can do. They can give advice and write letters; on occasion they will represent a claimant at a tribunal, or at

---

[8] www.adviceni.net.
[9] www.lawcentreni.org. Much of the information for this section has been gleaned from *Working for Your Rights*, the Law Centre (NI)'s Annual Report 2003-2004.

any rate help the claimant to present his or her case there, but they cannot otherwise do the work of practising lawyers. Their big advantage is that they do not charge for their services. To meet the need for an agency which not only does not charge but can operate almost as a firm of private solicitors, offices called Law Centres have been established throughout the United Kingdom. The first to be established was in North Kensington in London in 1970. Today there are about 60 of them around the country. The Belfast Community Law Centre began work in 1977. It changed its name to the Belfast Law Centre in 1980 and to the Law Centre (NI) a few years later.

The Law Centre (NI) reaches out to a larger geographical area than most other Law Centres in the United Kingdom and not many serve comparable populations. As well as its central office in Belfast it maintains a Western Area office in Derry / Londonderry. At present the organisation runs on an income of approximately £1.2 million per annum, about 40% of this being granted by the Department for Social Development. Other funders include the Northern Ireland Legal Services Commission, four health and social services boards and the Department of Employment and Learning. In August 2005 it employed about 30 staff in Belfast and nine in Derry / Londonderry. The Director is Mr Les Allamby.

The Law Centre states its purpose to be the promotion of social justice and the provision of specialist legal support to advice-giving organisations and disadvantaged individuals. It fulfils this by maintaining an advice line for its 450 or so member organisations every weekday morning, by providing a casework and representation service on referral from its members, by running training courses, by publishing relevant information and by supplying comments on proposed changes to law and policy. The member organisations elect the management committee of the Law Centre and must be independent advice groups: no government agency, statutory body or group with a vested interest may be a member.

Inquiries and casework

The latest annual report of the Law Centre shows that in 2004-05 there were 6,449 advice line inquiries. The largest proportion of queries related to immigration (33%), with social security accounting for as many as 29%, followed by employment (21%) and community care (12%). Housing issues were raised in just 2% of the inquiries. The

Centre has been granted a "waiver" by the Law Society, which in effect permits it to act as a firm of solicitors provided that it does not engage in the major areas of work in which private practitioners usually operate, such as buying and selling houses or dealing with wills, matrimonial disputes and criminal work. Generally speaking, the Law Centre will take on cases only if they have been referred to it by another advice agency, such as a Citizens' Advice Bureau or a firm of solicitors.

The sort of case which it will be most happy to deal with is a test case on some new point of law: if it can obtain a favourable ruling from a court or a tribunal, this will help many other people who may be encountering the same problem elsewhere in the United Kingdom. In concentrating on such cases the Centre comes close to advancing group interests, much in the way that in the United States of America "class actions" can be brought on behalf of a large number of people. This is a welcome development, for the legal system of Northern Ireland is otherwise a highly individualised one, that is, each problem has to be dealt with as and when it affects a particular person.

In 2003-04 the Law Centre worked on 485 cases and represented clients in 321 of these. The latter included 138 immigration appeals, 93 social security appeals and 53 employment cases in industrial tribunals. There were also 37 court cases, seven of which were heard in the Court of Appeal and one in the House of Lords. The Centre's overall success rate in its casework was an excellent 65%, which rose to 91% as far as cases in the industrial tribunals are concerned.

In one case in 2003 the Court of Appeal ruled that the Northern Ireland Housing Executive had not done enough to protect a family in Limavady from sectarian harassment emanating from their neighbours: the right to a private and family life under Article 8 of the European Convention had been breached.[10] In another case in 2002 a social security appeal tribunal held that a man who had "exported" his entitlement to the state retirement pension when he moved to live in the Republic of Ireland was also entitled to benefits automatically derived from that pension, such as the winter fuel payment: the requirement that a person claiming that payment had to be ordinarily resident in the United Kingdom was contrary to EC law. This decision was appealed and the view of the Social Security Commissioner is awaited. The Centre successfully challenged the rule that claims for bereavement

---

[10] *In re Donnelly's Application* [2003] NICA 55.

benefits must be made within three months of the death, its argument being that the strictness of the rule violated human rights standards.

Educational and campaigning role

The Law Centre has always set great store by its educative and preventative roles in society. It seeks to avoid potential problems becoming real ones by making people more aware of their rights and duties. For many years an especially important part of its work has been the provision of training and information to other groups giving advice, mainly in the area of welfare rights. Some staff are employed full-time on this work. As well as providing basic training for new advice workers the Centre runs specialist courses for established workers on topics such as debt, access to housing, disability and social security. A Certificate in Welfare Rights is available for those who are particularly dedicated (45 undertook this in 2004-05) and for two years the Law Centre has been working in partnership with Advice[ni] on the Advice Skills Learning (ASK) project, which can lead to the Welfare Rights Adviser Programme (WRAP) certificate. Further work has been done in conjunction with the Office of the Immigration Services Commissioner to ensure that those giving immigration advice in Northern Ireland are competent to do so.[11]

Along with Citizens Advice Northern Ireland and what is now Advice[ni] (see below), the Law Centre was instrumental in establishing an Advice Services Alliance, which aims to develop advice services throughout Northern Ireland by, for instance, encouraging liaison between agencies in the voluntary and statutory sectors. With a view to ensuring a high quality of advice-giving in the province, the Alliance publishes a booklet entitled *Standards and Guidelines for Advice Agencies*. The Law Centre itself supplements this guidance by distributing a variety of informational material in both hard copy and on-line. This includes an *Encyclopaedia of Rights*, a quarterly magazine (*Frontline*) and a Casework Bulletin issued three times a year. The Centre has also published *Rights in Progress*,[12] a very clear guide for advisers on case law stemming from the Human Rights Act 1998 and the European Convention on Human Rights.

---

[11] The OISC was set up under the Immigration and Asylum Act 1999 to regulate immigration advice workers. It is an offence to give such advice without registration or without being officially exempted from registration.

[12] 2nd ed., 2003.

In 2001 a research report on the detention of asylum seekers was published (updated in 2003)[13] and in 2004 a major new report was launched on the gaps in advice and support available for people with mental health problems in Northern Ireland.[14] In the same year staff co-authored a report on mental health and human rights published by the Human Rights Commission.[15] During 2003-04 the Government ceased its policy of detaining immigration detainees at Maghaberry prison, housing them instead at the Crumlin Road Working Out Centre in Belfast (males) and at Hydebank Wood Young Offenders Centre (females), but the Law Centre, along with many other organisations such as the Refugee Action Group, continues to campaign to have the policy of detention in prison environments abolished altogether (not least because it is not applied in England and Wales). The Law Centre recently succeeded in persuading the Northern Ireland Housing Executive to provide access to housing and housing benefit to nationals of new European Union countries who are registered for work and it is partnering the Rights in Community Care campaign to lobby for improvements to the system of paying for care in Northern Ireland.

The future

Funding for Law Centres in general is a constant problem, despite the efforts made by the Law Centres Federation (the umbrella organisation for law centres in the United Kingdom),[16] and the effect of recent reforms to the legal aid schemes has been to make even greater demands on the Centres (see 3.3 below). A development plan for the Law Centre (NI) covering the years 2005-08 has been published and takes into account the 10-year strategy on provision of advice and information which is due from the Department for Social Development in 2005. The Law Centre (NI) also plans to deepen its contact with the Irish Law Centres Network.

---

[13] V. Tennant, *Sanctuary in a Cell*. This examined the cases of 75 individuals who were detained in prison under immigration legislation in Northern Ireland over an 18-month period.

[14] J. Campbell and D. Wilson, *Unmet Need: A study of mental health legal advice and information services in Northern Ireland*.

[15] G. Davidson, M. McCallion and M. Potter, *Connecting Mental Health and Human Rights* (2004).

[16] www.lawcentres.org.uk.

Pressure groups

The distinction between an advice agency and a pressure group is not always a clear-cut one. In some respects it could be said that the Consumer Advice Centres, for example, are as much one as the other, for they combine their advisory work with some degree of campaigning about consumers' rights. Of the organisations which are primarily pressure groups, the most prominent in Northern Ireland on legal matters is the Committee on the Administration of Justice (the CAJ).[17] The group carries out research, publishes campaigning and informational materials and make submissions to the Government on suggested reforms. As a rule the organisation does not hold itself out as offering legal advice to individuals - because the Law Society has refused to grant a "waiver" to the CAJ's caseworker - but in some instances it has helped people to present their cases more persuasively to the authorities, including at the European Court of Human Rights.

The CAJ has been prominent in helping to establish other collectivities such as the Equality Coalition, the Human Rights Consortium and what is now known as the Coalition on Sexual Orientation (CoSO). There is now a vibrant Anti-Racism Network too.[18]

Some groups with headquarters in England have taken a keen interest in the Northern Ireland legal system – and not just in the emergency laws which have been introduced to deal with the troubles. Worthy of mention are Amnesty International,[19] British Irish Rights Watch,[20] the Howard League for Penal Reform,[21] Justice, the Legal Action Group, and Liberty (formerly the National Council for Civil Liberties).[22] Each of these groups has individual members in Northern Ireland. If you wish to join or be put in touch with local members, write to the offices in England at the addresses listed in Appendix 2.

---

[17] www.caj.org.uk. See too the Pat Finucane Centre in Derry/Londonderry: www.serve.com/pfc. These organisations are in effect the successor bodies to the now defunct Northern Ireland Civil Rights Association, the Association for Legal Justice and the Northern Ireland Association of Socialist Lawyers.

[18] www.amni.tk.

[19] www.amnesty.org.uk. (For the Northern Ireland office see www.amnesty.org.uk/ni/index.shtml).

[20] www.birw.org.

[21] See, *e.g.*, its *Suicide and Self-Harm Prevention: A Strategy for Northern Ireland* (2003).

[22] www.liberty-human-rights.org.uk.

3.2 THE LEGAL PROFESSIONS

Consulting a solicitor

Should your case be one which you want to take to a solicitor - perhaps after having been advised to do so by an advice agency - you will need to know how to deal with a solicitor and what the implications may be. Finding a solicitor should present no problem. You or your family may have dealt with one in the past and you may want to use the same person again; a friend or somebody at an advice agency may recommend someone to you; or you can simply cast your eye down the list of solicitors in the Yellow Pages of the telephone directory and choose one whose office is close to where you live. You can also search for a solicitor through the directory on the website of the Northern Ireland Legal Services Commission,[23] which also allows you to look for those solicitors undertaking particular types of work. It is best to call in person or by telephone in order to arrange an appointment. Bear in mind that some solicitors do not handle certain types of case, so you may have to shop around a little. Those firms which have met Law Society approved Practice Management Standards are entitled to display the "Lexcel" quality mark.

You should not be apprehensive about consulting a solicitor; he or she should be able to let you know quickly what your legal position is on the matter and what you should do next. But always prepare yourself well before arriving at the solicitor's office: rehearse your story with a friend beforehand and bring along all the relevant documents. If you are worried about the costs involved, you can ask if the solicitor will see you under the fixed-fee interview scheme, which provides you with a 30-minute interview for £5.00 (see 3.3 below). If the solicitor is unwilling to see you under that scheme, you can certainly ask when you make your appointment how much the initial interview will cost. If you are on income support, the cost may be covered by the legal advice and assistance scheme, also described in the next section. At each interview you can ask how much the proposed next step in the case is likely to cost and whether you will be eligible for legal aid, advice or assistance. You may even contact more than one solicitor and compare their estimated charges before you decide which to engage.

---

[23] www.nilsc.org.uk.

The Law Society of Northern Ireland

Solicitors became a distinct self-governing profession in Ireland with the creation of the Law Society of Ireland in 1830. In 1922 a Royal Charter was granted to solicitors in Northern Ireland to permit the setting up of the Incorporated Law Society of Northern Ireland.[24] Under a statute passed in 1938 (superseded by an Order in Council in 1976,[25] itself amended in 1989) the Law Society obtained the power to issue regulations governing the education,[26] the accounts and the professional conduct of solicitors. The current Practice and Accounts Regulations were issued, with the approval of the Lord Chief Justice, in 1987, and have since been amended many times, especially in 1998.

All solicitors must register with the Law Society every year (although they need not necessarily become members) and an annual practising certificate will be granted only if the Law Society is sure, amongst other things, that the solicitor is properly insured against loss wrongfully caused to clients. The Society operates through a Council of 30 members, all practising solicitors who serve on a voluntary basis.[27] As well as the 18 regional associations of solicitors which exist throughout Northern Ireland (the Belfast Solicitors' Association is over 50 years old), there are associations for solicitors interested in particular kinds of legal work, such as the Family Law Association and the misleadingly-named Criminal Bar Association.

Today, solicitors' offices are found throughout Northern Ireland; more than 400 firms are listed in the telephone directory and in mid-May 2005 there were 2,126 persons with practising certificates in the province.[28] The firms vary in size from the small one-person office to the large firm which may have several partners and employ several "assistant" solicitors - these are fully qualified solicitors who do not have a personal stake in the ownership of the firm. The firm will also employ secretarial staff and perhaps one or two apprentices; unlike English firms, solicitors in Northern Ireland do not employ assistants called legal executives. The size of the firm should not affect the quality of the service provided, nor should it greatly influence the

[24] www.lawsoc-ni.org.
[25] Solicitors (NI) Order 1976.
[26] See the Solicitors' Admission and Training Regs. (NI) 1988.
[27] The President of the Law Society for 2004-05 is Ms Attracta Wilson; in 2005-06 it will be Mr Rory McShane.
[28] Not everyone with a practising certificate will be in private practice, but the vast majority will be.

charges. Remember that solicitors are first and foremost professional business people, who need to pay overheads and make a profit. In a sense they are handicapped in this activity because the Law Society does not permit them to attract business through, for example, price-cutting or sharing offices with non-solicitors. Nor can they form themselves into limited companies, only partnerships. There are also restrictions on how solicitors can advertise themselves.[29] These rules exist in order to protect the interests of clients and to maintain the integrity of the profession as a whole.

The work of a solicitor

The daily work of a solicitor can be very varied. Most of it is office work, though solicitors do have what is called "the right of audience" in magistrates' courts and county courts (and occasionally in the Crown Court), which means that they can speak on behalf of their clients in those courts. Traditionally that is the role of barristers, who in Northern Ireland, as we shall see, retain the exclusive right of audience in the higher courts. In England and Wales all solicitors including those not in private practice can now address the higher courts if they first obtain a "certificate in advocacy",[30] but this is not yet possible in Northern Ireland. The largest single category of solicitors' work is conveyancing (*i.e.* the legal transfer of land and buildings), which occupies about one-third of their time and represents an even greater proportion of their income; the other important categories are matrimonial work, succession work (*i.e.* dealing with the consequences of a death), criminal work and accident compensation claims. If the firm is large enough it will probably have a litigation department to deal with those cases which may involve court actions; the vast majority of such actions are eventually "settled out of court" (*i.e.* a compromise is reached) and it is an essential part of a solicitor's function to try to arrange such settlements.

The time and cost involved in actually bringing matters to court are such that it is a step to be taken only as a very last resort. Even during the course of a court hearing the two sides to a dispute may agree to settle it, which then leads to a judgment by consent (see Chap. 6.1). In order to reduce the pressure on courts, and to keep down costs, the Law

---

[29] See the Solicitors' (Advertising, Public Relations and Marketing) Practice Regs. (NI) 1997.
[30] Under the Courts and Legal Services Act 1990.

Society has offered since 2002 an "alternative dispute resolution" (ADR) scheme for parties involved in commercial disputes.[31] Under this scheme, the parties share the fees.

Though varied, much of a solicitor's work is fairly routine. If it does not involve a dispute with another party, it is called non-contentious work, the charges for which are calculated on a different basis from that used for contentious work (see Chap. 3.4). All solicitors can now also function as Commissioners for Oaths, and 23 act as notaries public (they are listed on the Law Society's website). The former are required as witnesses for certain official documents, although they cannot witness documents prepared by themselves or by their opponents in a case. Notaries public are lawyers who can witness documents for use abroad. As regards two matters solicitors in Northern Ireland currently have a virtual monopoly: (i) the drawing up of a conveyance on the sale of land and (ii) the taking out of probate or letters of administration when someone dies. It is a criminal offence, with some minor exceptions, for anyone who is not a solicitor to undertake either of these tasks if payment is demanded for the work. In England the first of these monopolies was removed when the Administration of Justice Act 1985 provided for the licensing of non-solicitor conveyancers, but as yet this freedom of trade has not been extended to Northern Ireland and there is no immediate prospect of its occurring. Solicitors cannot provide expert financial advice but in 1988 a special company was set up in Northern Ireland - the Law Society (NI) Financial Advice Ltd - to provide a facility whereby clients can receive independent expert financial advice on referral by their solicitors.

Information relevant to the solicitors' profession in Northern Ireland is included in the Law Society's monthly magazine called *The Writ*, also available on-line. Every practising solicitor must now also undertake "continuing professional development" in the form of training course etc.[32]

---

[31] More details, including a downloadable leaflet about the scheme, are available on the Law Society's website.
[32] See the Solicitors' Training (Continuing Professional Development) Regs (NI) 2004, in force from 6 January 2005.

Complaints against solicitors[33]

If you wish to complain about a solicitor you should first of all discuss the matter thoroughly with the solicitor involved. You need to realise that, because technically they are officers of the Supreme Court, the primary duty of solicitors is not to their clients but to the courts. They certainly must act for you to the best of their ability but this does not allow them to conceal evidence or to ignore established procedures. However, if you are not satisfied with your solicitor's explanation in relation to your complaint you can write to the Law Society about the matter. All complaints are dealt with in the first instance by Society staff and the more serious cases are considered by the Professional Conduct Committee, on which four non-lawyers are entitled to sit.[34] Where it finds it merited, this Committee may reprimand the solicitor and / or direct him or her to take certain steps; if the complaint is about the solicitor's charges, the Committee can also determine the appropriate amount of money to be paid, provided the complaint was lodged within six months' of the solicitor's bill being sent to the client. The Committee cannot, however, award any compensation to the complainant. More serious cases can be referred to the Solicitors Disciplinary Tribunal, which is independent of the Law Society and again contains lay representatives. The Tribunal has the power, amongst other things, to strike a solicitor off the Solicitors' Roll, to impose a fine of up to £3,000 and to order the solicitor to pay back all or part of the legal fees for the work in question. An appeal against a decision of the Disciplinary Tribunal can be taken by any person affected by it to a judge of the High Court.

It is important to bear in mind that the Law Society's Professional Conduct Committee will consider complaints alleging negligence only if the behaviour being questioned, if proved to have occurred, would amount to professional misconduct or to inadequate professional services. Other cases of negligence must be processed in the ordinary way through the civil courts. It is important to note that as a result of a recent decision of the House of Lords a solicitor *can* now be sued if he or she conducts court proceedings negligently.

---

[33] The Law Society publishes leaflets entitled *Dissatisfied with your solicitor?* and *Unhappy about your bill?* They can be downloaded from the Society's website.

[34] In England and Wales a separate Office for the Supervision of Solicitors has been established.

The Lay Observer[35]

Since 1977 Northern Ireland has had an official called the Lay Observer,[36] a non-lawyer whose job it is to report on the nature of complaints made to the Law Society about the conduct of solicitors and the manner in which the complaints are dealt with by the Society. The reports are officially made to the Lord Chief Justice, the Government's Department of Finance and Personnel and the Council of the Law Society, but they are printed and can be purchased through The Stationery Office. The current Lay Observer is Mr Alasdair Maclaughlin. He was appointed in 2004 for just two years, as the Department of Finance and Personnel is currently considering what changes to make to the system of regulation for the provision of legal services in Northern Ireland.

In his report for 2003 the Lay Observer[37] revealed that there were 274 complaints against solicitors during the year ending in September 2003, a decrease of 12 compared with the previous year. This means that some 23% of solicitor firms had at least one complaint lodged against them in that year. Of these complaints, most related to work done on the buying or selling of homes, on personal injury claims or on matrimonial proceedings. The most frequent cause of complaint was undue delay (129 cases) but there were also 81 cases of alleged unethical behaviour. The Lay Observer was of the view that complaints to the Law Society were being handled promptly and efficiently but he nevertheless recommended that the Law Society should consider adopting the even better practices used in Scotland and the Republic of Ireland. In particular he advocated a more open approach to complainants and a more business-like approach to the management of relationships and communications with all clients.

In order to alleviate public anxiety at the lack of scrutiny of solicitors' and other legal services, the Government declared its intention in the early 1990s to appoint a Legal Services Ombudsman for Northern Ireland,[38] a post already in existence for England, Wales and Scotland thanks to the Courts and Legal Services Act 1990. Such an

---

[35] www.adrnow.org.uk/go/SubPage_76.html.
[36] Solicitors (NI) Order 1976, art. 42, as amended by the Solicitors (Amendment) (NI) Order 1989, art. 17.
[37] At that time the Lay Observer was Professor Vincent Mageean.
[38] See *Legal Services in Northern Ireland: The Government's Proposals*, Northern Ireland Court Service (1991).

Ombudsman, as befits his or her title (see Chap. 9.2), would have much greater investigative powers than those of the present Lay Observer, including the power to recommend the payment of compensation. As yet, however, no further steps have been taken to implement this proposal in Northern Ireland.

The Bar

In a small proportion of the cases handled by solicitors it will be necessary for the services of a barrister to be used. Barristers, or "counsel" as they are sometimes called, are experts in advocacy (*i.e.* oral argument) and have the sole right of audience in the High Court and above. They began to organise themselves in Ireland as a professional body (the Bar) as long ago as the thirteenth century and in 1541 their headquarters became the King's Inns in Dublin. Following the partition of Ireland in 1921, judges and practising barristers in Northern Ireland formed their own Inn of Court of Northern Ireland in 1926. The governing bodies of the profession are the Inn of Court's "benchers", who include all the Supreme Court judges, and (more importantly) the Executive Council of the Inn of Court. The Bar Council, elected by practising barristers, oversees standards within the profession and in effect acts as the profession's "trade union".[39]

In contrast with solicitors, who mostly work in firms, barristers are self-employed and are not permitted to form partnerships. In England they share premises known as chambers and are referred to as having tenancies in those chambers. In Northern Ireland (as in Scotland and the Republic of Ireland) the tradition is for all barristers to work out of a Bar Library, which is situated in Belfast beside the Royal Courts of Justice in Chichester Street.[40] That is usually where solicitors will contact them. There is therefore no need for barristers' clerks, who in England effectively act as business managers in each of the chambers and take a commission on the fees earned. In Northern Ireland the fees are negotiated directly between barrister and solicitor. As it is technically the solicitor who engages the barrister, even though the client may have asked for a particular barrister to be used, the barrister cannot sue the client for fees if they are not paid; indeed by legal custom the barrister cannot sue the solicitor either. A barrister who is offered a "brief" by a solicitor must undertake to work on the case

---

[39] Its current chairperson is Mr Peter Cush.
[40] www.barlibrary.com/nibl2005.pdf.

unless he or she does not have the time, or a proper fee is not offered, or he or she is in some way personally involved in the case; this is known as the "cab-rank principle". There is little specialisation at the Bar in Northern Ireland, so it is not common for a barrister to avoid work on the ground that it is not within his or her usual sphere of practice (therefore requiring too much time to perform properly). All barristers must now complete at least 12 hours' of "continuing professional development" each year.

A solicitor will need to consult a barrister whenever an expert's opinion is required as to the chances of successfully arguing a particular point in court. The client cannot approach the barrister directly: he or she must be briefed by a solicitor, a rule which is intended to filter out the less difficult cases so that barristers can concentrate on the more important ones. A written opinion by the barrister will often satisfy the client's needs, and even if the case does eventually come to court the client will probably meet the barrister there for the first time: only in a few cases is it deemed necessary for there to be a "conference" with the barrister and solicitor prior to the day of the trial. For cases being heard in the High Court (see Chap. 6.6) it is the barrister who drafts the pleadings. Once a barrister is involved in a case he or she will advise the client whether or not to accept an offer of settlement. Otherwise that advice can be given by a solicitor, though sometimes counsel is briefed purely to advise on settlement negotiations.

Queen's Counsel

Every few years experienced barristers in Northern Ireland are invited to apply to the Lord Chief Justice to "take silk", that is, to become a Queen's Counsel (QC). In 2000 a challenge was made to the wording of the declaration which QCs have to sign when they agree to become QCs[41] and this led to the Lord Chancellor altering the declaration by deleting the words "well and truly serve Her Majesty Queen Elizabeth II".[42] The current system for selecting QCs is at present under review[43] and further recruitment of QCs will be audited by the Commissioner

---

[41] *Re Treacy's Application* [2000] NI 330.
[42] The declaration now reads: "I [name] do sincerely promise and declare that I will well and truly serve all whom I may lawfully be called upon to serve in the office of one of Her Majesty's counsel learned in law according to the best of my skill and understanding."
[43] See the report of the Bar Council's committee dated April 2002: www.barlibrary.com/silk.

for Judicial Appointments (see Chap. 1.5). After appointment as a QC a barrister will not generally appear in court without a "junior", as all other barristers are called, and will charge higher fees. Juniors are said to be "led" by seniors. The distinction between senior and junior barristers is sometimes reflected in talk of the Inner and Outer Bars. Most judicial appointments are open only to practising barristers of a certain number of years' standing (see Chap. 1.5), so needless to say most of the judges are former QCs. The first ever female QC in Northern Ireland was appointed in 1989.

In August 2005 there were 61 QCs and 505 junior barristers registered as members of the Bar Library in Northern Ireland. There are in addition a few practising barristers who do not belong to the Bar Library and many more non-practising barristers whose membership of the Bar Library has lapsed. The Bar Library now publishes an annual Directory listing the contact details and interests of all barristers in Northern Ireland.[44]

Complaints against barristers

Barristers are meant to comply with the Bar's Code of Conduct.[45] Complaints that they have not done so should be directed to the Professional Conduct Committee of the Bar Council of Northern Ireland, which may conduct a hearing on the matter. No lay persons sit on this Committee, but if a serious complaint is received the Committee may refer the matter to a Disciplinary Committee of the Executive Council of the Inn of Court of Northern Ireland, which does have a lay member. Any decision to suspend or disbar a barrister in serious cases of misconduct can be taken only by the benchers. Again, as with complaints against a solicitor, if a client wishes to allege that a barrister has been negligent, he or she will need to begin a civil action in the courts. By virtue of a decision of the House of Lords in 1967,[46] barristers and solicitors used to be immune from being sued in respect of their performance as advocates in court (just as judges are immune in respect of their performance as adjudicators), although they could be sued in respect of pre-trial work. In 2000, however, the House of Lords refused to follow this precedent in *Arthur J S Hall (a firm)* v *Simons*.[47]

---

[44] Available at www.barlibrary.com/nibl2005.pdf.
[45] The latest version dates from 2003 and is available on-line at www.barlibrary .com/codeofconduct/code1.html.
[46] *Rondel* v *Worsley* [1969] 1 AC 191.
[47] [2002] 1 AC 615 (unusually, 7 Law Lords sat in this case).

The growth in qualified lawyers

As Table 6 below illustrates, there has been a dramatic increase in the numbers qualifying to practise law in Northern Ireland even in the last 10 years. In 1970 there were just 500 solicitors and about 74 barristers. Today there is one barrister in Northern Ireland for every 3,500 or so residents and one solicitor every 750 residents; in England and Wales and Scotland there are comparatively fewer lawyers. The number of would-be law students remains high throughout the United Kingdom, despite the sizeable expenses which must be incurred and the low incomes received during the lengthy training periods. The problem is a constant headache for the Council of Legal Education for Northern Ireland which, as the governing body of the Institute of Professional Legal Studies (see below), has the responsibility for deciding policies and setting standards concerning admission to the Institute.

TABLE 6: SOLICITORS AND BARRISTERS IN NORTHERN IRELAND 1994-2003[48]

	1994	1995	1996	1997	1998
Solicitors	1,513	1,499	1,556	1,618	1,694
Barristers	350	359	397	419	432
	1999	2000	2001	2002	2003
Solicitors	1,753	1,811	1,882	2,029	2,038
Barristers	452	477	509	534	555

Legal education

There is practically no instruction given in law to school-children in Northern Ireland. The province's Council for the Curriculum, Examinations and Assessment does not have a syllabus in law at either GCSE or "A" Level. Any examinable courses which are followed will therefore usually be organised from England and will deal with English law. There are Schools of Law at Queen's University, Belfast and at the University of Ulster (Jordanstown and Magee campuses). Both institutions offer a variety of degree, certificate and diploma courses, some taken through study at evening classes. Other colleges of further

---

[48] Source: Bar Council and Law Society publications.

education provide lower-level instruction in law. The Open University has recently begun to offer modules in law too, although only in English law.

To become a solicitor or barrister in Northern Ireland a person has to complete successfully the vocational course organised by the Institute of Professional Legal Studies,[49] which is currently part of Queen's University. You can apply for this course if you have a recognised law degree (of at least second class honours standard if you want to be a barrister) or if, having obtained another kind of degree, you have also completed a Bachelor of Legal Science degree at Queen's University (two years full-time or three years part-time). All applicants for the Institute, however, must sit an admissions test specifically designed to assess their aptitude for practising law and some candidates will be interviewed. In 2005 there were 120 places on the Institute's course, of which 25 were for prospective barristers and the remainder for trainee solicitors. Before 2004 some bursaries were available from the Department of Employment and Learning, but these have been discontinued. Applicants resident in Northern Ireland may, however, still apply for discretionary postgraduate awards from their local Education and Library Board. The Institute's fees for the year 2004-05 were £6,000, which did not include the costs of registering with the Law Society or Bar Council or course materials. Every year there are many more applicants than there are places (the ratio is usually about 4:1). Attempts to challenge the legality of the Institute's admission procedures have so far failed.[50]

For intending solicitors the Institute course is now a component part of a two-year "apprenticeship". "Apprentice" solicitors in Northern Ireland are the equivalent of what are termed "articled clerks" in England. The first four months of the two-year apprenticeship (September to December) are spent in a solicitor's office, the student having found a so-called "master" before gaining admission to the Institute. The next 12 months (except for University vacations, when the students are expected to be back in their offices) consist of lectures and vocational exercises at the Institute, at the end of which the student sits examinations for a Certificate in Professional Legal Studies. The service in a solicitor's office is then continued for a further eight

---

[49] www.qub.ac.uk/ipls, where much more detail about applying to the Institute is contained. This is the body which was directed by Professor Mary McAleese before she was elected President of Ireland in 1997.

[50] *Re CH* [2000] NI 62 and *Re Kelly's Application* [2000] NI 103.

months and the student is then qualified to hold a "restricted" practising certificate.[51] This means that for the next two years the solicitor cannot practise on his or her own account or in partnership, but only as an assistant solicitor in a firm or under a solicitor in a public body or government department. A solicitor in practice must also pay an annual fee to the Law Society for a practising certificate.

For intending barristers the Institute course runs for nine months, from October to June. They then obtain their Certificate in Professional Legal Studies and are "called to the Bar" in the following September. For a further 12 months they must serve a "pupillage", acting as "pupils" to experienced "masters" (barristers of at least eight years' standing at the Bar). During the first three months of this year they accompany their master to court and learn how things are done in practice; during the next three months they can take cases by themselves in the motions court (see Chap. 1.3), but only after the first half of the year can they accept other types of fee-earning work. It may be some months before they actually begin to receive an income from the briefs they have handled for solicitors. Barristers, too, must pay for an annual practising certificate as well as a fee for using the Bar Library.

In exceptional cases the arrangements just described for admission to the legal professions may be altered. This is particularly so for applicants who have already worked as a law clerk in a solicitor's office for seven years, who are university lecturers in law or who are professionally qualified in other jurisdictions. People who fully qualify as solicitors in England and Wales have the right to transfer their practising certificate to Northern Ireland, as do solicitors qualified in Ireland provided that they have practised for at least three years before transferring. Solicitors qualified in Scotland have first to do courses in wills and conveyancing at the Institute of Professional Legal Studies in Belfast. Barristers qualified in England and Wales can transfer to Northern Ireland provided that they have completed a 12-month pupillage under the supervision of a practising barrister in England and Wales. Barristers qualified in Ireland can transfer only if they are of at least three years' standing at the Bar in that jurisdiction. There are no

---

[51] Restrictions can be opposed for other reasons too. Appeals against these lie first to the Council of the Law Society and then to the Lord Chief Justice. See, *e.g.*, *In the matter of a Solicitor* [2001] NIJB 179.

reciprocal arrangements concerning the transfer of barristers qualified in Scotland.

Lawyers not in private practice

Not everyone who obtains a law degree or qualifies as a solicitor or barrister will actually want to practise law. Many will find employment in other positions where they can use their legal knowledge in less direct ways. Government departments (including the Northern Ireland Court Service), district councils, the Northern Ireland Housing Executive, public companies, watchdog bodies and teaching institutions all engage such persons in various capacities. On account of the smallness of the province, however, there is obviously not the variety of opportunities that there would be in Great Britain or in the Republic of Ireland. Few qualified solicitors or barristers who are so employed will want, or be permitted, to continue to hold a practising certificate. One disincentive is the requirement laid down by both the Law Society and the Bar Council that their members must at all times be covered by a professional indemnity insurance policy, the premium on which can be very costly.

The future of the professions

In December 1998 the Government published a White Paper on the future reform of legal services and the courts in England and Wales;[52] its proposals were later implemented by the Access to Justice Act 1999. Lawyers were henceforth permitted to practise in firms offering other business services and to supply legal services on a "no win, no fee" basis. Regarding the legal professions in Northern Ireland, however, the Government has proposed no further changes since the publication of its White Paper in 1991,[53] except that, as we shall see in 3.3 below, responsibility for administering the civil legal aid schemes has been removed from the Law Society of Northern Ireland and given to a new body, the Northern Ireland Legal Services Commission.

That the legal systems of England and Northern Ireland (and Ireland) should retain the division of labour between solicitors and barristers is an anomaly of history. Many other countries whose legal systems are

---

[52] See *Modernising Justice: The Government's Plans for Reforming Legal Services and the Courts* (Cm. 4155).

[53] See *Legal Services in Northern Ireland: The Government's Proposals*, Northern Ireland Court Service (1991).

based on the English "common law" system (see Chap. 1.1) - among them the United States of America and Canada - have long since abandoned the distinction. The main argument for fusing the two professions is that it would reduce costs for clients, but at the moment there are so many vested interests at stake that fusion is an extremely far-off ideal.

A tiny step in that direction, however, was taken by the European Communities (Services of Lawyers) Order 1978 which, under strict conditions, allows lawyers qualified in other EU states to provide services in the United Kingdom which could otherwise be provided only by barristers or solicitors. This cross-border legal activity was further facilitated by the creation of the Single European Market in 1993[54] and of course by the large expansion of the European Union in 2004 to 25 Member States.[55] Moreover, anyone who fully qualifies as a solicitor or barrister in England and Wales now has the right to be recognised as a practitioner in Northern Ireland as well, and vice versa.

In 2004 the Government asked Sir David Clementi to conduct an independent review of the regulatory framework for legal services in England and Wales. In his report published later in the year,[56] he recommended that the framework which would best promote competition, innovation and public and consumer interest in an effective, efficient and independent legal sector was one where the regulatory powers were vested in a body other than the frontline practitioner bodies. The Government has announced that it intends to follow this recommendation by creating a Legal Services Board for England and Wales to take over from the Law Society, the Bar Council and the Government itself the responsibility for regulating the legal professions and a Bill to achieve that is expected in the 2005-06 Parliamentary session.

---

[54] See EC Directive 89/48/EEC and the Establishment Directive 98/5/EC.
[55] See the European Communities (Lawyer's Practice) (Amendment) Regs. 2004.
[56] www.legal-services-review.org.uk.

3.3 STATE FUNDED LEGAL AID SCHEMES

Pro bono work[57]

The Northern Ireland Lawyers Pro Bono Unit is a joint venture sponsored by the General Council of the Bar of Northern Ireland and the Law Society of Northern Ireland. It aims to provide free legal advice and representation in deserving cases where legal aid or other funding is not available and where the applicant is unable to afford legal assistance. It is a registered charity and operates as a company limited by guarantee. Some 117 barristers (including 26 QC's) and more than 100 firms of solicitors have volunteered to join the pro bono panel and each has offered their services free of charge for up to three days or 20 hours each year. The cases most likely to meet the criteria for assistance are appeals, judicial review applications, tribunal hearings and advisory work. Cases that raise a specific issue of principle or test cases are particularly welcomed.

State schemes

There are three quite separate state schemes for the provision of financial assistance in legal matters, and the first of them has a variant which really constitutes a fourth scheme. By and large these schemes operate regardless of the nature of the legal problem involved, but a few special problems are not covered, such as libel and slander[58] or queries about the law outside Northern Ireland. Some matters are catered for by separate specially designed schemes, like the assistance which the Equality Commission for Northern Ireland, the Northern Ireland Human Rights Commission and the Northern Ireland Commissioner for Children and Young People (see Chap. 9.3, 9.6 and 9.7 respectively) are empowered to give in some cases of alleged discrimination or human rights abuse. Individuals may also receive financial assistance from purely private sources; your employer or trade union may help you, or a club to which you belong (*e.g.* the Automobile Association). It is also possible to take out insurance against the incurring of legal expenses (this is usually an option when insuring a car), although of course the policies will vary in the degree

---

[57] "Pro bono" is Latin meaning "for the public good". For more details see www.barlibrary.com/bono.

[58] Libel is the permanent (*e.g.* written) form of defamation of character; slander is the impermanent (*e.g.* spoken) form.

of protection they provide. If you have rights to such private help but resort instead to the state schemes, the state schemes may seek an "indemnity" (*i.e.* reimbursement) from the sources of private help; this applies mainly to insurance policies.

Probably the most attractive of the non-state schemes is the fixed-fee interview scheme, which many solicitors still operate.[59] Under this the client can receive half-an-hour's interview with a solicitor for a nominal flat fee (inclusive of VAT) of £5, an amount which has not changed in several years. This contrasts with the £30 or more which would normally be charged for such a period. Anyone can qualify for this assistance, although it is at the discretion of the solicitors participating in the scheme whether or not they will see a particular person under it. The names of the solicitors who may be prepared to give a fixed-fee interview are indicated in the Legal Aid Solicitors List, which is available from the Northern Ireland Legal Services Commission and from Citizens' Advice Bureaux, public libraries, etc. The scheme can even be used as a means of discovering whether you would be likely to qualify for help under one of the state schemes.

The three state schemes which provide funding for legal services are: (i) legal advice and assistance, (ii) legal aid for civil court proceedings and (iii) legal aid for criminal court proceedings. It is not possible to enjoy assistance under the first scheme at the same time as you are receiving aid under one of the other two schemes, but you can move from the first scheme to the second scheme if your case actually goes to court and aid under both the second and third schemes can be given to a person who is involved in both civil and criminal proceedings arising out of the same incident. Each of the schemes is described in more detail below. They operate on the basis of the Legal Aid, Advice and Assistance (NI) Order 1981 and numerous complex regulations made thereunder or under previous legislation. In recent years there have been radical reductions to the financial limits for the schemes, thereby drastically reducing the number of people eligible for assistance. The financial figures cited here are those which were valid for the 2005-06 financial year.

---

[59] Those that do are listed on the website of the Northern Ireland Legal Services Commission (look under "Solicitors").

The legal advice and assistance scheme

When this scheme was started in Northern Ireland in 1974 it was confined to the giving of oral advice. It was extended to written advice in 1978 and was sometimes referred to as "the £25 scheme", as that was the limit on the value of the assistance which could be granted under it. In 1980 this limit was raised to £40 and it now stands at £88. The scheme is popularly referred to as "the green form scheme", because of the colour of the appropriate application form. It is available to anyone aged 16 or over, provided that the financial eligibility criteria (see below) are also met.

The decision whether to grant legal advice and assistance is made by a solicitor. When you go for your initial interview, whether this is under the fixed-fee system or not (see above), you can ask the solicitor to calculate whether you qualify under the legal advice and assistance scheme. Solicitors can even accept applications from persons residing outside Northern Ireland, but they cannot grant assistance in any matter which has already attracted assistance unless they first obtain the permission of the Law Society.

Eligibility

The eligibility test applied by the solicitor is a purely financial one: the "merits" of your legal position are irrelevant. The stipulated financial limits are revised every year. According to the current rate you will not qualify if you have what is termed "disposable capital" of more than £1,000. This is an absolute disqualification, regardless of how low your weekly income is. "Disposable capital" basically means the savings you have in a bank, post office, building society or premium bonds, or any "valuables" such as jewellery; the value of capital assets such as a privately owned house, household furniture or personal clothing is ignored because these items are considered to be "indisposable", and the same applies to the value of the subject matter of the actual dispute (*e.g.* a car whose ownership is being contested). Even if your disposable capital *is* less than £1,000 you will qualify for advice and assistance only if you are in receipt of income support, income-based jobseekers allowance or a pensions credit (the so-called "passport benefits"), or if you have a "disposable income" of less than £203 per week.[60] "Disposable income" basically means your take-home pay

---

[60] Legal Advice and Assistance (Financial Conditions) Regs. (NI) 2005.

minus your regular living expenses (for rent, rates, hire-purchase payments and other necessary outgoings).

Your solicitor will help you to work out your disposable capital and disposable income. Normally the capital and weekly income of your husband or wife (or partner, whether same-sex or not[61]) must be included in the calculations as well. If you have dependants – such as a child – certain sums can be counted as indisposable capital (£335 for the first dependant, £200 for the second, and £100 for others). Weekly allowances are also made in the assessment of disposable income.[62] The solicitor will also be able to tell you whether you will be required to make a contribution to the advice and assistance granted to you and, if so, how much. You will have to contribute if your disposable income exceeds £86 per week, the size of the contribution depending on your exact income.[63] It will vary between £7 and £114, being always approximately £80 less than your disposal weekly income.[64] The solicitor will usually agree to the payment of these contributions by instalments, if that is necessary. In England and Wales the contributory part of the green form scheme was abolished in 1993, so only persons in receipt of the welfare benefits mentioned above, or having less than £203 weekly disposable income, are now eligible for assistance there, albeit free of charge.

A solicitor is entitled to give you £88 worth of advice and assistance under the green form scheme, which represents about two hours' work and excludes an allowance for VAT. If the work which needs to be done will be worth more than £88 the solicitor can apply to the Law Society for an extension on the upper value of the work he or she can do. The Law Society will grant the extension if it is satisfied that it is reasonable for the advice and assistance to be given and that the estimated amount of the costs to be incurred in giving it is fair and reasonable.

Since the introduction of the Police and Criminal Evidence (NI) Order 1989 (the PACE Order), a person detained in a police station is entitled to have access to a solicitor. To provide for such access the legal advice and assistance scheme has been amended to allow solicitors who attend

---

[61] Legal Aid (Assessment of Resources) (Amendment) Regs. (NI) 2004.

[62] Legal Aid (Assessment of Resources) Regs. (NI) 1981, as amended.

[63] Legal Advice and Assistance (Financial Conditions) Regs. (NI) 2005 and Legal Advice and Assistance (Amendment) Regs. (NI) 2005.

[64] *Ibid.*

such detainees (often, of course, at unsocial hours and at very little notice) to receive up to £200 without the need to apply for special authority from the Law Society.

Statistics on the use made of the green form scheme in the two most recent years for which figures are available are set out in Table 7, below. It can be seen that there was a rise of 32% in the number of claims registered, although only a 1% rise in the claims that were paid. Claims for work done under the Police and Criminal Evidence (NI) Order accounted in 2002-03 for 28% of all claims and 38% of all payments. The scheme is also widely used by people wishing to take legal advice about their entitlement to benefits or compensation, by solicitors who are asked to pay visits to prisoners and by parents who are in dispute over access to children. There is even a sizeable number of claims from those wanting to change their names by deed poll (145 in 2002-03 and 143 in 2001-02). In 2002-03 the Law Society's Legal Aid Department processed all claims for payment for work done under this scheme within 12 weeks, still quite a long time.

TABLE 7: THE LEGAL ADVICE AND ASSISTANCE SCHEME 2001-2003[65]

	2001-2002	2002-2003
Claims registered	41,949	55,292
Claims paid	38,586	39,028
PACE claims paid	10,742	11,519
Average cost of PACE claims	£132	£129
Total cost of PACE claims	£1,422,844	£1,483,544
Claims for government benefits	2,628	3,115
Criminal injury compensation claims	2,208	1,908
Prison visit claims	1,089	965
Claims for assaults by police or army	116	63
Children Order claims	1,068	967
Total cost of all claims	£3,738,869	£3,670,334
Average cost of all claims	£97	£94

---

[65] Source: *38th Annual Report of the Law Society's Legal Aid Department 2002-03*, HC 675 (2003-04), pp. 64-6. These were the latest published figures available at the time of writing.

Assistance by way of representation (ABWOR)

The solicitor can do all kinds of legal work under the legal advice and assistance scheme, including the preparation of applications for civil or criminal legal aid certificates (see below). He or she may write letters for you, draft documents (such as a will), negotiate with someone, take statements, get an opinion from a barrister, or prepare a case to help you appear before a tribunal. But before 1980 the solicitor could not personally represent an assisted person in court or before a tribunal. Since then such representation has been made possible in a limited range of situations, the most important of which are as follows.

(1)   A solicitor can apply for the approval of the Law Society to represent a client in certain civil proceedings in magistrates' courts (domestic cases, debt or land cases and some welfare cases). Since the coming into force of the Children (NI) Order 1995 in 1996 (see Chap. 7.1), this has been a particularly important type of assistance in family cases.[66] The Law Society will grant its approval only if it is shown that there are reasonable grounds for taking, defending, or being a party to the proceedings and that the application is not unreasonable in the particular circumstances of the case. This "merits" test distinguishes this variant of the legal advice and assistance scheme from situations not involving representative work.

(2)   If a person appearing before a magistrates' court or a county court is unrepresented, a solicitor who is within the precincts of the court may be asked, or may apply, to represent that person. As yet, however there is no *statutory* "duty solicitor" scheme in Northern Ireland.

(3)   Proceedings before the Mental Health Review Tribunal (see Chap. 8.4), provided that the application is reasonable, and some hearings held in respect of prisoners or detainees (see Chap. 4.3 and 4.6).

Representation under the legal advice and assistance scheme - or indeed under the legal aid schemes to be described shortly - is still not possible in any other kind of tribunal except the Lands Tribunal (see Chap. 8.5). The now defunct Legal Aid Advisory Committee (see below) argued for the extension of the representation scheme to

---

[66] Legal Advice and Assistance (Amendment No. 3) Regs. (NI) 1996.

industrial tribunals (as in Scotland), but the Government has not yet acceded to this. However, a solicitor can still give advice and assistance (short of representation) in a case which is due to come before any sort of tribunal. It seems, moreover, that the costs of briefing counsel in a case, or of obtaining the advice and opinions of counsel in connection with any funded steps in a case, are now also payable under the green form scheme.[67] In cases of ABWOR the disposable capital limit for eligibility is the same as for civil legal aid (£3,000). But the rule still applies that only £88 worth of assistance is obtainable unless the Law Society grants an extension.

TABLE 8: THE ASSISTANCE BY WAY OF REPRESENTATION SCHEME 2001-2003[68]

	2001-2002	2002-2003
Children Order claims made	5,708	5,999
Children Order claims paid	3,812	3,332
Contact order claims paid	1,596	1,345
Residence order claims paid	1,285	1,202
Children Order claims, total cost	£2,069,058	£2,131,907
Children Order claims, average cost	£543	£640
Other claims received	5,797	5,745
Other claims paid	4,306	4,171
Non-molestation order claims	2,912	2,954
Separation / maintenance claims	173	885
Mental Health Tribunal claims	75	84
Total costs of all other claims	£,1,662,541	£1,753,311
Average cost of all other claims	£386	£420

From Table 8, above, it can be seen that there has not been much change in the pattern of usage of the ABWOR scheme in recent years. It is worth noting that in each of the two years in question there were as

[67] *In re Hemsworth's Application (No. 2)* [2004] NIQB 26. Weatherup J also held in that case that the practice of not allowing such costs (which was changed only in March 2003) was, in the case of an inquest, a breach of Art. 2 of the European Convention on Human Rights.
[68] Source: 38th *Annual Report of the Law Society's Legal Aid Department 2002-03*, HC 675 (2003-04), pp. 66-9. No more recent figures had been published at the time of writing.

many claims for work done under the Children Order as there were for all other kinds of work, and in 2002-03 the total cost of Children Order claims paid was 21% higher than the total cost of all other claims. Most of the Children Order claims concerned attempts to obtain contact or residence orders. Work done in relation to non-molestation orders (which aim to protect people form being harmed by their partner or spouse) accounted for 51% of all other applications. In 2002-03 all applications for ABWOR, given their urgency, were processed by the Legal Aid Department within 24 hours; about 93% were granted.

How the legal costs are recouped

The difference between the value of the work done for a client under the advice and assistance scheme and the amount of contributions which the client may have to pay is recoverable by the solicitor out of (in order of priority): (i) the costs which the other side agrees, or is ordered by the court, to pay to the assisted person; (ii) the property which is recovered or preserved for the assisted person in the case, unless it is exempted property such as a house or maintenance payments; and (iii) the fund for civil legal services which is maintained by the Northern Ireland Legal Services Commission (see p.160 below). The debt owed to the solicitor constitutes a "charge" on these three funds, but the charge may not be enforced against (ii) if, on the application of the solicitor, the Law Society so authorises. The solicitor can make such an application whenever he or she thinks that enforcing this so-called "clawback" provision would cause grave hardship or distress to the client or would be unreasonably difficult because of the nature of the property.

In short, under the green form scheme if you win your case you will normally end up paying little or nothing towards the overall costs involved: any contribution you have already paid will be recouped by the award of costs made in your favour by the judge. If you lose your case, the cost to you should normally not exceed the amount of the contribution payable under the scheme. If a person who is assisted by representation is ordered by the court to pay the costs of the proceedings, he or she does not have to pay more than what the court thinks is reasonable having regard to all the circumstances. The other side may recover the balance of the costs from the Legal Services Commission.

The civil legal aid scheme

Legal aid for court proceedings in civil cases was not introduced in Northern Ireland until 1965, 16 years after its introduction in England and Wales. There are important differences between the civil aid schemes in the two jurisdictions.

If you are honestly contemplating civil court proceedings, whether as plaintiff or defendant, you should contact a solicitor. He or she can help you to fill in the relevant legal aid forms, but the decision whether to grant civil legal aid in any particular case is taken not by the solicitor but by officials at the Northern Ireland Legal Services Commission, to which the forms will be sent. Persons living outside Northern Ireland can apply for legal aid for civil proceedings which are to take place within Northern Ireland, but persons living inside the province who want aid for proceedings elsewhere - whether England, Scotland, the Republic of Ireland, or further afield - must apply to the authorities in those countries.

The financial and "merits" tests

An important difference between the civil legal aid scheme and the legal advice and assistance scheme (apart from ABWOR) is that for the former there is not only a financial eligibility test to be satisfied but also a "merits" test. As regards the financial limits, you will be eligible for civil legal aid as from April 2005 if your disposable capital is not more than £6,750 and your disposable income does not exceed £8,681 per annum. For cases involving personal injury claims these limits are increased respectively to £8,560 and £9,570.[69]

As the capital limit is quite high, more people qualify under this scheme than under the legal advice and assistance scheme. If your disposable capital is more than £6,750 you may still be granted aid if you cannot afford to proceed without legal aid because the costs of the case are likely to be too great, but the £8,681 limit on disposable income is absolute. Your disposable capital and income are calculated in similar ways to those already described for legal advice and assistance, except that the calculation is performed by the Legal Aid Assessment Office of the Social Security Agency. In calculating disposable capital no allowances are made for dependants, but allowances are made in calculating disposable income: they are the

---

[69] Legal Aid (Financial Conditions) Regs. (NI) 2005.

same as for legal advice and assistance claims, though converted from weekly into annual amounts.

Once you have shown that you are within the financial limits, the Northern Ireland Legal Services Commission must still be persuaded that you have reasonable grounds for being a party to the proceedings and that it is not unreasonable for you to receive legal aid in the particular circumstances of the case. So if the action is a trivial one, or if the cost to the Legal Services Commission would be disproportionate to the advantage you might gain from the litigation, legal aid may be refused even if you are financially eligible. This is the same "merits" test as needs to be satisfied in applications for representation under the legal advice and assistance scheme (ABWOR), and indeed civil legal aid may be refused if representation under that scheme would be more appropriate.

As it can take several weeks for both the financial and merits tests to be considered, there is a procedure for applying for an "emergency certificate", which can be granted at once provided you promise to pay whatever contributions are later assessed (see below). Approximately one-third of all applications received are emergency applications. But legal aid will be refused if the application is in connection with a cause or matter in which numerous persons have the same interest and it would be reasonable and proper for these other persons to bear the costs.[70]

If a civil or emergency certificate is refused on the ground that the merits test has not been satisfied, you may appeal to a committee of the Northern Ireland Legal Services Commission but not to a court. In 2002-03, the last full year of the existence of the former Legal Aid Committee of the Law Society, 1,450 such appeals were dealt with, of which 700 (48%) were successful. At many appeals applicants or their solicitors appeared in person. You may also seek judicial review of the Committee's refusal to grant you legal aid if you can show, for example, that no reasonable committee could have reached that decision[71] and the Legal Services Commission will even consider an application for legal aid to take such proceedings. This Commission is

---

[70] Legal Aid (General) Regs. (NI) 1965, reg. 5(11)(b). This was applied in *Re Hartley's Application* [2001] 3 BNIL 54, where a Sinn Féin councillor applied for legal aid in respect of judicial review proceedings relating to alleged discrimination against a group of Sinn Féin councillors on Belfast City Council.

[71] *In re Jordan's Application* [2003] NICA 30; for an example of an unsuccessful application in this context, see *In re Murphy's Application* [2003] NIQB 55.

not under a legal obligation to give reasons for all of its decisions but, like the Law Society's Legal Aid Committee before it, it should do so in appropriate cases.[72] In 2002-03 there were 10 applications for judicial review against decisions taken by the old Legal Aid Committee. From time to time judges deciding such cases give general guidance on how the legal aid schemes should be operated.

Financial contributions

Contributions towards the cost of civil legal aid have to be made by applicants whose disposable capital is between £3,000 and £6,750 or whose disposable income is between £2,931 and £8,681 (the respective maxima are £8,560 and £9,570 in cases where there is a claim in respect of personal injuries).[73] Any part of the excess capital can be requested as a contribution, but only one quarter of the excess income can be requested. The contributions can be required to be paid in one sum or in instalments, but as yet only for a period of 12 months: in due course the scheme in Northern Ireland may be brought into line with that in England and Wales, which requires contributions to be paid during the entire life of a civil legal aid certificate. Further contributions do not usually have to be paid if another application is made in respect of an appeal in the case to a higher court.

Coverage under the scheme

If the Northern Ireland Legal Services Commission considers that you have fulfilled both the financial and merits tests, it will grant you a civil legal aid certificate. This will cover legal services by a solicitor or barrister both before and during a court hearing. You are entitled to choose any solicitor (and, if needed, any barrister) to act in your case: you do not have to stick to the one who forwarded your application for legal aid to the Legal Services Commission or to the one from whom you may already have received legal advice and assistance.

Practically every type of hearing is within the civil legal aid scheme, with the exceptions of tribunals (other than the Lands Tribunal),[74] arbitrations (which include proceedings in a small claims court - see Chap. 6.3) and coroners' courts (see Chap. 7.3). In Northern Ireland

---

[72] *In re Jordan's Application, ibid.*
[73] Legal Aid (Financial Conditions) Regs. (NI) 2005.
[74] It may also soon be available for some challenges to the new Asylum and Immigration Tribunal: see the draft Legal Aid (Asylum and Immigration) Regs. (NI) 2005.

"care" proceedings regarding children and bail applications for scheduled criminal offences (see Chap. 4.3) are classified as civil matters for this purpose, as in fact are all appeals in the Court of Appeal on a case stated by a magistrates' court (even in what is otherwise undoubtedly a criminal case). The cost of taking proceedings in the Enforcement of Judgments Office (see 3.4 below and Chap. 6.8) or of referring an issue to the European Court of Justice (see Chap. 2.5) is also covered by the scheme. People who take cases to the European Court of Human Rights can benefit from a special legal aid scheme administered in Strasbourg. Particular types of case are excluded in all Northern Ireland courts, such as libel and slander claims,[75] admitted debts, and claims relating to elections.

While the case is progressing, your solicitor will be in regular contact with the Legal Services Commission. Before certain steps can be taken, such as the engagement of a barrister in a magistrates' court or a Queen's Counsel in a county court or High Court case, the permission of the Commission must be sought. But there is no £88 limit on the value of the legal work that can be done for you, as there is under the advice and assistance scheme.

TABLE 9: THE CIVIL LEGAL AID SCHEME 2001-2003[76]

	2001-2002	2002-2003
Applications registered	14,997	13,565
Divorce or nullity claims	2,745	2,650
Criminal injury claims	2,099	1,707
Negligence claims	2,163	2,427
Tripping claims[77]	1,096	869
Children Order claims	1,385	1,227
Road traffic accident claims	1,368	925
Claims paid	4,767	3,906
Total costs of claims paid	£10,3231,360	£11,636,145
Average cost of claims paid	£2,165	£2,979

---

[75] This has been held not to breach the European Convention on Human Rights: *In re Lynch's Application* [2002] 5 BNIL 44.

[76] Source: *38th Annual Report of the Law Society's Legal Aid Department 2002-03*, HC 675 (2003-04), pp. 70-6.

[77] These are also included in the figures for negligence claims.

Table 9, above, shows that in 2002-03, compared with the previous year, there were fewer claims made for civil legal aid, and fewer claims paid, but the total cost of the claims paid, and the average cost of each claim, were greater. The average cost, indeed, was about seven times that of claims paid under the ABWOR scheme. Claims were paid faster too: by the end of the financial year only those claims made during the previous month had not yet been paid. During 2002-03 there were 20,150 court cases decided where a party was in receipt of civil legal aid; of these, 6,335 were won by that party, 10,373 were settled and 3,442 were lost. This suggests that application of the merits test to claims for civil legal aid is reasonably accurate in predicting whether the case will be successful or not.

How the legal costs are recouped

The solicitor will be paid for the work, as will any barrister involved in the case, out of the Legal Services Commission's fund for civil legal services. In proceedings at or above High Court level the work will generally be paid for at 95% of the normal rate for work not legally aided. In county court proceedings the full rate will be paid if the costs are "taxed" (see 3.4 below). If the costs are not taxed, and in all magistrates' court proceedings, the sums paid will be in accordance with scales of remuneration laid down in regulations,[78] although in exceptional cases a judge can order that these scales should not apply.

Once the case is over, any sums recovered by the assisted person by virtue of a court order (or agreement[79]) for costs must be paid to the Legal Services Commission. If these exceed the sums paid out by that Commission on the assisted person's behalf the excess is retained by the Commission; if they are less, the balance is recouped from the assisted person's contributions, the amount unused, if any, being returned. If even the contributions are not enough to satisfy the debt owed to the Legal Services Commission, a "charge" may be imposed on any property recovered or preserved by the proceedings. This charge is similar to the solicitor's charge in connection with legal advice and

---

[78] The Legal Aid (Remuneration of Solicitors and Counsel in County Court Proceedings) (Amendment) Order (NI) 2003, effective from 3 March 2003, increased the maximum amounts allowable to lawyers acting for legally aided persons in the county court (to accord with the scale costs prescribed by the County Court (Amendment No. 2) Rules (NI) 2002).

[79] Such an agreement is usually part of any settlement (*i.e.* compromise) in the case.

assistance mentioned above, but unlike that charge it cannot be waived. The Legal Services Commission can, however, take its time over enforcing the charge and may accept an alternative charge on substitute property; certain forms of property, such as maintenance payments, are in any event exempt from the charge. If an assisted person happens to be insured against the legal expenses incurred, the insurance money received must be paid to the Legal Services Commission. If the Commission is still owed money after all this, the loss must be borne out of the public purse.

If an unassisted party wins a case against an assisted party the court may order the former's costs to be paid by the Legal Services Commission, provided that this is just and equitable in all the circumstances and that (except in appeals) the unassisted party would otherwise suffer financial hardship.[80]

The criminal legal aid scheme

Criminal legal aid has been available in one form or another for decades. The two distinguishing features of the present scheme are that the decision whether or not to grant aid is taken by the court itself (not by a solicitor, by the Law Society or by the Legal Services Commission) and that, if it is granted, the aid is *free*; unlike the scheme in England, no contributions are required from the aided person. However, if it transpires that the oral or written statement of means provided to the court by the applicant for legal aid is incorrect, the court may then take action to recover some or all of the costs from the applicant. Moreover, when the relevant provisions of the Access to Justice (NI) Order 2003 are brought into force, contributions towards the costs involved in criminal cases *may* be required from aided persons in Northern Ireland.[81]

The present scheme allows for a criminal legal aid certificate to be granted to persons who have been charged with a criminal offence (see Chap. 5.3) or who have been brought before a criminal court on a summons (see Chap. 5.1). It operates in the youth courts too, where parents or guardians can apply for aid on behalf of children or young persons. People who bring private prosecutions, however, cannot rely on the scheme, except when, after winning their case, the other side appeals against the decision.

---

[80] Access to Justice (NI) Order 2003, art. 19.
[81] Art. 31(2).

Applications are best made through a solicitor and preferably before the case is due to be heard in court. They can be made by letter addressed to the clerk of the petty sessions for the relevant district; if unsuccessful at that stage a later application can be made at the hearing itself. In practice in Northern Ireland most applications are made orally at the hearing. The applicant will usually be asked to fill in a form stating his or her means,[82] although there is no rigid financial eligibility test as there is for legal advice and assistance or civil legal aid. Having received an application the court may ask the Social Security Agency to inquire into the applicant's means and report back to the court; in that event the case will obviously be a little delayed. For aid to be granted it must simply appear to the court that the applicant's means are insufficient to obtain legal help in preparing and conducting a defence.

In appeals from the Crown Court to the Court of Appeal (or, further, to the House of Lords) legal aid is obtainable under provisions in the Criminal Appeal (NI) Act 1980; in these cases the legal aid is administered separately by the Northern Ireland Court Service and the fees payable are assessed by the Taxing Master (see Chap. 1.5).

Conditions of aid

As a "merits" test it must also appear to the court that it is desirable in the interests of justice that the applicant should have free legal aid. The sorts of factors which the court will take into account in applying this merits test (the so-called "Widgery" criteria because they were put forward by a Committee chaired by the Lord Chief Justice of England of that name[83]) are the gravity of the criminal charge, the ability of the applicant to present his or her own case and the nature of the defence. If a court has any doubts whether the applicant qualifies for aid, these must be resolved in favour of granting it, even when the applicant intends to plead guilty to the criminal charges. In cases where the charge is murder, or in situations where a court intends to sentence the defendant to imprisonment, detention in a young offenders' centre or a period in a training school, criminal legal aid *must* be offered.

The aid comes in the form of a criminal legal aid certificate. A solicitor and, where necessary, a barrister are assigned to the case by the court

---

[82] See the Sch. to the Legal Aid in Criminal Cases (Statement of Means) Rules (NI) 1999.
[83] Cm. 2934; 1966.

after it has taken into account any representations which the applicant may want to make on this matter. In a Crown Court trial the judge may request a solicitor or barrister to undertake the defence of a person who has not been granted a criminal legal aid certificate, in which event the case proceeds as if a certificate had in fact been granted.

How the legal costs are recouped

The costs payable to lawyers involved in cases where a criminal legal aid certificate has been issued are mostly regulated by the Legal Aid in Criminal Proceedings (Costs) Rules (NI) 1992, as amended.[84] These specify how much is to be paid in respect of work done in magistrates' courts, appeals to the county court and bail applications in the High Court. Different fees are listed for different types of work (preparation of the case, advocacy, travelling and waiting time, etc.), and usually on the basis of prescribed hourly rates. Costs in respect of work done for diversionary youth conferences and attendance at court-ordered youth conferences are paid in accordance with a regime set out in the Legal Aid for Youth Conferences (Costs) Rules (NI) 2003[85] and from 4 April 2005 costs in respect of legally aided work in the Crown Court are governed not by the 1992 Rules mentioned above but by the Legal Aid for Crown Court Proceedings (Costs) Rules (NI) 2005 (see 3.4 below).

Table 10, below, shows that, while the number of certificates issued in 2002-03 was higher than in 2001-02, as was the total cost of claims paid, the average bills paid to lawyers was considerably lower (by 10% for solicitors and 34% for barristers). But the average cost of counsel's fees in Crown Court cases increased from £4,887 to £5,239 (16%). By year's end the average time taken to process criminal legal aid claims was between 12 and 14 weeks.

---

[84] The Government keeps putting back the date after which certain types of legal work will be remunerated at discretionary instead of prescribed rates. It is currently 30 June 2006: Legal Aid in Criminal Proceedings (Costs) (Amendment No. 2) Rules (NI) 2005.

[85] *E.g.* a solicitor will receive £112 as a standard fee for preparing for and attending a diversionary youth conference lasting up to 1 hour.

TABLE 10: THE CRIMINAL LEGAL AID SCHEME
2001-2003[86]

	2001-2002	2002-2003
Criminal aid certificates registered	26,430	27,207
Certificates for magistrates' courts	22,752	23,080
Certificates for the Crown Court	1,489	1,644
Total cost of claims paid	£20,181,327	£22,221,579
Average bill paid to solicitors	£644	£582
Average bill paid to counsel	£1,662	£1,094

The Northern Ireland Court Service has issued draft Criminal Aid Certificate Rules (NI) 2005, which will revoke various rules issued as far back as 1966 and prescribe the new form of criminal aid certificates when free legal aid is granted for work in magistrates' courts, county courts or the Crown Court. Solicitors who are certified by the Law Society as being "Advanced Advocates" will be able to claim the sums that would otherwise be due to counsel in such criminal cases.

The administration of the state schemes

Since 1982 ministerial responsibility for legal aid, advice and assistance has rested with the Lord Chancellor rather than the Secretary of State for Northern Ireland, but under the Legal Aid, Advice and Assistance (NI) Order 1981 the Law Society retained responsibility for administering civil legal aid and administered criminal legal aid on behalf of the Court Service. The Law Society, however, had no control over the financial eligibility tests for the schemes, nor over the level of fees payable to lawyers in criminal cases. The Access to Justice (NI) Order 2003 transferred responsibility for the civil and criminal legal aid schemes to the new Northern Ireland Legal Services Commission (see below), although not all of the Order's provisions are yet in force so the provision of legal aid is still in a transitional phase.[87]

---

[86] Source: *38th Annual Report of the Law Society's Legal Aid Department 2002-03*, HC 675 (2003-04), pp. 77-9. No more recent figures had been published at the time of writing.

[87] There have been three commencement orders to date: SR 2003/344, SR 2003/440 and SR 2005/111.

The Law Society carried out most of its functions through an annually appointed Legal Aid Committee, which consisted of six to nine solicitors nominated by the Law Society, two barristers nominated by the Bar Council, and one barrister or solicitor nominated by the Lord Chancellor. The Committee served as a management board for the Law Society's Legal Aid Department, setting policies and objectives on legal aid matters. The Law Society submitted an annual report on the operation of all the state funded legal aid schemes to the Lord Chancellor, who in turn laid the report before Parliament. A Legal Aid Advisory Committee sent comments on the annual reports to the Lord Chancellor, which were also published. The Legal Aid Advisory Committee comprised about 10 persons, under the chairmanship of a county court judge (latterly Judge David Smyth QC). In the last few years of its existence the Advisory Committee made some very critical remarks about the performance of the Law Society's Legal Aid Department in administering the legal aid schemes. In his Foreword to the Committee's 2002-03 comments, for example, Judge Smyth wrote: "It would perhaps be inaccurate and a little unkind to describe 2002-2003 as being a year of unparalleled under performance...It has still to be said that the year we are reporting on once again is one of failure to meet targets....76% of targets have been missed."[88] The Advisory Committee was particularly critical of the delays in processing applications for legal aid, although it accepted that to some extent this was due to under-funding of the Legal Aid Department by the Northern Ireland Court Service.

The size of the Legal Aid Fund in Northern Ireland in 2002-03 (*i.e.* the amount allocated to the Law Society's Legal Aid Department by the Government for all the legal aid schemes here) was £45 million. There was an additional £3.58 million granted for administering the schemes. By the end of the year the Legal Aid Department had made payments of £46m and collected £1m in contributions from those legally aided. This represents an annual increase of 13% in civil legal aid (net of receipts) and of 9% in criminal legal aid. It still remains true that net expenditure on legal aid per head of the population is much less in Northern Ireland than it is in Scotland or in England and Wales.

---

[88] P. 83.

The Northern Ireland Legal Services Commission[89]

During 1998 a review of legal aid administration was carried out by officials in the Northern Ireland Court Service. Following this, a consultation paper was published in June 1999.[90] The proposals it contained took into account recent reforms of legal aid in England and Wales,[91] but they also supposedly reflected the differences between the two jurisdictions, such as the fact that a large majority of legal aid firms in Northern Ireland consist of only one or two solicitors and very few of them are specialist firms.[92]

The proposals were aimed at controlling the rate of increase of expenditure on legal aid in Northern Ireland. They suggested that the civil legal aid budget should be capped each year and that only those firms and organisations which had won contracts to provide legal services should be eligible to receive legal aid funding. Advice agencies would be able to apply for contracts just like firms of solicitors. There would be more monitoring of the quality of legal assistance provided and other ways of funding cases would be developed, such as conditional fees ("no win, no fee") and legal expenses insurance. Other means of settling disputes besides litigation would be explored. The responsibility for administering legal aid would be taken away from the Law Society (to end any appearance of a conflict of interest) and given instead to an independent body to be known as the Northern Ireland Legal Services Commission.

Both of the legal professions in Northern Ireland voiced their deep concern about a number of the specific proposals in the consultation paper, especially the capping of the civil legal aid budget. The Legal Aid Advisory Committee proposed[93] that non-traditional methods of resolving disputes, such as Alternative Dispute Resolution (ADR), should be funded by legal aid, that all initial diagnostic work should be free but that formal advice and assistance and full representation should be means tested, that the range of fixed fees for lawyers should be

---

[89] D. Capper, "The Legal Services Commission - Brave New World for Legal Aid" (2003) 54 NILQ 447.
[90] *Public Benefit and Public Purse: The Future of Legal Aid in Northern Ireland* (1999).
[91] See further *Modernising Justice* (Cm. 4155; 1998) and the Access to Justice Act 1999.
[92] See also B. Stewart (1999) 149 New LJ 85.
[93] The Committee's recommendations are summarised in App. 10 to its report on the *Legal Aid Annual Report 1998-1999*.

extended, that it was far too early to consider the contracting out of state funded legal services (especially for criminal defence work), that any large scale replacement of legal aid by conditional fees would be totally unjustified and that legal aid funding should be extended to the voluntary sector.

The Government's response to the views expressed on the consultation document was published in the form of a White Paper in September 2000.[94] Eventually this led to legislation in the form of the Access to Justice (NI) Order 2003.[95] Responsibility for the provision and reform of publicly funded legal services in Northern Ireland was assumed by the Northern Ireland Legal Services Commission on 1 November 2003.[96] There is a roughly comparable body in England and Wales.[97] The new Commission operates not just under the 2003 Order but also in accordance with regulations, direction and guidance issued by the Government's Department for Constitutional Affairs. It is chaired by Sir Anthony Holland and currently has 10 other members. The Commission has published a Corporate Plan for 2004-07, which includes target dates for the achievement of certain goals. Amongst these is the production (by November 2005) of a "funding code",[98] setting out the criteria according to which, in place of the existing "merits" test, decisions will be taken as to whether to fund civil legal services for an individual. In due course the Commission will also have to develop a code of conduct for those providing criminal defence services in Northern Ireland.[99] Panels of lawyers have been co-opted as sub-committee members of the Commission to deal with appeals against funding decisions.

---

[94] *The Way Ahead: Legal Aid Reform in Northern Ireland*, Cm. 4849. See too the report of the Northern Ireland Affairs Committee of the House of Commons: *Legal Aid in Northern Ireland*, 4th Report of 2000-01, HC 496.

[95] See L. Allamby, "Legal Aid Reform: A View from the Voluntary Sector" (2002) 53 NILQ 167.

[96] Access to Justice (NI) Order 2003, arts. 3-36 and Sch. 1.

[97] Also called the Legal Services Commission: see www.legalservices.gov.uk. The body in England and Wales, however, is much more developed, running both a Community Legal Service and a Criminal Defence Service. Art. 5 of the Access to Justice (NI) Order 2003 authorises the Secretary of State to replace the Northern Ireland Legal Services Commission with two separate bodies at some future date.

[98] In accordance with the Access to Justice (NI) Order 2003, art. 15.

[99] *Ibid.* art. 22. See Judge D. Smyth, "An Excellent Service and a Catalyst for Change: The Future Provision of Criminal Defence Services in Northern Ireland" (2002) 53 NILQ 179.

The Commission has an internal system for dealing with complaints but it is also subject, like most other public bodies, to oversight by the Parliamentary Commissioner for Administration (the Ombudsman) (see Chap. 9.2). One of its first actions was to commission research into the state of legal need in Northern Ireland, a report being submitted to it in July 2004.[100] Later the Commission will help to develop a wider range of standard fees for legally aided work (not necessarily based on existing fees). It will be able to set up its own salaried lawyer structure and to enter into contracts with legal service providers, including those in the voluntary sector, for specialist or new services. All such providers will have to register with the Commission and comply with codes of practice to ensure quality control.

One of the key questions for the new Legal Services Commission to consider will be the extent to which legal aid should continue to be made available for personal injury litigation. The Access to Justice (NI) Order 2003 makes provision for conditional fee agreements to be permitted, whereby lawyers will get paid only if they win, but commentators have predicted that this system will not work in a small jurisdiction like Northern Ireland.[101]

3.4 LEGAL COSTS

The cost of employing a professional lawyer can be very high. In cases of genuine hardship some form of legal aid may be available, as the previous section has explained, but the truth remains that the legal system of Northern Ireland is still a long way from ensuring free or subsidised legal help in all situations. If you do not qualify for legal aid or legal advice and assistance, or if your case is one for which the £5 fixed-fee interview is inadequate, the choice is stark: you must either try to conduct your legal affairs in person or else engage a solicitor and run the risk of incurring significant expenditure.

---

[100] T. Dignan, *Legal Need in Northern Ireland: Literature Review* (available on the Commission's website). The Legal Services Commission for England and Wales has an active division called the Legal Services Research Centre, the successor body to the Legal Aid Board Research Unit established in 1996 to inform legal aid policy. See now www.lsrc.org.uk/index2.htm.

[101] A. Morris, "Conditional Fee Agreements in Northern Ireland: Gimmick or Godsend?" (2005) 56 NILQ 38. See too D. Capper, "Personal Injury Litigation - The Case for Legal Aid" (2002) 53 NILQ 137, where a Contingency Legal Aid Fund is also canvassed.

Generally speaking it is inadvisable for a person who is untrained in the law to attempt to conduct his or her own legal affairs, or even to help a friend to do so. Rather drastic errors may be made, with the result that much greater expense is eventually incurred than it was originally hoped could be saved. In addition, in many situations it is actually a criminal offence for untrained persons to do legal work on other people's behalf if they ask payment for it. Some committed individuals do get as far as handling the conveyance of their house or conducting their own legal cases in court, but unless you have lots of free time and spare cash you could well find this to be so inconvenient as to be counterproductive. "Litigants in person", as such individuals are called if cases come to court, are few and far between.

The alternative of engaging a solicitor will not, however, always be unattractive. In particular, if the legal matter is one which involves a dispute with another person, rather than one (like drafting a will) which purely affects yourself, you may well stand a chance of getting back from the other person most of what you have to pay to your solicitor - provided that you win the dispute. As regards the solicitor's charges, the basic principle, as you would expect, is that the more work a solicitor does, the more he or she will require you to pay. The cost of a first visit should not be very high (perhaps around £30, although with increased competition this may even be free), and if the solicitor has to take any further action on your behalf you can ask to be kept informed about how much the work is going to cost. The bill, when it is finally received, should itemise all the work carried out and the corresponding charge. It will be made up differently depending on whether the work done was contentious or non-contentious, though there are no hard-and-fast rules as to when work becomes contentious.

Non-contentious work

Generally speaking, a solicitor's non-contentious work consists of all jobs done *excluding* those which relate to proceedings in court. It may be work of a more or less routine nature - like conveying a house or drafting a will - or work concerning a dispute which is settled before a date is fixed for a court appearance. The solicitor's bill in such non-contentious cases will be made up as follows:

(1)   a charge for "disbursements", or "outlays", such as the stamp duty on the value of a house or the fee for obtaining probate of a will;

(2)   a professional fee;

(3)   VAT, at 17.5%, on those items liable to it (which include the professional fee).

The size of the professional fee will depend on such factors as the time involved in handling the affair, the complexity of the affair, and the value of the property concerned. It is not unusual for a solicitor to charge at a rate of about £60 per hour for time spent on a case. In some matters, though not often, the fee is determined in accordance with guidelines laid down either by the Law Society, which is the governing body of the solicitors' profession, or by a local solicitors' association: the Belfast Solicitors' Association, for example, has guideline prices for the conveying of houses. The typical charge for the straightforward conveyance of a house priced at £50,000 will be in the region of £500 (which is somewhat more than in England); the charge for administering a deceased person's estate could be greater, perhaps around 2% of the estate's total value. Without going into the details of each case, which will vary greatly, it is impossible to be more precise in indicating likely charges, although solicitors acting in house conveyances must now provide a written statement of their proposed fees at the outset. Remember that help with the initial costs involved may occasionally be available under the legal advice and assistance scheme, which was described in the previous section of this book.

Challenging a solicitor's bill

If a client is dissatisfied with a bill provided by a solicitor for non-contentious work, two things can be done. He or she can require the solicitor to obtain what is called a Remuneration Certificate from the Law Society. This will state the charge which would be a fair and reasonable one for the work done in the case and the client will have to pay that amount. The Certificate has to be sought within one month from the date when the solicitor informs the client of the right to apply for one (as the solicitor is bound to do). It is supplied free of charge but in fact only about 30 are issued each year.

Alternatively, or in addition, the client can apply to have the costs officially assessed (*i.e.* "taxed") by an official of the Supreme Court called the Taxing Master (see Chap. 1.5). Applications must be made within three months of delivery of the bill to the client. The time limit can be extended - and this will usually be necessary if the client has first taken time to ask for a Remuneration Certificate - but the absolute limit is six months. There is a small initial fee for applying to the Taxing Master in the case of bills relating to non-contentious work, although after the Taxing Master has dealt with the case the person who loses the argument over the bill must pay an additional 15% of the amount in dispute by way of a fee to the Taxing Master's office. There are only a handful of these so-called "solicitor and client" applications each year.

Contentious work

A solicitor's contentious work consists of all the business which eventually leads to appearances in court. If judicial proceedings are begun, for example by the issuing of a writ or a summons, but are settled before the date fixed for the trial, all the work done up to then is usually classified as non-contentious. In considering how much a client will have to pay for contentious work it is essential to distinguish between criminal proceedings and civil proceedings. In both it is also essential to bear in mind the implications of the legal aid schemes.

Criminal proceedings

If you find yourself defending a prosecution for a criminal offence you will need to consider whether to apply for a criminal legal aid certificate (see 3.3 above). If a certificate is granted the costs are eventually met in the way described in the previous section. If you do not succeed in obtaining a criminal legal aid certificate it is not possible to appeal against the refusal to grant one, except during the course of an appeal in the case itself, and you yourself must therefore pay for the services of any solicitor or barrister whose services you engage. You can, of course, conduct your own defence, but in serious cases this is not at all wise. You can also have a friend in court to help you with your case (such people are called "McKenzie friends" after the name of the case where their appearance was first approved), but he or she is not usually permitted to speak on your behalf.[102] If you lose the case, however, it is very rare for an order to be made compelling you to contribute towards the prosecution's costs as well as paying your own. On the other hand, if you win the case and are acquitted it is also very rare in Northern Ireland for the prosecution to be ordered to pay your costs. It is only when the prosecution, or the defence, has been

---

[102] "McKenzie friends" may also be excluded from certain proceedings: see, *e.g.*, *Re D's Application* [2000] NIJB 248.

outrageously unsubstantiated that the costs will be ordered "to follow the event", that is, paid by the losing side.

If an order as to costs is made by a magistrates' court, the precise amount due will be calculated in accordance with the Magistrates' Courts (Costs in Criminal Cases) Rules (NI) 1988, as amended. These allow for up to £75 per lawyer per day, although the court can order payment of a greater sum if the proceedings are exceptionally long, difficult or complex. The principle to be applied is that the lawyer should be allowed "fair remuneration according to the work reasonably undertaken and properly done".[103] The recipient of the costs award will also be reimbursed the court fees which have had to be paid during the proceedings, these too being fixed by regulations.

Costs in respect of legally aided work in the Crown Court are now governed by the Legal Aid for Crown Court Proceedings (Costs) Rules (NI) 2005, which has introduced the supplementary principle that any costs awarded must have regard to "the cost to public funds...and the need to ensure value for money".[104] Schedule 1 sets out in some detail the method for determining the costs due in a "standard" case. A basic trial fee is supplemented by a refresher fee (paid on a daily basis), special additional fees (*e.g.* for late sittings) and a travel allowance, with the amounts in question differing depending on which of nine categories the offence being tried falls into. A trial for burglary, for example, will attract a basic trial fee of £1,900 for a solicitor, £2,275 for a junior counsel acting without a QC, and £3,500 for a QC, with the respective daily refresher fees being £500, £325 and £500. Lawyers who are unhappy with a decision by the Legal Services Commission as to how much they should be paid can ask for the Commission to review the decision; if they remain unhappy after the review they can appeal to the Taxing Master. Schedule 2 to the 2005 Rules sets out special hourly rates of payment in so-called "very high cost cases", which are trials likely to last for more than 25 days. The hourly rate payable for preparation work, for example, is £90 to £140 for a junior solicitor, £80 to £110 for a sole junior and £110 to £180 for a senior solicitor or QC. In these cases the exact amount payable will be determined by the Taxing Master. In all cases there can then be a final appeal against the decision of the Taxing Master to a judge of the High Court.

---

[103] Access to Justice (NI) Order (Commencement No. 3, Transitional Provisions and Savings) Order (NI) 2005.

[104] *Ibid.* Sch. 4, para. 6(3).

In criminal appeals, whether in a county court or the Court of Appeal, the precise amount payable by way of costs, in the absence of agreement between the parties, will usually be assessed by the Taxing Master, who is obliged by statute to allow such sums as are reasonably sufficient to compensate the party for the expenses properly incurred.

In all cases, of course, the costs actually awarded to a party may not be in line with those charged by the solicitor or barrister; the client is then left to bear the difference, although, as explained earlier, he or she can always apply to the Taxing Master for a reduction in the solicitor's bill.

An allowance is usually also made for the compensation of witnesses who, if they are professional people, can be allowed a professional fee in addition to out-of-pocket expenses. The allowances are changed every few years but are generally much less than the actual losses sustained (especially if the witness is a self-employed person). However the court can award higher amounts for attendance if it thinks that the claim is reasonable (and provided any loss of wages is certified by an employer).[105]

Civil proceedings

A person involved in civil proceedings, whether as plaintiff or defendant, should also consider whether to apply for a civil legal aid certificate (see 3.3 above). The costs, whether borne by the litigants themselves or by the fund administered by the Legal Services Commission, are calculated differently accordingly to the forum in which the proceedings are brought.

The Legal Services Commission will pay the following fees for work done under the green form scheme (these have not been upgraded for a number of years): £54.50 an hour for advocacy, £43.25 an hour for preparation call and attendances at meetings, £24.25 an hour for waiting and travelling, £10.75 for each telephone call when advice is given on the Police and Criminal Evidence legislation, and £3.35 for all letters (other than acknowledgements or fixing appointments) and for telephone calls (whether in or out). A one-third uplift is payable for unsociable hours on travel, waiting and attendance times.

After any contentious proceedings which have not been legally aided a party may apply to the Taxing Master for his or her solicitor's bill to be

---

[105] See generally the Magistrates' Courts (Costs in Criminal Cases) (Amendment) Rules (NI) 1994.

officially examined, provided that the application is made within 12 months of the bill's delivery. (In non-contentious cases, as we have seen, the time limit is usually just three months.) A party who is ordered to pay the other side's costs may, rather than agree them, insist on those being taxed too, this time within six months of the order.

The Taxing Master will arrange a date for a hearing to take place. He or she will then assess the costs at what is a reasonable amount in the light of all the relevant circumstances, referring of course to any appropriate regulations on the matter. A party, whether solicitor or client, who is dissatisfied with the Taxing Master's assessment may ask for a second review by the Master and for yet a further review by a judge. The costs of the taxing process are usually borne by the party paying the bill being taxed.

Proceedings in a magistrates' court

The amounts which can be in issue in civil cases in magistrates' courts are small (see Chap. 6.2). The fees for issuing a summons and for the various pieces of work which a solicitor or barrister might do are laid down in regulations (the Magistrates' Courts Fees Order (NI) 1996, as amended[106]). The fee for issuing a "process" for the recovery of a debt is just £9, service of a summons by post costs £13, and the application fee for the renewal of a liquor licence is £136. Parties are usually left to bear their own fees and lawyers' costs even if they win the case, but in a case involving family disputes it is more normal for the court to award costs against the loser of the case. In a typical case these might amount to £200.

Proceedings in a small claims court

The maximum sum which can be claimed in these so-called "arbitration" proceedings, which take place before a district judge, is £2,000 (see Chap. 6.3). At present the application fee for claims less than £150 is £16, for claims between £150 and £300 it is £36, for claims between £300 and £500 it is £52 and for claims larger than £500 it is £62. The other party (the "respondent") does not pay any fee for defending the case, unless he or she makes a counterclaim (in which event the fees are one-half of those payable by the claimant). Once again each side is usually left to bear his or her own costs, including the

---

[106] A full list of the fees payable from 1 September 2004 is on the website of the Northern Ireland Court Service.

cost of providing witnesses and (unless arranged by the district judge) expert reports; only the application fee itself will be recoverable by the winner from the loser. If a plaintiff makes a claim in a county court for a fixed amount less than £2,000 and the defendant insists upon fighting it in a small claims court but loses, the district judge may award to the plaintiff such costs as he or she would have received if the case had been heard in the county court.

Proceedings in a county court

Up to £15,000 can be claimed in most civil cases in a county court. However, for claims concerning matrimonial property or compensation for criminal damage to property there is no financial limit (see Chap. 6.4 and 6.5). The fees for commencing the proceedings (*i.e.* issuing and serving a "civil bill") and for summoning witnesses, as well as the costs for the work done by solicitors and barristers, are laid down in regulations (see the County Court Fees Order (NI) 1996, as amended). The amount payable often depends on the amount of money or the value of the property being claimed. For example, the cost of issuing an ordinary civil bill for a claim greater than £2,000 is £140, and for a similar counterclaim it is half of this. A witness summons costs £13, a decree *nisi* £62 and an application for a licence £216. A solicitor's costs for work done in a case where £4,500 is claimed will be approximately £1,200 and a barrister's costs will be about £260. A slightly lower sum is payable to the solicitor if he or she was acting for a defendant rather than a plaintiff. Counsel is also entitled to an allowance for travelling to the court. For each day or part of a day on which a trial or hearing is continued after the first day, counsel can get one-third of the scale fee for the first day and a solicitor in attendance can claim the same.

It is important to note that in a county court case the loser will have to pay the winner's costs unless the judge orders otherwise, but even this may not be enough to reimburse the winner completely for his or her outlay: the bill received from the solicitor will include an amount for the time and responsibility involved, which will not be wholly reflected in the fixed scale laid down in the regulations. In such instances the winner must bear the balance of the expense; this could be a significant fraction of the total expense, especially if what was claimed in the case was much more than he or she actually succeeded in winning.

To encourage settlements out of court the scales of costs in county court cases are greatly reduced if a defendant agrees to satisfy a claim within 14 days of the service of the plaintiff's civil bill or if he or she fails to defend the action. A defendant can also safeguard the position on costs by "paying into court" so much of the plaintiff's claim as the defendant is prepared to concede. If the plaintiff does not accept this payment but then does not succeed in getting a higher award from the court, he or she will have to pay virtually all the costs, both his or her own as well as the defendant's.

A plaintiff's costs in the county court may also be reduced if the amount recovered is less than £3,000. In that event the case should have been brought before a district judge and not a county court judge, so only half the scale cost for the amount of the successful claim is allowed. If the recovery is less than £2,000 then, whether the case was heard by a county court judge or by a district judge sitting in a county court, no costs at all will be allowed; the matter should have been dealt with by arbitration in a small claims court (see above and Chap. 6.3). Only in cases of misconduct by one party or in proceedings for a fixed amount of money may costs up to the county court scale be awarded. For further details on legal costs incurred in county courts see the County Court Rules (NI) 1981, Order 55 and Appendix 2 to the Rules, as amended.

Proceedings in the High Court

Any amount of money can be claimed in High Court proceedings. The court fees are again set out in regulations but lawyers' costs are not specified to the same extent as in county court proceedings. Appendix 3 to Order 62 of the Rules of the Supreme Court (NI) 1980, as amended, lays down fixed costs only for cases where, in effect, the defendant does not submit a defence to the claim. Naturally both fees and costs are higher than in county courts. The fee for a writ of summons is £175 and for a notice of appeal to the Court of Appeal it is £180. For an application for judicial review (see Chap. 6.7) the fee is £52 and if leave is granted for the review a further fee of £123 is payable. For further details on the level of fees, see the Supreme Court Fees Order (NI) 1996, as amended, and the Supreme Court Taxing Office Practice Direction 2004 No. 1.[107] Senior counsel (i.e. QCs) are more likely to be

---

[107] [2004] 4 BNIL 110. A full list of the fees payable from 1 September 2004 is on the website of the Northern Ireland Court Service.

involved; their charges are high, and the junior counsel who assist them usually get two-thirds of the fee paid to "the silk".[108] More will usually be payable if there have been pre-trial consultations between the barrister and the client and if the case is fought for a day or more. If a plaintiff recovers less than £15,000 in the High Court proceedings he or she will be restricted to costs on the county court scale.

The decision as to which side is to bear the costs in High Court proceedings is in the complete discretion of the judge, but in the vast majority of cases the loser will be ordered to pay most, if not all, of the winner's costs. (An exception is usually made to this in Northern Ireland in cases where a husband successfully petitions for divorce against his wife.) Once the judge has ordered who is to pay the costs, the actual amounts to be paid will be agreed between the parties or, in the absence of any agreement, assessed by the Taxing Master. The Master will allow costs only for work which was essential, or proper; any "extra" work must be paid for by the party requiring it to be done. This is termed the assessment of costs on a "party and party" basis. (If the winner of a case is legally aided, the costs will be taxed on what is called a "common fund" basis, which allows the winner to recover a reasonable amount for all expenses reasonably incurred.) A litigant in person in the High Court - someone who is unrepresented by a lawyer - can be allowed up to two-thirds of what the costs would have been if he or she had engaged a solicitor.

Proceedings in a tribunal

Tribunals (see Chap. 8) do not normally have the power to order one side to pay the other side's costs. As legal aid is not available for tribunal proceedings (except in the Lands Tribunal and for representation under the advice and assistance scheme in the Mental Health Review Tribunal and in some detention and immigration hearings - see 3.3 above) the parties usually end up paying their own costs. In some situations, however, the tribunal can make payments to cover travel expenses and loss of earnings. Exceptionally (*e.g.* if the respondent's arguments are considered frivolous or vexatious) a tribunal may order the respondent to pay the applicant's costs. This

---

[108] When junior counsel at the Bloody Sunday Inquiry were offered just 50% of QCs' rates (which is closer to the practice in England and Wales) they brought judicial review proceedings against the Tribunal: see *In re Kennedy and others' Application* [2001] 1 BNIL 52.

occurred in *Johnston* v *Chief Constable of the RUC*,[109] a case where female police reservists successfully complained of sexual discrimination.

Enforcement of judgment proceedings

As will be explained in Chapter 6.8, the cost of enforcing a judgment, if the losing side refuses at first to comply with it, can be quite substantial in relation to the size of the judgment itself. The fees payable to the Enforcement of Judgments Office are laid down by the Judgments Enforcement Fees Order (NI) 1996, as amended, and to these must be added the solicitor's fee for acting on the winner's behalf. The fee for lodging notice of intent to apply for enforcement of a judgment is just £20, but the fee for an actual application for enforcement grows with the size of the judgment in question. For instance, enforcement of a judgment for £1,000 will incur a fee of £181, which rises to £380 if the judgment is for £3,000 and to £645 if it is for £10,000. If the losing side can afford to pay the judgment debt, the enforcement costs are added to it; otherwise the enforcement costs must be written off by the "winning side" as another bad debt.

---

[109] [1987] QB 129.

CHAPTER FOUR

CRIME AND POLICING

4.1 CRIME LEVELS IN NORTHERN IRELAND

Statistics on offences committed in Northern Ireland are made available through the annual reports of the Chief Constable of the Police Service and through the Police Service's website.[1] The Northern Ireland Court Service also prepares a book entitled *Northern Ireland Judicial Statistics*, which deals mainly with the level of court business (criminal and civil) each year. The Northern Ireland Office publishes annually *A Commentary on Northern Ireland Crime Statistics*, where trends are identified and comparisons drawn, and also (from time to time) a comprehensive *Digest of Information on the Northern Ireland Criminal Justice System*, which presents much of its data in the form of graphs and charts.[2] Occasionally the Statistics and Research branch of the Northern Ireland Office produces a *Research Findings* booklet with important supplementary information. Every two or three years a Northern Ireland Crime Survey is conducted, the most recent being in 2003-04. The NIO's Statistics and Research branch reports the results of these surveys in its periodic booklets. Also worth consulting is the *Security and Justice* chapter of the *Northern Ireland Annual Abstract of Statistics*, now published by the Northern Ireland Statistics and Research Agency.[3]

Table 11, below, indicates the number of various types of serious offences recorded during the past three years. Attempting, conspiring, inciting, aiding, abetting, causing or permitting an offence is generally included under the heading of the offence itself. It must be remembered that recorded crime is not the same thing as actual crime, because for various reasons many offences never come to the notice of the police. Beneath the number of recorded crimes in Table 10 is the percentage which were "cleared" by the police. In the police's eyes an offence is "cleared" if it is one for which a person has been charged, summonsed or cautioned, or one which a court has taken into consideration when

---

[1] www.psni.police.uk. On this website some of the statistics in the most recent Chief Constable's Annual Reports appear only in the PDF version, not the Word version.
[2] The 4th ed. was published in March 2004. See www.nio.gov.uk./pdf/ digestinfo.pdf. Unfortunately some of its figures are up-to-date only to 2001.
[3] Most NISRA publications are available on its website: www.nisra.gov.uk.

sentencing someone for other crimes, or one which cannot be proceeded with because, although there is enough evidence of someone's guilt, the person is too young to be prosecuted or is dead. In other words, "cleared" offences are *not* the offences in respect of which persons have been found guilty and punished.

TABLE 11: RECORDED CRIME AND CLEARANCE RATES 2002-2005[4]

	2002-03	2003-04	2004-05
Offences against the person	28,455	28,982	29,339
Clearance rate (%)	51.4	57	53.1
Sexual offences	1,469	1,780	1,686
Clearance rate (%)	46.6	50.8	46.0
Burglary	18,659	16,389	13,388
Clearance rate (%)	9.9	12.2	14.8
Robbery	2,497	1,973	1,487
Clearance rate (%)	13.4	14.4	16.7
Theft	41,911	35,691	31,097
Clearance rate (%)	14.0	15.9	17.4
Fraud and forgery	8,801	6,273	5,198
Clearance rate (%)	28.4	32.4	36.0
Criminal damage	36,571	32,402	31,432
Clearance rate (%)	13.0	15.2	14.4
Offences against the state	1,771	1,292	1,185
Clearance rate (%)	33.4	41.6	45.9
Drug offences	1,308	2,589	2,622
Clearance rate (%)	68.0	71.6	73.5
All offences	142,496	127,953	118,124
Clearance rate (%)	23.0	27.4	28.2

The figures in Table 11 show that, while recorded crimes of violence and drug offences rose over the three-year period, the number of other crimes fell, especially theft and criminal damage. The clearance rate rose for every category except sexual offences, although ultimately only about one-quarter of all recorded crime was cleared. Compared with other jurisdictions crime rates are still low in Northern Ireland, at the rate of 76 per 1,000 of the population in 2003-04. Northern Ireland tends to have a higher rate of homicide and rape but lower rates in all other categories. The rate of commission of burglary, robbery and theft is approximately half the rate in England and Wales.

---

[4] Source: The website of the PSNI: www.psni.police.uk.

It should also be noted that racial incidents, as well as homophobic incidents and incidents of domestic violence, are all rising steeply in Northern Ireland. In 2004-05 there were 813 recorded racial incidents (compared with 453 in 2003-04), 196 recorded homophobic incidents (71 in 2003-04) and no fewer than 8,508 recorded domestic crimes (8,565 in 2003-04).

Organised crime

There is growing evidence that organised crime is now a serious phenomenon in Northern Ireland. Certainly the public perceive this to be the case, with 95% saying so in a recent survey.[5] Most (66%) were therefore in favour of the Organised Crime Task Force, which the Northern Ireland Office established in 2002.[6] This body comprises representatives from the Government, the police, Revenue and Customs, the Assets Recovery Agency and the National Criminal Intelligence Service[7] and is chaired by a government Minister. It has already identified 230 Northern Ireland-based organised crime gangs, 150 of which supposedly operate quite locally in the fields of vehicle theft, drug trafficking, fuel fraud, extortion and counterfeiting. The majority of the top level groups are, says the Task Force, either associated with or controlled by loyalist or republican paramilitaries, with cross-border smuggling being "by far" the most lucrative activity engaged in. The Organised Crime Task Force publishes an annual threat assessment of the scale and nature of the organised crime problem in Northern Ireland and its strategy for dealing with it.[8] Reports from the Independent Monitoring Commission (see below) have confirmed the involvement of paramilitary organisations in serious crime, although it should be remembered that that Commission does not have its own investigators - it is almost entirely dependent for its information on sources within the security forces.

Victimisation and the fear of crime

The Northern Ireland Crime Survey of 2003-04 found that 21.4% of all households had experienced at least one crime during the previous 12

---

[5] *Northern Ireland Omnibus Survey*, February 2003.
[6] www.octf.gov.uk.
[7] More details of the last two are supplied below.
[8] These can be viewed on the Task Force's website: see note 6 above.

months.[9] This was a rise from 19.7% in 2001 but a decrease from 23% in 1998. In England and Wales the figure for 2003-04 was 25.7% (down from 27.5% in 2001-02), so the statistics for Northern Ireland and England and Wales seem to be converging. The risk of being a victim of crime in Belfast is much higher than, say, in the west of the province (32% as opposed to 19%), but the most frequently experienced type of victimisation throughout Northern Ireland tends to be car vandalism, followed by theft from a car. Referrals by the police to Victim Support Northern Ireland, a charity which provides practical support to victims of crime, stood at 43,417 in 2002-03.[10] Its Court Witness Service, which provides support for adult victims and prosecution witnesses at court hearings, helped 483 people.

The Northern Ireland Crime Survey of 2003-04 revealed that 19% of female respondents and 11% of male respondents reported having been the victim of at least one incident of domestic violence at some time in their lives; again the figure was worse in Belfast (21%) than, say, in the west of the province (14%), and it was also slightly worse for Catholics (17%) than for Protestants (15%).[11] Most of the victims sustained injuries as a result of the "worst" incident they had experienced, yet the vast majority of "worst" incidents were not even reported to the police. In the 2003-04 Crime Survey some 47% said that they thought that the Government and its agencies were not doing enough to deal with domestic violence.

As in most societies, the fear of crime in Northern Ireland is in excess of the actual crime. In the 2001 Crime Survey 29% of respondents believed it was likely or very likely that they would be the victim of car theft, and 27% feared theft from a car (8 times the actual incidence of that crime). Some 55% reported that they believed crime had increased in their area in the previous two years. One in three said the biggest "anti-social behaviour" problems in their area were teenagers hanging around and vandalism or graffiti. Reassuringly, as many as 61% said that their lives were not really affected by fear of crime. On the other hand, the rate of actual crime is much higher than the rate of reported crime. The total number of recorded crimes in Northern Ireland in

---

[9] B. French and P. Campbell, *Crime Victimisation in Northern Ireland: Findings from the 2003-04 Northern Ireland Crime Survey*, Research Bulletin 4/2005 (NIO).

[10] The NIO funded Victim Support to the tune of £1.5 million in 2002-03.

[11] R. Freel and E. Robinson, *Experience of Domestic Violence in Northern Ireland: Findings from the 2003-04 Northern Ireland Crime Survey*, Research Bulletin 5/2005 (NIO).

2003-04 was 127,953 but, based on the results of the 2003-04 Northern Ireland Crime Survey, the estimated number of actual crimes was some 295,000; this means that only about 41% of actual crime was reported to the police.

Tables 12 and 13 (below) provide details of the proceedings taken in the criminal courts in Northern Ireland for the last three years for which figures are available.[12]

TABLE 12: CRIMINAL PROCEEDINGS IN MAGISTRATES' AND YOUTH COURTS 2001-2003

	2002	2003	2004
ADULTS			
Persons dealt with	42,929	50,996	53,340
Charges dealt with	84,011	94,462	111,872
Prison sentences	4,530	4,869	4,699
Fines	39,130	45,509	50,100
Community service and probation orders	2,706	2,826	3,132
JUVENILES			
Persons dealt with	2,009	1,915	1,969
Charges dealt with	3,565	3,657	4,083
Fines	290	358	539
Community service and probation orders	778	817	708
Training school orders	326	259	416
Attendance orders	197	274	296
Conditional discharges	931	843	710

[12] Source: *Northern Ireland Judicial Statistics 2002, 2003* and *2004*. The figures for 2002 do not always tally with those given in the *Digest of Information*, note 2 above, Chaps. 7 and 8, possibly because the latter focuses on numbers of persons while the former focuses on numbers of court orders. The Northern Ireland Court Service, from the first quarter of 2005, has started producing a provisional set of figures for magistrates' court work on a quarterly basis. This *Magistrates' Courts Bulletin* is available on-line at www.courtsni.gov.uk.

TABLE 13: CROWN COURT PROCEEDINGS 2002-2004

	2002	2003	2004
All defendants	1,131	1,209	1,570
Those in Diplock courts	113	111	77
% in Diplock courts	10%	9%	5%
Guilty pleas to all charges	651	738	953
% of all defendants	58%	61%	61%
Average weeks between	19 bail	15 bail	16 bail
committal and trial	13 custody	14 custody	13 custody
Persons totally acquitted	105	n/a	134
% of all defendants	9%	n/a	9%

The overwhelming majority of defendants in criminal cases, whether adults or juveniles, are male[13] and most plead guilty, thereby avoiding a full trial. In the Crown Court the delay before a trial starts can be several months, especially in cases where the persons being tried are allegedly connected with paramilitary organisations and the trials take place in so-called Diplock courts (see 4.2 below). By far the most common form of punishment for adults is a fine, with only about 8% of adult defendants in magistrates' courts being given immediate prison sentences. For juveniles the commonest punishment is a conditional discharge (*i.e.*, no penalty on condition that the young person in question commits no further wrongdoing over a stipulated period); community service orders or probation orders are the next most common punishment.

Terrorist crime

Table 14, below, gives a picture of the level of "terrorist" crime in Northern Ireland since 1969, as set out on the PSNI's website (other sources provide slightly different figures[14]).

---

[13] See further *Gender and the Northern Ireland Criminal Justice System* (NISRA, 1997). This contains information on victims, attitudes and fear of crime, offenders and court sentencing, as well information about those employed in the criminal justice system.

[14] *E.g.* in *Lost Lives* by D. McKittrick, S. Kelters, B. Feeney, C. Thornton and D. McVea (rev. ed. 2004), the authors calculate that 3,703 people died between 1969 and the end of 2003.

TABLE 14: TERRORIST CRIME IN NORTHERN IRELAND 1969-2004

YEAR	DEATHS				INJURIES	SHOOT-INGS	BOMBS[15]
	POL.	ARMY	CIVSs.	ALL			
1969	1	0	13	14	n/a	73	10
1970	2	0	23	25	n/a	213	170
1971	11	48	115	174	2,592	1,756	1,515
1972	17	131	322	470	4,876	10,631	1,853
1973	13	66	173	252	2,651	5,019	1,520
1974	15	37	168	220	2,398	3,208	1,383
1975	11	20	216	247	2,474	1,803	691
1976	23	29	245	297	2,729	1,908	1,428
1977	14	29	69	112	1,387	1,081	1,143
1978	10	21	50	81	985	755	748
1979	14	48	51	113	875	728	624
1980	9	17	50	76	801	642	402
1981	21	23	57	101	1,350	1,142	578
1982	12	28	57	97	525	547	368
1983	18	15	44	77	510	424	410
1984	9	19	36	64	866	334	258
1985	23	6	26	55	916	238	251
1986	12	12	37	61	1,450	392	275
1987	16	11	68	95	1,130	674	393
1988	6	33	55	94	1,047	538	466
1989	9	14	39	62	959	566	427
1990	12	15	49	76	906	557	319
1991	6	13	75	94	962	499	605
1992	3	6	76	85	1,066	506	497
1993	6	8	70	84	824	476	350
1994	3	3	56	62	825	348	337
1995	1	0	8	9	937	50	12
1996	0	1	14	15	1,419	125	29
1997	4	1	17	22	1,237	225	102
1998	1	1	53	55	1,652	211	263
1999	0	0	7	7	983	125	107
2000	0	0	18	18	1,064	302	157
2001	0	0	17	17	1,598	355	450
2002	0	0	13	13	1,161	350	242
2003	0	0	11	11	819	229	96
2004	0	0	4	4	718	185	97
All	302	655	2,402	3,359	46,518	37,215	18,576

[15] Including incendiaries.

As can be seen, at least 3,359 people had died by the end of 2004, the worst years by far being 1971-76. Approximately 60% of all deaths were caused by republican paramilitaries, 30% by loyalist paramilitaries and 10% by members of the security forces.[16] The worst single atrocity was the "Real IRA" bomb at Omagh in August 1998, which killed 29 people and unborn twins. Table 14 does not of course include the many people who died in Great Britain, the Republic of Ireland or other parts of Europe. In that category there were 51 British soldiers killed.[17] Approximately 2,000 of the killings are "unsolved" in the sense that no-one has been brought to justice for committing them. Additional resources have recently been given to the PSNI to allow investigators to determine whether even at this late stage criminal proceedings can indeed be initiated in any of these cases.

Independent Monitoring Commission[18]

Largely as a result of unionist political pressure, a body called the Independent Monitoring Commission (IMC) was established in January 2004 through a treaty which had been agreed between the United Kingdom and Ireland Governments. Powers were then conferred upon it by, in the UK's case, the Northern Ireland (Monitoring Commission etc.) Act 2003. The aim was to help establish a stable and inclusive devolved government in a peaceful Northern Ireland by creating a body which would report to the governments on activity by paramilitary groups, on the normalisation of security measures in the province and on claims by Assembly parties that other parties, or individuals Ministers in the Executive, were not living up to the standards expected of them. The Commission is precluded by statute[19] from doing anything which might prejudice the national security interests of either the United Kingdom or Ireland, put at risk the safety or life or any person or have a prejudicial effect on any present or future legal proceedings.

The IMC comprises four Commissioners (all men) - one from Northern Ireland (Lord Alderdice, the former Speaker of the Assembly), one from Great Britain, one from Ireland and one from the United States of America (a former Deputy General of the Central Intelligence Agency).

---

[16] F. Ní Aoláin, "Truth Telling, Accountability and the Right to Life in Northern Ireland" [2002] EHRLR 571.

[17] The last British soldier to be killed in Northern Ireland was Stephen Restorick, on 12 February 1997.

[18] www.independentmonitoringcommission.org.

[19] S. 2(1) of the Northern Ireland (Monitoring Commission etc.) Act 2003.

Together with their staff they have been granted certain privileges and immunities traditionally conferred on people working for bodies established under a treaty.[20]

By the end of May 2005 the IMC had delivered five reports to the two governments. In the third of these (November 2004[21]) it concluded that paramilitary violence remained at a "disturbingly high level"; it urged tighter regulation of charities in Northern Ireland so that they would find it harder to be involved in money-laundering, but it also expressed support for community restorative justice schemes, provided that these were not a cover for paramilitary groups. In its fourth report, an *ad hoc* report on the Northern Bank robbery in Belfast on 20 December 2004,[22] the Commission said that, had the Assembly not then been suspended, it would have recommended that Sinn Féin be suspended from the Assembly; because of the suspension all that it could actually recommend was that the Government should impose a financial penalty on the party, as had been done for both Sinn Féin and the Progressive Unionist Party after the IMC's first report.[23] That first report caused some controversy because at least one of its assertions was later proved to be false and some voluntary and community groups accused the Commission of advocating the political vetting of their work. But an attempt by one defendant to have the report suppressed failed in the Divisional Court.[24] The fifth report of the IMC confirmed that loyalist paramilitary groups remain responsible for more violence than republican groups but that dissident republican groups are the most committed to continuing terrorism.[25]

Commissions on Decommissioning and Victims' Remains[26]

Since 1992 there has also been an Independent International Commission on Decommissioning, led by General John de Chastelain from Canada. The Commission was the outcome of another international treaty between the United Kingdom and Ireland and it was

---

[20] Northern Ireland (Monitoring Commission etc.) Act 2003 (Immunities and Privileges) Order 2003.
[21] 2003-04, HC 1218.
[22] 2004-05, HC 308.
[23] 2003-04, HC 516.
[24] *In re Tolan's Application* [2004] NIQB 29.
[25] 2005-06, HC 46.
[26] Strangely, neither body has a website.

given specific power by the Northern Ireland Arms Decommissioning Act 1997 to operate a "decommissioning scheme" drawn up by the Secretary of State. This identifies an "amnesty period" (which is still running, having been extended several times[27]) during which unlawfully held arms can be deposited or destroyed with impunity. By section 5 of the 1997 Act no evidence of anything done, and no information obtained, in accordance with the decommissioning scheme can be admissible in criminal proceedings. To date, of course, very few arms have been decommissioned. Little hard information is available because part of the deal with the IRA appears to be that the Commission cannot publicly disclose what weapons have been put beyond use by that organisation. It was supposedly the failure to agree a method of recording the decommissioning planned to take place late in December 2004 that led to the breakdown in negotiations between the political parties earlier that month (see Chap. 1.2).

In an attempt to deal with the vexed question of "the disappeared" the United Kingdom and British Governments have also created an Independent Commission for the Location of Victims' Remains, upon which power has been conferred by the British Parliament through the Northern Ireland (Location of Victims' Remains) Act 1999.[28] Again, section 3 of that Act renders inadmissible in evidence in any criminal proceedings any relevant information provided to the Commission and any information obtained directly or indirectly as a result of such information being so provided. As with arms decommissioning, however, few bodies of the disappeared have yet been recovered.

"Punishment" attacks

In recent years paramilitary-style "punishment attacks" committed against those (mostly young men) supposedly responsible for "anti-social behaviour" have become very prevalent, as Table 15, below, shows.[29] Unfortunately neither the PSNI nor the Public Prosecution

---

[27] The Northern Ireland Arms Decommissioning Act 1997 (Amnesty Period) Order 2005 extends the period to 24 February 2006.
[28] And, in Ireland, by the Criminal Justice (Location of Victims' Remains) Act 1999.
[29] Source: PSNI website, www.psni.police.uk. See, generally, J. Darby "The Effect of Violence on the Irish Peace Process" in C. Harvey (ed.), *Human Rights, Equality and Democratic Renewal in Northern Ireland* (2001); C. Knox and R. Monaghan, *Informal Justice in Divided Societies: Northern Ireland and South Africa* (2002), and D. Feenan, *Informal Criminal Justice* (2002). Indications to date are that the number of such attacks occurring in 2005 will be significantly reduced.

Service is able to say how many people have been charged with these offences (let alone convicted).

TABLE 15: "PUNISHMENT" ATTACKS IN NORTHERN IRELAND 1995-2004

Year	Loyalist attacks		Republican attacks		All attacks	
	Shot	Beaten	Shot	Beaten	Shot	Beaten
1995	3	76	0	141	3	217
1996	21	130	3	172	24	302
1997	46	78	26	78	72	156
1998	34	89	38	55	72	144
1999	47	90	26	44	73	134
2000	86	78	50	54	136	132
2001	121	93	65	53	186	146
2002	117	89	56	50	173	139
2003	101	103	55	46	156	149
2004	89	75	23	41	112	116
Totals	665	901	342	734	1,007	1,635

At present the victims of loyalist paramilitary attacks outnumber those of republican attacks by approximately two to one. A significant amount of intimidation still exists too. The Northern Ireland Housing Executive reports that in 2003-04 it spent £45 million re-housing people who had been intimidated out of their homes.[30]

Developments in criminal proceedings

In July 1993, the Royal Commission on Criminal Justice - established in the wake of several high-profile instances of miscarriages of justice connected with the troubles in Northern Ireland, such as the Birmingham Six,[31] the Guildford Four,[32] the Maguire Seven[33] and

[30] Northern Ireland Housing Executive Annual Report 2003-04, p. 73.
[31] R v McIlkenny and others [1992] 2 All ER 417.
[32] R v Richardson and others, The Times, 20 May 1993.
[33] R v Maguire and others [1992] 2 All ER 433.

Judith Ward[34] - published its report.[35] While the Commission did not address any issues specific to the criminal justice system of Northern Ireland (its remit extended only to the law in England and Wales), several of its 352 recommendations have since been reflected in legislation extending to Northern Ireland. These include provision for the pre-trial disclosure of evidence,[36] a more clearly articulated system of sentence discounts in relation to early guilty pleas,[37] abolition of corroboration rules,[38] the re-drafting of the grounds on which an appeal can be taken from the Crown Court[39] and, perhaps most significant of all, the establishment, by the Criminal Appeal Act 1995, of a Criminal Cases Review Commission whose powers extend to Northern Ireland[40] (see 4.7 below).

In lieu of the Royal Commission, the Northern Ireland Office issued its own discussion paper, *Crime in the Community*, in March 1993. Some of the suggestions made in that paper have also been given legislative expression (*e.g.* the obligation to consider pre-sentence reports before a custodial sentence is imposed[41]), while others (such as the introduction of unit fines) have effectively been shelved. In 1997 the Northern Ireland Office published a further consultation paper entitled *New Criminal Justice Measures for Northern Ireland*. This set out five measures in then forthcoming Home Office legislation which were thought to be equally relevant to Northern Ireland.[42] All of these were implemented by the Criminal Justice (NI) Order 1998.

---

[34] *R* v *Ward* [1993] 2 All ER 577. See, generally, T. Ingman, The English Legal Process (10th ed., 2004), pp. 201-6.

[35] Cmnd. 2263. For a contemporaneous response, see *The Relevance to Northern Ireland of the Report of the Royal Commission on Criminal Justice*, Standing Advisory Commission on Human Rights, *19th Annual Report*, 1993-94, pp. 96-126.

[36] Cmnd. 2263, p. 199, nos. 124-8; ss. 3-11 of the Criminal Procedure and Investigations Act 1996.

[37] *Ibid.* p. 202, no. 156; Criminal Justice (NI) Order 1996, art. 33.

[38] *Ibid.* p. 206, no. 195; Criminal Justice (NI) Order 1996, art. 45.

[39] *Ibid.* p. 215, nos. 316-7; Criminal Appeal Act 1995, s. 2(2).

[40] *Ibid.* pp. 217-219, nos. 331-352.

[41] *Crime in the Community*, p. 46, and Criminal Justice (NI) Order 1996, art. 21.

[42] (i) The abolition of the rebuttable presumption that a child does not know the difference between right and wrong; (ii) the use of live television links at hearings for the purposes of remand; (iii) the creation of sex offender orders; (iv) the creation of drug treatment and testing orders; and (v) the Youth Court being able to proceed with offences without having to await the outcome of unrelated Crown Court proceedings.

Further Criminal Justice (NI) Orders have been enacted in the intervening years,[43] largely mirroring developments in England and Wales, but it should be remembered that, while efforts are made to maintain legislative parity between the two jurisdictions, the context in which the law has to operate often differs, and neither the analysis nor the prescriptions appropriate for England and Wales are necessarily valid in Northern Ireland. To match the creation of the Criminal Justice Consultative Council in England and Wales in 1992, a Criminal Justice Consultative Group was established in Northern Ireland in 1993. It was renamed the Criminal Justice Issues Group in 1998, under the chairmanship of Lord Justice Campbell.[44]

The Criminal Justice Review

Undoubtedly the most significant development in the criminal justice system of Northern Ireland in recent times has been the establishment of the Criminal Justice Review Group, provided for in the Belfast (Good Friday) Agreement of April 1998.[45] It comprised a five-member team of officials representing the Secretary of State for Northern Ireland, the Lord Chancellor and the Attorney General.[46] They were assisted by five independent assessors, who included both legal practitioners and academics. The Group began working in June 1998 and two months later launched a consultation paper.[47] Having consulted widely, the Group eventually reported to the Government in March 2000.[48]

The Review Group's report covers a wide range of institutional, procedural and substantive issues, including the prosecution system, the system for appointing judges, the involvement of lay people in the criminal justice system, restorative justice,[49] juvenile justice,

---

[43] There were two in both 2003 and 2004. Orders dealing specifically with criminal evidence were made in 1999 and 2004.

[44] For the Group's remit, see *CJIG news* - Newsletter of the Criminal Justice Issues Group of Northern Ireland, Issue 4, 1998, p. 12.

[45] J. Jackson, "Shaping the Future of Criminal Justice" in C. Harvey (ed.), *Human Rights, Equality and Democratic Renewal in Northern Ireland* (2001).

[46] The Chairman was Mr Jim Daniell, Director of Criminal Justice at the NIO.

[47] See also *Review of the Criminal Justice System in Northern Ireland: A Progress Report* (April 1999).

[48] www.nio.gov.uk/mainreport.pdf.

[49] This is an approach to crime which concentrates on restoring and repairing the relationship between the offender, the victim and the community at large. There are several schemes currently operating in Northern Ireland, some with police co-

community safety, the sentencing system and the position of victims and witnesses. It also considers some of the issues examined by the Macpherson Inquiry into the murder of the black teenager Stephen Lawrence in London.[50] At the same time the Review Group published no fewer than 18 research reports, which provide a huge amount of information about various aspects of the criminal justice system in Northern Ireland.

The core message running through the report was the need for the criminal justice system to protect human rights. One of the recommendations, for example, was that human rights issues should become a permanent part of the training programmes for all those who work within criminal justice agencies, the legal profession and the relevant parts of the voluntary sector. The report also suggested that the Government should publish a criminal justice plan every three years and set out how it will measure progress in meeting the plan's aims. In relation to the prosecution system, the report recommended a new Public Prosecution Service for Northern Ireland, which would be responsible for all the prosecutions formerly conducted by the police and by the Office of the Director of Public Prosecutions. An independent, statutory Judicial Appointments Commission was also proposed, comprising some judges and lawyers but also a number of lay people.

On juvenile justice the report suggested that 17-year-olds should be brought within the jurisdiction of the youth courts (at that time those courts could deal only with persons aged up to 16 years) and that children younger than 14 years should, if found guilty of a criminal offence, be provided for within the care system. A new Probation, Prisons and Juvenile Justice Advisory Board, a Community Safety Council and a Law Commission for Northern Ireland (to make proposals for law reform) were also recommended as a way of providing expert advice to the Government on all relevant policy matters.

Many of the reforms recommended in the Criminal Justice Review's report have since been implemented, by the Justice (NI) Acts 2002 and

---

operation and some not. For a study of two pilot restorative cautioning schemes used by the police in Ballymena and East Belfast, see the NIO's Research and Statistical Series Report No. 4 (2002).

[50] Cm. 4262-I and 4262-II; 1999.

2004.[51] They are detailed at the appropriate points in this book.[52] However some of the recommendations cannot be fully implemented until the responsibility for criminal justice is devolved to the Northern Ireland Assembly. At the time this book went to press, that looked a very dim prospect. Meanwhile the implementation process is being supervised by a Justice Oversight Commissioner, Lord Clyde (see 4.7 below).

4.2 TYPES OF CRIMINAL OFFENCE

The criminal law of Northern Ireland, like that of England, rests on two fundamental principles. The first is that any kind of behaviour is criminal only if it is *expressly* prohibited by the criminal law. The second is that no-one can be convicted of a crime unless the behaviour in question was prohibited at the time it occurred.[53] In recognition of these principles most of the criminal law has been embodied in statutes. Only a few offences – the most prominent of which is murder – are still regulated primarily by judge-made law, although of course the judges do still have to interpret the criminal law statutes whenever their provisions are ambiguous or unclear. It is occasionally a difficult *legal* question to decide if all the required elements of a crime are present in any particular case, but in most cases the issue is simply whether the prosecution has proved sufficient *facts* to establish the defendant's guilt.

With rare statutory exceptions, no accused person can be convicted of a crime unless the prosecution has proved his or her guilt "beyond reasonable doubt": since the accused person must be presumed innocent until proved guilty,[54] he or she must be acquitted if the court is not certain that he or she is guilty. There are rare occasions when, once

---

[51] See C. Fox, "New Hope for the Criminal Justice Review? A Commentary on the Implementation Process" (2003) 54 NILQ 438.

[52] *E.g.* for the new Public Prosecution Service and Judicial Appointments Commission see Chap. 1.5; for developments in community safety and probation see 4.4 and 4.6 below; for changes to the juvenile justice system see Chap. 7.1; and for the proposed Northern Ireland Law Commission see Chap. 9.14.

[53] This latter principle is also enshrined in Art. 7 of the European Convention on Human Rights, which is enforceable in the courts of Northern Ireland by virtue of the Human Rights Act 1998.

[54] This fundamental principle is protected under Art. 6(2) of the European Convention on Human Rights. See the *Fair Trials Manual* (Amnesty International, London; 1998), Chap. 15 - "The Presumption of Innocence". On-line at www.amnesty.org/ailib/intcam/fairtrial/indxftm_a.htm.

the prosecution has proved certain basic facts, the burden of proving that he or she is not guilty rests on the accused.[55] In such cases, however, it is usually enough for the accused to prove this on a "balance of probabilities". This is a lower degree of proof than "beyond reasonable doubt" and is the same standard as is required in all civil cases (these are dealt with in Chap. 6). It really means that the accused must prove that what he or she is saying is more likely to be true than not. Examples occur when the accused claims to have impaired mental responsibility or to be insane,[56] or when he or she has been charged with possession of certain types of prohibited articles.[57]

The law recognises that not all crimes are equally serious by providing two different forms of procedure and trial. Less serious offences are dealt with by a summary trial in a magistrates' court (sometimes called a court of petty sessions or a court of summary jurisdiction), and they involve no jury. More serious offences are tried on indictment in the Crown Court by a judge and jury (although there is also a preliminary step which takes place in a magistrates' court). Some offences must *always* be tried summarily and some *always* on indictment; others (often called "hybrid offences") may be tried in either way.

In addition, owing to the terrorist threat in Northern Ireland, certain offences (classified as "scheduled offences") are tried on indictment without a jury in the so-called Diplock courts. These courts were introduced following the report of a Committee chaired by Lord Diplock in 1972, which recommended a trial by judge alone in such cases.[58] While some offences must always be tried in Diplock courts, others may at times be tried either in Diplock courts or under the normal procedures. Other special features of Northern Ireland's anti-terrorism laws are described further in 4.3 below.

The various categories of offences will now be examined in a little more detail.[59]

---

[55] See J. Stannard, "A Presumption and Four Burdens" (2000) 51 NILQ 560.
[56] Criminal Justice Act (NI) 1966, s. 2(2).
[57] *E.g.* Terrorism Act 2000, s. 77.
[58] *Report of the Commission to consider legal procedures to deal with terrorist activities in Northern Ireland* (Cmnd. 5185; 1972). The scheduled offences are now listed in Sch. 9 to the Terrorism Act 2000.
[59] For a much more comprehensive survey of the relevant law and practice, see J. Stannard, *Northern Ireland Criminal Procedure* (2000).

Offences which *must* be tried summarily

These are relatively minor offences which have to be tried in a magistrates' court by a resident magistrate (an RM) sitting without a jury (see Chaps. 1.5 and 5.2). They have all been made triable in this way by a statute, not by the common law, and for most of them proceedings must be begun within six months of the offence being committed.[60] All the offences in this category are considered to be not serious enough to merit the extra time and expense required for a trial on indictment. A common example is careless and inconsiderate driving, which is an offence under article 12 of the Road Traffic (NI) Order 1995.

Even some offences under Northern Ireland's anti-terrorism laws have to be tried summarily, such as refusal to answer a soldier's questions concerning a recent explosion, which is an offence under section 89 of the Terrorism Act 2000.

Offences which *must* be tried on indictment

These are serious offences which have to be tried in the Crown Court by a judge and jury, although like all cases heard in the Crown Court they are originally dealt with at committal proceedings in a magistrates' court (see Chap. 5.3). There is usually no time limit on the commencement of proceedings. Murder, manslaughter, rape and robbery are all offences in this category. There are considered to be no circumstances which would justify trying such offences in full at the level of a magistrates' court.

Offences which may be tried summarily *or* on indictment

The position regarding this category of offence differs in Northern Ireland from that in England, where significant changes were introduced by the Criminal Law Act 1977. Besides, since the publication of the report of the Royal Commission on Criminal Justice (1993)[61] and the Nairey Review of Delay in the Criminal Justice System (1997),[62] consecutive UK Governments have indicated their intention to reduce, if not altogether abolish, the right of defendants in England and Wales to decide for themselves whether to be tried in a magistrates' court or the Crown Court in either-way cases.

---

[60] Magistrates' Courts (NI) Order 1981, art. 19.
[61] *Report of the Royal Commission on Criminal Justice* (Cmnd. 2263; 1993).
[62] M. Nairey, *Review of Delay in the Criminal Justice System* (Home Office, 1997).

In Northern Ireland, there is currently a choice of proceedings for three kinds of crime:

(1)　　A handful of offences which are normally tried summarily can be tried on indictment if two conditions are satisfied:[63] (i) the offence must be one for which a person, if convicted, can be sent to prison for more than six months, and (ii) the defendant himself must ask to be tried on indictment. An example of this type of hybrid offence is the improper importation of goods, which is a crime under section 45 of the Customs and Excise Act 1952.

(2)　　Some offences which are normally tried on indictment can be tried summarily if the resident magistrate who first hears the case at the committal stage (see Chap. 5.5) considers that it is not a serious one and if the prosecution and defendant have no objections to a summary trial.[64] The RM can take the initiative to try the case summarily at any stage of the proceedings, but he or she must first give the defendant 24 hours' written notice (or procure a waiver of this requirement).[65] Examples of such offences are theft, indecent assault and assault occasioning actual bodily harm.[66] Also in this category are instances where a child is charged with any indictable offence other than homicide.[67]

(3)　　In many cases the statute which creates a crime expressly states that it can be tried summarily or on indictment. It is then up to the prosecution, bearing in mind the seriousness of the particular case, to decide which form of trial to use. An example of this kind of offence is dangerous driving, which is a crime under article 10 of the Road Traffic (NI) Order 1995.

Scheduled offences under the anti-terrorist laws

These are the offences which are listed in Schedule 9 to the Terrorism Act 2000. They are the ones most commonly committed by terrorists in Northern Ireland and for which the UK Parliament has considered it

---

[63] Magistrates' Courts (NI) Order 1981, art. 29. For details of the procedure to be followed, see the Magistrates' Courts Rules (NI) 1984, r. 24.

[64] Magistrates' Courts (NI) Order 1981, art. 45. For details of the procedure to be followed, see the Magistrates' Courts Rules (NI) 1984, r. 45.

[65] *Ibid.* r. 44(2).

[66] These offences are listed in the Criminal Justice (NI) Order 1986, Sch. 2, which replaced the Magistrates' Courts (NI) Order 1981, Sch. 2.

[67] Criminal Justice (Children) (NI) Order 1998, art. 17.

necessary to establish special procedures. The distinction between scheduled and non-scheduled offences overlies that between summary and indictable offences, that is, not all scheduled offences will be tried on indictment. None of them is in the category of offences which *must* be tried summarily, but many of them, such as membership of a proscribed organisation or threats to destroy property, are in the category of hybrid offences and so will be tried summarily if the conditions outlined in (3) above are fulfilled.

While trials on indictment of scheduled offences depart significantly from standard procedures (see 4.3 below), the procedures for dealing with the summary trial of scheduled offences do not differ to any great extent from the ordinary procedures in magistrates' courts. The main differences are threefold. For scheduled offences:

(1)   the Director of Public Prosecutions must consent to the prosecution;

(2)   there are special arrangements for holding young persons in custody (whether on remand or after a finding of guilt); and

(3)   after the trial, a resident magistrate must, if finding the accused guilty, give a reasoned judgment, not just a decision.

To complicate matters further, the Attorney General may "de-schedule" some offences (if he or she believes that no element of terrorism was involved in their commission) by certifying in a particular case that the offence is not to be treated as a scheduled offence. This applies, in particular, to the offences of murder, manslaughter, riot, kidnapping, robbery, aggravated burglary, intimidation, throwing a petrol bomb, arson, bomb hoaxes and carrying a firearm in a public place.[68] If the Attorney General refuses to de-schedule an offence, it is not possible to appeal against that decision to a higher authority, but it is possible to challenge it on very limited grounds by way of judicial review proceedings (see Chap. 6.7).[69] Amongst the offences which *cannot* be de-scheduled are belonging to, or inviting support for, a proscribed organisation,[70] fund-raising for terrorist purposes and money-

---

[68] Terrorism Act 2000, Sch. 9, Pt. I, note 1.

[69] For an example of a failed challenge see *R v Shuker and others' Applications* [2004] NIQB 20.

[70] These are organisations which the Secretary of State has placed on a banned list (see Sch. 2 to the Terrorism Act 2000). An organisation can ask to be de-proscribed and if the Secretary of State refuses to do so the organisation can appeal to the Proscribed

laundering terrorist property, and giving or receiving training in the making or use of firearms, explosives or explosive substances.[71]

In 2004 the Attorney General considered applications from 558 accused persons to have a total of 740 offences de-scheduled; in the event, 629 of these offences (85%) were de-scheduled.[72] However, it is not possible to tell from the published statistics how many of the accused persons involved did not then have to undergo trial in a Diplock court. This is because section 75(4) of the Terrorism Act 2000 requires an accused person to be tried by a Diplock court so long as even *one* of the charges remains scheduled. In 2004, 77 people were dealt with by a Diplock court (see Table 13 on p. 178).

4.3 ANTI-TERRORISM MEASURES[73]

As mentioned in the previous section, the UK Parliament and, when it existed, the Parliament in Belfast, have enacted "emergency" laws for Northern Ireland to help deal with "the troubles".[74] In recent years these have been merged with permanent anti-terrorism laws enacted for the whole of the United Kingdom.[75] Other permanent measures aimed principally at paramilitary activity have also been enacted, such as the Protection of the Person and Property Act (NI) 1969 (strengthening the offence of intimidation), the Public Order (NI) Order 1987 as amended by the Public Processions (NI) Act 1998 (restricting the right to hold open-air public meetings) and the Criminal Evidence (NI) Order 1988 and Criminal Justice (NI) Order 1996 (altering the law on the right to silence - see Chap. 5.1). It is worth noting, on the other hand, that there are no special laws governing the use of force by security forces in

---

Organisation Appeals Commission, created by the Terrorism Act 2000. See the Proscribed Organisations (Applications for Deproscription) Regs. 2001 and the Proscribed Organisation Appeals Commission (Procedure) Rules 2001.

[71] Terrorism Act 2000, Sch. 9, Pt. I, para. 22.

[72] *Northern Ireland Statistics on the Operation of the Terrorism Act 2000: Annual Statistics 2004*, NIO, Research and Statistical Bulletin 9/2005. These statistics are also available on-line at www.nio.gov.uk/index/statistics-research.htm.

[73] See generally L. Donohue, *Counter-Terrorist Law and Emergency Powers in the United Kingdom 1922-2000* (2000), especially Chaps. 2, 4 and 6.

[74] See C. Gearty and J. Kimbell, Terrorism and the Rule of Law (The Civil Liberties Research Unit, King's College, London, 1995) and C. Walker, "The Commodity of Justice in States of Emergency" (1999) 50 NILQ 164.

[75] The Terrorism Act 2000, the Anti-terrorism, Crime and Security Act 2001 and the Prevention of Terrorism Act 2005.

Northern Ireland.[76] In the area of civil law there are special laws dealing with discrimination in employment on religious or political grounds (see Chap. 9.3).

The European Court of Human Rights has in the past concluded that the level of violence in Northern Ireland justifies derogations from (*i.e.* exceptions to) internationally accepted human rights standards, on the ground that a state of public emergency existed.[77] At present no such derogation specific to Northern Ireland is in place,[78] but if so-called "house arrest" control orders are issued anywhere in the United Kingdom under the Prevention of Terrorism Act 2005 a derogation *will* be required. While the level of terrorist crime in Northern Ireland has markedly decreased in recent years, a threat from dissident terrorist groups and individuals remains.

EPAs and PTAs

Prior to the enactment of the Terrorism Act 2000 anti-terrorism laws for Northern Ireland were enacted under the title Northern Ireland (Emergency Provisions) Acts (EPAs). They were the successors to the notorious Civil Authorities (Special Powers) Acts (NI) 1922-33 and were enacted in 1973, 1978, 1987, 1991, 1996 and 1998. Some other provisions - applying throughout the United Kingdom - were to be found in the Prevention of Terrorism (Temporary Provisions) Acts (PTAs). The PTA 1989, amended by the Criminal Justice and Public Order Act 1994 and the Prevention of Terrorism (Additional Powers) Act 1996, was the successor to earlier PTAs, beginning with the one enacted immediately after the Birmingham pub bombings in 1974. Following the Omagh bomb in 1998, the Criminal Justice (Terrorism and Conspiracy) Act 1998 was rushed through Parliament, further amending the current EPA and PTA to make it easier to draw inferences from an accused person's silence.[79] This Act also provided,

---

[76] See, *e.g.*, the judgments of the Law Lords in *R* v *Clegg* [1995] 1 AC 482.

[77] *Brannigan and McBride* v *UK* (1994) 17 EHRR 539 (see Chap. 2.5). See too C. Harvey and S. Livingstone, "Human Rights and the Northern Ireland Peace Process" [1999] EHRLR 162.

[78] One was in place for the whole of the UK on account of Pt. IV of the Anti-terrorism, Crime and Security Act 2001: see the Human Rights Act 1998 (Designated Derogation) Order 2001. But this was withdrawn when that Act was replaced in 2005: see the Human Rights Act 1998 (Amendment) Order 2005.

[79] The Offences Against the State (Amendment) Act 1998 was passed in the Republic of Ireland. The emergency legislation in the Republic was recently the subject of a review by a team led by Hederman J.

in relation only to Northern Ireland, that where a person is charged with the offence of membership of a proscribed organisation, a statement of opinion from a senior police officer that the person is or was a member of a "specified"[80] organisation is admissible as evidence of the offence, although it is insufficient by itself to convict the accused.

The Terrorism Act 2000

The Terrorism Act 2000 replaced the current EPA and the PTA and applies throughout the United Kingdom, but in Part VII it contains special provisions which apply only in Northern Ireland (see below). The EPA and PTA were supposedly "temporary" laws, each of them requiring a Parliamentary order to keep them in force from year to year, but the 2000 Act places anti-terrorist laws on a permanent footing in the United Kingdom, in line with recommendations made by Lord Lloyd in a report in 1996 and by a Home Office consultation paper in 1998.[81] It also alters the definition of terrorism, so that it now means the use or threat of action where: (i) the action involves serious violence against a person, serious damage to property, the endangering of a person's life, a serious risk to the health or safety of a section of the public or the serious disruption of an electronic system, (ii) the use or threat is designed to influence the Government or intimidate a section of the public, and (iii) the use or threat is made for the purpose of advancing a political, religious or ideological cause.[82]

For Northern Ireland the concept of scheduled offences and the juryless Diplock courts were retained, and the Act also preserved special procedures for nearly every stage in the criminal process whenever a scheduled offence is being dealt with. The provisions in Part VII (*i.e.* ss. 65-113), however, have to be renewed from year to year, and will lapse altogether in February 2006 unless new legislation is enacted to replace them.[83]

---

[80] A "specified" organisation is defined as an Irish terrorist organisation which the Secretary of State does not believe to be observing a complete and unequivocal ceasefire.

[81] *Inquiry into Legislation Against Terrorism*, Cm. 3420, and *Legislation Against Terrorism*, Cm. 4178.

[82] S. 1(1) and (2).

[83] By s. 112, Part VII ceases to have effect a year after it is brought into force unless, under s. 112(2), the Secretary of State makes a continuance order.

The 2001 and 2005 Acts on terrorism

After the attacks in the USA on 11 September 2001 the UK Government ensured that quite draconian additional legislation was introduced to aid in the fight against terrorism. The most controversial aspect of the Anti-terrorism, Crime and Security Act 2001 was that it permitted the indefinite detention without trial of non-British nationals who were reasonably suspected of involvement in international terrorism. In December 2004, however, a bench of nine Law Lords held (by a majority of 8 to 1) that this was a disproportionate and discriminatory response to the threat facing the United Kingdom.[84] As a consequence the Government had to present new legislation to Parliament, which was enacted after much debate as the Prevention of Terrorism Act 2005. This permits restrictions short of imprisonment to be imposed on any person who is reasonably suspected of involvement in international terrorism, although the more extreme restrictions, if and when they are applied, will require a derogation notice to be delivered to the Council of Europe to ensure compliance with the European Convention on Human Rights. To ensure enactment of the 2005 Act, and rather than include a "sunset clause" within it (*i.e.* a clause providing for the Act to lapse on a certain date), the Government gave an undertaking to Parliament that it would introduce new anti-terrorist legislation within the next year.[85]

Reviews of anti-terrorist legislation

Both the EPA and the PTA were the subject of annual reviews. From 1987, these were prepared by Viscount Colville of Culross QC, and he was succeeded in 1994 by Mr John Rowe QC. The reports were considered by Parliament before it decided whether to renew the Acts for another year. The Terrorism Act 2000 also requires the submission to Parliament of annual reports on how the Act has operated.[86] These are prepared by Lord Carlile of Berriew QC, who also reported to Parliament on the operation of the detention provisions in the Anti-terrorism, Crime and Security Act 2001 until they were repealed by the Prevention of Terrorism Act 2005. He has been asked to report also on the operation of that legislation.

---

[84] *A and others* v *Secretary of State for the Home Department* [2005] 2 WLR 87.
[85] Such legislation was notified in the Queen's speech on 17 May 2005.
[86] S. 126.

In addition to this periodic scrutiny, several more extensive inquiries have been commissioned over the years. A fundamental review of the EPA 1991 was completed by Mr John Rowe in 1994[87] and, as already noted, Lord Lloyd of Berwick was asked in 1995 to consider whether there would be any need for specific counter-terrorism legislation in the United Kingdom in the event of lasting peace in Northern Ireland. Lord Lloyd's report was published in October 1996[88] and it included a comparison of the provisions in the PTA and EPA with those in the general criminal law.[89] It also focused on the implications for anti-terrorist provisions of the European Convention on Human Rights. In 2003 a committee of Privy Counsellors published a review of the 2001 Act (as required by the Act itself)[90] and Parliament's Joint Committee on Human Rights also publishes analyses of anti-terrorist legislation from time to time. Increasingly it seems that the need to have effective anti-terrorist legislation in place for Northern Ireland is being eclipsed by the need to have effective anti-terrorist legislation in place for the United Kingdom as a whole. Some features of the anti-terrorist legislation currently in force in Northern Ireland are described in the following paragraphs. In August 2005 the Government announced that it hoped to be able to do away with Northern Ireland specific legislation in this field (including Diplock courts) within two years.

Power to stop and question

Under section 89 of the Terrorism Act 2000 there is an obligation to answer questions from a police officer or a soldier about one's identity, one's movements and what one knows concerning any recent explosion or any other recent incident endangering life, but the duty arises only after one has been stopped in the street by a police officer or soldier. It is an offence to refuse to answer such questions to the best of one's knowledge and ability. In 2003 the PSNI stopped and questioned 1,368 people (2,448 in 2002), while the army stopped and questioned 10,921 (9,873 in 2002). The figure is so much higher for the army because most of the stops took place in the counties of Fermanagh, Tyrone and Armagh, where dissident republicans are said to be most active and where the army take the lead in operating vehicle check points. In

---

[87] Cm. 2706.
[88] Inquiry into Legislation Against Terrorism, Cm. 3420.
[89] Ibid. App.B, pp.125-164, although this is now slightly dated.
[90] Anti-terrorism, Crime and Security Act 2001, s. 122. See Anti-terrorism, Crime and Security Act 2001: Review, HC 100.

addition it should be noted that in 2003 a total of 2,621 people (3,957 in 2002) were stopped and searched for guns or ammunition under section 84 of the Terrorism Act.

Power to arrest

As regards powers of arrest, under section 41 of the Terrorism Act 2000 the police anywhere in the United Kingdom may arrest without a warrant any person whom they reasonably suspect to be guilty of certain specified offences (including membership of a proscribed organisation[91]) or of being concerned in the commission, preparation or instigation of acts of terrorism. In addition, section 82 allows police officers in Northern Ireland to arrest without a warrant any person whom they reasonably suspect is committing, has committed or is about to commit a scheduled offence or any other offence created by the Act. Section 83 supplements this by allowing any soldier on duty to arrest without a warrant any person whom he or she reasonably suspects of committing, having committed or being about to commit *any* offence. Police officers remain under a common law duty to give the reason for an arrest at the time it is effected, but soldiers do not. In 2003, 359 people were detained by the PSNI under section 41 of the Terrorism Act in Northern Ireland (compared with 236 in 2002) and 121 of these (33%) were charged with some kind of offence. In the same year 39 people were arrested by the PSNI under section 82 (of whom at least 10 were charged with an offence) and just five people were arrested by soldiers under section 83.[92]

Power to detain

Persons arrested under the Terrorism Act in Northern Ireland are not detained in an ordinary police station but in a special "serious crime suite" at Antrim police station. Formerly there were three special "holding centres" (or "police offices"), at Castlereagh in East Belfast, at Gough Barracks in Armagh and at Strand Road in Derry / Londonderry. There was never any express statutory authority for using these premises as places of detention and persons held there were always taken to a proper police station if they were to be charged after

---

[91] As a result of the Criminal Justice (Terrorism and Conspiracy) Act 1998, s. 3.

[92] *Northern Ireland Statistics on the Operation of the Terrorism Act 2003*, NIO, Research and Statistical Bulletin 3/2004, Tables 3, 7 and 16. The figures for the first 9 months of 2004 are 182 arrests under s. 41, 6 under s. 82 and 5 under s. 83: Research and Statistical Bulletin 2/2005.

being questioned. The conditions at Castlereagh holding centre, in particular, were consistently criticised by independent and international observers,[93] but not by the Northern Ireland judiciary.[94] In one case the European Court of Human Rights described the conditions in Castlereagh as austere and intimidating and as "intended to be psychologically coercive and conducive to breaking down any resolve [the detainee] may have manifested...to remain silent".[95]

Persons arrested by the police under the Terrorism Act 2000 may be initially detained for 48 hours[96] but the police can apply to a designated county court judge or magistrate for permission to extend the detention by periods amounting to 12 days ("warrants of further detention"), making 14 days in all.[97] The fact that a judicial authority grants such extensions, rather than a government Minister as previously was the case under the PTA, means that the United Kingdom has been able to withdraw the derogation notice by which it exempted itself from the duty to comply with the provision in the European Convention on Human Rights protecting people's right to liberty (Art. 5). In 2003, only 14 of the 359 people arrested under section 41 of the 2000 Act were detained beyond the initial 48-hour period and only two were held for between six and seven days.[98] A person arrested by the army under section 83 of the 2000 Act may be detained for up to four hours, but may then be passed to the police for detention.

Power to intern without trial

From 1971 to 1975 people could be detained indefinitely without trial in Northern Ireland, and hundreds indeed were. Given the intensity of civil unrest in the province at the time, the practice of internment was held to be compatible with the European Convention on Human Rights,[99] but today most legal experts view it as not only a serious violation of basic human rights but also an ineffective way of

---

[93] Such as the United Nations' Committee Against Torture.
[94] E.g. Re Floyd's Application [1997] NI 414.
[95] Magee v UK (2001) 31 EHRR 35.
[96] S. 41(3).
[97] Sch. 8, Pt. III. The original maximum of 7 days' detention was doubled by an amendment made to the 2000 Act by s. 306 of the Criminal Justice Act 2003.
[98] Northern Ireland Statistics on the Operation of the Terrorism Act 2003, NIO, Research and Statistical Bulletin 3/2004, Table 6.
[99] Ireland v UK (1979-80) 2 EHRR 25, where the European Court of Human Rights said, at p. 91, para. 25, that the emergency in Northern Ireland was "perfectly clear from the facts".

countering terrorism (since it tends to act as a "recruiting sergeant" for paramilitary organisations). The safeguards initially put in place (*e.g.* having detention orders approved by judicial "commissioners" and allowing appeals to a separate tribunal) were found not to be working satisfactorily when investigated by a committee chaired by Lord Gardiner, a former Lord Chancellor,[100] although the measures put in place instead were little better.[101] The policy of interning people was therefore abandoned in 1975 but the Secretary of State's power to reactivate the policy remained on the statute book, ultimately in the form of section 36 of, and Schedule 3 to, the EPA 1996. These provisions were finally repealed by section 3 of the EPA 1998.

Remarkably, internment for foreign nationals suspected of having associations with Al Qa'ida was re-introduced throughout the United Kingdom by the Anti-terrorism, Crime and Security Act 2001, but in December 2004 the House of Lords declared this to be incompatible with the European Convention on Human Rights.[102] This led to the Prevention of Terrorism Act 2005, which no longer provides for internment.

Treatment during detention

Persons arrested under the Terrorism Act 2000 may be forcibly photographed and fingerprinted by the police in the same situations where this could occur under the PACE Order,[103] namely when a police superintendent is satisfied that it is necessary. But, unlike under the PACE legislation, the fingerprints taken do not later have to be destroyed if no charge is brought against the person concerned. The detained person may also be denied access to a solicitor for up to 48 hours,[104] which is 12 hours longer than in ordinary cases, and the grounds upon which such denial may be permitted are more numerous.[105] But no requests for access to a solicitor have been delayed during the last three years for which statistics are available.[106] The same

---

[100] Cmnd. 5847; 1975.

[101] Northern Ireland (Emergency Provisions) (Amendment) Act 1975, s. 12 and Sch. 1 (giving more power to the Secretary of State and his or her "Adviser").

[102] *A and others v Secretary of State for the Home Department* [2005] 2 AC 68.

[103] Terrorism Act 2000, Sch. 8, para. 10.

[104] *Ibid.* s. 41(3) and Sch. 8, paras. 7 and 8. See, *e.g., R v Chief Constable, ex parte Begley and McWilliams* [1997] 1 WLR 1475.

[105] Terrorism Act 2000, Sch. 8, para. 8(4).

[106] *Northern Ireland Statistics on the Operation of the Terrorism Act 2003*, NIO, Research and Statistical Bulletin 3/2004, Table 9.

variations exist in relation to the right to have a friend or relative informed of the arrest.[107] Once access to a solicitor is granted it does not automatically stretch to allowing the solicitor to be present during the periods when the detained person is being interrogated by the police (again, in contrast to PACE[108]), but since October 2000 (when the Human Rights Act 1998 came fully into force) the practice of the police in Northern Ireland has been to allow solicitors to be present during interviews with suspects.

Under section 99 of the Terrorism Act 2000 a Code of Practice has been issued by the Northern Ireland Office to govern the detention, treatment and questioning of detainees and the identification of persons. There are also Codes of Practice applying throughout the United Kingdom for examining officers (*e.g.* at ports) and for authorised officers (*e.g.* when investigating financial matters).

The recording of interviews

Interrogation sessions with detainees in holding centres are subject to both audio- and video-recording and Codes of Practice on how the recordings are to take place have been issued under the Terrorism Act 2000.[109] The Code on audio-recording closely mirrors the PACE Code, the main differences being as follows:

(1)   the written notice required to be given to the detainee at the end of an interview must, in the case of persons held under the Terrorism Act, stipulate (amongst other things) both the period of retention of the tape and the arrangements for its destruction; notice under the PACE Code does not state these arrangements;

(2)   the PACE code does not provide for the destruction of master tapes, which should usually occur after six years from the date of the interview in terrorist cases; both Codes, however, require working copies to be completely erased at the conclusion of criminal proceedings or in the event of a direction not to prosecute;

---

[107] Terrorism Act 2000, Sch. 8, paras. 6 and 8. In the years 2001, 2002 and 2003 only once was there a delay in allowing a detainee to have someone else informed about the detention: see Table 8 in Bulletin referred to in previous note.

[108] See paras. 6.8-9 of Code C of the revised *Police and Criminal Evidence (NI) Order 1989 (Articles 60 and 65) Codes of Practice* (1996).

[109] The Code of Practice on audio-recording applies throughout the UK, while the Code of Practice on video-recording with sound applies only in Northern Ireland.

(3)   a copy of the tape of a PACE interview must be supplied to the detainee as soon as is practicable if the detainee is charged or informed that he or she will prosecuted; in contrast, under the Terrorism Act code, a copy of the tape will be supplied only to the detainee's solicitor and only on application to the Sub-Divisional Commander for the area where the crime occurred;

(4)   a full transcript (as opposed to a summary only) is normally made of any interview considered to be significant in the case of terrorist suspects; under the PACE code, only admissions need be transcribed word for word.

While interviews of detainees held under the provisions of the PACE Order are not subject to video-recording, obligatory *silent* video recording of all interviews of detainees at holding centres was introduced under the EPA in 1998 and video-recording *with sound* has been introduced under the Terrorism Act. A Code of Practice for the latter has been published. The Code emphasises that video-recording is intended to protect both the detained person and the interviewing officers, and that even if the detained person objects to the interview being video-recorded, it must still occur.[110]

Bail, committal and Diplock courts

For scheduled offences tried on indictment, the law on bail is altered by section 67 of the Terrorism Act 2000 so as to permit only a judge of the High Court or of the Court of Appeal, or the judge at the trial itself, to grant bail. Resident magistrates have no power to grant bail in these cases, presumably in order to confine the judicial function to a small number of judges (whom it is easier to defend against terrorist attack). High Court judges will sometimes sit on a Saturday to consider such bail applications.

In committal proceedings for scheduled offences the prosecution is entitled to insist on a preliminary enquiry (PE) rather than a preliminary investigation (PI) (see Chap. 5.5), unless the court is of the opinion that in the interests of justice a preliminary investigation should be conducted into the offence.[111] In practice nearly all committals are conducted through the shorter PE process, which apart from anything else avoids a witness having to attend on two separate occasions to give

---

[110] Para. 3.3.
[111] Terrorism Act 2000, s. 66.

evidence in court (once at the committal proceedings and again at the trial itself).

Trials on indictment of scheduled offences take place before one judge sitting without a jury, the so-called Diplock courts.[112] It is felt that the risk of perverse verdicts, either through jury bias or the intimidation of jurors, is too great to allow continued use of jury trials. Even in 2004, apparently, such intimidation was on-going.[113] One implication of this is that when scheduled offences are involved, trials within a trial (see Chap.5.6) are not very different from the main trial: the judge who decides the *voir dire* issues will usually be the one who goes on to decide the issue of fact at the main trial. If the judge has held certain evidence to be inadmissible during the *voir dire* the judge is meant to put that evidence out of his or her mind when deciding the main issues; sometimes, because the judge realises how difficult this will be, he or she directs the main trial to be re-commenced before a different judge.

In 2004, of the 1,570 defendants dealt with by the Crown Court in Northern Ireland, 77 (5%) were processed through the Diplock courts. By the time their trial started 49 (64%) were on bail. Those on bail waited an average of nearly 15 weeks between being committed for trial and their trial starting, but those in custody waited on average almost twice as long.[114] In 2004 there were 1,769 applications for bail made by persons charged with scheduled offences (1,775 in 2003); obviously many of these were repeat applications by the same defendants; 48% of the applications were granted (49% in 2003).[115] Of the 77 defendants dealt with in Diplock courts in 2004, 27 pleaded guilty to all charges. Of the remaining 50 defendants, exactly one-half were convicted of at least some of the charges levelled against them.[116]

---

[112] *Ibid.* s. 75. See generally J. Jackson and S. Doran, *Judge without Jury* (1995). From December 1999 to July 2000 the Government conducted a review of the Diplock court system, but this did not lead to any significant change in the way the courts operate.

[113] In 2005, during a debate on the continuance of Pt. VII of the Terrorism Act 2000, the Minister for Security in Northern Ireland, Mr Ian Pearson MP, said that in 2004 there were 74 recorded incidents of either attempted or substantive witness intimidation, an increase of 27% on the 2003 figure: First Standing Committee on Delegated Legislation, 7 February 2005, col. 5.

[114] *Northern Ireland Judicial Statistics 2004*, Tables C.3 and C.4.

[115] *Northern Ireland Statistics on the Operation of the Terrorism Act 2004*, NIO, Research and Statistical Bulletin 9/2005, Table 11.

[116] *Northern Ireland Judicial Statistics 2004*, Table C.6.

Mainly because of guilty pleas, only 20%-30% of cases brought before the Diplock courts each year actually lead to a full trial.

The right to silence

The powers of detention are obviously designed to enable the security forces to place arrested persons under sustained questioning. By section 109 of the 2000 Act (replacing s. 2A of the PTA 1989 and s. 30A of the EPA 1996[117]), if an accused person, while being questioned by the police before being informed that he or she might be prosecuted for belonging to a proscribed organisation, fails to mention a material fact which he or she could reasonably be expected to mention, and provided that he or she was permitted to consult a solicitor, the court may draw adverse inferences from such a failure. The accused, however, cannot be committed for trial, be found to have a case to answer or be convicted solely on the basis of such inferences. This power to draw inferences, which applies only in Northern Ireland, goes beyond the normal power to draw inferences which exists under the ordinary criminal law of both Northern Ireland and England and Wales.[118]

Confessions and the burden of proof

One of the commonest reasons for holding a trial within a trial is to assess the admissibility of a confession. For many years the test for admissibility in scheduled cases was significantly altered from that applicable in non-scheduled cases (see Chap. 5.1): the confession was inadmissible unless, after a *prima facie* case had been raised by the defence alleging malpractice on the part of the investigating officers, the prosecution could show beyond reasonable doubt that the confession had *not* been extracted by torture, violence, threats of violence, or inhuman or degrading treatment inflicted in order to induce

---

[117] Inserted by ss. 1 and 2 of the Criminal Justice (Terrorism and Conspiracy) Act 1998, enacted in response to the Omagh bomb in August 1998. Parliament was recalled from its summer recess for the purpose.

[118] Criminal Evidence (NI) Order 1988, art. 3 and Criminal Justice and Public Order Act 1994, s. 34. These laws allow inferences to be drawn only if the accused fails to mention a material fact which he or she later wishes to rely on in his or her defence. S. 109 of the Terrorism Act 2000 allows inferences to be drawn if the accused fails to mention a material fact which he or she could reasonably have been expected to mention.

the defendant to make the confession.[119] In addition, though, as in non-scheduled cases, even if the prosecution discharged this burden of proof, the court could still exclude the confession from the evidence in order to avoid unfairness to the accused or otherwise in the interests of justice.[120] In 2002, following a recommendation by the reviewer of anti-terrorism legislation, Lord Carlile, Parliament removed the special rule for scheduled cases, leaving these cases to be dealt with in exactly the same way as non-scheduled cases under article 74 of the Police and Criminal Evidence (NI) Order 1989.[121]

In trials on indictment of non-scheduled offences the burden of proving the defendant's guilt is on the prosecution. In some trials on indictment of scheduled offences this principle has been qualified in that section 77 of the Terrorism Act 2000 appears to place the burden of proving their innocence on persons found to be in possession of explosives, firearms or ammunition. In fact, the judges in Northern Ireland have mostly interpreted this provision (and its predecessors) in a way which equates it with the ordinary law. To avoid any potential incompatibility with the Human Rights Act 1998,[122] section 118 of the Terrorism Act 2000 shifts the burden of proof in such cases back to the prosecution once the defendant has adduced evidence "which is sufficient to raise an issue with respect to the matter".

The right to appeal

All persons convicted of a scheduled offence tried on indictment in Northern Ireland can appeal against conviction to the Court of Appeal on any ground and without any leave.[123] This is largely because there is no jury in the case, an absent safeguard which the automatic right of appeal is intended in part to replace. Moreover, because the judge in a Diplock court, unlike a jury in an ordinary trial, is obliged to give reasons for his or her decisions,[124] it should be easier for a defendant to

---

[119] Terrorism Act 2000, s. 76, substantially re-enacting the Northern Ireland (Emergency Provisions) Act 1996, s. 12 (and first enacted as the Northern Ireland (Emergency Provisions) Act 1973, s. 6).

[120] *Ibid.* s. 76(6).

[121] Terrorism Act 2000 (Cessation of Effect of Section 76) Order 2002, effective from 26 July 2002.

[122] See *R v DPP, ex parte Kebeline* [2000] 2 AC 326, decided before the Human Rights Act 1998 came into force.

[123] Terrorism Act 2000, s. 75(8).

[124] *Ibid.* s. 75(7).

establish grounds for appeal. The risk of a miscarriage of justice is accordingly lessened.

4.4 THE POLICE SERVICE OF NORTHERN IRELAND[125]

The Royal Ulster Constabulary

The police in Northern Ireland are now called the Police Service of Northern Ireland, the successor body to the Royal Ulster Constabulary (RUC). The RUC was formed in 1922 to replace the Royal Irish Constabulary, which policed the whole of the island until partition. Following civil disturbances in 1968-69, an Advisory Committee was set up under the chairmanship of Lord Hunt to examine the recruitment, organisation, structure and composition of the RUC and to recommend whatever changes were required to provide for the efficient enforcement of law and order.[126] Some of Lord Hunt's recommendations were subsequently implemented through the Police Act (NI) 1970.[127] One of these was that the police in Northern Ireland should no longer be armed, but in view of the attacks they continued to suffer, this recommendation, while at first implemented, could not be sustained. Between 1969 and 1998, 200 police officers and 102 police reservists were killed in terrorist incidents, almost all the work of republican paramilitaries.[128] Following the signing of the Anglo-Irish Agreement in 1985, and again after various disputes over parades at Drumcree near Portadown (especially in 1996), there were numerous incidents of serious attacks and threats against RUC officers by loyalist paramilitaries. To recognise the collective courage and dedication to duty of all of those who served in the RUC and who accepted the

---

[125] For this section I have drawn on my own chapter on "Policing and Human Rights after the Conflict" in M. Cox, A. Guelke and F. Stephen (eds.), *A Farewell to Arms? From 'long war' to long peace in Northern Ireland* (2nd ed., 2005), forthcoming.

[126] *Report of the Advisory Committee on Police in Northern Ireland* (Cmnd. 535).

[127] See also A. Guelke, "Policing in Northern Ireland", Chap. 7 in B. Hadfield (ed.), *Northern Ireland: Politics and the Constitution* (1992).

[128] Each of the deaths is catalogued in C. Ryder, *The RUC: A Force Under Fire* (1989). The last to be killed was Frank O'Reilly, fatally injured by a blast bomb thrown by a Loyalist in Portadown on 6 October 1998. See also J. Brewer and K. Magee, *Inside the RUC: Routine Policing in a Divided Society* (1991), Sir John Hermon, *Holding the Line: An Autobiography* (1997) and C. Ryder, *The Fateful Split: Catholics and the RUC* (2004).

danger and stress this brought to them and their families, the Queen awarded the George Cross to the organisation in November 1999.[129]

Of course several controversies dogged the RUC between 1969 and 1999.[130] Certain interrogation practices used by the force were investigated in 1977 by the European Court of Human Rights and were found to be inhuman and degrading treatment (but not torture).[131] In 1978 a Committee of Inquiry headed by an English county court judge, Judge Bennett, made various recommendations for making the practices more acceptable;[132] once these were implemented, the system considerably improved. Alleged shoot-to-kill incidents in 1982 were the subject of the controversial (but unpublished) Stalker-Sampson report in 1987; this led to investigations of breach of discipline by police officers but not to any criminal prosecutions. There were also extensive allegations that police officers colluded with loyalist paramilitaries,[133] particularly in the murder of Belfast solicitor Patrick Finucane in 1989,[134] that they issued threats to solicitors representing republicans,[135] that they harassed people on the streets and during searches,[136] that they fabricated evidence or altered notes of interviews,[137] that they unnecessarily resorted to the use of plastic baton rounds and that they stood by and allowed Catholics to be attacked by

---

[129] Only one other collective award of this honour has been made - to the island of Malta in 1942.
[130] See, generally, S. Livingstone, "Policing, Criminal Justice and the Rule of Law" in J. Hayes and P. O'Higgins (eds.), *Lessons from Northern Ireland* (1990); A. Jennings (ed.), *Justice Under Fire: The Abuse of Civil Liberties in Northern Ireland* (1988).
[131] *Ireland v UK* (1979-80) 2 EHRR 25.
[132] *Committee of Inquiry into Police Interrogation Procedures in Northern Ireland* (Cmnd. 7947; 1979).
[133] A report on this by a senior police from England, Mr John Stevens (later the Commander of the Metropolitan Police), was completed in 1990, but only a summary of it was published. No police officer was charged as a result of the inquiry, only soldiers.
[134] A further report by John Stevens concluded in 2003 that state security forces did collude in this killing; a further investigation by retired Canadian judge Peter Cory confirmed this; a public inquiry has been promised by the British Government.
[135] Such as Rosemary Nelson, who was murdered by Loyalist paramilitaries in 1999. A public inquiry into this killing was formally opened in Craigavon on 19 April 2005: see www.rosemarynelsoninquiry.org.
[136] See R. McVeigh, *It's Part of Life Here* (Committee on the Administration of Justice, Belfast; 1995).
[137] E.g. in the case of the UDR Four, three of whom had their convictions quashed by the Court of Appeal in 1992. The fourth defendant's conviction was confirmed: *R v Latimer* [2004] NIJB 142.

Protestants.[138] In several cases the courts ordered the police to pay exemplary damages to people mistreated while in police custody.[139]

The Patten Commission

One of the elements of the Belfast (Good Friday) Agreement of 1998 was the establishment of a Commission on Policing. Its terms of reference required it to bring forward proposals for future policing structures and arrangements (including composition, recruitment, training, culture, ethos and symbols) "such that in a new approach Northern Ireland has a police service that can enjoy widespread support from, and is seen as an integral part of, the community as a whole". The person appointed to chair the inquiry was Mr Chris Patten, the last British Governor of Hong Kong. The Commission invited written submissions, organised a series of public meetings and visited several jurisdictions abroad, including New York and South Africa. It issued its report in September 1999[140] and amongst the most controversial of its recommendations were that the RUC should be renamed, its badge altered, the Union flag no longer flown at police stations and the focus of policing made the protection of human rights.[141]

Many of the recommendations of the Patten Report were translated into law by the Police (NI) Acts 2000 and 2003 and an Oversight Commissioner was appointed to ensure that implementation was thorough. Direct responsibility for managing the police's budget had already been passed to the Chief Constable from the then Police Authority on 1 April 1999. The Police (NI) Act 2000 also created a Northern Ireland Policing Board to replace the Police Authority for Northern Ireland[142] and the Board was tasked with appointing District Policing Partnerships in each of the 29 District Command Areas. Even before the Patten Report moves were afoot to create a Police Ombudsman's office. All of these institutions are described in more detail below.

---

[138] *E.g.* the case of Robert Hamill, killed in Portadown in 1997.
[139] *E.g. Adams* v *Chief Constable of the RUC* (1997), unreported.
[140] *A New Beginning: Policing in Northern Ireland.* See www.belfast.org.uk/report.htm.
[141] See too J. McGarry and B. O'Leary, *Policing Northern Ireland: Proposals for a new start* (1999).
[142] Ss. 2-13.

The Police Service of Northern Ireland[143]

The Police Service of Northern Ireland officially came into being on 4 November 2001, although as a concession to unionists the official title of the new service was stated by statute to be "the Police Service of Northern Ireland (incorporating the Royal Ulster Constabulary)".[144] The recruitment[145] and training[146] of new officers began almost immediately and the first batch of students to graduate as probationary constables did so in April 2002. By way of an exception to the law prohibiting discrimination on religious grounds in the employment of staff, the PSNI was required for a three-year period to draw 50% of its new recruits from the Catholic community.[147] In 2004 this period was extended for a further three years. By March 2005 the percentage of Catholic police officers had risen to 17%, compared with just 8% in 2001. It is projected to rise to 30% by 2011. The number of female police officers is rising too: in the March 2003 competition for new recruits 43% of the successful candidates were women. The recruitment process is overseen by an Independent Assessor. In 2004 plans were announced for a new Police College to be built by the end of 2007, in Desertcreat, near Cookstown.

Just after the establishment of the new Service the Chief Constable, Sir Ronnie Flanagan, announced that he would retire from his post within a few months, and indeed he left at the end of March 2002.[148] Mr Colin Cramphorn served as the Acting Chief Constable for six months before the appointment of Mr Hugh Orde, a Deputy Commander in the Metropolitan Police who had been handling the day-to-day running of

---

[143] Much of the recent information provided in this section is drawn from the *Annual Reports of the Chief Constable of the PSNI 2003-04* and *2004-05*, which are available on the PSNI website. See too L. Moore and M. O'Rawe, "A New Beginning for Policing in Northern Ireland?" in C. Harvey (ed.), *Human Rights, Equality and Democratic Renewal in Northern Ireland* (2001).

[144] Police (NI) Act 2000, s. 1(1).

[145] Police (Recruitment) Regs. (NI) 2001, as amended in 2002 and 2004 and supplemented by the PSNI (Recruitment of Police Support Staff) Regs. 2002.

[146] Police Trainee Regs. (NI) 2001.

[147] Police (NI) Act 2000, s. 46. This has been expressly permitted by a provision in an EC Directive and a challenge based on the European Convention on Human Rights failed in the Court of Appeal: *Re Parsons' Application for Judicial Review* [2004] NI 38.

[148] He took up a post with HM's Inspectorate of Constabulary in England and in 2004 he became the Chief Inspector.

the Stevens Inquiry into the murder of solicitor Patrick Finucane in 1989.

Since November 2003 the PSNI has been organised on the basis of two regions (Urban and Rural). The Urban Region covers the greater Belfast area, a population of about 800,000; it has 12 district command units (four for Belfast and eight for beyond Belfast); the Rural Region covers a population of some 900,000 and has 17 district command units mirroring the 17 district council areas involved. It also polices the 250 miles of the border with the Republic of Ireland. Each of the two regions is headed by an Assistant Chief Constable and there are also Assistant Chief Constables in charge of Crime Operations, Criminal Justice, Operational Support, and Corporate Development and Change Management. The Crime Operations Department includes the Intelligence Branch (formerly the Special Branch). A Deputy Chief Constable, currently Mr Paul Leighton, takes responsibility for matters such as finance, equal opportunities and internal discipline.

The maximum permitted size of the Service, as recommended by the Patten Report, is 7,500 officers, with a further 3,370 posts in the Reserve (2,500 of which are for part-time officers). In March 2005 there were actually 7,470 regular serving officers, 1,387 in the full-time Reserve and 917 in the part-time Reserve. Permission has been granted to delay the reduction in the full-time Reserve to the establishment figure of 870 until the Chief Constable can be sure that he has the personnel at his disposal to effectively fulfil the Service's goals. A generous severance scheme allowed nearly 2,000 officers to leave the police between 2001 and 2004 yet plans are now being laid to recruit a large number of part-time reservists. The police officers' representative bodies are the Superintendents' Association of Northern Ireland and, for lower ranks, the Police Federation for Northern Ireland. The Chief, Deputy and Assistant Chief Constables are members of ACPO, the Association of Chief Police Officers for England, Wales and Northern Ireland.[149]

The net revenue and capital expenditure on the PSNI in 2004-05 was no less than £931 million. This includes the compensation and costs due to people who successfully brought civil claims against the Chief Constable.[150] In 2004-05 some 658 of these were concluded.[151] Most

---

[149] www.acpo.police.uk.
[150] Police (NI) Act 1998, s. 29. All settlements have to be approved by the Policing Board.

were brought by members of the public in respect of "wrongful acts" committed by the police, such as using incorrect arrest procedures or causing minor injuries, or in respect of property damage, but there were also claims brought by police officers in respect of employers' liability (including for post-traumatic stress disorder). The total amount paid out was £1.3 million (40% less than in 2003-04). Approximately £1.1 million was spent on legal costs.

As regards internal discipline, in 2004-05 39 officers were charged with disciplinary or misconduct offences. Nine of the cases arose from complaints by members of the public;[152] the remainder were generated within the PSNI itself. Five officers were dismissed or required to resign, two were reduced in rank and 20 were fined or reduced in pay.

The PSNI's functions

As in other legal systems, the primary role of the police in Northern Ireland is to prevent and detect crime. Despite the troubles, the crime rate in Northern Ireland is comparatively low (see 4.2 above) and the clear-up rate is usually on a par with that of the United Kingdom's 51 other police forces[153] - in 2004-05 it was 28.2%. While crime overall is falling, crimes involving violence, racism and drugs are increasing. The police have been assisted in their public order related work during the past 35 years by the British Army, although the avowed policy since 1976 has been that the police have an independent responsibility in all areas and the soldiers are merely there to give support when needed. Since the second IRA ceasefire of 1997 the Army has been gradually reducing its police support role. There are currently about 12,000 members of the armed forces serving in Northern Ireland. The Government has said that it intends to reduce the number to 5,000.[154]

In England, the powers of prosecution which were formerly vested in the police forces were transferred to the Crown Prosecution Service by the Prosecution of Offences Act 1985. The police in Northern Ireland still possess such powers in minor cases but the Public Prosecution Service (see 1.5 above) currently deals with whichever offences the DPP considers appropriate. The PSNI are to lose their residual power to conduct prosecutions once the recommendations of the Criminal Justice

---

[151] Each case takes 2 or 3 years to process.
[152] See too the section on the Police Ombudsman in 4.5 below.
[153] There are 43 in England and Wales and 8 in Scotland.
[154] Statement by the Secretary of State, Peter Hain MP, 1 August 2005.

Review, published in 2000, are fully implemented. The police's continuing monopoly over the official *investigation* of crimes will always, however, be a limiting factor on a prosecutor's autonomy. If the state decides not to prosecute someone for an alleged offence, any person with a sufficient interest, or standing (*locus standi*), in the matter can initiate a private prosecution instead. But private prosecutions are time-consuming and expensive (no legal aid is available) and the Attorney General can always apply for them to be terminated if he or she does not feel that they are in the public interest (see Chap. 5.3). It seems that only one private prosecution has ever reached the trial stage in Northern Ireland, and in that case no conviction was obtained. As an alternative course of action, if an interested person feels aggrieved at the police's failure to investigate a crime, an application can be made to the High Court for the "prerogative order" of *mandamus* which, if granted, will compel the police to carry out their duty (see Chap. 6.7).[155]

It used to be thought that it was not possible for the victim of a crime, or his or her relative, to sue the police if the police were negligent in failing to prevent the crime,[156] but the European Court of Human Rights has held that such a blanket immunity from being sued is contrary to the right to a fair hearing conferred by Article 6 of the European Convention on Human Rights.[157]

In March 2004 a Serious Crime Review Team was established within the PSNI to carry out "progress reviews" into murders which remain undetected 28 days into the investigation and "deferred reviews" into unsolved murders over two years old. The team is establishing a secure central murder archive store for all case papers and exhibits. In February 2005 the Government announced that it was allocating an additional £30 million for this team's work. It was anticipated to take six years, since there are approximately 2,000 "old" unsolved murders. The review system is seen as one way of providing closure for some of the families who lost loved ones during the troubles.

It is to the Chief Constable of the PSNI that applications for firearm certificates must be made, although an appeal against a refusal lies to the Secretary of State for Northern Ireland. During 2003-04 the PSNI

---

[155] *R* v *Commissioner for the Metropolitan Police, ex parte Blackburn* [1968] 2 QB 118.
[156] *Hill* v *Chief Constable of West Yorkshire* [1989] AC 53.
[157] *Osman* v *UK* (1998) 29 EHRR 245.

processed 34,124 such applications, of which 2,742 were new. There are well over 100,000 legally held firearms in Northern Ireland, approximately 150 registered firearms dealers and several dozen firearms clubs and approved ranges.[158] In 2003-04 the police also supervised some 1,278 blast operations at quarries throughout Northern Ireland.

"Crimestoppers" is a UK national charity which works in conjunction will all UK police forces to encourage people to provide information (anonymously if they prefer) about suspected crimes. The freephone number it uses is 0800 555 111.

National policing

At the moment the PSNI is occasionally assisted in its work by the National Criminal Intelligence Service (NCIS),[159] a non-departmental public body which provides criminal intelligence to police forces and other law enforcement agencies throughout the United Kingdom (such as Revenue and Customs) and also by the National Crime Squad (NCS),[160] which tackles serious and organised crime throughout Great Britain (including drug trafficking, illegal arms dealing, money laundering and counterfeiting of currency).[161] But these two bodies are about to be abolished, by the Serious Organised Crime and Police Act 2005, and merged with that part of Her Majesty's Revenue and Customs which deals with drug trafficking and money laundering, to form the Serious Organised Crime Agency. This new Agency will have similar powers to those of the already existing Serious Fraud Office,[162] a government department which was created by the Criminal Justice Act 1987 to investigate and prosecute cases of complex fraud and can compel individuals to answer questions during interviews and produce documents on demand (on pain of being found guilty of a criminal offence). The 2005 Act also allows search warrants to be used in respect of more than one property owned by an individual and on more

---

[158] The relevant legislation is the Firearms (NI) Order 2004.
[159] www.ncis.gov.uk.
[160] www.nationalcrimesquad.police.uk.
[161] Both organisations are regulated by the Police Act 1997 (Pt. I: NCIS; Pt. II: NCS). The NCIS was set up in a non-statutory form in 1992.
[162] www.sfo.gov.uk. The Director (currently Mr Richard Wardle) is appointed by and is accountable to the Attorney General.

than one occasion; moreover it puts on to a statutory footing for the first time the concept of "turning Queen's evidence".[163]

There also exists a Criminal Records Bureau,[164] an Executive Agency of the Home Office based in Liverpool, which provides for disclosure to prospective employers and licensing bodies of information about a person's criminal record. There can be no disclosure without the consent of the person in question and he or she must be supplied with a copy of what is sent to the employer or licensing body.[165] As yet, however, the Bureau has no role within Northern Ireland, although there is currently a proposal to implement Part V of the Police Act 1997 in Northern Ireland.[166]

Community policing

The police's community policing strategy in Northern Ireland – implementing a series of recommendations in the Patten Report[167] – is set out in a policy document and implementation plan published in 2003.[168] The goal is to have a neighbourhood policing team within sectors in each district command unit. The system for consulting with members of local communities is much more developed than in the past in that there are now district policing and community safety partnerships in each district command unit (see 4.5 below).

As part of its efforts to improve community relations among young people, the police continue to run camping trips, football tournaments and discos. Its contact with school pupils is maintained through a road safety roadshow[169] and a programme called Citizenship and Safety Education (CASE). Designed for all ages of school children, this programme covers topics such as crime prevention, personal and community safety and young people and the law. "Globalclub" is a youth project addressing issues such as security, finance, the environment, enterprise, information technology, social inclusion and politics. The Youth Diversion Scheme, introduced in September 2003

---

[163] See Chap. 1.5. Ss. 71-75 of the 2005 Act provide for "restricted use undertakings" and "immunity notices" to be issued to informers.

[164] www.crb.gov.uk.

[165] Police Act 1997, Pt. V.

[166] *Safer Recruitment in Northern Ireland: A consultation document*, issued by the NIO in February 2005.

[167] Nos. 33 and 44-49.

[168] Available on the PSNI's website: www.psni.police.uk.

[169] In 2004-05 140 people died on the roads of Northern Ireland (142 in 2003-04).

in place of the Juvenile Liaison Scheme, provides a framework within which the PSNI respond to all those below the age of 17 who come into contact with the police on account of their wayward behaviour. It supplies an opportunity for diversion through "restorative" interventions such as warnings and cautions; in fact since 2001 all juvenile cautions have been administered by means of a conferencing process called a restorative caution.[170] In the seven months up to March 2004 there were 8,014 referrals under this new scheme, of which 1,231 were dealt with through a "restorative disposal".[171]

Perceptions of the police

In 2004 the Northern Ireland Policing Board published the results of a survey of public perceptions of the PSNI.[172] They showed that 56% of respondents thought that their local police were doing a very good or a fairly good job, the figure for Protestant respondents being 59% and that for Catholics 50%. The figures were higher when respondents were asked whether the police did a good job in Northern Ireland as a whole (62% of all, 67% of Protestants and 55% of Catholics). Conversely, respondents were more likely to think that the police treated the two communities equally in their own area than in Northern Ireland as a whole (73% as opposed to 68%). The proportion of Catholics who had at least some confidence in ordinary day-to-day policing stood at 75%, although this fell to 69% when the question was asked in relation to the police's handling of public disorder situations.

The Forensic Science Agency

Forensic Science Northern Ireland (FSNI) has been an executive agency sponsored by the Northern Ireland Office since 1995. It provides scientific advice and support to the police in the investigation of crime, to the office of the Police Ombudsman in its investigation of complaints against the police, to the legal professions and the courts when they require scientific evidence and to pathologists when they are investigating the causes of deaths.

---

[170] For further details see Chap. 7.1 and M. Decodts, *Juvenile Reconviction in Northern Ireland*, Research Bulletin 6/2005 (NIO).

[171] *Chief Constable's Annual Report 2003-04*.

[172] *Public Perceptions of the Police and the Northern Ireland Policing Board*, available on the Board's website: www.nipolicingboard.org.uk. Perceptions of the Board and of the DPPs are dealt with below (pp. 218-9).

The first forensic science laboratory in Northern Ireland was created in 1956. It later played a significant role in bringing to justice people who committed crimes during Northern Ireland's "troubles" and in 1992 its laboratory in South Belfast was destroyed by a van bomb. Contrary to popular belief, however, very few exhibits were lost in that explosion and it did not significantly affect the outcome of any individual case. The FSNI's current premises, in Carrickfergus, are due to be replaced by a new building in 2007.

In 2003-04 the Agency employed 145 staff and cost £6,878,000 to run (the vast majority of this was spent doing work for the police). It dealt with 563 cases concerning burglary, 531 concerning abuse of drugs, 387 concerning firearms, 170 concerning sexual assaults, 114 concerning explosives and 73 concerning murder or attempted murder. A report by the House of Commons' Northern Ireland Affairs Committee in 2003 found that by and large the Agency was doing a good job.[173]

The Assets Recovery Agency[174]

The Assets Recovery Agency (ARA) is based in London, but it has an office in Belfast directed by Mr Alan McQuillan, a former Assistant Chief Constable in the PSNI. The establishment of the Agency was a key aspect of the Proceeds of Crime Act 2002, which was itself based on a study conducted by the Cabinet Office's Performance and Innovation Unit in 2000. The ARA's aims are to disrupt organised criminal enterprises and to promote the use of financial investigation as an integral part of criminal investigative work. It operates in accordance with guidance issued by the Home Office, which was revised early in 2005.[175] Applications by the Agency to have certain property transferred to a trustee are civil, not criminal, proceedings.[176]

Given the prevalence of cross-border smuggling in Ireland, the Northern Ireland branch of the ARA liaises closely with its sister body in the Republic, the Criminal Assets Bureau.[177] The draft Criminal Justice (NI) Order 2005 contains proposals for enhancing the powers of

---

173 5th Report of 2002-03, HC 204.
174 www.assetsrecovery.gov.uk.
175 www.assetsrecovery.gov.uk/downloads/SOSrevisedguidanceFeb2005.pdf.
176 *In the matter of the Director of the Assets Recovery Agency and Walsh* [2004] NIQB 21.
177 Established under the Criminal Assets Bureau Act 1996.

the ARA by, for example, allowing it to have access to the contents of safe deposit boxes.

4.5 BODIES OVERSEEING POLICING

The Policing Oversight Commissioner[178]

The Police (NI) Act 2000 provided for a Commissioner to be appointed to oversee the implementation of changes in the policing of Northern Ireland.[179] Mr Tom Constantine, a former senior police officer from the USA, was first appointed on a non-statutory basis in the autumn of 2000, and he has since been succeeded by Mr Al Hutchinson, another American. The office will continue to exist at least until the end of May 2007.[180] The Oversight Commissioner has to make at least three reports per year to the Secretary of State on the implementation of the Patten recommendations and the Secretary of State must lay these reports before Parliament at Westminster and publish them. The thirteenth such report was published in June 2005.

The Northern Ireland Policing Board

Until 1970 the RUC was exclusively accountable to the Minister of Home Affairs in the Northern Ireland Government, but following the civil disturbances in 1969 an Advisory Committee under the chairmanship of Lord Hunt recommended the establishment of a Police Authority, free of direct political influence and with the task of monitoring the RUC's activities.[181] This body was duly created by the Police Act (NI) 1970, as amended by (in particular) the Police (NI) Act 1998.[182] In England and Wales, under the Police and Magistrates' Courts Act 1994, the police authorities comprise at least one-third local councillors. In Northern Ireland the UK Government's view until recently was that if elected representatives were appointed to the Police Authority it might quickly become politically partisan.

The Police Authority appointed senior officers in the RUC and until the establishment of the Police Ombudsman's office it was the disciplinary

---

[178] www.oversightcommissioner.org. This office should not be confused with that of the Justice Oversight Commissioner (see p. 243 below).
[179] Ss. 67-8 and Sch. 4.
[180] Police (NI) Act 2000 (Continuance of Office of Commissioner) Order 2005.
[181] *Report of the Advisory Committee on Police in Northern Ireland* (Cmd. 535; 1969).
[182] Mainly ss. 1-13.

authority for such officers. In 1988 it considered the position of senior officers involved in the shooting incidents investigated in the Stalker-Sampson report, but it found that none of them deserved to be disciplined. The Authority also had to keep itself informed as to the manner in which complaints from members of the public against junior police officers were dealt with by the Chief Constable. Prior to 1987, if a complaint appeared to affect the public interest, the Authority could require the Chief Constable to refer it to a tribunal for consideration and report, but this was done on only one occasion (in the *Rafferty* case, 1980). Article 8(2) of the Police (NI) Order 1987 , which had no equivalent in England and Wales, allowed the Authority to refer a matter which was not the subject of a complaint to the Independent Commission for Police Complaints, provided it appeared to the Authority that it was in the public interest that the Commission should supervise the investigation of the matter. The Authority could, in addition, require the Chief Constable to submit reports in writing on such matters as may be specified, but this power appears never to have been exercised. It was only in 1999 that the Police Authority first became obliged to issue an Annual Report. In its first two such reports it chided the RUC quite severely for not meeting some of the targets set in those years' policing plans.

The Policing Board replaced the Police Authority in November 2001.[183] Its chairperson is Sir Desmond Rea and it has eight other "independent" members as well as 10 members who are political representatives. In 2003-04 its budget was £5,774,000 and it employed about 50 staff. The Secretary of State continues to set long-term objectives for the police, after consulting with the Policing Board and others,[184] and he or she must lay these before both Houses of Parliament at Westminster,[185] but the Policing Board sets shorter-term objectives which must be so framed as to be consistent with the Secretary of State's objectives.[186] The Chief Constable must also submit to the Policing Board the draft of an annual policing plan; the Board itself must then review this draft and issue its own final policing

---

[183] www.nipolicingboard.org.uk.
[184] Police (NI) Act 2003, s. 1. The other consultees are the Chief Constable, the Northern Ireland Human Rights Commission and the Equality Commission for Northern Ireland.
[185] Police (NI) Act 2000, s. 24.
[186] *Ibid.* s. 25.

plan after consulting the Secretary of State.[187] The Board can require
the Chief Constable to report on any issue relating to policing,
including the reasons for, and effects of, operational decisions, and can
as a result initiate an inquiry into any aspect of policing.

The Secretary of State *may* issue codes of practice relating to the
Board's functions[188] and the Board *must* issue codes of practice relating
to the district policing partnerships' functions (see below). The Board
has already issued a code of ethics laying down standards of conduct
and practice for police officers and making them aware of the rights
and duties arising out of the European Convention on Human Rights.[189]
The Board has set up a Human Rights and Professional Standards
Committee, which oversees the monitoring of the PSNI's adherence to
human rights standards. In April 2005 the Board issued its first *Human
Rights Annual Report*, following substantial work undertaken by the
Board's human rights advisers, Keir Starmer QC and Jane Gordon. The
Secretary of State has been left with the power to regulate the emblems
to be used by the police, but the Policing Board wasted little time in
agreeing a new badge and uniform for the PSNI.[190] Complaints of
maladministration by the Policing Board can be taken to the UK
Ombudsman (see Chap. 9.2).

According to a recent survey commissioned by the Policing Board,[191]
49% of respondents thought that the Board was doing very well or well
in monitoring how the PSNI performs. This represents an average of
53% for Protestant respondents and 46% for Catholics. A rather low
27% thought that the Board was doing very well or well in consulting
the public on policing issues, and this figure was the same for both
Protestants and Catholics.

---

[187] *Ibid.* s. 26.
[188] *Ibid.* s. 27. Again he or she must first consult with the Board and others: Police (NI) Act 2003, s. 2.
[189] *Ibid.* s. 52. The code was made part of the discipline code for police officers by the PSNI (Conduct) Regs. 2003, which amended the RUC (Conduct) Regs. 2000, the RUC (Conduct) (Senior Officer) Regs. 2000 and the RUC (Unsatisfactory Performance) Regs. 2000.
[190] *Ibid.* s. 54.
[191] *Public Perceptions of the Police and the Northern Ireland Policing Board* (2004), available on the Board's website.

District Policing Partnerships

One of the most innovative suggestions in the Patten Report was that the Policing Board should be complemented by district policing partnerships (DPPs) in each of the 26 district councils in Northern Ireland. These have all now been created, with Belfast City Council having four of them[192] (making 29 altogether). They are actually committees of the district councils and a majority of the members are elected councillors, with the rest being chosen by the Board after quite a stringent selection process. These "independent" members must, like the councillors, sign a declaration that they are against terrorism.[193] Regrettably, several of them have been the targets of intimidation since taking up their posts.

There are monthly meetings between the DPPs and the district police commanders at which the police present reports and answer questions. The DPPs' views have to be taken fully into account by the police and the Policing Board when policing plans and strategies are being formulated at the central level. In the recent survey conducted for the Policing Board,[194] 66% of respondents had heard of DPPs and 72% had total, a lot of, or some, confidence that the DPPs would help address local policing problems, with no real difference between the views of Protestant and Catholic respondents.

The Criminal Justice Review, in 2000, recommended that a Community Safety Unit should be set up within the Northern Ireland Office (or, after devolution, within the Office of the First Minister and Deputy First Minister) to advise the Government and others on community safety policies. This has indeed occurred, with the Unit helping to develop an overall strategy on community safety, funding projects in the field and providing advice to the community safety partnerships which now exist in every district council in Northern Ireland.[195] There is obviously an overlap between the functions of these partnerships and those of the DPPs and there is a good case for merging the two.

---

[192] Police (NI) Act 2003, Sch. 1, para. 5.
[193] *Ibid.* s. 15.
[194] See note 191 above.
[195] See www.communitysafetyni.gov.uk.

HM's Inspectorate of Constabulary[196]

Her Majesty's Inspectorate of Constabulary for England and Wales acts as an advisory body to the Northern Ireland Office regarding such matters as recruitment and equipment for the police in Northern Ireland. It also carries out regular inspections of the PSNI: in 2003 it reviewed the PSNI's handling of finance and the following year it reported on best value arrangements within the PSNI (and also within the Policing Board). Later in 2004 it published a baseline assessment against which future performance by the PSNI will be monitored.[197] This report, in Appendix 1, contains useful statistics comparing the performance of the PSNI against the UK national average (on most indicators it scores higher). The PSNI is also included in the Inspectorate's periodic thematic reports; in 2004, for instance, it reported on, amongst other matters, police success in recovering assets from criminals and in investigating and prosecuting domestic violence. The Inspectorate is now headed by Sir Ronnie Flanagan, the Chief Constable of the RUC at the time of the Patten Commission's report.

Custody visitors

The Policing Board has taken over the responsibility previously vested in the Police Authority for a statutory "lay visiting" scheme in Northern Ireland.[198] This allows for the appointment of about 50 people who, in their spare time and for no payment except expenses, are entitled to visit any of the 20 or so "designated" police stations where people can be detained for between six and 36 hours under the Police and Criminal Evidence (NI) Order 1989 or for up to 48 hours under the Terrorism Act 2000. Formerly called "lay visitors", the custody visitors visit the stations in pairs and can call at any time of the day or night. Their job is to ensure that the detainees are being properly looked after in accordance with a Code of Practice issued under the 1989 Order. To that end they can speak with the detainees and examine their custody records (provided the detainee consents).

After each visit a report is submitted both to the Policing Board and to the Chief Constable. The Policing Board's Community Involvement Committee considers the visitors' reports at its monthly meetings. In 2003-04 no fewer than 973 visits were made, during which 466 of the

---

[196] www.homeoffice.gov.uk/hmic/hmic.htm
[197] www.homeoffice.gov.uk/hmic/psnibaseline0604.pdf.
[198] Police (NI) Act 2000, s.73.

947 persons then in detention were seen and spoken to by the visitors (some detainees refused the contact and some were talking with their solicitor and/or the police at the time). The visitors reported that 80% of the visits were entirely satisfactory. In some cases detainees complained about the meals they had received or the poor drinking water and in five instances there were complaints about injuries received while being arrested.[199] The visitors cannot themselves investigate complaints, but they can draw them to the attention of the relevant authorities.

The Independent Commissioner for Detained Terrorist Suspects

When lay visitors were first appointed the Government refused to allow them to visit detainees who had been arrested under the anti-terrorism laws. Instead the Government preferred to rely upon the work (since 1992) of an independent commissioner, at first called the Independent Commissioner for the Holding Centres but now known as the Independent Commissioner for Detained Terrorist Suspects. The current post-holder is Dr William Norris.[200] Although the post is a non-statutory one, the Commissioner has greater powers than lay visitors in that, not only can he visit the places of detention whenever he wishes, but he can also interrupt police interrogation sessions to make sure that the detainee is being properly treated and can remotely view and listen to such interrogations. All such sessions are now video- and audio-recorded. In recent years the Northern Ireland Office has acquiesced in custody visitors being allowed to visit detained terrorist suspects to check on their welfare, but they still cannot attend or observe interrogation sessions. It seems likely, however, that later in 2005 this will be made possible. The Commissioner's post may then be terminated.

Since 2003 terrorist suspects in Northern Ireland have been detained in the Serious Crime Suite at Antrim police station, where there is space for 10 detainees at any one time; an overflow facility exists at Grosvenor Road police station in Belfast. In 2004 there were 230 terrorist suspects detained and the Commissioner made 83 visits, speaking to 138 detainees. He did not find anything amiss. In his report for 2004 Dr Norris examined the way in which the identification parade

---

[199] See the Northern Ireland Policing Board's *Annual Report 2003-04*.
[200] Until 2000 it was Sir Louis Blom-Cooper QC.

system operates for detained terrorist suspects and he made one or two recommendations for tightening procedures.

The Police Ombudsman for Northern Ireland[201]

The system for dealing with complaints against the police in Northern Ireland has recently been radically changed. From November 2000 the body responsible for this area has been the Office of the Police Ombudsman. Formerly the key body was the Independent Commission for Police Complaints (ICPC), which was established by the Police (NI) Order 1987 and operated from 1988.[202] That Commission in turn replaced the Police Complaints Board, which had existed since 1977 and which many observers felt was not effective enough. The body operating in England is now the Independent Police Complaints Commission, which assumed the role of the former Police Complaints Authority in 2004.[203]

The ICPC consisted of seven members and had a staff of some 16 people. It could *supervise* investigations of complaints, which were otherwise conducted by police officers. The supervising Commissioner would then tell the Chief Constable whether the investigation was or was not conducted to the Commission's satisfaction[204] and until a statement of satisfaction was issued no disciplinary charge or criminal proceedings could be brought against the officer involved in the complaint. The Commission could direct the Chief Constable to refer a case to the DPP and could recommend or, if need be, direct the preferment of disciplinary charges.

It was following a widely acclaimed report on the subject by Dr Maurice Hayes,[205] a former Ombudsman for Northern Ireland, that

---

[201] See also M. O'Rawe, "Complaints Against the Police", Chap. 5 in B. Dickson and M. O'Brien (eds.), *Civil Liberties in Northern Ireland: The CAJ Handbook* (4th ed., 2003).

[202] The evolution of the police complaints process in Northern Ireland from 1970 to 1998 is explained in the *ICPC's Annual Report for 1998*, pp. 7-18.

[203] See www.ipcc.gov.uk. The IPCC was created by the Police Reform Act 2002. Its current chairperson is Mr Nick Hardwick.

[204] In 1999 it transpired that the Commissioner who was supervising the RUC's investigation of complaints made by and on behalf of Mrs Rosemary Nelson, who was later murdered by loyalist paramilitaries, had not been satisfied with the investigation. This led the Chief Constable to ask an officer from the Metropolitan Police, Mr Mulvihill, to reinvestigate the complaints.

[205] *A Police Ombudsman for Northern Ireland? A Review of the Police Complaints System in Northern Ireland* (1997).

the UK Government secured the enactment of new legislation, sections 50-65 of the Police (NI) Act 1998, which created a whole new system for dealing with complaints against the police in Northern Ireland. This, of course, was pre-Patten, but the legislation was further developed in 2000 as a result of recommendations in the Patten report.[206]

The current system

There is now a complaints system in Northern Ireland which, in theory at any rate, is second to none in the world. The Police Ombudsman (currently Mrs Nuala O'Loan), together with her officials, is able to conduct her own, completely independent, investigations into complaints brought against the police. No police investigators have to be involved at all. At the same time, the way in which complaints are classified has been altered, as has the standard of proof required.[207] The Police Ombudsman's expenditure in 2004-05 was £7,750,000.

To allow complaints which are not serious to be settled, and provided that the complainant and the police officer involved agree, the Police Ombudsman can, after investigating a complaint, attempt to act as a mediator between the two parties.[208] The Police Ombudsman can also investigate, and send to the Chief Constable and to the Northern Ireland Policing Board a report on, any matters concerning police practices and policies which come to her attention as a result of a complaint.[209] This is a significant power which has the potential to bring to light general malpractices which may lie behind an actual complaint. Since 2003 the Police Ombudsman has also been able to investigate a current police practice or policy - even if it has not come to her attention as a result of a complaint - if he or she has reason to believe that this would be in the public interest.[210]

The Ombudsman cannot, however, investigate complaints of misconduct by officers who have retired from the police (unless the misconduct is allegedly criminal), nor can he or she investigate complaints against soldiers, even when acting in support of the police (e.g. in controlling a riot). If a complainant is the object of a criminal prosecution, the prosecution should be completed before the Police

---

[206] Police (NI) Act 2000, ss. 62-6.
[207] RUC (Conduct) Regs. 2000; RUC (Conduct) (Senior Officer) Regs. 2000; RUC (Appeals) Regs. 2000.
[208] Police (NI) Act 1998, s. 58A, inserted by Police (NI) Act 2000, s. 62(1).
[209] Ibid. s. 61A, inserted by Police (NI) Act 2000, s. 63(1).
[210] Ibid. s. 60A, inserted by Police (NI) Act 2003, s. 13.

Ombudsman concludes an investigation of the complaint.[211] In grave and exceptional circumstances the Police Ombudsman will look into an issue which occurred more than a year before the complaint was made - in 2001, for example, a report was issued into the death of Samuel Devenny in 1969. The Police Ombudsman does not have to disclose to complainants documents examined during the course of an investigation.[212]

The Ombudsman's office does not itself take disciplinary proceedings against police officers. This is left to the police themselves, though the Ombudsman can direct the Chief Constable to bring such proceedings against officers up to the rank of chief superintendent. Hearings usually take place before disciplinary boards consisting of three officers, one of whom must be an assistant chief constable or commander.[213] Hearings into the conduct of senior officers will take place in a tribunal consisting of a single person appointed by the Policing Board (perhaps with one or more assessors to help).[214] The standard of proof required for a finding of guilt in these hearings used to be the same as in criminal proceedings, namely "beyond reasonable doubt". In practice this was very hard to achieve and so very few complaints from members of the public eventually led to a finding of breach of discipline. Today, for complaints relating to police conduct on or after 6 November 2000, the standard of proof is the balance of probabilities.[215]

Appeal tribunals can be set up to hear appeals from disciplinary boards.[216] If the officer appealing is a senior officer (chief superintendent or above) the tribunal will consist of a lawyer (as chairperson), a member of a police authority in Great Britain and someone who is or has been an inspector of constabulary or a former chief officer of another force - all of these being appointed by the Secretary of State. If the officer appealing is not a senior officer the tribunal will consist of a lawyer (as chairperson), a member of the Northern Ireland Policing Board, a former or current chief officer of

---

[211] *In re O'Callaghan's Application* [2003] NIQB 18.
[212] *In re an Application by the Committee on the Administration of Justice and Martin O'Brien* [2005] NIQB 25.
[213] RUC (Discipline and Disciplinary Appeals) Regs. 1988, Sch. 4
[214] RUC (Conduct) (Senior Officer) Regs., reg 14.
[215] RUC (Complaints etc.) Regs. 2001, reg. 11.
[216] RUC (Appeals) Regs. 2000, see especially reg. 8.

another force and a retired officer of appropriate rank - all of these being appointed by the Policing Board.

Table 16, below, presents the figures on complaints lodged against the PSNI during the last three years. Unfortunately it is not possible to deduce from the Police Ombudsman's annual reports how many complaints have led to officers being successfully disciplined or convicted of a criminal offence. It is therefore perhaps too early to say whether the Police Ombudsman's office is proving effective in dealing with poor standards of policing in Northern Ireland, but all the signs to date are that it is doing as good a job as any similar body elsewhere in the world. From the Chief Constable's *Annual Reports 2003-04* and *2004-05* we know that in those two years 87 officers were charged with disciplinary or misconduct offences, but in only 16 cases did the charges arise from complaints by members of the public. Of the 87 officers, 10 were dismissed or required to resign, two were reduced in rank and 27 were fined or reduced in pay.

TABLE 16: COMPLAINTS AGAINST THE PSNI 2000-05[217]

	2000-02	2002-03	2003-04	2004-5
New complaints received	5,129	3,193	2,976	2,885
Alleged serious or sexual assaults	80	51	27	21
Alleged other assaults	2,328	1,254	949	854
Alleged oppressive conduct or harassment	543	334	487	516
Complaints resolved informally	394	281	312	343
Files sent to the DPP with no recommendations	78	185	174	142
Files sent to the DPP recommending criminal charges	12	16	10	7
Cases where the Ombudsman recommended disciplinary action within the PSNI	n/a	41	76	57

When it was established the Police Ombudsman's office inherited 2,124 cases which were then with the Independent Commission for

---

[217] Source: annual reports of the Police Ombudsman's office. The office was established on 6 November 2000, so the first column covers the 17-month period from then until 31 March 2002.

Police Complaints; by April 2002 the investigations into all but 330 of those had been completed. In 2004-05 the office received 2,885 new complaints (comprising a total of 4,206 allegations, a slight decrease on the 2003-04 figure). It can be seen that the proportion of complaints which lead to recommendations that criminal charges be laid or disciplinary action taken is very small indeed: at present it is running at just under 3%. An even smaller proportion result in such charges or action actually materialising. In 2004-05 misconduct charges were heard against police officers in five cases (all pleaded guilty). However warnings and advice are sometimes issued instead; in 2004-05 the Ombudsman made 47 recommendations for changes in policing policy, practice, training or personnel management.

4.6   THE PROBATION AND PRISON SERVICES

The Probation Service[218]

The Probation Service in Northern Ireland is now administered by the Probation Board.[219] This was first set up in 1982 and has up to 18 members, appointed by the Secretary of State and drawn from a wide spectrum of the community.[220] The Board is serviced by a small secretariat based at its headquarters in Belfast. The Board's chairperson is currently Mr Ronnie Spence. The Board has a commitment to deal with persistent and/or violent offenders in a manner which reduces their offending and helps to integrate them into their communities. The Board is also meant to operate within a policy framework set by the Secretary of State, who in his latest Strategy Statement made it clear that the government wants the Probation Service to protect the public, to provide high quality information to the courts and to give value for money. In 2003-04 the cost of running the Probation Service was approximately £14 million, which was just 1.6% of the total amount spent on law and order in Northern Ireland during that year. The Board has been complaining for years that it is unable to give the service it would like to give because of a lack of financial resources.

---

[218] Information in this section is drawn in part from the Probation Board's *Annual Report 2003-04*, its *Corporate Plan 2005-08* and its *Business Plan 2005-06*. See also C. Blair, *Prisons and Probation*, Research Report No. 6 prepared for the Review of the Criminal Justice System in NI (2000).

[219] www.pbni.org.uk.

[220] Probation (NI) Order 1982. This was passed largely as a result of the *Report of the Children's and Young Persons' Review Group* (the Black Report), 1979.

There are about 30 probation offices throughout the province, all of which are listed in the telephone directory's yellow pages, and the Probation Service employs about 275 staff. Probation officers have a manual which covers in one volume those aspects of law and procedure affecting their work in the courts, the community and prisons. They also adhere to minimum standards of practice issued by the Board with regard to the supervision of probation orders and community service orders.

The chief aim of the Service is to prevent re-offending. It seeks to achieve this, in part, by trying to reduce the number of custodial sentences imposed by the courts. Probation officers, operating under the Criminal Justice (NI) Order 1996 and the Criminal Justice (Children) (NI) Order 1998, write pre-sentence reports (PSRs) on offenders found guilty in a court. These reports are expected to be called for when a court is considering whether to impose a community sanction such as a community service order or a supervision order, but they are compulsory - unless regarded as unnecessary in the circumstances (*e.g.* because the offence is so serious) - before a court decides that a custodial sentence is appropriate. The reports attempt to give an objective assessment of the offender to the judge or magistrate, set out the courses of action available to the court and make recommendations as to which would be most appropriate in the particular case. The Board acknowledges that use of PSRs in magistrates' courts varies noticeably between court locations and that there are wide variations in sentencing practice.

A court can place an offender on probation for a period between six months and three years. The order is not intended as a punishment but rather as an offer of rehabilitation. To that end the probation officer assigned to the case will befriend, give guidance to and supervise the offender. Supervision within the community is not only better for the offender, it is also vastly cheaper than containment in prison. The recidivism rate for those placed on probation (*i.e.*, the proportion of offenders who re-offend) is also much lower than for those who are given a custodial sentence. In the year ending March 2004 the Probation Service wrote some 8,267 PSRs (5% more than in 2002-03) and by the end of the year it was supervising 1,222 offenders on probation orders and 733 on custody probation orders.[221]

---

[221] Probation Board's *Annual Report 2003-04*, p. 39. The nature of custody probation is explained in Chap. 5.4 below. The number of custody probation orders issued in

Probation officers also help to run the community service order scheme, whereby offenders aged 17 or over can be required to perform a set number of hours of community service (see Chap. 7.1).[222] In the year ending March 2004 there were some 765 orders issued (5% more than in the previous year). They are a successful means of reintegrating offenders as law-abiding members of society. Various local initiatives have been developed to provide opportunities for community service: Northern Ireland, despite all its problems, may to some extent be better than elsewhere in this respect because of its comparatively low crime rate and its still vibrant family networks and local communities. In 2003-04 there were also 317 combination orders made: these require someone who is on probation to undertake community service at the same time (see Chap. 5.4 below)

From 2001-04 the Probation Board was the lead organisation in a multi-agency partnership in West Belfast delivering IMPACT - an "inclusive model of partnership against car theft". The programme provided structured diversionary activities for young people tempted to engage in such theft.

Rehabilitation of offenders

The Probation Service provides welfare services for prisoners, prisoners' families and people recently released from prison. In this capacity the officers act not so much as legal officials but as specialised social workers. Whenever life sentence prisoners are taking part in the "working out" scheme during the months before their release on licence, probation officers help to counsel them. They also maintain contact thereafter.[223]

The Board has a statutory responsibility to fund some voluntary projects operating in this field - in 2003-04 it distributed more than £1.5 million to some 100 organisations. The Northern Ireland Association for the Care and Resettlement of Offenders (NIACRO) and the Extern Organisation are the most prominent groups in the voluntary sector whose services overlap with those of the Probation Board and between them they received more than one-half of the Board's grants in 2003-04. The Board also helps to fund child-minding and family centre

---

2003-04 was 24% higher than in 2002-03. The Social Services Inspectorate completed a review of the custody probation system in 2004.

[222] See M. Allen and F. McAleenan, *Sentencing Law and Practice in Northern Ireland* (3rd ed., 1998, with Supplement 2003), pp. 58-62.

[223] See Prison Act (NI) 1953, s. 23.

facilities in prisons and it helps to finance hostels for ex-prisoners, the Rape Crisis Centre, the Youth at Risk programme and a growing number of victim support schemes throughout the province.

It is worth noting that under the Rehabilitation of Offenders (NI) Order 1978 an individual's sentence (whether or not it involved imprisonment) may in certain circumstances become "spent", which means that from then on that person must for most purposes be treated as someone who has not been convicted of, or even charged with, the offence in question. Such a rehabilitated person can even sue for libel or slander if someone later refers to the fact that he or she has been convicted of the offence, and the failure to disclose a spent conviction is not in law a proper ground for prejudicing a person as regards employment (except in relation to work with people under 18 years of age). The period which must elapse before a sentence becomes spent depends on the type and severity of the original sentence. For a prison sentence of up to six months, for instance, the rehabilitation period is seven years, while for sentences of between six and 30 months the period is 10 years. Prison sentences of more than 30 months are excluded altogether from the scheme. If a person is placed on probation the rehabilitation period runs simultaneously with the probation period, or for one year after the conviction, whichever is longer.

In 2004 the Northern Ireland Office issued a consultation paper with proposals for reforming the law on rehabilitation of offenders in Northern Ireland.[224] The proposals are modelled almost exactly on proposals for England and Wales and, surprisingly, do not take account of the higher proportion of ex-prisoners in Northern Ireland[225] or of the provisions in the Belfast (Good Friday) Agreement concerning the re-integration of prisoners into the community. Under the proposals, life sentenced prisoners would continue to be exempt from the rehabilitation provisions and employers would still not be obliged to abide by a code of practice relating to the employment of ex-prisoners.

The future

The Criminal Justice and Court Services Act 2000 makes changes to the law on probation in England and Wales. Amongst other things it replaces the term "probation order" with "community rehabilitation

---

[224] Available on the NIO's website.
[225] It has been estimated that there may be as many 25,000 individuals who have spent some time in prison as a result of Northern Ireland's "troubles" since 1969.

order" and provides for young people to be curfewed. Such changes have not yet been mirrored in Northern Ireland. The Review of the Criminal Justice System, published in March 2000, recommended that, when criminal justice is eventually devolved to the Northern Ireland Assembly, the Probation Service should become an agency comparable to the Prison Service (see below). The present Probation Board would be abolished and the Minister would instead be supported by an advisory board covering not just probation but also prisons and juvenile justice. These changes, too, have not yet been made. The Review recommended in addition that there be closer liaison between the Probation and Prison Services, especially in relation to the development of offending behaviour programmes. The two organisations do now work together more closely on such matters (including temporary release schemes).

The Prison Service[226]

The Northern Ireland Prison Service, although operating in a separate jurisdiction, is run along similar lines to its equivalent in England and Wales. Social and political factors, however, have led to some divergences. The Service is an executive agency of the Northern Ireland Office and it issues an annual report and annual accounts.[227] In 2003-04 the cost of running it was approximately £112 million. Given that the average number of prisoners on any one day in 2003-04 was 1,198, the cost per prisoner per year is more than £93,000. This is considerably higher than the cost of imprisonment in Great Britain.

The total number of people employed by the Prison Service at the end of January 2005 was about 2,050, of whom some 420 were civilians working as teachers, nurses, cleaners, etc. Nearly one-half of the staff work at Maghaberry Prison. The numbers are considerably reduced from what they were a few years ago, partly because the size of the prisoner population has fallen. Prison officers are trained at the Prison Service College in Millisle, County Down, and are unionised in the Prison Officers' Association.

---

[226] www.niprisonservice.gov.uk. Information in this section is drawn in part from the Northern Ireland Prison Service's *Annual Report and Accounts 2003-04*. See also C. Blair, *Prisons and Probation*, Research Report No. 6 prepared for the *Review of the Criminal Justice System in Northern Ireland* (2000) and J. Challis, *The Prison Service in Northern Ireland 1900-1990* (1999).

[227] Prison Act (NI) 1953, s. 5. The current Director General of the Prison Service is Mr Robin Masefield.

During the 30 years of the troubles in Northern Ireland, from 1969 to 1998, 29 prison officers were murdered by terrorists. There were also particularly serious incidents within Northern Ireland's prisons during the 1980s and 1990s. A hunger strike at the Maze Prison, following the long-running "blanket" and "dirty" protests, led to the deaths of 10 prisoners in 1981.[228] The European Commission of Human Rights rejected a case taken by the protesters, largely because their conditions were said to be self-inflicted, but the Commission did criticise the inflexibility of the prison authorities.[229] Some of the demands of the prisoners, such as the right to wear their own clothes, were eventually conceded. In 1983 there was a mass escape of 38 prisoners from the Maze Prison, the largest ever escape in British penal history. It was investigated by Sir James Hennessy, whose report recommended better inspection and self-assessment arrangements.[230] In 1997 a loyalist prisoner, Billy Wright, was murdered at the Maze Prison by republican paramilitaries[231] and in 1998 another prisoner, David Keys, was murdered by loyalist paramilitaries. In 2002, after staff contact details somehow fell into the hands of paramilitary organisations, more than £30 million was spent by the Northern Ireland Office in providing extra security measures for Prison Service staff. Even in 2003-04 there were more than 50 attacks on the staff's homes.

Today periodic inspections of the prisons are conducted by Her Majesty's Inspectorate of Prisons (see 4.7 below), by the European Committee for the Prevention of Torture[232] and by the Northern Ireland Human Rights Commission (see Chap. 9.6). Each prison also has a Board of Visitors (see 4.7). Issues highlighted in recent times by inspections have included the conditions in which female prisoners are held at Hydebank Wood (including the frequency of strip-searching), the continued use of "slopping out" at Magilligan and the procedures in place for preventing, and investigating, prison deaths. Facilities for ensuring that prisoners are given appropriate psychiatric care seem not to be in place and this may have contributed to the fact that in the past

---

[228] See D. Beresford, *Ten Men Dead* (1987).
[229] *McFeeley and others* v *UK* (1981) 3 EHRR 161.
[230] HC 203 (1983-84). See too C. Ryder, *Inside the Maze: The untold story of the Northern Ireland Prison Service* (2000), Chap. 12.
[231] Following a recommendation by Judge Peter Cory, this death is currently the subject of an inquiry led by Lord MacLean, a Scottish judge, being conducted under the Prison Act (NI) 1953, s. 7.
[232] www.cpt.coe.int/en/default.htm.

three years there have been at least seven suicides in Northern Ireland's prisons, including those of two female prisoners.[233]

Legal aid is granted for numerous applications for judicial review made by prisoners on a wide variety of issues (see Chap. 6.7), but few of these are ultimately successful.

The prison population[234]

There are at the moment three prison establishments in Northern Ireland: Magilligan Prison (on the North-West coast), Maghaberry Prison (near Lisburn) and Hydebank Wood Prison and Young Offenders Centre (on the outskirts of South Belfast). Magilligan is a medium-security prison, housing mainly shorter-term prisoners. Maghaberry is a high-security prison housing male long-term prisoners as well as male remand prisoners. The prison at Maze, also near Lisburn (and formerly known as Long Kesh), closed in 2000[235] and the Crumlin Road prison in Belfast closed in 1996, but some alleged illegal immigrants and asylum seekers are still detained in a facility near the old Crumlin Road prison in what is now categorised as a Belfast facility of the prison at Maghaberry.

The most dangerous offenders are held at Maghaberry, where, since March 2004, following a review conducted in August 2003 by a committee chaired by Mr John Steele, a former head of the Northern Ireland Prison Service, prisoners claiming allegiance to paramilitary organisations have been permitted to be housed in separate parts of the prison, away from each other and from other prisoners. Remand prisoners are held only at Maghaberry or Hydebank Wood; woman prisoners are held only at Hydebank Wood (having been transferred there from Mourne House at Maghaberry Prison in June 2004).

Unlike the position in many other countries, the prison population in Northern Ireland has declined in recent years, although it has just begun to rise again. It reached a peak of almost 3,000 in 1978, but in early August 2005 it was 1,296. These comprised 694 prisoners at

---

[233] See, generally, L. Moore and P. Scraton, *The Hurt Inside*, a report published by the Northern Ireland Human Rights Commission in 2004. The Prison Service later banned the Commission's representatives from conducting further research on the experience of women prisoners.

[234] See C. O'Loan and K Amelin, *The Northern Ireland Prison Population in 2004*, NIO, Research and Statistical Bulletin 8/2005. This examines trends in the prison population over the last 10 years.

[235] See C. Ryder, note 230 above.

Maghaberry, 369 at Magilligan and 233 at Hydebank Wood. Of this total, 449 were prisoners held on remand (*i.e.* not yet convicted), some 80 or so were "separated" prisoners (affiliated to paramilitary organisations) and 36 were women. In 2004 the average daily population of *sentenced* prisoners was 794 (6% higher than in 2003), of whom just 14 were female. Of the prisoners sentenced in 2004, 227 were imprisoned for crimes of violence, 230 for motoring offences, 264 for theft or burglary and 124 for robbery.[236] There were altogether 5,455 "committals" to prison during the year. Of these, 2,003 (37%) were prisoners on remand, 1,647 (28%) were people sent to prison for not paying a fine and 106 (2%) were imprisoned for not paying a civil debt (such as maintenance to an ex-wife) or for being an alleged illegal immigrant. In 2004 there were 122 "lifers" or "SoSPs" in Northern Ireland's prisons, three of whom were women.[237] According to Home Office research, in November 2003 Northern Ireland had 70 prisoners for every 100,000 people in the population. The figures for other countries included 85 for Ireland, 129 for Scotland, 141 for England and Wales and 701 for the USA.[238]

The prison régime[239]

The normal prison regime in Northern Ireland, although maligned in some quarters, actually compares quite favourably with that in other parts of the United Kingdom, Ireland and Western Europe. It is regulated partly by legislation (the Prison Act (NI) 1953 and the Prison and Young Offenders Centre Rules (NI) 1995) and partly by Standing Orders issued to prison governors by the Northern Ireland Office.[240] Prisoners will be categorised as being on a "basic", "standard" or "enhanced" regime depending on how well they adhere to the rules of the prison. The Prison (Amendment) (NI) Order 2004 made provision for compulsory alcohol and drug testing of prisoners in Northern

---

[236] Robbery is theft accompanied by violence or the threat of violence.
[237] Those sent to prison "at the Secretary of State's pleasure" are those who were under 18 years of age when they committed an offence carrying a life sentence (Criminal Justice (Children) (NI) Order 1998, art. 45). See also Chap. 7.1.
[238] *World Prison Population List* (5th ed., 2003), Home Office, Research Findings No. 234.
[239] For a general survey of the law affecting prisoners in Northern Ireland, see S. Livingstone, "Prisoners' Rights", Chap. 6 in B. Dickson and M. O'Brien (eds.), *Civil Liberties in Northern Ireland: The CAJ Handbook* (4th ed., 2003).
[240] The Standing Orders are available on the Prison Service's website.

Ireland and repealed an earlier provision[241] which had allowed prisoners on remand to buy foodstuffs for their own consumption. The rules require that prisoners should engage in useful work. Some are employed in servicing the prisons themselves, while others work in prison industries making items such as shoes, clothing and metalwork. As regards education, a lot of the prisoners, especially those allied to paramilitary organisations, enrol for courses, ranging from the most basic to Open University level.

The Young Offenders' Centre at Hydebank Wood, which opened in 1979, has places for 300 young men, mainly aged 17 to 21, who have been sentenced to less than three years in custody. The few females in this category are housed in a separate unit at the same establishment. The régime is officially described as "brisk", with the inmates gaining privileges by using their time in a positive and constructive way. The Centre offers extensive education, vocational training and physical recreation facilities. Young persons aged 15 or 16 are sometimes held in a juvenile unit at the Centre when a court has certified them to be unruly or guilty of serious misconduct, even though they may not have been convicted of any crime (see Chap. 7.1).

Discipline and welfare

Discipline in the prisons is now primarily the responsibility of the governors, the role of the Boards of Visitors in this regard having been removed in 2000.[242] But the most serious punishment which a governor can impose is loss of 28 days' remission. Any serious or repeated offence which a governor believes requires a more severe punishment may be referred to the Secretary of State and it is for him or her to decide how the case should be handled. The maximum penalties which can be imposed by the Secretary of State are loss of up to 180 days' remission and/or confinement in a prison cell for up to 56 days.

Prison governors have a discretion to allow prisoners to have legal representation in disciplinary hearings. Representation should be allowed where the charge is serious or the penalty might involve loss of remission, where points of law are likely to arise or where a prisoner might be unable to present his or her case properly. Judicial review (see Chap. 6.7) is available in respect of hearings, but there is otherwise no right of appeal.

---

[241] Prison Act (NI) 1953, s. 40.
[242] By the Prison and Young Offenders Centre (Amendment) Rules (NI) 2000.

Voluntary groups active in the area of prisoners' welfare include the Northern Ireland Association for the Care and Resettlement of Offenders, the Extern Organisation and the Prison Fellowship of Northern Ireland. The Butler Trust has also funded many worthwhile projects. There are active community organisations working on behalf of "political" ex-prisoners, notably Coiste na n-Iarchimí[243] and EPIC (the Ex-Prisoners' Interpretive Centre).

The "accelerated" release of prisoners

Even before the Belfast (Good Friday) Agreement in 1998, prisoners convicted in Diplock courts (see 4.2) were able to benefit from the more generous rules in Northern Ireland regarding remission of sentence: they could be released after serving just one-half of their sentence whereas in England prisoners had to serve at least two-thirds. But the Good Friday Agreement required each of the Governments of the United Kingdom and Ireland to put in place mechanisms for accelerating still further the release of prisoners convicted either of scheduled offences in Northern Ireland or of similar offences elsewhere. The UK Parliament accordingly enacted the Northern Ireland (Sentences) Act 1998, which provided for the appointment of Sentence Review Commissioners,[244] to whom prisoners could apply for a declaration of eligibility for early release.[245]

The pre-conditions for early release were: (i) that the prisoner had committed a scheduled offence before 10 April 1998 and the sentence imposed had been imprisonment for life or a term of at least five years; (ii) that the prisoner was not a supporter of a specified organisation (*i.e.* an organisation not on ceasefire[246]); (iii) that the prisoner would not be likely to become a supporter of a specified

---

243 This is, loosely, Irish for "Association of Ex-Prisoners".
244 www.sentencereview.org.uk. Ten Commissioners were appointed, the joint chairpersons being Sir John Blelloch and Mr Brian Currin, who is actually based in South Africa. For details as to their terms of office and procedure, see Schs. 1 and 2 to the Northern Ireland (Sentences) Act 1998. It has been held that the Commissioners are a sufficiently independent body for the purposes of Arts. 5 and 6 of the European Convention on Human Rights: *In re Sheridan's Application* [2004] NIQB 4.
245 Ireland enacted the Criminal Justice (Release of Prisoners) Act 1998, which set up a Release of Prisoners Commission.
246 The organisations currently specified are the Continuity IRA, the "Real" IRA, the Loyalist Volunteer Force, the Red Hand Defenders and the Orange Volunteers: Northern Ireland (Sentences) Act 1998 (Specified Organisations) Order 2004.

organisation or to become concerned in the commission, preparation or instigation of acts of terrorism connected with the affairs of Northern Ireland if released immediately; and (iv) that, if the prisoner was serving a life sentence, he or she would not be a danger to the public if released immediately.

The first group of seven prisoners to be released under these provisions left prison on 11 September 1998. A further 129 followed the following month and by July 2000 some 447 prisoners had been released (241 Republicans, 194 Loyalists and 12 "non-aligned"). Only 10 of these ex-prisoners have been recalled to prison because of an alleged breach of their release conditions. It is worth noting that under the Northern Ireland (Sentences) Act 1998 anyone convicted after July 2000 of a scheduled offence committed before Good Friday 1998, and who is a member of a paramilitary organisation which is on ceasefire, will have to spend no more than two years in prison (including time spent on remand).[247] The Government has also conceded that an amnesty will in due course be given to republicans who are "on the run" from the security forces.[248] These are people who, for example, fled the country when they knew they were under investigation for some troubles-related incident.

Remission and release on licence

There is no parole system in Northern Ireland, unlike in England and Wales. Instead, under Prison Rules, prisoners can earn up to 50% remission on their sentences. [249] They can also qualify for temporary release under a number of schemes. In 2003-04, for example, 2,030 prisoners were allowed out of prison under the Pre-Release Home Leave Scheme, 127 under the Christmas Home Leave Scheme and 66 under the Compassionate Temporary Release Scheme. The vast majority of prisoners return to prison after such periods of freedom, but at the time of writing there are still 15 who are "unlawfully at large". Remand prisoners used to leave prison quite frequently in order to attend court hearings, but today a large number of such "appearances"

---

[247] Annexes to the Commissioners' Annual Report for 2003-04 (HC 790) contain helpful guides on procedure for prisoners.

[248] See the annex to the Joint Declaration of the British and Irish Governments, 30 April 2003: www.nio.gov.uk/proposals_in_relation_to_on_the_runs_ (otrs).pdf

[249] For further discussion about remission generally, see M. Allen and F. McAleenan, *Sentencing Law and Practice in Northern Ireland* (3rd ed., 1998, with Supplement 2003), pp. 87-90, paras. 2.28-41.

take place through a video link (there were 9,750 such cases in 2003-04). Prisoners can also consult their lawyers through a video link (9,588 in 2003-04).

The system for reviewing life sentences in Northern Ireland was altered as a result of recommendations contained in the Criminal Justice Review, published in 2000. The new system applies to those life sentenced prisoners (and to those detained at the pleasure of the Secretary of State - SoSPs - *i.e.* people who were under 18 years of age when they committed a serious crime)[250] who cannot apply for early release to the Sentence Review Commissioners mentioned above. Instead, under the Life Sentences (NI) Order 2001, they can apply to the Life Sentence Review Commissioners (some of whom are the same individuals).[251] The Secretary of State appointed 25 such Commissioners in 2002, under the chairmanship of Mr Peter Smith QC. Seven are from a legal background, six from a background in psychiatry or psychology, three from a "criminological" background and three from a "rehabilitative" background. In taking their decisions the Commissioners must have "due regard" to the need to protect the public from serious harm from life prisoners and "regard" to the desirability of preventing the commission of further offences by life prisoners and securing the rehabilitation of life prisoners.[252]

The Order requires the court imposing a life sentence to determine in most cases the "tariff period" which must be served in order to satisfy the requirements of retribution and deterrence, having regard to the seriousness of the offence. On occasions the trial judge will sit with the Lord Chief Justice to hear arguments from barristers as to what the appropriate tariff period should be[253] and an appeal lies to the Court of Appeal against the term set.[254] Judges in Northern Ireland follow the guidelines on tariffs set out by the Lord Chief Justice of England and

---

[250] Legislation precludes them from receiving a life sentence: Criminal Justice (Children) (NI) Order 1998, art. 45.

[251] www.lsrcni.org.uk. Annex A to the Commissioners' Annual Report for 2003-04 (HC 789) contains a step-by-step guide for prisoners to the life sentence review process.

[252] For details as to the Commissioners' procedures, see the Life Sentence Review Commissioners' Rules (NI) 2001. The Commissioners' website contains a useful Guide to the process used when prisoners are being dealt with and it also carries the minutes of the Commissioners' plenary meetings.

[253] See, *e.g.*, *R* v *Larmour* [2004] NICC 4, *R* v *McParland* [2004] NICC 6 and *R* v *Gribben* [2004] NICC 7.

[254] Criminal Appeal (NI) Act 1980, s. 8.

Wales in 2002, where he talked of a "normal" starting point of 12 years and a "higher" starting point of 15/16 years.[255] In some particularly serious cases no such tariff period is set (so that a life sentence means, literally, "for life"), but the Secretary of State can (and, in cases where the offender was under 18 years of age when he or she committed the offence, must) at a later stage direct when the release provisions are to apply.[256]

After the tariff period has expired the prisoner can apply to the Life Sentence Review Commissioners for a release date. Any such date is usually about a year in advance so that during the pre-release period the prisoner can take part in a scheme of work and home leave. Even after release the prisoner remains on licence for the rest of his or her life and can be recalled to prison when the Secretary of State considers this necessary to avoid danger to the public. In fact the vast majority of persons released on licence in this way do not re-offend.[257]

Under section 68 of the Justice (NI) Act 2002 a scheme has been put in place whereby the victim of a crime (or a representative of the victim if the victim is dead) can apply to be kept informed by the Secretary of State about the temporary release and discharge of the person imprisoned for the crime.[258] In certain circumstances, however, the Secretary of State can refuse to provide the information and the scheme does not usually apply to the victims of offences committed by juveniles.

4.7 BODIES OVERSEEING CRIMINAL JUSTICE

The Criminal Justice Board

The heads or senior representatives of the seven main criminal justice agencies in Northern Ireland - the Public Prosecution Service, the Northern Ireland Court Service, the Northern Ireland Office, the Northern Ireland Prison Service, the Probation Board for Northern Ireland, the Police Service of Northern Ireland and the Youth Justice

---

[255] [2002] 3 All ER 412, adopted by the NICA in *R v McCandless and others* [2004] NICA 1.
[256] For the applicability of the new system to persons held "at the Secretary of State's pleasure" when the 2001 Order came into force, see *In re King's Application* [2002] NICA 48.
[257] See M. Allen and F. McAleenan, note 249 above, pp. 90-93, paras. 2.42-49.
[258] Prisoner Release Victim Information (NI) Scheme 2003.

Agency - meet regularly as the Criminal Justice Board. They seek to ensure that there is proper co-ordination between the activities of their agencies and that they are working to mutually supportive goals. In 2003 they published a strategy for developing the public information and education aspects to their work. The Board meets from time to time with a ministerial "trilateral" comprising Ministers from the Department for Constitutional Affairs, the office of the Attorney General and the Northern Ireland Office.

The Board also now produces what is called an "Annual Report of the Criminal Justice System in Northern Ireland", first published in 2004. This sets out how the different organisations within the criminal justice system have performed against the aims they set for themselves in 2003,[259] but is not meant to replace the annual reports of the individual agencies. The report is a useful source of up-to-date information about the trends and plans within the various agencies. One of the main concerns of the agencies has been to ensure better communication between themselves. A programme called Causeway has been set up to improve the exchange of information about, for example, individuals' criminal records.

The Criminal Cases Review Commission[260]

The Criminal Cases Review Commission (CCRC) is a body established under the Criminal Appeal Act 1995. It is one of the outcomes of the Royal Commission on Criminal Procedure, which reported in 1991. This in turn was partly prompted by a series of high-profile miscarriages of justice involving a number of people convicted by juries in England for crimes connected with the political affairs of Northern Ireland. The Commission is based in Birmingham and comprises a Chairman (Professor Graham Zellick), 15 other members (only one of whom is a woman) and about 100 staff. It operates in relation to England, Wales and Northern Ireland.[261] Scotland has its own separate Commission.[262] In 2003-04 the CCRC cost just over £7 million to run.

[259] www.nio.gov.uk/cjsni_annual_report_2004-2005.pdf.
[260] www.ccrc.gov.uk.
[261] See, generally, B. Dickson, "Miscarriages of Justice in Northern Ireland", Chap. 14 in C. Walker and K. Starmer (eds.), *Miscarriages of Justice: A Review of Justice in Error* (1999).
[262] www.sccrc.org.uk.

The CCRC's role is to conduct thorough reviews of convictions and sentences in suspected miscarriages of justice. If it considers that there is "a real possibility" that a conviction or sentence would not be upheld by an appeal court (even though an unsuccessful appeal has already taken place), it can refer the case to an appeal court. The Court of Appeal itself can also ask the CCRC to investigate and report to it on any matter and the Home Secretary can refer matters to it concerning the possible exercise of the Royal prerogative of mercy. For there to be "a real possibility" of an appeal against conviction succeeding there has to be an argument or evidence which was not raised during the trial or earlier appeal, or some other exceptional circumstances. A decision to refer a case can be made only by a committee of three members of the Commission, but this can follow an investigation conducted by the Commission's own caseworkers, by an outside expert appointed to the task or by the police. The Commission usually elects to interview witnesses itself but it takes no further part in cases that have been referred. A decision by the Commission not to refer a conviction to the Court of Appeal can be subjected to judicial review.[263]

In 2003-04, a typical year, the CCRC received 885 new cases for consideration and referred 30 to the Court of Appeal in England and Wales and Northern Ireland.[264] It receives fewer applications, proportionately, from Northern Ireland than it does from England Wales (there were a total of 96 between 1997 and 2004), but in turn a greater proportion of these applications lead to cases being referred back to the Northern Ireland Court of Appeal: of the 74 cases dealt with by March 2004, 13 had been referred back; nine of these had by then been dealt with by the Court of Appeal, leading to seven convictions being quashed and two upheld.[265] In one case, for example, the conviction of a man in 1987 for involvement in a murder was quashed by the Court of Appeal in 2002 after the CCRC referred it back on the basis that new medical knowledge now showed that it was possible that the accused's confessions were made at a time when he was suffering from "a non-diabetic hypoglycaemic episode".[266] In another prominent

---

[263] See, *e.g.*, *In re Torney's Application* [2003] NIQB 36.
[264] *Annual Report and Accounts 2003-04.*
[265] See, *e.g.*, the cases of two juveniles convicted in 1980 of killing a police officer: *R v Gorman and McKinney* [2001] 8 BNIL 35. For the case of Ian Hay Gordon see Chap. 5.7.
[266] *R v Green* [2002] 5 BNIL 28.

subsequent case, however, the conviction was not quashed.[267] In England and Wales there have been at least two cases where the convictions of men who were hanged for their crimes have been quashed.[268] Another of the English cases involved Danny McNamee, convicted in 1987 of conspiracy to cause explosions relating to affairs in Northern Ireland, for which he received a 25-year prison sentence. His conviction was quashed in December 1998. It must not be assumed, however, that every victim of a miscarriage of justice will be entitled to compensation. Compensation will not be paid if there has not been a failure of the judicial process but merely a new legal ruling on undisputed old facts.[269]

The Criminal Justice Inspectorate

The Review of Criminal Justice in Northern Ireland, in 2000, recommended that an independent statutory criminal justice inspectorate should be established with the responsibility of ensuring the inspection of all aspects of the criminal justice system in Northern Ireland other than the courts.[270] This was implemented by the Justice (NI) Act 2002, which provides for the creation of a Chief Inspector of Criminal Justice in Northern Ireland.[271] Mr Kit Chivers was appointed as the first Chief Inspector of Criminal Justice in August 2003.

The 2002 Act imposes a duty on the Chief Inspector to carry out inspections of the following organisations:[272] the Police Service of Northern Ireland, Forensic Science Northern Ireland, the State Pathologist's Department, the Public Prosecution Service for Northern Ireland, the Probation Board for Northern Ireland, the Northern Ireland Prison Service, the Youth Justice Agency, Health and Social Services Boards and Trusts[273] and the Compensation Agency. However, in recognition that some existing bodies, such as HM's Inspectorate of Constabulary (see 4.5 above), already carry out some inspections of these organisations, the Act goes on to say that the Chief Inspector must not carry out inspections if he or she is satisfied that the

---

[267] *R v Latimer* [2004] NIJB 142; the defendant was one of the so-called "UDR Four".
[268] Mahmood Mattan (hanged in 1952) and Derek Bentley (hanged in 1953).
[269] *In re Magee's Application* [2004] NIQB 57, which followed the quashing of the applicant's conviction: *R v Magee* [2001] 4 BNIL 15.
[270] Recommendation 263.
[271] S. 45 and Sch. 8. See www.cjsni.gov.uk/index.cfm.
[272] S. 46(1). This list has since been added to in minor ways.
[273] Only in so far as these Boards and Trusts provide secure accommodation for children the subject of custody care orders.

242 The Legal System of Northern Ireland

organisation is subject to adequate inspection by someone else.[274] It adds, indeed,[275] that before an inspection of the PSNI can take place the Chief Inspector must notify HM's Inspectorate of Constabulary which can, if it wishes, insist on being delegated the task of conducting the inspection. Even if HM's Inspectorate does not so insist, the Chief Inspector of Criminal Justice must still obtain the approval of the Secretary of State for the inspection

The Chief Inspector must consult with the Secretary of State and the Attorney General for Northern Ireland when preparing an inspection programme[276] and can also be required by the former to carry out an inspection or to review any matter relating to the criminal justice system in Northern Ireland.[277] But the Chief Inspector may not carry out inspections or reviews of individual cases.[278] Inspectors carrying the inspections can enter any premises at any reasonable hour and require documents to be produced for copying.[279] All inspections and reviews conducted must be reported to the Secretary of State, laid before Parliament and published, although the Secretary of State can exclude a part of the report from the copy laid or published if in his or her opinion this is in the public interest or is necessary to prevent jeopardising any person's safety.[280]

The Chief Inspector must also prepare an annual report for the Secretary of State, who again has to lay it before Parliament and arrange for it to be published.[281] The Inspectorate also now produces a periodic newsletter entitled *The Spec*.

HM's Inspectorate of Prisons[282]

For many years the London-based Inspectorate of Prisons has carried out inspections of prisons in Northern Ireland even though it has no express statutory power to do so. In recent times, especially under the leadership of the current Chief Inspector, Ms Anne Owers, these reports have been very detailed and have focused on whether the

---

[274] S. 46(2).
[275] In Sch. 8, para. 8.
[276] S. 47(1).
[277] S. 47(3) and (4).
[278] S. 47(6).
[279] S. 48(1) and (2). It is an offence to fail to comply.
[280] S. 49.
[281] Sch. 8, para.4.
[282] www.homeoffice.gov.uk/justice/prisons/insprisons.

prisons are safe and healthy environments for prisoners and staff alike. The conditions in the prisons are measured against "Expectations", which are based largely on international human rights standards in this field. The inspectorate's reports, which are available on its website, invariably make recommendations for improvements in the running of the prisons which the Prison Service has to consider and respond to. Now that there is Criminal Justice Inspectorate in Northern Ireland it is envisaged that future inspections of prisons in Northern Ireland will to some extent be jointly conducted.

HM Inspectorate of Probation[283]

In England and Wales this body reports to the Home Secretary on the work of the National Probation Service and of Youth Offending Teams, but it does not operate in Northern Ireland. The Criminal Justice Inspectorate (see above) now fills the gap in Northern Ireland.

The Justice Oversight Commissioner[284]

This non-statutory office was established in response to criticisms that without it there would be no means of ensuring that implementation of the Criminal Justice Review's recommendations would be thorough and swift. The person appointed, Lord Clyde, is a former Law Lord. His terms of reference require him to report on a six-monthly basis on progress achieved in implementing the Review and he has already produced three such reports. The latest, released in July 2005, records that "the overall picture is one of a major advance over the past six months". Reform of the prosecution service and of the youth justice system is continuing to be monitored.

The latest report also confirms that a number of the recommendations still await the devolution of criminal justice to Northern Ireland. In an appendix to his reports Lord Clyde sets out the current status of each of the 294 recommendations made by the Criminal Justice Review, indicating whether implementation has been begun, completed, verified and evaluated. By June 2005 implementation of 112 of the recommendations had been completed, verified and evaluated, but implementation of 31 others had not yet begun.

---

[283] www.homeoffice.gov.uk/justice/probation/inspprob.
[284] www.justiceoversight.com.

Prison Boards of Visitors

Each prison in Northern Ireland has a Board of Visitors, soon to be renamed an Independent Monitoring Board, which is appointed by the Secretary of State. The Board has to meet at least once a month, sending copies of its minutes to the Secretary of State, and the prison must be visited by one member of the Board at least once a fortnight. The Board's function is to satisfy itself on behalf of the general public as to the state of the prison premises, the administration of the prison and the treatment of the prisoners. Every Visitor has free access at all times to all parts of the prison. He or she can hear any complaint or request which a prisoner may wish to make, if necessary out of the sight and hearing of prison officers. The Boards draw the attention of the prison governors to particular matters as well as publishing annual reports (which are available on the Prison Service's website). For the Young Offenders' Centre there is a corresponding Visiting Committee.

The Prisoner Ombudsman[285]

In February 2005 Mr Brian Coulter was appointed as the first (non-statutory) Prisoner Ombudsman for Northern Ireland. His role is to consider any eligible complaint referred by a prisoner, or by a former prisoner (if no more than 21 days have elapsed since his or her release), regarding his or her treatment in prison. For the complaint to be eligible it must first have gone through the Prison Service's own three-stage complaints system and it cannot relate to a decision made by a Minister, a judge, the police or the Prosecution Service; nor can it relate to any ongoing criminal or civil court proceedings. The Ombudsman can, if he considers it fitting, make recommendations based on the complaint to the Secretary of State or to the Director General of the Prison Service, and the latter must respond within 21 days. An annual report has to be submitted to the Secretary of State.

In England and Wales there is a non-statutory Prisons and Probation Ombudsman (currently Mr Stephen Shaw).[286] Unlike his Northern Ireland counterpart, Mr Shaw can investigate deaths of prisoners and complaints made by residents of probation hostels and immigration detention centres. The Government is proposing to elevate this office into a statutory one in the near future.

---

[285] www.niprisonerombudsman.gov.uk.
[286] www.ppo.gov.uk.

CHAPTER FIVE

CRIMINAL PROCEEDINGS

5.1 SUMMONSES AND ARRESTS

Criminal proceedings are begun in one of three ways: (i) by the issue of a summons, (ii) by the issue of a warrant of arrest, or (iii) by an arrest without a warrant. A sizeable proportion of persons appearing in court do so after having been originally arrested but then released and later summonsed. Being summonsed and being arrested are, however, quite distinct processes.

Summonses

If the police (or anyone else for that matter) believe that a person is guilty of a summary offence, or a not very serious indictable offence, they can give the details in a "complaint" to a lay magistrate or to a clerk of petty sessions. If the lay magistrate or clerk of petty sessions is satisfied that there is sufficient evidence to suspect the person of having committed the offence, he or she will issue a summons giving details of the alleged offence and ordering that person to appear at a magistrates' court on a particular date to answer the complaint.[1] If the offence allegedly committed is a summary one, a summons should not be issued more than six months after the date of its commission;[2] if the offence is indictable, a summons can be issued at any time.

In previous years the summons was usually served by the police on the "defendant" (as the person being summonsed is called) a reasonable time before the case is to be heard in court. The Magistrates' Courts Rules (NI) 1984 have, however, been amended to allow for service of a summons by ordinary post.[3] The summons will tell the defendant the nature of the complaint being made against him or her, but will not set out the evidence on which the police intend to rely. The defendant may have to prepare a defence statement before appearing in court, although of course he or she may consult a solicitor and obtain legal representation, and the cost of advice or representation may be allowed to the defendant under the legal aid schemes described in Chapter 3.3.

---

[1] Magistrates' Courts (NI) Order 1981, art. 20.
[2] *Ibid.* art. 19.
[3] Rr. 11(3A), 12(A), 13 and 13(A).

Arrests

In more serious cases, or where a magistrate is satisfied that a person suspected of a summary offence cannot for some reason be served with a summons, the police may arrest a person, that is, take him or her into custody.[4] Arrests can lawfully be made in two different ways: (i) with a warrant or (ii) without a warrant. The latter are sometimes called summary arrests.

Arrests with a warrant

Like a summons, a warrant of arrest can be issued by a lay magistrate (but not a clerk of petty sessions) provided that he or she is satisfied that there is reasonable evidence to suspect a named person of a serious offence. The complaint to the lay magistrate must, however, be in writing and substantiated on oath.[5] The warrant is an order by the lay magistrate to the police to arrest the person named in the warrant and to take him or her before a court to answer the charges which may be brought. The details on the warrant must be completely accurate; if it gives the wrong home address for the person being arrested, for example, it may be invalidated.[6]

A magistrate or judge has power to issue a warrant when a person who has been summonsed does not appear in court when ordered to do so.[7] Such a warrant is known as a "bench warrant". Also, if a warrant is issued in one part of the United Kingdom (*e.g.* Northern Ireland) but is to be executed in another part (*e.g.* England), it is valid only if "backed" (*i.e.* endorsed) by a magistrate in the jurisdiction where it is to be executed.[8] A similar rule applies when a warrant is issued for the extradition of a suspect from the Republic of Ireland to any part of the United Kingdom.[9] In such cases judges usually take great care to ensure that the letter of the law is meticulously complied with before ordering a person's further detention.

---

4 Magistrates' Courts (NI) Order 1981, art. 20(5).
5 *Ibid.* art. 20(7).
6 *R* v *Leighton* [2002] NICC 10.
7 *Ibid.* art. 25(1).
8 Petty Sessions (Ir.) Act 1851, ss. 27-8.
9 Magistrates' Courts (Backing of Warrants from Republic of Ireland) Rules (NI) 1965.

Arrests without a warrant

The law on summary arrests is contained in the Police and Criminal Evidence (NI) Order 1989 (the PACE Order) which brought the law in Northern Ireland largely into line with that in England and Wales as set out in the Police and Criminal Evidence Act 1984. In both legal systems there are special arrest powers to deal with terrorist offences[10] and in some respects these are more extensive in Northern Ireland than in Great Britain; these special powers are outlined in Chapter 4.3. It should be noted that a warrant issued in England, Wales or Scotland for the arrest of a person charged with an offence may be "executed" (*i.e.* the person mentioned in the warrant may be arrested) by any member of the police in Northern Ireland.[11]

By article 26 of the PACE Order a police officer may arrest without a warrant in the following circumstances:

(1)   where a person is in the act of committing or is about to commit what is called an "arrestable offence";

(2)   where the officer has reasonable grounds for suspecting a person to be in the act of committing or to be about to commit an arrestable offence;

(3)   where, provided that the officer has reasonable grounds for suspecting that an arrestable offence has been committed, the officer has reasonable grounds for suspecting a person to be guilty of that offence; or

(4)   where a person is guilty of having committed an arrestable offence which has actually been committed or is someone whom the officer has reasonable grounds for suspecting to be guilty of that offence.

The concept of "arrestable offence" is defined in the same article as meaning:

(a)   any offence for which the sentence is fixed by law (*e.g.* life imprisonment for murder);

(b)   any offence for which a person aged 21 or over may be sentenced to five years' imprisonment (this would embrace all crimes of theft, including shoplifting, as well

---

[10]   Under the Terrorism Act 2000 (see Chap. 4.3).
[11]   Criminal Justice and Public Order Act 1994, s. 136.

as cases of criminal damage where the value of the property destroyed or damage caused is more than £2,000);

(c)   the specific statutory offences listed in article 26(2) of the PACE Order (these include taking a motor vehicle without authority and going equipped for stealing).

There are two other categories of offence for which a person can be arrested without a warrant but which are not, strictly speaking, arrestable offences within the definition of article 26. One of these categories comprises the offence of breach of the peace: an arrest can occur here if harm is likely to be done to any person or to his or her property in his or her presence. The other category comprises the statutory offences listed in Schedule 2 to the PACE Order as amended, which include breaking a personal protection order (see Chap.6. 2), illegal immigration, impersonation at a polling booth, provocative conduct in a public place, at a public meeting or at a procession, driving with excess alcohol and loitering or importuning by a prostitute. The statutory offences often require particular conditions to be satisfied before the power of summary arrest can legitimately be exercised. A police officer may also arrest without a warrant for a non-arrestable offence if it appears to him or her that service of a summons is impracticable or inappropriate because, for instance, the name of the person to be arrested cannot be readily ascertained by the officer.[12] In 2004-05 the police made 27,748 arrests under the PACE Order (2% more than the previous year); 87% of these were males.

As far as the powers of private citizens to make arrests are concerned, article 26 makes it clear that they are in two respects more limited than those of the police: (i) only if an arrestable offence has *in fact* been committed can a person arrest someone who is reasonably suspected of being guilty of the offence, and (ii) a person has no power to arrest someone who is reasonably suspected of being *about to* commit an arrestable offence.

Persons who are arrested have five important rights. In the first place, they must be told at the time of their arrest why they are being arrested;[13] secondly, after their arrest they must be allowed access to a solicitor (although in certain circumstances access can be delayed for as

---

[12] Police and Criminal Evidence (NI) Order 1989 (PACE Order), art. 27.
[13] *Ibid.* art. 30(3).

long as 36 hours[14]); thirdly, they can require a friend or relative to be informed of their arrest;[15] fourthly, they must be released from custody as soon as it becomes apparent to the police that grounds for detaining them no longer exist;[16] finally, they have the right to consult any of the statutory codes of practice.[17]

If it appears to the police that it may be necessary to keep an arrested person in police detention for more than six hours, he or she must be taken to one of 22 "designated" police stations[18] in Northern Ireland, where "custody officers" will be responsible for their welfare. Detention without charge is permissible for 24 hours but this can be extended to 36 hours if the authority of a police superintendent is obtained and if the offence in question is a "serious" one.[19] The PACE Order defines "serious" in terms of the loss or harm caused by the offence and lists some offences as always being in this category (*e.g.* rape or kidnapping). In the year 2004-05, only eight people were detained for longer than 24 hours but then released without charge.[20] Detention beyond 36 hours is permissible only on the authority of a magistrates' court;[21] it can be extended by that court up to 72 hours, and then again to 96 hours,[22] but that is the absolute maximum. In 2004-05, there were 28 applications to magistrates' courts for these extensions of detention, 25 of which were granted; 18 people were later charged with an offence as a result.[23]

---

[14] *Ibid.* art. 59. In 2004-05 there were 4 cases where a delay was authorised by a police superintendent: *Chief Constable's Annual Report 2004-05.* See further J. Jackson, "The Rights of Detainees", Chap. 4 in B. Dickson and M. O'Brien (eds.) *Civil Liberties in Northern Ireland: The CAJ Handbook* (4th ed, 2003). The House of Lords has ruled that compensation is not payable if the police wrongly deny access to a solicitor: *Cullen v Chief Constable of the RUC* [2003] 1 WLR 1763.

[15] *Ibid.* art. 57. The exercise of this right can also be delayed on the authority of a police superintendent; this occurred 12 times in 2004-05: *Chief Constable's Annual Report 2004-05.*

[16] *Ibid.* art. 35(2).

[17] PACE Code C, para. 3.1.

[18] See also the section about custody visitors in Chap. 4.5.

[19] PACE Order, arts. 42-3.

[20] *Chief Constable's Annual Report 2004-05.*

[21] PACE Order, art. 44.

[22] *Ibid.* art. 45.

[23] *Chief Constable's Annual Report 2004-05.*

Arrest and questioning

We cannot here go into all the complexities of the law on arrest and questioning, but the following points should be noted. In several respects the provisions of the anti-terrorist laws are different (see Chap. 4.3). Also of general note is the Code of Practice issued under the authority of section 23(1) of the Criminal Procedure and Investigations Act 1996. This applies to all criminal investigations (*i.e.* including investigations prior to arrest[24]) and covers such matters as the recording of information, the retention of material obtained during the course of investigations and the preparation by the disclosure officer (see 5.3 below) of material for the prosecutor.

Attendance at a police station

No person is under a legal obligation to accompany a police officer to a police station unless that person has been formally arrested (with or without a warrant). People who are simply "helping the police with their inquiries" are present at the police station of their own free will and must be allowed to leave the station if they want to.[25]

Use of force

The police may use reasonable force to effect an arrest.[26] The use of excessive force will make the arrest unlawful and, although not necessarily requiring the arrested person's immediate release, will justify a claim for compensation for assault.

Citizens' powers

Although ordinary citizens can arrest people under certain circumstances (see above), they can detain people only if a breach of the peace would otherwise be likely. The arrested person should be taken to a police station as soon as possible, otherwise the arresting citizen may be committing the civil wrong of "false imprisonment" and could be sued for compensation.

---

[24] "Criminal Investigation" is defined in para. 2.1 of the Code.
[25] PACE Order, art. 31.
[26] *Ibid.* art. 88.

Right to silence

The general rule is that no-one is legally obliged to volunteer information or to answer questions put by the police (or army). But by virtue of the Criminal Evidence (NI) Order 1988 this right to silence has been qualified in that prosecutors, judges and juries are permitted to draw inferences about guilt from an accused's silence in the face of questioning. Furthermore, the abolition of the "corroboration rules"[27] (whereby judges were required to warn juries about the dangers of "uncorroborated" - *i.e.* unsupported - evidence) means that the prosecution, while still having to prove the accused's guilt beyond reasonable doubt, may now place greater reliance upon such adverse inferences (see 5.3 below).[28] As a result of the Criminal Evidence (NI) Order 1999, however, inferences cannot be drawn if the accused has not had the opportunity to be advised by a solicitor.[29] This reform implemented a recommendation made in a research report prepared for the Northern Ireland Office in October 2000.[30] The research found that drawing inferences from silence is much more frequently an issue in Diplock trials than in other Crown Court trials but that in both contexts the issue was raised less frequently in the years after 1990. Judges in Diplock trials had not, it seems, been drawing inferences mechanically in every case where the issue had arisen: inferences were drawn in about one-third of the cases where the issue was raised. The researchers concluded that there was little evidence to show that the 1988 Order had had the effect of convicting people who would otherwise have been acquitted.

It should be noted that, under article 175 of the Road Traffic (NI) Order 1981, there is a duty to report certain accidents and under section 89 of the Terrorism Act 2000 there is a duty to answer certain police or army questions (see Chap. 4.3). It is also a criminal offence under section 5(1) of the Criminal Law Act (NI) 1967 (as amended) to fail to give

---

[27] By the Criminal Justice (NI) Order 1996, art. 45.

[28] See *Annual Reports of the Independent Commissioner for the Holding Centres for 1997 and 1998*, pp. 29 and 19 respectively; J. Jackson, "The Rights of Detainees", Chap. 4 in B. Dickson and M. O'Brien (eds.), *Civil Liberties in Northern Ireland: The CAJ Handbook* (4th ed., 2003), pp. 72-74.

[29] The equivalent provision in English law is the Youth Justice and Criminal Evidence Act 1999, s. 58.

[30] J. Jackson, M. Wolfe and K. Quinn, *Legislating Against Silence: The Northern Ireland Experience*.

information about an arrestable offence committed by some other person, although prosecutions for this seem to be extremely rare.

Police cautions

Until December 1988 the questioning of persons by the police in Northern Ireland was regulated by the so-called Judges' Rules, which dated from 1976. As mentioned in Chapter 2.2, these did not have the full force of law, but they were meant to be adhered to in practice. Answers to questions asked in contravention of the Rules were still admissible as evidence in a court, subject to the judge's discretion to exclude them. As a consequence of the making of the Criminal Evidence (NI) Order 1988, which altered the law on a suspect's right to silence, the judges rescinded the 1976 Rules and they were replaced by written guidance issued by the Secretary of State for Northern Ireland to the RUC's Chief Constable. This guidance has itself since been amended,[31] and requires the police to caution a person being questioned in the following terms:

> "You do not have to say anything, but I must caution you that if you do not mention when questioned something which you later rely on in court, it may harm your defence. If you do say anything it may be given in evidence."

Under the PACE Order, a Code of Practice has been issued dealing with the detention, treatment and questioning of persons by police officers,[32] and a similar Code exists concerning questioning under the emergency laws.[33] These Codes require the new caution to be given to all persons who are arrested. However, under article 66 of the PACE Order, a breach of the PACE Codes will not of itself render the officer liable to criminal or civil proceedings, although, of course, if a complaint is lodged, it may render a police constable liable to disciplinary proceedings (see Chap. 4.5). Furthermore, evidence obtained as a result of a breach will *not* automatically be declared

---

[31] Code C of the revised *Police and Criminal Evidence (NI) Order 1989 (Articles 60 and 65) Codes of Practice* (1996), para. 10.5.

[32] Code C of the revised *Police and Criminal Evidence (NI) Order 1989 (Articles 60 and 65) Codes of Practice* (1996) - "The detention, treatment and questioning of persons by police officers".

[33] Code I of the *Prevention of Terrorism (Temporary Provisions) Act 1989, Codes of Practice* - "The detention, treatment, and questioning of persons".

inadmissible as evidence in court proceedings later brought against the victim of the breach.[34]

Recording of interviews

Tape-recording is intended to help eliminate disputes over whether a detained person was physically or verbally abused while being questioned, as well as over the precise content of statements made by the detainee. As required by the PACE Order, the Secretary of State has issued a Code of Practice governing the tape-recording of interviews. It details the requisite procedure for the changing of tapes or taking a break during an interview etc.[35] Interviews with PACE detainees are not, however, video-recorded, unlike interviews with persons arrested under the anti-terrorist laws (see Chap. 4.3).

Fingerprinting

Under article 61 of the PACE Order, as amended by the Criminal Justice (NI) Order 2004, fingerprints can be taken without the consent of the detained person if he or she has been arrested and if a police officer of at least the rank of superintendent gives written authorisation for them to be taken. Article 64(3) requires that if the detained person ceases to be a suspect, or if a decision is taken not to prosecute him or her, or if he or she is cleared of the offence, the fingerprints must be destroyed as soon as practicable. However, if someone from whom a sample was taken has been convicted for the offence, the samples need not be destroyed so long as they are not used in evidence against, or for the purposes of any investigation of, a person entitled to their destruction under article 64(3).[36]

Where a person has been arrested on suspicion of being involved in a recordable offence, or has been charged with such an offence, or has been informed that he will be reported for such an offence, the police may conduct a "speculative search" by checking their fingerprints against any other fingerprints contained in police records.[37] The same

---

[34] See, *e.g.*, *R v Cross* [1997] 5 BNIL 18.

[35] Code E of the revised *Police and Criminal Evidence (NI) Order 1989 (Articles 60 and 65) Codes of Practice*, 1996 - "The tape recording of interviews by police officers at police stations with suspected persons".

[36] PACE Order, art. 64(3A), as inserted by the Police (Amendment) (NI) Order 1995, art. 13.

[37] PACE Order, art. 63A, as inserted by the Police (Amendment) (NI) Order 1995, art. 12, and amended by the Criminal Procedure and Investigations Act 1996, s. 64.

applies to any other sample or information derived from samples taken under any power conferred by Part VI of the PACE Order.

Searches of detained persons

The PACE Order regulates in detail the searching of detained persons and distinguishes between intimate and non-intimate body searches. Intimate searches are physical examinations of body orifices (except the mouth[38]). They can be carried out without consent only if there are grounds for believing that the person may have a concealed weapon or drug. Only a handful of such searches are conducted each year in Northern Ireland (there were none at all in 2004-05).

Taking samples

The PACE Order, as amended by article 8 of the Police (Amendment) (NI) Order 1995 and by the Criminal Justice (NI) Order 2004, also distinguishes between the taking of intimate and non-intimate body samples. The former can be taken only with the person's consent; they include blood and urine samples and dental impressions. In 2004-05 there were no such samples taken.[39] Non-intimate samples, such as hairs from the head, saliva or footprints, do not require the person's consent. Article 10 of the 1995 Order also makes provision for the police to take an intimate sample (with consent) from a person who is *not* in police detention but from whom, in the course of an investigation, two or more non-intimate samples suitable for the same means of analysis have been taken but have proved insufficient. A non-intimate sample may likewise be taken from a person not in police detention *without* his or her consent if the person has been convicted of, charged with, or informed that he or she will be reported for a recordable offence.[40] Special rules apply to persons suspected of road traffic offences.[41]

Confessions as evidence

If a person makes a statement confessing to a crime, this is admissible as evidence in a court only if, when challenged to do so, the prosecution proves beyond reasonable doubt that the confession was

---

[38] Police (Amendment) (NI) Order 1995, art. 5.
[39] *Chief Constable's Annual Report 2004-05.*
[40] PACE Order, art. 63(3A) as inserted by the Police (Amendment) (NI) Order 1995, art. 11(2).
[41] PACE Order, art. 62(11), as amended.

not obtained by oppression or in consequence of anything said or done which was likely to render it unreliable.[42] But even if a confession is declared inadmissible under this rule, any facts discovered as a result of the confession *can* be admitted in evidence (contrary to what is termed "the fruit of the poisoned tree" principle, which is commonly applied in the United States). Generally, though, a court should exclude a confession if there is a reasonable doubt that the defendant would not have made it if he or she had been cautioned in accordance with the PACE Code.[43] Judges also have a discretion to refuse to consider any prosecution evidence which they feel "would have such an adverse effect on the fairness of the proceedings that the court ought not to admit it".[44]

Suing the police

A person who has been arrested unlawfully, or unlawfully treated while in detention, can bring a civil action for compensation against the police (see Chap. 6.4 and 6.6). The police will be guilty of the civil wrongs (known as "torts") of false imprisonment and/or assault. The Court of Appeal of Northern Ireland has stated that the starting point for compensation in a straightforward case of false imprisonment is about £600 for the first hour of deprivation of liberty, while a period of 24 hours would normally attract an award of some £4,000 to £5,000.[45] But the wrongful police behaviour is not of itself a defence to a criminal charge brought against the victim of that behaviour: the person arrested can still be found guilty of an offence.

5.2 BAIL AND REMAND

Usually a person arrested with a warrant is held in custody pending a first appearance in court, but when issuing the warrant the lay magistrate may authorise the police to release the accused on bail once he or she has been arrested.[46] This means releasing the accused in exchange for a promise to return to the police station, or to attend at a

[42] *Ibid.* art. 74.
[43] *R v McKeown* [2000] NIJB 139; *R v Caraher and McGinn* [2001] 4 BNIL 42.
[44] PACE Order, art. 76. For a case where the judge refused to exercise this discretion even though the confession was made to a journalist who swore to keep it secret, see *R v McKeown* [2003] NICC 3 (not the same case as in the previous note).
[45] *Dodds v Chief Constable of the RUC* [1998] NI 393.
[46] Magistrates' Courts (NI) Order 1981, art. 129, as amended by the PACE Order, art. 48(12).

magistrates' court, on a certain day. This promise, or the money which may have to be forfeited if the promise is broken, is called a "recognisance".[47] Under the Criminal Justice (NI) Order 2004, police officers can now grant bail to persons following their arrest without the need to take them first to a police station (this is known as "street bail").

Persons arrested with or without a warrant may also be released on what is called police bail. The custody officer at the station to which the arrested person is brought must release any person who has been charged (see 5.3 below) - either on bail or without bail - unless, where the person is an adult, one of four conditions is met: (i) his or her name or address cannot be ascertained; (ii) in the case of a person arrested for an imprisonable offence, there are reasonable grounds for believing that detention of the person is necessary to prevent him or her from committing an offence; (iii) there are reasonable grounds for believing that continued detention is necessary for the detainee's own protection or to prevent him or her from causing injury or damage to any person or property; or (iv) there are reasonable grounds for believing that the detainee will fail to appear in court or to answer bail, or will interfere with the administration of justice or with the investigation of any offence.[48] Where a juvenile is concerned, continued detention can be justified under (i) above or if the custody officer has reasonable grounds for believing that the juvenile ought to be detained in his or her own interests. Where the custody officer releases the person on bail, he or she may require the person to enter into a recognisance.[49]

In summary proceedings, when a person who has been charged eventually appears in a magistrates' court, the prosecution or the defence may still not have fully prepared its case and the resident magistrate will then be asked to "adjourn" (*i.e.* postpone) the hearing. In such circumstances the RM also has to decide whether to release or to "remand" the accused, and, if the latter, whether to remand him or her in custody or on bail. In practice the views of the police are highly influential on these points. The factors which are meant to be taken into account include the character of the accused, the nature of the alleged

---

[47] See the Magistrates' Courts (NI) Order 1981, arts. 135-9, and the Magistrates' Court Rules (NI) 1984, rr. 150-3. Also, M. Allen and F. McAleenan, *Sentencing Law and Practice in Northern Ireland* (3rd ed., 1998, with Supplement 2003), pp. 9-14, paras. 1.22-1.46.

[48] PACE Order, art. 39, as amended by the Police (Amendment) (NI) Order 1995, art.6.

[49] PACE Order, art. 48.

offence and the strength of the evidence against the accused. Having considered such factors, the court should grant bail unless it is satisfied that the accused will not turn up again at court, will commit another offence or will try to obstruct the course of justice by, for instance, putting pressure on witnesses.[50] Some research, now a little dated, has shown that approximately one-quarter of defendants convicted in magistrates' courts were actually on bail for other offences when they committed the offence for which they were being sentenced.[51]

Remands in custody

Remands in custody cannot normally be for more than eight clear days, but they can be for 28 days in a case where the accused is already serving a prison sentence or is detained in a young offenders' centre or juvenile justice centre.[52] The period of remand can also be extended for up to 28 days if: (i) the accused has previously been remanded in custody for the same offence and is before the court; (ii) the prosecution and accused have been given an opportunity to make representations; and (iii) the court has set a date for sentencing.[53] Before the end of each period of remand the defendant must again be brought before a court; he or she can then reapply for bail but this will usually be refused unless there has been a significant change of circumstances.

Appeals in bail cases

If bail is refused in a magistrates' court, a further application can be made later, relying upon changed circumstances.[54] It is also possible for the defendant to exercise a common law right to apply to a judge of the High Court for bail, but there will be great reluctance to overturn a magistrate's previous refusal. If the magistrate has awarded bail but at such a sum or on such conditions as to make it impossible for the defendant to accept release on those terms, the defendant can apply to the High Court to have the sum or conditions altered: excessive bail

---

[50] Magistrates' Courts (NI) Order 1981, art. 133.
[51] Research Findings 1/98 - *The Use of Bail and Levels of Offending on Bail in Northern Ireland*, NIO, Statistics and Research Branch (1998).
[52] Magistrates' Court (NI) Order 1981, art. 47(2), as amended by the Criminal Justice (Children) (NI) Order 1998, Sch. 5, para. 19.
[53] Magistrates' Court (NI) Order 1981, art. 47(3), as substituted by the Criminal Justice (NI) Order 1996, art. 35. See further M. Allen and F. McAleenan, note 47 above, pp. 273-279, paras. 6.52-6.70.
[54] See, *e.g.*, *Re Donaldson* [2002] NIQB 68.

was made unlawful by the Bill of Rights 1689. In such circumstances the defendant can also apply for a writ of *habeas corpus*, which can lead to a declaration by the Divisional Court (a court within the High Court's Queen's Bench Division) that the continued detention of the accused is unlawful.[55] *Habeas corpus* may nowadays also be available if a suspect is mistreated while detained. Rather oddly, all applications to the High Court for bail or *habeas corpus* are considered as civil, not criminal, proceedings. They therefore qualify for civil, not criminal, legal aid.

The Justice (NI) Act 2004[56] has for the first time given the prosecution the right to appeal to the High Court against the grant of bail by a magistrates' court. In such instances the prosecution must give oral notice of the appeal at the conclusion of the magistrates' court proceedings and the court must then remand the person in custody until the appeal is determined.[57]

Where the accused is charged with an indictable offence, the Crown Court may admit to bail any person who has been committed for trial or who is in the custody of the Crown Court pending the disposal of his or her case.[58] There can be no appeal by either side against the decision of a Crown Court to grant or not grant bail. A person who has already been convicted can, however, apply for bail to the court which is hearing an appeal in the case.

Time limits

The Criminal Justice (NI) Order 2003 empowers the Secretary of State to set time limits for the prosecution to complete the preliminary stages of criminal proceedings or a maximum period during which an accused person may be held in custody while awaiting completion of those preliminary stages. There is a similar power with specific regard to preliminary proceedings for scheduled offences.[59] As yet, however, neither power has been exercised. The position in other parts of the United Kingdom is different.[60]

---

[55] See Rules of the Supreme Court (NI) 1980, O. 54.
[56] S. 10.
[57] Magistrates' Courts (Amendment No. 3) Rules (NI) 2004.
[58] Judicature (NI) Act 1978, s. 51(4)-(8).
[59] Terrorism Act 2000, s. 72.
[60] In Scotland defendants have to be tried no later than 110 days after being arrested. A whole new set of Criminal Procedure Rules for England and Wales came into force

5.3 CHARGES AND PROSECUTIONS

Being charged

When the police officer in charge of the police station believes that there is enough evidence to show that the suspected person has committed an offence, the officer should either prefer a charge against that person or tell him or her that he or she may later be prosecuted for that offence (*e.g.* by the issue of a summons). At that time the accused should again be cautioned in the following terms:

> "You are charged with the offences(s) shown below. You do not have to say anything, but I must caution you that if you do not mention when questioned something which you later rely on in court, it may harm your defence. If you do say anything it may be given in evidence."[61]

Questions relating to an offence should not be put to a person after he or she has been charged with committing it, unless the questions are necessary to prevent harm to some other person or to clear up an ambiguity in a previous answer, or new information has come to light since the person was charged and it is in the interests of justice that he or she should be given an opportunity to comment upon it.[62] Before such extra questions are put, the accused must once again be told of the "right" to remain silent.

Even a person who has not already been arrested can in this way be charged, or informed that he or she may be prosecuted, although if the police want to detain the arrested person in custody they should formally arrest the person immediately before notifying the charge.

Being formally cautioned

If the police decide not to charge or prosecute a suspect he or she can instead be formally cautioned by a senior police officer and will not then have to appear in court. Such a caution will usually be administered only if the suspect has admitted guilt of an offence and if the police believe that the person's own interests as well as those of society can just as well be served by a formal caution as by forcing an

---

on 4 April 2005; they are designed to produce greater efficiency in the handling of cases, as has been achieved by the Civil Procedure Rules.

[61] Code C of the revised *Police and Criminal Evidence (NI) Order 1989 (Articles 60 and 65) Code of Practice* (1996), para. 16.3A.

[62] *Ibid.* para. 16.6.

appearance in court. Cautioning is especially common in relation to juvenile offenders (see Chap. 7.1). Research has shown that the offence most likely to result in a caution of this kind is shoplifting and that some 20% of juveniles and 14% of adults do in fact "re-offend" after being cautioned.[63] If the police decide not to charge or formally caution the suspect, he or she should be released.

Being prosecuted

Once a person has been charged or summonsed for an offence the process of prosecution has begun. If at any stage it becomes clear that it is not going to be possible to prove the accused's guilt beyond reasonable doubt the charge should be dropped or ordered by a court to be withdrawn.

In Northern Ireland the Police Service currently acts as the prosecuting authority for many minor criminal offences. Indeed about three-quarters of all prosecutions in Northern Ireland are conducted by the police. The police's own officers will do all the paperwork and present the case in court. But the prosecution of major criminal offences and certain types of less serious cases is the responsibility of the Public Prosecution Service (PPS), headed by the Director of Public Prosecutions (DPP). As explained in Chapter 1.5, this is an independent office created in 1972[64] as a further safeguard against unjustified prosecutions and to relieve the then RUC of some of its workload. Its main function is to consider any information brought to its notice with a view to initiating or continuing any criminal proceedings. The Service is in the process of being reorganised and will soon be taking over all of the police's responsibility for prosecuting minor crimes.

At present, when the police have completed their investigations into a less than minor offence, during which time the accused may have been remanded in custody or on bail (see 5.2 above) or may not have been charged at all, they will pass the investigation file to the PPS. It will be considered by a member of that Service under the supervision of an Assistant Director, and a decision will be taken as to the offences, if any, for which the accused should be prosecuted. The PPS can consider information from sources other than the police if it is sent directly to the PPS, and while it cannot carry out more investigations into the case

---

[63] Research Findings 4/98: *Cautioning in Northern Ireland*, NIO, Statistics and Research Branch (1998).
[64] By the Prosecution of Offences (NI) Order 1972.

itself, it can ask the police to do so[65] (as, for instance, it did in a case involving a woman facing prosecution for serious driving offences who claimed that she had been drugged and then raped and had no recollection of hitting another car or of being chased by the police[66]). To help it decide whether to prosecute, the PPS will often seek the opinion of an experienced barrister. The tests to be applied are whether there is more than a 50-50 chance of proving the case beyond reasonable doubt and whether a prosecution would be in the public interest.

If the PPS decides that no prosecution is justified, a direction is issued that no evidence should be offered against the accused and the charges must then be dropped. It is very difficult to succeed in an application for judicial review of a decision not to prosecute (see Chap. 6.7), since such applications examine only the process used in making the decision, not the merits of the decision.[67] Moreover, decisions taken prior to 2 October 2000, when the Human Rights Act 1998 came into force, did not have to comply with all of the requirements of the European Convention on Human Rights, and these cannot be revived now by asking the Director of Public Prosecutions to reconsider its former decision.[68]

If the PPS decides that a prosecution is justified it will direct which charges are to be pressed (usually these will be similar to those which may already have been preferred by the police) and (if a choice is available - see Chap. 4.2) whether the trial is to be summary or on indictment. If a trial on indictment is directed, the committal proceedings (see 5.5 below) will be arranged and conducted on the prosecution's side almost entirely by the PPS. If the accused person is then committed for trial to the Crown Court the committal papers (including all the evidence submitted at the committal proceedings) and the police investigation files are sent by the PPS to Crown Counsel. It is this barrister who will draw up the required form of indictment (see 5.6 below) and act as the chief representative of the prosecution in the trial on indictment. In less serious cases a junior barrister alone will be employed; in more serious cases he or she will be led by senior counsel. The PPS will serve as the prosecuting solicitors in the case.

---

[65] This is not a power which the DPP has in England and Wales.
[66] *Sunday Life*, 8 August 1999, p. 6.
[67] See, *e.g.*, *In re Thompson's Application* [2004] NIQB 62; *In re Boyle's Application* [2004] NIQB 63.
[68] *In re Jordan's Application* [2003] NI 198.

Pre-trial disclosure and plea-bargaining

The Criminal Procedure and Investigations Act 1996 created a new scheme for pre-trial disclosure.[69] During all criminal investigations, a disclosure officer examines material retained by the police and is responsible for revealing material to the prosecutor and disclosing material to the accused at the request of the prosecutor.[70] The prosecutor must disclose to the accused - unless, on an application by the prosecutor, the court orders that it is not in the public interest to do so - any prosecution material which in the prosecutor's opinion might undermine the case for the prosecution.[71] The accused, if charged with an indictable offence, *must* give a defence statement to the court and the prosecutor. In summary proceedings, however, the accused is not required to give a defence statement, but may do so voluntarily. A defence statement is a written statement which sets out in general terms the nature of the accused's defence (including the particulars of any alibi and any information about possible witnesses who may be able to give evidence in support of the alibi), indicates the matters on which the accused takes issue with the prosecution, and explains why. If a defence statement is given, the prosecution is under a further duty to disclose to the accused any material which might reasonably be expected to assist the accused's defence as outlined in that statement. Indeed, the prosecution has a continuing duty to keep under review whether or not there is prosecution material which has not been disclosed and which might undermine the prosecution's case.

In theory there is not meant to be any bargaining between the prosecution and the defence as to the offences, if any, to which the accused should plead guilty. In practice, however, it is acknowledged that such "plea bargaining" does occur (as it does quite openly in the United States), but the rule is maintained that a trial judge must not indicate to the accused, or to a lawyer acting for the accused, the severity of the sentence which he or she intends to impose.[72] That said, a guilty plea will often lead to a sentence discount and article 33 of the

---

[69] Sch. 4 to the Act contains the Northern Ireland amendments. See further J. Sprack, *A Practical Approach to Criminal Procedure* (2004).

[70] *Criminal Procedure and Investigations Act 1996, s. 23(1) Code of Practice*, NIO, p. 2.

[71] Criminal Procedure and Investigations Act 1996, s. 3.

[72] Code of Conduct for the Bar of Northern Ireland, ss. 16.24 and 16.26. See also M. Allen and F. McAleenan, *Sentencing Law and Practice in Northern Ireland* (3rd ed., 1998, with Supplement 2003), pp. 256-58.

Criminal Justice (NI) Order 1996[73] now specifically provides for courts, in discounting sentence, to consider the stage at which a guilty plea is entered and the circumstances in which this is done. If, as a result of taking such matters into account, the court imposes a punishment which is less severe than the punishment which it would otherwise have imposed, it must state openly that it has done so (although it need neither reveal the amount of discount given nor explain the reasons for not giving discount where such a position is adopted[74]).

Private prosecutions

In addition to "public" prosecutions by the police and the PPS, it is theoretically possible to bring a "private" prosecution. Any individual can pursue a private prosecution but legal aid is not available for the process and it is believed that to date only one such case has ever reached the Crown Court in Northern Ireland (where it failed). In Great Britain, however, there have been successful private prosecutions for manslaughter and rape.

The Director of Public Prosecutions has the power to take over or abort a private prosecution if he or she thinks fit to do so at any stage of the proceedings, and any prosecution, whether public or private, can be brought to an end by the Attorney General entering what is called a *nolle prosequi* ("unwilling to proceed"). This has the effect of preventing further consideration of the charge against the accused in that particular trial but it does not operate as a formal acquittal, so in theory the accused could be prosecuted later for the same offence.

It must be remembered, of course, that whoever is called the prosecutor, the actual representations in court will in the vast majority of cases be made by solicitors or barristers engaged by the prosecutor. Many official bodies and private companies employ staff to detect and investigate offences; when they think that they have sufficient evidence against a suspect they pass the case to the police or the PPS. This happens, for instance, in cases of shoplifting, where large stores employ detectives but suspected culprits are dealt with by the police. Other common examples are the so-called "departmental" prosecutions, although in England many of these are prosecuted entirely by

---

[73] This mirrors s. 48 of the Criminal Justice and Public Order Act 1994 in England and Wales.
[74] See M. Allen and F. McAleenan, note 72 above, pp. 317-20.

employees of the government departments concerned. Examples commonly occurring in Northern Ireland are prosecutions instigated by the Social Security Agency (for non-payment of national insurance contributions or making false claims for social security benefits – there were 340 of the latter in 2002-03), the Driver and Vehicle Licensing Agency (5,099 proceedings instituted in 2002-03, leading to 1,697 convictions), the National TV Licence Records Office (5,984 cases in Northern Ireland in 2002-03), the Rate Collection Agency (36,923 court processes issued in 2002-03) and Translink (157 prosecutions in 2002-03 for failure to show a ticket).[75] It can be just as difficult to challenge the decision of one of these bodies not to prosecute someone as it can be to challenge such a decision by the Director of Public Prosecutions.[76]

5.4 SUMMARY TRIALS IN A MAGISTRATES' COURT

Usually the official name for a magistrates' court is a court of petty sessions, that is, a court of summary jurisdiction which sits at regular specified times and is presided over by a resident magistrate (see Chap. 1.5). But a magistrates' court may also be constituted by a resident magistrate (RM) or lay magistrate sitting "out of petty sessions". Magistrates' courts deal with criminal cases in two different ways: (i) they try persons accused of summary offences or indictable offences being dealt with summarily (see Chap. 4.2), and (ii) they undertake an initial examination of the case against persons accused of offences being tried on indictment. This latter sort of hearing is called "committal proceedings" because its object is to decide whether the defendant should be "committed" (*i.e.* sent) for trial on indictment in the Crown Court. It is discussed in the next section. In the present section we concentrate on summary trials.[77]

The vast majority (around 98%) of all criminal offences dealt with in Northern Ireland (as in England and Wales) are tried summarily in magistrates' courts. More than half of all the charges tried summarily are motoring offences. Even where the defendant has a choice between

---

[75] All figures from the *Digest of Information on the Northern Ireland Criminal Justice System* (4th ed., 2004), p. 53.

[76] See, *e.g.*, *In re D's Application* [2003] NICA 14 (where a man failed to get the Department for Regional Development to prosecute a Loyal Orange Lodge for allegedly erecting an Orange arch unlawfully).

[77] See further B. Valentine and A. Hart, *Criminal Procedure in Northern Ireland* (1989), pp. 167-181, paras. 16.00-16.42.

summary trial and trial on indictment (see Chap. 4.2), approximately three out of every four cases are dealt with summarily, and indictable offences triable summarily usually account for about 10% of all charges dealt with by the magistrates' courts. Summary trial is quicker, less expensive and subject to less publicity - advantages which usually outweigh the fact that in a summary trial there is no jury. Furthermore, if the defendant pleads guilty or is convicted, the sentence which the RM can impose is likely to be much less severe than the sentence which could be imposed by a judge in the Crown Court. If the case is one which is being tried summarily but which might have been tried on indictment, the RM can send the accused to the Crown Court for sentencing if he or she does not think that a magistrate's powers are sufficient in this regard, but this is a very rare occurrence.

Pleading

A criminal trial in a magistrates' court begins with the clerk of the court (the clerk of petty sessions) explaining to the defendant (if he or she is present) the details of the offence for which he or she has been summonsed or charged. If the offence is one for which the defendant can choose to be tried by a jury in the Crown Court, the defendant must be there in person to indicate his or her choice to the magistrate. Similarly, if the case is one which the prosecution can claim to have tried by jury this claim must be made immediately. If the summary trial is to go ahead, the clerk of petty sessions will then ask whether the defendant wishes to plead guilty or not guilty.[78]

If the defendant has been summonsed for an offence which must be tried summarily - but in no other situation - a plea of guilty can be entered by post.[79] The defendant can then be tried without having to appear in court, and unless a custodial sentence is to be imposed he or she can even be sentenced while absent. A plea of not guilty cannot, technically, be accepted through the post, but if no plea of guilty is received it will be assumed that the accused is not admitting the offence. If the accused does not turn up in court on the day in question, a warrant can be issued for his or her arrest or there can be a trial in the defendant's absence.

[78] Magistrates' Courts (NI) Order 1981, art. 22.
[79] *Ibid.* art. 24.

Procedure in a summary trial

If the defendant chooses to plead guilty, the prosecutor will outline the facts of the case to the resident magistrate and hand over a list of the defendant's previous convictions, if any. After listening to defence arguments for leniency - "a plea in mitigation" - the magistrate will pronounce sentence.[80]

If the defendant chooses to plead not guilty, the prosecutor will outline the facts and then call witnesses to give their evidence. If the defendant's legal representative is not available at the time of the hearing, it may be appropriate for the magistrate to adjourn the proceedings until he or she becomes available.[81] The Court Service has produced a leaflet containing useful information for those who are called as witnesses in a criminal court.[82] In limited circumstances evidence of the defendant's bad character can be presented,[83] but generally speaking any previous criminal record of the defendant cannot be revealed unless and until he or she has been found guilty of the latest offence - it then becomes relevant to the sentencing process. Where the court considers that the evidence of a child is likely to involve matter of an indecent or immoral nature, it should direct that the court be cleared during the taking of that evidence.[84]

Reforms to the way evidence from vulnerable or intimidated witnesses can be heard were introduced in England and Wales by the Youth Justice and Criminal Evidence Act 1999 and in Northern Ireland by the Criminal Evidence (NI) Order 1999.[85] These provide that a witness in criminal proceedings who is under the age of 17 at the time of the hearing will be eligible for assistance, which may include the screening of the witness from the accused, giving evidence by live link or in private, the removal of wigs and gowns, video-recorded cross-examination, examination through an intermediary, and aids to communication. Each of these measures is available (where facilities

---

[80] For the order of proceedings in a summary trial, see the Magistrates' Courts Rules (NI) 1984, r. 23.

[81] *In re Doherty's Application* [2001] 10 BNIL 79.

[82] Available on-line.

[83] Criminal Justice (Evidence) (NI) Order 2004.

[84] Art. 21 of the Criminal Justice (Children) (NI) Order 1998. See also 5.6 below and the Children's Evidence (NI) Order 1995, art. 5.

[85] Arts. 4-21.

allow) by means of a "special measures direction",[86] and the court must determine whether a direction would be likely to improve the quality of evidence given by the witness. Moreover, where young witnesses are concerned, the court *must* give a special measures direction allowing any video-recording of an interview of the witness to be admitted as evidence-in-chief, unless to do so would not be likely to maximise the quality of the child's evidence. The court must also allow a child's evidence (other than that already adequately dealt with in the child's recorded testimony) to be given by means of a live link. The court may vary a special measures direction of its own motion if it considers it to be in the interests of justice to do so and, if there has been a material change of circumstances in the case, a party to the proceedings may apply for such a variation to be made.

The defendant or the defendant's lawyer can cross-examine any of the prosecution witnesses. At the end of the prosecution case the defendant can apply for a direction, that is, submit that he or she ought to be acquitted because the prosecution has failed to produce any evidence to establish an essential element of the offence or because the evidence adduced is so weak that no reasonable jury (if one had been involved) would convict the accused. If the RM grants the direction, that is the end of the case and the defendant is free to go. He or she is not, however, formally acquitted, and so may be prosecuted later for the same offence. If the application is rejected, the defence can either rest its case on that point or go on to call its own witnesses including, usually, the defendant.

The defendant used to have the right to make an unsworn statement from the dock, but this was taken away by the Police and Criminal Evidence (NI) Order 1989. By virtue of the Criminal Evidence (NI) Order 1988 an accused person must indicate at the start of his or her defence that he or she intends to give evidence or, if this is not done, the defendant must be told that he or she will be called upon to give evidence for the defence. If the defendant then refuses to testify or without good cause refuses to answer any question, the court or jury may draw such inferences from the refusal as appears proper.

The prosecution can cross-examine all the defence witnesses (including of course the defendant) but if it wants to introduce any new evidence to contradict anything proved or said on behalf of the defence it must

---

[86] Though this part of the Order was "commenced" for committal and Crown Court proceedings only on 1 December 2003 and for county courts only on 1 January 2004.

first ask the magistrate's permission to do so. With the consent of the other side either party to the proceedings can also submit written statements made by any person; if necessary, the maker of the statement can be called to give oral evidence to supplement what is related in the written statement. When all the evidence has been given, the defence may make a final address to the magistrate outlining its arguments.

Criminal proceedings (whether in magistrates' courts, the Crown Court or appeal courts) are "adversarial" in nature. This means that each side is engaged in a battle against the other with the magistrate or judge acting as a neutral umpire. The purpose is not necessarily to arrive at the truth but to win a game. In continental Europe a much more investigative (or "inquisitorial") function is given to the judge. Opinions differ as to which system is the better.

The magistrate's decision and sentencing powers[87]

The Criminal Justice (NI) Order 1996 introduced a new sentencing framework into Northern Ireland.[88] The Order makes it clear that the sentence must be proportionate to the seriousness of the offence. It further details the procedures which a court must observe before imposing certain sentences. The RM may give a decision on the spot or take a few hours or days to make up his or her mind. In 2004 the average time that elapsed between an adult being summonsed for an offence and the magistrates' court issuing its sentence was 21 weeks; for juveniles it was even longer, at 29 weeks.[89]

If the RM decides that the defendant is guilty then the defendant's previous convictions,[90] if any, are considered and a plea in mitigation is submitted by the defence before the RM passes sentence.[91] The defendant may also ask for other offences which he or she admits to

---

[87] See generally *Sentencing Trends in Northern Ireland 1993-1997* (NIO, 2000), especially Chaps. 5 and 7.

[88] See further M. Allen and F. McAleenan, *Sentencing Law and Practice in Northern Ireland* (3rd ed., 1998, with Supplement 2003), pp. 298-301, paras. 6.127-6.135; the Magistrates' Court (Amendment No. 2) Rules (NI) 1997. For useful, if slightly dated, research reports see *Sentencing Trends in Northern Ireland 1993-1997* and *Northern Ireland Sentencing Patterns by Court Division 1993-1997*, NIO's Research and Statistical Series, Report Nos. 2 (2000) and 3 (2001).

[89] *Northern Ireland Judicial Statistics 2004*, Tables E.5 and E.10.

[90] Criminal Justice (NI) Order 1996, art. 37(1). See M. Allen and F. McAleenan, note 88 above, pp. 271-3, paras. 6.46-6.51.

[91] See M. Allen and F. McAleenan, *ibid.* pp. 281-2, paras. 6.76-6.79.

having committed to be "taken into consideration" (TICs).[92] A court, before forming its opinion as to whether an offence is serious enough to merit only a custodial sentence, is now required to obtain and consider a pre-sentence report - unless it considers this to be unnecessary, whereupon its reasons must be openly stated in court.[93] Under the Criminal Justice (No. 2) (NI) Order 2004 a sentence can be increased if the offence in question was aggravated by hostility based on the victim's actual or presumed religion, race, disability or sexual orientation. In such cases the magistrate or judge must again state the reason for the increase in open court.

A magistrates' court (like the Crown Court) may also, under article 3 of the 1996 Order, defer passing sentence (only once, and for a period not longer than six months) to allow the defendant's conduct *after conviction* to be taken into account when determining his or her sentence.[94] The court should follow this procedure only with the offender's consent if it is satisfied that to do so would be in the interests of justice. Whenever the court wishes to sentence an offender whose sentence has been deferred, it can issue a summons requiring the offender to appear before the court or, alternatively, issue a warrant for his or her arrest. A court which defers passing sentence on an offender cannot on the same occasion remand that person.

Generally speaking, the most serious punishment which a magistrate has power to impose is a fine of £5,000 or six months in prison, or both, although if the offence is an indictable one being tried summarily the maximum prison sentence is 12 months, and this may extend to 18 months if consecutive terms of imprisonment are imposed for more than one indictable offence.[95] Article 24 of the 1996 Order introduced the custody probation order - a sentence unique to Northern Ireland, where there is no provision for granting prisoners parole. This new order is available where the court is of the opinion that a convicted person should serve a custodial sentence of 12 months or more, and requires the person to serve a (shorter) custodial sentence and, on release from custody, to be supervised by a probation officer for

---

[92] Criminal Justice Act (NI) 1953, s. 4. See further *ibid.* pp. 279-81, paras. 6.71-6.75.

[93] Criminal Justice (NI) Order 1996, art. 21.

[94] See M. Allen and F. McAleenan, note 88 above, pp. 28-34, paras. 1.91-1.114 and Judge Smyth, "Deferral of Sentence: Principles, Practice and Proposals" (2000) 51 NILQ 48.

[95] Magistrates' Courts (NI) Order 1981, art. 56.

between one and three years as specified in the order.[96] The reduction in custody should not be materially greater or less than the probation period imposed.[97] Prison sentences may also be "suspended" for between one and three years[98] (between one and two years in England[99]), which means that they may be "activated" only if the convicted person commits another imprisonable offence within that period. While, in relative terms, immediate custodial sentences are much less frequently imposed in magistrates' courts (about 5% of all disposals) than they are in the Crown Court (more than 50%), and this reflects the less serious nature of the offences dealt with, the aggregate number of adult offenders receiving an immediate custodial sentence from the magistrates' courts (4,699 in 2004)[100] is always several times higher than the equivalent figure in the Crown Court.

Community sentences

The Criminal Justice (NI) Order 1996 sought to emphasise the value of "community sentences".[101] Probation orders, community service orders, supervision orders and attendance centre orders all fall within this category. Community service orders have become popular with magistrates and about 750 are issued each year.[102] The 1996 Order also introduced a new community sentence called a "combination order".[103] This effectively combines the provisions of a probation order and a community service order and requires the offender to: (i) be under the supervision of a probation officer for a specified period of between one and three years, and (ii) perform between 40 and 100 hours of unpaid work as specified by the court. As with other sentences, the test which the court must use is that of whether the sentence is commensurate with the seriousness of the offence. In 2004 the magistrates' courts issued 1,186 community service orders against adults and 185 against

---

[96] See M. Allen and F. McAleenan, note 88 above, pp. 96-97, paras. 2.59-2.63.
[97] *R v McDonnell* [2000] 4 BNIL 83 (CA).
[98] Treatment of Offenders (NI) Act 1968, s. 18(1).
[99] Powers of Criminal Courts Act 1973, s. 22(1).
[100] *Northern Ireland Judicial Statistics 2004*, Table E.4. There were also 3,879 suspended prison sentences and just 8 custody probation orders.
[101] See *Crime and the Community: A discussion paper on criminal justice policy in Northern Ireland*, HMSO, 1993, p. 50, para. 7.11.
[102] See M. Allen and F. McAleenan, note 88 above, pp. 58-62, paras.1. 201-1.220.
[103] Art. 15.

juveniles, 1,712 probation orders against adults and 523 against juveniles, and 226 combination orders against adults.[104]

In a sense, disqualification from driving is a community sentence because it serves to protect the community against bad drivers. In 2004 there were no fewer than 14,857 disqualifications issued against adults and 301 against juveniles. Moreover 1,041 adults and 17 juveniles were bound over to keep the peace.

Fines

The most common punishment in magistrates' courts is a fine.[105] In 2004 it was imposed in nearly one-half of the cases (50,100 out of 102,576 disposals).[106] Since 1984 there have been five scales for fines, the limits of these being set by secondary legislation from time to time. The current limits are set out in article 3(2) of the Criminal Justice (NI) Order 1994: £200 for Level 1; £500 for Level 2; £1,000 for Level 3; £2,500 for Level 4; and £5,000 for Level 5. The maximum fine which a magistrates' court can impose on a child under the age of 14 is £250; for any other child, the maximum is £1,000.[107] If legislation says that a person can be fined "the prescribed sum" this means £5,000 unless a different amount is specified.[108]

Compensation orders

Magistrates also have the power to make compensation orders against a convicted person.[109] In 2004, this power was exercised in magistrates' courts in respect of 1,920 charges faced by adults and 98 faced by juveniles - roughly 2% of the total number of disposals.[110] These orders - which can be made in addition to or instead of any other sentence - require a person to pay compensation for any personal injury, loss or damage, or to make payments for funeral expenses or bereavement in respect of a death, resulting from any offence for which the court has

---

[104] *Northern Ireland Judicial Statistics 2004*, Tables E.4 and E.9.
[105] M. Allen and F.McAleenan, *Sentencing Law and Practice in Northern Ireland* (3rd ed., 1998, with Supplement 2003), pp. 15-27, paras. 1.48-1.90.
[106] *Northern Ireland Judicial Statistics 2004*, Table E.4.
[107] Criminal Justice (Children) (NI) Order 1998, art. 34.
[108] Fines and Penalties (NI) Order 1984, art. 4(8), as amended by the Criminal Justice (NI) Order 1994, art. 3(1).
[109] Criminal Justice (NI) Order 1994, art. 14. See further M. Allen and F. McAleenan, note 105 above, pp. 134-151, paras. 3.01-3.59 and pp. 151-155, paras. 3.60-3.81 (Restitution Orders).
[110] *Northern Ireland Judicial Statistics 2004*, Tables E.4 and E.9.

convicted that person, or from any other offence which the court took into consideration when sentencing him or her. Losses arising from road traffic accidents are excluded from the scheme, unless the vehicle has been stolen or unless the offender is uninsured and compensation is not payable through the Motor Insurance Bureau Agreement relating to uninsured drivers. The maximum which can be ordered to be paid in respect of any one offence is £5,000, although compensation for bereavement can amount to £7,500.[111] Sums paid are deducted from any award of damages later obtained by the victim of the crime in civil proceedings but are additional to any sum ordered to be paid by way of a fine. The court must also give reasons if it does *not* grant a compensation order whenever it has the power to do so. Property used for the purposes of crime (including vehicles involved in the commission of any imprisonable offence under the Road Traffic (NI) Order 1981) can be ordered to be forfeited[112] and under the Theft Act (NI) 1969[113] any property which has been stolen, or its proceeds, can be ordered to be restored by the defendant to the victim of the theft by way of a restitution order. New laws on divesting criminals of the proceeds of their crimes were introduced in 1996 and 2002.[114]

Enforcement of fines and compensation orders

Compensation, restitution and forfeiture orders, as well as fines, are all enforceable in the same way, namely by issuing a warrant of "distress" or a warrant of commitment to prison. Distress is the process whereby property belonging to the defendant is seized and sold in order to pay the sums owing. Imprisonment is a last resort, but one which is quite often needed; the duration of the imprisonment will depend on the amount of the sums owing. Under article 4(1) of the Criminal Justice (NI) Order 1994 a person fined by a magistrates' court can, for instance, be sent to prison for seven days if the unpaid fine is up to £200, or 28 days if the unpaid fine is between £500 and £1,000, or three months if the unpaid fine is between £2,500 and £5,000. As pointed out in Chapter 4.6, many of the people sent to prison in Northern Ireland receive that punishment because they have failed to

---

[111] Fatal Accidents (NI) Order 1977, art. 3A(3).
[112] Criminal Justice (NI) Order 1994, art. 11.
[113] S. 27 as amended by the Criminal Justice (NI) Order 1980, arts. 6 and 12(2). See further M. Allen and F. McAleenan, note 105 above, pp. 151-155, paras. 3.60-3.81.
[114] Financial Investigations (NI) Order 2001 and Proceeds of Crime Act 2002, Pt. IV (ss. 156-239).

pay a court fine (1,540 out of 5,411 prison committals in 2003-04 - 28%).

It was partly to avoid fines which defendants could not afford to pay that, in England and Wales, the Criminal Justice Act 1991 created the system of "unit fines". This was meant to ensure that a fine would be related to a defendant's own personal financial circumstances. But the system was so severely criticised by magistrates and others in England and Wales that it was repealed by section 65 of the Criminal Justice Act 1993. In Northern Ireland the magistrates' court in Newtownards made experimental use of a unit fine system for the first six months of 1992, but it has never since been introduced province-wide. Instead, under article 29 of the Criminal Justice (NI) Order 1996, when fixing the amount of any fine, the RM should consider, among other things, the financial circumstances of the offender, and this can effect a reduction *or* an increase in the amount of the fine that would otherwise be imposed.

Imminent reforms

At the time of writing the Northern Ireland Office is considering what changes to make to the sentencing framework in Northern Ireland.[115] It is proposing to alter the rules and guidance on matters such as post-release supervision, discretionary release, intermittent custody, electronic monitoring, deferred sentences, restorative justice and fine defaulting. If these proposals are implemented they will bring the sentencing system in Northern Ireland more into line with that in England and Wales.

Discharges and acquittals

Two further types of "sentence" which a magistrate might impose are those for the conditional discharge or absolute discharge of the convicted person.[116] The former is like a probation order: the convicted person is released without punishment but may be sentenced at a later date if he or she commits an offence during the period specified in the order (which cannot exceed three years). An absolute discharge means no punishment at all (although disqualification from driving can still be

---

[115] This follows publication of a consultation document, *Review of the Sentencing Framework in Northern Ireland* (2005), available on www.nio.gov.uk.
[116] Criminal Justice (NI) Order 1996, art. 4.

imposed): it is not an acquittal, however, so technically the defendant still stands convicted of the offence.

It is worth noting at this point that if a person serves time in prison, after having been convicted of an offence, and it is later proved that he or she did not in fact commit the alleged offence, there may then be the possibility of claiming compensation from the state. The Criminal Justice Act 1988[117] set up a limited statutory scheme for the whole of the United Kingdom. It applies whenever a convicted person is pardoned or the conviction is quashed after an appeal beyond the normal time limit for appealing. A specially appointed assessor[118] will decide how much compensation should be paid and usually this takes months if not years to calculate. The mechanism for getting alleged miscarriages of justice corrected - through the Criminal Cases Review Commission - is further described at Chapter 4.7 (and at p. 276 below).

For further details of a magistrate's sentencing powers in cases involving juveniles, see Chapter 7.1.

Appeals by the defendant

When a criminal case is tried summarily and the defendant is convicted, as the vast majority of them are, the defendant has the right to appeal within 14 days.[119] A notice of appeal must be given to the prosecution and a copy of the notice to the clerk of petty sessions of the court where the defendant was convicted. (Appeals are not the same as applications for judicial review, for which see Chap. 6.7.)

The defendant may wish to appeal against conviction, against sentence, or against both - though obviously there cannot be an appeal against conviction if the defendant pleaded guilty at the trial. If the defendant pleaded not guilty at the trial and wishes to appeal against conviction, or if (whether or not he or she pleaded guilty) the defendant wishes to appeal against sentence, there is a choice of two procedures: (i) an appeal to a county court, or (ii) an appeal by way of case stated to the Court of Appeal. The right of appeal on both grounds is preserved until

---

[117] S. 133.
[118] Sch. 12 to the Act governs the making of such appointments.
[119] Magistrates' Courts (NI) Order 1981, art. 144. The County Court (Amendment) Rules (NI) 1994, however, enable a county court, on application, to extend this time limit either before or after it expires. Opposition to any such application must be notified within 14 days.

such time as any application for a case to be stated has actually been granted.[120]

Appeals to a county court

An appeal to a county court[121] will be heard by the county court judge who sits for the area in which the magistrates' court itself sits. If it is against conviction the appeal takes the form of a complete rehearing of the case: witnesses are called again and all the written statements are reconsidered. The facts, in other words, have to be re-established. The county court judge (sitting without a jury) can reverse the conviction or confirm it - even on grounds different from those given by the magistrate. In these proceedings the judge can also increase or decrease the accused's sentence, even though this was not specifically appealed against.[122] If the appeal to the county court is only against sentence, all that is required is a review of the accused's previous convictions, if any, and a reconsideration of his or her plea in mitigation.

In 2002 the number of criminal appeals dealt with by the county courts was 1,743 (the numbers have been decreasing over the last 10 years or so). Of these, 1,269 (73%) were against sentence only, while the rest were against conviction only or against conviction and sentence. In 46% of appeals the original decision was confirmed, in 48% the original sentence was varied and in only 6% was the conviction quashed.[123]

Appeals to the Court of Appeal

An appeal by way of case stated to the Court of Appeal can be used only where there is a disputed point of law.[124] If it is the facts which are disputed, the defendant must appeal to a county court. Points of law can be raised in appeals to a county court as well as in appeals by way of case stated to the Court of Appeal, but the latter procedure *must* be used if only a point of law is involved. If this distinction between points of

---

[120] Magistrates' Courts (NI) Order 1981, art. 146(8), as interpreted by the Court of Appeal in *Wallace* v *Stokes* [2003] NICA 33.
[121] *Ibid.* art. 140 and Magistrates' Court Rules (NI) 1984, rr. 154-7, as amended.
[122] County Courts (NI) Order 1980, art. 28(3).
[123] *Digest of Information on the Northern Ireland Criminal Justice System* (4th ed., 2004), pp. 107-8.
[124] Magistrates' Courts (NI) Order 1981, art. 146 and Magistrates' Court Rules (NI) 1984, rr. 158-60, as amended. See further, B. Valentine and A. Hart, *Criminal Procedure in Northern Ireland* (1989), pp. 190-5, paras. 17.26-17.41.

law and points of fact is applied to appeals against sentence, it means that a complaint that the magistrate had, for instance, no power to order disqualification from driving for the offence which the accused has committed would be an appeal on a point of law, whereas a complaint that the magistrate disqualified the accused for too long a period, given the circumstances of the case, would be considered as an appeal on a point of fact.

Under the procedure by way of case stated, the resident magistrate is asked by the side appealing (the appellant) to pose a question to the Court of Appeal for its opinion on what the law is on a particular point.[125] The Court of Appeal answers the question and on the basis of that answer affirms, reverses or varies the decision appealed from.[126] It may also consider any points of law not considered in the court below or give directions on what the law is and remit the case to the lower court for a further hearing. But it may not increase the defendant's sentence, least of all in cases where the appeal was only against conviction. All that the Court of Appeal can do to increase a sentence is decide to discount a period spent in custody pending the appeal.[127] There are only a few of these cases stated each year, most appeals going to the county court instead.

Appeals by the prosecution

All the appeal procedures so far considered have been concerned with appeals by the defendant. The prosecution has fewer rights of appeal. If the defendant is acquitted by a magistrates' court, or if a conviction is reversed by the county court, the prosecution cannot appeal against those decisions on the ground that the facts were wrongly found by the resident magistrate or the county court judge. The only avenue open to the prosecution is to appeal directly to the Court of Appeal on a point of law by way of case stated.[128] Even then the appeal can only be against an acquittal, not against too lenient a sentence.

Further appeals

The Criminal Appeal Act 1995 established the Criminal Cases Review Commission (CCRC), which is further described in Chapter 4.7. Under

---

[125] *E.g. Clinton* v *Bradley* [2000] NI 196.
[126] Magistrates' Courts (NI) Order 1981, art. 147.
[127] *Ibid*. art. 153(1)(b).
[128] *Ibid*. art. 146.

section 12 of the Act, the CCRC may refer a conviction by a magistrates' court, and/or any sentence imposed then or in subsequent proceedings, to the county court. The CCRC should make a reference either if: (i) an appeal against the conviction or sentence has been unsuccessfully determined or leave to appeal has been refused and the CCRC considers that there is "a real possibility" of over-turning the conviction (because of an argument or evidence not raised in the proceedings) or the sentence (because of an argument on a point of law or information not yet raised); or if (ii) there are exceptional circumstances which justify doing so. Cases in which the applicant has not exhausted the normal appeals process make up the vast majority of applications determined to be ineligible for review. On such a reference, the county court may not award a punishment more severe than that originally given.[129]

If the accused has appealed to a county court the main way in which the case can be taken further is by either side stating a case from that court to the Court of Appeal.[130] But if the county court acquits a defendant in an appeal, the prosecution may get the original conviction restored if it is successful in an application for judicial review (see Chap. 6.7).

All decisions of the Court of Appeal on appeals are in turn appealable to the House of Lords,[131] the highest court in the land. Before this can happen, however, the permission (or "leave") either of the Court of Appeal or of the House of Lords must be granted, and this leave will not be obtained unless two conditions are satisfied: (i) the Court of Appeal must certify that a point of law of general public importance is involved, and (ii) it must appear to the Court of Appeal or to the House of Lords that the point is one which ought to be considered by the latter.[132] All appeals to the House of Lords are therefore on points of law only. If leave is refused once it may still be possible to apply again.[133] Understandably, it is very rare for a case which has been tried summarily in Northern Ireland's magistrates' courts to travel as far as the House of Lords, but two examples are *McEldowney* v *Forde*[134] (see

---

[129] Criminal Appeal Act 1995, s. 12(6).
[130] County Courts (NI) Order 1980, art. 61(1).
[131] Judicature (NI) Act 1978, s. 41(1)(b) and Criminal Appeal (NI) Act 1980, s. 31.
[132] *Ibid.* s. 41(2).
[133] The point was left undecided by the Court of Appeal in *R* v *McBride* [2002] 3 BNIL 19.
[134] [1970] NI 11.

Chap. 2.2) and *Seay* v *Eastwood*.[135] If an appeal is unsuccessful in the Court of Appeal the convicted person can still try to take advantage of the mechanism for correcting miscarriages of justice provided by the Criminal Cases Review Commission.

5.5   COMMITTAL PROCEEDINGS IN A
MAGISTRATES' COURT

The other type of criminal case which a magistrates' court deals with is committal proceedings. These are held for persons charged with indictable offences which are not triable summarily or which, although triable summarily, the defendant or prosecution has elected to have tried on indictment (see Chap. 4.2). The purpose of committal proceedings is to decide if there is a *prima facie* case (*i.e.* a case "on the face of it") for the accused to answer. A finding that there is such a case simply means that the defendant is then committed for trial to the Crown Court: it does not imply any presumption that the accused is guilty. In 2004 magistrates' courts committed 1,705 defendants to the Crown Court.[136]

Committal proceedings take the form of either a preliminary investigation (a PI),[137] where witnesses attend and give their evidence by word of mouth on oath in court (although a video-recording of an interview with a child witness is also admissible[138]), or - as in the majority of cases - a preliminary enquiry (a PE),[139] where copies of witnesses' written statements are simply presented to the court and, if either side so requests, read out aloud. When evidence is given by word of mouth on oath it is written down in court and is then called a deposition. Witnesses are then "bound over" to attend and give evidence if required at the main trial.[140] In all non-scheduled cases the defendant can opt for either form of proceeding, although in practice he or she rarely objects to a PE. Where the accused is charged with a scheduled offence, the court must conduct a PE if requested by the

---

[135] [1976] 3 All ER 153.
[136] *Northern Ireland Judicial Statistics 2004*, Table E.11 (18 were juveniles).
[137] Magistrates' Courts (NI) Order 1981, art. 30. For the procedure, see also the Magistrates' Courts Rules (NI) 1984, rr. 25-30.
[138] Under the Police and Criminal Evidence (NI) Order 1989, art. 81(A), as inserted by the Children's Evidence (NI) Order 1995, art. 5. See further 5.6 below.
[139] Magistrates' Courts (NI) Order 1981, arts. 31-4. See also Magistrates' Courts Rules (NI) 1984, rr. 31-42.
[140] *Ibid*. art. 39.

prosecution, unless the court believes that a PI is required in the interests of justice.[141]

Occasionally there can be a mixture of both types of committal proceedings - a PE where the defendant nevertheless insists that the evidence of certain witnesses be taken down by way of deposition. Under article 4 of the Children's Evidence (NI) Order 1995, the Director of Public Prosecutions can issue a "notice of transfer", which has the effect of bypassing committal proceedings altogether where there is a child witness and the alleged offence was one of the violent and sexual offences specified in the Order and one which the Crown Court can try. There are similar special transfer procedures for certain categories of fraud and war crimes.[142]

In committal proceedings the prosecution does not have to reveal all of its evidence and the accused will usually reserve his or her defence by saying nothing at all but trying to assess the strength of the prosecution's case by cross-examining some of the Crown's witnesses. Indeed, until recently the only situation in which a defendant was obliged to disclose any part of his or her defence in advance of the main trial was where he or she intended to rely on an "alibi", that is, a defence that the defendant was somewhere else at the time when the offence was committed. However, the Criminal Procedure and Investigations Act 1996 introduced new provisions regarding pre-trial disclosure (see 5.3 above). Under this Act, following initial disclosure by the prosecution, a person charged with an indictable offence who is committed for trial must provide a defence statement to both the court and the prosecutor in advance of the main trial.

Discharging the accused

If the resident magistrate considers that there is not enough evidence to require the accused to answer the charge brought by the prosecution, he or she will not commit the accused for trial.[143] This is called "discharging" the accused, or "refusing an information". It occurs infrequently, certainly in less than 1% of cases. The defendant is then free to go, although because there has not been a formal acquittal he or she *may* be charged again with the same offence at a later date.

---

[141] Terrorism Act 2000, s. 66.
[142] See the Criminal Justice (Serious Fraud) (NI) Order 1988 and the War Crimes Act 1991.
[143] Magistrates' Courts (NI) Order 1981, art. 37.

The prosecution cannot appeal against a discharge but it can apply to a judge of the Court of Appeal, High Court or Crown Court for permission to present an indictment notwithstanding the absence of any committal by a magistrates' court.[144] This is known as a "voluntary" indictment and is very rare in Northern Ireland. It has been used in cases where no committal proceedings at all have taken place (because, *e.g.*, the chief prosecution witness was an alleged accomplice of the defendant and the prosecution wished to protect him or her before the main trial), but it may also be used where there have been committal proceedings and the magistrate has discharged the defendant. In either case, it is then a matter for the judge to decide whether or not there is a *prima facie* case against the defendant and, if so, whether to permit a "voluntary" indictment to be presented to an appropriate Crown Court.

Reviews of committals

If a resident magistrate does commit the accused for trial the accused or his or her barrister can, before arraignment in the Crown Court (see 5.6 below), apply to the trial judge to have the committal reviewed or the proposed venue changed. Under this procedure (which has never had any parallel in English procedure), if the judge is satisfied that the evidence does not disclose a sufficient case to justify trying the accused for an indictable offence, he or she can order an entry of "No Bill" in the Crown Court book, thereby discharging the accused without requiring any further answer from him or her. From the accused's point of view this is not as good as a formal acquittal because he or she can still be indicted again in the future on the same facts or evidence. The same applies if the accused successfully brings judicial review proceedings on account of some irregularity at the committal hearing.[145] If the review application is unsuccessful the trial will proceed.

The future

Reforms introduced by the Criminal Justice and Public Order Act 1994 built on the recommendations of the Royal Commission on Criminal Justice[146] and provided for the replacement of committal proceedings in England and Wales with an entirely new transfer procedure. However

---

[144] Grand Jury (Abolition) Act (NI) 1969, s. 2(2)(e).
[145] For an unsuccessful attempt to seek judicial review of a committal, see *Re Martin's Application* [2000] 7 BNIL 9.
[146] Cmnd. 2263; 1993, pp.198-9, nos. 116-121.

the Government then decided that the new procedure would not lead to the efficiency gains it had anticipated and it therefore repealed the provisions of the 1994 Act before they ever came into force.[147] By the Crime and Disorder Act 1998 committal proceedings in England and Wales were eventually abolished. Adults appearing before magistrates charged with such offences are now automatically sent for trial, although the person charged can still apply to a Crown Court judge to have the charge dismissed if there appears to be insufficient evidence for a jury to convict.

In 1995 the Northern Ireland Office issued a discussion paper outlining a number of possible future arrangements including an accelerated route for those pleading guilty (as in Scotland) and - if committal proceedings were to continue - a right on the part of defendants to waive them. None of these proposals was taken forward but in 2004 the Northern Ireland Office published a further consultation paper putting forward two options for reform: (i) a presumption that a defendant should be transferred to the Crown Court, but with a right in the defendant to elect for committal proceedings if he or she so wishes, or (ii) complete abolition of committal proceedings entirely, with a right in the defendant to make a submission of "no case to answer" once the case gets to the Crown Court. The outcome of this consultation is still awaited.

5.6   TRIALS ON INDICTMENT IN THE CROWN COURT

Trial on indictment involves two distinct court stages. There must, first, be committal proceedings in a magistrates' court or leave given for the presentation of a voluntary indictment (see 5.5 above). There is then the main trial in the Crown Court, which is the stage described in this section.

When a person has been committed by a magistrates' court for trial, it is the responsibility of the Public Prosecution Service (see Chaps. 1.5 and 5.3) to prepare a formal document known as "the form of indictment", sometimes referred to inaccurately as "the bill of indictment". This contains details of the specific charge or charges against the accused arising out of the committal proceedings. Each offence charged in the indictment is known as a "count", and each

---

[147] By the Criminal Procedure and Investigations Act 1996.

count must contain a statement of the offence and particulars indicating the person indicted, the person (if any) injured and the necessary ingredients of the offence. A copy of the indictment must be given to the defendant to let him or her know precisely for what offences he or she is being tried. The trial should start no sooner than eight days and no later than 14 weeks[148] (8 weeks in England[149]) after the date of the accused's committal. During 2003 the average delay between committal and arraignment was just over six weeks (even in Diplock cases; see Chap. 4.2 above), and an average of eight weeks (14 in Diplock cases) elapsed between arraignment and the actual start of the hearing.[150]

The Crown Court

The Crown Court was created as a branch of the Supreme Court of Judicature of Northern Ireland in April 1979 (see Chap. 1.3). It sits at 11 different places in the province (see Table 2 on p. 20) and often there are several sittings occurring at the same time. The court can be presided over by the Lord Chief Justice (who is the President of the Court), a judge of the Court of Appeal, a High Court judge or a county court judge, but the Lord Chancellor has directed that some offences (*e.g.* murder) must be tried by at least a judge of the High Court. In 2003 the Crown Court dealt with 1,570 defendants (21% more than in 2002); 953 (57%) defendants pleaded guilty to all charges against them, which meant that only 608 were actually tried.[151]

In all cases there will be a jury of 12 persons, except when the offence being dealt with is a scheduled offence (*i.e.* one liable to be committed by terrorists), which is tried by a judge sitting alone in a so-called Diplock court (see Chap. 4.2). The trial of non-scheduled offences takes place at the sitting of the Crown Court determined by the magistrate who committed the accused, although this venue can be altered by a ruling of the Crown Court itself. Usually, non-scheduled

---

[148] Judicature (NI) Act 1978, s. 48(5) and Crown Court Rules (NI) 1979, r. 44. By a Crown Court Practice Direction of 12 October 1998 [1998] 8 BNIL 58 the target time lapse between committal and arraignment is 6 weeks and the target time lapse between arraignment and trial is 12 weeks.

[149] Supreme Court Act 1981, s. 77 and Crown Court Rules 1982, r. 24.7.1.1.

[150] *Northern Ireland Judicial Statistics 2004*, Tables C.3 and C.4.

[151] *Northern Ireland Judicial Statistics 2004*, Fig. C.2 and Table C.6. In 2005 the Northern Ireland Court Service began issuing a quarterly Crown Court Bulletin (available on its website) which gives provisional figures for defendants dealt with, the outcome of charges, waiting times, etc.

offences are tried at the Crown Court acting for the county court division in which the offence is alleged to have been committed, but a different venue can be arranged on account of special circumstances such as the convenience of witnesses, security reasons or the need to speed up the proceedings.[152]

Arraignment

Proceedings in a Crown Court commence with the "arraignment" of the accused,[153] that is, with the court clerk reading the indictment to the accused and asking the accused how he or she pleads on each count. If the accused pleads guilty to all counts there will be no need for a jury to be sworn: the prosecution will outline the facts and the judge will pass sentence after considering the accused's previous convictions, if any, and any plea in mitigation by his or her barrister. An accused who pleads guilty can ask the Crown Court judge at any time before sentence to "vacate" (*i.e.* change) that plea.[154] If the accused pleads not guilty to any count, and if the offence is not a scheduled offence, a jury must be sworn from the panel already summoned to the Court for that day. Technically the trial begins only with the swearing of the jury. In 2004, 73% of Crown Court defendants were on bail at the time of their arraignment.[155]

If the question of the defendant's mental fitness to be tried arises at the arraignment stage it is decided by the jury empanelled for the trial, but only after it has heard oral evidence from a medical practitioner appointed for the purpose by the Mental Health Commission and also the written or oral evidence of another medical practitioner. If the jury decides that the accused is fit to be tried the trial itself must be heard by a different jury.[156] If the jury decides that the accused is not fit to be tired another jury will then determine whether the accused did in fact do the act alleged. If it decides that he did do the act the court can make

---

[152] S. 48(1)-(4) of the Judicature (NI) Act 1978. See B. Valentine and A. Hart, *Criminal Procedure in Northern Ireland* (1989), p. 74, para. 7.27.

[153] See further B. Valentine and A. Hart, *ibid.* Chap. 8, pp. 75-82.

[154] *R v Lees* [2002] 9 BNIL 16.

[155] *Northern Ireland Judicial Statistics 2004*, Table C.3.

[156] Mental Health (NI) Order 1986, art. 49, as amended by the Criminal Justice (NI) Order 1996, art. 48.

a hospital order, a guardianship order, a supervision and treatment order or an order for his or her absolute discharge.[157]

Juries

Under the Juries (NI) Order 1996, jurors are selected from "the Divisional Jurors Lists" by the Juries Officer of each county court division. These lists are drawn up annually from registers prepared by the Chief Electoral Officer for Northern Ireland (see Chap. 9.11). Every registered elector aged between 18 and 70 is qualified for inclusion, although certain individuals (such as any person who in the last five years has been placed on probation) are disqualified from serving[158] and others (by reason of their jobs, such as lawyers, ministers of religion, doctors, nurses and chemists) are either ineligible[159] or excusable as of right.[160]

People called for jury service are paid allowances and a claim form is sent out together with the jury summons. They can find out more about what is involved in being a juror by consulting the Court Service's leaflet on the topic and they can also read and listen to materials on-line, including a short video. The Juries Officer selects a jury to serve not just for one particular trial but for all the hearings in a particular court or place over a prescribed period of time. To keep the size of a jury panel manageable the judge of any court may divide the selected jurors into two or more sections and may excuse from attendance jurors whose names appear in any one or more of those sections.[161]

When the members of a jury panel are being "empanelled", that is, sworn in to serve a particular trial, a defendant can, without giving reasons, object to any 12 of them. This is called the right to a peremptory challenge and those members must then stand down.[162] Such challenges were abolished in England and Wales by the Criminal Justice Act 1988 but are still possible in Northern Ireland. After 12 peremptory challenges the defendant can challenge would-be jurors only if reasons are given, and the jurors will have to stand down only if

---

[157] *Ibid.* arts. 49A and 50A, inserted by the Criminal Justice (NI) Order 1996, arts. 49 and 51. In 2003 there were only 9 defendants who were found unfit to be tried: *Northern Ireland Judicial Statistics 2004*, Table C.6.

[158] Juries (NI) Order 1996, Sch. 1, lists all those disqualified from jury service.

[159] *Ibid.* Sch. 2.

[160] *Ibid.* Sch. 3.

[161] *Ibid.* art. 10.

[162] *Ibid.* art. 15.

the judge considers the reasons to be satisfactory. The prosecution has no right of peremptory challenge but can require any would-be juror to "stand by", that is, to wait on one side until the rest of the jury group has been gone through to see if a full jury can be sworn.[163] If by then a full jury has not been sworn the prosecution can prevent a juror who has been stood by from serving only if it provides the judge with good reasons why this should be so. Even if the defence or the prosecution does not object to a particular juror, the judge may personally excuse jurors who have already participated in a trial of an exceptionally exacting nature and a juror may always apply to be excused on the grounds of hardship or ill-health.

In England and Wales the Attorney General has laid down guidelines for what amounts to acceptable "jury-vetting" by either side in particularly sensitive trials. In Northern Ireland, juries would tend not to be involved in such trials anyway. It should be noted that article 47 of the Criminal Justice (NI) Order 1996 creates a new offence of intimidation of witnesses, jurors and others, and a person convicted of this may be sent to prison for up to five years.

Procedure in a trial on indictment

Once a jury has been empanelled for the case in hand - and it must be stressed that no jury will be sworn in trials on indictment of scheduled offences (see Chap. 4.2) - it is the duty of the prosecution to prove beyond reasonable doubt that the defendant committed the offence. This means that the jury has to believe that the evidence produced shows that the accused committed the offence and that there is no real doubt about that. Only in exceptional cases is there any burden on the defendant to prove his or her innocence: for instance, when he or she claims to be of impaired mental responsibility or insane,[164] these matters must be proved "on the balance of probabilities". Examination, cross-examination and re-examination of witnesses take place as in a magistrates' court, but will usually be conducted in more detail and with the utmost attention to the law's many rules of evidence. If the judge interferes by asking too many questions of the defendant rather

---

[163] See, *e.g.*, *R v Christie* [1998] 1 BNIL 15 and *R v King and Wilson*, Belfast Crown Court, 7 May 1997, which affirmed the Crown's right of stand by: [1998] 1 BNIL 15.

[164] Criminal Justice (NI) Act 1966, ss. 5(3) and 2(2).

than leaving this to the barristers involved, this may render the trial unfair.[165]

In trials on indictment (as well as in committal proceedings, appeals to the Court of Appeal, hearings of references under section 10 of the Criminal Appeal Act 1995 and proceedings in youth courts), the court may grant leave for evidence to be tendered by way of a video-recording of an interview with a child[166] and any further cross-examination of a child who has given evidence in this way should be conducted by way of a live television link.[167] All witnesses may remain in court during the hearing of evidence, unless a special application to exclude some of them is granted by the judge. This differs from the practice in England, where, more sensibly, witnesses remain outside the courtroom during the taking of other evidence.

Trials within a trial

If at any stage of the trial either side wishes to produce evidence which may not, according to the strict rules of evidence, be admissible, the judge will ask the jury to withdraw while the judge hears the evidence and decides whether or not it is admissible. Technically it is for the defendant to decide whether the jury should be present or not, but in practice the judge controls this. This is an example of what is called a *"voir dire"* hearing, or a trial within a trial. If the judge decides that the evidence is admissible the jury will be recalled and the trial will proceed with the evidence being presented. If the judge decides that the evidence is not admissible the jury will be recalled and the trial will proceed with no mention being made of the inadmissible evidence. In this way the jury is protected from hearing evidence which, for one reason or another, the law considers to be improper.

Hearsay evidence, which is evidence given by A about what B said, rather than direct evidence given by B, is generally inadmissible

---

165 *R* v *Roulston* [2001] 3 BNIL 21.
166 Police and Criminal Evidence (NI) Order 1989, art. 81(A), as inserted by the Children's Evidence (NI) Order 1995, art. 5, and further amended by the Criminal Procedure and Investigations Act 1996, Sch. 4, para. 25. The NIO has issued a *Memorandum of Good Practice* in relation to how these interviews should be conducted (1997).
167 PACE Order, art. 81(B), as inserted by the Children's Evidence (NI) Order 1995, art. 5.

because it tends to be inaccurate.[168] Another commonly recurring example of questionable evidence is a confession extracted by dubious methods. As explained in Chapter 4.3, in trials of non-scheduled offences such a confession is inadmissible if it may have been obtained by oppression or as a result of anything said or done which was likely to render it unreliable. The defendant's previous convictions will not be made known to the jury unless the prosecution is allowed to refer to them because the precise manner in which the earlier offences were committed bears a striking resemblance to the offence now being alleged against the accused.

The verdict in trials on indictment

After all the evidence in a Crown Court trial has been presented, the lawyers representing prosecution and defence make final speeches summarising their points. The judge must sum up the whole case for the jury by drawing its attention to the rival versions of the relevant facts and directing it on the relevant law to be applied to those facts. In long trials the judge's summing-up may last for days.[169]

The jury's verdict should be unanimous, but need not be so if it has been deliberating for at least two hours and, in a case where there are not less than 11 jurors, 10 of them agree on the verdict, or where there are 10 jurors, nine of them agree on the verdict - this is called "a majority verdict".[170] If the jury finds it impossible even to arrive at a majority verdict the judge may discharge that jury and order a new trial before a different jury. If the jury's verdict is "not guilty" the accused must be acquitted and cannot be held in custody or tried again in connection with the offence charged. If charged again for the same offence the accused is said to have the defence of "*autrefois acquit*" (*i.e.* formerly acquitted) and to be protected by the principle which forbids a person being subjected to "double jeopardy".[171] If the verdict is "guilty", the judge will pass sentence. Before doing so the judge will consider the defendant's previous convictions, if any, and may be addressed by the defence on points of mitigation as well as being

---

[168] See B. Valentine and A. Hart, *Criminal Procedure in Northern Ireland* (1989), p. 107, para. 12.22.

[169] *Ibid.* pp. 127-131, paras. 13.13-23.

[170] Criminal Procedure (Majority Verdicts) Act (NI) 1971, s. 1(1), as substituted by the Juries (NI) Order 1996, art. 32(1). A jury may have fewer than 12 members because one or more have been discharged on account of illness etc.

[171] See B. Valentine and A. Hart, note 168 above, pp. 79-82, paras. 8.16-21.

assisted by reports from probation officers, welfare officers, doctors, etc.

Sentencing in the Crown Court[172]

The sentencing powers of the Crown Court embrace all of those exercisable by resident magistrates but include as well other powers conferred by the common law and statutes. The new sentencing framework introduced by the Criminal Justice (NI) Order 1996 applies equally to the Crown Court as it does to magistrates' courts (see 5.5 above). In England and Wales, following a report by the Law Commission,[173] further clarification has been introduced by the Powers of Criminal Courts (Sentencing) Act 2000. In that jurisdiction there is a Sentencing Guidelines Council,[174] chaired by the Lord Chief Justice. The Council issues guidelines on sentencing after receiving advice based on research and consultation conducted by a Sentencing Advisory Panel, currently chaired by Professor Martin Wasik. The guidelines indicate the factors which judges should bear in mind when calculating what the appropriate sentence should be in a particular case. The Northern Ireland Court of Appeal has said that sentences in Northern Ireland should apply the starting points recommended by that Council.[175]

The most common sentence, whether in Northern Ireland or in England and Wales, is immediate imprisonment, which, if we include detention in a young offenders' centre (see Chap. 7.1), was imposed in 48% of Crown Court cases in Northern Ireland in 2001 (444 out of 933).[176] The average sentence length in that year (excluding life sentences) was just under 30 months. In a further 250 or so cases a suspended prison or detention sentence was given.[177] A suspended sentence must not exceed

---

[172] See generally *Sentencing Trends in Northern Ireland 1993-1997*, NIO, (2000), especially Chaps. 4 and 6.

[173] *Sentencing Law Clarified*, Report No. 264 (1999). For the Law Commission see Chap. 9.14.

[174] www.sentencing-guidelines.gov.uk.

[175] *Attorney General's Reference (No. 2 of 2004)* [2004] NICA 15. See too *Attorney General's References (Nos. 2, 6, 7 and 8 of 2003)* [2004] NI 50, in relation to sentences for causing death or grievous injury by dangerous or careless driving.

[176] *Digest of Information on the Criminal Justice System of Northern Ireland* (4th ed., 2004), pp. 84-5. Figures for years after 2001 do not yet seem to have been published. The annual *Judicial Statistics* provide such information only in respect of sentences imposed in magistrates' courts.

[177] *Ibid.* p. 96.

seven years and the period of suspension must be between one and five years;[178] the sentence *may* be activated if the offender commits another imprisonable offence during the period of suspension. Prior to the Treatment of Offenders (NI) Order 1989, Crown Court judges in Northern Ireland (like their counterparts in Ireland, but not in Great Britain) also exercised a self-professed power to impose "recorded" sentences. These allowed a prison term of *any* length to be suspended for *any* period and to be activated automatically if there was *any* breach of the suspension. They were abolished by the 1989 Order.

The precise sentence which a convicted person will receive will depend on a number of factors. Some of these relate to the nature of what the accused actually did at the time of or immediately after the crime - whether it was particularly brutal, malicious or dishonest, whether he or she acted with premeditation, whether there was a degree of co-operation with the police investigation, etc - while others relate to the kind of person the defendant is - whether he or she has an otherwise unblemished record, is genuinely remorseful, is easily influenced by others, is mentally unstable, etc. Each crime is subject to a maximum possible sentence, but not to any minimum. Under the Criminal Justice (NI) Order 1996, the court should look first at the seriousness of the offence and then decide what sentence is the most appropriate. Proportionality is the principal sentencing aim and while, for instance, a judge might wish to deter others from perpetrating similar crimes, such an outcome must be secondary and incidental to the imposition of a sentence commensurate with the gravity of the offence.[179] It is notoriously difficult to compare sentences in different cases because the precise factors to be taken into account are unique to each case. If a dispute arises at the sentencing stage over the precise facts surrounding the offence in question, a further oral hearing (called a "Newton hearing")[180] may be required to settle the matter.

There are many offences for which the maximum punishment laid down by statute is life imprisonment, but the only offences for which

---

[178] Treatment of Offenders Act (NI) 1968, s. 18, as amended by the Treatment of Offenders (NI) Order 1989, art. 9(1) and the Criminal Justice (NI) Order 1996, art. 23. See further M. Allen and F. McAleenan, *Sentencing Law and Practice in Northern Ireland* (3rd ed., 1998, with Supplement 2003), pp. 101-115, paras. 2.78-128.

[179] See M. Allen and F. McAleenan, *ibid.* pp. 298-301, paras. 6.127-135.

[180] After *R* v *Newton* (1982) 77 Cr App R 13.

that sentence *must* be imposed are murder[181] and genocide.[182] The death penalty was to all intents and purposes abolished in Northern Ireland in 1973, the last execution having taken place in 1964. The system now in place for considering when life sentenced prisoners should be released from prison has been described in Chapter 4.6.

If a person is found not guilty by reason of mental illness, or if the court believes that a guilty defendant requires treatment in a mental hospital, he or she can be made the subject of a hospital order and sent to a mental hospital.[183] Such a person can also be made the subject of a restriction order, limiting his or her discharge from the hospital.[184] Until recently, seriously mentally disturbed defendants might have had to be sent to England or Scotland (especially to Carstairs in Lanarkshire) because there was no adequately secure unit in Northern Ireland. In April 2005, however, the Shannon Clinic was opened at Knockbracken Healthcare Park in South Belfast. This can accommodate up to 34 patients, providing assessment, care, treatment and rehabilitation in a secure environment.

5.7 APPEALS IN CROWN COURT CASES

Appeals by the defendant

Under the Criminal Appeal Act 1995, when a criminal case is tried on indictment the accused person can appeal against conviction if the trial judge grants a certificate that the case is fit for appeal or if the leave of the Court of Appeal is obtained.[185] Prior to the 1995 Act the accused could appeal on a point of law alone *without* obtaining the permission of any court. The new law, however, abolished the distinction between questions of law and questions of fact as the determinant of the appropriate appeal procedure. Appeal courts had generally been very reluctant to interfere with the findings of fact made by a lower court, although it was often a nice question whether a disputed point was indeed one of pure fact, or of mixed law and fact, rather than one of

---

[181] Northern Ireland (Emergency Provisions) Act 1973, s. 1.
[182] Genocide Act 1969, s. 1.
[183] Mental Health (NI) Order 1986, art. 44.
[184] *Ibid.* art. 47. Arts. 53 and 54 provide for the transfer to mental hospital of prisoners who become ill.
[185] Criminal Appeal (NI) Act 1980, s. 1, as substituted by Criminal Appeal Act 1995, s. 1(2). In this field see, generally, the Criminal Appeal (NI) Rules 1968, as amended.

pure law. But requests for leave to appeal, when leave is required, are usually turned down (63% in the period 1998-2002).[186]

Under section 10 of the 1995 Act, the Criminal Cases Review Commission (CCRC)[187] may refer a conviction by a Crown Court and/or any sentence imposed then or in subsequent proceedings, or a decision of not guilty on the ground of insanity, or a finding that a person is unfit to be tried, to the Court of Appeal. On such a reference, the Court of Appeal may not award a punishment more severe than that originally given in the Crown Court.[188] The Commission's powers replace those previously vested in the Secretary of State for Northern Ireland under section 14 of the Criminal Appeal (NI) Act 1980. It was as a result of a reference to the Court of Appeal made by the CCRC that Mr Ian Hay Gordon was finally acquitted in 2000 of the murder of Patricia Curran, a judge's daughter, in 1952.[189]

There is no case stated procedure (see 5.4 above) for trials on indictment, nor is the judicial review procedure available (see Chap. 6.7), because it lies only in respect of proceedings in tribunals or "inferior" courts (*i.e.* magistrates' courts and county courts).

Appeals by the prosecution

As far as the prosecution is concerned, there is no right of appeal against the acquittal of a defendant who has been tried on indictment. But following a recommendation made by the Macpherson Inquiry into the murder of the black teenager Stephen Lawrence in London, the Law Commission considered whether changes should be made to the legal rules concerning double jeopardy.[190] As a result the Government ensured that the law was indeed slightly altered. The Criminal Justice (NI) Order 2004 now provides[191] that, if the prosecution obtains leave from either the trial judge or the Court of Appeal, it can appeal to the

---

[186] *Digest of Information on the Northern Ireland Criminal Justice System* (4th ed., 2004), p. 103.
[187] See also Chap. 4.7.
[188] Criminal Appeal Act 1995, s. 10(5).
[189] See too the cases of William Gorman and Patrick McKinney, convicted of the murder of an RUC officer in 1980; their convictions were referred back to the Court of Appeal by the CCRC in 1998 because of new evidence concerning the police interview notes and in 1999 the Court of Appeal quashed the convictions.
[190] See *Double Jeopardy and Prosecution Appeals* (Report 267; 2001), which followed two separate consultation papers in 2000 (Nos. 156 and 158).
[191] In Pt. IV; the equivalent legislation in England and Wales is the Criminal Justice Act 2003.

Court of Appeal, prior to the judge's summing up, against a ruling by the judge that has the effect of terminating the trial prematurely or, prior to the opening of the defence case in relation to certain offences, against a ruling on points of evidence which significantly weakens the prosecution case. But there can still be no appeal against the decision of a jury to acquit a defendant.

All that can be done at present is that the Attorney General can refer a point of law to the Court of Appeal for its opinion.[192] This is only a reference and not an appeal as such, and there are very few applications.[193] Even if the Court of Appeal considers that the trial judge made an error of law which resulted in an undeserved acquittal, the acquittal still stands; once a person has been formally acquitted he or she cannot be tried again for the same offence. The Court of Appeal's opinion will simply guide the prosecution in the trials of other defendants in the future.

The Criminal Justice Act 1988 has also conferred on the Attorney General in both Northern Ireland and England and Wales the power to refer a case to the Court of Appeal if he believes that the sentence imposed by the Crown Court is "unduly lenient".[194] This provision was provoked by highly publicised cases in England where violent sex offenders were given comparatively light sentences by trial judges. Each year a handful or so of cases are referred in Northern Ireland.[195]

The powers of the Court of Appeal

Pending the determination of an appeal the Court of Appeal can permit the defendant to be released on bail, although this rarely occurs. The Court should allow the appeal if it thinks that the defendant's conviction is unsafe.[196] There are, in fact, four possible outcomes. The court may: (i) allow the appeal and acquit the defendant;[197] (ii) allow the appeal but substitute a verdict of guilty of one or more other

---

[192] Criminal Appeal (NI) Act 1980, s. 15.
[193] See, *e.g. Reference under s. 15 of the Criminal Appeal Act (NI) Act 1980* [1993] 7 NIJB 88.
[194] S. 36.
[195] *E.g. Attorney General's Reference (No. 3 of 2004)* [2004] NICA 20 (where a sentence of 7 years' custody and 2 years' probation for a firearms offence was not changed) and *Attorney General's Reference (No. 6 of 2004)* [2004] NICA 33 (where a 12-year minimum tariff for a brutal murder was increased to 15 years).
[196] Criminal Appeal (NI) Act 1980, s. 2(1), as substituted by Criminal Appeal Act 1995, s. 2(2).
[197] *Ibid.* s. 2(2)

offences, in which event the Court of Appeal can reduce, vary or even increase the appellant's sentence;[198] (iii) allow the appeal but order a retrial;[199] or (iv) dismiss the appeal. In any appeal against sentence the Court of Appeal can also alter the sentence up or down. From time to time it issues sentencing guidelines for the lower courts.[200] In 2004, 94 appeals in criminal cases were lodged with the Court of Appeal - 85 of these were in ordinary cases and nine in "Diplock" cases (see Chap. 4.2). More than two-thirds of the appeals lodged (70) were against sentence only, five were against conviction only and 19 were against both. The Court of Appeal managed to dispose of 61 criminal appeals during the year, 16 of which were successful from the defendant's point of view.[201]

Further appeals

Decisions of the Court of Appeal relating to trials on indictment can be further appealed *by either the prosecution or the defence* to the House of Lords. But, as with appeals after summary trials, the leave of either the Court of Appeal or the House of Lords is first required, and this is granted only if the Court of Appeal certifies that a point of law of general public importance is involved and if the Court of Appeal or the House of Lords thinks that the point is one which ought to be considered by the House.[202] There are on average only one or two such appeals each year from Northern Ireland. A "reference" under section 15 of the 1980 Act (see above) can also be further referred by the Court of Appeal to the House of Lords, but the decision of that House can still not reverse the original acquittal. Likewise a decision by the Court of Appeal under the Criminal Justice Act 1988 in relation to an "unduly lenient" sentence (see above) may be referred to the House of Lords if there is a point of law of general public importance at issue.

The appeal system for criminal proceedings is resented diagrammatically in Table 17, below. Note that the avenues available

---

[198] Criminal Appeal (NI) Act 1980, ss. 3 and 4. See too the Criminal Justice Act 2003, s. 317.

[199] *Ibid.* s. 6.

[200] In England and Wales a Sentencing Advisory Panel was established in 1999 under the Crime and Disorder Act 1998. This is an independent advisory and consultative body which provides fully researched, objective information to the Court of Appeal to assist it in framing or revising sentencing guidelines.

[201] *Northern Ireland Judicial Statistics 2004*, Tables A.2. and A.3. In addition some defendants had their sentences varied (up or down).

[202] Criminal Appeal (NI) Act 1980, s. 31(2).

for appeal differ depending on whether the case is a summary one or an indictable one and whether the disputed point is one of fact or of law.

TABLE 17: THE APPEAL SYSTEM IN CRIMINAL CASES

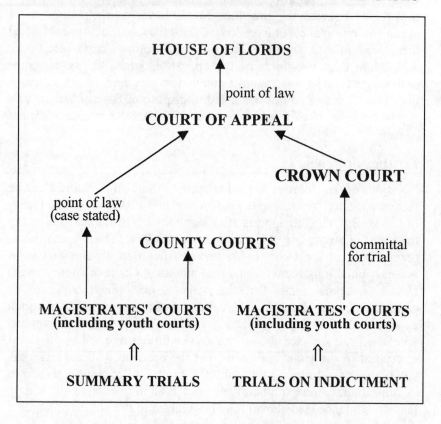

CHAPTER SIX

CIVIL PROCEEDINGS

6.1 THE NATURE OF CIVIL PROCEEDINGS

Civil proceedings have to be distinguished from criminal proceedings (see Chaps. 2.6 and 6.1). Perhaps the best way to understand the difference is to consider the legal proceedings that may be taken after a road accident, where one person's careless driving has damaged another person's car. The careless driver may receive a summons from the police, which means that *criminal* proceedings are being taken in a magistrates' court with the object of punishing the driver if he or she is found guilty of the crime of careless driving. But this will not help the other person to pay for the repairs to his or her car. Even if the careless driver is fined by the magistrates' court, the money paid will go to the state and not to the other car-owner. Unless the careless driver or an insurance company pays up voluntarily, the other car-owner must commence *civil* proceedings against the careless driver in a county court or in the High Court (depending on the amount involved), claiming "damages" (*i.e.* compensation) to cover the cost of repairing the car. The same distinction is apparent whenever some property is stolen. The owner of the property may well sue the culprit for the recovery of the property or its value, but the state - in the shape of the police or the Public Prosecution Service - may also prosecute the defendant for the crime of theft.

It can be seen, therefore, that one incident can give rise to both criminal and civil proceedings, but the person initiating the proceedings and the object of the proceedings are different, and the courts hearing the cases are also different (although the judges may be the same). Criminal courts do have some powers to award civil law remedies in the course of criminal proceedings, but these powers are limited and are not frequently exercised (see Chap. 5.4). There also exists a right, moreover, to claim compensation from the state for losses suffered through violent criminal action. This kind of claim must be processed through the *civil* courts and is described in more detail in 6.5 below. A diagram illustrating the civil court system in Northern Ireland, and the avenues of appeal within it, appears in Table 18. The workload of the various courts over the past four years is reflected in Table 19, the figures in which are derived from the *Northern Ireland Judicial Statistics* published annually by the Northern Ireland Court Service.

TABLE 18: THE APPEAL SYSTEM IN CIVIL CASES

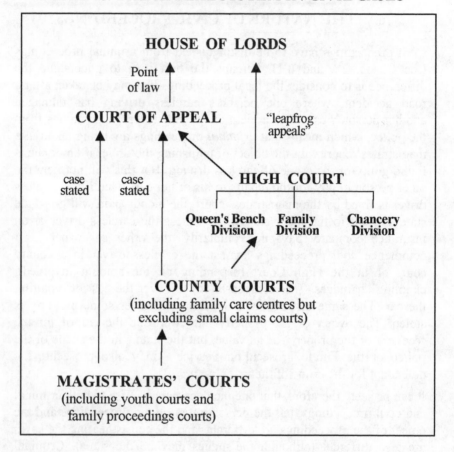

Settlements

Once criminal proceedings have begun they must go to court unless the charges are dropped. Even if the person accused (the "defendant") pleads guilty, and there is therefore no trial, the court must impose an appropriate sentence. But in civil proceedings (with some rare exceptions, most notably divorces) the plaintiff and the defendant can at any time - even after the court has started to hear the case, or when the case has reached an appellate court - agree between themselves that actions are in fact settled before they ever see the inside of a court.

TABLE 19: CIVIL CASES DEALT WITH IN NORTHERN IRELAND 2000-2003

	2000	2001	2002	2003
Court of Appeal				
Appeals disposed of	34	74	77	79
Queen's Bench Division				
Appeals from county courts	369	440	395	372
Appeals from Masters	87	147	94	131
Bail applications	1,686	1,846	2,478	2,783
Actions begun	5,944	5,980	6,078	6,250
Actions tried	38	36	48	30
Judgments by default	901	956	869	1,056
Judicial review applications	242	254	316	340
JR applications granted	34	34	26	49
Chancery Division				
Mortgage suits begun	1,717	1,604	1,625	1,710
Other land / property suits begun	272	287	287	327
Company proceedings begun	280	234	226	260
Bankruptcy proceedings begun	1,853	1,466	1,619	2,085
Family Division				
Divorce decrees *nisi*[1]	1,277	1,322	1,147	1,329
County courts				
Civil appeals heard	88	80	118	96
Divorce decrees *nisi*	1,207	1,320	1,324	1,322
Criminal injury cases	3,346	3,905	3,582	2,722
Defended civil bills	12,023	12,674	10,783	8,977
Small claims courts				
All cases dealt with	10,730	12,521	14,765	10,194
Cases dealt with in Belfast	4,242	5,251	7,590	4,530
Magistrates' courts				
Total number of applicants	39,338	37,323	40,222	40,787
Licence applications	615	567	n/a	628
Domestic cases	1,609	1,568	1,211	1,071
Non-molestation and occupation	5,732	6,672	6,749	5,974
Debts and ejectments	23,442	20,236	n/a	22,892
Enforcement of judgments				
Notices of intention to enforce	17,325	16,240	20,598	19,859
Enforcement orders made	10,195	9,343	10,567	15,207
Cases of unenforceability	639	475	513	474
Money recovered	£3.16m	£3.03m	£3.33m	£ 3.85m

---

[1] These figures include the very few decrees of nullity and judicial separation issued each year.

Once civil proceedings have actually started, the court must be officially notified of any settlement (so that "judgment by consent" can be decreed) and it must grant its approval before a civil action involving a person under the age of 18 can be settled. The question of who is to bear the costs of a settled action is usually made part and parcel of the settlement agreement, but failing this the court can order the costs to be "taxed" (*i.e.* assessed by a court official - see Chap. 3.4).

If the case is not settled there are currently three main courts in which civil proceedings can be started, depending largely on the amount of money or value of property at stake. They are: (i) the magistrates' courts, (ii) the county courts and (iii) the High Court. Each of these will be examined in turn, together with the procedures for appealing to higher courts (see 6.2 to 6.6 below). We will then consider how judgments in civil cases are enforced (see 6.7 below). The specially constituted family proceedings courts and family care centres also deal with civil matters, but only in relation to children; they are explained in Chapter 7.1 First, though, a word about possible reforms to the civil justice system.

The Civil Justice Reform Group

The civil justice system in England and Wales has undergone major reform in recent years, following the publication of the Woolf reports,[2] the review of civil justice by Sir Peter Middleton[3] and the wider implications of the Access to Justice Act 1999. New Civil Procedure Rules, common to both county courts and the High Court have been issued,[4] and a Civil Justice Council has been established.[5]

In 1998 the Lord Chancellor set up a Civil Justice Reform Group in Northern Ireland, chaired by Lord Justice Campbell. It issued its final report in 2000.[6] The Review of the Civil Justice System made

---

[2] See *Access to Justice: Interim Report* to the Lord Chancellor on the Civil Justice System in England and Wales (1995) and *Access to Justice: Final Report* (1996). For earlier discussions see the *Final Report of the Review Body on Civil Justice* (Cm. 394; 1988) and the joint report of the Law Society and Bar Council, *Civil Justice on Trial - The Case for Change* (the Heilbron-Hodge Report, 1993).

[3] See the *Review of Civil Justice and Legal Aid* (1997).

[4] Civil Procedure Rules 1998 issued under the Civil Procedure Act 1997, s. 1 and Sch. 1. The Rules are available on-line at www.dca. gov.uk/ civil/procrules_fin.

[5] *Ibid.* s. 6. See www.civiljusticecouncil.gov.uk.

[6] Civil Justice Reform Group, *Review of the Civil Justice System in Northern Ireland: Interim Report* (1999) and *Final Report* (2000). Both reports are available on-line at www.nics.gov.uk/pubsec/courts/courts.htm. See too D. Capper, "Final Report of the

recommendations regarding three levels of court for civil proceedings: (i) the "lower tier" (the small claims court), (ii) the "medium tier" (county courts) and (iii) the "upper tier" (the High Court). The distinction between the three tiers is roughly similar to that between the three "tracks" proposed by Lord Woolf (the "small claims track", the "fast track" and the "multi track") but, unlike the reforms in England and Wales, the report for Northern Ireland did not propose the adoption of common rules of procedure for county courts and the High Court.

The civil bill procedure (see 6.4 below) continues to operate in the county courts in Northern Ireland, with the main procedural changes taking place in the High Court. And to date no Civil Justice Council has been set up in Northern Ireland. The Council in England and Wales (in existence since 1998) ensures that the future development of the civil justice system there is kept under review. The report of the Civil Justice Review also covered a number of general matters, including the evidence of experts, the operation of additional schemes for alternative dispute resolution (ADR)[7] and the future role of information technology. Details of some of the recommendations are mentioned at the appropriate points later in this chapter. Family matters (and therefore most of the civil jurisdiction of magistrates' courts), the enforcement of judgments in civil cases, the work of tribunals hearing civil disputes and the provision of legal services were all matters excluded from the review, but the last of these topics has recently been the subject of a separate reform initiative (see Chap. 3.3) and a review of tribunals which was conducted for England and Wales[8] may in due course lead to similar reforms in Northern Ireland.

6.2 CIVIL PROCEEDINGS IN A MAGISTRATES' COURT

The powers of a magistrates' court in relation to civil proceedings are much less important than those in relation to criminal proceedings (see Chap. 5.4 and 5.5). Resident magistrates spend only about one quarter of their time on civil work, but in both spheres it is a local court, mainly dealing with *comparatively* unimportant matters arising within

---

Civil Justice Reform Group - Still Keeping Woolf from the Door" (2000) 51 NILQ 619.

[7] The report recommends that a pilot scheme should be established to evaluate the feasibility of a voluntary form of ADR by way of mediation in commercial and medical negligence cases in the Queen's Bench Division.

[8] By a team led by Sir Andrew Leggatt. See www.tribunals-review.org.uk and also Chap. 8.1.

the petty sessions district where the court sits. At the moment there are 20 magistrates' courts in the province, all of which are listed in Table 2 on page 20. They sit at intervals varying from every working day (in Belfast) to once a month. As implied in Chapter 5.4, where the criminal jurisdiction of magistrates' courts is described, the jurisdiction of these courts is called summary because the procedure used in them is simple, informal and speedy; in civil matters there is none of the elaborate procedure normally found in the High Court cases or to a lesser extent in county courts. When a case comes to a magistrates' court it is dealt with by a resident magistrate sitting without a jury. The litigants are often represented by solicitors rather than barristers, although witnesses are examined and cross-examined in the same way as in a higher court. Because there is often not a great deal at stake in the case, compared with proceedings in a higher court, the proceedings do not usually take much time and most decisions are announced straightaway.

The main types of civil cases which a magistrates' court can deal with are "domestic" cases, claims to recover small debts, claims to deprive someone of the occupation of land ("ejectment proceedings"), and applications for licences. Of the 33,307 civil applications dealt with during 2003, approximately 25% related to domestic matters, while some 69% concerned small debts or ejectment. A few words will be said about each type of case. For further details readers are referred to the intricacies of the Magistrates' Courts (NI) Order 1981 and the Magistrates' Courts Rules (NI) 1984, both of which have been frequently amended in subsequent years.[9]

Domestic cases

Domestic cases are those involving family matters. Many legal remedies (but not decrees of divorce or nullity) are available in a magistrates' court to a husband or wife whose marriage is not working out very happily. Remedies for domestic violence or for disputes over the care of children are available to co-habitees as well as to people who are married. A resident magistrate may grant any of the following orders.

---

[9] The Northern Ireland Court Service, from the first quarter of 2005, has started producing a provisional set of figures for magistrates' court work on a quarterly basis. This *Magistrates' Courts Bulletin* is available on-line at www.courtni.gov.uk. In the first three months of 2005 some 6,641 civil applications were dealt with.

Financial provision orders

If things are going badly between a husband and wife it is obviously very important that proper financial provision is made for both spouses and for any children. Provision for children is now usually obtained through the Child Support Agency but a spouse will have to apply to a magistrates' court regarding his or her own maintenance. In many instances the court may have to compel these arrangements to be carried out. If the spouses have agreed in writing between themselves that one of them should pay an amount of money to the other, or to a child of the family, the court can confirm this agreement and order the payments to be made. Similarly, if the parties are living apart by agreement and one of them has been paying money to the other or to a child of the family for at least three months, these voluntary payments can be ordered by the court to be continued.

If a person contests the duty to pay anything at all to the other spouse, the latter can apply under the Domestic Proceedings (NI) Order 1980 for a financial provision order to compel such payment. This last course of action is possible, however, only if one of a number of grounds is first satisfied: these are: (i) that the spouse has failed to provide reasonable maintenance for the applicant or a child of the family, (ii) that he or she has committed adultery, (iii) that he or she has deserted the applicant, or (iv) that he or she has behaved in such a way that the applicant cannot reasonably be expected to live with that spouse. In all of these situations the financial provision which a magistrate can order to be made may take the form of a regular weekly or monthly sum, or one single lump sum not exceeding £1,000.

Non-molestation orders and occupation orders

Under the Family Homes and Domestic Violence (NI) Order 1998,[10] a non-molestation order may be granted to prevent a person from molesting another person who has or had some kind of relationship with the first person (an "associated person") or a relevant child. It is possible for divorcees, former co-habitees and even close relatives, including parents and brothers and sisters, to apply for protection. In deciding whether to grant a non-molestation order, the magistrate will

---

[10] This largely mirrors the Family Law Act 1996 for England and Wales; see generally J. Murphy, "Making Private Violence Public" (1999) 50 NILQ 186. The Northern Ireland Court Service has an explanatory leaflet on the Order (which is also available on-line).

take a number of factors into account including the health, safety and well-being of the other party or child. The order restrains the violent party from generally threatening, pestering or harassing the other person or from acting in a particular way such as making abusive telephone calls. A non-molestation order can last for a fixed period of time or indefinitely. If the order is disobeyed, a police officer can arrest the guilty party without a warrant.[11]

Under the Family Homes and Domestic Violence (NI) Order 1998 an occupation order can be granted on its own or in conjunction with a non-molestation order. It is available to a wide range of associated persons, including spouses, former spouses and co-habitees, as well as others who have an interest in the ownership of the property in question. The terms of an occupation order can prevent a party from doing a number of things, including entering the family home, other specified premises or some area in which the family home or those specified premises are situated. It can remain in force for up to 12 months but can be extended if necessary (unlike in England and Wales). It is a criminal offence to disobey an occupation order and again the guilty party can be arrested without a warrant.

These two remedies replaced what were formerly called personal protection orders and exclusion orders. They are usually applied for in a magistrates' court unless the parties are already involved in family proceedings in a different court (*e.g.* a divorce hearing in a county court), in which case the application will be dealt with in that other court. In appropriate cases a resident magistrate can decide to transfer an application to a different court; for further details, see the Family Homes and Domestic Violence (Allocation of Proceedings) Order (NI) 1999.

A resident magistrate can grant a non-molestation order or an occupation order in cases of emergency without notifying the other party; this is called an *ex parte* application. The other party will be given the opportunity to present his or her side of the story at a later stage. It is possible for children under the age of 18 to apply for a non-molestation order or, in some cases, an occupation order (if they are entitled to occupy the home), but such applications can be dealt with *only* in the High Court and not by a resident magistrate. If a child

---

[11] See art. 26 of the 1998 Order and the Police and Criminal Evidence (NI) Order 1989, art. 26(2)(g).

applicant is under the age of 16, the judge must also be satisfied that he or she understands what is involved.

In 2003, there were 3,823 applications for non-molestation orders, 1,000 applications for occupation orders and 1,151 applications for combination occupation and non-molestation orders. The total number of orders actually made, after cases were dismissed, withdrawn or adjourned, was 4,220. Of these 23% were made by consent.

Future reforms

A number of consultations on domestic violence and the effectiveness of the law in protecting the victims of abuse have been launched since the Family Homes and Domestic Violence (NI) Order 1998 came into effect in 1999. One of these was a consultation paper issued by the Northern Ireland Office entitled *Tackling Violence Against Women*, which highlighted the growing problem of violence against women generally, and another was a discussion paper regarding ownership of the family home and other property, issued by the Law Reform Advisory Committee in 1999.[12] The Office of Law Reform (see Chap. 9.14) also conducted research among legal and other professionals on how the Family Homes and Domestic Violence (NI) Order 1998 was actually working in practice. The findings, published in late 2003, concluded that the 1998 Order was generally working satisfactorily, although some changes were required to make the Order compliant with human rights obligations. These are now contained in the Law Reform (Miscellaneous Provisions) (NI) Order 2005 which, amongst other things, extends the protection of the 1998 Order to same-sex partners.[13] In October 2003, the Department for Social Development launched a consultation on "Tackling Violence at Home" aimed at further strengthening and harmonising the law in relation to domestic violence. The Department's final proposals in this regard are expected in 2005.

---

[12] *Matrimonial Property* (Discussion Paper No. 5, 1999). For the work of the LRAC see Chap. 9.14.

[13] The Order also abolishes three old rules affecting matrimonial property: (i) the presumption that property transferred by a husband to his wife is for her own personal use (known as the presumption of "advancement"), (ii) the rule that a husband must maintain his wife and (iii) the rule that savings out of housekeeping money given by a husband to his wife still belong to the husband.

Orders concerning children[14]

The powers of magistrates and of other judges in civil matters relating to children were significantly altered by the Children (NI) Order 1995. Under this law a magistrates' court can decide where children should live and with whom they should have contact, and whether a child should be placed under the supervision of or committed to the care of the Department of Health, Social Services and Public Safety. A resident magistrate can also resolve disputes between parents regarding their children's upbringing (*e.g.* which school they should attend) and in some cases the court can prevent the parents from taking certain steps regarding their children without first obtaining its approval (*e.g.* taking the children abroad on holiday).

All of these powers concerning children can, however, be exercised only in connection with other domestic proceedings already taking place in a magistrates' court (*e.g.* if the court is considering financial provision arrangements between the spouses). Proceedings involving children are otherwise begun in a special "family proceedings court", although if necessary they will be transferred to a "family care centre" (a county court) or even to the Family Division of the High Court. For further details on how such cases are distributed among the different courts, see the Children (Allocation of Proceedings) Order (NI) 1996.[15] In 2004, only four applications concerning children were dealt with in Northern Ireland's magistrates' courts during the course of other domestic cases (so-called "connected proceedings")[16], but as many as 5,332 applications were dealt with on a "free standing" basis.[17]

Magistrates also have the power to make orders granting "parental responsibility" to unmarried fathers. Following an Office of Law Reform consultation paper on the topic,[18] the Northern Ireland Assembly passed the Family Law Act (NI) 2001, which makes it easier for such fathers to acquire parental responsibility. Magistrates do not, however, have jurisdiction to grant adoption orders: for those the applicant has to go to a county court (see Chap. 6.4).

---

[14] For criminal proceedings concerning children see Chap. 7.1.
[15] See Chaps. 2 and 6 and the useful summary provided by Higgins J. in *S* v *S* [1998] 2 BNIL 39.
[16] *Northern Ireland Judicial Statistics 2004*, Table F.3.
[17] *Ibid.* Table F.1.
[18] *Parental Responsibility for Unmarried Fathers and Court Procedures for the Determination of Paternity* (1999).

Procedures in general

The party who wants any of these domestic remedies in a magistrates' court (the complainant or applicant) can begin the civil proceedings in one of two ways, depending on the type of order being sought. In cases concerning financial provision, the complainant starts the process by stating the facts (in a "complaint") to a lay magistrate or clerk of petty sessions. In all other cases, the applicant sets out the details on an application form and sends it together with certain documents to the court office. A summons will then be issued and served on the respondent ordering him or her to come before a magistrates' court on a certain day. If the applicant is seeking a non-molestation order, occupation order or any of the orders concerning children, a copy of the application form is attached to the summons and the respondent must be given at least two days' notice of the court date (or seven days for orders concerning children). Of course it is always wise to seek proper legal advice before deciding to start proceedings. It should be noted that during the course of domestic proceedings a resident magistrate can decide to make a non-molestation order, occupation order or any of the orders concerning children even if the parties involved have *not* made an application.

Domestic cases are heard at different times from other cases and *in camera* (*i.e.* with the general public excluded). For further details on rules of procedure in these cases see the Magistrates' Courts (Domestic Proceedings) Rules (NI) 1996 and the Magistrates' Courts (Children (NI) Order 1995) Rules (NI) 1996, both as amended.[19]

Small debts

Claims to recover small debts are a second common type of civil case in a magistrates' court. Examples of such cases are claims for arrears of income tax, national insurance contributions, VAT, rates and rent. Generally speaking, the debt in question must be for a fixed amount and less than £100. If the claim is for the balance of an account - say you still owe £120 on a bill for £240 - you can be proceeded against in this way provided the total bill is for no more than £250. Larger sums are also recoverable, but only if a statute so provides (as the Rent (NI) Order 1978 does in the case of rent).

---

[19] See the Magistrates' Courts (Domestic Proceedings) (Amendment) Rules (NI) 1999 and the Magistrates' Courts (Children (NI) Order 1995) (Amendment) Rules (NI) 1999.

Proceedings for debt recovery are initiated not by way of complaint or summons but by way of a "process", which is a form filled in and served by the creditor or the creditor's solicitor. It can be issued at any time within six years after the debt falls due. The jurisdiction of magistrates' courts to deal with cases of debt overlaps with that of small claims courts, which are really a branch of the county courts (see 6.3 below), and the Civil Justice Reform Group recommended that this duality should continue.[20] Numerically the recovery of small debts is the largest part of the civil jurisdiction of magistrates, but legally they are not the most difficult of cases to resolve.

Land cases

Claims to deprive someone of the occupation of land are in this context known as "ejectment proceedings". They can be brought by landlords to get rid of tenants who are no longer entitled to stay on the premises. But unless a statute provides otherwise, a magistrates' court has jurisdiction in such matters only when premises have been let at a rent which is less than £110 per year. Most commercial and residential tenancies would therefore not be affected by this procedure were it not for the fact that the Housing (NI) Order 1981 confers special recovery rights upon housing associations and the Northern Ireland Housing Executive. In these matters proceedings are begun by a process, just as in claims to recover small debts. In 2003 there were as many as 22,892 applications for small debt recovery and ejectment in Northern Ireland's magistrates' courts (see Table 19 on p. 297).

Licences and appeals

Magistrates also have the important functions of renewing licences authorising the sale of alcohol as well as gamekeepers' and general dealers' licences, and granting or renewing registered club certificates.[21] They deal too with appeals against certain decisions taken by bodies such as education authorities. For instance, if an Education and Library Board refuses to issue a licence to someone under the age of 16 years to allow the child to participate in public performances on

---

[20] *Review of the Civil Justice System in Northern Ireland, Final Report*, (2000), para. 21, and *Interim Report*, para. 7.29.

[21] The relevant legislation includes the Betting, Gaming, Lotteries and Amusements (NI) Order 1985, the Licensing (NI) Order 1996 and the Registration of Clubs (NI) Order 1996. The Department for Social Development publishes guides to the law on these matters and also on Sunday trading.

the stage, an appeal can be heard by a magistrate. Under the Magistrates' Courts (Betting, Gaming, Lotteries and Amusements) (No. 2) (Amendment) Rules (NI) 2004, magistrates no longer have jurisdiction to consider applications for bookmaking (*i.e.* betting) licences; these applications must now be made to a county court.[22] Since 1997 applications to a magistrates' court for the renewal of licences authorising the sale of alcohol or for registered club certificates are made every five years rather than annually.[23]

As Table 19 on page 297 shows, 628 applications for licences were dealt with by magistrates in 2003. The document which is used to bring any of these applications to a magistrates' court is itself called a "notice" rather than a complaint or a process.

Appeals from a magistrates' court

As in criminal cases (see Chap. 5.4), if either side is dissatisfied with the decision of a court of summary jurisdiction in a civil matter it may appeal against that decision in one of two ways: (i) by way of ordinary appeal to a county court (where there will be a complete rehearing of the factual *and* legal issues), or (ii) by way of "case stated" to the Court of Appeal (where only points of law will be considered). If the first course is taken, there is then a further right of appeal for either side on a point of law - by way of case stated - to the Court of Appeal. The procedure by way of case stated and the composition of the Court of Appeal are described in more detail in Chapters 5.4. and 1.5 respectively. (For the different, but related, procedure known as judicial review, see 6.7 below.) Of the 2,454 appeals from magistrates' courts heard in county courts in 2003, only 4% related to civil cases.[24] There are usually just a few cases stated to the Court of Appeal by resident magistrates each year.[25]

---

[22] These Rules are a consequence of the Betting and Gaming (NI) Order 2004, which amended the Betting, Gaming, Lotteries and Amusements (NI) Order 1985.

[23] For details of the rules of procedure to be followed, see the Magistrates' Courts (Licensing) Rules (NI) 1997 and the Magistrates' Courts (Registration of Clubs) Rules (NI) 1997. More generally, see D. McBrien, *Liquor Licensing Laws in Northern Ireland* (1997).

[24] *Northern Ireland Judicial Statistics 2003*. The 2004 figures were not available at the time of writing.

[25] According to Table A.4 in *Northern Ireland Judicial Statistics 2004*, only 15 cases were set down in 2004.

In civil appeals the decision of the Court of Appeal is to all intents and purposes final. The only occasion when a civil case begun in Northern Ireland's magistrates' courts (or indeed county courts) can be taken to the House of Lords is when it involves a question as to the validity of a piece of legislation passed by the Northern Ireland Parliament.[26]

6.3 SMALL CLAIMS COURTS

The small claims court is dealt with at this stage because it is the popular name given to a type of proceeding which in fact is a special county court procedure provided for by the County Court Rules.[27] The jurisdiction is exercised by officials called district judges, formerly known as circuit registrars, four of whom have been appointed under the Judicature (NI) Act 1978 to serve in the court circuits into which the province has been divided - the Northern, Southern, Eastern and Belfast. The chief task of the district judges, who must be solicitors of at least seven years' standing, is to deal with claims which are for less than £2,000[28] (in England and Wales this figure was raised in 1996 to £3,000). District judges also hear undefended county court claims for sums up to £15,000 and they frequently sit as deputy county court judges to hear other claims. If the value of the money or property claimed is between £2,000 and £5,000 a district judge will deal with the claim just as a county court judge would deal with a larger one, but if the value of the claim does not exceed even £2,000 then a much simpler procedure - known technically, though misleadingly, as "arbitration" - is followed. It is this type of hearing which is popularly called a small claims court.

Some types of dispute involving less than £2,000 cannot be resolved in a small claims court in Northern Ireland at all and must still be taken to a county court in the normal way. These "excepted proceedings" are disputes involving personal injuries, road accidents,[29] libel or slander, a gift under a will or an "annuity" (a fixed sum paid each year), the ownership of land, the property rights of married couples, and matters referred to the county court from the High Court. No claim can be

---

[26] Judicature (NI) Act 1978, s. 42(6).
[27] County Court Rules (NI) 1981, O. 26. See too the County Courts (NI) Order 1980, art. 30(3).
[28] County Court (Financial Limits) Order (NI) 2001.
[29] As to what constitutes a road accident, see *Pedlow* v *Dept for Regional Development* [2003] 3 BNIL 108.

made for an "injunction" to stop someone doing something. Debt claims up to £2,000 can be brought either as a small claim or as a "civil bill" (see 6.4 below), but they must be treated as a small claim if either party so wishes. It is possible to make a claim against someone outside Northern Ireland if the incident giving rise to the claim occurred in this jurisdiction, but adopting this course of action could prove very costly and this may defeat the purpose of doing so. All other cases involving £2,000 or less *must* now be brought under the small claims procedure.

The current procedure[30]

To make a claim in a small claims court the applicant sets out the details of the case on an application form and sends it with two copies to a county court office. The fee is £16 for a claim not exceeding £150, £36 for a claim between £150 and £300, £52 for a claim between £300 and £500 and £62 for a larger claim.[31] The fees for counterclaims are 50% of these amounts and if either side wishes to appeal a fee of £175 must be lodged. A copy of the application form and a notice as to when and where the hearing is to take place will be returned to the applicant. Another copy is sent to the person against whom the claim is being made (the respondent) to find out if he or she intends to dispute the claim. If the respondent wishes to submit a counterclaim there is a fee of between £8 and £31 depending on the size of the counterclaim (see also Chap. 3.4).

About 20% of claims are usually settled out of court but if they are not they will be heard by a district judge on the day specified for the hearing. The hearing itself should take place within three months of the application being submitted and recent figures show that most cases are dealt with quickly with delays of longer than four months occurring in less than 5% of cases. Over one-half of all applicants tend to win their case at the hearing.

The procedure at the hearing is intended for use by individual applicants without the need for legal or lay representation. In practice, however, solicitors are present in up to 30% of the cases and advice workers would occasionally represent claimants (in England and Wales claimants have a *right* to be represented by another lay person in small

---

[30] The Northern Ireland Court Service publishes a helpful leaflet explaining the procedure used in small claims courts; it is also available on-line.

[31] Information on all court fees is available on the Northern Ireland Court Service's website, under the heading "Court Fee Code List".

claims proceedings[32]). Legal aid is *not* available, although some claimants may be entitled to advice under the green form scheme (see Chap. 3.3). Compared with proceedings in a proper court, the hearing will be informal and the normal rules of evidence will not apply; it will sometimes take place in a small room of the courthouse.[33] If the parties agree, the district judge may even decide the claim on the basis of written evidence only. Witnesses are usually required to be heard; there may be no witness box as such, but the swearing of a formal oath is usually demanded. If a witness is reluctant to attend, the party wishing to call the witness can oblige him or her to attend by applying to the district judge for a witness summons. If a district judge makes a ruling on an interlocutory matter in a small claims case (*i.e.* on a preliminary issue) this cannot be appealed to a county court judge but must be taken to the High Court either by way of judicial review (see 6.7 below) or by way of case stated.[34]

Neither of the parties can (except rarely) recover his or her costs from the other party in a small claims arbitration (except the fee payable with the application form), so any travel expenses incurred by witnesses and the charge of any lawyers who are engaged for the case will have to be borne by the party calling the witness or employing the lawyer. This applies also to the cost of engaging an expert (*e.g.* a building contractor) to report on some matter, but the district judge may ask for a report from an independent expert to clarify a technical point and the cost of this will then be borne by the court office and not by the parties. The only occasion on which a district judge may award costs to one party is where the other party's conduct has been unreasonable.

The district judge's decision will usually be announced as soon as the hearing is over. It may be issued even in the absence of the losing party. If the losing party does not comply with whatever order is made, the winner can take the case to the Enforcement of Judgments Office (see Chap. 5.8). If one party wishes to appeal against the decision of a district judge, he or she can only ask for a case to be stated on a point of law, not fact, to the Court of Appeal (until April 2004 appeals lay to

---

[32] See Courts and Legal Services Act 1990, s. 11 and the Lay Representatives (Rights of Audience) Order 1992.

[33] Though in a recent case decided by the European Court of Human Rights it was held that small claims proceedings should invariably be held in public: *Scarth* v *UK* (1998) 28 EHRR CD 47.

[34] *Cooper* v *Royal British Legion* [2004] NICty 1.

the High Court).[35] The rights of appeal are deliberately restricted so as to prevent undue consideration of what are, relatively speaking, minor matters.

The small claims procedure remains very popular.[36] During 2003 a total of 10,261 applications were dealt with, with Belfast accounting for 45% of the business. Most of the cases, however, were claims brought by shops and companies against consumers, rather than *vice-versa*. The vast majority of small claims which go to a hearing in Northern Ireland are undefended; in England such cases do not lead to a hearing at all.

The future reform of the small claims court

The Review of the Civil Justice System in Northern Ireland recommended a number of reforms to the small claims court.[37] These included introducing a default judgment procedure where a claim is not being disputed, giving claimants a right to be represented by another lay person, allowing a district judge to remove certain cases from the small claims court to the county court and publishing a separate set of procedural rules in plain English. These reforms have not yet been initiated. The Review also recommended that claims for personal injuries should continue to be excluded from the small claims court, as should claims for property damage arising from road traffic accidents.

6.4 CIVIL PROCEEDINGS IN A COUNTY COURT

With the establishment of the Crown Court in 1979 (see Chap. 5.6) county courts became almost exclusively civil courts. However they still hear appeals from criminal cases tried summarily in magistrates' courts, and some judges who sit as county court judges also sometimes sit as Crown Court judges (see Chaps. 1.5 and 5.6).

The civil work of county courts is much more varied than that of magistrates' courts, but it is still subject to restrictions as regards both type and size of claim. We shall first of all list the main types of case dealt with in a county court and then look at a few typical procedures. Further details are to be found in the County Courts (NI) Order 1980 and the County Court Rules (NI) 1981, both as amended.[38]

---

[35] Justice (NI) Act 2002, s. 74, amending County Courts (NI) Order 1980, art. 30(4)(b); see too the Rules of the Supreme Court (NI) (Amendment) 2004.

[36] J. Baldwin, "Is there a Limit to the Expansion of Small Claims?" [2003] CLP 313.

[37] *Final Report* (2000), Chap. 2.

[38] See also B. Valentine, *Civil Proceedings: The County Court* (1999).

It should be noted that a county court can deal with any debt claim for a "liquidated" (*i.e.* certain) amount of money even though the sum involved is greater than that laid down as the normal upper limit for a county court, provided that the parties themselves agree to this. County courts must also deal with any cases which for one reason or another are transferred to them by the High Court. If county court cases are contested they will normally be determined by county court judges if the amount in dispute is above £5,000; contested disputes for lesser amounts, and uncontested disputes over amounts up to £15,000, will usually be heard by district judges (see Chap. 1.5).

Types of case

At the moment the main types of case, or "action", heard in the county courts in Northern Ireland are the following:

(1)   actions in tort, or for breach of contract, where the amount claimed is less than £15,000 (£3,000 in libel or slander claims); an action in tort is what lawyers call a claim for compensation for personal injury or damage to property caused by the defendant - it is the kind of legal action taken by the victims of assaults, thefts or accidents at work or on the roads; libel and slander (which together form the tort of defamation) allow compensation for damage to a person's reputation - libel is the permanent form (*e.g.* a letter in a newspaper), slander the transient form (*e.g.* a speech at a meeting);

(2)   actions for the recovery of land or involving disputed claims to the ownership of land where, generally speaking, the land does not have an annual rateable value of more than £500[39] (this covers, for instance, disputes between landlords and tenants or between neighbours) or £4,060 if the land is wholly or partly uninhabited;

(3)   Chancery work, such as the management of funds held in trust, the enforcement of mortgages, the ending of partnerships and the supervision of contracts for the sale of land, provided that in all these cases the sum of money or value of property involved is less than £45,000 or the annual rateable value of any land

---

[39] In some cases (*e.g.* under "Deasy's Act" 1861), the figure is £1,000. The figure for commercial property was amended to £3,250 by the Revaluation (Consequential Provisions) Order (NI) 1997.

involved is less than £500 (in the county courts, Chancery work is always referred to as "Equity" business - see Chap. 1.3);

(4) disputes as to the validity of a will and as to who is to act as executor under a will, or administrator of the estate of someone who dies without making a will, provided that in such cases the estate does not exceed a value of £45,000 after payments of all taxes, etc.; this heading includes disputes over "legacies" (*i.e.* gifts of goods or money in a will), where the legacy claimed has a value of less than £15,000;

(5) undefended petitions for divorce, and certain applications for a share in matrimonial property (regardless of the value of the property);

(6) applications to adopt children;[40]

(7) equality of opportunity and discrimination cases brought under the Equal Pay Act (NI) 1970, the Sex Discrimination (NI) Order 1976, the Disability Discrimination Act 1995, the Race Relations (NI) Order 1997 or the Fair Employment and Treatment (NI) Order 1998, although cases alleging discrimination in employment practices are dealt with by industrial tribunals (see Chap. 8.3);

(8) applications brought under the Consumer Credit Act 1974, for instance, to re-open a credit agreement of less than £15,000 on the ground that its terms are extortionate;

(9) applications for licences to sell intoxicating liquor (applications to renew or to transfer licences are made to a magistrates' court: see Chap. 5.4);

(10) actions to recover rates under the Rates (NI) Order 1977 and applications to determine the proper rent for a protected tenancy under the Rent (NI) Order 1978 (see also Chap. 8.5);

(11) appeals against decisions of the Secretary of State for Northern Ireland on certain issues connected with compensation for criminal injuries or criminal damage (these are considered to be civil claims even though they arise out of the commission of a crime; they can be for any amount: see 6.5 below);

(12) applications concerning the care and welfare of children;

---

[40] 160 adoption applications were processed in 2003: *Northern Ireland Judicial Statistics 2003*, p. 31.

(13)   applications in cases involving domestic violence.

Undefended divorce cases

County court cases concerning family matters are begun either by issuing a summons (as with domestic cases in magistrates' courts - see 6.2) or by lodging a "petition". Since 1981 county courts have been able to grant divorces, but only in undefended cases. From 1992 it has not even been necessary for the petitioner to appear personally in court: like petitioners in England since much earlier, he or she can in effect get a divorce by post. Legal aid is available to cover divorce cases, whether defended or undefended (see Chap. 3.3). As Table 19 on page 297 indicates, in 2003 there were 1,322 divorces granted by the seven county court divisions in Northern Ireland; more than 60% of these were at the request of women. Of *all* divorce decrees granted in Northern Ireland in 2003, 50% were obtained in the county courts and 50% in the High Court. For further details on the procedure adopted in these cases see the Family Proceedings Rules (NI) 1996, as amended.[41] Important research on the way in which divorce law operates in Northern Ireland was published in 1999,[42] as was a consultation paper issued by the Office of Law Reform (see Chap. 9.14).[43] No legislative reform has yet occurred, however, partly because of the suspension of the Northern Ireland Assembly since October 2002.

Civil bills

Other county court cases are usually begun by the plaintiff, or the plaintiff's solicitor, issuing a document called a "civil bill". This can be delivered by hand or posted to the defendant.[44] The civil bill is a way of proceeding which is peculiar to Ireland and dates back to mediaeval times. It is more straightforward than the procedures used until recently in the county courts in England, requiring much less resort to "interlocutory" (*i.e.* preliminary) proceedings and not demanding any carefully worded pleadings as in High Court proceedings (see 6.6 below). The case raised by the civil bill is dealt with by a judge sitting

---

[41] A consolidated version of these 1996 Rules, as amended, was published by The Stationery Office in 2004 (at a cost of £100).

[42] C. Archbold, C. White, P. McKee, L. Spence, B. Murtagh and M. McWilliams, *Divorce in Northern Ireland: Unravelling the System*.

[43] *Divorce in Northern Ireland - A Better Way Forward*.

[44] See the 1981 Rules as amended by the County Court (Amendment No. 2) Rules (NI) 1995.

without a jury and the emphasis is on speed and cheapness. During 2003 (see Table 19 on page 297), 8,977 defended civil bills were dealt with by the county courts).

If the defendant wishes to contest the civil bill, he or she has a period of three weeks within which to notify the plaintiff and the court by handing in or posting a document called a notice of intention to defend. The plaintiff has a further six months in which to inform the court and the defendant that the case is ready for hearing by delivering a "Certificate of Readiness" to the chief clerk and serving a copy on the defendant; otherwise the matter will be referred to a judge who can: (i) set a date for hearing, (ii) "stay" (*i.e.* stop) the proceedings or (iii) dismiss the case.[45] This system, introduced in 1995, ensures that cases in the county court are processed more quickly. In general it seems to work well, although there is some evidence that it is not vigorously enforced in equal measure throughout all of the county courts in the province.[46]

In debt cases, if the defendant decides not to defend the civil bill or fails to serve the appropriate notice, the plaintiff can apply to the court for a judgment against the defendant without the need for a hearing. To do this the plaintiff must lodge a number of documents with the chief clerk including an "affidavit" (*i.e.* a sworn statement) specifying the amount of money owed plus any interest. The judgment, if granted, will be for this amount. This is called "a judgment in default of notice of intention to defend".[47]

However, in cases where the amount of compensation claimed in the civil bill is uncertain (*i.e.* a claim for "unliquidated damages"), the plaintiff can apply for an "interlocutory" (or provisional) judgment for an amount to be assessed afterwards by a district judge. If this is granted, the plaintiff must send any supporting evidence to the chief clerk, who then issues a summons which is served on the defendant at least seven days before the assessment of the damages is due to take place. If the defendant wishes to give evidence at the assessment, both the plaintiff and the court must be notified of this in writing. A district

---

[45] See the 1981 Rules as amended by the County Court (Amendment No. 3) Rules (NI) 1995.

[46] *Review of the Civil Justice System in Northern Ireland, Interim Report*, para. 8.34. See also Certificates of Readiness: County Court Practice Note No. 9 of 2004 [2004] 5 BNIL 72.

[47] See O. 12, substituted in the 1981 Rules by the County Court (Amendment No. 2) Rules (NI) 1995.

judge gives a "decree" (or final judgment) for the amount assessed. This procedure can also be used in certain other cases, including claims for the detention of goods or the possession of land. (It is not possible, however, to apply for a default judgment against a minor or a hospital patient, and the approval of the court is necessary for judgments against the Crown or in cases where a debtor wishes to re-open a credit agreement under the Consumer Credit Act 1974). During 2003 there were 3,760 default judgments (1,881 liquidated claims, 440 unliquidated claims and 1,439 other claims).[48]

Generally speaking, as you would expect, the proceedings in county courts are more formal than in magistrates' courts but less formal than in the High Court. It must also be remembered that at any stage the parties to a civil dispute can agree to sink their differences and settle the action between themselves. If this does not happen a county court judge usually delivers a judgment as soon as the parties have completed the submission of their arguments. In only a few cases will judgment be "reserved" until a later date.

Appeals to and from a county court

County courts hear appeals from civil as well as criminal cases heard in magistrates' courts, although the criminal workload is by far the more demanding: in 2003 there were just 96 civil appeals but 2,343 criminal appeals, a ratio of about 1:24. Not counting appeals which were withdrawn, appeals against conviction resulted in the conviction being reversed or the sentence varied in 59% of cases, while appeals against sentence only were allowed in 54% of cases. Civil appeals were successful in 78% of cases.[49] As in criminal cases (see Chap. 5.4) there will be a complete rehearing in the county court, which can uphold, vary or reverse the decision of the magistrates' court. As mentioned above, county courts also hear appeals on certain issues connected with claims for compensation for criminal injury and criminal damage (see also 6.5 below)

A person aggrieved by a decision of a county court in the exercise of its "original" (*i.e.* non-appellate) civil jurisdiction may appeal either by way of a full rehearing to the High Court or by way of case stated on a point of law to the Court of Appeal. The High Court can itself then state a case on a point of law for the opinion of the Court of Appeal.

---

[48] *Northern Ireland Judicial Statistics 2003*, Table D.10.
[49] *Ibid.* p. 57.

Whichever path is followed the decision of the Court of Appeal is final. In 2003 there were 372 county court appeals to the High Court, 6% fewer than in 2002. There were no cases stated by county court judges.[50]

The future reform of the county courts

The Final Report of the Review of the Civil Justice System (see Chap. 5.1) was generally supportive of the county court system in Northern Ireland and it made only a few recommendations for change.[51] These include allowing district judges to deal with civil bills up to the value of £5,000 as well as disputes involving road accidents, libel or slander, a gift under an annuity, the ownership of land, the property rights of married couples and the matters referred to the county court from the High Court. The Report also wanted it to be made easier for cases to be transferred from a county court to the High Court and from a district judge's civil bill list to a county court judge's list. It suggested that the current financial limits on the county court's jurisdiction should be retained, as well as the system of scale fees prescribed by the County Court Rules Committee (provided they are regularly reviewed) but it believed that the right of a party to apply for judicial review of a decision of a county court judge (see 6.7 below) should be removed if a statutory right of appeal against such a decision already exists. To date most of the recommendations requiring action have not yet been implemented.

Overall, the county court system in Northern Ireland is relatively cheap and speedy and the Civil Justice Reform Group which conducted the Review found that it already compares quite favourably with the "fast track" procedure proposed by Lord Woolf for England and Wales.[52] As stated in the Interim Report (and confirmed in the Final Report): "The Certificate of Readiness procedure, if properly followed and applied, provides an efficient and workable compromise between strong judicial intervention and complete litigant autonomy."[53] It is unlikely, therefore that any future reforms will be as drastic as those introduced in England and Wales by the Access to Justice Act 1999.

---

[50] *Ibid.* Tables A.4 and B.17.
[51] Final Report (2000), Chap. 3.
[52] See Judge A. Hart, "Complexity, Delay and Cost - County Courts in Northern Ireland" (2002) 53 NILQ 125.
[53] *Interim Report*, Provisional Recommendation No. 36.

6.5 COMPENSATION FOR CRIMINAL OFFENCES

This section deals with one particular type of claim which, at least until recently, was commonly dealt with by a county court. As pointed out in Chapters 2.6 and 5.1, the law makes a basic distinction between civil wrongs and crimes. The former are acts for which private individuals can seek redress, whereas crimes are acts by which the state is offended. Even though one and the same act can constitute both a civil wrong and a crime, the two forms of misbehaviour are processed quite differently in the legal system of Northern Ireland (and other common law countries). The victim of a civil wrong *sues* the perpetrator of the act for *damages*; the state *prosecutes* and *punishes* him or her for the crime. In a perfect world both the victim and the state would be satisfied and the offender would pay his or her debt to the individual and to society alike.

For a number of reasons things may not work out so neatly, certainly from the point of view of the victim. In the first place, the perpetrator of the act may never be caught; secondly, even if caught, the perpetrator may not be convicted because he or she is very young, has a mental disability or is immune from prosecution, or because the evidence is insufficient; and thirdly, whether or not caught and convicted for the crime, the perpetrator may not be able to afford to compensate the victim. In these circumstances it would be unjust to expect the victim to bear the loss alone. For a very long time, therefore, the state has operated compensation schemes to which the victims of some crimes can have recourse, and these can be used even if no-one has been prosecuted or convicted for the crimes in question.

In Northern Ireland, because of the heavy incidence of violent crime, there are in fact four such schemes, each of them long-established. One deals with crimes that cause injuries, another deals with crimes that cause damage to property, a third deals with losses suffered as a result of activities by the security forces in their fight against terrorists and a fourth compensates people who have had to leave their jobs because of intimidation. Some statistics on recent applications for criminal compensation are supplied in Table 20.

TABLE 20: CRIMINAL COMPENSATION CLAIMS
2000-2004

	2000-01	2001-02	2002-03	2003-04
Criminal injury claims				
Under the 1988 Order	13,939	14,363	2,416	275
Under the 2002 Order	0	0	8,102	7,997
Criminal damage claims	2,043	1,844	1,675	1,026
Terrorism Act claims	4,542	6,338	7,796	1,633
Appeals to the courts	3,346	3,905	3,582	2,722

Criminal injuries compensation

In 1998, the Secretary of State for Northern Ireland set up an independent review body under the chairmanship of Sir Kenneth Bloomfield, a former head of the Northern Ireland Civil Service, to examine the system then in place for awarding criminal injuries compensation in Northern Ireland.[54] The detailed report which followed in 1999 recommended that the Northern Irish criminal injuries scheme should be made more like the scheme in England and Wales[55] by having most injury claims decided on a tariff basis.[56] It also proposed increasing the amount of compensation paid where the victim dies to £10,000 to the closest relative and £5,000 to each of certain other relatives, making a payment of up to £10,000 to the families of the

---

[54] Sir Kenneth Bloomfield was formerly the Northern Ireland Victims Commissioner and in his report entitled *We Will Remember Them* (1998), at para. 5.11, he recommended the establishment of just such an independent review of the criminal injuries system.

[55] The Criminal Injuries Compensation Scheme 1996, made under the Criminal Injuries Compensation Act 1995.

[56] *Report of the Review of Criminal Injuries Compensation in Northern Ireland* (1999). In the same year the UK Government published a consultation paper on possible changes to the criminal injuries compensation scheme in England and Wales. It that paper it restated its commitment to the tariff scheme and ruled out any likelihood of fundamental change in the near future: See *Compensation for Victims of Violent Crime: Possible Changes to the Criminal Injuries Compensation Scheme*, Home Office (1999).

"disappeared" (*i.e.* people in Northern Ireland who have almost certainly been murdered by terrorists and buried at unknown locations)[57] and re-opening cases in certain circumstances (but not cases concerning injuries sustained before the new tariff scheme comes into effect).

Most of these recommendations were accepted by the Government in 2000 and were put into effect through the Criminal Injuries Compensation (NI) Order 2002 (despite the fact that not one MLA or MP from Northern Ireland voted in favour of such a change when the Order was debated in the Assembly and at Westminster). The amount of compensation received is now governed by the Northern Ireland Criminal Injuries Compensation Scheme,[58] which applies to all incidents occurring on or after 1 May 2002. The Scheme is administered by the Compensation Agency (see below),[59] and a copy is available on the Agency's website.[60] It should be stressed that the claims made under all the schemes are civil, not criminal, claims. They are not like the compensation and restitution orders which can be made during criminal proceedings (see Chap. 5.4) but are direct actions against the state.

The Compensation Agency

Until 1992 the claims were dealt with by the Criminal Compensation Division of the Northern Ireland Office, but in that year the Division became the Compensation Agency, the first Executive Agency to be set up in Northern Ireland. Today the Agency employs some 150 staff under a Chief Executive (currently Ms Anne McCleary) and it publishes a corporate plan, a business plan, an annual report and leaflets explaining the various compensation schemes it administers. In 2003-04 the Compensation Agency cost £4.25 million to administer.

The House of Commons' Northern Ireland Affairs Committee recently conducted an appraisal of how the Agency goes about its business. It was by and large complimentary, but it suggested that the Government should act urgently to ensure that there is no barrier to compensation for child sex abuse victims.[61] It also found that, although the 2002

---

[57] These cases are outside the existing and proposed criminal injury schemes and the Compensation Agency is not involved in processing them.

[58] Made under art. 3 of the 2002 Order.

[59] www.compensationni.gov.uk.

[60] www.compensationni.gov.uk/pdf/nicics02.pdf.

[61] *The Compensation Agency*, 3rd Report of 2003-04 (HC 271).

Scheme took away claimants' rights to be legally aided when claiming compensation, more than half of the recent claimants were still using solicitors to help them with their claims and were having to pay the solicitors' fees out of whatever compensation was awarded. Help under the legal advice and assistance scheme is available for claimants who meet the tight financial eligibility requirements (see Chap. 3.3).

Applying for criminal injuries compensation

In general the following conditions must be met before an application for compensation will be considered:

(1)   the applicant must be a victim of a crime of violence (including arson or an act of poisoning), or injured in some other way covered by the Scheme - a street-mugging would be a typical example; traffic offences, however, are excluded and where the violence has occurred within a household (*e.g.* child abuse) certain further conditions must be satisfied before compensation can be claimed;

(2)   the applicant must have been physically and/or mentally injured as a result; it is enough if the injury is suffered while trying to arrest an offender or prevent an offence; mental illness or trauma caused by reaction to a violent crime (called in law "nervous shock") is covered, but in most cases only if the person was actually present when the crime was committed;

(3)   the applicant must have been in Northern Ireland at the time when the injury was sustained;

(4)   the applicant must have been injured seriously enough to qualify for at least the minimum award available under the Scheme (currently £1,000), or be a dependant or relative of a victim of a crime of violence who has since died, or who has had a close relationship of love and affection with the victim; and

(5)   the injury must have been sustained within the past two years (unless in the particular circumstances of the case it is reasonable and in the interests of justice to consider older cases);[62] this two-year time limit is one year less than the period allowed for personal injury claims brought directly against the person who

---

[62] See para. 2.3 of *A Guide to the Northern Ireland Criminal Injuries Compensation Scheme* (2002), available from the Compensation Agency's website at www.compensationni.gov.uk.

caused the injury,[63] but a lot longer than the previous tight time limit for criminal injury claims of just three months; claims made outside the time limit are said to be "statute barred".

A number of other important factors are identified in paragraphs 14(a)-(e) of the Scheme as having an impact on an applicant's success in making an application. These include whether or not the police were informed of the crime at the earliest possible opportunity, whether the applicant helped or was prepared to help the police in their efforts to prosecute the offender, whether or not the applicant has co-operated fully with the Compensation Agency, how the applicant conducted him- or herself before, during or after the incident and whether the applicant has a criminal record. Fear of reprisals by the perpetrator of the offence will not, generally speaking, be considered an excuse for not co-operating with the police in their efforts to bring the offender to justice. A scale of penalty points is used to assess any reduction in an award as a result of the applicant's previous or spent convictions. For example, if the applicant has received a custodial sentence of three years and makes a claim 10 years later in relation to an unconnected incident, he or she could face a 50% reduction in the award.[64]

Calculating criminal injuries compensation

The Scheme sets out a "tariff" for compensation, dependent on the nature of the injury sustained. There are 28 tariff levels, ranging in monetary terms from £1,000 to £255,000. In a standard case a perforated ear drum will attract compensation of £2,000 (level 4), a broken lower arm £3,500 (level 7), attempted rape £10,000 (level 14) and loss of one eye £60,000 (level 22). Additional sums can be paid in respect of loss of earnings and other special expenses, and in cases of fatal injury a bereavement support payment can be made to acknowledge the grief and sorrow caused by the death of that person and the loss of that person's care, guidance and society. In place of making legal aid available for such claims the 2002 Order, in the face of stiff opposition from the Law Society of Northern Ireland, required

---

[63] Limitation (NI) Order 1989, art. 7.
[64] For further information consult paras. 8.15-8.17 of *A Guide to the Northern Ireland Criminal Injuries Compensation Scheme* (2002) or contact the Compensation Agency at the address cited in Appendix 2. The applicant should be told what particular factors influenced the decision to refuse compensation: *In re McCallion and others' Applications* [2001] 8 BNIL 16.

the Secretary of State to designate a body able to provide advice, assistance and support to claimants. The Secretary of State has since designated Victim Support (NI) for this purpose.

If compensation is paid but the Agency then discovers that the claimant did not make full and true disclosure, the Secretary of State can apply to a county court for reimbursement from the recipient. Likewise, if someone is later convicted of the criminal offence which caused the criminal injury, the Compensation Agency can apply to a county court for an order that this person must reimburse to the Agency the whole or a part of the compensation already paid to the victim.

In 2004, following high profile instances involving victims of the 1998 Omagh bomb, a review was published of the practice of lawyers viewing victims' scars during the process of attempting to settle applications for compensation for criminal injuries. Professor Desmond Greer, the author of the review,[65] recommended, amongst other things, that in every case the applicant's consent to a viewing should be a fully *informed* consent.

Challenging a decision on compensation

The 2002 Scheme allows for decisions on compensation to be reviewed and goes on to provide for appeals against decisions taken on reviews to be submitted within 90 days to adjudicators on an Appeals Panel appointed for that purpose by the Secretary of State.[66] The Panel has 24 members, drawn mainly from the legal and medical professions, plus a chairperson (Mr Oliver Loughran, a solicitor), seven staff and a budget in its first full year of £433,000. It was appointed in August 2002 and began hearing appeals in November 2003. By April 2004 it had heard 30 appeals (having received a total of 162 by that time).[67] The existence of the Appeals Panel relieves the county court of its role in hearing such appeals but that court still has jurisdiction to hear claims by the Secretary of State for the recovery of money from the person who committed the crime in question or (in cases where the victim has been doubly compensated as a result of other court proceedings) from the

---

[65] Summarised at [2004] 1 BNIL 16.
[66] There are equivalent panels in England and Wales: see www.cicap.gov.uk.
[67] *Criminal Injuries Compensation Appeals Panel, Accounts 2003-04*, HC 352 (2004-05). See too www.cicapni.org.uk.

victim him- or herself.[68] Decisions taken by the Criminal Injuries
Compensation Appeals Panel can be subjected to judicial review (see
6.7 below)[69] but otherwise they cannot be challenged on their merits.
However, if an injured person's condition deteriorates after an award of
compensation has been made he or she may ask the Compensation
Agency to review its earlier decision.

Criminal damage compensation

The scheme for compensating people who have suffered criminal
damage is a little more technical than the criminal injuries scheme. The
legislation now applicable is the Criminal Damage (Compensation)
(NI) Order 1977. The scheme for property damage compensation in
England and Wales - under the Riot (Damages) Act 1886 - remains
different from and less extensive than that in Northern Ireland. In fact
Northern Ireland's system compares favourably with those in most
other countries.[70]

Except in relation to agricultural buildings and property, compensation
for damage is available only if it has been caused by three or more
persons who have "unlawfully, riotously or tumultuously assembled
together", or by an act committed maliciously by a person acting for an
organisation engaged in terrorism. Compensation for unlawful removal
of property (*i.e.* "looting") is restricted to situations where the removal
takes place in the course of a riot causing more than £200 worth of
damage to the building where the property was located.

To qualify for compensation a person must serve on the Secretary of
State (as represented by the Compensation Agency) and on the police,
within 10 days of the damage being caused, a notice of intention to
apply for compensation. This notice must fully and truthfully disclose
certain facts. Within a further four months the application itself must be
made. The Compensation Agency decides what amount of
compensation, if any, should be paid having regard to all such
circumstances as are relevant and in particular to the conduct of the
applicant and whether all reasonable precautions were taken to reduce
or avoid the loss.

---

[68] Criminal Injuries Compensation (NI) Order 2002, arts. 14 and 15. The county court
also continues to hear appeals in cases of compensation under the Terrorism Act
2000 (see below).
[69] See, *e.g.*, *In re Skelly's Application* [2004] NIQB 53.
[70] See D. Greer (ed.), *Compensating Crime Victims: A European Survey* (1996).

Anyone who at any time has been a terrorist or a member of an organisation engaged in terrorism is barred from recovering compensation, with the exception that the Secretary of State may in any particular case make an *ex gratia* payment in the public interest. No compensation at all is provided for the first £200 of any loss, and it cannot be paid for lost money or jewellery or for any loss for which the applicant has already received adequate compensation under a statute or at common law (as in a civil action for damages). There are special provisions for dealing with situations where more than one person with an interest in property suffers loss through its damage or removal (*e.g.* when a house is mortgaged or a car is being bought on hire-purchase).

Appeals against the Compensation Agency's decisions on criminal damage claims still go to the county court, not to an Appeals Panel, and have to be lodged within six weeks.

Compensation under the anti-terrorism legislation

If any property is taken, occupied, destroyed or interfered with by security forces acting under the Terrorism Act 2000 - formerly the Northern Ireland (Emergency Provisions) Act 1996 (see Chap. 4.3) - compensation must be paid by the Secretary of State, again acting through the Compensation Agency.[71] The only exception is that no person who has been convicted of a scheduled offence (see Chap. 4.2), or of an offence under the 2000 Act, has a right to compensation in respect of acts done in connection with that offence. Applications for compensation have usually to be submitted within 28 days of the act which is the subject of the complaint (before 2000 the time limit was four months). Failing acceptance of the amount offered as compensation, the claimant can appeal to a county court. The county court judge will process the application as if it were an equity civil bill (see 6.4 above), except that no limit applies as to the amount which can be claimed.

As Table 20 on page 319 indicates, in the year 2003-04 the Compensation Agency received 1,633 claims for this kind of compensation, a huge decrease from the 2002-03 figure of 7,796 claims (which was itself more than twice the figure for 2001-02). The Northern Ireland Office's statistics on the operation of the Terrorism Act 2000 in 2003 reveal that in that calendar year total payments of

---

[71] Terrorism Act 2000, s. 102 and Sch. 12.

£1,885,697 (including solicitors' and assessors' fees) were made in respect of property damaged or requisitioned by the security forces.

In its report on the work of the Compensation Agency published in 2004,[72] the Northern Ireland Affairs Committee of the House of Commons stated that there had been "blatant exploitation and abuse" of the compensation provisions in the anti-terrorism legislation, especially in the two years following the coming into force of the 2000 Act – the very time when activity by the security forces under the anti-terrorism legislation was diminishing. The Committee had heard evidence that this was because some people systematically submitted fraudulent claims and were now doing so much more frequently given the shorter time limits for claims. The Committee estimated that £5 million had been lost through such fraud. The lower number of claims for 2003-04 would suggest that steps taken by the Compensation Agency to frustrate such fraudulent claims are proving successful.

Compensation for intimidation of employees

Since 1970 a non-statutory scheme has operated under which applications can be made to a Compensation Tribunal by employees who, having been in continuous employment for two years, have been dismissed by their employer or ceased employment voluntarily because of threats or other reasons directly attributable to civil disturbances in Northern Ireland. The scheme is administered by the Department of Enterprise, Trade and Investment (formerly the Department of Economic Development) and is applied to only a handful of cases each year.

6.6   PROCEEDINGS IN THE HIGH COURT

Unlike that of the inferior courts (magistrates' courts and county courts), the jurisdiction of the High Court is limited neither geographically nor by the value of the claim. If the matter is one which could also be dealt with in a magistrates' court or in a county court, the proceedings should be begun there because they will be cheaper and quicker; if they are begun in the High Court the judge can transfer them to a lower court and the plaintiff can be penalised as regards costs (see Chap. 3.4).

---

[72] *The Compensation Agency*, 3rd Report of 2003-04 (HC 271). For the role of the NIAC, see Chap. 9.1.

The High Court can deal with any subject-matter, but for reasons of administrative convenience its business is roughly distributed between its three divisions as follows.

(1)   *Queen's Bench Division*: claims for compensation for personal injury or for damage caused to a person's property or reputation (these are called "tort" claims); claims for breach of contract; claims concerning ships ("Admiralty actions"); all business not specifically assigned to another division (including various appeals).

(2)   *Chancery Division*: disputes concerning the distribution of a deceased person's property; difficulties arising out of the management of trust funds, including a charity's funds; the enforcement of mortgages and other securities; problems concerning partnerships and companies; bankruptcies; copyright; the supervision of contracts for the sale of land; the correction of deeds.

(3)   *Family Division*: petitions for divorce or nullity; property claims between married couples; disputes over a person's marital status or illegitimacy; applications concerning the wardship, adoption or guardianship of persons under the age of 18; applications regarding the care and welfare of children;[73] applications under the Family Homes and Domestic Violence (NI) Order 1998;[74] applications for the right to carry out the terms of a person's will or to manage the property of someone who dies intestate (*i.e.* without having made a will); matters affecting persons who have a mental illness.

The High Court in England and Wales is currently comprised of the same three divisions, but there are in addition some informally organised sub-divisions. In Northern Ireland there are only two of these, namely the Companies Court within the Chancery Division and the Commercial Court within the Queen's Bench Division. The Restrictive Practices Court is a separate court in its own right, on the same level as the High Court. It operates for the whole of the United Kingdom; its members comprising five judges (including one Supreme

---

[73] Proceedings under the Children (NI) Order 1995 are assigned to the Family Division by the Children (Allocation of Proceedings) Order (NI) 1996.
[74] Proceedings under the Family Homes and Domestic Violence (NI) Order 1998 are assigned to the Family Division.

Court judge nominated by the Lord Chief Justice of Northern Ireland) and 10 lay members, although usually only one judge and two lay members sit in any particular case. When it hears cases originating from Northern Ireland - this does not yet seem to have occurred - appeals lie to the Court of Appeal of Northern Ireland.

It is also necessary to note the existence of so-called Divisional Courts, not to be confused with the courts of the three separate divisions (see also Chap. 1.3). A Divisional Court is a court *within* a division and usually comprises two, or three, judges. It hears special appeal cases or deals with a particular type of case as a court of first instance. In England there are currently Divisional Courts within all three divisions; two of them carry out the very important task of hearing appeals from magistrates' courts in criminal and family law matters. The Divisional Court of the Queen's Bench Division also deals with applications for judicial review in criminal cases (see 6.7 below). It is mainly to deal with important examples of this last type of case that the Divisional Court of the Queen's Bench Division also exists in Northern Ireland, but it hears only a few cases each year.[75] The decisions of Divisional Courts, being still decisions of the High Court, are not as authoritative, according to the system of precedent, as decisions of the Court of Appeal (see Chap. 2.3).

Proceedings in the High Court can be begun in a variety of ways, depending on the type of claim being made. We shall first of all look at a typical Queen's Bench action and then briefly consider actions in the Chancery and Family Divisions.[76] It will be clear from the description of the Queen's Bench action that proceedings at a High Court trial can be rather formal and ponderous. Despite all the documentation, great emphasis is still laid on hearing the oral evidence of witnesses in the courtroom. The system is designed to ensure that the plaintiff and the defendant feel satisfied that the trial in open court leaves no stone unturned in the dispute between them. It is an "adversarial" system, where the parties fight each other, rather than an "inquisitorial" or "investigative" system (like those on the continent of Europe), where the court itself takes the initiative in seeking the truth.

---

[75] In 2003 it heard just two: *Northern Ireland Judicial Statistics 2003*, Table B.25.
[76] For further details see B. Valentine, *Civil Proceedings: The Supreme Court* (1997) and *Supplement* (2000).

Pleadings in a Queen's Bench action

Proceedings in the High Court can be begun in a variety of ways, depending on the type of claim being made. In the Queen's Bench Division the most typical claim is one made following an accident on the roads or at work. The claimant, who is called "the plaintiff", sets the ball rolling by issuing a writ of summons, which warns the defendant that a claim is being made and states the general nature of that claim. The writ will be delivered by hand or special delivery post.

If the defendant wishes to have a chance to contest the plaintiff's claim he or she should, within 14 days, "enter an appearance" with the court by handing in or posting the appropriate document. If the defendant does not do this the plaintiff can obtain a judgment without further argument, provided that it is proved that the writ of summons was properly delivered. This is called "a judgment in default of appearance". Even after an appearance has been entered, the plaintiff may be so confident of the defendant's lack of defence to the claim (except perhaps as to the *amount* of compensation being claimed) that he or she will apply for what is called a "summary judgment", that is, judgment without a full-scale hearing. (In a few types of action, however, such as those involving libel, slander or fraud, it is not possible to apply for a summary judgment.) Another way in which cases can be brought to a conclusion without a full hearing taking place is if the defendant pays a sum of money into the relevant court office and the plaintiff, within three weeks, decides to accept this amount in settlement of the claim. This "stays" (*i.e.* stops) the proceedings. If a payment into court has been made but not accepted, the judge and jury must not be told about it in case it prejudices their decision on whether and to what extent the defendant is liable.

If the defendant enters an appearance and the plaintiff does not apply for summary judgment, the plaintiff should, within six weeks, send the defendant a document called a statement of claim, which specifies the precise facts and law on which the claim is based and asks for particular remedies. The statement of claim will specify, for instance, where and how the accident occurred, why the defendant is legally liable and what injury was suffered. The defendant should respond to this, within three weeks, by sending to the plaintiff a defence. This document will deny most of the allegations made in the statement of claim and may well be accompanied by a counterclaim which makes allegations against the plaintiff. Within a further three weeks the plaintiff should produce a reply to the defence and, if necessary, a defence to the counterclaim. All these documents are called "pleadings", and the general rule is that points not raised in the written pleadings cannot later be argued orally in court. For a Northern Ireland case in the House of Lords where the failure of the plaintiff's lawyers to plead certain points ultimately led to rejection of the plaintiff's case, see *Farrell* v *Secretary of State for Defence.*[77]

At this juncture the pleadings are normally "closed", although further documents can be served with the special permission of the court, and in most cases either side can apply to the court at an earlier stage to have the action tried without the exchange of any further pleadings. Pleadings are meant to serve the purpose of making each side aware, before the case comes to trial, of what exactly the other side is arguing. In practice, however, the lawyers drafting these documents often prefer to hedge their bets, so that when the case does come to court they will not be prevented from arguing a certain point just because it was not mentioned in their pleadings. The time limits for serving the various pleadings are, as well, usually ignored in practice, by agreement of both sides. It is therefore a widely held view that the system of pleadings does little to reduce the length and cost of a High Court action. As explained in 6.2 and 6.4 above, civil cases in magistrates' courts and county courts are not hampered in the same way.

Interlocutory proceedings

Once the pleadings in a Queen's Bench action have been closed, the plaintiff can apply within six weeks to have the case set down for trial at a date some time in the future. But further pre-trial procedures can still be taken to ensure that when the case does reach the trial stage it will be dealt with as efficiently as possible. These further proceedings are called "interlocutory proceedings". Although well intentioned, they do add to the length, cost and complexity of the action. Examples are applications for the "discovery" of documents or for the serving of "interrogatories": these help a party to prepare for the trial by, respectively, giving access to certain vital papers or providing answers to important preliminary questions. There is also a right to apply for disclosure of documents held by persons not involved in the court

---

[77] [1980] 1 WLR 172.

case.[78] The process known as an application for a summons for directions, where a party seeks a ruling from a judge on a preliminary point, is commonly used in England but is not known in Northern Ireland.

The decision-making process

If the case eventually comes to trial - and this will be many months or even years after the issue of the writ - it will usually be held in the presence of a judge sitting alone. Until 1987 it was quite common in Northern Ireland for cases to be heard by a judge sitting with a jury (of seven persons), but the province then adopted the English rule whereby trials without a jury are the norm unless special circumstances warrant otherwise. Only actions such as claims for libel will now be heard by a jury, or if the judge accedes to a particular application.[79] Although it is highly likely that moving away from juries has shortened the average length of the trial of a personal injury claim in the High Court, this may have been counteracted to some extent by, for example, the increased use of expert witnesses.

When a judge *does* sit with a jury it is the judge's task to make sure that the trial is properly conducted and that the jury understands what law must be applied to the facts. The jury decides which version of the facts to believe, whom to hold liable and what amount of compensation (if any) is to be paid. This power to decide what remedy to give distinguishes the role of the civil jury from the roles of the criminal jury (see Chap. 5.6) and the coroner's jury (see Chap. 7.3). If there is no jury and the judge deems it necessary for a detailed assessment to be made of the compensation due, the matter will be referred to a High Court Master (see Chap. 1.5).

In most cases the judge will award compensation by referring to the Judicial Studies Board of Northern Ireland's "Green Book", which sets out guidelines for the assessment of damages in personal injury cases. These are based on what are believed to be the rates currently used in

---

[78] See *O'Sullivan* v *Herdmans Ltd.* [1987] 1 WLR 1047. See too the Law Reform Advisory Committee's Report, *Third Party Discovery in Civil Proceedings* (2003), which recommends that there should be rules of court in Northern Ireland (as there are in England and Wales) on this matter.

[79] The Court Service has produced an explanatory leaflet, also available on-line, for people who are called to serve on a High Court jury.

the negotiation and settlement of claims.[80] There is general agreement that compensation awards are on average slightly higher in Northern Ireland than in comparable cases in England and Wales, a factor contributing to higher insurance premiums in Northern Ireland.

Other cases and the overall caseload[81]

It should be remembered that the Queen's Bench Division also handles some applications for bail (and is the only court that can handle such applications in cases where a person has been charged with a scheduled offence - see Chap. 4.2). In 2003 there were 2,783 High Court bail applications (up 12% from 2002), 46% of which were granted. The same Division handles applications for judicial review (see 6.7 below) and in 2003 there were 340 of these, 173 of which were granted leave to continue; of the 139 applications which had a final hearing, 49% were successful. In the same year there were 372 appeals from county courts (including criminal injury claims), a 6% drop on the 2002 figure, and 131 appeals from decisions by Masters, 39% up on 2002.

At present, only about 2% of all the cases begun in the Queen's Bench Division actually culminate in a full-scale trial. The remainder are withdrawn or are settled before or during the course of the trial. In 2003 a total of 6,250 actions were initiated (3% up on the 2002 figure), but only 2,157 (4% up on 2002) were set down for trial and only 1,424 were disposed of in court in any way (excluding the 99 cases dealt with in the commercial court). Default judgments were issued in 1,056 cases (22% up on 2002). Of the writs issued, 981 were for claims lower than £15,000 (and so could have been heard in the county court instead), 434 were for claims higher than £15,000 and 4,832 were for "unliquidated" (*i.e.* unspecified) amounts. Of the judgments issued in cases where the claim was for an unliquidated amount, the amount awarded was less than £15,000 in 82% of them. Of the writs disposed of in court some 35% concerned claims for negligence, breach of statutory duty or nuisance. The average waiting time between a case being set down for trial and the trial actually beginning was 31 weeks, down massively from 50 weeks in 2002. Judgment was issued in favour of the plaintiff in 79% of the cases.

---

[80] *Guidelines for the Assessment of General Damages in Personal Injury Cases in Northern Ireland* (2nd ed., 2002).

[81] All the figures in these paras. are taken from *Northern Ireland Judicial Statistics 2003*, Pt. B. The figures for 2004 were not available at the time of writing.

Actions in the Chancery and Family Divisions

High Court proceedings in the Chancery and Family Divisions may be just as cumbersome as those in the Queen's Bench Division, but because in such cases there is often little argument about the relevant facts giving rise to the action - the dispute being really about whether some legal rule applies - the legal procedures are sometimes speedier and more informal. Again, many such actions are settled out of court. Chancery actions - such as claims that a contract for the sale of a house should be enforced - are usually started by a document called "an originating summons", which does not then lead to an exchange of pleadings. The matter is heard in the absence of a jury by a Master (see Chap. 1.5) or by a High Court judge sitting in chambers (*i.e.* the judge's own private office). Witnesses usually do not have to be present at the hearing because the evidence is presented in the form of written statements, called "affidavits", rather than as oral testimony. (Affidavits are documents sworn by the maker to be true in the presence of a Commissioner for Oaths - all solicitors are also Commissioners for Oaths).

During 2003,[82] as in previous years, the principal form of business in the Chancery Division were claims concerning mortgages (where a lender of money takes an interest in property as security for the loan). There were 1,710 of these, leading to 819 possession orders being made in favour of the lenders when the mortgagors could not keep up their mortgage repayments. There were also 1,057 bankruptcy petitions, although these were all dealt with by a Master rather than a High Court judge, and 260 proceedings concerning the management of companies (*e.g.* for winding-up orders). Only 53 Chancery writ actions were set down for trial during 2003. A list of the 19 Practice Directions currently governing the work of the Chancery Division (spanning the period from 1969) was published in 2004.[83]

An action in the Family Division,[84] such as a request for a divorce, is usually begun by the petitioner lodging a petition with the court and serving a copy of it on the respondent by having it handed over personally or posted. The petitioner is no longer *required* to appear in open court in every case in order to give an oral account of the grounds

---

[82] See note 81 above.

[83] See [2004] 1 BNIL 68. Several of them are summarised at [2003] 10 BNIL 102-9.

[84] See K. O'Halloran, *Family Law in Northern Ireland* (1997), though out of date in some respects.

for the petition, but this does usually still occur. There will of course be no jury involved. Many family actions are undefended, which obviously allows them to be processed more quickly and cheaply. What might delay the proceedings is the necessity for the judge to be satisfied that, when the parties to the action have children, the welfare of these children is being protected. There may also be complications over the division of the family property, a matter which is usually dealt with by a Master or a judge in chambers. Applications by a married person for an award of money against his or her partner are made by originating summons and not by petition.

During 2003,[85] a total of 3,231 divorce petitions were filed in Northern Ireland's High Court Family Division (up 9% from 2002); 2,117 of these (66%) were lodged by wives. Of the 1,445 petitions disposed of during the year, 95% were undefended and the commonest ground for divorce (in 41% of the cases) was two years' separation of the spouses coupled with their consent to a divorce). The High Court issued 1,329 decrees *nisi* of divorce, 16% more than in 2002. As many people now get divorced in the High Court as in the county courts.

Appeals from the High Court

For cases begun in the High Court, appeals lie directly to the Court of Appeal. The appeal takes the form of a full rehearing, without the re-examination of witnesses but usually with a word-for-word transcript of the evidence being placed before the judges. The Court of Appeal can overturn the decision on whether or not the defendant is liable, but it cannot recalculate the damages to be awarded. That issue has to be sent back to the High Court for retrial. The total number of civil appeals disposed of by the Court of Appeal in Northern Ireland during 2004 was 91 (compared with 65 criminal appeals); the main source of civil appeals was the Queen's Bench Division of the High Court (37 cases) but there were also 19 "cases stated" (7 from industrial or fair employment tribunals, 6 from RMs, 2 from county court judges, 2 from district judges and 2 from the Social Security Commissioners), three appeals from the Family Division and four appeals from the Chancery Division.[86]

There is then a further avenue of appeal, provided either the Court of Appeal or the House of Lords gives its permission, to the House of

---

[85] See note 81 above.
[86] *Northern Ireland Judicial Statistics 2004*, Table A.4.

Lords. Usually only one or two such cases arise in Northern Ireland each year. An even rarer procedure is that provided for by the Administration of Justice Act 1969, whereby in certain cases there can be a direct appeal straight from the High Court in Northern Ireland to the House of Lords, by-passing the Court of Appeal. This "leapfrog" procedure is possible only if all the parties to the case agree to it and if the proposed appeal raises a question of law of general public importance involving either the interpretation of a piece of legislation or an issue on which the High Court must follow a precedent laid down by the Court of Appeal or the House of Lords (see Chap.2.3). It would appear that no such appeal has ever been made from the High Court of Northern Ireland.

For the composition of the Court of Appeal and House of Lords see Chapter 1.5, and for the procedure known as judicial review (not to be confused with appeal procedures strictly so called) see 6.7 below. The complete system of appeals for civil cases is represented diagrammatically in Table 18 on page 288 above.

The future reform of the High Court

Partly on account of the delays and expense engendered by the present system, the Final Report of the Civil Justice Review in Northern Ireland recommended a number of (mainly procedural) changes to the High Court.[87] These included the proposals that pleadings should be simplified by replacing the writ of summons and statement of claim with a single form (which should be served within four months) and that there should be only one form for contesting the plaintiff's claim, that the "Certificate of Readiness" system - which has proved effective at speeding up cases in the county courts - should also be adopted in the High Court (in preference to Lord Woolf's "multi- track" system introduced in England and Wales), that parties should have at most nine months from the date the defence is filed in which to have their case ready for hearing (except for cases in the commercial list and in the Chancery Division), that if this deadline is not met the matter should be automatically listed before a judge who should be entitled to make whatever directions he or she thinks fit, that the amount of time experts spend in court giving oral testimony should be reduced by encouraging the use of written reports instead, that the summary judgment procedure should be available in more cases, that "pre-action

---

[87] *Final Report* (2000), Chap. 4.

protocols" should be introduced to help the parties settle their dispute earlier, that the parties should be allowed to make offers to settle as well as making payments into court before the hearing, and that the use of scale costs in the High Court should be increased (see Chap. 3.4). Regrettably, not all of these reforms have so far been implemented.

6.7 JUDICIAL REVIEW PROCEEDINGS[88]

The nature of the proceedings

The High Court's supervisory jurisdiction is exercised through the granting of applications for judicial review, a procedure which has given rise to many of the developments in what is now called "administrative law". The procedure outlined below would have been initiated in only a handful of cases 20 years ago, but by 2003 there were 340 such cases lodged in Northern Ireland alone.[89] Of these, 173 were successful to the extent that leave was given to proceed with them; in 49 cases the application was successful on the merits.

In general, a judicial review application can be brought against all persons or bodies exercising a judicial, quasi-judicial or administrative function. However, as far as courts of law are concerned, decisions made by the superior courts (the Crown Court, the High Court and above) are all exempt from judicial review; only decisions by magistrates' courts and county courts can be reviewed. The orthodox view is that the procedure is also unavailable in respect of some kinds of tribunal, namely the ones which are predominantly private bodies, like those involved when individuals are in dispute with trades unions, professional bodies or universities. But a decision of the House of Lords permitting the procedure to be used in relation to the City Panel on Mergers and Takeovers cast some doubt on this view.[90] Tribunals established by statute, such as the Law Society's Disciplinary Tribunal, *are* subject to the judicial review procedure. Decisions by

---

[88] See generally M. Fordham, *Judicial Review Handbook* (4th ed., 2004); P. Craig, *Administrative Law* (5th ed., 2003), Chaps. 12-20; Lord Woolf, J. Jowell and A. Le Sueur, *de Smith, Woolf and Jowell's Principles of Judicial Review* (1999); T. Ingman, *The English Legal Process* (10th ed., 2004), pp. 486-522.

[89] *Northern Ireland Judicial Statistics 2003*, Table B.24. In 1974 there were 160 applications in England and Wales but by 2004 the figure had risen to 4,207 (more than 50% of these being immigration cases): Department for Constitutional Affairs, *Judicial Statistics Annual Report 2004*, Table 1.13.

[90] *R v Panel on Take-overs and Mergers, ex parte Datafin* [1987] QB 815.

Parliamentary officials are not capable of being judicially reviewed.[91] This type of proceeding should also not be used if there is an effective alternative remedy available to the applicant; complaints of discrimination, for example, which often turn on the specific facts in dispute, are usually better dealt with by tribunals.[92] And the general rule is that judicial review proceedings should not be allowed to continue if the issues in question have become academic by the time of the hearing.[93]

The procedure can also be used to challenge the validity of secondary legislation (see Chap. 2.2), which, after all, is itself the product of decisions taken by one or more public authorities.[94] The Government is so conscious that civil servants can easily leave themselves open to judicial review that it issues to every senior official a booklet entitled *The Judge Over Your Shoulder*.[95] This explains in some detail the relevant law and highlights the principles of good administration which the courts expect Government officials to apply.

A high proportion of the applications involve claims by prisoners, and many of these are noted in the *Bulletin of Northern Ireland Law*. Indeed it was a precedent set by the Northern Ireland Court of Appeal[96] which persuaded the House of Lords to rule that decisions by prison governors in England and Wales should be open to judicial review.[97] In one recent case a republican prisoner lost his challenge to a ruling that he was not allowed to wear an Easter lily;[98] in another a prisoner lost his challenge to the removal of additional home leave privileges when he was discovered with a broken key ring taken from a shop where he was working.[99] Other recent examples of applications for judicial review in Northern Ireland include a challenge to a magistrate's

---

[91] *E.g. Re McGuinness' Application* [1997] NI 359 (Kerr J), where Mr Martin McGuinness MP sought to review a ruling by the Westminster Speaker that he could not use the facilities at Westminster unless he swore an oath of allegiance to the Queen.

[92] *In re Ruane* [2001] 6 BNIL 1; *In re Kirkpatrick's Application* [2003] NIQB 49.

[93] *In re Nicholson's Application* [2003] NIJB 30; but see *In re E's Application* [2003] NIQB 288.

[94] *E.g.* the (unsuccessful) challenge to the Solicitors Admission and Training Regs. (NI) 1988 in *Re Kelly's Application* [2000] NI 103.

[95] 3rd ed., 2000. Available on the website of the Treasury Solicitor's Dept, www.open. gov.uk/ tsd/judge.htm.

[96] *In re McKiernan* [1985] 6 NIJB 6.

[97] *Leech v Parkhurst Prison Deputy Governor* [1988] 1 All ER 485.

[98] *In re Byers' Application* [2004] NIQB 23.

[99] *In re Matthews' Application* [2004] NIQB 9.

decision ordering a defendant to pay the costs of an investigation into his activities,[100] an attempt to overturn the Secretary of State's decision that the IRA's ceasefire was holding,[101] a complaint against the way in which a coroner had conducted an inquest,[102] a challenge to the Minister for Health's decision to centralise Belfast maternity services at the Royal Victoria Hospital,[103] a challenge to the suspension of a pupil from school[104] and an objection to the Lord Chancellor's decision to use a certain forms of words in the declaration which new Queen's Counsel have to sign.[105]

The procedure

For details of the procedure used in judicial review applications, see the Rules of the Supreme Court (NI) 1980, Order 53. In the High Court the office which processes such applications is called the Crown Office.

Permission to make an application for judicial review in respect of an administrative tribunal cannot be granted unless the applicant is deemed to have a sufficient interest, or standing (*locus standi*), in the matter to which the application relates. The law on what constitutes adequate standing for this purpose is still in a state of flux, but in matters directly affecting the general public - such as the levying of rates - it seems that virtually any person may be justified in applying. The application for permission must be made to a High Court judge "promptly", and in any event no later than three months after the proceeding complained of, unless the judge is satisfied that the granting of relief after this time would not cause hardship to, or unfairly prejudice, the rights of any person. The test applied by a judge when deciding whether to grant permission to make an application is whether he or she is satisfied "that there is a case fit for further investigation at a full *inter partes* hearing of the substantive application for judicial review".[106] If the application for permission is unsuccessful, an appeal

---

[100] *Re Caffrey's Application* [2000] NI 17. See too *Re DPP for Northern Ireland's Application* [2000] NI 49, where the DPP applied to overturn a magistrate's decision which had rescinded a defendant's conviction for driving without insurance.
[101] *Re Williamson's Application* [2000] NI 281.
[102] *Re Mullan's Application* [2000] 9 BNIL 14.
[103] *Re Buick's Application* [2000] 7 BNIL 47.
[104] *In re M's (A Minor) Application* [2004] NIQB 6.
[105] *Re Treacy's Application* [2000] NI 330; see too Chap. 3.2.
[106] *Re Jones' Application* [1996] 9 BNIL 84.

can be lodged with the Court of Appeal.[107] Once permission to apply is granted, the judicial review application itself will usually be considered by one judge of the High Court, again with appeals lying to the Court of Appeal. In some cases, particularly those involving criminal matters, the High Court will sit as a court of two or even three judges; this is the Divisional Court mentioned in Chapters 1.3 and 5.6. The High Court judge who currently hears most of the judicial review applications in Northern Ireland is Mr Justice Weatherup; formerly it was Mr Justice Kerr, who was appointed Lord Chief Justice in 2004.

To succeed in an application for judicial review[108] the applicant has to show that the decision being questioned was: (i) illegal, in that it was, for example, beyond the powers of the body which took it; (ii) improper, in that it was, for example, taken without first consulting the appropriate people; (iii) irrational, in that no reasonable decision-maker in the same position could have arrived at the same decision (this is know as *Wednesbury* unreasonableness, after a leading case[109]); or (iv) contrary to the European Convention on Human Rights, a ground added by the Human Rights Act 1998.[110] It is only when this last ground is relied upon that there is a requirement that the decision in question should be "proportionate" to the mischief it was trying to deal with; "proportionality" is otherwise not yet a ground for judicial review in itself.

Remedies obtainable

In an application for judicial review the applicant can seek a number of remedies: (i) "*certiorari*", an order that a decision must be quashed, (ii) "prohibition", an order that a body must decline to deal with a matter, (iii)"*mandamus*", an order that compels the performance of some public duty, (iv) an "injunction", an order that requires someone to act or stop acting in a certain manner, and (v) a "declaration", an order that clarifies someone's legal position by stating clearly what the law is on a particular point. The first three of these remedies used to be officially

---

[107] For an example of a failed appeal see *Omagh District Council* v *Minister for Health, Social Services and Public Safety* [2004] NICA 10.
[108] See, in particular, the judgment of Lord Diplock in the GCHQ case, *Council of Civil Service Unions* v *Minister for the Civil Service* [1985] AC 374.
[109] *Associated Provincial Picture Houses Ltd.* v *Wednesbury Corporation* [1948] 1 KB 223, a decision of the English Court of Appeal.
[110] S. 3.

known as "prerogative orders" and are sometimes still referred to as
such.

Injunctions and declarations can be obtained not only through
applications for judicial review but also through the issuing of a civil
bill (see Chap. 5.4) or a writ (see Chap. 5.6).[111] These conventional
processes allow aggrieved persons to query even the private, domestic
proceedings which cannot be subjected to judicial review (see above).
In such situations the remedy will not be obtained as quickly, directly
or cheaply; on the other hand the conventional processes are not so
constrained by time limits, they do not require prior judicial
permission, they allow for more effective emergency relief and they
provide for a fuller trial of all the issues.

Damages (*i.e.* compensation) cannot be awarded to a successful
applicant for judicial review: unlike some other countries, neither
England and Wales nor Northern Ireland provide such a remedy for
breach of a public law right. An applicant will receive compensation
only if the "misconduct" of the public body in question is also a
recognised legal wrong, such as a breach of contract or a tort (*e.g.* the
torts of breach of statutory duty or misfeasance in public office).[112]

The future reform of judicial review proceedings

In 1994 the Law Commission made a number of recommendations for
reform of judicial review procedure in England and Wales[113] and in
April 2000 a further review was published.[114] The Government then
produced a consultation paper inviting comments on proposed new
rules, the aim of these being to allow unmeritorious cases to be
disposed off early and to minimise delays and costs. To coincide with
the coming into force of the Human Rights Act 1998 on 2 October
2000, new Civil Procedure Rules were introduced in England and
Wales from that date.[115] In particular, new names have been given to

---

[111] The challenge brought by Ulster Unionist Party MPs in 2003 to the laying of
disciplinary charges against them by officers of the Ulster Unionist Council seems
to be an example of this: see *Donaldson and others* v *Ulster Unionist Council*
[2003] NIQB 52.
[112] See M. Fordham, *Judicial Review Handbook* (4th ed., 2004), pp. 511-27.
[113] See *Administrative Law: Judicial Review and Statutory Appeals*, Law Comm. No.
226, 1994.
[114] Sir Jeffrey Bowman, *Review of the Crown Office List*.
[115] See Civil Procedure (Amendment No. 4) Rules 2000. The full set of Rules is
available on-line at www.dca. gov.uk/civil/procrules_fin.

various terms. What was formerly the "Crown Office" is now known as the "Administrative Court";[116] "applications" for judicial review are now "claims" for judicial review; "applicants" and "respondents" are now "claimants" and "defendants"; and "the relief of mandamus, prohibition or certiorari" is now "the remedy of a mandatory, prohibiting or quashing order".[117]

During 1995-96 the Law Reform Advisory Committee for Northern Ireland examined the Law Commission's proposals but did not recommend any significant changes to the law and practice in Northern Ireland. Further reform to bring the position more into line with that in England and Wales is still awaited.

6.8 THE ENFORCEMENT OF CIVIL JUDGMENTS[118]

The fact that a court order has been issued in favour of the winner of litigation does not necessarily mean that he or she will receive the money (or whatever else is awarded) from the other side. Sometimes the loser is not willing to pay and has to be forced to do so. Ensuring that the loser of litigation complies with a court order can often be as difficult as obtaining that order in the first place. Since 1971, however, the task has been simplified in Northern Ireland through the creation of the Enforcement of Judgments Office (the EJO), which is part of the Northern Ireland Court Service and under the overall control of the Lord Chancellor. It handles virtually all types of money judgments, the principal exceptions being most judgments issued in criminal proceedings and those against a spouse ordering him or her to make maintenance payments to the other spouse or to a child. The Office keeps a register of judgments, which can be searched, on payment of a small fee, by anyone who needs to know whether a particular person or company has an unpaid judgment debt against his or her name. The EJO enforces civil judgments of magistrates' courts and county courts (including small claims courts) as well as of the High Court, whereas in England and Wales the judgments of each of these courts are enforced in different ways. For details see the Judgments Enforcement (NI)

---

[116] The leading judge of this court now makes an annual statement about the court's workload. See, *e.g.*, Practice Statement (Administrative Court: Annual Statement) [2004] 1 All ER 322.
[117] For more details see M. Fordham, "Judicial Review: the New Rules" [2001] PL 4.
[118] See generally D. Capper, *The Enforcement of Judgments in Northern Ireland* (2004).

Order 1981 and the Judgments Enforcement Rules (NI) 1981, as amended.

The person ordered by a court to pay money to another is called a judgment debtor; he or she is under a legal duty to pay the money within a reasonable time after the judgment has been delivered. If the person who is owed the money (the judgment creditor) thinks that more than a reasonable time has elapsed, he or she may get the Enforcement of Judgments Office to send the debtor a document called "a notice of intent to enforce". This orders the debtor to pay the money within 10 days. If the debtor still refuses to pay after that period has elapsed, the creditor may apply to the EJO for actual enforcement of the judgment. This can cost quite a bit of money (*e.g.* £261 in respect of a £1,600 judgment),[119] so before good money is thrown after bad the creditor should make sure that the debtor does in fact have assets out of which the value of the judgment can be realised. Money spent on enforcing a judgment is added to the amount owed by the judgment debtor, so that in the event of success the judgment creditor will get back the fees paid to the EJO. Interest on the judgment debt is also payable.

In response to an enforcement application the EJO will interview the debtor to assess his or her means and will proceed to enforce the award in whichever of a number of ways it thinks fit. It may, for instance, make an order that property belonging to the debtor should be seized and sold, an order that goods on premises occupied by the debtor should be deemed to be in the custody and possession of the EJO, or an order that the debtor's earnings should be "attached" so that an employer must make periodical deductions from wages or salary and pay them directly to the EJO on the creditor's behalf.

The EJO may postpone enforcement if it thinks that the debtor's property ought to be administered for the benefit of all the creditors and not just those who have applied for enforcement. Or if the EJO thinks that enforcement within a reasonable time is impossible, it must issue a notice to that effect and, after hearing the parties, grant "a certificate of unenforceability". In these circumstances, or if the EJO otherwise fails to extract any money from the debtor, the creditor is not allowed to resort to self-help and must come to terms with the fact that the judgment in his or her favour is worthless.

---

[119] See the Judgments Enforcement Fees Order (NI) 1996, as amended.

Against some of the EJO's orders, such as an order for the transfer of possession of land or attachment of earnings, an aggrieved party may appeal to the High Court; against the rest an appeal may be made, on a question of law only, to the Court of Appeal. In both instances the decision of the court in which the appeal is heard is final.

During 2004 there were 17,551 notices of intention lodged with the EJO and 7,734 accepted applications for enforcement. There were 13,609 enforcement orders made (1,941 of which were for the possession of land, 2 for goods, 4,720 for the recovery of money and the remainder for miscellaneous reasons). There were 458 certificates of unenforceability. The net fee income was £2.56 million.[120]

The EJO is currently involved in a programme of modernisation known as "The Growth and Change Programme". As part of this the EJO has initiated several measures to promote both efficiency and accessibility, including the launch of a case-tracking system on the Court Service's website.[121] The system is in the early stages of implementation but it is hoped that it will provide an invaluable source of up-to-date information for creditors, debtors and other interested parties, including solicitors. The EJO has also reformed its structure to accommodate a "one process" approach to case management, which means that one team will manage a case from the initial stages until enforcement is obtained or the case is closed.

---

[120] For more details see *Northern Ireland Judicial Statistics 2004*, Pt. H.

[121] www.courtsni.gov.uk. The Court Service also has a useful leaflet, available on-line, about the work of the EJO.

CHAPTER SEVEN

SPECIALISED COURTS

7.1 COURTS DEALING WITH CHILDREN

Recent legislative developments have done much to establish child law as a specialist field requiring special courts. These are able to take account of the special vulnerability of children and to ensure that the legal system does not operate to their disadvantage. Underpinning the current structure of the children's court system is the belief that a clear distinction should be made between proceedings where the care of children is at issue and those where the responsibilities of children under the criminal law are in question. While such a separation had been strongly recommended in Northern Ireland as long ago as 1979 in the *Report of the Children and Young Persons Review Group* (the Black Report), it was not implemented until 1996, when the Children (NI) Order 1995 came into force.

Before 1996 the juvenile court (a court of summary jurisdiction) dealt with nearly all matters concerning children and young persons. The Children (NI) Order 1995 stipulated that when dealing with the care of children a juvenile court should from then on be known as a family proceedings court.[1] At county court level, family care centres were established to hear appeals from family proceedings courts, but there is no further right of appeal to the High Court.[2] Civil proceedings which do not relate to their care can still be brought by children in the ordinary civil courts (magistrates' courts, county courts and the High Court - see Chap. 6), and such children will almost invariably qualify for civil legal aid for those proceedings (see Chap. 3.3).

Criminal proceedings concerning children under the age of 17 continued to be heard in the juvenile court until the Criminal Justice (Children) (NI) Order 1998 came into force in 1999. This abolished the distinction between "children" and "young persons" and juvenile courts were renamed "youth courts". Appeals from the youth court, like those from the magistrates' court in criminal proceedings involving adults (see Chap. 5.7), go to the county court, the only difference being that in such cases lay magistrates are appointed to sit as assessors with a

---

[1] Children (NI) Order 1995, art. 164(4).
[2] *Ibid*. art. 166.

county court judge when an appeal is being heard. The Justice (NI) Act 2002 extended the jurisdiction of youth courts to 17-year-olds. The operation of the criminal justice system in respect of children is the responsibility of a juvenile justice unit within the Northern Ireland Office and a Youth Justice Agency[3] advises the Government on the provision of community based services, youth conferencing and secure custody. The Agency publishes a quarterly magazine called *Youth Justice Connections*.

The respective powers of family proceedings courts, family care centres and youth courts are examined more fully below. In many important respects they differ from those applying in the equivalent courts dealing with adults (the magistrates' courts and the county courts). There is an active Northern Ireland Youth and Family Courts Association; twice a year it publishes an informative *Lay Panel Magazine*.

Children Order Advisory Committee

The operation of the Children (NI) Order 1995 is supported by the Children Order Advisory Committee (currently chaired by Mr Justice Gillen), the role of which is to "advise the Lord Chancellor and the Secretary of State on the progress of Children Order cases through the court system with a view to identifying special difficulties and reducing avoidable delay". The Committee is itself further supported by three Family Court Business Committees, each chaired by a family care centre judge, which "examine the process of litigation and court procedures under the Children Order to ensure that cases are managed efficiently, effectively and expeditiously". In 2003 the Advisory Committee published very useful *Best Practice Guidance* for Children Order cases and the following year it produced a report on *Delay in Children Order Cases in the Court System*. Its fifth report, covering the period April 2003 to March 2004, was published in October 2004.[4]

For further information on the operation of the Children (NI) Order 1995, see the annual reports on the Order issued by the Department of Health, Social Services and Public Safety in accordance with article

---

[3] www.youthjusticeagencyni.gov.uk. The Chief Executive is Dr Bill Lockhart. The Agency replaced the Juvenile Justice Board on 1 April 2003. The Youth Council for Northern Ireland is a different body. It focuses on the education and training needs of young people (up to 25): see www.youthcouncil-ni.org.

[4] These are all available on the website of the Northern Ireland Court Service.

181 of the Order and the *Northern Ireland Judicial Statistics* issued by the Northern Ireland Court Service.[5]

Child Protection Registers

At the end of March 2004, as Table 21 below indicates, there were no fewer than 1,417 children on Child Protection Registers in Northern Ireland. These are children who have been abused or who are considered to be at risk of abuse. The figure represents a registration rate of 3 per 1,000 children. If a Health and Social services Trust decides to place a child's name on the Register the child's parents can appeal to an appeals panel and they can then seek judicial review of the appeals panel's decision if they disagree with it.[6]

TABLE 21: CHILDREN ON CHILD PROTECTION REGISTERS IN NORTHERN IRELAND 2001-04[7]

	2001	2002	2003	2004
Neglect, physical abuse and sexual abuse	13	11	9	11
Neglect and physical abuse	87	104	119	122
Neglect and sexual abuse	28	29	23	30
Physical and sexual abuse	35	32	28	31
Neglect only	526	625	651	509
Physical abuse only	340	359	376	330
Sexual abuse only	189	159	178	164
Emotional abuse only	196	212	224	220
Total of all abuse	1,414	1,531	1,608	1,417

Children's rights

The Children (NI) Order 1995 brought the law concerning children in Northern Ireland largely into line with that in England and Wales under

---

[5] Pt. F.
[6] See, e.g., *A and B* v *Hospitals Trust* [2004] NIQB 22.
[7] NSPCC and Department of Health, Social Services and Public Safety, *Community Statistics* (2004).

the Children Act 1989.[8] It also, to some extent at least, incorporated principles laid down in the United Nations' Convention on the Rights of the Child 1989, the most widely ratified of all the world's human rights treaties. Article 3 of the Order stipulates that (i) in any court proceedings the welfare of the child is to be the paramount consideration, (ii) courts should ensure that delay is avoided and (iii) courts should issue a court order only if to do so is better for the child than making no order at all. Courts dealing with children are now more conscious than ever of the need to reach their decisions in a way which complies with the human rights of the children involved.

In Northern Ireland there is also a strong network of voluntary and community organisations working with and for children to help ensure that their rights are protected. In 1997 a Children's Law Centre was established, with the help of a grant from what was then the Department of Health and Social Services. It has developed a range of advisory services for children, parents and carers. Other prominent non-governmental organisations active in the field are Save the Children, Barnardos, the NSPCC and Include Youth. "Children in Northern Ireland" is an umbrella group which tries to ensure that there is co-ordination of activities in this area and Children's Services operates a useful website on children's issues for those within the statutory and the voluntary sectors (especially on adoption).[9] Children's organisations have recently campaigned collectively to try to achieve a ban on the smacking of children, a matter which was the subject of a consultation paper issued by the Office of Law Reform in 2001 (see Chap. 9.14). The Government, however, does not seem keen to pursue this reform. In 2003 a statute-based Commissioner for Children and Young People in Northern Ireland was appointed. His functions are outlined in Chapter 9.7.

Family proceedings courts and family care centres

Family proceedings courts (like youth courts) normally consist of a bench of three members, one of whom will be a resident magistrate acting as the chairperson. The others will be lay (*i.e.* non-lawyer) magistrates, including at least one woman.[10] The lay magistrates are

---

[8] See generally M. Long and G. Loughran, *The Law of Children in Northern Ireland: The Annotated Legislation* (2004) and K. O'Halloran, *Child Care and Protection: The Law and Practice in Northern Ireland* (2003).

[9] www.childrensservicesnorthernireland.com.

[10] Children and Young Persons Act (NI) 1968, Sch 2.

selected for cases by the clerk of petty sessions from a panel appointed by the Lord Chancellor. There are at present about 250 persons on the panel, each of whom must retire at the age of 70 (see Chap. 1.5). They will usually possess no legal qualifications but before assuming their responsibilities they will have attended a training programme organised by the Northern Ireland Court Service. They perform a valued and important public function - particularly as they may have to deal with emergency applications for the protection of children arising outside normal court hours. The chairperson of the family proceedings court may sit alone (although this should be a rare occurrence) and has a casting vote if only one lay magistrate is present; otherwise decisions are reached by majority vote. The court itself will sit in the same building as the district's magistrates' court.

Family care centres are presided over by a county court judge who, likewise, will have received training in Children Order work. Although they are distinct courts in their own right, family care centres generally sit in the same building as the designated county court (where child-friendly waiting facilities now exist). A family proceedings court may hear a case in total privacy if it considers it expedient to do so in the interests of the child.[11] Unless the court directs otherwise, no report or picture in any newspaper or broadcast can reveal the identity of any child involved, in whatever capacity, in either care[12] or criminal[13] hearings.

In Northern Ireland there are currently seven family proceedings courts (one for each county court division) and four family care centres.[14] The jurisdiction of family proceedings courts is set out in the Children (NI) Order 1995 and procedure is governed by the Magistrates' Courts (Children (NI) Order 1995) Rules (NI) 1996, as amended. The procedure to be followed in family care centres is contained in Part IV of the Family Proceedings Rules (NI) 1996, as amended. The Children (Allocation of Proceedings) Order (NI) 1996 provides for the commencement and transfer of proceedings between the various competent courts.

---

[11] Magistrates' Courts (Children (NI) Order 1995) Rules (NI) 1996, r. 17(7).
[12] Children (NI) Order 1995, art. 170(2).
[13] Criminal Justice (Children) (NI) Order 1998, art. 22.
[14] Their locations are listed in Schs. 1 and 2 to the Children (Allocation of Proceedings) Order (NI) 1996, as amended. The care centres are in Belfast, Craigavon, Dungannon and Derry/Londonderry.

Applications to these family courts

Applications may be classified as "free-standing" (such as an application for a parental responsibility order by an unmarried father - see below) or "connected" (where there are other family proceedings pending which may affect the child[15]). Connected proceedings should be commenced in the same court as the related proceedings. In 2004 there were just four such cases.[16] In contrast, most free-standing cases ought to be commenced in a family proceedings court.[17] The main exception here is where a previous court order will be affected, in which case the proceedings should be commenced in the court which made that order.[18] The vast majority of free-standing applications dealt with in 2004 (4,731 out of 5,332: 89%) were dealt with in family proceedings courts, with just 275 (5%) dealt with in family care centres and 326 (8%) in the High Court.[19] Of the 4,001 applicants in free-standing cases, 1,929 (48%) were fathers, 1,289 (32%) were mothers, 452 (11%) were one of the 11 Health and Social Services Trusts,[20] 164 (4%) were grandparents and just 30 were Education and Library Boards.[21] A total of 3,947 children were involved in free-standing Children Order applications in 2004, of whom 36% were aged between 0 and 4 years of age.[22]

A further contrast can be drawn between public law and private law applications. Public law proceedings occur when the state intervenes through, for example, one of the Health and Social Services Trusts. Typical cases involve youngsters who fail to attend school regularly or who are suffering or at risk because of a lack of parental care or

---

[15] The term "pending proceedings" was clarified by Higgins J. in the case of *S v S* [1998] 2 BNIL 39. The court should ask itself whether there remains a live genuine issue for the court to decide or rule upon - see [1998] 2 BNIL 39. See also, C. Archbold, "The Children Order 1995: *S v S* and the Commencement Conundrum" (1998) 49 NILQ 180, at 184-5.

[16] *Northern Ireland Judicial Statistics 2004*, Table F.3.

[17] See art. 3 of the Children (Allocation of Proceedings) Order (NI) 1996. See further W. McCarney, "The Children's Court System in Northern Ireland", in *Lay Panel Magazine*, vol. 41, April 1999, pp. 14-21; and C. Archbold, note 15 above.

[18] Children (Allocation of Proceedings) Order (NI) 1996, art. 4. The effect of art. 4 was limited by Higgins J. in *S v S* [1998] 2 BNIL 39.

[19] *Northern Ireland Judicial Statistics 2004*, Table F.1.

[20] North and West Belfast, South and East Belfast, North Down and Ards, Down and Lisburn, Foyle, Armagh and Dungannon, Sperrin Lakeland, Homefirst, Causeway, Newry and Mourne, Craigavon and Banbridge.

[21] *Northern Ireland Judicial Statistics 2004*, Table F.6.

[22] *Ibid.* p. 97.

because a member of their household has committed an offence directly linked to the safety of children. A Health and Social Services Trust has a duty to investigate when there is reasonable cause to suspect that a child in its area is suffering, or is likely to suffer, significant harm.[23] The authority will submit a report on the home surroundings, school record, physical and mental health and the character of the child or young person. In reaching its decision in any case, the court must take such reports into consideration in fulfilment of its statutory duties to have regard to the welfare of the child and, if appropriate, to take steps to remove the child from undesirable surroundings and to secure that proper provision is made for his or her education and training.

Private law applications are those made in the course of domestic proceedings and matrimonial causes or where parents are otherwise in dispute about their children.[24] The Children Order Advisory Committee has recommended that in private law cases Health and Social Services Trusts should consider providing mediation services at family proceedings courts, resulting in possible savings both in court time and to the legal aid budget, as well as helping reduce the inevitable trauma of divorce and separation cases.[25] Private law business accounted for 87% of all the applications dealt with in 2003-04.[26]

It is important to note that the Family Division of the High Court or *any* magistrates' or county court can make any of the orders available under the Children (NI) Order if such issues arise in the course of other business, for instance maintenance proceedings (see Chap. 6.2) or divorce proceedings (see Chap. 6.4 and 6.6). In this way, the three court levels have "concurrent jurisdiction". Where a family proceedings court considers that the proceedings are exceptionally grave, important or complex[27] the proceedings should be transferred to a family care centre, and if a court of summary jurisdiction refuses to transfer a case, a party may apply to a family care centre for an order granting transferral.[28] Where the family care centre believes that the

---

[23] Children (NI) Order 1995, art. 66.

[24] Definitions of "public law" and "private law" extracted from *The Children Order Advisory Committee First Annual Report*, October 1998, DHSS and Northern Ireland Court Service, p. 7, note 1.

[25] *Ibid.* p. 29, paras. 7-8.

[26] 5,604 applications out of a total of 6,534: Fifth Report of Children Order Advisory Committee, p. 52.

[27] Guidelines for assessing "complexity" are listed in the Children (Allocation of Proceedings) Order (NI) 1996, art. 5(1).

[28] *Ibid.* art. 9.

case is suitable for hearing in the High Court, it may, in turn, transfer it to the High Court.[29] In 2003-04 only 113 cases were transferred from a family proceedings court to a family care centre and only 58 were transferred from a care centre to the High Court.[30]

Cases may also be transferred back to a lower court if the related proceedings with which the transferred proceedings were to be heard have already been determined, or if the higher court is of the opinion that the criterion cited for transfer no longer applies. Even if proceedings are commenced or transferred incorrectly, they will not be invalid, and no appeal can be made on this basis alone.[31]

Guardians ad litem

In certain public law proceedings under the Children Order, as well as in adoption proceedings under the Adoption (NI) Order 1987, an independent person called a "guardian *ad litem*" may be appointed by the court under article 60 of the 1995 Order to represent the child's interests. The Northern Ireland Guardian *Ad Litem* Agency (NIGALA)[32] was set up by the Government in 1996.[33] The current chairperson is Mr Jim Currie. It is charged with the recruitment, management and administration of a regional guardian *ad litem* panel and is an Executive Agency, that is, it is administratively independent from the Department of Health, Social Services and Public Safety. This differs from the situation in England and Wales, where the service is managed by local authorities.

Guardians *ad litem* are experienced social workers whose function in Children Order cases is to make sure that the applications put forward by the Health and Social Services Trusts actually meet the needs of the children in question. They appoint a solicitor to act for the child (unless one has already been appointed) and to provide a report to the court, at least seven days in advance of the final hearing, advising on the child's interests.[34] The investigation carried out by the guardian *ad litem* might involve looking at, amongst other things, the child's health and

---

[29] *Ibid.* art. 10.
[30] Fifth Report of Children Order Advisory Committee, p. 53.
[31] Children (NI) Order 1995, art. 16.
[32] www.nigala.n-i.nhs.uk. *Ad litem* is Latin for "for the case".
[33] In accordance with art. 60(7) of the Children (NI) Order 1995 and the Guardians *Ad Litem* (Panel) Regs. (NI) 1996.
[34] Magistrates' Courts (Children (NI) Order 1995) Rules (NI) 1996, r. 12 and Family Proceedings Rules (NI) 1996, r. 4.12.

physical growth, the parents' abilities and commitment to change, the level of attachment between parents and child, and any other important people in the child's life. Between April 1998 and March 1999, guardians *ad litem* were appointed in 480 cases involving 718 children.[35] Of the 480 cases, 146 involved adoption proceedings and the remaining 334 were specified public law cases under the Children Order. The normal provisions as to legal aid and advice apply (see Chap. 3.3).

Court orders

The Children Order also introduced a completely new range of court orders, the most common of which are briefly described below. In 2003-04 a total of 3,560 final orders were made (the numbers given after the article numbers below represent the numbers of orders of that type made in that year).

(1) *Contact order* (art. 8; 1,620). This is an order requiring the person with whom a child lives to allow the child to visit, stay or otherwise have contact with the person named in the order. Where the court is considering making a contact order in favour of a person who is, or the court considers should be, prohibited from molesting another person by a non-molestation order made under the Family Homes and Domestic Violence (NI) Order 1998 (see Chap. 6.2), the court must ask itself whether the child has suffered, or is at risk of suffering, any harm through seeing or hearing the ill-treatment of another person by the prohibited person.[36] The same question should also be asked where the court is considering making a residence order.

(2) *Residence order* (art. 8; 989). This order sets out the arrangements to be made concerning the person with whom a child is to live. Under article 12, if a residence order is made in favour of the father of a child and the father does not already have parental responsibility, the court must also make an order under article 7 giving him that responsibility - see (5) below.

---

[35] *The Northern Ireland Guardian Ad Litem Agency, First Annual Report*, p. 8. See also the *Report on the Children Order*, DHSS (1999), Chap. 3.
[36] Children (NI) Order 1995, art. 12A as inserted by Family Homes and Domestic Violence (NI) Order 1998, art. 28.

(3)   *Care order* (art. 50; 297). These make up the bulk of public law applications. They aim to have a child placed in the care of a designated authority. A court may make such an order only if it is satisfied that the child is suffering, or is likely to suffer, significant harm, and that that harm stems either from the care currently being given to the child (which is not what it would be reasonable to expect a parent to give the child) or a contention that the child is beyond parental control. Often an *interim* care order is granted while a fuller assessment is made of the child's position: in 2003-04 there were as many as 3,983 such orders granted. The Children (Leaving Care) Act (NI) 2002, one of the few Acts passed by the Northern Ireland Assembly when it sat between 2000 and 2002, gives further rights to children in care.

(4)   *Emergency protection order* (art. 63; 33). In cases where a child or young person is considered to be the victim of abuse he or she can be removed to a place of safety and made the subject of an emergency protection order. This can last for a maximum of eight days and may be extended once only for a further seven days.[37] If the situation is not deemed urgent enough for the emergency protection procedure, a child can be made the subject of a child assessment order,[38] which allows an investigation to be conducted into the child's safety and well-being.

(5)   *Parental responsibility order* (art. 7; 220). This order applies only where the child's father and mother were not married to each other at the time of his or her birth. Article 5 states that in such circumstances the mother shall have parental responsibility for the child. However the court may, on an application made by the father under article 7, order that he shall have parental responsibility for the child, or the father and mother may by agreement provide for the father to undertake responsibility ("a parental responsibility agreement"). A child of sufficient understanding may, with the leave of the court, him- or herself apply to have a parental responsibility order brought to an end by an order of the court.

(6)   *Prohibited steps order* (art. 8; 53). This is an order that no step which could be taken by a parent in meeting his or her parental responsibility for a child, and which is of a kind specified in the

---

[37] Art. 64(2), (3), (4) and (5).
[38] Art. 62.

order, shall be taken by any person without the consent of the court.

(7) *Supervision order* (art. 54; 27). This kind of order requires someone with parental responsibility for a child or someone with whom the child is living to take all reasonable steps to ensure that the child complies with certain specified directions. Such orders normally lapse after one year, but can be extended for a maximum period of three years.[39] Article 55(1) of the Children (NI) Order enables an Education and Library Board to apply for an education supervision order. This requires the Board to "advise, assist and befriend, and give directions to the supervised child and his or her parents in such a way as will, in the opinion of the supervisor, secure that he or she is properly educated".[40] There were 18 of these in 2003-04.

(8) *Secure accommodation order* (art. 44; 21). The Children Order also introduced a new statutory framework regulating the use of secure accommodation (defined as "accommodation provided for the purpose of restricting liberty") by Health and Social Services Trusts. Trusts must satisfy certain statutory criteria before placing a child in secure accommodation, and must also seek the permission of a court if they wish to extend any placement beyond a period of 72 hours. Under the Children (Secure Accommodation) Regulations (NI) 1996, secure accommodation must be provided by *statutory* children's homes, of which there is only one in Northern Ireland - Shamrock House Secure Unit located at the Lakewood Centre in Bangor (previously the care unit of Rathgael Training School).

Youth courts

Juvenile justice was examined as part of the Criminal Justice Review, the report of which was published in 2000. In implementation of the Review's recommendations, various legislative changes were made by the Justice (NI) Act 2002. Section 53 of that Act states that the principal aim of the youth justice system is to protect the public by preventing offending by children. It goes on to say that all persons operating the system must encourage children to recognise the effects of crime and to take responsibility for their actions but that they must also have regard to

---

[39] Children (NI) Order 1995, Sch. 3, para. 6.
[40] *Ibid.* Sch. 4, para. 2(1)(a).

the welfare of children and to the furtherance of their personal, social and educational development. Efforts are made to keep the number of criminal proceedings against children to a minimum and "restorative" justice schemes have been devised to help divert children from court and from detention.[41] If the police believe that a child may be in need of advice, guidance or assistance they are required to inform the local social services office, and if they suspect children of the commission of some offence they often prefer to rely on informal words of advice or official cautions rather than bring the matter before a court.[42]

Youth courts are courts of summary jurisdiction which deal with persons aged 10-17.[43] There is a presumption in law that no child under the age of 10 can be guilty of an offence (this is commonly referred to as the "age of criminal responsibility").[44] Under the Children and Young Persons Act (NI) 1968, a child aged between 10 and 13 was also presumed to be *doli incapax* (*i.e.* incapable of wickedness), a presumption which could be overturned by the prosecution, but that rule has now been abolished.[45] Children *can* be punished for committing criminal offences, although not in the same way as adults, and even the words "conviction" and "sentence" must not be used in relation to children dealt with summarily: the expressions "finding of guilt" and "order made on a finding of guilt" must be used instead.[46] An exception is made when a child is charged jointly with an older person: such charges must initially be heard by an ordinary magistrates' court and the ordinary terminology can be employed.[47]

Youth courts should sit at different times from other hearings in a magistrates' court so that there is little chance of children coming into contact with adult offenders,[48] and proceedings in youth courts are held in private with only court officials, the parties to the case, the parties' representatives, the parents or guardians of the child, representatives of the press and such other persons as the court may authorise, being

---

[41] Justice (NI) Act 2002, ss. 57-61.
[42] See further *Research Findings 4/98 - Cautioning in Northern Ireland*, NIO, Research and Statistics Branch (1998).
[43] The courts' jurisdiction was extended to 17-year-olds by the Justice (NI) Act 2002, s. 63 and Sch. 11.
[44] Criminal Justice (Children) (NI) Order 1998, art. 3. The threshold in Northern Ireland is amongst the lowest in the world (although in Scotland it is just 7 years).
[45] *Ibid.*
[46] *Ibid.* art. 5.
[47] *Ibid.* art. 28(3).
[48] *Ibid.* art. 27(3).

present.[49] There are restrictions on what the press can report about the case.[50]

As Table 12 on page 177 indicates, the number of juveniles proceeded against in Northern Ireland has remained fairly constant in the recent years. In 2003 some 1,915 juveniles were dealt with by youth courts and a total of 3,657 were examined.[51] The majority of the charges brought against juveniles are usually related to theft.

Procedures in youth courts

The procedures to be followed in youth courts are governed by the Magistrates' Courts (Criminal Justice (Children)) Rules (NI) 1999 and the Youth Conference Rules (NI) 2003. Any youth who has been arrested and charged should be released if he or she, or a parent or guardian, enters into a recognisance (see Chap. 5.2), unless the charge is for a "serious arrestable offence"[52] or the custody officer believes that the child should not be released for the protection of the public.[53] If the youth is not released, he or she must be detained by the police in Rathgael Juvenile Justice Centre before being brought before a magistrates' court.[54]

Where a court remands or commits a child for trial, there is a presumption of bail:[55] the child must be released on bail unless the court considers that a remand in custody is necessary to protect the public *and* the offence is a violent or sexual offence, is one for which an adult would be liable on conviction on indictment to be sent to prison for 14 years or more, or is an arrestable offence and the child was either already on bail when he or she committed it or has been found guilty of an arrestable offence within the last two years.[56] A

---

[49] *Ibid.* art. 27(4).

[50] *Ibid.* art. 22(2).

[51] The Northern Ireland Court Service, from the first quarter of 2005, has started producing a provisional set of figures for youth court work on a quarterly basis. This *Magistrates' Courts Bulletin* is available on-line at www.courtni.gov.uk.

[52] For a definition, see Police and Criminal Evidence (NI) Order 1989, art. 87, as amended.

[53] Criminal Justice (Children) (NI) Order 1998, art. 6(3).

[54] *Ibid.* art. 8(3).

[55] *Ibid.* art. 12.

[56] It is noteworthy that as far as remands in custody are concerned, the requirement that custody is necessary to protect the public must be satisfied in *all* cases. The restrictions on imposing custodial sentences are less demanding, only requiring that

remand in custody during the course of a hearing must also be to Rathgael; it can be to Hydebank Young Offenders' Centre only if the child is aged 15 or over and the court considers that the child is likely to injure him- or herself or other persons.[57] The Police and Criminal Evidence (NI) Order provisions concerning bail (see Chap. 5.2), and the provisions concerning legal aid and advice (see Chap. 3.3) which apply to suspected adult offenders, apply similarly in cases involving children.

A youth court can try children summarily or can conduct preliminary enquiries or preliminary investigations into indictable offences (see Chap. 5.5). A youth court can also deal summarily with any indictable offence other than homicide if it thinks that such a course is expedient and if both the prosecutor and the child (or, in the case of a child under the age of 14, the child's parent or guardian) consent.[58] In such a case the youth court, on making a finding of guilt, may make any order which might have been made if the case had been tried by the Crown Court on indictment. It may therefore impose a much more serious sentence than an ordinary magistrates' court. If tried in a Crown Court a child may still be sent back to the youth court for sentencing.[59] A youth court can also proceed with sentencing a child for an offence even if there are other (unrelated) charges against him or her pending in the Crown Court.[60]

It is worth noting that the controversial Anti-social Behaviour (NI) Order 2004 allows magistrates to issue anti-social behaviour orders (ASBOs) against children as well as adults if an application has been made by the police, a district council or the Northern Ireland Housing Executive. These are *civil law* orders but if they are breached the person in question can be convicted of a criminal offence. For that reason the law requires magistrates to apply a high standard of proof before agreeing to issue such an order.[61]

---

custody be necessary to protect the public where the offence is violent or serious in nature (art. 19 of the Criminal Justice (NI) Order 1996).

[57] Criminal Justice (Children) (NI) Order 1998, art. 13(1)(b).

[58] *Ibid.* art. 17(1).

[59] *Ibid.* art. 32(1)(b).

[60] Criminal Justice (NI) Order 1996, art. 4, which inserts a new art. 30(A) into the Criminal Justice (Children) (NI) Order 1998.

[61] *R (on the application of McCann)* v *Crown Court at Manchester* [2003] 1 AC 787.

Punishment

The sentencing framework established by the Criminal Justice (NI) Order 1996 (see Chap. 5.4 and 5.6) applies equally to cases involving children. The guiding principle, therefore, is that the sentence imposed must be commensurate with the seriousness of the offence.[62] As in care proceedings, the youth court must consider all medical and welfare reports relating to the child and can choose from a wide selection of available remedies. As explained below, the Justice (NI) Act 2002 added to these by providing for reparation orders, community responsibility orders and custody care orders.[63] Corporal punishment (whether of juveniles or adults) is completely outlawed.[64]

While children *can* be fined for any offence other than murder, they are less likely to be fined than adults. A child under the age of 14 cannot personally be made to pay more than £200 (including costs) and any older child cannot be made to pay more than £1,000.[65] If the offender is under the age of 17, the amount payable in compensation to the victim of the offence is also limited to £1,000 (as opposed to the adult maximum of £5,000).[66] The child's parent or guardian will be ordered to pay the fine or compensation if the child is under the age of 16, and may be ordered to do so in any other case.[67] Children are also less likely than adults to receive a suspended sentence, or be released on a recognisance. In cases where no custodial or community sentence is passed, or where the child is found not guilty, the court reserves the power to notify the social services of any matters it thinks fit, provided it considers that the welfare of the child requires this.[68]

By significantly amending the Criminal Justice (Children) (NI) Order 1998,[69] the Justice (NI) Act 2002 introduced the idea of youth conferencing into Northern Ireland, whereby young people who admit

---

[62] Of particular relevance are art. 19 (restrictions on imposing custodial sentences) and art. 37 (regarding the effect of previous convictions and of offending while on bail).

[63] Ss. 54-56.

[64] Treatment of Offenders Act (NI) 1968, s. 22. It was abolished in public schools by the Education (Corporal Punishment) (NI) Order 1987.

[65] Criminal Justice (Children) (NI) Order 1998, art. 34 and Criminal Justice (NI) Order 1994, art. 3(2).

[66] Criminal Justice (NI) Order 1994, art. 14(11), as amended by Criminal Justice (Children) (NI) Order 1998, Sch. 5, para. 41(b).

[67] Criminal Justice (Children) (NI) Order 1998, art. 35.

[68] *Ibid.* art.33.

[69] See the new arts.3A-3C, 10A-10D, 33A-33E, 36A-36L and Sch.1.

their involvement in certain criminal behaviour, or are found guilty in a court, can be brought face-to-face with the victims of their crimes so that an action plan can be developed to prevent further offending and make amends to the victim. When prosecutors refer young people to the Youth Conference Service,[70] rather than proceed with a prosecution, the resulting meetings are called diversionary youth conferences. Otherwise references are by the youth court. Youth conferencing is still in its early stages of development in Northern Ireland so it is not yet possible to say how effective it is as a means of dealing with young offenders. A general leaflet explaining the work of the Youth Conference Service, called *a Balanced Approach*, has been published.[71]

The main features of the other sentencing options available to the youth court are set out below.

Detention in a young offenders' centre[72]

This option is available only for persons aged at least 16.[73] As with juvenile justice centre orders (below), it is subject to the restrictions placed on the imposition of custodial offences contained in the Criminal Justice (NI) Order 1996 - primarily, that the offence is so serious that only a custodial sentence can be justified or it is of a violent or sexual nature and only a custodial sentence would protect the public from harm.[74] The 1996 Order also includes the proviso that where the offender is aged under 17 the court *must*, where the offence is a summary one, or is triable either way, have regard to the most recent pre-sentence report obtained in respect of the offender (see Chap. 1.6).[75] Child offenders must also be legally represented.[76] If the offence involved is one which is punishable in the case of an adult with 14 years' imprisonment (or five years if it is a scheduled offence - see Chap. 4.3), the detention of the offender may be ordered to be in such place and for such time as the Secretary of State for Northern Ireland

---

[70] This is a service overseen by the Youth Justice Agency. Its Director is Ms Alice Chapman.

[71] Available on-line at www.youthconferenceserviceni.gov.uk.

[72] See further the Prisons and Young Offenders' Centre Rules (NI) 1995, as amended.

[73] See Treatment of Offenders Act (NI) 1968, s. 5, as substituted by Treatment of Offenders (NI) Order 1989, art. 7.

[74] Criminal Justice (NI) Order 1996, art. 19.

[75] *Ibid.* art. 21(3).

[76] *Ibid.* art. 18.

may direct. These include the "SoSPs" mentioned in Chapter 4.6.[77] Otherwise the maximum permissible period of detention in a young offenders' centre is four years.[78] The only Young Offenders' Centre in Northern Ireland is at Hydebank Wood in South Belfast. In the year ending 31 March 2004, the average number of persons held at Hydebank Wood on any one day was 182.[79]

A juvenile justice centre order

This custodial sentence was introduced by the Criminal Justice (Children) (NI) Order 1998 and replaced the training school order as the main custodial sentence available to the court. Juvenile justice centre orders should be used where a child is found guilty of an offence which, if an adult had committed it, would be punishable by imprisonment.[80] They require a child to be detained for a set period followed by an equal period of supervision by a probation officer (or other person designated by the Secretary of State). They differ from the old training school order in two further respects. First, they are determinate sentences, the normal duration of which is six months (*i.e.* three in detention and three under supervision), although the court can specify a period of up to two years.[81] Secondly, the period of detention should be reduced by any period already spent on remand in custody.[82]

There is now just one juvenile justice centre in Northern Ireland, at Rathgael near Bangor. It can hold up to 43 young people at any one time. A new purpose-built facility is due to be completed on the same site in 2006. In the year ending 31 March 2004 the total number of admissions to Rathgael was 269 (including 129 females), but most of these were remands while further investigations were being conducted.[83] Only 15 children were committed to the Centre after a trial.[84] This is in line with one of the principles underpinning the

[77] Criminal Justice (Children) (NI) Order 1998, art. 45.
[78] See note 73 above.
[79] *Northern Ireland Prison Service Annual Report and Accounts 2003-04*, App. 1, p.34.
[80] Criminal Justice (Children) (NI) Order 1998, art. 39(1).
[81] *Ibid.* art. 39(2).
[82] *Ibid.* art. 39(6).
[83] The *Northern Ireland Judicial Statistics 2004* say, in Table E.9, that in 2004 the youth court issued 416 "training school orders". This presumably refers to the number of juveniles ordered to be detained, however temporarily, in the juvenile justice centre.
[84] *Annual Report of the Youth Justice Agency 2003-04*, p. 24. Of the 15 committals, 1 was a 14-year old, 5 were 15, 8 were 16 and 1 was 17.

Criminal Justice (Children) (NI) Order 1998, namely that "court disposals should have regard to the best interests of the child, with custody being used to the minimum extent possible".[85]

In a report published in 2005[86] the Northern Ireland Office showed that, of the juveniles who were discharged from the juvenile justice centre into the community in 2001, 36% were reconvicted of an offence within one year. The reconviction rate for those not sent to custody was 22%, with the rate for juveniles who were given a community supervision order being 27% and the rate for those who were fined being 16%. In all cases the reconviction rate after two years was about twice what it was after one year.

An attendance centre order

Article 37 of the Criminal Justice (Children) (NI) Order 1998 provides for attendance centre orders and the Attendance Centre Rules 1995 and National Standards[87] which apply to England and Wales are closely followed by the Attendance Centres in Northern Ireland. The orders require the offender to attend a Centre for a fixed number of hours every Saturday. A session of physical education is usually followed by a lecture (*e.g.* on first aid), employment in handicrafts, or other instruction. A child cannot be required to attend for a total of more than 24 hours, but a child aged 14 to 16 must attend for at least 12 hours.[88] During 2004 there were 296 attendance centre orders made throughout Northern Ireland.[89]

A probation order[90]

This type of order places a child under the supervision of a probation officer for a period between six months and three years and can require a child to comply with any requirements which the court considers desirable in the interests of securing his or her rehabilitation, of protecting the public from harm or of preventing the child from committing further offences. A court can attach an extra condition to a probation order whereby the probationer is required to attend at a

---

[85] *Draft Children Justice (Children) (NI) Order 1998: Revised Explanatory Document*, Criminal Justice Policy Division, NIO (1998) para. 3.
[86] M. Decodts, *Juvenile Reconviction in Northern Ireland*, Research Bulletin 6/2005.
[87] Home Office (1995).
[88] Criminal Justice (Children) (NI) Order 1998, art. 37(2).
[89] *Northern Ireland Judicial Statistics 2004*, Table E.9 .
[90] Criminal Justice (NI) Order 1996, art. 10 and Sch. 1; see also Chap. 1.6.

specified place for up to a maximum of 60 days.[91] If a probation order is breached, the child may then be dealt with as if found guilty of the original offence for which he or she was placed on probation.[92] If a child aged 14 to 16 does not wish to be placed on probation the youth court must resort to some other punishment.[93] There are also some offences which by statute cannot be dealt with in this way. In 2004, a total of 523 juveniles were given a probation order, representing 14% of the total juvenile disposals.[94] There was a 30% decline in the number of probation orders issued to juveniles between 2001 and 2004.

A community service order[95]

These orders are available only for persons aged 16 or over. They require a person to undertake a specified service for a specified number of hours (between 40 and 240). In 2004 there were 185 such orders issued against juveniles, 14% of the total number issued.[96]

A reparation order

These orders were introduced by the Justice (NI) Act 2002,[97] which inserts relevant new provisions into the Criminal Justice (Children) (NI) Order 1998.[98] They require the child to make reparation for the offence to a specified person (if he or she agrees) or to the community at large, otherwise than by paying compensation. They can be issued only after the court has considered a report by a probation officer or social worker indicating, for example, the attitude of the victim of the offence to the proposed order, and they require the child's consent. They cannot be combined with a custodial sentence, a community service order or a community responsibility order and they cannot require more than 24 hours' activity by the offender. The reparation will be supervised by, usually a probation officer or social worker and must be completed within six months of the order being made. If the reparation order is breached the child can be given an attendance centre

---

[91] *Ibid.* Sch. 1, para. 4.
[92] *Ibid.* Sch. 2, para. 3.
[93] *Ibid.* art. 10(3).
[94] *Northern Ireland Judicial Statistics 2004*, Table E.9.
[95] Criminal Justice (NI) Order 1996, art. 13.
[96] *Northern Ireland Judicial Statistics 2004*, Table E.9.
[97] S. 54 and Sch. 10.
[98] Art. 36D and Sch. 1A.

order or can be dealt with for the original offence as if he or she had just been found guilty of it.

A community responsibility order

These orders, also introduced by the Justice (NI) Act 2002,[99] which inserts further new provisions into the Criminal Justice (Children) (NI) Order 1998,[100] require the child offender to attend at a specified place for a number of hours of instruction in citizenship (no more than 40) and to undertake specified practical activities. The instruction is to include information about the responsibilities which a person owes to the community and the impact of crime on victims and it must be received within six months of the order being made. The orders cannot be combined with any other punishment and require the child's consent. If they are breached the child can be given an attendance centre order or a community service order or can be dealt with for the original offence as if he or she had just been found guilty of it.

A custody care order

These orders, again new under the Justice (NI) Act 2002,[101] allow a child under the age of 14, instead of being given a custodial sentence, to be placed in secure accommodation for a set period of up to two years, followed by a period of supervision. If the child will become 14 years of age during the period to be spent in secure accommodation the court may require him or her to be detained thereafter in Rathgael Juvenile Justice Centre. While being kept in secure accommodation the child must benefit from certain provisions of the Children (NI) Order 1995 (as if he or she were in care) but if a child runs away from such secure accommodation he or she can be arrested and the custody care order can be lengthened by up to 30 days; alternatively the child can be dealt with for the original offence as if he or she had just been found guilty of it. There are also penalties for breaching the supervision part of the custody care order.

7.2 COURTS-MARTIAL

Courts-martial are a relic from the days when, in addition to the ordinary courts of law, there were many other courts dealing with

---

[99] S. 55 and Sch. 10.
[100] Art. 36E and Sch. 1A.
[101] S. 56, which inserts art. 44A into the Criminal Justice (Children) (NI) Order 1998.

special matters. Ecclesiastical courts are another example, but they are too specialised to warrant expanded treatment in this book.[102]

Courts-martial apply military law,[103] a special body of rules addressed only to persons serving in the Army, and they apply a similar body of rules addressed to members of the Air Force. Auxiliary and reserve forces are affected as well, as are civilians employed by the armed forces abroad. The Royal Navy operates a comparable system, but it differs in a number of important ways: in particular, there is only one type of naval court-martial - equivalent to a general court-martial (see below) - which tends to deal with only the most serious cases.[104] The rules are published officially in the *Manual of Military Law*, but derive ultimately from Acts of Parliament and from Regulations issued under the Crown Prerogative (see Chap. 2.1). They provide for many internal disciplinary offences, but all offences under the criminal law of England and Wales are also offences under military law if committed by a member of the armed forces. Moreover, there is a policy of bringing service law and procedure into line with civilian law and procedure where it is sensible and practical to do so.

Some very serious offences, such as murder, manslaughter and rape, must be tried in ordinary civilian courts if committed within the United Kingdom. Recent high profile cases have included the two Scots Guards convicted of the murder of Peter McBride in North Belfast in 1992,[105] as well as Private Lee Clegg whose conviction for the murder of Karen Reilly in 1990 was subsequently quashed.[106] Once a trial has occurred in either of the court systems there cannot be a second trial on the same or a similar charge in the other court system. In practice, in Northern Ireland as well as in Great Britain, the vast majority of criminal offences committed by members of the armed forces during

---

[102] For an example of the jurisdiction of one of these courts, the Consistory Court, see *Re Holy Trinity, Bosham* [2004] 2 All ER 820 (which concerned the putative grave of King Harold).

[103] See G. Rubin, "United Kingdom Military Law: Autonomy, Civilianisation, Juridification" (2002) 65 MLR 36.

[104] A. Lyon, *After Findlay: A Consideration of Some Aspects of the Military Justice System* [1998] Crim LR 109, at pp. 109-10, note 2.

[105] James Fisher and Mark Wright. The family of Peter McBride has been seeking to have these two soldiers dismissed from the Army, but the Army Board has so far successfully resisted all such pressure. See, *e.g.*, *In re McBride's Application* [2003] NICA 23 and [2003] NIQB 72.

[106] *R v Clegg* [2000] 8 BNIL 20 (CA). This was after the original conviction had been confirmed by the House of Lords: *R v Clegg* [1995] 1 AC 482.

peacetime are tried in the ordinary way by civilian courts; only if the defendant has since been posted abroad, or if the incident did not in any way affect civilians, might a court-martial be held.

Servicemen below the rank of warrant officer can be dealt with summarily by the commanding officer of the battalion or regiment for a number of minor military offences. The severest punishment which can be imposed is 60 days' military detention or the forfeiture of 28 days' pay.[107] The accused is not allowed to have any form of representation at these summary hearings, but, in all cases, has the right to call for a court-martial. Following criticisms made by the European Court of Human Rights,[108] summary appeal courts have now been established to hear appeals in these minor cases.[109]

Trials

More serious charges must be investigated to see if the accused should be sent for trial by court-martial. The decision regarding how best to proceed with any charge is taken by the commanding officer (with or without advice from the Advisory Branch[110]) on the basis of a *prima facie* test. The commanding officer can dismiss the charge, deal with it summarily (subject to certain restrictions) or refer the case to a higher authority (usually Brigadier level).[111] If the higher authority considers a court-martial to be appropriate, the papers will be passed to the Prosecuting Authority,[112] which operates in a similar way to the Crown Prosecution Service in England and Wales.

The prosecutor may order a formal preliminary examination.[113] This is comparable to committal proceedings in ordinary magistrates' courts (see Chap. 5.5), though without the accused being entitled to representation. At the court-martial itself there can be representation by a lawyer nominated from civilian life or by a regimental officer; representatives from the forces are often preferred because they are more familiar with service standards and jargon. Legal aid under the

---

[107] See Army Act 1955, s. 76C, inserted by Armed Forces Act 1996, Sch. 1, para. 2.
[108] See, *e.g.*, *Hood* v *UK* (2000) 29 EHRR 365.
[109] See Armed Forces Discipline Act 2000. A suspect can no longer be held in custody unless this is approved by a judicial officer.
[110] See further Lyon, note 104 above, pp. 115-6.
[111] Army Act 1955, s. 76, as substituted by Armed Forces Act 1996, Sch. 1, para. 2.
[112] *Ibid.* s. 76A(1). For the powers and functions of the Prosecuting Authority, see s. 83B of the 1955 Act, as inserted by the 1996 Act, Sch. 1, para. 14.
[113] Courts-Martial (Army) Rules 1997, rr. 5 and 6.

Northern Ireland criminal legal aid scheme is not available for military proceedings in the province, but a special scheme administered by the Ministry of Defence and based on the English civilian scheme has been set up in its place. One consequence of this is that the Army scheme (to be distinguished from the Army Legal Aid Scheme which now applies only to legal aid for matrimonial and similar work) does not ensure free legal aid: the accused may be compelled to contribute an amount depending upon his or her savings and annual income.

In peacetime there are two basic types of court-martial. One is a District Court-Martial, which consists of a bench of three officers usually presided over by a major or lieutenant-colonel and the judge advocate (see below). It tries ordinary soldiers and non-commissioned officers, with powers to imprison convicted defendants for up to two years. More than 90% of courts-martial are tried as District Courts-Martial.[114] The other is a General Court-Martial, which has a bench of at least five officers presided over by a colonel or higher-ranking officer and the judge advocate.[115] It can try any member of the forces and impose any sentence prescribed by military law. The judges for General Courts-Martial are appointed for one case at a time, but the Presidents of District Courts-Martial (of whom there are five in the United Kingdom) are appointed on a long-term basis for a particular area. The accused has the right to object to a particular officer being appointed to hear his or her case.[116] The trial of civilians in a court-martial must be before Crown servants rather than military officers (with the exception of the court's President). The courts sit at irregular intervals (every four to six weeks) and in makeshift courtrooms. Each year there are about 1,000 District Courts-Martial and between 30 and 40 General Courts-Martial throughout the United Kingdom.

Judge Advocates

No court-martial sits with a jury, but the officers on the bench are assisted by a lawyer employed in the Office of the Judge Advocate General. This is an independent civilian office with general responsibility for supervising the handling of legal matters affecting the armed forces. As well as the Judge Advocate General himself, and the

---

[114] Lyon, note 104 above, p. 111, note 7.
[115] Army Act 1955, s. 84D, as inserted by the 1996 Act, Sch. 1, para. 19.
[116] *Ibid.* s. 92, as amended.

Vice-Judge Advocate General, there are (for the United Kingdom) four judge advocates. They are barristers who function in a similar way to the advocates-general in the European Court of Justice (see Chap. 2.5); they sum up the evidence,[117] advise the court on questions of law and are responsible for the conduct of the trial in accordance with the law of England and Wales.[118] On some matters the court is bound to follow the judge advocate's advice, but the actual decision in the case must be taken by a majority vote among only the officers on the bench.

As well as being continuously under the supervision of the Office of the Judge Advocate General, the proceedings of a court-martial can be subjected to the judicial review procedures described in Chapter 6.7 and writs of *habeas corpus* can be issued to put an end to any unauthorised detention.

Reviews and appeals

The court-martial's decision will be to find the defendant guilty or not guilty. By way of punishment it can fine, detain or imprison; it cannot grant a conditional discharge, make a probation order or impose a suspended sentence. In response to a ruling by the European Court of Human Rights,[119] the Armed Forces Act 1996 abolished the earlier requirement that a higher-ranking officer must "confirm" the findings of a court-martial.[120] Instead, every finding of a court-martial is now subject to automatic review[121] by the Reviewing Authority, and the accused can petition the Authority in order to draw attention to particular points. Formally speaking, this body is comprised of the Army Board of the Defence Council but its function can be delegated. The Authority can overturn a finding of guilt and/or any sentence, substituting its own judgment for that of the court-martial. It cannot, though, impose an alternative sentence which is more severe than that passed in the first instance.[122]

Until recently a member of the armed forces had no right to appeal against his or her sentence to the Courts-Martial Appeal Court (CMAC). Section 17(2) of the Armed Forces Act 1996, however,

---

[117] Courts-Martial (Army) Rules 1997, r. 69.
[118] *Ibid.* r. 32.
[119] In *Findlay* v *UK* (1997) 24 EHRR 221.
[120] S. 15 and Sch. 7, Pt. II.
[121] *Ibid.* s. 16 and Sch. 5.
[122] *Ibid.* s. 113AA, as inserted by the 1996 Act, Sch. 5, para. 4.

introduced such a right of appeal,[123] and this complements the existing right of appeal against conviction, thereby bringing the court-martial system into line with the ordinary criminal system. Furthermore, the Secretary of State can now refer the sentence of any person convicted (rather than civilians only) to the CMAC,[124] and appeals can also be brought or continued where the person convicted has died.[125]

The CMAC was set up in 1951 and is staffed by all the English Court of Appeal judges and by such English, Northern Irish and Scottish judges as are nominated for the purpose. It usually sits in London as a bench of three judges, although it may in fact sit anywhere in the United Kingdom or even abroad. Its powers are similar to those of the Northern Ireland Court of Appeal (see Chap. 5.7), although it can order a retrial only where there is fresh evidence to consider (not where there has been a wrong decision of law or a material irregularity in the course of the court-martial). Only a handful of appeals are heard each year. In 1999 the CMAC laid down new guidelines for sentencing decisions in courts-martial.[126]

There is a further channel of appeal for either side to the House of Lords, but one of the two courts must first grant permission for this appeal and the Courts-Martial Appeal Court must certify that a point of law of general public importance is involved. The last such appeal was in 2002.[127]

Independent Assessor of Military Complaints Procedures

There is also a system for dealing with complaints against soldiers lodged by members of the public in Northern Ireland. The Army maintains two brigades in Northern Ireland, the 8 and 39 Infantry Brigades. In April 2004 there 14,030 army personnel committed to Northern Ireland, including 2,110 full-time and 1,300 part-time Royal

---

[123] See D. Richards, *Appeal against Court-Martial Sentences: Has Anything Changed?* [1999] Crim LR 480.

[124] Courts-Martial (Appeals) Act 1968, s. 34(4), as amended by the 1996 Act, s. 17.

[125] *Ibid.* s. 48(A), as inserted by the 1996 Act, s. 19.

[126] *R v Cooney* [1999] 3 All ER 173.

[127] *R v Spear* [2003] 1 AC 734. In this case the House of Lords confirmed that the trial of a civil offence by court-martial in the UK was compatible with the European Convention on Human Rights, as was the role of the permanent presidents of District Courts-Martial. On the latter point it argued that the European Court of Human Rights had not ruled to the contrary in *Morris v UK* (2002) 34 EHRR 1253.

Irish Regiment "home service" soldiers, 970 Royal Air Force personnel and 30 Royal Navy or Royal Marine personnel.[128]

Any complaints alleging criminal conduct by members of these forces are investigated by the PSNI; formal non-criminal complaints are handled by the Community Relations Office at Army Headquarters in Lisburn; informal complaints are dealt with by the local "Civil Representative", who will conduct an investigation locally and report back to the complainant.[129]

Since 1997 Mr James McDonald has served as the Independent Assessor of Military Complaints Procedures.[130] This post is unique to Northern Ireland and requires the holder to keep under review the procedures adopted by the General Officer Commanding Northern Ireland (currently General Philip Trousdell) for responding to complaints. There were just eight formal non-criminal complaints lodged in 2004 (the same number as in 2003), of which five alleged harassment or abuse.[131] Six were found to be not substantiated, one required no further action to be taken and one was substantiated. In addition there were 395 other complaints which were resolved informally (compared with 543 in 2003).[132]

7.3 CORONERS' COURTS

In Northern Ireland coroners are today appointed by the Lord Chancellor from among barristers or solicitors of five or more years' standing.[133] (In England and Wales and the Republic of Ireland[134] they are appointed by local authorities. There is an altogether different system in Scotland, where they rely not on coroners but on chairpersons of "fatal accident inquiries"). Before 1959 doctors were also eligible to be appointed, and they still can be in England and

---

[128] www.dasa.mod.uk/natstats/ukds/2004/c7/sec1tab72.html.
[129] See also the leaflet *How to make a complaint against the Armed Forces in Northern Ireland*, which is freely available from Army Units and the Civil Representatives.
[130] The post is now provided for by the Terrorism Act 2000, s. 98 and Sch. 11.
[131] *Annual Report for 2004*, App. B.
[132] *Ibid.* App. C
[133] Coroners Act (NI) 1959, s. 2(3).
[134] In September 2004 Ireland's Minister for Justice, Equality and Law Reform published a detailed report of a Working Group on the Review of the Coroner Service: see www.justice.ie/80256E010039C5AF/vWeb/flJUSQ65 GET5-ga/$File/CoronerRvw.pdf. It proposes the creation of a Coroner Agency.

Wales and the Republic of Ireland. Coroners are meant to act completely independently of the Government, the police and the medical profession. At present there are seven in Northern Ireland but this number is soon to be reduced to three. The coroner for Greater Belfast, Mr John Leckey, is full-time and he is assisted by two temporary full-time deputy coroners. The coroners outside Greater Belfast are part-time. By the end of 2005 all the part-time districts should be amalgamated with Greater Belfast and Northern Ireland will become a single coroner's district.[135]

The relevant legislation is the Coroners Act (NI) 1959 and the Coroners (Practice and Procedure) Rules (NI) 1963, as amended. The textbook, *Coroners' Law and Practice in Northern Ireland*, by John Leckey and Desmond Greer (1998), provides comprehensive coverage of the subject and in 2004 the Northern Ireland Court Service published a useful 20-page booklet entitled *A Guide to the Coroners Service*.[136]

The chief function of coroners is to investigate unexpected, unexplained, violent or suspicious deaths. Formerly the investigations were carried out with a view to uncovering unsuspected homicide, but with the development of the police service and medical science one of the main objects today is the accurate determination of the cause of death. To assist in determining the cause of death, the coroner can order a *post mortem* examination to be carried out by a government-approved doctor, and this is done in almost half the cases investigated. If the investigation indicates that death was due to an unnatural cause the coroner will usually hold an inquest. Even if a coroner decides not to hold an inquest, the same or another coroner can order one to occur at a later stage if new information comes to light.[137] In England and Wales and the Republic of Ireland an inquest can be held even though the death occurred abroad, provided that the body has since been returned to the coroner's district, but inexplicably the law does not permit such an inquest to be held in Northern Ireland.

---

[135] In a dispute over the alleged unlawful discrimination against part-time coroners regarding their rate of pay, a High Court judge ruled that it was not a matter appropriate for judicial review proceedings (but rather for an industrial tribunal): see *In the matter of an application by HM Coroner for South Down for Judicial Review* [2004] NIQB 86. The dispute was settled in 2005.

[136] Available on the Northern Ireland Court Service's website.

[137] *In the matter of an application by Michael Millar* [2005] NIQB 34.

TABLE 22: CORONERS' BUSINESS IN
NORTHERN IRELAND 2000-03[138]

	2000	2001	2002	2003
Deaths reported	3,615	3,752	3,563	3,280
Inquests held	303	198	230	226[139]

Inquests

As can be seen from Table 22, above, there are around 3,500 deaths reported to the coroner each year in Northern Ireland and inquests are held in less than 10% of these. They usually take place in recognised courthouses and do not normally involve a jury, but if it appears to the coroner that there is reason to suspect that the death occurred in prison, in an accident or in circumstances prejudicial to the safety of the public, a jury of between seven and 11 persons must be summoned.[140] (In England a jury must also be summoned if the death results from an injury supposedly caused by a police officer in the execution of his or her duty. Inquest juries in England comprise 12 jurors.)

The purpose behind an inquest is to determine who the deceased person was, and how, when and where he or she came to die. It must be held in public. The coroner plays a more leading role than a judge would do in a regular court of law in that he or she has a wide-ranging discretion as to which witnesses should be called, compelling their attendance if necessary (even that of someone who has been, or is likely to be charged in connection with the death[141]) and the coroner will take an active part in examining them.[142] The witnesses are placed under oath and may also be questioned by other interested parties such as the family of the deceased person. There is no absolute right for these parties to be legally represented in the proceedings. Applications can be made under the legal advice and assistance scheme (see Chap. 3.3) for

---

[138] Source: *Judicial Statistics for Northern Ireland 2003*, Figure G.1. The figures for 2004 were not available at the time of writing.

[139] This figure does not include a handful of inquests held in two of the seven districts, which had not returned statistics in time for the report.

[140] Coroners Act (NI) 1959, s. 21.

[141] Coroners (Practice and Procedure) (Amendment) Rules (NI) 2002, reversing the effect of *Devine* v *Attorney General for Northern Ireland* [1992] 1 WLR 262.

[142] See *Re Bradley's Application (No. 2)* [1996] 8 BNIL 10 and *Re Mullan's Application* [2000] 9 BNIL 14.

financial help with preparing for an inquest and there is now an extra-statutory scheme for covering the cost of representation in "exceptional" cases, but otherwise state legal aid is not available.[143] Speeches cannot be made to the jury except by the coroner in his or her summing-up. However, in the case of a death at the hands of the police, the family of the deceased has the right to obtain copies of relevant evidence submitted to the coroner in advance of the inquest.[144] The practice of Mr Leckey, the coroner for Greater Belfast, is to provide these on request to any properly interested person. Inquest proceedings, in short, are more inquisitorial than adversarial (see Chap. 6.1).

The conclusions at an inquest

Within five days of the end of the inquest the coroner must send the particulars of death to the appropriate registrar of deaths. Where the circumstances appear to the coroner to disclose that a criminal offence may have been committed the coroner must also, as soon as practicable, furnish the Public Prosecution Service with a written report of those circumstances,[145] but neither the coroner nor the jury may express any opinions on questions of criminal or civil liability. Coroners are not judges in a trial, and nothing in proceedings before a coroner should prejudice proceedings which might be taken in another court; for this reason inquests are often delayed until any criminal proceedings connected with the death have run their course. In Northern Ireland delays in holding an inquest have often endured for years. In recent times a further delay has been caused by the need to wait for a definitive ruling from the House of Lords as to whether deaths occurring before the date when the Human Rights Act 1998 came into force (2 October 2000) had to be investigated in a way which fully complied with Article 2 of the European Convention on Human Rights. In *Re McKerr*[146] the answer was given that they do not, so the backlog of cases may now dissipate.

---

[143] The scope of the extra-statutory scheme was considered in *In re Hemsworth's Application* [2003] NIQB 5. The Lord Chancellor made a further exception to the rule on non-availability of legal aid at the inquest into the Omagh bomb of August 1998, which took place in September 2000. The Justice (NI) Act 2002, s. 76, allows the Lord Chancellor to direct that legal aid is to be available in connection with proceedings which are otherwise excluded from the state schemes.

[144] *Re Jordan's Application* [1996] 7 BNIL 15.

[145] Prosecution of Offences (NI) Order 1972, art. 6(2).

[146] [2004] 1 WLR 807.

Until 1981 the coroner or jury had to record the death in one of five ways: (i) natural causes, (ii) the result of an accident or misadventure, (iii) the deceased's own act (adding, if appropriate, "whilst the balance of his mind was disturbed"), (iv) execution of sentence of death or (v) an open verdict. This last verdict was used when none of the others was appropriate. Since 1981 coroners or juries in Northern Ireland have simply had to list their "findings", a procedure which in theory ought to have allowed for more informative conclusions but which still precluded any verdict (such as is possible in England) of "unlawful killing". However an important decision by the House of Lords in 2004 means that when coroners and juries are determining "how" a person died they must now set out not just the means of death but also the circumstances in which it occurred.[147] In some recent inquests the coroner for Greater Belfast has put specific questions to the jury to enable them to be quite specific about how a person died.

There cannot be any appeal against the decision at a coroner's inquest, but the proceedings can be made the object of an application for judicial review (see Chap. 6.7), which might lead to a new inquest if at the earlier one the coroner, for instance, failed to call a jury when one should have been called, or failed properly to sum up the evidence to the jury. In 1988 the Northern Ireland Court of Appeal ordered a new inquest to be held in respect of a shooting incident in 1982: at the first inquest the coroner had applied a rule of evidence which the Court of Appeal said was *ultra vires* (*i.e.* beyond the powers conferred by) the Coroners Act (NI) 1959. A year later the House of Lords reversed this decision (*McKerr* v *Armagh Coroner*[148]). In England, but not in Northern Ireland, the Attorney General retains a power to refer a coroner's inquest to the High Court, which can order a second inquest to be held.

The future reform of coroners' courts

Some of the most controversial inquests occurring in Northern Ireland are those into deaths caused by members of the security forces[149] and in important decisions in 2001 the European Court of Human Rights ruled

---

147   *R (Middleton)* v *West Somerset Coroner* [2004] 2 AC 182.
148   [1990] 1 WLR 649.
149   *Inquests and Disputed Killings in Northern Ireland* (Committee on the Administration of Justice, Belfast; 1992); F. Ní Aoláin, *The Politics of Force: Conflict Management and State Violence in Northern Ireland* (2000); B. Rolston, *Unfinished Business: State Killings and the Quest for Truth* (2000).

that inadequacies in the inquest system in such cases meant that there had been a breach of Article 2 of the European Convention on Human Rights, which protects the right to life.[150] Some changes have been made to the inquest system in Northern Ireland as a result of those decisions (*e.g.* the removal of a suspect's right not to give evidence at the inquest[151]) and at the same time a more systematic review has been conducted by a distinguished committee.[152] This review proposed that the seven coroners districts in Northern Ireland should be amalgamated into one district and that it should be headed by a High Court judge with one full-time coroner and two full-time deputy coroners.

In 2004 a consultation paper by the Northern Ireland Court Service presented a range of relatively minor administrative reforms aimed at improving the service provided for bereaved families[153] and in April 2005 the Court Service announced that it would be modernising the Coroners Service by indeed creating a single Northern Ireland Coroners jurisdiction, introducing a full-time coroners judiciary and establishing a Coronial Council and Coroners Service Inspectorate.[154] It seems that the Court Service will not be introducing coroners' officers in Northern Ireland, a type of administrator well known in England and Wales,[155] but "family liaison officers" are to be appointed in the near future.

Treasure

Coroners also have jurisdiction to hold inquests into the finding of treasure, that is, (i) any object at least 300 years old when found which has metallic content of which at least 10 per cent by weight is precious metal or which is one of at least ten coins in the same find which are at least 300 years old at that time, and (ii) any object at least 200 years old when found which belongs to a class designated by the Secretary of State as being of outstanding historical, archaeological or cultural importance.[156] Property qualifying as treasure normally belongs to the Crown, subject to any prior interests and rights deriving from the time

---

[150] *Jordan* v *UK* (2003) 37 EHRR 52, *Kelly and others* v *UK* App. 30054/96, *McKerr* v *UK* (2002) 34 EHRR 553 and *Shanaghan* v *UK* App. 37715/97.

[151] Coroners (Practice and Procedure) (Amendment) Rules (NI) 2002.

[152] *Fundamental Review of Death Certification and Coroner Services in England, Wales and Northern Ireland* (Cm. 5831; 2003) (The Luce Report).

[153] *The Coroners Service of Northern Ireland: Proposals for Administrative Redesign.*

[154] Further details are available on www.courtsni.gov.uk.

[155] At the time of writing a government White Paper on reforming the death certification system in England and Wales was still awaited.

[156] Treasure Act 1996, ss. 1 and 2. See also the Treasure (Designation) Order 2002.

when the treasure was originally hidden or abandoned. The Crown will usually donate the treasure to a museum. Before the transfer takes place, the Secretary of State must determine whether an *ex gratia* reward is to be paid by the museum to any person involved in the find, or any occupier of, or person who had, or who has since acquired, an interest in the land on which the treasure was found.[157]

When treasure is found, the finder must notify the coroner in the district of the find within 14 days of his or her first having reason to believe that the object is treasure[158] and the coroner should take reasonable steps to notify the finder of any subsequent inquest. A coroner proposing to conduct an inquest *must* also notify the Department of the Environment for Northern Ireland and must give any interested persons who have been notified an opportunity to examine witnesses at the inquest.[159]

A revised code of practice for treasure cases in Northern Ireland was published in 2002 by the Environment and Heritage Service of the Department of the Environment[160] and this was supplemented by a circular issued to coroners by the Northern Ireland Court Service in the same year.[161] These documents provide for the close involvement of the Ulster Museum in any case involving treasure. Naturally enough an inquest of this type is very rare.

7.4 ELECTION COURTS

The statutes governing elections in Northern Ireland allow for the establishment of election courts to try election petitions. These petitions are challenges to the election of a Member of Parliament or a local councillor on the basis that there was some material irregularity in the course of the election. They must be presented within 21 days of the election or within 28 days of any alleged corrupt practice. Each year the judges of the High Court and the Court of Appeal must select two of their number to be the judges to sit in these election courts, from which (unlike in England and Wales) there can be no appeal. They do not sit with a jury.

---

[157] *Ibid.* s. 10(1) and (2).
[158] *Ibid.* s. 8.
[159] *Ibid.* s. 9.
[160] *The Treasure Act 1996: Northern Ireland Code of Practice.*
[161] Treasure Act 1996 (Circular No. 39/97).

Naturally enough, election petitions are rare. One example is that brought to determine the validity of the election of Mr Joe Hendron as the SDLP MP for West Belfast in the April 1992 general election. The court found, as it was entitled to do under the Electoral Law Act (NI) 1962, that illegal practices had occurred (*e.g.* spending £782 in excess of the allowed limit) but that these were of too limited a character to justify a report to the Speaker of the House of Commons to the effect that the election must be declared void.[162] After the 2001 general election a petition was raised challenging the election of Sinn Féin's Michelle Gildernew as MP for Fermanagh and South Tyrone on the ground that the presiding officer had allegedly allowed votes to be cast after the poll should have closed at 10pm. The court held that even if such irregularities did occur (which was undecided), they did not affect the result of the election and the petition was therefore dismissed.[163]

It is also possible for an elector to appeal against his or her registration or non-registration on the electoral register. The appeal is first heard by an official called the Revising Officer but it can be further dealt with by a county court. There were two such county court appeals in Northern Ireland in 1992, the first since 1976. Electoral issues can also arise before the High Court in judicial reviews. In one recent case an administrative officer in the Northern Ireland Civil Service challenged unsuccessfully the rule that he could not stand for election to the Northern Ireland Assembly unless he resigned from his job (with no guarantee of reinstatement if he was not elected).[164]

---

[162] *McGrory v Hendron* [1993] 5 BNIL 48.
[163] *In the matter of the Parliamentary Election for Fermanagh and South Tyrone* [2002] NIJB 415.
[164] *In re McKinney's Application* [2004] NIQB 73. This case was part-funded by the Northern Ireland Human Rights Commission.

CHAPTER EIGHT

TRIBUNALS

8.1 TRIBUNALS IN GENERAL

In Chapters 5 and 6 we examined the workings of the criminal and civil courts in Northern Ireland. These can be called ordinary courts of law. Elsewhere in the book we have mentioned what might be called special courts of law: the Judicial Committee of the Privy Council (see Chap. 1.4), the European Court of Justice and the European Court of Human Rights (see Chap. 2.5), the Restrictive Practices Court (see Chap. 6.6), family proceedings courts and youth courts (see Chap. 7.1), courts-martial (see Chap. 7.2) and election courts (see Chap. 7.4). With coroners' courts (see Chap. 7.3) we encountered an institution which is called a court but which in fact differs markedly in its procedures and powers from all other courts; the Planning Appeals Commission (Chap. 8.5) and the Proscribed Organisation Appeals Commission (see Chap. 4.2) are other such bodies. At this point it is necessary to turn our attention to other institutions which do not bear the name of courts but which officially adjudicate on some quite important issues. These institutions are called tribunals. They constitute a most significant sector in the legal system of Northern Ireland.

Tribunals are created by legislation. Among the first to be established were those which settled disputes arising out of the pension, health and unemployment insurance schemes set up by the Old Age Pensions Act 1908 and the National Insurance Act 1911. Some even see the Special Commissioners of Income Tax, created in the early nineteenth century, as the first tribunal of all.[1] In the last 60 years or so many dozens of different kinds of tribunal have been formed throughout the United Kingdom, largely on account of the development of the welfare state. There are now some 70 tribunals in England and Wales, administered by 10 Government departments and by local authorities. They deal with over one million cases a year and range in size from the Appeals Service, which deals with over 270,000 social security appeals, to the

---

[1] Today these are governed by the Special Commissioners (Jurisdiction and Procedure) Regs. 1994, as amended. See too the General Commissioners (Jurisdiction and Procedure) Regs. 1994, as amended. For more information on tax and financial tribunals see www.financeandtaxtribunals.gov.uk, which has leaflets on all of them.

20 or so regulatory tribunals that rarely sit. Recently created tribunals operating in Northern Ireland include the Care Tribunal[2] and the Information Tribunal[3] and more are always in the pipeline. The ordinary citizen is therefore much more likely to confront a tribunal than a court of law. The number of cases dealt with by tribunals certainly far exceeds that disposed of at county court level or in a higher court.

There are many reasons why tribunals have become such popular institutions. On the whole they provide justice which is quicker, cheaper, less formal and more private. But essentially they are preferred because the conventional judicial system is ill-suited to dealing with their particular kinds of problem, notably those which arise in the administration of a complex statutory scheme. Judges cannot be experts in every walk of life or field of law; some issues demand a particular expertise possessed by other persons which it would be wasteful to ignore when disputes arise. There are also issues which are peculiarly factual in nature and for which it would be both unnecessary and inappropriate to resort to the traditional paraphernalia associated with courts of law. It has to be conceded, though, that there sometimes appears to be little logic in the way in which some issues are allocated to courts of law and others to tribunals.

Tribunals are normally composed of three members, with only the chairperson being legally qualified. The pernickety rules of etiquette and of evidence, so beloved by judges and professional lawyers, are for the most part ignored.[4] Representation is usually permitted, but it is often undertaken by someone other than a solicitor or barrister – something practically unheard of in the ordinary courts. Civil legal aid for representation at tribunals is generally not available, as the objective is to "de-legalise" proceedings as much as possible. But the legal advice and assistance scheme *can* be used (see Chap. 3.3). Decisions are more frequently arrived at on the spot than in courts of law, and the costs are kept to a minimum. Courts do, however, still play a significant background role: they decide questions specifically reserved to them by the legislation governing the administrative scheme involved, they deal with some appeals and they supervise tribunals by hearing complaints that they have denied natural justice to

---

[2] See the Health and Personal Social Services Act (NI) 2001 and Chap. 9.8.
[3] Freedom of Information Act 2000, s. 18(2); it replaces the Data Protection Tribunal.
[4] As they are in small claims courts: see Chap. 6.3.

one of the parties or have committed some elementary error of law (such as hearing a case which they had no authority to deal with). This supervisory jurisdiction is exercised through the judicial review procedure, explained in Chapter 6.7.

The last detailed examination of tribunals in England and Wales was begun in 2000, when Sir Andrew Leggatt, a former Lord Justice of Appeal, led a team undertaking a wide-ranging review. His committee also looked at other administrative and regulatory bodies which decide disputes. The review was partly prompted by the need to ensure that the decision-making processes within all of these bodies are compliant with the European Convention on Human Rights, which was incorporated into UK law as from 2 October 2000 by the Human Rights Act 1998 (see Chap. 2.5). The Leggatt Review was published in 2001[5] and after engaging in further consultation the Lord Chancellor announced in 2003 that the Government would be setting up a unified Tribunal Service for the main government tribunals.

A White Paper followed in July 2004.[6] This provides for a new Tribunals Service agency to be created, bringing the administration of central government tribunals together within the Department for Constitutional Affairs. Over the period 2006-08 the Tribunals Service will take over responsibility for employment tribunals, social security tribunals, the Mental Health Review Tribunal, the Criminal Injuries Compensation Appeals Panel and the Special Educational Needs and Disability Tribunal. Lord Justice Carnwath has been appointed as the Senior President-designate of the new agency. A Courts and Tribunals Bill is to be enacted within the next year or so. This will create a Tribunals Procedure Committee to prepare rules and will transform the Council on Tribunals (see below) into an Administrative Justice Council. Part of the aim behind these reforms is "to lead the common law world in establishing beyond doubt the independence of tribunals from the executive".[7]

---

[5] *Tribunals for Users - One System, One Service*. A prior consultation paper had been issued in June 2000. The Leggatt Review, the Report on Access to Justice by Lord Woolf (1996) and the Review of the Criminal Courts by Lord Justice Auld (2001) are the three main pillars of reform of the English legal system in recent years. Northern Ireland will probably benefit from all of them in due course.

[6] *Transforming Public Services: Complaints, Redress and Tribunals*.

[7] Lord Falconer (the Lord Chancellor) in a speech at the Council on Tribunals Conference, London, 25 November 2004: www.dca.gov.uk/speeches/2004/lc251104.htm.

Tribunals in Northern Ireland

Although for most purposes Northern Ireland constitutes an independent legal system with its own laws, courts and tribunals, there are still some fields of law which are uniformly administered either throughout the United Kingdom or at least throughout England, Wales and Northern Ireland. Many of these fields are ones which were never within the domain of the Parliament of Northern Ireland because they were excepted or reserved matters under the Government of Ireland Act 1920 (see Chap. 1.2). Any tribunal system existing within such fields will be a nationwide system, so that a tribunal sitting in Belfast will apply the same laws and operate in the same way as a tribunal sitting in, say, Birmingham.

Examples of this phenomenon are the Banking Appeal Tribunals, the Income Tax Tribunals (composed of Special and - from 1989 - General Commissioners of Income Tax),[8] the VAT Tribunals, the Misuse of Drugs Tribunal, the Information Tribunal and the Copyright Tribunal. All of these, and many other tribunals, are supervised by the Council on Tribunals, a body set up in 1958 to keep under review the workings of most tribunals throughout Great Britain.[9] The Council can make recommendations to government Ministers as to who should be appointed to sit on a tribunal and it must usually be consulted before rules of procedure are laid down for a tribunal. Some UK-wide tribunals do not, however, fall within the jurisdiction of the Council on Tribunals, for example, the Interception of Communications Tribunal[10] and the Intelligence Services Tribunal.[11] If courts need to be involved in such fields, to hear appeals, answer referred questions or exercise a supervisory jurisdiction, the courts of Northern Ireland will deal with proceedings originating within the province, but the tribunals will still remain part of the UK system. Most of the general rules concerning the

---

[8] The Special Commissioners hear appeals concerning decisions of the Revenue relating to all direct taxes, *e.g.* income tax, corporation tax, capital gains tax and inheritance tax. They mostly sit in London but will sit elsewhere if there is a good reason for this. Appellants can, if they wish, be represented. The Special Commissioners are legally qualified and usually sit alone, but occasionally in pairs. Appeals go to the High Court.

[9] The remit of the Council on Tribunals is determined by Sch. 1 to the Tribunals and Inquiries Act 1992, which currently lists 80 different tribunals.

[10] Created by the Interception of Communications Act 1985, s. 7.

[11] Created by the Intelligence Services Act 1994, s. 9.

functioning of tribunals throughout the United Kingdom are now contained in the Tribunals and Inquiries Act 1992.

Occasionally, as in the case of the Asylum and Immigration Tribunal[12] and the Foreign Compensation Commission (which deals with claims for compensation regarding British-owned property confiscated abroad), hearings will take place at centres in England, Wales or Scotland even though the case has something to do with Northern Ireland. If courts have to be involved in these cases they may be English, Welsh or Scottish courts. Sometimes this causes inconvenience to applicants, but the system seems to tolerate this.[13] Appeals from the Asylum and Immigration Tribunal go to the Court of Appeal in Northern Ireland but to the High Court in England.[14] If the tribunal refuses leave to appeal, this can be judicially reviewed.[15] The Special Immigration Appeals Commission, which determines whether keeping someone out of the United Kingdom is "conducive to public good" or "in the interests of national security", also sits as a UK body; it is chaired by a High Court judge and appeals from it go to the Court of Appeal.[16]

For most matters, however, Northern Ireland retains its own independent tribunal systems. The law applied by the tribunals may well be virtually identical to the law in the rest of the United Kingdom, and the procedures they adopt may also be indistinguishable, but they nevertheless constitute separate systems. They are not subject to the supervision of the Council on Tribunals. It is to be expected, however, that in due course Northern Ireland will follow the lead being set in England and Wales (see above) as regards bringing together within one Tribunals Service the responsibility for all tribunals in the province.

It would be impossible to examine here the jurisdiction and procedures of all such tribunals, but the remaining sections of this chapter describe the ones which are most prominent - those dealing with social security

---

[12] This unified tribunal replaced the previous immigration adjudicators and Immigration Appeal Tribunal from 4 April 2005. See the Asylum and Immigration (Treatment of Claimants, etc) Act 2004, s. 26, and the Asylum and Immigration Tribunal (Procedure) Rules 2005.

[13] *In re Mang Yun Gao and another's Application* [2004] NIQB 16.

[14] *Ibid.*, interpreting the Nationality, Immigration and Asylum Act 2002, s. 101.

[15] See, *e.g.*, *In re Razeghi's Application* [2002] NIQB 66.

[16] See the Special Immigration Appeals Commission Act 1997. It allows for "special advocates" to be appointed to represent the interests of applicants during closed hearings, but those advocates are not allowed to disclose to the applicant anything which is said at those hearings.

or with children (see 8.2), those dealing with employment disputes (see 8.3), mental health review tribunals (see 8.4) and tribunals concerning land, rent and planning (see 8.5).

Tribunals of inquiry

The tribunals dealt with in this chapter should, however, be distinguished from the tribunals of inquiry set up on an *ad hoc* basis under the Tribunals of Inquiry (Evidence) Act 1921. These are created by resolution of both Houses of Parliament and they entrust to a judge the task of inquiring into some alleged scandal or disaster. Examples are the Widgery Tribunal of Inquiry appointed in 1972 to investigate the killing of 14 unarmed demonstrators in Derry/Londonderry on so-called "Bloody Sunday"[17] and the Saville Tribunal of Inquiry set up in 1998 to re-examine the events of that day.[18] From time to time a judge or other senior figure is appointed to conduct a less official inquiry and with less extensive powers. For example, a retired Canadian judge, Peter Cory, was asked by the British and Irish Governments in 2001 to re-examine a number of disputed killings in Northern Ireland and the Republic of Ireland with a view to assessing whether they should then be the object of full-scale public inquiries. He concluded that they should,[19] although before proceeding to set up one of these public inquiries - that into the murder of Patrick Finucane in 1989[20] - the Government has altered the way such a tribunal would operate by securing the enactment of the Inquiries Act 2005, which contains "reforms" that Judge Cory has publicly disowned. The 2005 Act repeals the 1921 Act as well as some provisions in other statutes allowing for inquiries to be held.[21]

---

[17] See, generally, D. Walsh, *Bloody Sunday and the Rule of Law in Northern Ireland* (2000).

[18] The proceedings of this inquiry can be viewed on-line at www.bloody-Sunday-inquiry.co.uk. Several judicial review applications were made in relation to decisions taken while the inquiry was sitting, some of which ere heard in England. See, *e.g.*, *In re Donaghy's Application* [2002] 5 BNIL 84. Note too the inquiries into BSE by Lord Scott and into the Harold Shipman case by Mrs Justice Smith. In all, only about 30 tribunals of inquiry have been set up since 1921.

[19] His reports are available on the NIO's website: www.nio.gov.uk.

[20] The European Court of Human Rights held that the investigation in this case had not complied with the requirements of Art. 2 of the European Convention on Human Rights: *Finucane* v *UK* (2003) 37 EHRR 656.

[21] Such as the Prison Act (NI) 1953, s. 7, under which an inquiry into the 2001 murder of Billy Wright in the Maze Prison was established.

A tribunal of inquiry has all the powers of the High Court as regards enforcing the attendance of witnesses, examining them on oath and compelling the production of documents. If a witness refuses to give evidence he or she can be held in contempt and, in a serious case, imprisoned.[22]

The Northern Ireland Act Tribunal

This tribunal has been set up under section 91 of the Northern Ireland Act 1998.[23] It deals with appeals against certificates issued by the Secretary of State saying that an act which discriminated against a person on the ground of religious belief, political opinion, gender or race was justified on the basis of national security or the need to protect public safety or public order. The tribunal can either uphold or quash the certificate; if it is upheld (or not appealed against in the first place) the certificate is "conclusive evidence of the matters certified by it".[24]

Parties to a tribunal hearing can be legally represented, but legal aid is not available (only advice and assistance: see Chap. 3.3). The appellant can be denied access to the full particulars of the reasons for the issue of the certificate and he or she, and their legal representative, can also be excluded from the tribunal proceedings, in which case the Attorney General can appoint a person (known as a "special advocate") to represent the interest of the appellant in the proceedings; such an advocate, however, "shall not be responsible to the party whose interest he represents".[25] Any party to the tribunal proceedings can appeal to the Court of Appeal on a point of law, but only with the permission either of the tribunal or of the Court of Appeal.[26]

The tribunal was created because in more than one case the European Court of Human Rights had ruled that the then inability to challenge a national security certificate issued by the Secretary of State under section 42 of the Fair Employment (NI) Act 1976 was a breach of the right to a fair trial guaranteed by Article 6 of the European Convention on Human

---

[22] Such contempt proceedings are criminal rather than civil: *Lord Saville of Newdigate* v *Harnden* [2003] NICA 6.

[23] See too Sch.11. For gender discrimination see art. 53ZA of the Sex Discrimination (NI) Order 1976, inserted by art. 96 of the Fair Employment and Treatment (NI) Order 1998. For race discrimination see art. 41A of the Race Relations (NI) Order 1997, inserted by art. 98 of the Fair Employment and Treatment (NI) Order 1998.

[24] Northern Ireland Act 1998, s. 90(4).

[25] *Ibid*. s. 91(8)(b).

[26] *Ibid*. s. 92(1) and (2).

Rights.[27] The Lord Chancellor has appointed a chairperson, a deputy chairperson, eight part-time lay members and three part-time legal members to be available to sit on the tribunal. Procedural rules for it have also been produced,[28] as far back as 1999. So far, however, the tribunal has not had any sittings!

8.2   TRIBUNALS CONCERNING SOCIAL SECURITY AND CHILDREN

The system for making decisions and dealing with appeals in social security and child support matters has recently been reformed. Prior to the coming into force of the Social Security (NI) Order 1998, the initial decision on whether or not a claimant qualified for a particular benefit or payment was taken by independent adjudication officers, social fund officers or child support officers. There were also separate appeal procedures depending on whether the claim in question was for a particular benefit or child support. Under the Social Security (NI) Order 1998, all decisions in social security and child support matters are now made by officials in the Department for Social Development, and what were previously known as the Social Security Appeal Tribunals, Disability Appeal Tribunals, Medical Appeal Tribunals, Child Support Appeal Tribunals and Vaccine Damage Tribunals have been incorporated into a single unified Appeal Tribunal.[29]

Local offices of the Social Security Agency or Child Support Agency can provide information as to the conditions to be fulfilled before you are entitled to any payment; the conditions change frequently, usually in April of each year.[30] These offices can also explain precisely what to do if you disagree with the assessment of your entitlement; the present section can give only an outline of what might happen in such a situation.[31] In 2001 the post of Independent Case Examiner was created. This person's role is to investigate cases where customers of

---

[27] *Tinnelly and McElduff* v UK (1998) 27 EHRR 249, *Devlin* v UK (2002) 34 EHRR 1029 and *Devenney* v UK (2002) 35 EHRR 643.

[28] Northern Ireland Act Tribunal (Procedure) Rules 1999.

[29] Social Security (NI) Order 1998, art. 5. The heading of the article uses the word "unified", but it does not appear elsewhere in the Order.

[30] See further details in the Child Poverty Action Group's, *Welfare Benefits and Tax Credits Handbook* (7th ed., 2005). The Department for Work and Pensions also has a useful website providing details about all benefits and services: www.dwp.gov.uk/lifeevent/benefits/index.asp.

[31] The relevant legislation is arts. 9-44 of the Social Security (NI) Order 1998.

the Social Security Agency or the Child Support Agency, having gone through the existing internal complaints procedures of these bodies, are still dissatisfied. Ms Jodi Berg is the current holder of the position.

Claims for benefits[32]

Most of the law concerning entitlement to social security benefits derives from the Social Security Contribution and Benefits Act (NI) Act 1992, as amended, and regulations made under the authority of that Act. The initial decision as to whether or not a claimant qualifies for a particular benefit is taken by an official within the Social Security Agency, a non-departmental public body within the Department for Social Development. It is also possible for assessments and decisions to be made by computer. The decisions cover eligibility for contributory benefits (for which you help to pay through subscriptions to the national insurance fund deducted from your wages or salary), non-contributory benefits and means-tested benefits. Contributory benefits include statutory sick pay (which are normally paid by an employer), statutory adoption, maternity and paternity pay, maternity allowance, bereavement allowance, incapacity benefit, industrial injuries disablement benefit and the retirement pension. Non-contributory benefits include child benefit, disability living allowance, attendance allowance and carer's allowance. The best known of the means-tested benefits is income-based jobseekers allowance, which is designed to provide income to people who are not in full-time employment (but who are required to search for work) and whose income, if any, whether from other benefits or from private resources, is not enough to meet their requirements. Income support is still available to people who are not expected to work, such as single parents or full-time carers. Other means-tested benefits include housing benefit, social fund payments, working tax credit and child tax credit (tax credits and child benefit are administered by HM Revenue and Customs, not the Social Security Agency).

All benefit authorities should process a claim promptly. The Northern Ireland Housing Executive is legally required to process claims for housing benefit within 14 days, or as soon as practical afterwards, once it has received all the information it needs. There are no similar

---

[32] The website of the Department for Social Development carries an electronic version of the so-called Blue Volumes, *The Law Relating to Social Security for Northern Ireland*: www.dsdni.gov.uk/benefitlaw/benefitlaw.asp. The Orange Volume (*The Law Relating to Child Support*) is still only available in hard copy.

statutory requirements on the Social Security Agency and HM Revenue
and Customs, though an interim payment can be made in certain
circumstances where there is a delay in paying a social security benefit
or tax credit. There is no right of appeal against a decision not to make
an interim payment but leave to make an application for judicial review
can be sought.

In most cases the claimant can ask for the official's decision to be
revised on any grounds; the revision will be automatic if requested
within one month of the original decision, otherwise specific grounds
for the revision (such as an official error or a mistake about or
ignorance of facts) must be provided. There is a right to appeal against
a decision, including a revised decision, within a further one month.

After an appeal has been lodged the decision in question may be looked
at again and revised. If this happens and the decision is changed the
appeal may lapse, even if the claimant has not got everything he or she
wants. If still unhappy the claimant must appeal again.

Appeals are dealt with by one of the unified Appeal Tribunals. A
tribunal will be made up of one, two or three members depending on
the benefit or issue under appeal. By way of example, appeals
regarding disability living allowance or attendance allowance are heard
by a lawyer, a medically qualified person and a person with experience
of disability.

"Lay" members of tribunals are drawn from a panel appointed by the
President of the Appeal Tribunals, but chairpersons are appointed by
the Lord Chancellor. The current President of Appeal Tribunals is Mr
Conal MacLynn. Part of his role is to ensure that chairpersons and
panel members are adequately trained and informed, that procedures
are kept fair and easy to understand, and that the arrangements for
holding tribunals are properly made. In status and salary the President
is of equal rank with a county court judge. The Appeals Service is the
name given to the office over which he presides. On 31 March 2004,
apart from the President of Appeal Tribunals, there was one full-time
panel member and 222 part-time members (including 97 with medical
expertise and 53 with legal expertise).[33]

The tribunal hearing

An appeal to a tribunal must be in writing - you simply fill in a form and return it to your local social security office or, for tax credits and child benefit, your local Revenue and Customs office - and it will usually be heard within two or three weeks of the tribunal receiving the papers. Tribunals in this sphere are meant to be, as well as to *seem*, completely independent of the Department for Social Development. For this reason the tribunal hearings are not conducted on Departmental premises. Members of the public can attend tribunal hearings just as they can attend hearings in a court of law, although of course they rarely do so. If intimate personal or financial circumstances or public security considerations are involved, the chairperson can direct the hearing to be held in private. The proceedings are meant to be informal and uncomplicated, with the chairperson having a wide discretion as to how to run things. With a little forethought a claimant ought to be able to conduct his or her own case (it is, after all, a personal problem and no-one knows all the circumstances better than the claimant), but research has shown that claimants stand a far greater chance of winning their cases if they are legally represented (see Chap. 3.1). At the very least claimants ought to ensure that they turn up in person at their hearings: cases can be dealt with in their absence but the vast majority of these will be lost.

Most controversially, legal aid is not available for people who are too poor to pay for representation by a solicitor, although the legal advice and assistance scheme (see Chap. 3.3) can make £88 worth of solicitor's help available short of actual representation; this could cover most of the cost of the paperwork involved in preparing a case for hearing. Alternatively, or additionally, a Citizens' Advice Bureau worker, an independent advice centre worker, a friend or a relative is allowed to represent the claimant free of charge: in tribunals, unlike courts, there are no restrictions on who can act as a legal representative. Some people believe it is a good thing that legal aid is not available for representation because otherwise the proceedings would inevitably become too legalistic; others hold that the denial of legal aid is blatant discrimination against the underprivileged. Imminent reforms to the legal aid system may address some of the injustices in this context by allowing legal aid money to be paid to advisers working in the voluntary sector (see Chap. 3.3).

A claimant can obtain reimbursement of travelling expenses and compensation for loss of wages incurred through attendance at a tribunal. Witnesses can be called and questioned by both sides, but a tribunal has no power, as a court of law would have, to compel the attendance of witnesses, the swearing of oaths or the production of documents. The tribunal's decision is given in a short note. To appeal further to be a Social Security Commissioner (see below) a claimant must normally have a record of the proceedings and a statement of reasons for the decision. A request for these must normally be made within one month of receiving the short decision note.

Social Security and Child Support Commissioners

From the decision of an appeal tribunal there is the opportunity of a full appeal within one month of the claimant receiving the full written decision, by either the claimant or the Department for Social Development or HM Revenue and Customs, to a Social Security Commissioner. But the permission of the chairperson of the tribunal is required before an appeal can go ahead and in all cases there must be a question of law in dispute, not just a question of fact. If the chairperson refuses permission to appeal, a request can be put directly to a Commissioner. Commissioners have to be barristers or solicitors of at least 10 years' standing, which also puts them on a footing with county court judges. Apart from the Chief Commissioner (Judge Martin QC) there is one other full-time Social Security Commissioner in Northern Ireland and on occasions a Commissioner from Great Britain will also hear cases in Northern Ireland. The conduct of the proceedings before a Commissioner is regulated by the Social Security Commissioners (Procedure) Regulations (NI) 1999.[34] The Appeals Service has published an information leaflet describing what happens when an appeal is forwarded to the Service, and it is available on-line.[35]

A Social Security Commissioner may or may not hold an oral hearing into the case, but he or she must always fully reconsider the case and give a decision in writing. This is normally supplied to the parties a few weeks after the oral hearing (if there is one). A new decision can be substituted for that of the original tribunal, or the case can be referred back to a tribunal with instructions as to how to determine it. Reports of

---

[34] See too the Social Security Commissioners (Procedure) (Tax Credits Appeals) Regs. (NI) 2003 and the Child Support Commissioners (Procedure) Regs. (NI) 1999.
[35] www.dsdni.gov.uk/publications/documents/tas_information_leaflet(2).pdf.

some decisions by the Commissioners are published, and decisions by Commissioners in Northern Ireland are binding on tribunals, while decisions by Commissioners in Great Britain are not binding but are strongly persuasive. A few decisions are noted from time to time in the *Bulletin of Northern Ireland Law* (see Chap. 2.3) and there is a selection available on-line through the websites of the Department for Social Development[36] and the British and Irish Legal Information Institute.[37] In 2004 the Social Security and Child Support Commissioners dealt with 163 applications for leave to appeal (6 after a hearing) and 81 actual appeals (20 after a hearing).[38]

Child Support Commissioners are appointed under the Child Support Act 1991 and they hear appeals from appeal tribunals handling child support claims. In Northern Ireland the same people serve as Social Security and Child Support Commissioners.

A further appeal can lie from either kind of Commissioner, although again only with permission and on points of unclear law, to the Court of Appeal; usually only two or three of these arise each year.[39]

Pensions Appeal Tribunals

These tribunals deal with claims that certain pensions (especially war pensions) have been wrongly denied to the claimant. They are regulated by the Pensions Appeal Tribunals Rules (NI) 1981, as amended. Appeals go the Social Security Commissioners (who are then known as Pensions Appeal Commissioners).[40] In 2004 the tribunals dealt with 54 appeals against the amount to be awarded by way of a pension (43 after a hearing) and 25 appeals against a decision that there was no entitlement to a pension at all (18 after a hearing).[41]

There is also a Pensions Regulator and a Pensions Regulator Tribunal,[42] appeals from which lie to the Court of Appeal. The main purpose of the Regulator is to ensure that pension providers are properly accountable.

---

[36] www.dsdni.gov.uk/benefitlaw/ni-caselaw-digest.asp.
[37] www.bailii.org/recent-accessions-nie.html#nie/cases/NISSCSC.
[38] *Northern Ireland Judicial Statistics 2004*, p. 102 and Tables G1 to G3.
[39] See, *e.g.*, *Chief Adjudication Officer* v *Creighton* [2000] NI 222 (a case taken, successfully, by the Law Centre (NI) - see Chap. 3.1) and *Quinn* v *Department for Social Development* [2004] NICA 22 (a case on disability living allowance).
[40] Pensions Appeal Tribunals (NI) (Amendment) Rules 2005.
[41] *Northern Ireland Judicial Statistics 2004*, Tables G.4 and G.5.
[42] This was established in April 2005 under s. 102 of the Pensions Act 2004. See also the Pension Regulator Tribunal Rules 2005.

In 2002 the Government established a Pensions Commission,[43] under the chairmanship of Mr Adair Turner, to review the UK's private pension system and to assess its effectiveness. The Commission's second main report is due to be published in the autumn of 2005.

The Social Fund Commissioner[44]

In the case of discretionary social fund payments there can be no appeal to a Social Security Commissioner: in those areas final decisions are taken by the Social Fund Commissioner, which is a body independent of government departments. Regulated payments under the Social Fund, such as funeral payments, Sure Start maternity grants and winter fuel payments, can be appealed to an appeal tribunal. The Department for Social Development's Annual Report on the Social Fund 2003-2004[45] reveals that in that year there were 2,928 awards of funeral payments, 73,438 cold weather payments, 9,295 sure start maternity grants, 30,939 community care grants, 91,718 budgeting loans and 85,010 crisis loans. Some 57% of applications for a review of community care grants led to the grant being revised (4,458 out of 7,836). More than 280,000 people in more than 200,000 households received a winter fuel payment. The budget for crisis loans for 2004-05 is £44.8 million and the budget for community care grants is £12.64 million.

The Social Fund Commissioner also appoints social fund inspectors, monitors the quality of their decisions, gives advice to them on how to improve the standard of their decisions and arranges for their training. He or she must submit an annual report to the Department for Social Development. The office also participates in social policy research that contributes to the wide debate about the Social Fund and related issues. At present the Social Fund Commissioner responsible for Northern Ireland is Sir Richard Tilt (he also serves in Great Britain[46]).

---

[43] www.pensionscommission.org.uk.
[44] www.osfcni.org.uk.
[45] Made under Social Security Administration (NI) Act 1992, s. 146.
[46] Where his office is called the Independent Review Service: www.irs-review.org.uk.

The Social Security Advisory Committee[47]

The Social Security Advisory Committee (SSAC) was set up in 1980 for the whole of the United Kingdom when what was then known as the supplementary benefit scheme was being substantially altered. It is an independent body charged with the task of advising the Secretary of State for Social Security, and the equivalent devolved Departments, on UK social security matters. Although the chairperson and the dozen or so members[48] are appointed by the Secretary of State, they do not automatically agree with the government line when giving an opinion on social security issues, which they may do either at the Government's request or on their own initiative. Most social security regulations, when they are at the drafting stage, have to be submitted to the SSAC for its comments. Before producing a report on the draft regulations the SSAC usually undertakes a public consultation exercise and the Government must publish the SSAC report when it lays the regulations before Parliament for consideration.

Education Tribunals

Education and Library Boards in Northern Ireland have Schools Admissions Tribunals to hear complaints regarding a pupil's failure to be admitted to their preferred school.[49] The decision of these tribunals can in turn be judicially reviewed,[50] but there is otherwise no right of appeal to any judicial body.

The Special Educational Needs and Disability Tribunal[51] was first created by the Education (NI) Order 1996[52] but was given extra powers by the Special Educational Needs and Disability (NI) Order 2005. It hears complaints against the "statementing" of a child's educational needs and, unusually, appeals lie to the High Court.[53] Education and Library Boards are required to comply with the tribunal's orders within

---

[47] www.ssac.org.uk. There is also an Industrial Injuries Advisory Council (www.iiac.org.uk/) and a Disability Living Allowance Advisory Board (www.dlaab.org.uk).

[48] Including Mr Les Allamby, Director of the Law Centre (NI): see Chap. 3.1.

[49] Education (NI) Order 1997, art. 15. See the Schools Admission (Appeal Tribunals) Regs. (NI) 1998 and L. Lundy, *Education Law, Policy and Practice in Northern Ireland* (2000), pp. 123-7.

[50] See, *e.g.*, *In re H's Application* [2001] 9 BNIL 21.

[51] See generally L. Lundy, note 49 above, pp. 257-66.

[52] Art. 22.

[53] *Ibid.* art. 24.

prescribed periods. Unfortunately, however, no legal aid is available for representation at hearings before the tribunal, although "green form" advice and assistance can be applied for (see Chap. 3.3). The current President of the Tribunal is Mr Damian McCormick.

8.3 INDUSTRIAL TRIBUNALS AND THE INDUSTRIAL COURT

Industrial tribunals (now called employment tribunals in England and Wales) deal with disputes relating to individual employment contracts. More general collective disputes (those between employers and trade unions) are the concern of the Industrial Court and statutory bodies such as the Labour Relations Agency. To deal with the particular problem of religious and political discrimination in employment in Northern Ireland, the Fair Employment Tribunal has been created. Watchdog bodies with a role to play in matters concerning employment or industrial relations are outlined in the following chapter (see, especially, Chap.9.3, 9.4 and 9.5).

Industrial tribunals

Industrial tribunals have operated in Northern Ireland since 1965 and are now established under the Industrial Tribunals (NI) Order 1996, as amended. Their procedures are now governed by the Industrial Tribunals (Constitution and Rules of Procedure) Regulations (NI) 2004. They are staffed by a President (Ms Eileen McBride), a Vice-President, five full-time and one part-time chairpersons, and approximately 270 lay members. A full-time chairperson earns the equivalent of what a Resident Magistrate or district judge earns.[54] Industrial Tribunals sit all year round in six different venues in Northern Ireland, the headquarters now being in Waring Street in Belfast. The chairpersons and lay members are appointed by the Department for Employment and Learning, but of course they are meant to act completely independently of the Government.

Most of the various employment rights which industrial tribunals protect are enshrined in the Employment Rights (NI) Order 1996, as amended, together with a number of other pieces of legislation. The most frequently recurring types of case are those which concern redundancy, unfair dismissal, discrimination or activities on behalf of a

---

[54] Currently £90,760. See Table 3 in Chap. 1.5.

trade union. The Employment (NI) Order 2003 made changes to the way in which disputes about these rights are handled by, for example, promoting the early resolution of disputes at work (so that claims can now be rejected at the tribunal if an effort has not been made to solve the dispute internally first). These changes are expected to produce something like a net reduction of 20%-25% in the caseload of the tribunals.[55] Some new regulations came into effect in 2004 and others are due to come into force in 2005.[56] The latter mainly deal with grievance, disciplinary and dismissal procedures in the workplace.

Proceedings for a tribunal hearing are begun by the applicant sending an application to the Office of Industrial Tribunals and the Fair Employment Tribunal.[57] All applications will then be automatically referred to the Labour Relations Agency (see Chap. 9.4) to see if the matter can be resolved with the help of one of its conciliation officers. If a tribunal hearing does eventually take place the evidence will be presented through the testimony of witnesses or the production of documents; written representations may also be made. The tribunal is expressly authorised to regulate procedure in whatever way is deemed best. The chairperson, who is legally qualified and normally sits with two lay persons with industrial relations experience, has considerable power to control the strictness or otherwise of the procedure to be adopted. Proceedings are meant to be informal, but since some hearings are conducted in county court rooms the atmosphere of informality is not always easy to engender. In certain types of case the chairperson may sit alone or with only one lay member.

The two sides can be legally represented at tribunal hearings but cannot obtain legal aid for this purpose. They will have to bear the cost themselves unless their representative is, for instance, a volunteer, a trade union official or a lawyer paid for by the Equality Commission. Legal advice and assistance, however, is still available to those who are financially eligible (see Chap. 3.3). Only in exceptional circumstances, as where one party has asked for a postponement of the proceedings or has been vexatious, will one of the parties be made to bear the other's costs after the case is over. The Police Authority, for example, had to

---

[55] Industrial tribunals are now also able to issue default judgments in cases which are uncontested.

[56] Useful information can be found on the website of the Department for Employment and Learning: www.delni.gov.uk/docs/pdf/DR%20Employer%20Guidance%20Final .pdf. See too the Employment (NI) Order 2003 (Dispute Resolution) Regs (NI) 2004.

[57] www.industrialfairemploymenttribunalsni.gov.uk.

pay the costs of female reservists who successfully brought a sex discrimination claim against the Chief Constable during the 1980s (*Johnston* v *Chief Constable of the RUC*[58]). Tribunal costs, however, will not normally be as high as those in a court case.

Decision and challenge

The industrial tribunal's decision may be given at the end of the hearing or reached later and notified to the parties. Written reasons must be given and in cases concerning disability discrimination either party can ask the tribunal for extended reasons. If the tribunal decides that the applicant is in the right, the particular remedy afforded will depend on the nature of the application. For instance, if the claim is in respect of redundancy or maternity pay the tribunal may assess the amount of payments due; if it is a claim in relation to unfair dismissal the tribunal can order the reinstatement of the employee, or compensation, or both; if the complaint relates to discrimination an order can be issued requiring the discrimination to be stopped. A register of all decisions is open for general public inspection at the Office of Industrial Tribunals and the Fair Employment Tribunal and copies of a selection of the decisions are available on the website of the British and Irish Legal Information Institute.[59]

There are three ways of challenging an industrial tribunal's decision: (i) asking for a review by the tribunal itself, (ii) applying for judicial review by the High Court (see Chap. 6.7), or (iii) asking for a case to be stated for the opinion of the Court of Appeal on a point of law (see Chap. 6.2 and 6.4).[60] A decision by the Court of Appeal can again be appealed to the House of Lords.[61] In each of these cases care has to be taken to make the challenge within the specified time limit. There is no appeal, as there is in social security cases, to a higher tribunal or to a Commissioner. In particular, there is no Employment Appeal Tribunal in Northern Ireland such as exists in Great Britain. If a tribunal refuses to state a case for the opinion of the Court of Appeal, that very refusal can itself be made the object of an application for judicial review.[62] If

[58] [1987] QB 129; see also Chap. 2.5.
[59] www.bailii.org/recent-accessions-nie.html#nie/cases/NIIT.
[60] For a recent Court of Appeal decision in a case stated by an industrial tribunal, see *Perceval-Price* v *Department of Economic Development* [2000] NI 141.
[61] As in *Murray* v *Foyle Meats Ltd.* [2000] 1 AC 51.
[62] As in (albeit unsuccessfully) *Re the University of Ulster's Application* [2000] 2 BNIL 31.

an industrial tribunal makes an award of money to one of the parties, and that party proves unwilling to pay, the award may be enforced through an application first to a county court, and then, if necessary, to the Enforcement of Judgments Office (see Chap. 6.8).

Statistics on the workload of the industrial tribunals are not as easy to access as the figures for courts and tribunals which fall under the aegis of the Northern Ireland Court Service.[63] In 2003-04 there were 11,328 claims registered; this was a huge rise on the figure for 2002-03 (4,856) but this was because 6,250 related claims were submitted against one employer. The industrial tribunals dealt with 4,672 cases, but 1,069 of these (23%) were settled through conciliation organised by the Labour Relations Agency (see Chap. 9.4), 871 (19%) were settled by the parties themselves and 1,800 (39%) were withdrawn. The majority of claims (56%) concerned complaints under the Working Time Regulations. The other claims alleged unfair dismissal (16%), unlawful deduction of wages (7%), sex discrimination (5%), disability discrimination (2%) and race discrimination (1%). Altogether there were 953 claims of discrimination (excluding those dealt with by the Fair Employment Tribunal - see below). Hearings took place in 704 cases and the applicant was successful in 346 of these (49%).

The Fair Employment Tribunal

This tribunal (the FET) was set up by the Fair Employment (NI) Act 1989 to adjudicate upon individual complaints of discrimination on grounds of religious belief or political opinion and to enforce against employers affirmative action plans directed by the then Fair Employment Commission. Shortly after its inception a difficulty arose with regard to section 30 of the 1989 Act, which in some situations criminalised the disclosure of information concerning a person's religious background. It was only after this section was repealed by the Fair Employment (Amendment) (NI) Order 1991 that the FET was able to resume hearing cases.

The relevant legislation in this area has been consolidated in the Fair Employment and Treatment (NI) Order 1998, which extends protection against religious or political discrimination into the spheres of property

---

[63] Here I have drawn upon the Regulatory Impact Assessment produced by the Department for Employment and Learning in March 2005 in relation to proposed reforms of the tribunal system: www.delni.gov.uk/consultDebate/files/IT-FET Final?RIAPhase2-AnnexC.pdf. The annual reports of the Labour Relations Agency (see Chap. 9.4) are also useful.

sales and the provision of goods, facilities and services. The governing rules are now the Fair Employment Tribunal (Rules of Procedure) Regulations (NI) 2004. Hearings are conducted in public, although some categories of evidence, such as information originally provided in confidence, can be presented in private.

The FET can request an employer to take action to eliminate the effects of discrimination and can award damages up an unlimited amount to individual complainants. The compensation can include an amount for injured feelings. If an employer refuses to implement an affirmative action plan the tribunal can also impose an unlimited fine. Since October 1999 the functions of the Fair Employment Commission have been transferred to the Equality Commission for Northern Ireland, which was set up under the Northern Ireland Act 1998 (see Chap. 9.3). As with industrial tribunals, all decisions of the FET can be appealed on a point of law by way of case stated to the Court of Appeal.[64]

In 2003-04 there were 467 cases registered with the FET (down from 501 in 2002-03). The new dispute resolution procedures required to be put in place by employers by April 2005 will mean a reduction in the annual caseload. In 2003-04 there were 78 cases heard and determined, of which just 16% resulted in a finding in favour of the applicant.

The Industrial Court

The Industrial Court for Northern Ireland, which is the counterpart of the Central Arbitration Committee in Great Britain, was provided for by the Industrial Courts Act 1919 but was not actually constituted until 1964, when it was required to give effect to the Terms and Conditions of Employment Act (NI) 1963. As in the case of tribunals, a sitting of the Court comprises one independent chairman (the President of the Court) plus two lay members selected from panels representing both sides of industry. The current Chairman of the Court is Mr Richard Steele.

The jurisdiction of the Industrial Court is fairly limited. Until recently it dealt with failure to comply with a recommendation made by the Labour Relations Agency for trade union recognition (see Chap. 9.4). Under the Equal Pay Act (NI) 1970 it can amend collective agreements, pay structures or wages orders whenever they contain discriminatory provisions applicable to men or women only. Further functions relating

---

[64] See, e.g., *Chief Constable of the RUC* v *Sergeant A* [2000] NI 261.

to trade union recognition were conferred by the Employment Relations (NI) Order 1999 and the Court was formally reconstituted as a result.[65] Certain of the Court's decisions, while not in themselves enforceable in ordinary courts, lead to the incorporation of new terms into individual contracts of employment.

In 2003-04 the Industrial Court dealt with only four applications. In December 2003 it successfully defended itself in a judicial review application brought by an employer who was unhappy at the way in which the Court had refused to disclose information concerning the identity of certain workers in the company.[66]

8.4 THE MENTAL HEALTH REVIEW TRIBUNAL

The jurisdiction and operation of the Mental Health Review Tribunal (MHRT), which has existed in Northern Ireland since 1962, are set out in the Mental Health (NI) Order 1986 and the procedures used are governed by the Mental Health Review Tribunal (NI) Rules 1986. The Tribunal has no powers or functions outside those granted by this legislation. Its members are all appointed by the Lord Chancellor and at present there are eight legal members, eight medical members and eight lay members. Two of the legal members have been appointed as Chairperson and Deputy Chairperson and a legal member always presides at each sitting of the MHRT. At such sittings there will also be a medical member and a lay member. The panels are appointed by the MHRT's Chair. The cost of operating the MHRT during the year 2004-05 was £108,390.

The 1986 Order updated the law in Northern Ireland on the detention, guardianship, care and treatment of patients suffering from mental disorder and on the management of the property and affairs of such patients. The MHRT hears applications for discharge made by or on behalf of patients who are liable to be detained, who are subject to guardianship or who have been placed under a restriction order by a criminal court (people in this last category are called restricted patients). The MHRT cannot itself instigate hearings about patients' cases: it can only react to applications made to it. As regards long-stay patients, Health and Social Services Trusts (or, in the case of restricted patients, the Secretary of State) are under a duty to refer cases to the

---

[65] Art. 25 inserts new arts. 91, 91A, 92 and 92A into the Industrial Relations (NI) Order 1992.

[66] *In re James E McCabe Ltd's Application* [2003] NIQB 77.

MHRT at least once every two years. In the case of restricted patients the MHRT can order the person's absolute discharge or make the discharge subject to conditions.

Hearings

On receipt of an application the MHRT sends notice of it to the responsible authority (usually the Health and Social Services Trust administering the hospital in which the patient is detained), to the patient (if he or she is not the applicant) and, if the patient is a restricted patient or a conditionally discharged patient, to the Secretary of State. The Trust is required to forward to the MHRT up-to-date reports on the medical and social circumstances of the applicant. Information can be withheld from the applicant (or, where he or she is not the applicant, from the patient) on the ground that its disclosure would adversely affect the health or welfare of the patient or anyone else. In such cases the information will be provided in a separate document in which the reasons for believing that its disclosure would have such an effect will be set out.

As soon as is practicable the MHRT sends a copy of every relevant document it receives to the parties. Where it is minded not to disclose any document to a patient it must nevertheless disclose it as soon as practicable to that person's authorised representative, a registered medical practitioner or a person who, in the opinion of the Tribunal, is a suitable person by virtue of his or her experience or professional qualification. On the day of the hearing the MHRT may decide to disclose some or all of the information withheld by the Trust.

The MHRT must give all parties concerned (including the patient's nearest relative, as defined in art. 32 of the 1986 Order) at least 14 days' notice of the date, time and venue of the hearing. It has a discretion to exclude any person from the hearing (which is heard in private) but may appoint some person to act as the applicant's or patient's authorised representative (in cases where the patient does not wish to conduct his own case and does not authorise a representative). Representation under the legal advice and assistance scheme (see Chap. 3.3) has been available since 1980.

At any time before the hearing the medical member of the MHRT must examine the patient and take such other steps as he or she considers necessary to form an opinion about the patient's mental condition. For this purpose the patient may be seen in private and all his or her medical records may be examined by the medical member, who may take such notes and copies as he or she may require for use in connection with the application. The MHRT may also interview the patient and is required to do so if the patient so requests. Written arguments can be presented, in addition to the oral testimony of witnesses. The attendance of witnesses or the production of documents can be compelled as in other courts, but strict rules of evidence do not apply.

The Tribunal's decision is based on the written and oral evidence adduced to it at hearing and the burden of showing why detention or guardianship should continue remains firmly on the responsible authority. The Mental Health (Amendment) (NI) Order 2004 amended the 1986 Order to ensure that the burden of proving why detention should not continue does not rest on the patient. This followed a High Court declaration in an English case that the previous rule applied by the MHRT in that jurisdiction was incompatible with Article 5 of the European Convention of Human Rights, which protects the right to liberty.[67] Other challenges to the compatibility of the procedures used in Northern Ireland with the European Convention have so far failed,[68] although a report prepared for the Northern Ireland Human Rights Commission suggests that reforms are still necessary.[69]

Decisions and appeals

Decisions of the MHRT can be by majority vote. They must be communicated in writing, together with reasons, within 14 days of the hearing, unless the MHRT considers that this would adversely affect the health or welfare of the patient or any other person.

The MHRT has power to order the continued detention of a patient, but if it is not satisfied that the patient continues to suffer from mental illness or severe mental impairment of a nature or degree which

---

[67] *R (on the application of H) v Mental Health Review Tribunal of the North and East London Region* [2002] QB 1.

[68] See, *e.g., Re Laurence McGrady* [2003] NIQB 15, where the applicant unsuccessfully challenged rr. 11 and 12 of the MHRT Rules (NI) 1986, which require the medical member of a tribunal to disclose privately to the non-medical members his or her opinion of the patient's mental condition; this was held to be tolerable provided the medical member expressed no view at that time concerning whether the patient should or should not be discharged.

[69] G. Davidson, M. McCallion and M. Potter, *Connecting Mental Health and Human Rights* (2004).

warrants his or her detention in hospital for medical treatment, or that discharge would create a substantial likelihood of serious physical harm to the patient or to any other person, it must order the patient's discharge. With a view to facilitating discharge on a future date the MHRT may recommend leave of absence for the patient or transfer to another hospital.

The only way of appealing against a decision of the MHRT is by requesting a case to be stated for determination by the Court of Appeal (see Chap. 6.2 and 6.4.). As only questions of law can be stated in this way, such appeals are rare. The substance of the law in this area is fairly clear: it is in its application to the facts, and in the ascertainment of those facts, that the difficulties lie. There can be no further appeal beyond the Court of Appeal. Of course, judicial review proceedings might also be available (see Chap. 6.7).

During the year ending 31 March 2005, the MHRT fully processed 216 cases. Of these, 116 cases did not proceed to a hearing: 13 were invalid applications, 26 were withdrawn and 77 were from persons who were re-graded as voluntary patients. Of the 100 cases determined at a hearing, 62 resulted in the applicant's detention, 22 left the applicant subject to guardianship, nine cases were adjourned and seven patients were discharged.[70]

The property of mental patients

It should be noted that the MHRT has no remit regarding the management of the property of mentally disordered patients. Prime responsibility for this lies with the Office of Care and Protection, an office within the Family Division of the High Court (which is also responsible for wardship, guardianship and adoption proceedings). At any one time about 1,200 people have property which is being managed by this office. It is the Master (Care and Protection) who decides whether any step needs to be taken to deal with a patient's property; if necessary the Master will appoint a Controller to manage a patient's affairs. In 2003, 730 patients were referred to the Office of Care and Protection under the Mental Health (NI) Order 1986 (8% more than in 2002) and the total caseload during the year was 1,212.[71] A patient living in a hospital or other statutory accommodation can have amounts

---

[70] Information supplied by the MHRT.
[71] *Northern Ireland Judicial Statistics 2003*, Table B.35.

of money up to £20,000 managed by the Health Board on his or her behalf without needing to involve the Office of Care and Protection.

The Mental Health Commission

The Mental Health Commission for Northern Ireland (MHC) was set up under the Mental Health (NI) Order 1986, largely as a result of one of the recommendations made by the Northern Ireland Review Committee on Mental Health Legislation (the MacDermott Committee), which reported in 1981. At present the Commission has 19 part-time members (including the chairperson), their period of appointment being at the discretion of the Minister for Health, Social Services and Public Safety. They include a general practitioner, a psychologist, an occupational therapist, two lawyers, two social workers, two nurses, four psychiatrists and six lay persons. The current chairperson is a barrister, Ms Daphne Elliott. The MHC publishes an annual report and both a triennial Strategic Plan and an annual Business Plan. As yet, however, it does not have a website. Like most public bodies in Northern Ireland, it can in turn be subject to investigation by the Commissioner for Complaints (see Chap. 9.2).

The MHC has a duty to keep under review the care and treatment of people in Northern Ireland who have a learning disability or mental health needs. In meeting this responsibility, it provides a number of key services. Multi-disciplinary teams of Commission members undertake announced and unannounced visits to learning disability hospitals, psychiatric hospitals and community facilities. The MHC appoints doctors who can legally detain people in hospital or recommend their reception into guardianship and it also appoints independent doctors to provide second opinions for people who require specific treatment, such as electroconvulsive therapy. The MHC reviews all the legal documentation regarding the detention and guardianship of patients to ensure that there has been compliance with the 1986 Order and it reviews of all serious "untoward events" involving individuals with mental health needs or a learning disability. Finally, the MHC reviews the treatment plans for patients who are detained for longer than three months. The plans are scrutinised for their clinical acceptability as well as for evidence of consent or the need for a second opinion.

In performing these various functions the MHC is in effect monitoring the operation of the powers and duties placed by the 1986 Order on the Health and Social Services Trusts, the Department of Health, Social

Services and Public Safety, the Secretary of State and persons running private hospitals. When it thinks fit to do so, the MHC may refer to the Mental Health Review Tribunal the case of any patient who is liable to be detained under the 1986 Order.[72] But the MHC's role is not confined to detained patients: it also covers voluntary patients and anyone else suffering from mental disorder.

In 1992, after consulting with the MHC, the then Department of Health and Social Services published a Code of Practice which gives guidance to medical practitioners, staff of the Health and Social Services Trusts, hospital staff and approved social workers concerning the admission into hospital of patients suffering from mental disorder and their treatment there. The 1986 Order does not impose a legal duty to comply with the Code but a breach of the Code can be cited as evidence in legal proceedings. One chapter of the Code is devoted to the handling of patients who are or have been involved in criminal proceedings.

During 2003-2004 the MHC visited all psychiatric and learning disability hospitals in Northern Ireland. In the course of the visits 28 patients and five relatives or carers requested interviews with Commissioners. Visits were also made to 29 community facilities and the work of 28 community mental health or learning disability teams was reviewed. There were reviews of 106 reported "untoward events" (including a number of deaths) and 13 people were interviewed who had complaints in respect of their treatment and care. In 49 instances (3% of all admissions) the MHC was of the view that people had been improperly detained or received into guardianship. Such events are immediately raised with the respective Trust. A total of 345 drug treatment plans were independently reviewed.

In 2002 the Government announced a Review of Mental Health and Learning Disability in Northern Ireland, to be conducted under the chairmanship of Professor David Bamford.[73] The review is to bear in mind the personal dignity of people with mental health needs as well as new laws on human rights and equality. It is to make recommendations on future policy and service priorities, reflecting the needs of both users and carers. The Legal Issues Sub-group is charged with making recommendations in respect of the future of the MHC. Initial reports

---

[72] Art. 86(3).
[73] www.rmhldni.gov.uk.

have so far been issued on adult mental health and on learning disability and the final report is due by the end of 2005.

8.5 TRIBUNALS CONCERNING LAND, RENT AND PLANNING

The Lands Tribunal[74]

The Lands Tribunal for Northern Ireland was set up by the Lands Tribunal and Compensation Act (NI) 1964. It is technically not a tribunal at all but a proper court, although it is not always presided over by a judge and it is not serviced by the Northern Ireland Court Service. Persons serving on it are barristers or solicitors of seven years' standing or persons experienced in the valuation of land. They are assisted by a registrar (currently Mr Gary Shaw[75]) and a small clerical staff. There are at present only two members; one of these is a High Court Judge and serves as part-time President of the Tribunal (Mr Justice Coghlin), the other is a chartered surveyor and serves in a full-time capacity (Mr Michael Curry).[76]

The functions of the Lands Tribunal are varied. One of its most important is to resolve disputes over the amount of compensation to be paid for the compulsory acquisition of land or for the injury caused to land by, for instance, the making of roads.[77] Another important function is the hearing of appeals and references concerning the valuation of land for rate relief purposes,[78] a job which frequently entails deciding whether a particular organisation is or is not a charity (it is in this context that such decisions are usually made in Northern Ireland, where there is no public register of charities[79]). The Tribunal must also deal

---

[74] www.landstribunalni.org.

[75] To whom I remain grateful for assistance with this section.

[76] Salaries are set by Parliament. See Lands Tribunal (Salaries) Order (NI) 2005, which fixes the President's salary from 1 April 2004 at £116,515 and the member's at £112,116.

[77] *E.g.* under the Land Commission (NI) Order 1982. See too N. Dawson, "Modification and Extinguishment of Land Obligations under the Property (NI) Order 1978" (1978) 29 NILQ 223 and *Ward* v *Northern Ireland Housing Executive* [2004] 2 BNIL 65.

[78] Under the Rates (NI) Order 1977, which provides for appeals against decisions of the Commissioner of Valuation to be taken to the Lands Tribunal.

[79] There is a proposal to create a Northern Ireland Register of Charities and a Northern Ireland Charity Commission: see *Consultation on the Review of Charities Administration and Legislation in Northern Ireland*, issued by the Department for

with the renewal of business tenancies,[80] consent for alterations to land, assignments and agreements to surrender, and the modification of legal obligations which are allegedly impeding the enjoyment of land, such as rights of way.[81] Parties can, moreover, agree to ask the Lands Tribunal to sit in private as an arbitrating body to settle disputes concerning the value, use or development of a piece of land (*e.g.* in the context of a rent review dispute). In all cases there is no limit to the value of land which may be at issue, in contrast, say, with the jurisdiction of the county court in land matters (see Chap. 6.4).

The rules of procedure for the Tribunal are laid down in the Lands Tribunal Rules (NI) 1976, as amended, but in most cases the parties themselves are invited to agree a timetable for the handling of their dispute. Prior to any hearing the parties usually provide each other with all the facts upon which they intend to rely and the experts involved exchange their reports showing how they arrived at their conclusions. Such an open approach is intended to encourage the parties to arrive at a settlement of the dispute prior to the hearing itself. Indeed the Lands Tribunal does not regard its role as confined to processing the cases according to law, it actively encourages flexible prevention and resolution of disputes. The Registrar will advise practitioners on the procedures normally adopted. The forms most frequently used in Lands Tribunal work can be downloaded from the Tribunal's website.

The Lands Tribunal has its own courtroom and offices in the Royal Courts of Justice in Belfast, but it will also sit in a courthouse convenient to the location of the land concerned whenever the parties prefer such a venue for the hearing. Usually the surveyor member of the Tribunal will hear the case, with the President joining him if the case involves particularly sensitive or complex issues. The President has a casting vote if the two members disagree. Members of the public can attend hearings and legal aid is available for some types of cases. The parties may represent themselves or employ a solicitor, a barrister or (in suitable cases, and only with the Tribunal's permission) a valuer.

Decisions are usually given in writing, and must contain reasons. They are final as regards the determination of facts, but they can be appealed

---

Social Development in February 2005. More generally, see K. O'Halloran and R. Cormacain, *Charity Law in Northern Ireland* (2001).

[80] Under the Business Tenancies (NI) Order 1996. See N. Dawson, *Business Tenancies in Northern Ireland* (1994).

[81] See generally S. Witchell, *Residential Property Law in Northern Ireland* (2000).

to the Court of Appeal within a week on a point of law by way of case stated. As the Tribunal is a court, an award of costs usually follows the event. Apart from arbitration awards, all written decisions of the Lands Tribunal are published and can be treated as precedents. Summaries appear in the *Bulletin of Northern Ireland Law* and the most important cases are reported in the *Estates Gazette* or the *Rating and Valuation Reporter*, which are English journals. A Table of Cases from 1990 (plus a few earlier ones) is on the Tribunal's website.[82] All recent decisions as well as most of the important earlier cases are available on the *Lexis* database (see Chap. 2.3) or from the Registrar, by email, free of charge.[83]

In 2004 the Lands Tribunal dealt with about 200 cases. Some 160 of these were settled before a hearing date was fixed and about five were settled at or during the hearing. Summary decisions (*i.e.* decisions given there and then) were delivered in about 20 cases and in another 12 or so the decision was given after a delay. About 150 of the cases that year concerned commercial tenancies, and about 10 cases concerned valuation of land for rating purposes. The volume of rating cases is cyclical – it follows the five-yearly pattern of general commercial revaluations. Current proposals for reform of the water rates and domestic rating systems in Northern Ireland may lead to a temporary surge in cases over the next few years.

The Rent Officer and Rent Assessment Panel

Northern Ireland has a complex system for controlling the level of rents in the private housing sector. If on 1 October 1978 the dwelling was not let at a rent controlled under the Rent Restriction Acts, it still today cannot be subjected to control. But if the dwelling was so controlled it is now subject to the Rent (NI) Order 1978.

Under that Order the Department for Social Development for Northern Ireland[84] will, upon application, register an increased rent if the net annual value of the dwelling is more than £60 or, when the NAV is less than £60, if the district council has certified that the dwelling meets certain standards. If either the landlord or the tenant disagrees with the registered rent, appeal against it can be made to a rent assessment committee.

---

[82] www.landstribunalni.org/Table_of_Cases.dot.
[83] Lands.tribunal@dfpni.gov.uk.
[84] Formerly the responsibility lay with the Department of the Environment.

The appeal is first of all sent to the Rent Officer, who is an official independent of the Government.[85] He or she makes the necessary arrangements for a survey of the premises and for the determination of the issue by a rent assessment committee at a hearing if either the landlord or the tenant so desires. The committees are composed of members drawn from a Rent Assessment Panel of about 17 people (all appointed by the Department for Social Development and chaired by the Rent Officer) and they sit throughout Northern Ireland.[86] The Rent Officer appoints one chairperson for each committee and usually one or two other members.

At the hearing the landlord and tenant can be heard either in person or by a representative (a barrister, solicitor or any other authorised person such as a person from the Housing Rights Service). The proceedings are meant to be informal and uncomplicated, with no state legal aid being available. In determining the appropriate rent the committee will have regard to the report of its surveyor, its own inspection and the rents of houses let by the Northern Ireland Housing Executive. These public sector rents in turn mostly depend at present on the age of the premises and the number of persons they can accommodate. The committee will disregard any improvements made by the tenant.

Rent assessment committees also hear applications for the reassessment of registered rents in cases where there has been a change in circumstances relating to either the dwelling-house or the tenancy. This is in effect the only way of challenging a rent assessment committee's original assessment of rent. In March 2004 there were 5,626 "regulated" tenancies in Northern Ireland and just 360 so-called "restricted" tenancies.[87] Each year rent assessment committees hear about 50 appeals against rent levels and in about one-half of these the rents are reduced as a result. In 2003-04 the service cost about £69,000 to run.[88]

---

[85] For more details see www.dsdni.gov.uk/housing/rent-officer.asp. The current holder of the post is Ms Joan McCrum.
[86] For more details see www.dsdni.gov.uk/housing/rent-assess-panels.asp and the Rent Assessment Committees Regs. (NI) 1978.
[87] Department for Social Development, *Northern Ireland Housing Statistics 2003-04*, p.59: www.dsdni.gov.uk/publications/documents/Housing_Statistics_2003-04.pdf.
[88] For the Rent Officer Service Annual Report 2003-04, see www.dsdni.gov.uk/rent_ofice_annual_report_0304_.pdf. (sic).

The Planning Appeals Commission[89]

In Northern Ireland all applications for planning permission must be made to the Department of the Environment rather than to a local authority as in England and Wales. Not all need to be advertised in the press.[90] The Department has a duty to consult with district councils and other affected bodies but the decision whether to grant planning permission is for it alone to take. If the permission is refused, or granted subject to conditions, the applicant may appeal to the Planning Appeals Commission (PAC) within six months (or such longer period as the Commission may allow). But anyone who objects to a planning application has, at present, no right to appeal against the granting of permission.[91]

The PAC is one of those bodies which, like rent assessment committees, does not call itself a tribunal but in fact operates in much the same way as those which do. It was first established in 1973 by the Planning (NI) Order 1972, although the relevant legislation is now the Planning (NI) Order 1991.[92] According to its website it has no fewer than 37 functions conferred by the 1991 Order and a further 30 functions conferred by other pieces of legislation.

The PAC consists of a Chief Commissioner (currently Mr John Warke) and such number of other members as the Office of the First Minister and Deputy First Minister may determine. At present, in addition to the Chief Commissioner, there are 15 full-time Commissioners and four part-time panel Commissioners. An appeal is generally heard by one Commissioner appointed by the Chief Commissioner, and the hearing usually takes place at a venue near to the location of the relevant land. The actual decision on the appeal, however, is taken by the PAC as a whole. Some of the more important decisions are noted in the *Bulletin of Northern Ireland Law* (see Chap. 2.3).

As full reasons for the refusal of planning permission are not always given at the time when the refusal is first announced, the hearing before a Commissioner may be the applicant's earliest opportunity to discover

---

[89] www.pacni.gov.uk. The PAC doubles up as the Water Appeals Commission, in which capacity it deals with matters such as appeals against decision on sewerage services or trade effluent discharges.

[90] See the Planning Applications (Exemption from Publication) Order (NI) 1991.

[91] *Re Ronald Foster's Application* [2004] NIQB 1.

[92] See further W. Orbinson with A. Farningham, *Northern Ireland Planning Policy, Vol.1 (Policy) and Vol.2 (Index)* (2003).

what the details of those reasons are. The Department consequently presents its case first at these hearings, even though it is technically the respondent. No official rules have been made to govern the conduct of proceedings at a hearing, but they are kept as informal as possible.[93] Legal aid is not available. There is an alternative "written representation" procedure available to appellants; this avoids the need for a hearing and is used for some of the apparently straightforward appeals.

In 2003-04 there were just under 33,060 applications for planning permission in Northern Ireland (up from 27,941 in 2002-03) and of those which were considered during the year (23,751) 93% were granted.[94] The Planning Appeals Commission received 522 appeals (up from 330 in 2002-03 - a 58% increase),[95] of which 472 (89%) were actually planning appeals.[96] Some 50% of the planning appeals actually decided (191 out of 385) were allowed.[97] There were 21 formal hearings and 168 informal hearings, but the success rate was identical for each. Obviously each appeal takes several months to process. The Commission's website lists all the appeals received during the previous three months as well as all of the decisions made within the previous six months. If you know the PAC appeal reference number you can even view the decision letters.

The PAC also has a duty to conduct public local inquiries (in order to consider objections made against development plans) as well as hearings or inquiries which may arise from planning applications which the Department of the Environment judges to be of major significance. There are usually only two or three of these each year. Normally one member of the PAC will conduct such an inquiry or hearing and will report to the PAC as a whole. Having considered the matter, the PAC prepares its collective recommendations and submits them to the Department of the Environment. It is the Department which makes the final decision.

---

[93] Care needs to be taken that the informality is not such as to breach the right to a fair hearing guaranteed by Art. 6 of the European Convention on Human Rights: *In re Stewart's Application* [2003] NICA 4.

[94] See note 87 above, p. 26. Details are also provided in the following pages there as to the kind of applications made and geographical variations.

[95] See the *Planning Appeals Commission Chief Commissioner's Annual Report 2003-04*, Table 5.

[96] The remainder were appeals concerning enforcement and advertisements etc.

[97] See note 95 above, Tables 6A and 6B.

There can be no further appeal against a decision of the Planning Appeals Commission, only an application for judicial review (see Chap. 6.7). In 2003-04 there were four such challenges, but they were all unsuccessful.

In 2004 the Department of the Environment consulted the public on proposed reforms to the planning legislation in Northern Ireland. These include proposals to reduce the normal life of planning permissions and listed building consents from five years to three, to make disabled access a primary consideration at the start of every development process, to confer new powers to protect buildings in conservation areas from demolition before designation takes effect and to allow planning decisions to be made by a single member of the Planning Appeals Commission. Legislation to enact some of these changes is expected in 2005 or 2006.

CHAPTER NINE

OFFICIAL WATCHDOGS

9.1 QUANGOS AND ACCOUNTABILITY

It would be misleading to create the impression that the Northern
Ireland legal system, any more than other legal systems, consists only
of the courts and tribunals surveyed in Chapters 5, 6, 7 and 8. On the
contrary, there are many other bodies whose function it is to oversee
the administration of the law in Northern Ireland (or in the UK as a
whole). Some of them even help to enforce the law. This chapter
briefly describes a number of these official bodies. Some are
accountable to Parliament, others are not; some have real powers to
change the law or practice, others may only advise. All act as official
watchdogs so that the general public can have greater confidence in the
fairness and justness of the legal system in various fields. The popular
name for these bodies is "quangos" - quasi-autonomous non-
governmental organisations.

Some of the bodies deserving to be included in this chapter have
already been described at earlier points in this book. The role of the
Lay Observer, *vis-à-vis* complaints against solicitors, was dealt with in
Chapter 3.2, the Northern Ireland Legal Services Commission in
Chapter 3.3, the Police Ombudsman in Chapter 4.5, the Prisoner
Ombudsman and the Criminal Justice Inspectorate in Chapter 4.7, the
Social Security Advisory Committee in Chapter 8.2, the Mental Health
Commission for Northern Ireland in Chapter 8.4. In many other spheres
there are unofficial lobbying organisations which try to keep the law in
step with prevailing views in society; reference to a few of these has
already been made in Chapter 3.1 under the heading "pressure groups".
The "supervisory" jurisdiction of the High Court, exercised through
judicial review (see Chap. 6.7), must also not be forgotten.

The role of Parliament

Persons who are particularly well placed to maintain an oversight of
quangos are Parliamentarians (MPs and peers). They can do so through
asking parliamentary questions (PQs) of government Ministers or
through working on Parliamentary committees. MPs and peers have
considerable freedom to ask numerous and searching PQs, prominent

exponents of the art at present being Mr Norman Baker (Liberal Democrat MP) and Lord Laird of Artigarvan (Ulster Unionist peer). But Select Committees have considerable power to conduct their own probing investigations and their reports have the potential to cause great embarrassment, if not worse, to those persons and institutions that are the object of them. In the present context the work of the House of Commons' Select Committee on Northern Ireland Affairs is worth highlighting.

In the Parliamentary sessions 2001-05 that Committee had 13 members (all men) and the Chair was held by Mr Michael Mates MP, a former Minister of State in the Northern Ireland Office. It produced a total of 51 reports, including 23 which were a reply to the Government's official response to an earlier report of the Committee. Amongst the topics examined, mostly in considerable detail, were the Northern Ireland Prison Service,[1] the Parades Commission (three times),[2] relocation following paramilitary intimidation,[3] legal aid,[4] the Forensic Science Agency,[5] the illegal drugs trade,[6] the separation of prisoners,[7] hate crime (twice),[8] the Compensation Agency,[9] social housing provision,[10] electoral registration,[11] the Police Ombudsman,[12] the Policing Board[13] and the position of victims and survivors regarding ways of dealing with Northern Ireland's past.[14] Very often the evidence submitted to the Committee is also published. These volumes of evidence, as well as the reports themselves and the Government's official responses to the reports, are illuminating repositories of information concerning key aspects of Northern Ireland's legal system.

---

[1] 2000-01, 1st Report, HC 263.
[2] 2000-01, 2nd Report, HC 120-I; 6th Report, HC 521; 2004-05, 2nd Report, HC 172-I.
[3] 2000-01, 3rd Report, HC 59-I.
[4] 2000-01, 4th Report, HC 444.
[5] 2002-03, 5th Report, HC 204.
[6] 2002-03, 8th Report, HC 1217-I.
[7] 2003-04, 2nd Report, HC 302.
[8] 2003-04, 5th Report, HC 615; 2004-05, 9th Report, HC 548-I.
[9] 2003-04, 4th Report, HC 271.
[10] 2003-04, 6th Report, HC 493-I.
[11] 2004-05, 1st Report, HC 131.
[12] 2004-05, 5th Report, HC 344.
[13] 2004-05, 7th Report, HC 108.
[14] 2004-05, 10th Report, HC 303-I.

The Commissioner for Public Appointments[15]

The Commissioner for Public Appointments for Northern Ireland monitors government appointments to many public bodies and deals with complaints about the appointment process if the complainant is dissatisfied with the response of the government department in question. But the Commissioner will not investigate how a body is run. The Commissioner has issued a Code of Practice for public appointments[16] and advertisements for those posts in Northern Ireland must carry the Commissioner's kitemark. Each year the performance of government departments is measured against the Code of Practice and is assessed in the Commissioner's annual report. The current Commissioner is Mrs Felicity Huston. Her office is known as OCPA - the Office of the Commissioner for Public Appointments.

9.2 THE NORTHERN IRELAND OMBUDSMAN[17]

The term "ombudsman", deriving from Scandinavia, is used to describe both official (*i.e.* government-appointed) and unofficial positions. Industries such as banks, building societies, insurance firms and investment companies, and even publishers of newspapers and suppliers of coal, have all established their own unofficial ombudsmen, but these tend to operate on a UK basis with no separate or special role in Northern Ireland. In England and Wales there is a statutory Legal Services Ombudsman, but no such post yet exists in Northern Ireland. Northern Ireland does, however, have a Judicial Appointments Ombudsman (see Chap. 1.5), a Police Ombudsman (see Chap. 4.5) and a Prisoner Ombudsman (see Chap. 4.7). For helpful information on the range of Ombudsmen operating throughout the United Kingdom and Ireland, contact the British and Irish Ombudsman Association.[18]

In Northern Ireland there are two official ombudsman posts for the independent investigation of complaints about public maladministration. One is the Assembly Ombudsman for Northern Ireland and the other is the Northern Ireland Commissioner for Complaints. Both posts have always been held by the same person, the current incumbent, in place since 2000, being Mr Tom Frawley. The

---

[15] www.ocpani.gov.uk.
[16] In March 2005. See www.ocpani.gov.uk/newcodemarch05.pdf.
[17] www.ni-ombudsman.org.uk.
[18] www.bioa.org.uk.

salary of the post-holder, like that of a judge, is protected against interference by the Government[19] and the retirement age is 65.[20] The title of the first post was changed by the Ombudsman (NI) Order 1996 from Northern Ireland Parliamentary Commissioner for Administration to Assembly Ombudsman for Northern Ireland.[21] The legislation governing the second post is the Commissioner for Complaints (NI) Order 1996. An annual report on the work carried out in both posts has to be submitted to the Northern Ireland Assembly, although during periods of direct rule they go to the House of Commons at Westminster. That House has a Select Committee on the Parliamentary Commissioner for Administration, which from time to time issues a report on the work of the Northern Ireland official. In 2003-04 the costs of running the Ombudsman's two offices, apart from his salary, was £1,105,000, mainly covering the cost of employing 21 staff. In 2003 consultants carried out a review of the Ombudsman's role on behalf of the Office of the First Minister and Deputy First Minister, the first such review since 1969; there will be public consultation on the OFMDFM's proposals for reform following this review.

The workload for each of the posts is now roughly the same. No matter which of the two hats is being worn, the Ombudsman's job is to examine the procedures by which administrative decisions are reached, not to assess the merits of those decisions in the absence of maladministration. The term "maladministration" is not defined in the legislation, but it does not simply mean "a mistake"; it refers to action which has been influenced by improper considerations, which is totally unreasonable or which is incompetent, malicious, discriminatory or negligent. The Ombudsman, therefore, does not usually investigate complaints in respect of which the complainant has, or had, a right to take proceedings in a court of law, or to appeal to a tribunal,[22] and for this purpose the Equality Commission for Northern Ireland (see 9.3 below) and the Police Ombudsman (see Chap. 4.5) are treated as tribunals. Someone who is complaining about being refused income support, for instance, must take the grievance to an Appeal Tribunal (see Chap. 8.2). Only if he or she is unhappy with the manner in which

---

[19] From 1 April 2005 it is £116,515: Salaries (Assembly Ombudsman and Commissioner for Complaints) Order (NI) 2005.
[20] Ombudsman (NI) Order 1996, arts. 5(6) and 4(2)(c).
[21] Art. 3(1). Pending devolution the holder was also entitled to be called the Parliamentary Ombudsman for Northern Ireland: art. 3(3).
[22] Ombudsman (NI) Order 1996, art. 10(3).

the claim was processed before or after the decision was made will a complaint to the Ombudsman be permissible.

The Assembly Ombudsman for Northern Ireland

This post was first created by the Parliamentary Commissioner Act (NI) 1969, two years after a similar post was established for UK government departments. Appointments are now made under the Northern Ireland Constitution Act 1973.[23] The function of the Assembly Ombudsman is to investigate written complaints about maladministration within any of the Northern Ireland government departments and several other bodies, including government agencies like the Child Support Agency and the Planning Service, North-South Bodies, and even some tribunals (as regards their administrative practices).[24] Unlike the ombudsmen in Great Britain, the Assembly Ombudsman in Northern Ireland also has the power to investigate complaints about personnel matters in the civil service, a role which the previous holder of the office was in favour of giving up because there are now other ways in which public servants can seek protection against discriminatory treatment.[25] There are, however, some matters which cannot be made the subject of a complaint even in relation to the bodies listed, for example the commencement or conduct of any civil or criminal proceedings before a court of law in the United Kingdom.[26]

As the Northern Ireland Court Service and the Northern Ireland Office are departments of the UK Government, complaints about them should be sent to the UK Parliamentary Commissioner for Administration, who is based in London;[27] the same applies to national public bodies such as the Revenue and Customs and the Post Office, and to bodies which are themselves accountable to the Northern Ireland Office, such as the Northern Ireland Human Rights Commission.[28] At present the UK Ombudsman is Ms Ann Abraham.

---

[23] S. 36(1).
[24] The full list is set out in Sch. 2 to the Ombudsman (NI) Order 1996, as amended, and is available on the Ombudsman's website.
[25] *Annual Report of the Parliamentary Commissioner for Northern Ireland 1998-99*, p. 5.
[26] The full list of matters not subject to investigation is in the Ombudsman (NI) Order 1996, Sch. 4.
[27] www.ombudsman.org.uk.
[28] For the full list of bodies subject to the UK Parliamentary Commissioner, see the Parliamentary Commissioner Order 2005.

Complaints about maladministration can be made by anyone who claims to have sustained injustice as a result of it. In the first instance the complaint should be made to a Member of the Legislative Assembly (MLA),[29] who should then pass it on to the Ombudsman, but if the Ombudsman receives a complaint which has not first been passed through an MLA, he or she will in practice refer it to an MLA nominated by the complainant and ask the latter to act as a sponsor for the complaint.

A complaint must normally be made within 12 months of the date when the aggrieved person first had notice of the matters alleged in the complaint.[30] The Ombudsman may, however, investigate a complaint made at a later date if he or she thinks there is a special justification for doing so.[31] In all cases except those which clearly fall outside his or her jurisdiction, or which are withdrawn, the Commissioner invites the comments of the body complained about, examines papers, and interviews persons privately. He or she has all the powers of a High Court judge to secure the examination of witnesses and the production of documents,[32] and, most importantly, no-one can refuse to supply information because of some other legal obligation to maintain secrecy or some legal right to claim "privilege".[33]

The Ombudsman sends a report on the investigation to the MLA who has sponsored the complaint, to the body complained about and to any person involved in the allegations made in the complaint. If the Ombudsman finds that a complaint is justified, he or she seeks to obtain a settlement of the grievance on the complainant's behalf; this may involve the granting of an apology, the remedying of some situation or even the payment of compensation. But if no settlement can be reached the complainant cannot take the matter any further. Like all the official Ombudsmen in the United Kingdom, the Assembly Ombudsman has the power to make a special report to Parliament, but this power is very rarely exercised.

As can be seen from Table 23 on page 420, the caseload of the Assembly Ombudsman increased by 10% between 2001 and 2004, and the number of full reports issued went up by 67%. As a result, the

---

[29] Ombudsman (NI) Order 1996, art. 9(2). Before devolution the complaints had to be sent through an MP.

[30] *Ibid*. art. 11(5).

[31] *Ibid*. art. 11(6).

[32] *Ibid*. art. 14(2).

[33] *Ibid*. art. 14(3) and (4).

average time taken to complete each investigation also went up, by some 50%, to 23 weeks. The most complained about bodies in 2003-04 were, as usual, the Department of the Environment (92 complaints) and the Department for Social Development (67). Complaints against the Child Support Agency in Northern Ireland remained fairly common too (at 20). All manner of maladministration was alleged in the complaints lodged during 2003-04, but it is worth noting that once again there was not one allegation of religious discrimination. That is a matter, though, which is more usually taken to the Equality Commission (see 9.3 below). In four of the cases the complaint was fully upheld and in 10 it was partially upheld. Settlements were achieved in all of the fully upheld cases and in each of them the agency concerned apologised to the complainant and made consolatory payments of between £100 and £500. In the partially upheld cases the Ombudsman criticised the Department or agency concerned in seven cases. Details of all the investigations conducted each year are supplied in the Ombudsman's Annual Report.

The Northern Ireland Commissioner for Complaints

The function of the Commissioner for Complaints is to investigate written complaints made directly by persons claiming to have suffered injustice through maladministration on the part of public bodies other than those of, or sponsored by, central government. The office therefore covers such bodies as Education and Library Boards, Health and Social Services Boards, Councils and Trusts, district councils, the Labour Relations Agency and the Mental Health Commission.[34] Like that of the Parliamentary Commissioner, the office was created in 1969.[35] It has a similar, but by no means identical, role to that of the Local Administration Ombudsmen in Great Britain. Among the matters which cannot be investigated are the conduct of legal proceedings, the behaviour of the police, and the financial interests of district councillors.[36]

This kind of complaint does not have to be processed through a Member of the Legislative Assembly, but it still usually needs to be made within 12 months of the complainant getting to know of the

---

[34] The full list of bodies which are subject to the Commissioner's oversight is provided in the Commissioner for Complaints (NI) Order 1996, Sch. 2. See too the office's website: www.ni-ombudsman.org.uk.

[35] By the Commissioner for Complaints Act (NI) 1969.

[36] The full list is in the Commissioner for Complaints (NI) Order 1996, Sch. 3.

action he or she is complaining about.[37] Investigations are conducted in the same way as described for the Assembly Ombudsman, with reports made to the complainant, the body concerned and any other person involved in the complaint.

TABLE 23: THE WORK OF THE NORTHERN IRELAND OMBUDSMAN 2001-2004[38]

	2001-02	2002-03	2003-04
As Assembly Ombudsman			
Complaints received	250	262	278
Complaints about planning	74	73	75
Complaints about benefits	41	24	35
Complaints about staffing	46	47	32
Cases concluded	229	255	285
Average time taken[39]	15 weeks	18 weeks	23 weeks
Full reports issued	23	34	39
Complaints upheld	14	14	14
As Commissioner for Complaints			
Complaints received	303	298	337
Complaints about housing	125	105	144
Cases concluded	292	292	338
Average time taken	14 weeks	15 weeks	19 weeks
Full reports issued	52	59	44
Complaints upheld	22	22	20
As Health Service Commissioner			
Complaints received	107	103	94
Social work complaints	19	23	17
Mental health complaints	13	12	13
Cases concluded	98	96	89
Average time taken	16 weeks	22 weeks	31 weeks
Full reports issued	6	4	6
Complaints upheld	2	2	4

---

[37] Commissioner for Complaints (NI) Order 1996, art.10(6).
[38] All figures in this Table are taken from the *Northern Ireland Ombudsman Annual Reports 2001-04*, available on the Ombudsman's website.
[39] *I.e.* for a full investigation.

An important difference between the two procedures, however, is that if the Commissioner for Complaints upholds a grievance but is unable to obtain a satisfactory settlement, the complainant can then apply to a county court for compensation.[40] The Commissioner for Complaints may also seek an injunction or declaration in the High Court to restrain a body from persisting in action which has been found to amount to maladministration.[41] Such remedies, it should be noted, are not available in Great Britain.

In the year ending March 2004 the main body complained against, as in previous years, was the Northern Ireland Housing Executive, the main concerns being waiting lists and access to housing grants. In 105 cases the matter was referred to the body concerned to be dealt with under its own complaints procedure. Of the 44 full investigation reports, 19 related to mistakes in employment practices, such as shortlisting or grievance procedures, and another 14 related to housing issues. Settlements were achieved in 12 of the 14 cases upheld, involving an apology in all but one case and consolatory payments of between £100 and £1,000 in all of them. Again, details of the formally investigated cases are given in the Commissioner's Annual Report.

In 1997 the Commissioner for Complaints acquired the right to deal with complaints against health service providers, including complaints about clinical judgments and hospital and community nursing services.[42] The work of dentists, opticians and chemists is included too. The equivalent post in Great Britain is that of the Health Service Ombudsman. In his capacity as the Health Service Commissioner Mr Frawley was able to achieve a settlement in three of the four cases where a complaint was upheld last year: details are set out in the 2003-04 Annual Report. The Commissioner highlighted in that report that there was an emerging trend regarding the arbitrary removal of people from the patient list of their general health service provider. In one case his recommendation that an apology should be made to the complainant in a certain way and that a consolatory payment should be offered was ignored by the medical practice in question. The Commissioner therefore recommended that the Department of Health, Social Services and Public Safety should seek a change to the law to ensure that the Commissioner's recommendations are fully complied with in future.

---

[40] Commisioner for Complaint (NI) Order 1996, art 16.
[41] *Ibid.* art. 17.
[42] Commissioner for Complaints (Amendment) (NI) Order 1997.

9.3   THE EQUALITY COMMISSION FOR NORTHERN IRELAND[43]

In 1998 the UK Government issued a consultation document, *A Partnership for Equality*, suggesting that a unified Equality Commission should be created in Northern Ireland. A month later the Belfast (Good Friday) Agreement confirmed this intention and the Commission was eventually provided for in section 73 of the Northern Ireland Act 1998. The Commission finally came into being on 1 October 1999. The Commissioners, of whom there can be up to 20,[44] are appointed by the Secretary of State following public advertisement and are to be as representative of the community in Northern Ireland as is practicable.[45]   Mr Bob Collins is the current full-time Chief Commissioner and Ms Anne O'Reilly is the part-time Deputy Chief Commissioner. The other Commissioners give approximately two days per month to the work of the Commission.

The Equality Commission's functions derive from those previously exercised by the Fair Employment Commission for Northern Ireland, the Equal Opportunities Commission for Northern Ireland, the Commission for Racial Equality for Northern Ireland and the Northern Ireland Disability Council (all of which were dissolved on 1 October 1999), and the new Commission is obliged to divide its resources appropriately between these four areas.[46] In addition, the Equality Commission is charged with enforcing the new statutory duties placed on public authorities in Northern Ireland to promote equality of opportunity and good relations.[47] There is provision for the Commission to receive advice on the exercise of its functions from a "consultative council", but such a body has not yet been formed.[48] The Commission is also looking forward to the enactment by the Northern Ireland Assembly of the so-called Single Equality Act,[49] which will

---

[43] www.equalityni.org. Statistics in this section are taken from the Equality Commission's Annual Report for 2003-04, available on the website.

[44] S. 73(2) of the Northern Ireland Act 1998.

[45] *Ibid.* s. 73(4).

[46] *Ibid.* s. 74(3)(a).

[47] *Ibid.* s. 75(1) and (2) and Sch 9.

[48] *Ibid.* s. 74(3)(b) and (4). The Commission issued a consultation paper on the topic in 2004.

[49] This was foreshadowed in the Executive's Legislative Programme announced in September 2000.

harmonise the various pieces of legislation governing discrimination in the province. The Office of the First Minister and Deputy First Minister issued consultation documents on this proposed legislation in 2001 and 2005.

During 2003-04 the Equality Commission received a government grant of £6,937,000. Some 52% of this was spent on Commissioners' fees and the salaries of the 122 staff, leaving £3,329,000 for operating costs. The Commission considered 727 applications for assistance with individual cases that year, granting 12% of them. Ninety cases were completed, of which 77 were settled, four were upheld at a tribunal and nine were dismissed at a tribunal. At the year's end the Commission was in the process of assisting just over 350 cases. After identifying pressure in relation to expenditure on casework, the Commission revised its Legal Assistance Strategy in 2002, leading it to assist more cases itself directly, rather than through solicitors, and by the end of March 2004 it was supporting 67% of cases in this manner (as opposed to just 30% in May 2003). Summaries of many of the Commission's cases are provided in Appendix 3 to the Commission's Annual Report. In addition, some 4,943 employers received advice from the Equality Commission in 2003-04.

Religious and political discrimination[50]

The Equality Commission continues the work of the pre-existing Fair Employment Commission for Northern Ireland, which in turn was the successor body to the Fair Employment Agency set up by the Fair Employment (NI) Act 1976 (a Westminster statute) with the general functions of promoting equality of opportunity in Northern Ireland and eliminating unlawful discrimination on the grounds of religious belief or political opinion. For this purpose atheism and agnosticism are religious beliefs but "political opinion" does not include an opinion which involves acceptance of the use of violence for political ends connected with Northern Ireland affairs.

During the 1980s the Fair Employment Agency was considered by many to have insufficient powers to deal effectively with religious and political discrimination and following extensive research conducted for

[50] For a general account of the relevant law, see S. Livingstone, "Religious and Political Discrimination", Chap. 12 in B. Dickson and M. O'Brien (eds.), *Civil Liberties in Northern Ireland: The CAJ Handbook* (4th ed., 2003). See too R. Cormack and R. Osborne, *Discrimination and Public Policy in Northern Ireland* (1991) and D. Smith and G. Chambers, *Inequality in Northern Ireland* (1991).

the Standing Advisory Commission on Human Rights (see 9.6 below) the law in this area was reformed by the Fair Employment (NI) Act 1989.[51] One consequence was the replacement of the Agency by the Fair Employment Commission. As well as retaining the duties to promote equality of opportunity and eliminate unlawful discrimination, the Commission had to promote affirmative action to help redress existing imbalances. The Government undertook to commission a comprehensive review of the 1989 legislation within five years of its introduction, a task which was again allocated to the Standing Advisory Commission on Human Rights. This review resulted in the publication in 1996 of three books containing detailed research studies on aspects of fair employment[52] and in the production of a report with a set of recommendations.[53] The Government responded by issuing a White Paper[54] and introducing the Fair Employment and Treatment (NI) Order 1998, a law which consolidates previous laws but also adds to them significantly by, for instance, authorising the use of positive discrimination to help people who are unemployed and outlawing religious and political discrimination in access to goods, facilities and services.

Equality of opportunity and fair participation

The 1998 Order does not make inequality of opportunity or unlawful discrimination on religious or political grounds a criminal offence, but the Equality Commission can require employers to take action to ensure that for the employees in their workforce there is both equality of opportunity and fair participation. To this end the Department of Economic Development[55] published a Code of Practice on Fair Employment, the contents of which the Equality Commission encourages employers and vocational organisations to adopt, and enforcement bodies rely upon the Code as good evidence of best practice. The Commission also keeps a register of trades, businesses

---

[51] Religious and political discrimination in Northern Ireland was felt to be such an important issue in the 1970s and 1980s that it was legislated for by Act of Parliament rather than by Order in Council (see Chap. 2.1 and 2.2).
[52] D. Magill and S. Rose (eds.), *Fair Employment Law in Northern Ireland: Debates and Issues*; E. McLaughlin and P. Quirk (eds.), *Policy Aspects of Employment Equality in Northern Ireland*; J. McVey and N. Hutson (eds.), *Public Views and Experiences of Fair Employment Issues in Northern Ireland*.
[53] *Employment Equality: Building for the Future* (1997).
[54] *Partnership for Equality* (Cm. 3890; 1998).
[55] Now the Department of Enterprise, Trade and Investment.,

and other activities in which people are employed; this describes the business in general terms and gives the name and address of the employer and the number of employees. The 1998 Order requires all private sector employers with more than 10 employees to register with the Commission. Public authorities are automatically registered. At the end of March 2004 the register had 3,959 entries. It is a criminal offence to fail to register when required to do so.

Certain forms of employment, such as serving as a cleric, a school-teacher or in a private household remain exempt from control in this field.[56] The exemption for school-teaching is particularly controversial, as it is seen by some as a hindrance to the development of integrated education in Northern Ireland. The Commission launched a strategic investigation into the exemption in 2003 and published its report in December 2004.[57] In 2004 the Equality Commission lent its support to the renewal of the positive discrimination provision in favour of the recruitment of Catholics to the Police Service of Northern Ireland, imposed by law after the Patten Commission report in 1999.[58] This will be in place until at least 2006 (see Chap. 4.4).

All registered employers must "monitor" the religious make-up of their workforce and send details of this to the Commission each year.[59] In addition, each public sector employer and each private sector employer with more than 250 employees must return information on the perceived religion of *applicants* for jobs.[60] The Commission in turn publishes a report summarising the returns, which now cover about 72% of the workforce as a whole. The aim of monitoring is to make it easier to identify job categories where there are fewer workers or applicants from one religious community than might otherwise be expected. Again it is a criminal offence to refuse to supply information which must be monitored or to disclose it to anyone other than the Commission; in 2003-04 there were three convictions for failure to submit a monitoring return. A registered employer must also review the employment practices within the firm at least once every three years

---

[56] Fair Employment and Treatment (NI) Order 1998, Pt. VIII (arts. 70-80).

[57] Under the Fair Employment and Treatment (NI) Order 1998, art. 71. The investigation found that in controlled (state) schools 85% of the teachers were Protestants and 5% were Catholics, in maintained (Catholic) schools 98% were Catholic and 1% Protestant, and in integrated schools 48% were Protestants and 43% Catholic.

[58] Police (NI) Act 2000, s. 46.

[59] Fair Employment and Treatment (NI) Order 1998, art. 52.

[60] *Ibid.* art. 54.

(this is known as an "article 55 review"). It should be stressed, moreover, that even if an employer employs too few people to have to register or monitor the workforce, he or she is still bound by the law's requirement not to discriminate against a person, directly or indirectly, on the basis of his or her religious belief or political opinion.

The Equality Commission has power under article 11 of the 1998 Order to investigate the employment practices of particular employers to see what action ought to be taken to promote equality of opportunity. Under this power the former Fair Employment Commission undertook dozens of investigations into private sector companies as well as several public bodies such as district councils and Education and Library Boards. If the Commission finds a failure to afford equality of opportunity it can determine what steps should be taken to secure it and can ask for undertakings from employers or give them directions.[61] If such directions are not complied with within a reasonable period the Commission can apply to the Fair Employment Tribunal (see below) for an enforcement order. If this in turn is not complied with, the Tribunal can fine the employer up to £30,000 and can disqualify the employer from eligibility for government grants and contracts (this is the notion of "contract compliance"). It can even refer the employer's case to the High Court, which has greater powers to fine and can imprison for contempt of court.

The Equality Commission often seeks to promote affirmative action programmes with employers. The sorts of measures recommended include the ending of informal selection methods (such as word of mouth recruitment), the establishment of a neutral or harmonious working environment as regards religious and political emblems, and the setting of goals and timetables with respect to improvements to the religious balance of the workforce. There is some evidence that affirmative action programmes have had an effect in reducing inequality.[62] Of course some of these measures have to contend with the so-called "chill factor" - some people will be reluctant even to apply for jobs in an environment where they might feel threatened.

---

[61] *Ibid.* arts. 12-4.
[62] C. McCrudden, R. Ford and A. Heath, "Legal Regulation of Affirmative Action in Northern Ireland: An Empirical Assessment" (2004) 24 OJLS 363.

Claims from individuals

To help eliminate unlawful discrimination on the grounds of religious belief or political opinion the Equality Commission can receive complaints from any person claiming to be a victim and can investigate the matter. Even positive or reverse discrimination can be unlawful under the Order, although affirmative action programmes will generally not be. The Fair Employment (NI) Act 1989 made indirect discrimination just as unlawful as direct discrimination, although no compensation is payable for the former unless it was intentional. Until the coming into force of the 1998 Order, discrimination on religious and political grounds was unlawful only in an employment context;[63] now it is unlawful as well in the context of access to goods, facilities and services.[64]

A complaint of unlawful discrimination must be made to the Fair Employment Tribunal[65] (another product of the 1989 Act[66]) within three months of the discrimination occurring. The Tribunal will first refer the complaint to the Labour Relations Agency (see 9.4 below) to see if an amicable settlement can be reached. If it cannot, a hearing will in due course take place before the Tribunal, where the procedures are essentially the same as in the industrial tribunals (see Chap. 8.3). As in cases of alleged sex discrimination (see below), the burden of proof on the complainant is relatively easy to discharge. No legal aid is available but under article 45 of the Fair Employment and Treatment (NI) Order 1998 the applicant can ask the Equality Commission not just for initial advice but also for free legal representation before the Fair Employment Tribunal. The Tribunal can order unlimited compensation if it upholds the complaint, including an award for injured feelings,[67] something not usually allowable in cases heard by industrial tribunals.

---

[63] In *Kelly and Loughran* v *Northern Ireland Housing Executive* [1999] 1 AC 428 the House of Lords had to decide exactly what was meant in the Act by the term "employment".

[64] Fair Employment and Treatment (NI) Order 1998, arts. 28-31.

[65] Which is part of the Office of Industrial Tribunals and the Fair Employment Tribunal: see Chap. 8.3.

[66] It is now governed by the Fair Employment and Treatment (NI) Order 1998, arts. 81-90.

[67] *Ibid.* art. 39(4). In *Shaw* v *Greenan Inns Ltd., trading as Balmoral Hotel* (22 May 1998) the Fair Employment Tribunal awarded as much as £10,000 by way of injury to feelings (*Fair Employment Commission Annual Report 1998-99*, p. 33). Guidance was given by the Court of Appeal of Northern Ireland in *Baird* v *Cookstown DC* [1998] NI 88.

The Tribunal can also specify what other remedial action needs to be taken to correct the discrimination. An appeal lies on a point of law to the Court of Appeal. In 2003-04 the Equality Commission received 222 applications for assistance in this area; it granted initial assistance in 19 cases and more than initial assistance in a further 156 cases. In 35 cases the Commission helped the applicant to obtain a favourable settlement.

Under article 80 of the 1998 Order, investigations into individual complaints have to be curtailed if the Secretary of State for Northern Ireland issues a certificate that an allegedly discriminatory act has been done for the purpose of safeguarding national security or protecting public safety or public order. To deal with appeals against such certificates a special tribunal has been created, although it has not yet sat (see Chap. 8.1).

Promotional work and the future

As well as dealing with the matters above, the Equality Commission has a significant educational and research role in the area of religious and political discrimination. It sees itself as the guardian of fair practice, emphasising to employers the economic, social and industrial advantages which flow from fair and lawful practices in recruitment and promotion, etc. It visits employers to give training courses and advice on employment practices; it conducts seminars, shows videos and runs publicity campaigns. It has the additional task of looking out for discriminatory advertisements. If it believes that an advertiser is likely to continue to publish such adverts it can apply to the High Court for an injunction restraining their publication.

As a whole, the laws on religious and political discrimination in Northern Ireland are widely viewed as the most radical employment equity laws enacted anywhere in Europe.[68] They have clearly had some impact on the employment differential between Catholics and Protestants in Northern Ireland, but the unemployment differential

---

[68] However dissatisfaction with the Fair Employment (NI) Act 1976 led to the formulation in 1984 of the so-called MacBride Principles, drawn up by a group of civil rights activists led by Sean MacBride, a Nobel Peace Price laureate. The Principles were inspired by the Sullivan Principles, which were designed to encourage responsible employment practices by American firms operating in South Africa. Several state legislatures in America endorsed the MacBride Principles by threatening to disinvest from American companies which refused to abide by them. The UK Government and the Fair Employment Commission strongly condemned the Principles.

remains stubbornly resistant to change. Today the unemployment rate for male Catholics is 1.7 times that for male Protestants.[69] According to its *Fourteenth Monitoring Report* (2004) the overall composition of the workforce in Northern Ireland in 2003 was 58.3% Protestant and 41.7% Catholic; this means that the proportion of Catholics in the workforce was close to the proportion of Catholics of working age and available for work in the population as a whole (42.7%). A recent book ably demonstrates, indeed, that a great deal has been achieved in this domain over the past 25 years or so.[70]

Sex discrimination[71]

The Equality Commission also continues the work of the Equal Opportunities Commission for Northern Ireland, which was set up under the Sex Discrimination (NI) Order 1976 to work for the elimination of discrimination on the grounds of sex or marriage and to promote equality of opportunity between men and women generally. It has a duty to keep under review the workings of the Equal Pay Act (NI) 1970, the Sex Discrimination (NI) Order 1976, the Equal Pay (Amendment) Regulations (NI) 1984 and such parts of the health and safety legislation which require men and women to be treated differently. In this context discrimination can refer to one of two practices: (i) treating a person of one sex less favourably than a person of the other sex solely because of the first person's sex, or (ii) treating a married person less favourably than a single person solely because the first person is married. It does not encompass less favourable treatment of single persons, but through other legislation transsexuals *are* now protected,[72] as are homosexuals.[73] Indirect discrimination, if intentional, is covered.

---

[69] See I. Shuttleworth and S. Lavery, *Initial Results from the 2001 Census of Population* (2004), a report prepared for the Equality Commission. See too the *Northern Ireland Labour Force Survey* (30 June 2004): www.detini.gov.uk/cgi-bin/down doc?id=684.

[70] B. Osborne and I. Shuttleworth, *Fair Employment in Northern Ireland: A Generation On* (2004).

[71] For a general account of the relevant law, see B. Jones, "Sex Discrimination", Chap. 13 in B. Dickson and M. O'Brien (eds.), *Civil Liberties in Northern Ireland: The CAJ Handbook* (4th ed., 2003).

[72] Sex Discrimination (Gender Reassignment) Regs. (NI) 1999.

[73] Employment Equality (Sexual Orientation) Regs. (NI) 2003.

Research and education

As well as having power to submit proposals to the Government for amending the legislation it reviews, the Commission has extensive powers covering education and research. In campaigning for fairer treatment of women it is not satisfied with pious statements of intent concerning equal opportunities policies but requires them to be matched with affirmative action, something which is not unlawful under the legislation. Employers, for instance, can legally train more women than men for occupations in which women have previously been under-represented. The conditions of work of part-time employees are a particular concern of the Commission, since (in 2003-04) 73% of part-time workers in Northern Ireland are women. Furthermore, women's average earnings (when payments for overtime are included) are still only about 75% of those of men.

The Commission conducts research projects and helps to finance some external projects. It also publishes leaflets, posters, booklets and reports, most of which are available free of charge. European Union law is ever more important in the area of gender discrimination and the Equality Commission seeks to ensure that it is fully implemented in Northern Ireland.

Enforcement

To fulfil its role as an enforcement body in this area the Commission may initiate its own formal investigations into suspected instances of discrimination and may serve non-discrimination notices, which require the provisions of the 1970 Act and the 1976 Order, as amended, to be complied with; they are eventually enforceable in a county court. Decisions to initiate formal investigations may be challenged by way of judicial review.[74] A register of non-discrimination notices is available for public inspection at the Commission's offices in Belfast, although none are currently in existence. The Commission also has the sole right to initiate action in relation to persistent discrimination, discriminatory advertisements and instructions, or pressure to discriminate.

In the 12 months up to April 2004 the Equality Commission received 811 complaints or inquiries relating to alleged sex discrimination. Under article 75 of the 1976 Order, the Commission can provide personal and financial assistance to complainants in cases which are

---

[74] See, *e.g.*, *In re Belfast Telegraph Newspaper Ltd's Application* [2001] NI 178.

complex or involve a question of principle. This can be particularly valuable in employment cases, as the civil legal aid and legal advice and assistance schemes (see Chap. 3.3) do not provide for state-funded representation in industrial tribunals. Again, complaints of sex discrimination have to be lodged with the tribunal within three months of the incident in question having occurred, but the tribunal can extend this period if it is just and equitable to do so.[75] In 2003-04 the Equality Commission received 138 new applications for assistance with sex discrimination claims, and granted 26 (but awarded assistance in 125 existing cases after a review). In 30 cases a settlement was reached.

Probably the best known of the cases supported in the past by the Equal Opportunities Commission was that taken by 31 female police reservists who complained that the Chief Constable of the RUC had discriminated against them by not renewing their contracts. The industrial tribunal dealing with this case referred it to the European Court of Justice, which delivered its judgment in 1986 (*Johnston and others* v *Chief Constable of the RUC*[76]). The decision led to a settlement payment of £1.2 million and resulted in the Sex Discrimination (Amendment) (NI) Order 1988, which changed the 1976 Order so as not to allow a claim of national security automatically to prevent a future legal action based on sex discrimination.[77] The Chief Constable, most unusually for a tribunal case, was ordered to pay the applicants' legal costs. Another significant victory was won by the EOC when it successfully challenged the Department of Education's arrangements for selection of pupils after the 11-plus examination; these were held to be discriminatory against girls[78] and extra places in grammar schools had accordingly to be made available.

Racial discrimination[79]

Amazingly, it was only with the enactment of the Race Relations (NI) Order 1997 that racial discrimination became unlawful in Northern Ireland. To help enforce the law the Order set up the Commission for

---

[75] See, *e.g.*, *E and others* v *A and others* [2004] 6 BNIL 51, where a claim which was some 18 months out of time was nevertheless allowed to proceed.

[76] [1987] QB 129.

[77] For comparable cases in the area of religious and political discrimination, but which were decided by the European Court of Human Rights, see Chap. 8.1.

[78] *In re EOC for Northern Ireland* [1988] NI 223.

[79] For a general account of the relevant law, see C. White, "Race Discrimination", Chap. 14 in B. Dickson and M. O'Brien (eds.), *Civil Liberties in Northern Ireland: The CAJ Handbook* (4th ed., 2003).

Racial Equality for Northern Ireland in 1997, one of the four bodies which merged to form the Equality Commission in 1999. In this field the Commission works towards the elimination of racial discrimination and promotes equality of opportunity and good relations between members of different races. It can again support applicants who wish to complain to a tribunal or court about racial discrimination.[80] In 2003-04 the Commission received 337 complaints or inquiries about racial discrimination and 83 applications for assistance with tribunal or court cases. It granted initial assistance in 16 new cases (and in a further 51 existing cases after a review); seven cases were settled during the year. Northern Ireland law does not require all public authorities to produce race equality schemes in the same manner as public authorities in Great Britain have to do,[81] but the section 75 equality schemes (see below) do go some way towards filling this gap.

The 2001 census suggested that fewer than 1% of the population of Northern Ireland is from a minority ethnic background.

Disability discrimination[82]

The Northern Ireland Disability Council was established in 1996 at the time of the introduction of the Disability Discrimination Act 1995, a piece of legislation which did not go as far as many campaigners would have wished in protecting people with disabilities against discriminatory treatment. Just as the Act did not extend to matters such as education, so the Disability Council was not given the powers to help people take cases to court. It existed merely to advise the Government on how to eliminate discrimination against people with disabilities. During its three years of existence the Northern Ireland Disability Council commissioned research, collected information on the economic activity of disabled people, advised the Government on a number of consultation papers and helped with the revision of Codes of Practice to guide employers and service-providers in their obligations under the law.[83] It monitored the public's awareness of the Disability Discrimination Act and the number of complaints made to industrial tribunals.

---

[80] Race Relations (NI) Order 1997, art. 64.

[81] As a result of the Race Relations (Amendment) Act 2000.

[82] For a general account of the relevant law, see G. Kilpatrick, "Disability Discrimination", Chap. 15 in B. Dickson and M. O'Brien (eds.), *Civil Liberties in Northern Ireland: The CAJ Handbook* (4th ed., 2003).

[83] For further details see the Council's Annual Reports.

TABLE 24: THE EQUALITY COMMISSION AND
INDIVIDUAL APPLICANTS 2001-2004[84]

	2001-02	2002-03	2003-04
Legal complaints received			
Religious/political discrimination	901	n/a	35
Gender discrimination	1,144	n/a	811
Race discrimination	308	n/a	337
Disability discrimination	328	n/a	505
Sexual orientation discrimination	n/a	n/a	5
Total	2,681	n/a	2,393
Applications granted[85]			
Religious/political discrimination	289	164	175
Gender discrimination	160	160	151
Race discrimination	100	79	67
Disability discrimination	112	89	110
Sexual orientation discrimination	n/a	n/a	1
Total	661	492	504
Applications refused			
Religious/political discrimination	122	135	270
Gender discrimination	31	178	164
Race discrimination	40	63	64
Disability discrimination	7	89	142
Sexual orientation discrimination	n/a	n/a	0
Total	200	465	640

The Disability Council was also represented on the Disability Rights Task Force, a UK-wide body charged with making proposals on what more needed to be done by the Government to ensure comprehensive civil rights for disabled people. A more powerful Disability Rights Commission was formally established for Great Britain in April 2000.[86] The same additional powers were extended from that date to the Equality Commission for Northern Ireland.[87] Moreover, from October

---

[84] Source: the Equality Commission's *Annual Reports 2001-04*.

[85] For the years 2002-03 and 2003-04 these figures include cases where assistance was granted after a review or re-examination had occurred.

[86] www.drc-gb.org/drc.

[87] By the Equality (Disability, etc) (NI) Order 2000.

1999 it has been unlawful anywhere in the United Kingdom to discriminate against people with a disability not only as regards employment (covered since 1996) but also as regards access to goods, facilities and services; from October 2004 it has also been unlawful to discriminate as regards physical access to buildings. The Special Educational Needs and Disability (NI) Order 2005 outlaws disability discrimination in the field of education. No date has yet been fixed by which public sector transport facilities must be provided on a non-discriminatory basis.[88]

In May 2003 the Equality Commission issued a Code of Practice on the Disability Discrimination Act 1995 and in October 2003 it published a Code of Practice on Access. In the same year it also produced *Enabled?*, a review of the Disability Discrimination Act 1995, which makes 34 recommendations for reform to the law. In 2003-04 the Commission received 505 complaints or inquiries relating to disability and 171 applications for assistance with proceedings. It granted initial assistance in 25 cases (plus in a further 85 existing cases after a review). In 17 cases a settlement favourable to the applicant was reached.

The section 75 duties

Section 75(1) of the Northern Ireland Act 1998 obliges designated public authorities in Northern Ireland[89] to have due regard to the need to promote equality of opportunity between:

- persons of different religious belief, political opinion, racial group, age, marital status or sexual orientation;

- men and women generally;

- persons with a disability and persons without; and

- persons with dependants and persons without.

Section 75(2) likewise obliges such authorities to have regard to the desirability of promoting good relations between persons of different religious belief, political opinion or racial group. For these purposes "public authority" includes all those bodies listed in Schedule 2 to both the Ombudsman (NI) Order 1996 and the Commissioner for

---

[88] Disability Discrimination Act 1995, Pt. V.
[89] For a full list see the Northern Ireland Act 1998 (Designation of Public Authorities) Order 2004.

Complaints (NI) Order 1996 (see 9.2 above).[90] The Secretary of State can also designate other bodies as public authorities, and has already done so as regards the Police Service of Northern Ireland and the Northern Ireland Policing Board.[91]

Public authorities covered by section 75 have to produce an "equality scheme" demonstrating how they are complying with their duties. This needs to be submitted to, and approved by, the Equality Commission. If the Equality Commission does not feel able to approve it, the scheme is referred to the Secretary of State for Northern Ireland, who has the powers to request the authority to make a revised scheme or to make a scheme him- or herself for the authority. To gain approval from the Equality Commission the scheme has to address a number of points, in particular it has to state the authority's arrangements for assessing the likely impact (as regards equality of opportunity) of policies proposed to be adopted by the authority and for monitoring any adverse impact of policies which are adopted.

The Equality Commission has issued guidelines as to the desirable form and content of equality schemes,[92] and also practical guidance on equality impact assessment,[93] but has stopped short of publishing a model scheme. It is also clear from section 75 itself that the duty to promote equality of opportunity takes precedence over the duty to promote good relations. The Commission publishes annual reports on implementation of the section 75 duties. If an equality scheme is breached a complaint can be lodged with the Equality Commission and an investigation can be launched. In 2004 the Commission published reports on five such investigations. But the Commission has limited powers to apply any sanctions if the complaint is substantiated.

Discrimination on the basis of age is still not unlawful anywhere in the United Kingdom, but as a result of the EU's Framework Employment Directive of 2000 it will need to be made unlawful in the field of employment before December 2006. In Ireland there are already two comprehensive Acts dealing with age and a range of equality issues - the Employment Equality Act 1998 and the Equal Status Act 2000.

---

[90] Northern Ireland Act 1998, s. 75(3)(b) and (c).
[91] *Ibid.* s. 75(3)(a) and (d). S. 74 and Sch. 5 also amend the anti-discrimination laws as they apply to the police.
[92] *Guide to the Statutory Duties* (rev. ed. 2005).
[93] *Section 75 of the Northern Ireland Act 1998 - Practical Guidance on Equality Impact Assessment* (2005).

9.4   THE LABOUR RELATIONS AGENCY[94]

The Labour Relations Agency was created by the Industrial Relations (NI) Order 1976 and continued by a further such Order in 1992. Like the equivalent body in England and Wales - the Advisory, Conciliation and Arbitration Service (ACAS)[95] - it is a body independent of government and operating under the direction of a Board comprising representatives of employers, employees and others. There are at present nine part-time members together with a part-time chairman (Mr Patrick Macartan), all appointed, after consultations, by the Department for Employment and Learning. A report on the Agency's activities is presented each year to that Department and can be obtained free of charge from the Agency's offices in Belfast and Derry/Londonderry or from its website. There are about 45 full-time members of staff employed in Belfast, with a small additional group based in Derry/Londonderry. The Belfast office also accommodates the Certification Officer for Northern Ireland, whose job it is to ensure that trades unions and employers' associations comply with relevant statutory requirements (see p. 466 below).

The cost of running the Labour Relations Agency in 2003-04 was approximately £2,313,000. It was the busiest year for employment relations yet recorded, due to the rise in high-profile industrial disputes (*e.g.* at Shorts Bombardier, the Fire Service and the Northern Ireland Civil Service) and the number and complexity of individual claims taken to tribunals. According to the Chairman's Foreword in the 2003-04 Annual Report, at one point some 10% of the workforce in Northern Ireland was directly involved in conflict at work (given that there were some 14,000 individual cases pending before tribunals!).

The Agency's mission is to contribute to economic prosperity and organisational effectiveness in Northern Ireland through promoting best practice, fostering good employment relations, providing accurate advice and information, and preventing and resolving disputes. It carries out this mission in the following ways.

Giving general advice and information

To help avoid industrial relations problems, the Agency provides confidential, free, expert advice on all aspects of employment

---

[94] www.lra.org.uk.
[95] www.acas.org.uk.

relationships. As can be seen from Table 25 below, the Agency advises about 400 organisations each year on best practice in employment policies and procedures, mostly in relation to terms and conditions of employment, disciplinary rules and procedures, and notification of absence procedures.

TABLE 25: THE WORK OF THE LABOUR RELATIONS AGENCY 2001-2004[96]

	2001-02	2002-03	2003-04
Advice and information			
Organisations advised	398	465	374
Persons making inquiries	29,109	28,432	29,943
Individual conciliation			
Individual cases referred [97]	5,968	6,094	5,673
Cases dealt with	4,807	5,507	4,725
Cases withdrawn	2,727	2,612	2,633
Cases settled by conciliation	1,473	2,039	1,885
Cases referred to a tribunal	607	856	687
Cases referred as % of total	13%	16%	15%
Cases about dismissals	1,589	2,086	1,865
Cases about minimum wages	999	767	695
Alleged breach of contract	543	682	570
Alleged sex discrimination	588	608	624
Sectarian discrimination[98]	321	434	480
Disability discrimination	56	145	162
Alleged racial discrimination	30	126	106
Cases about equal pay	203	126	91
Cases on-going at year's end	12,921	13,514	13,982
Arbitration/collective disputes			
Independent arbitration cases	37	22	24
Arbitration scheme cases	n/a	1	5
Collective disputes dealt	20	50	27

[96] All figures are from the *Annual Reports of the Labour Relations Agency 2001-2004*.
[97] The figures in this row are the aggregates of the figures for non-FET cases and FET cases.
[98] *I.e.* discrimination based on religious belief or political opinion.

In 2003-04 the Agency also ran 36 workshops throughout Northern Ireland on similar topics and hosted 60 good practice seminars (attended by 900 people). Its staff spoke at 73 events not organised by the Agency. About 30,000 callers a year get in touch with the Agency with all manner of employment law queries, especially about contractual rights, disciplinary procedures and holiday entitlement. (In 2003-04 58% of these came from employees, 42% from employers.) The Agency's website carries useful summaries of, and links to, all the employment legislation currently applying in Northern Ireland, some of it dating back to 1871.

In addition to all this the Labour Relations Agency issues codes of practice. Codes have so far been published on disclosure of information to trade unions for collective bargaining purposes, on disciplinary and grievance procedures, on time off for trade union activities and on redundancy procedures.[99] The Codes have no actual legal force but are taken into account by industrial tribunals when deciding disputes. In 1998 the then Department of Economic Development issued an important Code of Practice on picketing[100] and in 2000 the then Department of Higher and Further Education, Training and Employment issued a draft Code on industrial action ballots.

The Agency has published three Advisory Guides, *Collective Dispute Resolution* (1999), *Bullying at Work* (2000) and *Varying a Contract of Employment* (2000),[101] a series of Information Notes and (together with Invest Northern Ireland and the Equality Commission) *The Employers' Handbook - Guide to Employment Law and Good Practice* (2002).

Conciliating individual workers' complaints

If there is a dispute involving an individual's employment rights the matter will be automatically referred to the Labour Relations Agency by the Office of Industrial Tribunals and the Fair Employment Tribunal (see Chap. 8.3), unless it relates to a claim for redundancy payment or for written particulars of a contract of employment. A conciliation officer in the Agency will try to arrive at a mutually agreed settlement,

---

[99]   These can all be downloaded from the Agency's website. The first two are being reviewed in light of the Employment (NI) Order 2003, many provisions in which come into effect on 3 April 2005. See the Industrial Tribunals (Constitution and Rules of Procedure) Regs. (NI) 2004 and the Fair Employment Tribunal (Rules of Procedure) Regs. (NI) 2004.

[100]   Under the Industrial Relations (NI) Order 1992, art.95.

[101]   Available on the Agency's website.

a service which is again free and confidential. Table 25 on page 437 indicates clearly that the conciliation process helps to reduce drastically the number of disputes which actually reach a tribunal, with only about one in six surviving the reference to the Agency. About a third of all the cases dealt with by the Agency relate to alleged unfair dismissals and about a quarter relate to discrimination of one kind or another (29% in 2003-04). A very worrying feature is the number of cases left pending at the end of each year: with a current backlog of nearly 14,000 cases it is little wonder that many believe the tribunal system to be hopelessly log-jammed.[102]

If its conciliation process is unattractive or unsuccessful, the Agency can try to resolve industrial disputes by referring them to independent arbitration. During 2003-04 there were 24 cases where decisions were issued as a result of independent arbitration. In addition, under the Employment Rights (Dispute Resolution) (NI) Order 1998 and the Fair Employment and Treatment (NI) Order 1998,[103] the Labour Relations Agency is empowered to set up arbitration schemes for specific types of complaint; it has already done so, since April 2002, for complaints of unfair dismissal and in 2003-04 five such cases were arbitrated. An arbitration scheme for complaints about time off for flexible working is currently being developed. These statutory schemes are welcome alternatives to the resolution of disputes by the industrial tribunals or the Fair Employment Tribunal. The sooner a scheme can be devised for discrimination complaints, the better.

A further alternative is for the Agency to hold a formal inquiry into the issues raised by an individual dispute, this being an effective way of proceeding where there may be considerable public interest or concern in the dispute. A formal inquiry does not require the consent of the parties, but it occurs very rarely. Likewise, the introduction of legislation on equal pay for work of equal value[104] has provided industrial tribunals with great problems in assessing whether different forms of work are indeed of equal value. The Labour Relations Agency assists the tribunals by maintaining a list of independent experts available to examine such claims. There are currently six names on this list, but in recent years there have been virtually no requests to the Agency for this service.

---

[102] At the end of March 2004 there were 1,475 claims of religious or political discrimination still pending before the Agency.

[103] Art. 89.

[104] See the Equal Pay (Amendment) Regs. (NI) 1984.

Conciliating collective disputes

If there is a dispute between an employer and a group of employees the Agency can attempt collective conciliation. One of its conciliation officers meets with the parties and attempts to narrow their differences to vanishing point. During 2003-04 the Agency received 33 requests for such conciliation and dealt with 27 of them, of which 13 had been initiated by a trade union. One-half of all the cases (16) concerned disputes within the manufacturing industry and obviously most of the cases were about conditions of employment and/or rates of pay. Unfortunately the Agency's annual reports do not reveal how many of these collective disputes are actually conciliated, and with what results, or how many lead to a stoppage of work.

9.5 THE HEALTH AND SAFETY EXECUTIVE[105]

The Health and Safety at Work (NI) Order 1978 extended the protection of the health and safety legislation to all persons at work (except domestic servants in private households) and placed new basic duties regarding safety on employers, the self-employed, employees, and those manufacturing and supplying articles and substances for use at work. The Order protects not just persons at work but also the general public outside places of work. By virtue of the Reporting of Injuries, Diseases and Dangerous Occurrences Regulations (NI) 1986, duties are imposed concerning the reporting of accidents. There are also a Health Protection Agency and an Environment Agency, both with remits far beyond the workplace, but they operate only in England and Wales, not Northern Ireland.[106]

Responsibility for implementing the 1978 Order was conferred upon a Health and Safety Agency. This was similar to the Health and Safety Commission in Great Britain but, rather than having direct executive control over the authorities which enforced health and safety legislation, the Agency had mainly advisory functions. To help raise the profile of occupational safety and to allow more effective targeting of resources, in 1999 the Agency was replaced by a new Health and Safety Executive for Northern Ireland, which also took over the

---

[105] www.hseni.gov.uk.

[106] See the Health Protection Agency Act 2004 and www.hpa.gov.uk, and the Environment Act 1995 and www.environment-agency.co.uk. Also S. Turner and K. Morrow, *Northern Ireland Environmental Law* (1997).

functions previously carried out by the Health and Safety Division and the Employment Medical Advisory Service within what was then the Department of Economic Development. The current Chairperson of the Health and Safety Executive is Mr Liam McBrinn; there is also a deputy chairperson and eight other members. All the members are now appointed by the Department of Enterprise, Trade and Investment; they represent district councils, employers or employees. A Workplace Health Support Group has been formed within the Executive to raise the profile of health at work: it is reckoned that some 70,000 people in Northern Ireland suffer from a work-related health problem every year, estimated to cost the economy some £330 million. The cost of running the Health and Safety Executive in 2003-04 was £3,344,000.

The Executive's general task is to promote health and safety at work. It fulfils this by inspecting places of work, investigating accidents, making recommendations to government departments, arranging for research, training and the provision of information, and issuing and approving codes of practice. The recommendations made to government departments will often relate to regulations proposed by those departments or by the Executive itself for health and safety at work. The Executive cannot itself actually issue such regulations, but it has to be consulted about their content. Recent examples include the Control of Asbestos at Work Regulations (NI) 2003 and the Control of Substances Hazardous to Health Regulations (NI) 2003. Its codes of practice have a semi-legal status in that a breach of them is evidence of dubious practices but no offence in itself. Examples are codes on occupational asthma, the control of lead at work and the use of pesticides for non-agricultural purposes.

In 2002-03 the Health and Safety Executive made 2,891 inspection visits to places of work and conducted a further 1,310 investigation visits. There were 11 prosecutions initiated,[107] 49 improvement notices issued and 120 prohibition notices issued. Twenty-one people died in accidents at work, six more than the annual average for the previous four years and worse than the rate in Great Britain. There were 836 "major injury accidents" reported and 3,563 "over three day injury accidents".[108] The Executive received 580 complaints relating to unsatisfactory working conditions and work-related activities.

---

[107] Five were completed during the year and are summarised in the HSE's *Annual Report for 2002-03*, p.125. One company was fined £15,000.
[108] These figures include accidents reported to district councils (see next para.).

Responsibility for enforcement of the 1978 Order as regards factories, farms and offices in the public sector, now also rests with the Executive. But health and safety in shops, and in offices in the private sector, remains a matter for the environmental health officers of district councils. The rise in the number of small businesses in Northern Ireland has made this responsibility a heavy one.[109] An annual report on how the district councils perform their responsibilities in this area is now also issued.

Where prosecutions have to be brought for breach of safety regulations the Executive monitors the fines imposed to see if they are of real deterrent value. Its predecessor, the Health and Safety Agency, called more than once for an increase in the maximum penalty. As awareness of the importance of safety at work increases, it is likely that the average fine will rise significantly in due course. It is estimated that each year more than 50,000 people in Northern Ireland suffer from ill-health caused or made worse by work and the total cost to the UK economy of workplace accidents and ill-health is supposedly around 4% of Gross Domestic Product.[110]

The Health and Safety Executive is able to conduct investigations and can commission research. It provides training and it promotes safety at work through producing short films for television, publishing leaflets, conducting seminars, running competitions and issuing a bulletin (called *Health, Safety and You*) describing recent developments in health and safety at work. It also publishes guides to relevant new legislation, such as its *Guide to Balancing Disability Rights with Health and Safety Requirements* and *Guide to Workplace Health and Safety*.

9.6 THE NORTHERN IRELAND HUMAN RIGHTS COMMISSION[111]

The Northern Ireland Human Rights Commission (NIHRC) is another of the institutions foreshadowed in the Belfast (Good Friday) Agreement of 1998.[112] The parties to that Agreement would have been

---

[109] The precise division of labour between the HSE and district councils is set out in the Health and Safety (Enforcing Authority) Regs. (NI) 1999.

[110] Figures taken from the HSE's Corporate Plan 2002-05.

[111] www.nihrc.belfast.org.

[112] Like the Northern Ireland Assembly, the Northern Ireland Executive, the Equality Commission, the Northern Ireland Victims Commission, the North/South

aware that Human Rights Commissions had been established in many other parts of the world, especially in societies emerging from conflict, such as South Africa.[113] Their plan was to provide for a Commission which had more teeth than the already existing Standing Advisory Commission on Human Rights (SACHR), a body which had been operating since 1973 but whose views on issues of human rights had been largely ignored by successive UK Governments.[114]

Standing Advisory Commission on Human Rights

Strictly speaking the statutory function of SACHR was to advise the Secretary of State only on the adequacy and effectiveness of the law in preventing discrimination based on religious belief or political opinion in Northern Ireland. SACHR frequently pressed for its statutory remit to be officially widened and in 1984 the then Secretary of State gave a written undertaking that this would happen. No action was ever taken on this, although in practice no constraints were placed on the Commission if it wished to examine *any* topic concerning human rights. Indeed the Commission was encouraged by successive Secretaries of Sate to review the operation of the "emergency" legislation enacted to deal with the civil unrest in Northern Ireland (see Chap. 4.3). Much to its disappointment, however, the Commission was frequently not consulted about new legislative initiatives which clearly had human rights implications.[115] By 1998 SACHR had a very small annual budget of about £250,000. It presented annual reports to the Secretary of State; in its later years these included, in a series of Annexes, a variety of reports commissioned by the Commission during the course of each year.

SACHR played a significant role in getting the Fair Employment (NI) Acts enacted in 1976 and 1989. As mentioned in 8.2 above, it was also entrusted with conducting the five-year review of the 1989 Act,[116]

Ministerial Council, the North/South implementation bodies, the British-Irish Council (also known as the Council of the Isles) and the British-Irish Intergovernmental Conference.

[113] The General Assembly of the UN approved the so-called "Paris Principles" in 1993 to indicate what features *national* human rights institutions should display.

[114] The creation of SACHR pre-dates the establishment in the late 1970s of the first generation of fully-fledged Human Rights Commissions in Australia, Canada and New Zealand.

[115] *E.g.* the right to silence legislation introduced in 1988, and the anti-terrorist legislation introduced after the bomb in Omagh in August 1998.

[116] *Employment Equality: Building for the Future* (1997).

which led to the Government's White Paper[117] and to the enactment of the Fair Employment and Treatment (NI) Order 1998. In its final few years SACHR also looked closely at the law on the use of lethal force by police officers and soldiers, the system for handling complaints against the police, the rights of prisoners, arrangements for supporting victims of crime, plans for improving community relations, access to education, legal aid, inquests, abortion, race relations and the rights of disabled persons.

SACHR also undertook significant work on a Bill of Rights for Northern Ireland. Its report on the subject in 1977 remains one of the best studies of the topic.[118] Originally its view was that a Bill for the United Kingdom as a whole, based on the European Convention on Human Rights (see Chap.2.5), should be introduced as a matter of urgency. In 1992 it changed its position so as to advocate a Bill of Rights for Northern Ireland alone, again based on the European Convention.

The Northern Ireland Human Rights Commission[119]

The Northern Ireland Human Rights Commission (NIHRC) was formally established on 1 March 1999, under section 68 of the Northern Ireland Act 1998, and its duties and powers are set out in section 69 of that Act.[120] The Act does not specify how many Commissioners there should be, but all of them are part-time[121] except for the Chief Commissioner, who is currently Professor Monica McWilliams. Appointments are made by the Secretary of State after applicants are interviewed. The budget of the Commission for 2005-06 is £1.35 million and it employs some 17 staff. Its current Strategic Plan

[117] *Partnership for Equality* (1998).
[118] *The Protection of Human Rights by Law in Northern Ireland* (Cmnd. 7009). SACHR also argued strongly elsewhere for the incorporation of the European Convention on Human Rights into UK law: see, *e.g. Annual Report 1983-84*, pp. 6-15 and *Annual Report 1992-93*, pp. 3-6 and Annex C.
[119] See, generally, S. Livingstone, "The Northern Ireland Human Rights Commission" (1999) 22 *Fordham International Law Journal* 1465; C. Harvey, "Building a Human Rights Culture in a Political Democracy: The Role of the Northern Ireland Human Rights Commission" in C. Harvey (ed.), *Human Rights, Equality and Democratic Renewal in Northern Ireland* (2001), Chap. 5.
[120] See generally B. Dickson, "Northern Ireland", Chap. 6 in A. Lester and D. Pannick, *Human Rights Law and Practice* (2nd ed., 2004).
[121] The part-time Commissioners are expected to give approximately one day per week to the Commission's work.

(covering 2003-06) is due to be reworked for 2006-09. Answerable to the Secretary of State for Northern Ireland, its annual report is lodged in Parliament at Westminster (and, like all other Commission publications, placed on its website[122]).

The NIHRC's main duties[123] are to promote understanding and awareness of the importance of human rights in Northern Ireland, to review the adequacy and effectiveness in Northern Ireland of law and practice relating to the protection of human rights, to advise the Secretary of State and the Executive Committee of the Assembly of measures which ought to be taken to protect human rights, to advise the Assembly whether a Bill is compatible with human rights, to advise the Secretary of State on what should be contained in a Bill of Rights for Northern Ireland and to do all that it can to establish a Joint Committee with the Human Rights Commission in the Republic of Ireland.[124] The NIHRC also has four important powers: (i) to assist individuals with court or tribunal proceedings involving law or practice relating to the protection of human rights, (ii) to bring proceedings of this nature itself,[125] (iii) to conduct such investigations as it considers necessary or expedient (provided these are for the purpose of exercising the Commission's other functions), and (iv) to publish its advice and the outcome of its research and investigations.

The Commission sets great store by its educational work and its casework. As part of the former the Commission is continuing to seek views on what should be contained in a Bill of Rights for Northern Ireland. This project was initiated in 2000, but by April 2005 the Commission had still not been able to achieve consensus amongst the local political parties in Northern Ireland as to the Bill's content.[126] The

---

122 www.nihrc.org.
123 The Commission must also make recommendations to the Secretary of State within two years as to how its effectiveness could be improved: s. 69(2) of the Northern Ireland Act 1998.
124 Membership of the Republic's Commission was announced in December 2000; the President is currently Dr Maurice Manning, a former leader of Fine Gael in the Seanad.
125 The Commission may or may not have a common law power to submit an *amicus curiae* brief (*i.e.* a "friend of the court" report) when a matter involving human rights comes before any court or tribunal.
126 Issues 3 and 4 of the 2001 issue of the Northern Ireland Legal Quarterly (vol. 52) are devoted to the Bill of Rights; see also C. Harvey, "The Politics of Rights and Deliberative Democracy: the Process of Drafting a Northern Irish Bill of Rights" [2001] EHRLR 48; A. Smith, "The Drafting Process of a Bill of Rights for Northern Ireland" [2004] PL 526.

Belfast (Good Friday) Agreement requires the Bill of Rights to go beyond what is already contained in the European Convention on Human Rights, which in any event is already binding on the Northern Ireland Assembly and Executive by virtue of the Northern Ireland Act 1998[127] and on all other public authorities in Northern Ireland by virtue of the Human Rights Act 1998. The Bill of Rights must "reflect the particular circumstances of Northern Ireland, drawing as appropriate on international instruments and experience"; more specifically, it must "reflect the principles of mutual respect for the identity and ethos of both communities and parity of esteem".[128] The Commission has to date published two drafts of a possible Bill of Rights. It also has a video and a training manual for use by individuals and groups who want to discuss the topic, not to mention a set of Bill in Rights in Schools (BORIS) materials, prepared in co-operation with the Department of Education. In 2005 the Commission published guides to Articles 2 and 3 of the European Convention on Human Rights, which guarantee the right to life and the right not to be subjected to torture or inhuman or degrading treatment or punishment.

Through its casework the Commission can assist individual applicants as well as take cases in its own name. In 2003-04, for example, it granted assistance to 11 individuals (10 in 2003-03) and intervened in seven other cases (including three in the House of Lords). To win the right to intervene in cases as an interested third party the Commission had to challenge in the House of Lords a ruling by the Northern Ireland Court of Appeal.[129] In 2003-04 it rejected 38 applications from individuals for assistance (55 in 2002-03). This was largely because they did not fit with the Commission's strategic priorities, which at the time were the right to life, the right not to be subjected to inhuman or degrading treatment, the right to a fair trial, the right to freedom from discrimination and the right to education.

Amongst the investigations conducted by the Commission have been those into the rights of children held in juvenile justice centres and the

---

[127] Ss. 6(2)(c) (Assembly) and 24(1)(a) (Executive).

[128] Para. 4 of the section headed "Rights, Safeguards and Equality of Opportunity" in Strand Three of the Belfast (Good Friday) Agreement 1998.

[129] *Re Northern Ireland Human Rights Commission* [2002] NI 236. See L. Blom-Cooper, "Third Party Intervention and Judicial Dissent" [2002] PL 602 and A. Smith "Access to Intervene: The Northern Ireland Human Rights Commission and the Northern Ireland Act 1998" [2003] EHRLR 423.

rights of women and girls in prison.[130] During research for the latter the Northern Ireland Office banned the Commission from conducting any further research in either Rathgael Juvenile Justice Centre or Hydebank Wood, to where female prisoners were transferred from Maghaberry prison in June 2004. The Commission has also submitted innumerable papers commenting on proposed changes to law and policy made by various government departments (*e.g.* on terrorism, anti-discrimination measures and anti-social behaviour orders), but its experience has been that the Government pays little heed to the recommendations made. A better venue for the Commission to be effective is probably the international plain,[131] where interventions can be made at the UN Commission on Human Rights and at the various UN treaty-monitoring bodies such as the Committee Against Torture, the Committee on the Rights of the Child and the Committee on the Elimination of Racial Discrimination.

In 2001 the Commission issued a report to the Secretary of State on whether the powers it had been given by the Northern Ireland Act were adequate and effective.[132] In this, it asked in particular for the power to compel the disclosure of information to the Commission (a power already vesting in most other human rights commissions around the world).[133] Late in 2004 the Government indicated that it was willing to confer this power, and the relevant legislation is awaited. Evaluations have been published of the work done by the Commission with the limited powers it has at present.[134] By and large these have been positive, despite disruptions caused to that work by some Commissioners resigning or "withdrawing" in 2002 and 2003 over differences of opinion on the strategic direction of the Commission and its funding of a court challenge to the way in which the police handled the Loyalist "protest" at Holy Cross Girls' Primary School in Ardoyne in 2001.[135] To date the Commission has taken the view that non-state

---

[130] *In Our Care* (2002) and *The Hurt Inside* (2004).

[131] B. Dickson, "The Contribution of Human Rights Commissions to the Protection of Human Rights" [2003] PL 272.

[132] As required by the Northern Ireland Act 1998, s. 69(2).

[133] See, *e.g.*, Ireland's Human Rights Commission Act 2000, s. 9.

[134] *Work of the Northern Ireland Human Rights Commission*, 14th Report, 2002-03, HL 132 and HC 142. See too S. Livingstone and R. Murray, "The Effectiveness of National Human Rights Institutions", Chap. 6 in S. Halliday and P. Schmidt (eds.), *Human Rights Brought Home* (2004).

[135] *Re E's Application* [2003] NIJB 288; an appeal to the Court of Appeal is pending in this case.

agents, such as paramilitary organisations, should also be expected to respect human rights standards and it has highlighted their failure to do so in recent annual reports.[136] This is in line with the approach adopted by most other human rights commissions in the world (although not by some local human rights organisations) and is approved by the office of the UN High Commissioner on Human Rights.

9.7 THE NORTHERN IRELAND COMMISSIONER FOR CHILDREN AND YOUNG PEOPLE[137]

This office (NICCY) was created by the Commissioner for Children and Young People (NI) Order 2003 and the first Commissioner, Mr Nigel Williams, took up his post on 1 October 2003.[138] He has extensive powers to safeguard and promote the rights and best interests of children and young people (defined as those under 18 years of age[139]) in Northern Ireland. As regards promoting rights, he takes his lead from the United Nations' Convention on the Rights of the Child (1989). He can help children and their parents or guardians with any complaints they might have about public services for children, he can carry out formal or informal inquiries and he can conduct research. The first major research report, commissioned mainly from researchers based at Queen's University, was on the state of children's rights in Northern Ireland and was submitted in 2004.[140] In 2004 the Commissioner failed in an application for judicial review of the Government's decision to put before Parliament the proposed Anti-social Behaviour (NI) Order 2004.[141]

The Commissioner is also under a duty to review the adequacy and effectiveness of services and the law relating to children and young people and to advise Ministers accordingly. In that capacity Mr

---

[136] See, generally, K. McEvoy, "Human Rights, Humanitarian Interventions and Paramilitary Activities in Northern Ireland" in C. Harvey (ed.), *Human Rights, Equality and Democratic Renewal in Northern Ireland* (2001), Chap. 9.

[137] www.niccy.org.

[138] There are now similar commissioners in other jurisdictions in these islands, but their duties and powers differ significantly. The Derry Children's Commission is an unofficial body. There is also a European network of such offices: see www.ombudsnet.org.

[139] But he can help young people with a disability, or those leaving care, up to the age of 21.

[140] Available on the Commissioner's website.

[141] *In re the Northern Ireland Commissioner for Children and Young People's Application* [2004] NIQB 40.

Williams has criticised the Government's spending plans for Northern Ireland as they affect children and has recommended that the draft strategy[142] for this sector, issued by the Office of the First Minister and Deputy First Minister at the end of 2004, be reviewed in the light of the research report mentioned above. The Commissioner strongly recommended that a Minister for Children and Young People should be appointed in Northern Ireland with a responsibility cutting across all other government departments and the power to oversee and implement the government's strategy. Lord Rooker was in fact appointed to this position in August 2005. The Children Act 2004 created a Children's Commissioner in England (Professor Al Aynsley-Green), and he or she can promote the views and interests of children in Northern Ireland in relation to non-devolved matters. There is also a Children's Commissioner in Wales.

There is not yet a Commissioner for Older People in Northern Ireland, but there are proposals to appoint such an official in both Scotland and Wales.

9.8 SOCIAL CARE BODIES

Inspection of social services provision in Northern Ireland is conducted by the Social Services Inspectorate,[143] a unit within the Department of Health, Social Services and Public Safety. By the Health and Personal Social Services (NI) Order 1972, as amended, and other related Orders,[144] this unit is empowered to inspect the organisation, management and quality of the services, to advise government Ministers on what changes to make to policy in this area and to devise effective strategies for the training and development of staff. The inspectorate aims to ensure that social work and social care services are responsive to the needs of the population and are of the highest standards given the resources available. It places its reports, or at least summaries of them, on its website. Among its recent publications are a report on mental health services in Northern Ireland and a historical review of child care provision.[145]

---

[142] *Making it R Wrld 2*: www.allchildrenni.gov.uk/strategy.pdf.

[143] www.dhsspsni.gov.uk/hss/ssi/index.asp. At present the Chief Inspector is Mr Paul Martin.

[144] Principally the Probation (NI) Order 1982, Adoption (NI) Order 1987, Registered Homes (NI) Order 1992 and Children (NI) Order 1995.

[145] *Inspection of Social Work in Mental Health Services* (2004) and *A Better Future - 50 Years of Child Care in Northern Ireland 1950-2000* (2000).

The Northern Ireland Social Care Council[146] was set up by the Health and Personal Social Services Act (NI) 2001 as an organisation to regulate the social work profession, whose members number about 30,000 in Northern Ireland. It replaced the Central Council for Education and Training in Social Work. Like its predecessor the new body seeks to maintain educational and training standards, but it also regulates standards of conduct and practice. The new Council has published a code of practice for social care workers and their employers and it is beginning to keep a Register of such workers. It will soon be a criminal offence to claim to be a social worker if one is not registered as such. The current chairperson of the Social Care Council is Dr Jeremy Harbison, a retired senior civil servant.[147]

The Northern Ireland Health and Personal Social Services Regulation and Improvement Authority was set up by the Health and Personal Social Services (Quality, Improvement and Regulation) (NI) Order 2003.[148] Its current chairperson is Mr Brian Coulter (who is also the Prisoner Ombudsman). It has the general duty of keeping the Government informed about the availability and quality of health and social services in Northern Ireland and must encourage improvement in the quality of such services. The 2003 Order also reforms the law regarding registration of institutions such as children's homes,[149] residential care homes and nursing homes.

Medical workers in Northern Ireland fall under the jurisdiction of the Health Boards and Trusts. Complaints against registered professionals in this domain (doctors, dentists and ophthalmic opticians) can be heard by a tribunal set up under the Health and Personal Social Services (NI) Order 1972.[150] The tribunal can strike any such worker off the register, although there is a right of appeal to the Court of Appeal against its decisions.[151] The Lord Chief Justice appoints the chairperson of the tribunal but its other two members are appointed by the Department of Health, Social Services and Public Safety.[152] The General Medical Council, based in London,[153] also has power to prevent a doctor from

---

[146] www.niscc.info.
[147] Further details about the Council are in Sch. 1 to the 2001 Act.
[148] Further details about the Authority are in Sch. 1 to the 2003 Order.
[149] Now regulated by the Children's Homes Regs. (NI) 2005.
[150] Arts. 65, 106(b) and Sch. 11. See too the Tribunal Regs. (NI) 2004, consolidating and amending previous regulations.
[151] *Ibid.* Sch. 11, para. 4.
[152] *Ibid.* paras. 11 and 12.
[153] www.gmc-uk.org.

practising, or can place conditions on the kind or practice he or she can engage in. Nurses and midwives are regulated by the Northern Ireland Practice and Education Council for Nursing and Midwifery (chaired by Mrs Maureen Griffith), which was created by the Health and Personal Social Services Act (NI) 2002.

To hear appeals against some decisions of the Social Care Council and the Regulation and Improvement Authority a new Care Tribunal has been established.[154] This will deal, for example, with challenges to decisions concerning the registration of homes, the registration of workers and the employment of workers who are caring for vulnerable people. Further protections for such people were put in place by the Protection of Children and Vulnerable Adults (NI) Order 2003. Appeals against decisions of the Care Tribunal lie to the High Court, but only on points of law, not fact.[155]

Northern Ireland has a Chief Medical Officer (currently Dr Henrietta Campbell). Her annual reports are a mine of fascinating information about the health of the people living in Northern Ireland.[156]

9.9 THE PARADES COMMISSION[157]

Special measures have been introduced in Northern Ireland in an effort to control public disorder arising from parades and associated protests.[158] Prior to 1998, the law governing parades and protests was contained solely in the Public Order (NI) Order 1987. Under this Order, the power to impose conditions on public processions resided with the RUC. A senior police officer could impose conditions if he or she reasonably believed that the circumstances in which the parade was being held might result in serious public disorder, serious damage to property or serious disruption to the life of the community.[159] These criteria, however, were widely criticised because they gave primacy to the potential for disorder, and thus, effectively, put tremendous pressure on the police to yield to the greatest threat from whichever side that came.

---

[154] Health and Personal Social Services (Quality, Improvement and Regulation) (NI) Order 2003, art. 44 and Sch. 2. See too the Care Tribunal Regs. (NI) 2005.
[155] *Ibid.* art. 44(6).
[156] They are available at www.dhsspsni.gov.uk.
[157] www.paradescommission.org.
[158] See further B. Dickson and M. Hamilton, "Meetings and Marches", ch. 8 in B. Dickson and M. O'Brien (eds.), *Civil Liberties in Northern Ireland* (4th ed., 2003).
[159] Art. 4.

In 1996, after the second year of disturbances in Portadown, the Government established the Independent Review of Parades and Marches, chaired by Dr Peter North of Oxford University. The group was tasked to review "the current arrangements for handling public processions and open-air public meetings and associated public order issues in Northern Ireland"[160] and it reported early in 1997. The principal recommendations were the establishment of an independent Parades Commission, which would take over the police's decision-making powers in relation to public processions, and an extension of the statutory criteria under which conditions could be imposed on parades. The recommendations of the Report were largely implemented by the Public Processions (NI) Act 1998, although the Parades Commission was actually first established on a non-statutory basis in March 1997. It did not have power to rule on parades until February 1998.

Two years later the Parades Commission was reconstituted. It now comprises seven persons, all men,[161] under the chairmanship of Sir Anthony Holland, an English solicitor.[162] In 2003-04 the cost of running the Commission was £1,292,000. At talks in Weston Park in the summer of 2001 the British Government agreed to review the Parades Commission and the 1998 Act and in November 2001 Sir George Quigley was appointed to conduct such a review. He reported a year later,[163] but two years after that the Government largely rejected his recommendation that responsibility for key decisions on parades should be returned to the police.

In addition to issuing determinations relating to proposed parades, section 2 of the Public Processions (NI) Act 1998 places the Parades Commission under a duty to promote greater understanding about public processions and to promote and facilitate mediation as a means of resolving disputes. The Commission fulfils its role of facilitating mediation largely through its "Authorised Officers", of whom there are currently 12. The Act also requires the Commission to produce a Code of Conduct (providing guidance to persons organising public

---

[160] Foreword to the *Independent Review of Parades and Marches* (The North Report) (1997).

[161] An application for judicial review of the appointments to the Commission was unsuccessful: *Re White's Application* [2001] 2 BNIL 50.

[162] All of its determinations are published on its website. Sir Anthony is retiring from the chairmanship in 2005.

[163] www.nio.gov.uk/quigreport.pdf.

processions or protest meetings), a set of Procedural Rules (regulating the procedure which the Commission must follow in exercising its functions) and a Guidelines document (expanding on the statutory criteria in s. 8(6) of the Act).[164] These three documents were most recently revised with effect from 15 April 2005 and are available on the Commission's website. In addition, the Commission has provided marshal training for stewards at processions and listed the help of a private organisation, the Mediation Network of Northern Ireland, to help with the training of the authorised officers. It also employs monitors to observe and report back on parades.

Until recently there existed a two-tier decision-making structure which rested upon the distinction between "processions", which fall within the remit of the Parades Commission, and "open-air public meetings" (*including* what s. 17 of the 1998 Act defines as "related protest meetings"), which remained within the operational jurisdiction of the police under the Public Order (NI) Order 1987. The Commission had no power to impose conditions on protest meetings. The Public Processions (Amendment) (NI) Order 2005, however, has changed this, largely as a result of serious disturbances which took place in Ardoyne in Belfast on 12 July 2004, when some "supporters" of a parade were not required to comply with the restrictions imposed upon the marchers themselves.[165] But only the Secretary of State will be able to ban a meeting.

Organisers of all public processions (except funerals and Salvation Army processions) are required to give the police 28 days' notice[166] and organisers of any related protest must give 14 days' notice.[167] A copy of these notices is then passed to the Parades Commission. If it is not reasonably practicable to give the required notice, notice must be given as soon as it is so. Before it reaches a decision on contentious parades or protest meetings the Commission will invite written and oral evidence. If conditions need to be imposed on the parade or protest, the Parades Commission will aim to issue a determination to that effect at least five days before the parade.

---

[164] Ss. 3, 4 and 5.
[165] See *Report on the Policing of the Ardoyne Parades 12 July 2004*, prepared for the Policing Board by Keir Starmer QC and Jane Gordon.
[166] The notice requirement had been 7 days until it was increased by the Public Order (Amendment) (NI) Order 1997.
[167] Public Processions (NI) Act 1998, ss. 6 and 7.

The criteria which the Commission may consider when deciding whether or not to issue a determination are contained in sections 8(6) and 9A(6) of the Public Processions (NI) Act 1998. These refer (as well as to the potential for public disorder and disruption to the life of the community) to any impact which the procession may have on relationships within the community, any failure of the organiser of, or a participant in, any parade or protest meeting to comply with the Code of Conduct and (in the case of parades only) the desirability of allowing a procession customarily held along a particular route to be held along that route. The compatibility of these criteria with the European Convention on Human Rights was unsuccessfully challenged in a case concerning a proposed Orange Order parade in Dunloy in County Antrim.[168]

Rule 6 of the Parades Commission's revised Procedural Rules provides for the Commission itself to amend or revoke a determination where fresh information has come to light. The Secretary of State may, too, if requested by the Chief Constable, review a determination of the Commission and either amend, repeal or confirm the determination. The only other means of challenging a decision of the Commission is by way of judicial review (see Chap. 6.7). In a judicial review application concerning the Commission's decision to allow an Orange Order parade on the Lower Ormeau Road in July 1998, the Court of Appeal held that by "community" the Public Processions (NI) Act 1998 intended to refer not just to the people living in the area through which the parade was to pass but also to the wider community in Northern Ireland.[169] The Commission also survived judicial reviews of its decision in 1999 to re-route a "Civil Rights March" between Lurgan and Portadown[170] and to impose restrictions on a march in Portadown.[171] But in 2004 the Commission was ordered to disclose to an Orange Order Lodge police reports and reports from authorised officers which the Commission took into account before banning a parade by the Lodge on Easter Sunday that year in Dunloy, County Antrim.

According to the Commission's Annual Report for 2003-04, in that year there were about 3,120 parades notified to the police (a 4% drop on the 2002-03 figure), of which 70% were loyalist parades, 3.5% were nationalist parades and 26.5% were other civic parades, galas or

[168] *Re Tweed's Application* [2001] NI 165.
[169] See *Annual Report of the Parades Commission* 1999-2000.
[170] *Re McConnell's Application* [2000] 4 BNIL 71.
[171] *Re Farrell's Application* [1999] NIJB 143.

marches by ex-service organisations. Only 231 of the parades (7%) were contentious, with 50 of these, as in previous years, being the parades which are notified each week by an Orange Order Lodge from Portadown in relation to a request to march down the Garvaghy Road in that town. Only 7% of the contentious parades were nationalist parades. But even 69 of the contentious parades (29%) were allowed by the Parades Commission to proceed; some of these, together with the remainder, were subject to restrictions, mostly relating to the route of the march but sometimes to the music to be played or the timing of the march.

The Secretary of State retains the power in exceptional circumstances to prohibit individual parades, a class of parades or protest meetings,[172] but so far as is known this power has not been exercised since August 1996 when Sir Patrick Mayhew prohibited all public processions along a stretch of the city walls in Derry/Londonderry.

9.10   THE COMMUNITY RELATIONS COUNCIL[173]

Strange as it may seem, the Community Relations Council is not a statutory body but a registered charity. Now sponsored by the Community Relations Unit of the Office of the First Minister and Deputy First Minister, it was created in 1990 to help improve relations between the Protestant and Catholic communities in Northern Ireland and to encourage cultural diversity. It follows earlier failed experiments with a Community Relations Commission in the early 1970s and the setting up of a Ministry of Community Relations within the old Stormont administration in 1969.

The current chairperson of the Council is Mr Eamonn McCartan and there are 17 other members, all appointed for a three-year period but receiving no pay for their work of about one day per month. Two-thirds of the members are selected by the Council (following a public advertisement seeking nominations) and the remaining one-third are appointed by the Government. Since 1990 the Council has published numerous booklets, organised many conferences and, perhaps most importantly, granted funding to a huge variety of organisations wanting to engage in community relations work. There are something like 130 organisations dedicated to community relations and peace work in

---

[172]   Public Processions (NI) Act 1998, ss.11 and 11A.
[173]   www.community-relations.org.uk.

Northern Ireland. The Council has, for example, helped to create mobile phone networks for community workers so as to reduce the chances of conflict erupting across the community divide and recent topics of concern have been tensions at interface areas[174] and racist attacks.[175] In 1999 it began administering a support scheme for victims of violence, funded by the Government, and in 2003 it began making core funding grants for such work (64 applications were received and 46 granted).

In 2003-4 the Council operated 10 different funding schemes and gave grants to some 500 projects. In all it distributed £12.2 million, £8.7 million of which was from the European Union's Special Support Fund for Peace and Reconciliation (so-called Peace II funding). The Council employed 31 staff and had running costs of £712,000. A Community Relations Information Centre is maintained in the centre of Belfast and a newsletter, *CRC News*, is published three times a year.

9.11 ELECTION BODIES

The Electoral Office for Northern Ireland[176]

This is the office which supports the work of the Chief Electoral Officer for Northern Ireland (Mr Denis Stanley). It advises people on matters such as how to register to vote, how to apply for a postal vote and what kind of proof of identity is required when voting. Each year (during the first two weeks of December) the Chief Electoral Officer must also arrange for the selection of a sufficient number of jurors from the electoral register to enable the empanelling of juries for the following year.[177] The full electoral register can be made available only to specified people and organisations and they can use it only for specified purposes, although these include the prevention of crime and the vetting of people's creditworthiness.[178] In Northern Ireland a single transferable vote variety of proportional representation is used for European, Assembly and district council elections, but for Westminster elections the more traditional first-past-the-post system is maintained.

---

[174] See N. Jarman, *Demography, Development and Disorder: Changing Patterns of Interface Areas* (2004).

[175] In the last 9 months of 2004 there were 474 racist attacks reported across Northern Ireland.

[176] www.electoralofficeni.gov.uk.

[177] Juries (NI) Order 1996 (Amendment) Regs. 2003.

[178] Representation of the People (NI) (Amendment) Regs. 2002.

For an excellent website detailing the results of all elections in Northern Ireland since 1885, see www.ark.ac.uk/elections.

The Electoral Commission[179]

This is a body independent of the Government which was established by Parliament to foster public confidence and participation by promoting integrity, involvement and effectiveness in the democratic process. Although based in London it has an office in Belfast and one of the Commissioners (Mr Karamjit Singh) has a particular brief for this part of the country. The chairperson is Lord Younger. Generally the Commission engages in creative thinking about elections and tries to ensure that those which are held are run fairly. It produces four-page briefing documents for politicians and other policy-makers, two-page information factsheets for more general use (in schools, for example), policy and research reports and reports on elections after they have taken place. Amongst its research and policy reports published in 2004 are those entitled *The Marked Electoral Register, The Funding of Political Parties, Gender and Political Participation* and *Age of Electoral Majority*. In this last report it revealed that in an opinion survey 78% of respondents were against the idea that the voting age for general elections in the United Kingdom should be lowered from the current 18 years to 16 years. Even a minority of people under or just above the age of 18 were against such a change.

9.12 AUDIT BODIES

Amongst the most effective methods of overseeing a public body is to examine closely the way it spends its money. For public bodies in Northern Ireland there are three organisations which specialise in such scrutiny.

The National Audit Office

The National Audit Office, headed by the Comptroller and Auditor General Sir John Bourn, ensures that public money is indeed spent on the things it was allocated for by Parliament. Despite having primarily a Great Britain focus, some of its reports also impact, directly or indirectly, on Northern Ireland. Recent examples would be its reports on how government agencies interact with citizens,[180] on how to deal

---

[179] www.electoralcommission.gov.uk.
[180] 2002-03, HC 1145.

with defendants who fail to attend court[181] and on what redress people have if things go wrong with public services.[182] The National Audit Office also spends some time looking at how European Union money is spent in the United Kingdom, but this is primarily the responsibility of the European Court of Auditors. Local authorities and health service bodies in England and Wales are audited by yet another body, called the Audit Commission.

The Northern Ireland Audit Office

The Northern Ireland Audit Office (NIAO), in a nutshell, does for the devolved administration in Northern Ireland what the National Audit Office does for the whole of the United Kingdom.[183] There are equivalent bodies for Scotland and Wales. It looks at the expenditure not just of government departments but also of agency bodies and non-departmental public bodies. The Comptroller and Auditor General for Northern Ireland is Mr John Dowdall.[184] When the Northern Ireland Assembly is sitting the NIAO reports to it, but at other times it reports to Parliament at Westminster. Some of its staff work as local government auditors and report to the Department of the Environment. The chief local government auditor can seek a declaration from a court that certain expenditure was contrary to law, as when Newry and Mourne District Council spent money on a staff Christmas party in 1999.[185] Like its national parent organisation the NIAO undertakes both financial audits and value for money audits. Amongst its recent reports have been those on *Northern Ireland Tourist Board Accounts 2000-01* (2002), *Use of Consultants by Northern Ireland Government Departments* (2004), *Improving Pupil Attendance at School* (2004) and *Waiting for Treatment in Hospitals* (2004).

The Committee of Public Accounts

This House of Commons Select Committee, colloquially known as the PAC, has the role of examining those accounts which show how sums granted by Parliament to meet public expenditure have in fact been

---

[181] 2003-04, HC 1162.

[182] 2004-05, HC 21.

[183] For relevant legislation see the Audit (NI) Order 1987, the Government Resources and Accounts Act (NI) 2001 and the Audit and Accountability (NI) Order 2003.

[184] His salary is set by Parliament: see Salaries (Comptroller and Auditor-General) Order (NI) Order 2005. It was £122,435 from 1 April 2004.

[185] *In re the Local Government Auditor's Application* [2003] NIJB 207.

spent and also such other accounts laid before Parliament as the Committee may itself think fit to examine. It is a prestigious and highly respected body. Its chairperson in the 2001-05 Parliament was the Conservative MP Mr Edward Leigh. Clearly its work overlaps with that of the statutory audit offices, but this is no bad thing because the need for careful oversight in the area of expenditure is very great. From time to time the PAC issues reports which relate specifically to Northern Ireland, such as those on the management of industrial sickness absence by the Department for Regional Development (with particular reference to the Roads Service and the Water Service)[186] and on excess money required by the Department of Education in Northern Ireland for the pension scheme it administers.[187]

9.13 CONSUMER PROTECTION BODIES

There are several bodies with the job of looking after the interests of consumers. Some of these are branches of the Government at the central or local level; others are independent of the Government but receive government funding; a third group operates on an entirely voluntary basis.

The Office of Fair Trading[188]

Of government bodies the most important is probably the Office of Fair Trading (OFT). This was first established in 1973[189] but was re-launched under the Enterprise Act 2002, which considerably strengthened the law throughout the United Kingdom relating to consumer education and protection, codes of practice and market investigations. Other important pieces of legislation are the Consumer Credit Act 1974, the Estate Agents Act 1979,[190] the Competition Act 1980, the Control of Misleading Advertising Regulations 1988, the Unfair Terms in Consumer Contracts Regulations 1999[191] and the Consumer Protection (Distance Selling) Regulations 2000. The OFT's chairperson (from October 2005) is Mr Philip Collins, who is supported

---

[186] 2003-04, 50th Report, HC 561.
[187] 2004-05, 6th Report, HC 311.
[188] www.oft.gov.uk.
[189] By the Fair Trading Act 1973.
[190] Estate agents do not need licences but there is a register of people who have been banned from working in that role.
[191] In 2003-04 there were 1,102 complaints under these Regs., leading to 1,541 terms being altered or abandoned.

by six other Board members and a staff of some 700. In 2003-04 the organisation's budget was £49 million.

The Office collects evidence relating to business practices which may adversely affect the economic, health, safety or other interests of consumers. It can make recommendations to the Secretary of State for Trade and Industry on proposed regulation of these practices (*e.g.* the banning of "no refund" notices). It can also consider "super-complaints"[192] referred to it by designated consumer protection bodies: the General Consumer Council for Northern Ireland, for example, has referred to it a super-complaint about the market for personal banking services in Northern Ireland and the OFT may refer this in turn to the Competition Commission (see below). In June 2004 the OFT submitted proposals to the Government in response to a consultation paper issued by the Independent Review on Regulatory Framework for Legal Services in England and Wales (the Clementi Review: see Chap. 3.2). Needless to say the OFT is in favour of regulation which is less restrictive but more effective.

The OFT also has a Consumer Codes Approval Scheme, under which it has approved codes issued by the Society of Motor Manufacturers and Traders, the Vehicle Builders and Repairers Association and the Direct Selling Association.[193] The OFT does not deal directly with complaints received from individual members of the public, except in so far as these suggest a course of conduct detrimental to consumers as a whole, which the OFT can then try to have altered, if necessary through court proceedings.[194] In addition, most organisations giving credit to consumers can only do so if licensed by the OFT under the Consumer Credit Act 1974 (in 2003-04 nearly 17,000 new licences were issued).

The OFT receives a lot of information from the local agencies which enforce legislation dealing with hygiene and with weights and measures (now called trading standards). In Northern Ireland the responsibility for supervising and enforcing trading standards (including trade descriptions) rests with what is now the Trading Standards Service,[195] while the control of food hygiene is part of the duties of the local district councils (see 9.13 below) and there is a

---

[192] Defined in the Enterprise Act 2002, s. 11(1).

[193] All available on the OFT's website.

[194] In 2003-04 the OFT opened 45 court cases under the Consumer Protection (Distance Selling) Regs. 2000.

[195] www.tssni.gov.uk. There are offices in Belfast and in Armagh, Ballymena, Derry/Londonderry and Enniskillen.

branch of the UK's Food Standards Agency in Belfast.[196] These are the bodies which instigate prosecutions under the relevant legislation. Local government is also responsible for the establishment of consumer advice centres. In Northern Ireland there is at present only one such centre, in Belfast. Its job is to advise consumers rather than represent them or enforce consumer protection law. Its work is supplemented, of course, by that of the Citizens' Advice Bureaux (see Chap. 3.2).

The Competition Commission[197]

By virtue of the Competition Act 1998 the Competition Commission replaced the former Monopolies and Mergers Commission on 1 April 1999.[198] Also a government body, like the OFT, the Commission comprises between a Chairperson (Professor Paul Geroski) and (currently) some 35 other members appointed by the Secretary of State for Trade and Industry. It has its headquarters in London and had running costs in 2003-04 of some £20 million. There are about 90 staff.

The Commission's main function is to investigate and report on matters referred to it by the Secretary of State or, more commonly, by the OFT. Appeals against some of its determinations on anti-competitive practices are heard by the Competition Appeal Tribunal,[199] the President of which is Sir Christopher Bellamy.

The matters referred to the Commission will relate to mergers, monopolies, anti-competitive practices, the regulation of utilities, the costs and general efficiency of nationalised industries and the performance of public sector bodies. An inquiry was recently conducted, for example, into the use of store credit cards in the United Kingdom (on a reference from the OFT). The aim of such investigations may simply be to examine the facts, or it may be to assess whether the action in question will operate against the public interest. In the latter event the Commission will have to take into account, amongst other things, the interests of consumers, the need to reduce costs and the importance of developing new manufacturing techniques. The Commission's reports usually take several months to prepare as its investigations are thorough. It holds formal confidential

---

[196] www.food.gov.uk/northernireland.
[197] www.competition-commission.gov.uk.
[198] This body had been created by the Fair Trading Act 1973, and itself replaced the Monopolies and Restrictive Practices Commission established in 1948.
[199] www.catribunal.org.uk. It was created on 1 April 2003 by the Enterprise Act 2002, s. 12 and Sch. 2.

hearings at which witnesses will be examined and interested parties represented by barristers. The reports are laid before Parliament and published but the Government is not obliged to heed the recommendations.

Among the practices condemned by the Commission's predecessor body were the restrictions placed by the Law Society on advertising by solicitors and the rule whereby a Queen's Counsel cannot work in court without the assistance of a junior barrister. Some changes in these practices were made as a result. The new Commission has established panels on, for example, newspapers, telecommunications, water and utilities.

The General Consumer Council[200]

This body, functioning under the General Consumer Council (NI) Order 1984, came into full operation in 1985. It is independent of government, although its members are appointed by the Department of Enterprise, Trade and Investment and it is funded by that Department. In 2002-03 its total income was £1,272,000.

The General Consumer Council consists of a part-time chairperson (Mr Stephen Costello), a deputy chairperson and, at present, 12 other members. There is a supporting staff of 26 employees. The members represent a wide range of organisations and interests, such as the trade union movement, advice centres, local authorities and women's groups. Together these representatives make up a central body of consumer opinion, watching over consumer interests and speaking on the consumer's behalf to the Government, nationalised and private industries, and commercial enterprises of all sorts. The Council liaises closely with the National Consumer Council (of which its chairperson is a member) as well as with the Consumer Councils for Scotland and Wales. It is a member of the Consumers in Europe Group.

The Council has a general duty to promote consumer interests. To this end it has powers to carry out research, provide information and investigate matters of consumer concern. As it has particular responsibilities in the realms of food, transport, gas, coal and, since April 2003, electricity,[201] it maintains special groups working in those areas. In 2003-04 the Council received 153 representations about transport, 168 about gas and 26 about coal. It cannot receive complaints

---

[200] www.gccni.org.uk.
[201] As a result of the Energy (NI) Order 2003.

about food issues, which are the responsibility of district councils' environmental health officers. If consumers contact the Council to complain about areas for which it has no responsibility it will give basic advice or redirect them to other bodies (see Chap.3.1).

In recent years the General Consumer Council has commissioned and published incisive reports on such matters as buying a home, private rented housing for students, remedies for consumer complaints, coal prices, food safety and taxi services. It has also published a guide to fundamental consumer protection measures in Northern Ireland, entitled *Buying, Selling and Borrowing*. The National Health Service has its own statutory scheme to deal with complaints about the services of a general medical or dental practitioner, as well as established procedures for handling complaints about the services or treatment in hospitals; the Assembly Ombudsman also now has a role in this area (see 9.2 above).

Unfortunately the General Consumer Council does not possess the power to compel other bodies to act on its views. It seeks to influence rather than to enforce. Through developing its consumer education service and publishing a full annual report (submitted to the Department of Enterprise, Trade and Investment), it makes consumers aware of their legal rights. The need for easily accessible consumer advice agencies in Northern Ireland is great: the province has proportionally more consumer complaints than any other region in the United Kingdom and, of those consumers who take some action on their complaint, those in Northern Ireland have the highest level of residual dissatisfaction.

Responsibility for regulating most aspects of the telecommunications industry throughout the United Kingdom has recently been transferred to the Office of Communications (OFCOM),[202] created by the Office of Communications Act 2002 and given additional functions by the Communications Act 2003.[203] It can have up to nine non-executive members and its current chairperson is Mr David Currie. It has taken over the regulatory tasks formerly performed by the Broadcasting Standards Commission, the Director-General of Telecommunications, the Independent Television Commission and the Radio Authority. Under the Energy (NI) Order 2003 the Office for the Regulation of Electricity and Gas (OFREG) was replaced from 1 April 2003 by the

---

[202] www.ofcom.org.uk.
[203] Ss. 1-31.

Northern Ireland Authority for Energy Regulation[204] (of which the current chairperson is Mr Douglas McIldoon). But it is still popularly known as OFREG.

The Financial Services Authority

The Financial Services Authority (FSA)[205] is an independent non-governmental body, given statutory powers by the Financial Services and Markets Act 2000. It is financed by the financial services industry but the Board, consisting of a chairperson (currently Mr Callum McCarthy) and 15 other members, is appointed by the Government. The Authority has a wide range of rule-making, investigatory and enforcement powers and now regulates the whole of the financial services industry in the United Kingdom, including banking, insurance and investments. It does not, however, deal with personal loans or credit cards (these are still the concern of the Office of Fair Trading) nor with pensions (now the concern of the Pensions Regulator – see Chap. 8.2). The 2000 Act requires it to maintain confidence in the industry and promote public understanding of it, to ensure that consumers are properly protected and to reduce financial crime. The FSA's inspectors visit registered financial bodies of all types and scrutinise their annual reports. Recommendations can be made to government departments on what reforms are required. The public are allowed to examine the registers maintained by the Authority and it will answer day-to-day inquiries. Complaints about matters falling within the remit of the FSA can now be taken to the Financial Services and Markets Tribunal,[206] which can direct what action the FSA should take on a particular issue.

The FSA has taken over the work of the Friendly Societies Commission and the Registrars of Friendly Societies and of Credit Unions. These supervised the activities of industrial and provident societies (such as co-operatives and housing associations), credit unions and trade unions. There is no statutory definition of a "friendly society" but it is generally a society the membership of which contributes to a fund that is to be used to assist the members when they are in need. The functions which can be undertaken by a registered friendly society include offering its members most forms of life

---

[204] www.ofreg.nics.gov.uk.
[205] www.fsa.gov.uk.
[206] Financial Services and Markets Act 2000, s. 152.

insurance, annuity, and unemployment and health insurance. The rules governing credit unions and industrial and provident societies are about to be revised in Northern Ireland, following a consultation document issued in 2004 by the Department of Enterprise, Trade and Investment. In March 2005 a proposal for a draft Industrial and Provident Societies (NI) Order 2005 was issued.

The Financial Services Ombudsman

The Financial Services Ombudsman now acts as the industry's own dispute resolving mechanism (as an alternative to the courts).[207] It has been set up under statute by the Financial Services Authority (see above)[208] and covers the fields of insurance, banking, mortgage lending, credit unions, friendly societies, investments and stockbroking (but not private moneylending). It has taken over the role of the Insurance Ombudsman's Bureau (first set up in 1981), the Banking Ombudsman (1986) and the Building Societies Ombudsman (1987). It has nothing to do with the statutory ombudsmen offices described in 9.2 above and it cannot deal with complaints about the way particular investments have performed or the commercial judgement of companies.

There are now hundreds of companies which are subject to the ombudsman scheme. If you have a complaint against one of them which is not dealt with satisfactorily by the company's own complaints procedure you can send your complaint to the Financial Services Ombudsman within six months of the final decision by the company concerned. Even charities, trusts and small businesses (if they have an annual turnover of less than £1 million) can lodge complaints. The Ombudsman's staff will look into the matter, if necessary ordering the firm to produce all the inter-office memos and files relating to the case (failure to comply is tantamount to contempt of court).[209] If some settlement cannot be arrived at, a formal adjudication will be made by the Ombudsman and his or her decisions are binding on the firm in question up to the amount of £100,000.

There can be no recourse against any of the Ombudsman's decisions to the courts, but legal rights are otherwise unaffected by the scheme. The

---

[207] www.financial-ombudsman.org.uk. There is no one person acting as the Financial Services Ombudsman, but rather a panel of ombudsmen.
[208] Financial Services and Markets Act 2000, s. 225 and Sch. 17.
[209] *Ibid.* ss. 231-2.

service is free and confidential - the Ombudsman will not publish the names of either complainants or the companies complained against. Nor does the Ombudsman have any say over what rules the financial firms *have* to follow in their activities: this is a matter for the regulating body, Financial Services Authority (see above).

The Financial Services Ombudsman manages to resolve about 40% of complaints informally at an early stage. Some 50% require a more formal investigation and report, with recommendations. The remaining 10% will need a final decision by the Ombudsman. Every year about 40% of these final decisions are in favour of the complainant. At present the service is dealing with a flood of complaints about the way endowment mortgages were sold to customers.

There also exists an Independent Housing Ombudsman Service,[210] an Ombudsman for Estate Agents[211] and a Pensions Ombudsman.[212] The last of these deals with complaints about the way pension schemes are run, while complaints about the marketing of such schemes are dealt with by the Financial Services Ombudsman. For complaints about the Revenue and Customs there is an official called an Adjudicator,[213] based in London. He or she looks into allegations of excessive delay, mistakes, discourtesy of staff and the use of discretion, but does not examine issues of law or tax liability.

The Northern Ireland Certification Office

The role of the Northern Ireland Certification Office[214] is to supervise the activities of trade unions and employers' associations.[215] He or she receives the annual financial returns of these organisations and deals with trade union members' complaints about political funds, amalgamations and elections. The Office reimburses unions for certain costs incurred in conducting secret ballots. Decisions of the Certification Office can be appealed to the High Court and from there

---

[210] www.ihos.org.uk.
[211] www.oea.co.uk.
[212] www.pensions-ombudsman.org.uk. Decisions of the Pensions Ombudsman can be appealed to the Court of Appeal. For a Northern Irish example, see *Ewing* v *Trustees of Stockham Valve Ltd. Staff Retirement Benefits Scheme* [2000] 9 BNIL 50.
[213] www.adjudicatorsoffice.gov.uk.
[214] www.nicertoffice.com. The website carries the Office's annual reports, its hearing procedures and its decisions and orders..
[215] See the Employment Relations (NI) Order 1999, art. 28 and Sch. 6, amending the Industrial Relations (NI) Order 1992.

to the Court of Appeal. At the end of 2002 the total membership of trade unions with headquarters in Northern Ireland was 46,752 (more than 40,000 of these were in the Northern Ireland Public Service Alliance) and there were 14,662 members in Northern Ireland of unions based in the Republic of Ireland (including 7,500 in the Irish National Teachers' Organisation). There were also 64,906 members in Northern Ireland of unions with headquarters in Great Britain. At the time of writing the Certification Officer was Mr Roy Gamble.

Voluntary bodies

Of the purely voluntary organisations which act as watchdog bodies for all consumers, the best known are probably the Consumers' Association and the National Federation of Consumer Groups. Both of these have members, although no groups, in Northern Ireland. The former publishes *Which?*, the magazine providing information about the range of products and services available to consumers. The National Federation of Consumer Groups is a body representing groups of consumers as well as individuals throughout the United Kingdom; it too provides information to its members concerning all aspects of consumer affairs.

Many private bodies exist to help consumers in relation to particular industries or professions. Trade associations, such as those for jewellers or manufacturers of electrical appliances, often run their own complaints machinery. The insurance industry, eager to polish up its tarnished image, has established an Insurance Ombudsman Bureau, described below. The Press Complaints Commission[216] can deal with complaints about newspaper articles, including those printed by local and provincial newspapers in Northern Ireland, although someone who complains to it must give a written undertaking that he or she will not begin a legal action against the newspaper at some later date, and the Commission is powerless to award any effective remedy to the complainant. Complaints about advertisements in newspapers, on television or at the cinema can be made to the Advertising Standards Authority,[217] while OFCOM (see below) now handles complaints about the content of television and radio programmes. Again, however, neither of these bodies can grant remedies to complainants beyond

---

[216] www.pcc.org.uk.
[217] www.asa.org.uk.

condemning what was done, although their pronouncements should help to ensure that the same sort of conduct does not occur in future.

9.14 LAW REFORM BODIES[218]

As explained in Chapters 1 and 2, the two main sources of law in Northern Ireland are legislation and case law. Case law is obviously an unsatisfactory medium for making changes to the law because it comes into being only when persons choose to take particular disputes to court, and judges have neither the time nor the authority to expound on parts of the law which are not the precise subject of the litigation before them. Legislation is therefore the preferred medium for law reform and to help Parliament and the Government to design new legislation there exist various law reform agencies.

The Office of Law Reform[219]

The most important such body for Northern Ireland is the Office of Law Reform (OLR). This was originally constituted in 1965 as a separate branch of the Office of Legislative Counsel in Northern Ireland, that also being the year when the Law Commissions for England and Scotland, described below, were established. The OLR's remit at that time was to consider matters within the legislative powers of the Stormont Parliament, while bodies such as the English Law Commission retained power to consider matters falling outside Stormont's legislative capacity. The OLR initiated a survey of land law in Northern Ireland, and during its first five years was instrumental in having legislation enacted on, amongst other things, theft,[220] compensation for criminal injuries, preliminary enquiries in committal proceedings, misrepresentations, the age of majority and the enforcement of judgments.

During the short existence of the first Northern Ireland Assembly in 1974, the OLR in effect became a separate department of the Executive, with a Minister at its head (Sir Oliver Napier). Its remit was confined to reform of the civil law, criminal law being the responsibility of the Northern Ireland Office. Since the Assembly's demise. the OLR has functioned as a branch of what is now the Department of Finance and Personnel in the Northern Ireland Office. It

---

[218] See generally M. Zander, *The Law-Making Process* (6th ed., 2004), Chap. 9.
[219] www.olrni.gov.uk.
[220] Theft Act (NI) 1969.

has a director (Mrs Ethne Harkness) and eight other permanent members of staff. From time to time it engages the assistance of consultants who have expertise in specific fields.

The OLR no longer publishes regular reports on its activities, but its role is to consider what changes should be made in any part of the law on devolved matters in Northern Ireland. It has so far worked mainly in the areas of family law, property law, trust law, the law on mental incapacity, landlord and tenant law, contract and tort law and private international law. The province is still a separate legal jurisdiction, but whenever changes are under consideration for the law in England and Wales, thought is always given as to whether similar changes should be made in Northern Ireland. The OLR therefore keeps a close eye on the reports produced by other law reform bodies such as the English Law Commission. It also looks at suggestions for reform emanating from other common law jurisdictions, especially Canada, Australia and Ireland. It sometimes reacts as well to proposals for reform put forward by pressure groups or dissatisfied individuals: the Law Society, for instance, has a parliamentary and law reform committee, which sometimes submits ideas for change.

The OLR must inevitably work closely with the Office of the Legislative Counsel, commenting on draft legislation and making specific recommendations for new legislation. It is also involved in preparing consolidating Orders in Council, that is, Orders which bring together in one enactment the various provisions already relating to a certain topic without making any changes in the substance of the law. Recently the OLR was instrumental in securing law reform on domestic violence and it has since reviewed the legislation in question.[221] It also sponsored important research on divorce law,[222] resulting in the Family Law (Divorce etc.) Bill (NI), a piece of legislation which was under debate whenever the Northern Ireland Assembly was suspended in October 2002 but which has still not been enacted.

In 2003 the OLR consulted on new rights for transsexual people and on partnerships between same-sex couples (in each case because reforms on these topics were already in the pipeline for England and Wales through the Gender Recognition Bill and the Civil Partnership Bill. In

---

[221] The Family Homes and Domestic Violence (NI) Order 1998 was amended by the Law Reform (Miscellaneous Provisions) Order (NI) 2005.

[222] C. Archbold, C. White, P. McKee, L. Spence, B. Murtagh and M. McWilliams, *Divorce in Northern Ireland: Unravelling the System* (2000).

2001 it issued a consultation paper on physical punishment in the home and two-and-a-half years later, in 2004, it issued a paper analysing the responses to the consultation paper. On the basis of the majority views expressed it seems that the Government is reluctant to press ahead with reforms in this area

The Law Reform Advisory Committee for Northern Ireland[223]

The absence of an independent law reform body specifically for Northern Ireland was widely lamented for many years. In April 1989, however, the Government appointed a non-statutory Law Reform Advisory Committee for Northern Ireland, under the chairmanship of Mr Justice Carswell and with up to eight other members each appointed for three years and serving part-time. The Committee's secretary is provided by the Office of Law Reform. The current chairperson is Mr Justice Morgan.

The Law Reform Advisory Committee's remit is to scrutinise the civil law of Northern Ireland, except for those matters which are "excepted" or "reserved" under the Northern Ireland Constitution Act 1973 (see Chap. 1.2), and to put forward proposals for reform. It obtained approval for its First Programme of Law Reform in 1990, on which it is still working. It must also consider any aspect of the civil law referred to it by the Secretary of State, one such referral, in January 1998, being the law on marriage law (on which a report was published in December 2000). Responsibility for considering reforms to the criminal law remains with the Northern Ireland Office.

To date the Law Reform Advisory Committee has undertaken work on matters such as the law relating to business tenancies, evidence in civil proceedings, legal actions arising out of insidious diseases such as asbestosis, injuries on unadopted roads, defective premises, the enforcement of contracts by third parties, matrimonial property law, unincorporated associations and the rules relating to unsealed deeds (which are called "escrows").[224] It has published several discussion papers and considered many reports issued by the Law Commission for England and Wales. The Committee's work paved the way for the Business Tenancies (NI) Order 1996, for the Civil Evidence (NI) Order 1997 and for part of the Law Reform (Miscellaneous Proceedings) (NI)

---

[223] www.olrni.gov.uk/advisory_committee.
[224] See the Committee's *14th Annual Report* (covering 2003).

Order 2005. It is currently working on topics concerning leases of land and inheritance law. Copies of its annual reports can be obtained from the Committee's secretary (see Appendix 1 for an address).

The Law Commission of England and Wales[225]

Of the English law reform agencies which may have some impact on the law in Northern Ireland, by far the most important is the Law Commission, created under the Law Commissions Act 1965. This has offices in London and is chaired by a High Court judge (currently Mr Justice Toulson), who works with four full-time Commissioners appointed by the Lord Chancellor. It runs at a cost of about £5.1 million per year. The first chairperson was Mr Justice Scarman, as he then was. He helped to give the institution a high profile right from the start.

The Law Commission considers topics referred to it by the Department for Constitutional Affairs or adjudged by itself to require attention. At any one time it is engaged on about 20 different projects of law reform. Although the 1965 Act requires the Commission to keep "all the law" under review, it focuses mainly on trust and property law, criminal law, contract and tort law, commercial law, the law relating to "damages" (compensation) and landlord and tenant law. In March 2005 it published its Ninth Programme of Law Reform, which will be implemented over the following four years. This commits the Commission to working on, amongst other things, the rights of cohabiting people when their relationship ends, ways to ensure the more responsible letting of homes, a more coherent system for providing remedies against public authorities, insurance law, codification of the law on criminal evidence and a study of the best methods of scrutinising legislation after it has been enacted to see if it has had the effects intended.

In recent years the Law Commission has issued reports on, for example, partnership law,[226] defences to murder[227] and unfair contract

---

[225] www.lawcom.gov.uk. All of the Law Commission's consultation papers and reports are available on-line. The 1965 Act also created a Scottish Law Commission, which functions in a similar way to the Commission for England and Wales; it too has been very active and some reports are issued jointly by the two Commissions.

[226] Report 283 (2003).

[227] Report 290 (2004).

terms.[228] The Commission normally issues consultation papers for general discussion before publishing final reports. Recent examples are the consultation papers on the implications of the Human Rights Act 1998 for the law relating to bail and on the workability of the rules relating to company security interests.[229] The Commission's reports often include draft Bills designed to show how the proposed changes in the law might be enacted. Recent reports include those on claims for wrongful death, compensation for personal injuries, the duties of company directors, and the duties and powers of trustees. In 2000 it produced a particularly useful study of the way in which compensation has to date been awarded by the European Court of Human Rights for breaches of the European Convention on Human Rights, this being of great interest to UK judges as they implement the Human Rights Act 1998.

By the beginning of 2005, when the Commission was entering its 40th year, it had produced a total of 175 consultation papers and 291 reports (including its annual reports). Over 100 (*i.e.* more than two-thirds) of the Commission's law reform reports have been implemented by Parliament. Laws which have resulted from them include the Consumer Protection Act 1987, the Children Act 1989, the Computer Misuse Act 1990, the Family Law Act 1996, the Trustee Act 2000 and the Land Registration Act 2002. Increasingly, however, the Commission has to rely on Private Members' Bills or Private Peers' Bills to get its recommendations turned into law. The House of Lords now has special standing committee procedures to deal with Bills which are not contentious in a party political sense and this may facilitate the enactment of Law Commission Bills in the future. In addition to proposing substantive legal reforms, the Law Commission makes suggestions for tidying up the statute book. It drafts Statute Law (Repeals) Bills,[230] which since 1965 have repealed approximately 5,000 enactments.

---

[228] Report 292 (2005).

[229] Consultation Papers 157 and 176 respectively. The former led to Report 269 (2001), which concluded that the existing legislation could be applied in a way which was compatible with the European Convention. It made three recommendations for clarifying the law, which were implemented by the Criminal Justice Act 2003.

[230] Its 17th Report on Statute Law Revision was published in 2003 (Report 285) and this led to the Statute Law (Repeals) Act 2004. The next report is due around the end of 2008.

The Commission also makes recommendations for the codification of law, that is, putting all the relevant legislation on a certain topic into one single Act. It was responsible, for example, for the Income and Corporation Taxes Act 1988 which, at over 1,000 pages is still the largest statute ever enacted in the United Kingdom. It applies as much in Northern Ireland as in the rest of the United Kingdom. In 1989 the Commission produced a Criminal Code Report,[231] the culmination of its long-standing project to put into one code all of the important criminal law. Although this Report contained a draft Bill, no legislation has yet ensued. Supplementary reports aimed at codifying the criminal law have been published by the Law Commission, dealing, for instance, with offences against the person, intoxication, conspiracy to defraud, giving assistance or encouragement to crimes and corruption. The Government has said that it sees the enactment of a Criminal Code as an important part of its plans to modernise the criminal justice system and the Commission has therefore issued a further consultation paper on the topic in 2005. Family law has, to all intents and purposes, already been codified through a series of separate pieces of legislation in recent years.

A core of 15 civil service lawyers are employed at the Commission, together with four draftspersons serving on secondment from the Office of Parliamentary Counsel.[232] From time to time university academics and research assistants are also engaged. Three times a year the Commission issues a bulletin called *Law under Review*, which gives up-to-date summaries of *all* government law reform projects. This is available on-line at the Law Commission's website.[233]

The Law Commission has no direct responsibility for law reform in Northern Ireland, but many of the changes which it succeeds in getting introduced in England are later made in Northern Ireland as a matter of course. As noted above, the Office of Law Reform and the Law Reform Advisory Committee each pay particularly close attention to recommendations emanating from the Law Commission.

---

[231] Report 177.
[232] This is the name given to what in Northern Ireland is referred to as the Office of Legislative Counsel.
[233] www.lawcom.gov.uk/70.htm.

The Northern Ireland Law Commission

This body does not yet exist but, as a result of recommendations contained in the Criminal Justice Review, published in March 2000,[234] statutory provision for it has already been made.[235] It is to be chaired by a High Court judge and to have four other Commissioners, all appointed by the Secretary of State. The four Commissioners are to include a barrister, a solicitor and a teacher of law in a university. The Commission will be under a duty to keep under review the law of Northern Ireland with a view to its systematic development and reform, including through its simplification and modernisation, but in performing its duties the Commission will have to consult with the Law Commission of England and Wales, the Scottish Law Commission and the Law Reform Commission of Ireland. Annual reports must be laid before Parliament at Westminster.

At the time of writing the Government envisaged establishing the Northern Ireland Law Commission by April 2007, by when funding will be secured not just for its creation but also for its maintenance.[236] Criminal justice may possibly be devolved by that time, although the Criminal Justice Review stated that the Commission did not need to await the devolution of justice to the Northern Ireland Assembly. The Review also suggested that amongst the topics which the Law Commission should examine early in its life should be the disclosure provisions under the Criminal Procedure and Investigations Act 1996, plea-bargaining, domestic violence and the production of a comparative guide to criminal law and procedure in Northern Ireland and the Republic of Ireland for the benefit of legal practitioners in the two jurisdictions.

Other review bodies for the United Kingdom

Until recently two other committees sat from time to time in England to review particular aspects of the law which were referred to them. They were the Law Reform Committee and the Criminal Law Revision Committee. The former was appointed in 1952 as the successor to the Law Revision Committee, set up in 1934; it considered matters specifically assigned to it by the Lord Chancellor; its last report, in 1984, was on the topic of suing for latent damage. The Criminal Law

---

[234] Recommendations 244-255.
[235] Justice (NI) Act 2002, ss. 50-52 and Sch. 9.
[236] See the *Fourth Report of the Justice Oversight Commissioner* (July 2005), p. 168.

Revision Committee was created in 1959 and issued 17 reports, the last, on prostitution, in 1985. The Committee was accountable to the Home Secretary rather than the Lord Chancellor.

On occasions a body is appointed by the Government of the day to look into matters of specific or of general concern. The best example of the latter type are Royal Commissions, which conduct large-scale inquiries into affairs with wide-ranging social and legal implications. They are usually chaired by judges or high-ranking public servants. Recent Royal Commissions have included the Runciman Commission on Criminal Justice[237] and the Commission on Long Term Care for the Elderly.[238] The Royal Commission on Environmental Pollution is now a standing body which has already issued more than 25 reports since it was first established;[239] it gives advice to the Government on a range of environmental issues. The reports of these bodies extend to hundreds of pages and are based on considerable empirical research. An example of a less formal investigation is that known as the Civil Justice Review, conducted under the auspices of the Lord Chancellor's Department between 1985 and 1988; it looked into ways of improving the administration of the civil courts in England and Wales and was the stimulus for the appointment of a similar review group in Northern Ireland (see Chap. 6.1). A further example is the Report of the Independent Commission on the Voting System, which was compiled by Lord Jenkins and others and published in 1998.[240] Other government departments, or interdepartmental working parties, frequently issue green or white papers suggesting reforms,[241] and commissions of inquiry are sometimes set up under the Tribunals of Inquiry (Evidence) Act 1921, recently replaced by the Inquiries Act 2005 (see Chap. 8.1).

---

[237] Cmnd. 2263; 1993.
[238] Cmnd. 4192-I; 1999.
[239] www.rcep.org.uk.
[240] Cm.4090-1. See, too, the Pensions Commission (referred to in Chap. 8.2).
[241] See the Law Commission's regular bulletin called *Law under Review* (note 236 above.

APPENDIX 1

SAMPLE SOURCES OF LAW

(1) An Act of Parliament: the Theft Act (NI) 1969 (pages 477-482)

(2) An Order in Council: the Theft (NI) Order 1978 (pages 483-485)

(3) A statutory rule: Employer's Liability (Compulsory Insurance) (Amendment) Regulations (NI) 2004 (pages 486-489)

(4) A reported case: *Campbell* v *Armstrong and others* (pages 490-493)

(1) An Act of Parliament

Theft Act (Northern Ireland) 1969

1969 Chapter 16

An Act to revise the law of Northern Ireland as to theft and similar or associated offences; and for purposes connected therewith.
[10th July 1969]

Be it enacted by the Queen's most Excellent Majesty, and the Senate and the House of Commons of Northern Ireland in this present Parliament assembled, and by the authority of the same, as follows:—

Definition of "theft"

1.-(1) A person is guilty of theft if he dishonestly appropriates property belonging to another with the intention of permanently depriving the other of it; and "thief" and "steal" shall be construed accordingly. | Basic definition of theft

(2) It is immaterial whether the appropriation is made with a view to gain, or is made for the thief's own benefit.

(3) The five following sections shall have effect as regards the interpretation and operation of this section (and, except as otherwise provided by this Act, shall apply only for purposes of this section).

2.-(1) A person's appropriation of property belonging to another is not to be regarded as dishonest— | "Dishonestly"

(*a*) if he appropriates the property in the belief that he has in law the right to deprive the other of it, on behalf of himself or of a third person; or

(*b*) if he appropriates the property in the belief that he would have the other's consent if the other knew of the appropriation and the circumstances of it; or

(*c*) (except where the property came to him as trustee or personal representative) if he appropriates the property

in the belief that the person to whom the property belongs
cannot be discovered by taking reasonable steps.

(2) A person's appropriation of property belonging to
another may be dishonest notwithstanding that he is
willing to pay for the property.

3.-(1) Any assumption by a person of the rights of an
owner amounts to an appropriation, and this includes,
where he has come by the property innocently or not)
without stealing it, any later assumption of a right to it by
keeping or dealing with it as owner.

(2) Where property or a right or interest in property is
or purports to be transferred for value to a person acting in
good faith, no later assumption by him of rights which he
believed himself to be acquiring shall, by reason of any
defect in the transferor's title, amount to theft of the
property.

4.-(1) "Property" includes money and all other
property, real or personal, including things in action and
other intangible property.

(2) A person cannot steal land, 6r things forming part
of land and severed from it by him or by his directions,
except in the following cases, that is to say—

(*a*) when he is a trustee or personal representative, or
is authorised by power of attorney, or as liquidator of a
company, or otherwise, to sell or dispose of land belonging
to another, and he appropriates the land or anything
forming part of it by dealing with it in breach of the
confidence reposed in him; or

(*b*) when he is not in possession of the land and
appropriates anything forming part of the land by severing
it or causing it to be severed, or after it has been severed;
or

(*c*) when, being in possession of the land under a
tenancy, he appropriates the whole or part of any fixture or
structure let to be used with the land.

For purposes of this subsection, "land" does not
include incorporeal hereditainents; "tenancy" means a
tenancy for years or any less period and includes an
agreement for such a tenancy, but a person who, after the
end of a tenancy, remains in possession as statutory tenant
or otherwise is to be treated as having possession under the
tenancy, and "let" shall be construed accordingly.

(3) A person who picks mushrooms growing wild on
any land, or who picks flowers, fruit or foliage from a
plant growing wild on any land, does not (although not in
possession of the land) steal what he picks, unless he does
it for reward or for sale or other commercial purpose.

For purposes of this subsection, "mushroom" includes
any fungus, and "plant" includes any shrub or tree.

(4) Wild creatures, tamed or untamed, shall be
regarded as property; but a person cannot steal a wild
creature not tamed nor ordinarily kept in captivity, or the

"Appropriates"

"Property"

carcase of any such creature, unless either it has been reduced into possession by or on behalf of another person and possession of it has not since been lost or abandoned, or another person is in course of reducing it into possession.

(sections 5-29 omitted)

30.-(1) The following offences are hereby, abolished for all purposes not relating to offences committed before the commencement of this Act, that is to say—

    (*a*) any offence at common law of larceny, robbery, burglary, to offences. receiving stolen property, obtaining property by threats, extortion by colour of office or franchise, false accounting by public officers, concealment of treasure trove and, except as regards offences relating to the public revenue, cheating; and

    (*b*) any offence under an enactment mentioned in Part I of Schedule 3, to the extent to which the offence depends on any section or part of a section included in column 3 of that Schedule;

but so that the provisions set out in Schedule 1 (which respectively preserve with modifications the offence under the Larceny Act 1861 of taking or killing deer, the offence under the Summary Jurisdiction (Ireland) Act 1862 of unlawful possession of the carcase, hide or other part of a sheep and the offence under the Pawnbrokers Act (Ireland) 1788 of defacement, etc., before sale at auction, of name or marking on watch or plate) shall have effect as there set out.

(2) Except as regards offences committed before the commencement of this Act, and except in so far as the context otherwise requires,—

    (*a*) references in any enactment passed before this Act to an offence abolished by this Act shall, subject to any express amendment or repeal made by this Act, have effect as references to the corresponding offence under this Act; and, in any such enactment, the expression "receive" (when it relates to an offence of receiving) shall mean handle, and "receiver" shall be construed accordingly; and

    (*b*) without prejudice to paragraph (*a*), references in any enactment, whenever passed, to theft or stealing (including references to stolen goods), and references to robbery, blackmail, burglary, aggravated burglary or handling stolen goods, shall be construed in accordance with the provisions of this Act, including those of section 23.

31.-(1) The enactments mentioned in Schedule 2 shall have effect subject to the amendments there provided for.

(2) The enactments mentioned in Schedule 3 (which include in Part II certain enactments related to the subject matter of this Act but already obsolete or redundant apart from this Act) are hereby repealed to the extent specified in column 3 of that Schedule.

Marginal notes:

Effect on existing law and construction of references to offences

c.96
c.50

c.49

Miscellaneous and consequential amendments, and repeal

Supplementary

32.-(l) Sections 4 (1) and 5 (1) shall apply generally for purposes of this Act as they apply for purposes of section 1.

(2) For purposes of this Act—

(*a*) "enactment" means any statutory provision within the meaning of section 1(*f*) of the Interpretation Act (Northern Ireland) 1954;

(*b*) "gain" and "loss" are to be construed as extending only to gain or loss in money or other property, but as extending to any such gain or loss whether temporary or permanent; and—

(i) "gain" includes a gain by keeping what one has, as well as a gain by getting what one has not; and

(ii) "loss" includes a loss by not getting what one might get, as well as a loss by parting with what one has; and

(*c*) "goods" includes money and every other description of property except land, and includes things severed from the land by stealing.

Inter-pretation

c.33

33.-(1) This Act shall come into force on the 1st August 1969 and, save as otherwise provided by this Act, shall have effect only in relation to offences wholly or partly committed on or after that date.

(2) Sections 26 and 27 shall apply in relation to proceedings for an offence committed before the commencement of this Act as they would apply in relation to proceedings for a corresponding offence under this Act, and shall so apply in place of any corresponding enactment repealed by this Act.

(3) Subject to subsection (2), no repeal or amendment by this Act of any enactment relating to procedure or evidence, or to the jurisdiction or powers of any court, or to the effect of a conviction, shall affect the operation of the enactment in relation to offences committed before the commencement of this Act or to proceedings for any such offence.

Commence-ment and transitional provisions

34. This Act may be cited as the Theft Act (Northern Ireland) 1969.

Short title

SCHEDULES
SCHEDULE 1

OFFENCES OF TAKING, ETC., DEER, UNLAWFUL POSSESSION OF CARCASE, ETC., OF SHEEP AND DEFACEMENT, ETC., BEFORE SALE AT AUCTION, OF NAME OR MARKING ON WATCH OR PLATE

Section 30(1)

Taking or killing deer

1.-(l) A person who unlawfully takes or kills, or attempts to take or kill, any deer in inclosed land where deer are usually kept shall, on summary conviction, be liable to a fine not exceeding fifty pounds or, for an offence committed after a previous conviction for an offence under this paragraph, to imprisonment for a term not exceeding three months or to a fine not exceeding one hundred pounds, or to both.

(2) Any person may arrest without warrant anyone who is, or whom he, with reasonable cause, suspects to be, committing an offence under this paragraph.

Unlawful possession of carcase, etc., of sheep

2. Where the carcase of any sheep or lamb, or the head, skin or any part thereof, or any fleece thereof, is seized by any person pursuant to section 25(3), any person in whose possession or on whose premises any such carcase, head, skin, part or fleece is found may be arrested without warrant by any constable; and, if that person fails to satisfy a court of summary jurisdiction that he came lawfully by such carcase, head, skin, part or fleece, he shall, on summary conviction, be liable to imprisonment for a term not exceeding six months or to a fine not exceeding one hundred pounds, or to both.

Defacement, etc., before sale at auction, of name or marking on watch or plate

3. Any person who changes, alters or defaces, or causes to be changed, altered or defaced—

(*a*) any name engraved upon any watch as the maker or owner thereof, or the number of such watch, or the place where the same was made, or any coat of arms or crest thereon; or

(*b*) any name, cypher, crest or arms engraved upon any article or piece of family plate (whether gold or silver);

without the consent in writing of the owner thereof or of some person duly authorised to sell the same or to give such consent, shall, unless such watch or article or piece of family plate shall, before such change, alteration or defacement, have been sold at a public auction duly advertised, be deemed, until the contrary is proved, to have handled stolen goods knowing or believing them to be stolen goods.

(remainder of Schedule 1 omitted)

SCHEDULE 2

MISCELLANEOUS AND CONSEQUENTIAL AMENDMENTS

Enactments of United Kingdom Parliament

Act amended	Amendment
The Vagrancy Act 1824. 5 Geo. 4, c. 83.	In section 4 — (*a*) for paragraph (*i*) there shall be substituted the following— "(*i*)being armed with any dangerous or offensive weapon, or having upon him any instrument, with intent to commit any arrestable offence; or"; and (*b*) the word "implement", where last occurring, shall be omitted.

The Gaining Act 1845. 8 & 9 Vict., c. 109.	In section 17, for the words from "be deemed guilty" onwards there shall be substituted the words— "(*a*) on conviction on indictment, be liable to imprisonment for a term not exceeding two years; or (*b*) on summary conviction, be liable to imprisonment for a term not exceeding six months or to a fine not exceeding two hundred pounds, or to both.".
The Visiting Forces Act 1952 15 & 16 Geo. 6 & 1 Eliz. 2, c. 67.	In the Schedule— (*a*) in paragraph 1 (*a*), there shall be inserted after the word "buggery" the word ", robbery"; and (*b*) in paragraph 3, there shall be added at the end— "(*g*) the Theft Act (Northern Ireland) 1969, except section 8 (robbery)."

(remainder of Schedule 2 omitted)

SCHEDULE 3
REPEALS
PART I
PENAL ENACTMENTS SUPERSEDED BY THIS ACT
Enactments of United Kingdom Parliament

Session or Year and Chapter	Title or Short Title	Extent of Repeal
3 Edw. 1.	The Statutes of Westminster; the First.	Chapters 26 and 31.
50 Geo. 3, c. 59.	The Embezzlement by Collectors Act 1810.	The whole Act, so far as unrepealed.
7 Geo. 4, c. 16.	The Chelsea and Kilmainham Hospitals Act 1826.	Section 25. In section 34, the words from "and, if any pensioner" onwards, except the words from "such mark, stamp or brand" to "commissioners", where next occurring. Section 38.
20 & 21 Vict., c. 60.	The Irish Bankrupt and Insolvent Act 1857.	Section 379.

(remainder of Schedule 3 omitted)

(2) An Order in Council
1978 No. 1407 (N.I. 23)
NORTHERN IRELAND
The Theft (Northern Ireland) Order 1978

Made	*29th September 1978*
Laid before Parliament	*9th October 1978*
Coming into Operation	*30th November 1978*

ARRANGEMENT OF ORDER

Article
1. Title and commencement.
2. Interpretation.
3. Obtaining services by deception.
4. Evasion of liability by deception.
5. Making off without payment.
6. Punishments.
7. Supplementary.

At the Court at Balmoral, the 29th day of September 1978

Present,
The Queen's Most Excellent Majesty in Council

Whereas this Order in Council operates only so as to make for Northern Ireland provision corresponding to the Theft Act 1978 **[1]**:

Now, therefore, Her Majesty, in exercise of the powers conferred by paragraph 1 of Schedule 1 to the Northern Ireland Act 1974 **[2]** (as modified by section 6 of the Theft Act. 1978) and of all other powers enabling Her in that behalf, is pleased, by and with the advice of Her Privy Council, to order, and it is hereby ordered, as follows:-

Title and commencement

1. This Order may be cited as the Theft (Northern Ireland) Order 1978 and shall come into operation on the expiration of two months after the day which it is made.

Interpretation

2. The Interpretation Act (Northern Ireland) 1954 **[3]**) shall apply to Article and the following provisions of this Order as it applies to a Measure of the Northern Ireland Assembly

Obtaining services by deception

3.-(l) A person who by any deception dishonestly obtains services from another shall be guilty of an offence.

(2) It is an obtaining of services where the other is induced to confer a benefit by doing some act, or causing or permitting some act to be done, on the understanding that the benefit has been or will be paid for.

Evasion of liability by deception

4.-(1) Subject to paragraph (2), where a person by any deception—

(*a*) dishonestly secures the remission of the whole or part of any existing liability to make a payment, whether his own liability or another's; or

(*b*) with intent to make permanent default in whole or in part on any existing liability to make a payment, or with intent to let another do so, dishonestly induces the creditor or any person claiming payment on behalf of the creditor to wait for payment (whether or not the due date for payment is deferred) or to forgo payment; or

(*c*) dishonestly obtains any exemption from or abatement of liability to make a payment;

he shall be guilty of an offence.

(2) For purposes of this Article "liability" means legally enforceable liability; and paragraph (1) shall not apply in relation to a liability that has not been accepted or established to pay compensation for a wrongful act or omission.

(3) For purposes of paragraph (1)(*b*) a person induced to take in payment, a cheque or other security for money by way of conditional satisfaction of a pre-existing liability is to be treated not as being paid but as being induced to wait for payment.

(4) For purposes of paragraph (1)(*c*) "obtains" includes obtaining for another or enabling another to obtain.

Making off without payment

5.-(1) Subject to paragraph (3), a person who, knowing that payment on the spot for any goods supplied or service done is required or expected from him, dishonestly makes off without having paid as required or expected and with intent to avoid payment of the amount due shall be guilty of an offence.

(2) For purposes of this Article "payment on the spot" includes payment at the time of collecting goods on which work has been done or in respect of which service has been provided.

(3) Paragraph (1) shall not apply where the supply of the goods or the doing of the service is contrary to law, or where the service done is such that payment is not legally enforceable.

(4) Any person may arrest without warrant anyone who is, or whom be, with reasonable cause, suspects to be, committing or attempting to commit an offence under this Article.

Punishments

6.-(1) Offences under this Order shall be punishable either on conviction on indictment or on summary conviction.

(2) A person convicted on indictment shall be liable—

(*a*) for an offence under Article 3 or Article 4, to imprisonment for a term not exceeding five years; and

(*b*) for an offence under Article 5, to imprisonment for a term not exceeding two years.

(3) A person convicted summarily of any offence under this Order shall be liable to a fine not exceeding £1,000 or to imprisonment for a term not exceeding six months or to both.

Supplementary

7.-(l) For purposes of Articles 3 and 4 "deception" has the same meaning as in section 15 of the Theft Act (Northern Ireland) 1969 **[4]** ("the Act of 1969"), that it to say, it means any deception (whether deliberate or reckless) by words or conduct as to fact or as to law, including a deception as to the present intentions of the person using the deception or any other person.

(2) Sections 29(1) (effect on civil proceedings) and 32 (interpretation) of the Act of 1969, so far as they are applicable in relation to this Order, shall apply as they apply in relation to that Act.

N. In the Visiting Forces Act 1952 **[5]**, in paragraph 3 of the Schedule which defines for Northern Ireland (as well as for England and Wales) "offence against property" for purposes of the exclusion in certain cases of the jurisdiction of United Kingdom courts) there shall be added at the end of sub paragraph (*j*) (which refers to offences punishable under the Theft Act 1978) the words "and the Theft (Northern Ireland) Order 1978".

(4) In the Act of 1969 section 16(2)(*a*) is hereby repealed.

N. E. Leigh,
Clerk of the Privy Council.

EXPLANATORY NOTE
(*This Note is not part of the Order.*)

This Order makes for Northern Ireland provision corresponding to the Theft Act 1978 by replacing section 16(2)(*a*) of the Theft Act (Northern Ireland) 1969 (obtaining pecuniary advantage by deception in certain cases) with other provision against fraudulent conduct.

[1] 1978 c.31
[2] 1974 c.28
[3] 1954 c.33 (NI)
[4] 1969 c.16 (NI)
[5] 1952 c.67

(3) A statutory rule

2004 No. 449

EMPLOYER'S LIABILITY

Employer's Liability (Compulsory Insurance) (Amendment) Regulations (Northern Ireland) 2004

Made 25th *October 2004*
Coming into operation 29th *November 2004*

The Department of Enterprise, Trade and Investment[1], in exercise of the powers conferred by Article 7(c) and 10(1) of the Employer's Liability (Defective Equipment and Compulsory Insurance) (Northern Ireland) Order 1972[2] and now vested in it[3] and of all other powers enabling it in that behalf, hereby makes the following Regulations:

Citation and commencement
1. These Regulations may be cited as the Employer's Liability (Compulsory Insurance) (Amendment) Regulations (Northern Ireland) 2004 and shall come into operation on 29th November 2004.

Amendment of the Employer's Liability (Compulsory Insurance) Regulations (Northern Ireland) 1999
2. For Schedule 2 to the Employer's Liability (Compulsory Insurance) Regulations (Northern Ireland) 1999[4] there shall be substituted the Schedule set out in the Schedule to these Regulations.

Revocation
3. The Employer's Liability (Compulsory Insurance) Exemption (Amendment) Regulations (Northern Ireland) 2003[5] are hereby revoked.

Sealed with the Official Seal of the Department of Enterprise, Trade and Investment on 25th October 2004.

L.S.

Michael J. Bohill
A senior officer of the Department of Enterprise, Trade and Investment

SCHEDULE

Regulation 2

SCHEDULE TO BE SUBSTITUTED FOR SCHEDULE 2 TO THE EMPLOYER'S LIABILITY (COMPULSORY INSURANCE) REGULATIONS (NORTHERN IRELAND) 1999

"SCHEDULE 2

Regulation 9

EMPLOYERS EXEMPTED FROM INSURANCE

1. Any district council.

2. Any Education and Library Board established under Article 3 of the Education and Libraries (Northern Ireland) Order 1986[6].

3. Any employer to the extent that he is required by paragraph (1) of Article 5 of the 1972 Order to insure and maintain insurance against liability for personal injury suffered by his employee when the employee is -

(i) carried in or upon a motor vehicle; or

(ii) entering or getting on to, or alighting from, a motor vehicle,

in the circumstances specified in that paragraph and where that personal injury is caused by, or arises out of, the use by the employer of a motor vehicle on a road; and the expressions "road" and "motor vehicle" have the same meanings as in Part I of the Road Traffic (Northern Ireland) Order 1995[7].

4. Any Health and Social Services Board established under Article 16 of the Health and Personal Social Services (Northern Ireland) Order 1972[8].

5. Any subsidiary of any such body as is mentioned in Article 7(b) of the 1972 Order (which exempts any body corporate established by or under any statutory provision for the carrying on of any industry or part of an industry, or of any undertaking, under public ownership or control) and any company of which two or more such bodies are members and which would, if these bodies were a single body corporate, be a subsidiary of that body corporate.

6. Economic Research Institute of Northern Ireland Limited.

7. General Consumer Council for Northern Ireland.

8. Ilex Urban Regeneration Company Limited.

9. Invest Northern Ireland.

10. Northern Ireland Medical and Dental Training Agency.

11. Northern Ireland Tourist Board.

12. Planning Appeals Commission.

13. Strategic Investment Board.

14. The Fire Authority for Northern Ireland.

15. The Guardian Ad Litem Special Agency.

16. The Local Government Staff Commission for Northern Ireland.

17. The Mental Health Commission for Northern Ireland.

18. The Northern Ireland Blood Transfusion Service Special Agency.

19. The Northern Ireland Central Services Agency.

20. The Northern Ireland Council for the Curriculum, Examinations and Assessment.

21. The Northern Ireland Local Government Officers' Superannuation Committee.

22. The Northern Ireland Practice and Education Council For Nursing and Midwifery.

23. The Northern Ireland Social Care Council.

24. The Regional Medical Physics Agency.

25. The Staffs Council for Health and Personal Social Services."

EXPLANATORY NOTE

(This note is not part of the Regulations.)

These Regulations amend the Employer's Liability (Compulsory Insurance) Regulations (Northern Ireland) 1999 ("the 1999 Regulations"). The 1999 Regulations specify employers who are exempted from the requirements of Part III of the Employer's Liability (Defective Equipment and Compulsory Insurance) (Northern Ireland) Order 1972 ("the 1972 Order") to insure and maintain insurance against liability for personal injury suffered by their employees and arising out of and in the course of their employment. The specified employers are certain public bodies; the specified classes of employer include any employer to the extent that he is required to insure under a compulsory motor insurance scheme by virtue of the fact that his employees are carried on, or are alighting from or are entering into, a motor vehicle. The exemptions specified in the 1999 Regulations are additional to those contained in Article 7 of the 1972 Order.

These Regulations remove The National Board for Nursing, Midwifery and Health Visiting for Northern Ireland and the Northern Ireland Council for Postgraduate Medical and Dental Education from, and add the following bodies to, the exemptions specified in the 1999 Regulations, that is to say –

Economic Research Institute of Northern Ireland Limited;
General Consumer Council for Northern Ireland;
Ilex Urban Regeneration Company Limited;
Invest Northern Ireland;
Northern Ireland Medical and Dental Training Agency;
Northern Ireland Tourist Board;
Strategic Investment Board; and
The Northern Ireland Practice and Education Council for Nursing and Midwifery.

Notes:

[1] Formerly the Department of Economic Development; *see* S.I. 1982/846 (N.I. 11), Article 3 and S.I. 1999/283 (N.I. 1) Article 3(5)

[2] S.I. 1972/963 (N.I. 6)
[3] By S.R. & O. (N.I.) 1973 No. 504, Article 6 and Schedule 3
[4] S.R. 1999 No. 448
[5] S.R. 2003 No. 426
[6] S.I. 1986/594 (N.I. 3); Article 3 was amended by S.I. 1989/2406 (N.I. 20)
[7] S.I. 1995/2994 (N.I. 18)
[8] S.I. 1972/1265 (N.I. 14)

(4) A reported case

CAMPBELL v. ARMSTRONG AND OTHERS[1]

Highway-Negligence-Vehicle struck large stones on verge of road - Whether highway out of repair - Whether duty of care arises - Road (Liability of Road Authorities for Neglect) Act (Northern Ireland) 1966 (c.11),ss.1,2.

The plaintiff's son was killed while a passenger in a motor car driven by the defendant which crashed when it struck a large stone or stones which had fallen on to the grass verge bordering the road from a stone wall which marched alongside it. The defendant joined the Department of the Environment, the road authority as a third party. In a preliminary issue to determine if the Department is liable to indemnify the defendant against the plaintiffs claim or make contribution to it,

Held that a highway is not out of repair because stones lie on its grass verge and the operation of removing such stones does not amount to repairing it. Accordingly there is no liability on the roads authority arising from the Roads (Liability of Road Authorities for Neglect) Act (Northern Ireland) 1966. There is also no liability on the roads authority under the neighbour principle in *Donoghue* v. *Stevenson* [19321 A.C.562 as that principle does not extend the liability of a highway authority for non-feasance beyond the 1966 Act.

The following cases are referred to in the judgment:

Donoghue v. *Stevenson* [1932] A.C. 562

Forsythe v. *Evans* [1980] N.I. 230

Haydon v. *Kent County Council* [1978] Q.B. 343; [1978] 2 W.L.R. 485; [1978] 2 All E.R.97

Hedley Byrne and Co. v. *Heller & Partners* [1964] A.C. 465; [1963] 3 W.L.R. 101; [1963] 2 All E.R.575

Hereford and Worcester County Council v. *Newsman* [1975] 1 W.L.R. 901; [1975] 2 All E.R. 673

Home Office v. *Dorset Yacht Co.* [1970] A.C. 1004; [1970] 2 W.L.R. 1140; [1970] 2 All E.R. 294

Lagan v. *Department of the Environment* [1978] N.I. 120

PRELIMINARY ISSUE. The facts appear sufficiently from the judgment of Kelly J.

R.L. McCartney Q.C. and *M.A. Morrow* for the defendant *R D. Carswell Q.C.* and *B.F. Kerr* for the Department of the Environment.

KELLY J. The pleadings in this action raise a point of law for determination as a preliminary issue. It concerns the civil liability of a highway authority for injury loss and damage caused by obstructions on the grass verge of a road maintainable by the authority.

---

[1] In the Queen's Bench Division before Kelly J; January 22, March 13, 1981

The facts out of which the action arises can be stated shortly. On the 21 October 1977 the plaintiffs son was killed while a passenger in a motor car driven by the defendant which crashed when overtaking another car on a straight stretch of the Aughnacloy-Castlecaulfield road, County Tyrone. While overtaking the other car, part of the defendant's vehicle went on to the grass verge bordering the road and one or more of its wheels struck there a large stone or stones which had fallen on to the verge from a stone wall which marched alongside it.

The plaintiff as administratrix of her son's estate sues the defendant for damages under the Fatal Accident Order 1976 (sic) and the Law Reform (Miscellaneous Provisions) Act (Northern Ireland) 1937 alleging negligent driving. The defendant denies negligence and brings in as third parties to the action claiming indemnity or contribution against them, the Department of the Environment for Northern Ireland (hereinafter called "the Department") who is admittedly the road authority responsible for maintaining the roadway and grass verge in question and William Montgomery Buchanan who is the owner of the stone wall. This preliminary issue does not, however, concern the second-named third party.

It is the Department who disputes in law the defendant's claim that being the body responsible for the inspection maintenance repair and control of the grass verge and negligent in that duty in failing to keep it free of the stone or stones the Department is liable to indemnify the defendant against the plaintiffs claim or make contribution to it. The submission of the Department is that they cannot be made liable in damages.

I consider first their possible liability in damages for a breach of statutory duty. In this, one is drawn at once to the statutory duty of a highway authority in respect of obstructions on its roads contained in section 2 of the Roads (Liability of Road Authorities for Neglect) Act (Northern Ireland) 1966 which reads:

> "2. (1) If an obstruction occurs in a road from accumulation of snow or from the falling down of banks on the side of the road, or from any other cause, the road authority by whom the road is maintainable shall remove the obstruction.
>
> If a road authority fail to remove an obstruction which it is their duty under this section to remove, a court of summary jurisdiction may, on a complaint made by any person, by order require the authority to remove the obstruction within such period (not being less than twenty-four hours) from the making of the order as the Court thinks reasonable having regard to all the circumstances of the case."

But anyone who has suffered loss and damage from a breach of this section is stopped from embarking on a civil claim for damages by the clear prohibition of sub-section 6 of the section, which states;

> "(6) it is hereby declared that nothing in this section shall operate to confer on any person a right of action in tort against a road authority for failing to carry out any duty imposed on them under this section."

A civil remedy in damages against a road authority is of course earlier given by section 1 of the same Act, which states:

> "1. (1) Any rule of law which operates to exempt a road authority from liability for non-repair of roads is hereby abrogated."

The Legal System of Northern Ireland

but the language of section 1 has been held to confine the remedy to cases of strict non-repair of the highway (see Lagan v. Department of Environment [1978] N.I. 120, 124). Following this, it seems to me that it cannot be seriously argued that a highway is out of repair because stones lie on its grass verge or that the operation of removing a stone or stones from it amounts to repairing it.

This view is reinforced by dicta of Cairns L.J. in *Hereford and Worcester County Council* v. *Newman* [1975] 1 W.L.R. 901 and of Lord Denning M.R. in *Haydon* v. *Kent County Council* [1978] 2 W.L.R. 485. Cairns L J. said at page 910:

> "In relation to a highway I am of opinion that in ordinary speech nobody would speak of the mere removal of an obstruction from the highway as being in itself a repair. I respectfully agree with Lord Widgery C.J. in saying that if a builder chose to dump tons of rubble on a footpath thus rendering it impassable, it would be an abuse of language to say that the highway authority had allowed the footpath to become out of repair.

> It is I think striking that in all the Highway Acts from 1835 to 1959 repair and removal of obstructions are separately dealt with...

> I consider that a highway can only be said to be out of repair if the surface of it is defective or disturbed in some way."

Lord Denning M.R. in *Haydon's* case said at page 491:

> "'Repair' means making good defects in the surface of the highway itself ..."

and at page 492:

> "An 'obstruction' to a highway occurs when it is rendered impassable, or more difficult to pass along it by reason of some physical obstacle. It may be obstructed without it being out of repair at all. If a tree falls across a road, it may not injure the surface at all, it may even straddle it without touching the surface, the road is then 'obstructed' but it is not out of repair....

> 'Maintain' does not, however, include the removal of obstructions, except when the obstruction damages the surfaces of the highway and makes it necessary to remove the obstruction so as to execute the repairs."

The Act of 1966 does not therefore by any of its provisions give a civil remedy in the circumstances of this case and that appears to exhaust any possible remedy under statute.

Has the Department also immunity from civil liability at common law? It seems to me it has. Misfeasance cannot arise on the facts, but the defendant sought to apply the neighbour principle of *Donoghue* v. *Stevenson* [1932] A.C. 562 as a means of relief, encouraged no doubt by such well-known dicta as:

> "The criterion of judgment must adjust and adapt itself to the changing circumstances of life; the categories of negligence are never closed." (Lord MacMillan in *Donoghue* v. *Stevenson* (supra) at page 619) and

"English law is wide enough to embrace any new category or proposition that exemplifies the principle of proximity." (Lord Devlin in *Hedley Byrne & Co. Ltd.* v. *Heller & Partners Ltd.* 119641 A.C. 465, at page 531).

But I think it is wise before any new application or expansion of the neighbour principle is attempted to heed the caution expressed by Lord Diplock in *Home Office* v. *Dorset Yacht Co. Ltd.* [1970] A.C. 1004. At page 1060 in a reference to Lord Atkin's neighbour principle, he said:

"Used as a guide to characteristics which will be found to exist in conduct and relationships which give rise to a legal duty of care this aphorism marks a milestone in the modern development of the law of negligence. But misused as a universal, it is manifestly false.

The branch of English law which deals with civil wrongs abounds with instances of acts and more particularly, of omissions which give rise to no legal liability in the doer or omitter for loss and damage sustained by others as a consequence of the act of omission, however reasonably or probably that loss or damage might have anticipated."

Immunity from civil liability for non-repair of highways continued after the decision in *Donoghue* v. *Stevenson* in 1932. There is no reported decision that I know of, thereafter, to show that the neighbour principle was successfully applied in a case of non- repair, up to the time when statutory exemption from liability for non-repair was cancelled in England by the Highways (Miscellaneous Provisions) Act 1961 and by the Act of 1966 here. And since the passing of the 1966 Act, despite the comparatively confined meanings given to "non-repair" and "failure to maintain" in section 1 (see *Logan* v. *Department of the Environment* (supra)) no reported case has applied the neighbour principle to extend the liability of a highway authority for non-feasance outside that section. Therefore the acts of omission on the part of a highway authority would seem not to give rise to a cause of action for damages if they fail outside the highway authority's duty under section 1 on the principle, presumably, that where there is no duty to act, an omission to act gives no remedy.

And there may be sound reasons of public policy for refusing to expand the statutory duty of a road authority outside strict repair. I have stated possible considerations in a judgment in *Forsythe* v. *Evans, Charges Brand & Co. Ltd., v. The Department of the Environment* [1980] N.I. 230 (an issue concerning the civil liability of a road authority in respect of injury caused by icy roads) some of which I think are in point here. In the instant case it seems to me quite unreasonable that a duty of care should arise that obliges a road authority to inspect grass verges and free them from obstructions for the unimpeded passage of traffic, vehicular or pedestrian.

I hold that the defendant's statement of claim does not disclose a cause of action by the defendant against the Department. I give judgment for the first Third Party, the Department, against the defendant, with costs.

Order accordingly

Solicitors for the defendant: *Wilson & Simms*
Solicitors for the Department of the Environment: *Crown Solicitor*

APPENDIX 2

USEFUL ADDRESSES

Advice Centres (selected)

Ardoyne Association Advice
Centre
111 Etna Drive
Belfast BT14 7NN
Tel: 028 9071 5165

Ashgrove Community Centre
Garvaghy Road
Portadown
Co. Armagh BT62 1ED
Tel: 028 3833 1650

Ballybeen Women's Group
34 Ballybeen Square
Belfast BT16 2QE
Tel: 028 9048 1632

Ballynafeigh Community
Development Association
283 Ormeau Road
Belfast BT7 3GG
Tel: 028 9049 1161

Belfast Consumer Advice Centre
6 Callender Street
Belfast BT1 5BN
Tel: 028 9032 8260

Belfast Housing Aid
92 Victoria Street
Belfast BT1 3GN
Tel: 028 90245640

Childline Northern Ireland
PO Box 1111
Belfast BT1 2DD
Freephone: 0800 1111

Craigavon Independent Advice
Centre
Moylin House
21 Legahory Centre
Lurgan
Co. Armagh BT65 5BE
Tel: 028 3832 4945

East Belfast Independent Advice
Centre
85 Castlereagh Street
Belfast BT5 4NF
Tel: 028 9096 3003

Falls Community Council
275-277 Fall Road
Belfast BT12 6FD
Tel: 028 9020 2030

Highfield Community Advice
Centre
113 Highfield Drive
Belfast BT13 3RP
Tel: 028 9072 9916

Newry Welfare Rights Advice
Centre
28 Cornmarket
Newry
Co. Down BT35 8BG
Tel: 028 3026 7631

North Belfast Community Project
Enterprise House,
55-59 Adelaide Street
Belfast BT2 8FE
Tel: 028 9072 6014

Omagh Independent Advice
Centre
15 High Street
Omagh BT78 1BA
Tel: 028 8224 3252

Shankill Legal Advice Centre
Shankill Community Council
177 Shankill Road
Belfast BT13 1FD
Tel: 028 9032 5536

Upper Springfield Resource
Centre
Frank Cahill Building,
195 Whiterock Road,
Belfast BT12 7FW
Tel: 028 9058 5755

Other Agencies

Advertising Standards Authority
Mid City Place
71 High Holborn
London WCIV 6QT
Tel: 020 7492 2222

Advice[ni]
1 Rushfield Avenue
Belfast BT7 3FP
Tel: 028 9064 5919

Age Concern
3 Lower Crescent
Belfast BT7 1NR
Tel: 028 9024 5729

AIDS Helpline
7 James Street South
Belfast BT2 8DN
Tel: 0800 137 437

Amnesty International NI
397 Ormeau Road
Belfast BT7 3GP
Tel: 028 9064 3000

Assets Recovery Agency
Attorney General's Office
9 Buckingham Gate
London SW1E 6JP
Tel: 020 7271 2412

Bar Council of Northern Ireland
Bar Library
91 Chichester Street
Belfast BT1 3JQ
Tel: 028 9056 2349

British and Irish Ombudsman
Association
24 Paget Gardens
Chislehurst,
Kent BR7 5RX
Tel: 020 8467 7455

British-Irish Inter-Parliamentary
Body
7 Millbank
London SW1P 3JA
Tel: 020 7219 6800

Building Societies Commission
Victory House
30-34 Kingsway
London WC2B 6ES
Tel: 020 7663 5360

Carers Northern Ireland
58 Howard Street
Belfast BT
Tel: 028 9043 9843

Central Office of Industrial
Tribunals and the Fair
Employment Tribunal
Long Bridge House
Waring Street
Belfast BT1 2DY
Tel: 028 9032 7666

Central Services Agency
25-27 Adelaide Street
Belfast BT2 7FH
Tel: 028 9032 4431

Certification Officer for
Northern Ireland
10-12 Gordon Street
Belfast BT1 2LG
Tel: 028 9023 7773

Charity Commission for
England and Wales
St Alban's House
57-60 Haymarket
London SW1Y 4QX
Tel: 0870 333 0123

Child Care (NI)
216 Belmont Road
Belfast BT4 2AT
Tel: 028 9065 2713

Child Poverty Action Group
12 Queen Street
Derry / Londonderry BT48 7EG
Tel: 028 7126 7777

Children in Northern Ireland
216 Belmont Road
Belfast BT4 2AT
Tel: 028 9065 2713

Children's Law Centre
3rd floor, Philip House
123-137 York Street
Belfast BT15 1AB
Tel: 028 9024 5704

Chinese Welfare Association
133-135 University Street
Belfast BT7 1HP
Tel: 028 9028 8277

Citizens Advice Northern Ireland
11 Upper Crescent
Belfast BT7 1NT
Tel: 028 9023 1120
*(Addresses of local CABx are listed
in the telephone directory)*

Civic Forum Secretariat
11-13 Bloomfield Avenue
Belfast BT5 5HD
Tel: 028 9052 8841

Civil representatives (of the army):

BELFAST:
c/o PSNI Station
Woodburn
Stewartstown Road
Belfast BT11 9JQ
Tel: 028 9061 7700

Building 14A,
Girdwood Park
Belfast BT14 6BE
Tel: 028 9074 1474

PORTADOWN:
c/o PSNI Station,
Mahon Road
Portadown
Co. Armagh BT62 3EH
Tel: 028 3836 1460

OMAGH:
Lisanelly Barracks,
Omagh
Co. Tyrone BFPO 804
Tel: 0 28 8225 8661

BALLYKELLY:
Shackleton Barracks
Tel: 028 7772 1633

Coalition on Sexual Orientation
c/o The Rainbow Project
2-6 Union Street
Belfast BT1 2FJ
Tel: 028 9031 9030

Coiste na n-Iarchimí
10 Beechmount Avenue
Belfast BT12 7NA
Tel: 028 9020 0770

Commission of the European
Communities
Windsor House
9-15 Bedford Street
Belfast BT2 7EG
Tel: 028 9024 0708

Commission for Judicial
Appointments (England and
Wales)
7th floor, Millbank Tower
London SW1P 4RD
Tel: 020 7217 4470

Commission for Racial Equality (GB)
St.Dunstan's House
201-211 Borough High Street
London SE1 1GZ
Tel: 020 7939 0000

Commissioner for Judicial
Appointments
Headline Building
10-14 Victoria Street
Belfast BT1 3GG
Tel: 028 9072 8930

Committee on the
Administration of Justice
45-47 Donegall Street
Belfast BT1 2BR
Tel: 028 9096 1122

Community Relations Council
6 Murray Street
Belfast BT1 6DN
Tel: 028 9022 7500

Community Relations Council
Resource Centre
21 College Square East
Belfast BT1 6DE
Tel: 028 9022 7555

Community Safety Unit
4th floor, Millennium House
19-25 Great Victoria Street
Belfast BT2 7AQ
Tel: 028 9082 8555

Companies Registry
Waterfront Plaza
Laganbank Road
Belfast BT1 3LX
Tel: 0845 604 8888

Compensation Agency
Royston House
34 Upper Queen Street
Belfast BT1 6FX
Tel: 028 9024 9944

Competition Commission
Victoria House,
Southampton Row
London WCIB 4AD
Tel: 020 7271 0100

Consumers Association
2 Marylebone Road
London NWI 4DF
Tel: 084 5530 7400

Council on Tribunals
81 Chancery Lane
London WC2A 1BQ
Tel: 020 7855 5200

Court of Justice of the European
Communities (ECJ)
Boulevard Konrad Adenauer
L–2925 Luxembourg
Tel: 00 352 43 03 1

Court Funds Office
3rd Floor Bedford House
Bedford Street
Belfast BT2 7FD
Tel: 028 9072 8888

Court Service Headquarters
(GB)
5th floor, Clive House
Petty France
London SW1H 9HD
Tel: 020 7189 2000

Criminal Cases Review
Commission
Alpha Tower
Suffolk Street
Queensway
Birmingham B1 1TT
Tel: 0121 623 1800

Criminal Injuries Compensation
Appeals Panel
The Corn Exchange Building
31 Gordon Street
Belfast BT1 2LG
Tel: 028 9092 4400

Criminal Justice Inspectorate of
Northern Ireland
14 Great Victoria Street
Belfast BT2 7BA
Tel: 028 9025 8000

Criminal Records Bureau
(England and Wales)
Customer Services
PO Box 10
Liverpool L69 3EF
Tel: 0870 9090 811

Crown Prosecution Service
(England and Wales)
50 Ludgate Hill
London EC4M 7EX
Tel: 020 7796 8000

Crown Solicitor's Office
Royal Courts of Justice
Chichester Street
Belfast BT1 3JY
Tel: 028 9054 2555

CRUSE – Bereavement Care
Piney Ridge
Knockbracken Healthcare Park
Saintfield Road
Belfast BT8 8BH
Tel: 028 9079 2419

HM Customs and Excise
Northern Ireland Collection
Custom House
Custom Square
Belfast BT1 3ET
(National Advice Service
Tel: 0845 010 9000)

Departmental Solicitors Office
Victoria Hall
12 May Street
Belfast BT1 4NL
Tel: 028 9025 1251

Department of Agriculture and
Rural Development
Dundonald House
Upper Newtownards Road
Belfast BT4 3SB
Tel: 028 9052 0100

Department of Culture, Arts and
Leisure
Interpoint
20-24 York Street
Belfast BT15 1AQ
Tel: 028 9025 8825

Department of Education
Rathgael House
43 Balloo Road
Bangor BT19 7PR
Tel: 028 9127 9279

Department of Enterprise, Trade
and Investment
Netherleigh House
Massey Avenue
Belfast BT4 2JP
Tel: 028 9052 9900

Department of the Environment
Clarence Court
10-18 Adelaide Street
Belfast BT2 8GB
Tel: 028 9054 0540

Department of Finance and
Personnel
Rathgael House
43 Balloo Road
Bangor BT19 7NA
Tel: 028 9127 9279

Department of Health, Social
Services and Public Safety
Castle Buildings
Stormont estate
Belfast BT4 3SQ
Tel: 028 9052 0500

*(local social security offices are
listed in the current telephone
directory under "Social Security
Agency")*

Department of Employment and
Learning,
Adelaide House
39-49 Adelaide Street
Belfast BT2 8FD
Tel: 028 9025 7777

Department for Constitutional
Affairs
Selborne House
54-60 Victoria Street
London SW1E 6QW
Tel: 020 7210 8500

Department for Regional
Development
Clarence Court
10-18 Adelaide Street
Belfast BT2 8GB
Tel: 028 9054 0540

Department for Social
Development
Lighthouse Building
1 Cromac Place
Gasworks Business Park
Ormeau Road
Belfast BT7 2JB
Tel: 028 9056 9100

Disability Action
Portside Business Park
189 Airport Road West
Belfast BT3 9ED
Tel: 028 9029 7880

Electoral Commission
Seatem House
28-32 Alfred Street
Belfast BT2 8EN
Tel: 028 9089 4020

Electoral Office for Northern
Ireland
6-10 William Street
Belfast BT1 1PR
Tel: 028 9044 6688

Enforcement of Judgments
Office
6th floor, Bedford House
16-22 Bedford Street
Belfast BT2 7FD
Tel: 028 9024 5081

Environment and Heritage
Service
Commonwealth House
35 Castle Street
Belfast BT1 1GU
Tel: 028 9025 1477

Ex-Prisoners Interpretive Centre
c/o 182 Shankill Road
Belfast BT13 2BH
Tel: 028 9032 6233

Equal Opportunities
Commission (GB)
Arndale House
Arndale Centre
Manchester M4 3EQ
Tel: 0845 601 5901

Equality Commission for
Northern Ireland
Equality House
7-9 Shaftesbury Square
Belfast BT2 7DP
Tel: 028 9050 0600

Estates Agents Ombudsman
Beckett House
4 Bridge Street
Salisbury
Wiltshire SP1 2LX
Tel: 01722 333306

European Commission
Rue de la Loi 200
Brussels
B-1049 Belgium
Tel: 00 32 22 11 11
(*Freephone*: 00 800 6789 1011)

European Commission Office
Windsor House
9-15 Bedford Street
Belfast BT2 7EG
Tel: 028 9024 0708

European Court of Auditors
External Relations Department
12, rue Alcide De Gasperi
L-1615 Luxembourg
Tel: 00 352 4398 45410

European Court of Human
Rights
Council of Europe
F – 67075 Strasbourg – Cedex
France
Tel: 00 33 3 88 41 20 18

European Ombudsman
1 Avenue du Président Robert
Schumann
BP403
F – 67001 Strasbourg – Cedex
France
Tel: 00 33 3 88 17 23 13

The Extern Organisation
Graham House
1-5 Albert Square
Belfast BT1 3EQ
Tel: 028 9024 0900

Family Planning Association
113 University Street
Belfast BT7 1HP
Tel: 028 9032 5488

or

2nd floor, Northern Counties
Building
Custom House Street
Derry / Londonderry BT48 6AE
Tel: 028 7126 0016

Financial Ombudsman Services
South Quay Plaza
183 Marsh Wall
London E14 9SR
Tel: 0845 800 1800

Financial Services Authority
25 The North Colonnade
Canary Wharf
London E14 5HS
Tel: 020 7964 1000

Food Standards Agency (NI)
10A-C Clarendon Road
Belfast BT1 3BG
Tel: 028 9041 7700

Forensic Science Agency of
Northern Ireland
151 Belfast Road
Carrickfergus
Co. Antrim BT38 8PL
Tel: 028 9036 1888

Funeral Ombudsman Scheme
26-28 Bedford Row
London WC1R 4HE
Tel: 020 7430 1112

General Consumer Council
Elizabeth House
116 Hollywood Road
Belfast BT4 1NY
Tel: 0845 601 6022

General Medical Council
Regent's Place
350 Euston Road
London NW1 3JN
Tel: 0845 357 3456

Gingerbread Northern Ireland
169 University Street
Belfast BT7 1HR
Tel: 028 9023 1417

Health Promotion Agency for
Northern Ireland
18 Ormeau Avenue
Belfast BT2 8HS
Tel: 028 9031 1611

Help the Aged
Ascot House
Shaftesbury Square
Belfast BT2 7DB
Tel: 028 9023 0666

HM Coroner for Greater Belfast
Coroner's Office
Courthouse
Old Town Hall Building
80 Victoria Street
Belfast BT1 3FA
Tel: 028 9077 8202

Home Office
2 Marsham Street
London SW1P 4DF
Tel: 0870 000 1585

Housing Rights Service
4th floor, Middleton Buildings
10-12 High Street
Belfast BT1
Tel: 028 9024 5640

Howard League for Penal
Reform
1 Ardleigh Road
London N1 4HS
Tel: 020 7249 7373

Human Fertilisation and
Embryology Authority
21 Bloomsbury Street
London WC1B 3HF
Tel: 020 7291 8200

Immigration Advisory Service
190 Great Dover Street
London SE1 4YB
Tel: 020 7967 1200

Include Youth
Alpha House
3 Rosemary Street
Belfast BT1 1QA
Tel: 028 9031 1007

Independent Assessor of
Military Complaints Procedures
Hampton House
47-53 High Street
Belfast BT1 2AB
Tel: 028 9023 7822

Independent Case Examiner (for
social security and child support
matters)
PO Box 1245
Belfast BT2 7DF

Independent Commissioner for
Detained Terrorist Suspects
Hampton House
47-53 High Street
Belfast BT1 2AB
Tel: 028 9023 7822

Independent Monitoring
Commission
PO Box 709
Belfast BT2 8YB
Tel: 028 9072 6117

Independent Tribunal Service
3 Donegall Square North
Belfast BT1 5GA
Tel: 028 9051 8518

or

12 Dublin Road
Omagh
Co. Tyrone BT78 1ES
Tel: 028 8224 9595

Indian Community Centre
86 Clifton Street
Belfast BT13 1AB
Tel: 028 9024 9746

Industrial Court
Room 203, Adelaide House
39-49 Adelaide Street
Belfast BT2 8FD
Tel: 028 9025 7599

Information Commissioner for NI
Room 101
Regus House
33 Clarendon Dock
Belfast BT1 3BG
Tel: 028 9051 1270

Inspectorate of Court
Administration
8th floor, Millbank Tower
London SW1P 4QP
Tel: 020 7217 4355

Institute of Professional Legal
Studies
Queen's University
Lennoxvale
Belfast BT9 5BY
Tel: 028 9033 5567

International Court of Justice
The Peace Palace
2517 KJ
The Hague
The Netherlands
Tel: 00 31 70 302 23 23

Inter Trade Ireland
The Old Gasworks Business
Park
Kilmorey Street
Newry
Co Down BT34 2DE
Tel: 028 3083 4100

Irish Council for Civil Liberties
14 Exchequer Street
Dublin 2
Tel: 00 353 1077 9813

Judge Advocate-General of the
Forces
81 Chancery Lane
London WC2A 1BQ
Tel: 020 7218 8077

Judicial Studies Board (GB)
9th floor, Millbank Tower
Millbank
London SW1P 4QU
Tel: 020 7217 4779

Judicial Studies Board of NI
c/o Northern Ireland Court
Service
Windsor House
9-15 Bedford Street
Belfast BT2 7EH
Tel: 028 9032 8594

Justice
59 Carter Lane
London EC4V 5AQ
Tel: 020 7329 5100

Justice Oversight Commissioner
10 Cromac Place
Cromac Wood
Belfast BT7 2JB
Tel: 028 9033 3256

Juvenile Justice Centre for
Northern Ireland
School Avenue
Newtownards Road
Bangor
Co. Down BT19 1TB
Tel: 028 9127 2244

Labour Relations Agency
2 Gordon Street
Belfast BT2 2LG
Tel: 028 9032 1442

or

1-3 Guildhall Street
Derry / Londonderry BT48 6BJ
Tel: 028 7126 9639

Land Registers
Lincoln Building
27-45 Great Victoria Street
Belfast BT2 7SL
Tel: 028 9025 1515

Law Centre (NI)
124 Donegall Street
Belfast BT1 2GY
Tel: 028 9024 4401

or

9 Clarendon Street
Derry / Londonderry
BT48 7EP
Tel: 028 7126 2433

Law Centres' Federation
Duchess House
18-19 Warren Street
London W1T 5LR
Tel: 020 7387 8570

Law Commission for England
and Wales
Conquest House
38-39 John Street
Theobald's Road
London WC1N 2BQ
Tel: 020 7453 1220

Law Reform Advisory
Committee for Northern Ireland
Lancashire House
5 Linenhall Street
Belfast BT2 8AA
Tel: 028 9054 2909

Law Reform Commission of
Ireland
Ardilaun Centre
111 St Stephen's Green
Dublin 2
Tel: 00 3531 715699

Law Society of Northern Ireland
90 Victoria Street
Belfast BT1 3GN
Tel: 028 9023 1614

Lay Observer for Northern
Ireland
1st floor, Lancashire House
5 Linenhall Street
Belfast BT2 8AA
Tel: 028 9054 2900

Legal Services Ombudsman
3rd floor, Sunlight House
Quay Street
Manchester M3 3JZ
Tel: 0845 601 0794

Liberty
21 Tabard Street
London SE1 4LA
Tel: 020 7403 3888

Mediation NI
83 University Street,
Belfast BT7 1HP
Tel: 028 9043 8614

MENCAP
Segal House
4 Annadale Avenue
Belfast BT7 3JH
Tel: 028 9069 1351

Mental Health Commission for
Northern Ireland
Elizabeth House
118 Hollywood Road
Belfast BT4 1NY
Tel: 028 9065 1157

Motor Insurers' Bureau
Linford Wood House
6-12 Capital Drive
Linford Wood
Milton Keynes MK14 6XT
Tel: 01908 830001

Multi-Cultural Resource Centre
9 Lower Crescent
Belfast BT7 1NT
Tel: 028 9024 4639

National Association of Citizens
Advice Bureaux
Myddelton House
115-123 Pentonville Road
London N1 9LZ
Tel: 020 7833 2181

National Audit Office
157-197 Buckingham Palace Road
London SW1W 9SP
Tel: 020 7798 7000

National Consumer Federation
180 High Street
West Molesey KT8 2LX

National Consumer Council
20 Grosvenor Gardens
London SW1W 0DH
Tel: 020 7730 3469

National House Building
Council
59 Malone Road
Belfast BT9 6SA
Tel: 028 9068 3131

National Minimum Wages
Helpline (NI)
11 Upper Crescent,
Belfast BT7
Tel: 0845 650 0207

National Society for the
Prevention of Cruelty to
Children (NSPCC)
Arnott House,
12-16 Bridge Street
Belfast BT 1 1LU
*(Child Protection Helpline 0800
800500)*

Nexus Institute
119 University Avenue
Belfast BT7 1HP
Tel: 028 9032 6803
  (Derry / Londonderry
  028 7126 0566
  Enniskillen 028 6632 0046
  Portadown 028 3835 0588)

Northern Ireland African
Cultural Centre
60 Lisburn Road
Belfast BT9 6AF
Tel: 028 9023 8742

Northern Ireland Assembly
Parliament Buildings
Stormont
Belfast BT4 3SW
Tel: 028 9052 1137

Northern Ireland Association for the
Care and Resettlement of Offenders
(NIACRO)
169 Ormeau Road
Belfast BT7 1SQ
Tel: 028 9032 0157

Northern Ireland Association for
Mental Health
80 University Street
Belfast BT7 1HE
Tel: 028 9032 8474

Northern Ireland Audit Office
106 University Street
Belfast BT7 1EU
Tel: 028 9025 1000

Northern Ireland Child Support
Agency
Great Northern Tower
17 Great Victoria Street
Belfast BT2 7AD
Tel: 028 9089 6666

Northern Ireland Commissioner
for Children and Young People
(NICCY)
Millennium House
19-25 Great Victoria Street
Belfast BT2 7AQ
Tel: 028 9031 1616

Northern Ireland Committee of
the Irish Congress of Trade
Unions (NIC-ICTU)
3 Crescent Gardens
Belfast BT9 6DJ
Tel: 028 9024 7940

Northern Ireland Council for
Ethnic Minorities
3rd floor, Ascot House
24-31 Shaftesbury Square
Belfast BT2 7DB
Tel: 028 9023 8645

Northern Ireland Council for
Integrated Education
13-19 University Road
Belfast BT7 1NA
Tel: 028 9023 6200

Northern Ireland Council for
Voluntary Action
61 Duncairn Gardens
Belfast BT15 2GB
Tel: 028 9087 7777

Northern Ireland Court Service
Windsor House
9-15 Bedford Street
Belfast BT2 7LT
Tel: 028 9032 8594

Northern Ireland Federation of
Housing Associations
38 Hill Street
Belfast BT1 2LB
Tel: 028 9023 0446

Northern Ireland Gay Rights
Association
46 Malone Road
Belfast BT9 6ER
Tel: 028 9066 5257

Northern Ireland Housing
Executive
The Housing Centre
2 Adelaide Street
Belfast BT2 8PB
Tel: 028 9024 0588
(Addresses of district offices are listed in the telephone directory under "NIHE")

Northern Ireland Human Rights
Commission
Temple Court
39 North Street
Belfast BT1 1NA
Tel: 028 9024 3987

Northern Ireland Judicial
Appointments Commission
Headline Building
Victoria Street
Belfast BT1 3GG
Tel: 028 9072 8551

Northern Ireland Legal Services
Commission
2nd floor, Waterfront Plaza
8 Laganbank Road
Mays Meadow
Belfast BT1 3BW
Tel: 028 9024 6441

Northern Ireland Office
Block B, Castle Buildings
Stormont
Belfast BT4 3XX
Tel: 028 9052 0700
(Confidential freephone 0800 666999)
or

11 Millbank
London SW1P 4QE
Tel: 020 7233 3000

Northern Ireland Office
Statistics and Research Branch
Massey House
Stormont Estate
Belfast BT4 3SX
Tel: 028 9052 7534

Northern Ireland Ombudsman
Progressive House
33 Wellington Place
Belfast BT1 6HN
Tel: 028 9023 3821
(Free call information service: 0800 343424)

Northern Ireland Policing Board
Waterside Tower
Clarendon Road
Belfast BT1 3BG
Tel: 028 9023 0111

Northern Ireland Practice and
Education Council for Nursing
and Midwifery
Centre House
79 Chichester Street
Belfast BT1 4JE
Tel: 028 9023 8152

Northern Ireland Prison Service
Dundonald House
Upper Newtownards Road
Belfast BT4 3SU
Tel: 028 9052 5922

Northern Ireland Social Care
Council
7th floor, Millennium House
19-25 Great Victoria Street
Belfast BT2 7AQ
Tel: 028 9041 7600

Northern Ireland Statistics and
Research Agency
McAuley House
2-14 Castle Street
Belfast BT1 1SA
Tel: 028 9034 8104

Northern Ireland Transport
Users Committee
55 Royal Avenue
Belfast BT1 1FX
Tel: 028 9024 4147

Northern Ireland Women's Aid
Federation
129 University Street,
Belfast BT7 1HP
Tel: 028 9024 9041
*(24 hour helpline: 028 9033
1818)*

North-South Ministerial Council
39 Abbey Street
Armagh
Co. Armagh BT61 7EB
Tel: 028 3751 8068

Office of Care and Protection
Royal Courts of Justice
Chichester Street
Belfast BT1 3JZ
Tel: 028 9023 5111

Office of Communications
(OFCOM)
Riverside House
2a Southward Bridge Road
London SEI 9HA
Tel: 0845 456 3000

or

Landmark House
The Gasworks
Ormeau Road
Belfast BT7 2JD
Tel: 028 9041 7500

Office of the Commissioner for
Public Appointments for
Northern Ireland
Room A5.34, Castle Buildings
Stormont Estate
Belfast BT4 3SR
Tel: 028 9052 3201

Office of the Committee on
Standards in Public Life
Community Relations Council
6 Murray Street
Belfast BT1 6DN
Tel: 028 9022 7500

Office of Fair Trading
Fleetbank House
2-6 Salisbury Square
London EC4Y 8JX
Tel: 08457 22 44 99

Office of the First Minister and
Deputy First Minister
Castle Buildings
Stormont Estate
Belfast BT4 3SR
Tel: 028 9052 8400

Office of Law Reform
1st floor, Lancashire House
5 Linenhall Street
Belfast BT2 8AA
Tel: 028 9054 2900

Office of Legislative Counsel
Department of Finance and
Personnel
Stormont
Belfast BT4 3SW
Tel: 028 9076 3210

Organised Crime Task Force
Stormont House, Stormont Estate
Belfast BT4 3TA
Tel: 028 9052 0700

Parades Commission
Windsor House,
9-15 Bedford Street
Belfast BT2 7EL
Tel: 028 9089 5900

Parents Advice Centre
Franklin House
12 Brunswick Street
Belfast BT2 7GE
Tel: 028 9031 0891

Parliamentary and Health
Service Ombudsman (UK)
Millbank Tower
Millbank
London SW1P 4QP
Tel: 0845 015 4033

Pensions Appeal Tribunal
Headline Building
10-14 Victoria Street
Belfast BT1 3GG
Tel: 028 9032 6594

Pensions Commission
4th floor, Adelphi
1-11 John Adam Street
London WC2N 6HT
Tel: 020 7962 8641

Pensions Ombudsman
11 Belgrave Road
London SW1V 1RB
Tel: 020 7834 9144

Pensions Regulator
Napier House
Trafalgar Place
Brighton BN1 4DW
Tel: 0870 606 3636

Planning Appeals Commission
Park House
87 Great Victoria Street
Belfast BT2 7AG
Tel: 028 9024 4710

Planning Service
Headquarters
Millennium House
19-25 Great Victoria Street
Belfast BT2 7BN
Tel: 028 9041 6700

Police Ombudsman for
Northern Ireland
New Cathedral Buildings
11Church Street
Belfast BT1 1PG
Tel: 028 9082 8600
(For complaints: 0845 601 2931)

Police Service for Northern
Ireland (PSNI)
Headquarters
Brooklyn
65 Knock Road,
Belfast BT5 6LE
Tel: 028 9065 0222
*(The locations of police stations are
listed in the telephone directory
under "Police")*

Press Complaints Commission
1 Salisbury Square
London EC4Y 8JB
Tel: 020 7353 1248
(Helpline: 020 7353 3732)

Prisoner Ombudsman for
Northern Ireland
22nd floor, Windsor House
9-15 Bedford Street
Belfast BT2 7FT
Tel: 028 9044 3998

Prisons and Probation
Ombudsman (GB)
Ashley House
2 Monck Street
London SW1P 2BQ
Tel: 020 7035 2876

Probation Board for Northern
Ireland
80-90 North Street
Belfast BT1 1LD
Tel: 028 9026 2400

Public Prosecution Service
Royal Courts of Justice
93 Chichester Street
Belfast BT1 3JR
Tel: 028 9054 2444

Public Record Office of
Northern Ireland
66 Balmoral Avenue
Belfast BT9 6NY
Tel: 028 9025 5905

Queen's University Belfast
School of Law
28 University Square
Belfast BT7 1NN
Tel: 028 9027 3451

Rainbow Project
2-6 Union Street,
Belfast BT1 2JF
Tel: 028 9031 9030

Rape Crisis and Sexual Abuse
Centre
29 Donegall Street
PO Box 46
Belfast BT
Tel: 028 9032 9001

Rate Collection Agency
Oxford House
49-55 Chichester Street
Belfast BT1 4HH
Tel: 028 9072 6700

Registrar of Births, Marriages
and Deaths
General Register Officer
Oxford House
49-55 Chichester Street
Belfast BT1 4HL
Tel: 028 9025 2000

Relate
76 Dublin Road
Belfast BT2 7HP
Tel: 028 9032 3454
   (Derry / Londonderry
      028 7137 1502
   Newry 028 3025 2636)

Relatives for Justice
235A Falls Road
Belfast BT12 4PE
Tel: 028 9022 0100

Revenue and Customs Northern
Ireland
Beaufort House
31 Wellington Place
Belfast BT
Tel: 0845 302 1469

Review of Public Administration
McKelvey House
25 Wellington Place
Belfast BT1 6GD
Tel: 028 9027 7675

Rivers Agency
Hydebank
4 Hospital Road
Belfast BT8 8JP
Tel: 028 9025 3355

Roads Service
Clarence Court
10-18 Adelaide Street
Belfast BT2 8GB
Tel: 028 9054 0540

Royal Courts of Justice
Chichester Street
Belfast BT1 3JF
Tel: 028 9023 5111
(The telephone numbers of local courts are listed in the telephone directory under "Government")

Sentence Review
Commissioners
5th floor, Windsor House
9-15 Bedford Street
Belfast BT2 7SR
Tel: 028 9054 9412

Social Fund Commissioner
Scottish Amicable Building
11 Donegall Square North
Belfast BT1 5JE
Tel: 028 9024 7202

Social Security Advisory
Committee New Court
48 Carey Street
London WC2A 2LS
Tel: 020 7412 1506

Social Security Agency
1 Cromac Place
Gasworks Business Park
Ormeau Road
Belfast BT7 2JB
Tel: 028 9082 9000

Social Security
Commissioners and Child
Support Commissioners
Headline Building
10-14 Victoria Street
Belfast BT1 3GG
Tel: 028 9032 6594

Stationery Office
16 Arthur Street
Belfast BT1 4QG
Tel: 028 9023 8451

Trading Standards Branch
Department of Enterprise, Trade
and Investment
176 Newtownbreda Road
Belfast BT8 4QS
Tel: 028 9025 3900

Training and Employment
Agency
Adelaide House
39-49 Adelaide Street
Belfast BT2 8FD
Tel: 028 9025 7777

Treasury Solicitor's Department
Queen Anne's Chambers
28 Broadway
London SW1H 9JS
Tel: 0207 210 3000

University of Ulster at
Jordanstown
School of Law
Shore Road
Jordanstown
Co. Antrim BT37 OQB
Tel: 028 9036 6184

UK Immigration Service
Belfast International Airport,
Belfast BT29 4AB
Tel: 028 9445 2500

Valuation and Lands Agency
Queen's Court
56-66 Upper Queen Street
Belfast BT1 6FD
Tel: 028 9054 3920

VAT and Duties Tribunals
15-19 Bedford Avenue
London WC1B 3AS
Tel: 020 7612 9700

Victim Support (NI)
Annsgate House
70-74 Ann Street,
Belfast BT1 4EH
Tel: 028 9024 4039

Water Service
Northland House
3-5 Frederick Street
Belfast BT1 2NR
Tel: 028 9024 4711

Waterways Ireland
5-7 Belmore Street
Enniskillen
Co Fermanagh BT74 6AA
Tel: 028 6634 6286

Women's Information Group
 Women's Resource and
Development Agency
6 Mount Charles
Belfast BT7 1NZ
Tel: 028 9024 4119

Women's National Commission
1 Victoria Street
London SW1 OET
Tel: 020 7238 0386

Worker's Educational
Association
(Northern Ireland District)
1 Fitzwilliam Street
Belfast BT9 6AW
Tel: 028 9032 9718

or

1st floor, 28 Cornmarket
Newry
Co. Down BT38 8BG
Tel: 028 3026 8679

Youth Council for Northern
Ireland
Forestview
Purdy's Lane
Belfast BT8 7AR
Tel: 028 9064 3882

Youth Justice Agency of
Northern Ireland
41-43 Waring Street
Belfast BT1 2DY
Tel: 028 9031 6400

GLOSSARY[1]

absolute discharge
The release of a convicted person from the custody of a court, without imposing any punishment on him or her (except, perhaps, an order to pay compensation or a disqualification from driving).

adjectival law
The branch of law which focuses on practice and procedure in the courts. The opposite of "substantive law".

affidavit
A written statement the truth of which is sworn to, or affirmed, by the maker of the statement in front of an official.

affirmative action
Action which deliberately discriminates in favour of members of a particular group in order to help them to overcome historical or systemic disadvantages.

alibi
Evidence that a person was at a certain place at a certain time.

amicus curiae
Literally "a friend of the court", it refers to a lawyer (usually the Attorney General or his or her representative) who is asked by the judge(s) to give advice on how the law stands on a particular topic.

arraignment
The stage in criminal proceedings when charges are put to the defendant in court and he or she is asked whether he or she wishes to plead guilty or not guilty.

bail
The release of a person from the custody of a law officer or a court on condition that he or she will return to custody on a specified day.

bench warrant
A warrant for someone's arrest issued by a court while it is sitting.

---

[1] Only very brief explanations of the terms listed are given. For more details readers should consult the text of this book itself and/or a good law dictionary. The glossary draws in particular on E. Martin (ed.), *A Dictionary of Law* (5th ed., 2002), S. Bone (ed.,), L. Curzon, *Dictionary of Law* (6th ed., 2002), *Osborn's Concise Law Dictionary* (9th ed., 2001) and P. Collin, *Dictionary of Law* (3rd ed., 2000).

bill of indictment
A formal written accusation that someone has committed a serious ("indictable") offence.

binding over
Ordering someone to adhere to a specified commitment (*e.g.* to keep the peace) on pain of receiving further punishment.

brief
The document by which a solicitor instructs a barrister to appear for a client in court.

byelaw
A type of secondary legislation made mostly by district councils.

case stated
A written statement of the facts in a case presented by a magistrates' court, county court or tribunal for the opinion of a higher court (in Northern Ireland, usually the Court of Appeal) on how the law should be applied to those facts.

certiorari
A court order quashing (*i.e.* overturning) a decision already taken by a public body.

commencement order
A type of secondary legislation which indicates when another piece of legislation, primary or secondary, is to come into force.

committal proceedings
Proceedings in a magistrates' court in which a decision is taken on whether a defendant should be sent to the Crown Court for trial.

common law
(1)   A legal system based on Anglo-Saxon as opposed, for example, to ancient Roman legal principles.
(2)   Law made by judges, as opposed to law set out by Parliament in legislation.
(3)   Legal rules which are derived from "the King's courts", as opposed to those which are derived from what were formerly known as "courts of equity".

conditional discharge
The release of a convicted person from the custody of a court provided that he or she complies with certain conditions.

conditional fee agreement
An agreement to pay a lawyer's fee only if the lawyer wins the case in question.

contempt of court
Disobedience of a court order which can itself lead to the imposition of a fine or even a prison sentence.

conveyancing
Transferring the ownership of interests in land or in buildings on land.

corroboration
Evidence which tends to confirm the truth of other evidence.

counsel
A barrister.

count
A paragraph in an indictment for an indictable offence (*q.v.*) referring to one particular allegation of criminal misconduct.

decree *nisi*
Literally, a decree "unless", referring to a decree of divorce or nullity which is not final until more time has elapsed (usually six weeks).

defendant
The name given to the person who is being prosecuted by the state in a criminal case or sued by the plaintiff in a civil case.

deposition
A statement by, or evidence given by, a witness which is officially recorded and/or signed by the witness.

derogation
An "opt-out" from an international treaty obligation.

de-scheduling
Changing an offence from one which must be tried by a juryless Diplock court to one that can be tried by a normal Crown Court sitting with a jury.

direct rule
The governing of Northern Ireland by the Government in London rather than (in part at least) by the Executive Committee of the Northern Ireland Assembly.

doli incapax
Literally, "incapable of evil", referring to the rule that a child under 10 cannot be guilty of a criminal offence.

double jeopardy
Being tried twice for the same offence.

enabling Act
An Act of Parliament which authorises a public body (usually a government department) to make secondary legislation.

equity
The set of more flexible legal rules which were originally devised by the Lord Chancellor and the Court of Chancery but which are now "fused" with the rules devised by the King's courts (common law rules).

exemplary damages
Compensation awarded with a view not just to replacing the losses suffered by the plaintiff but to punishing the defendant.

family care centre
A county court which has been designated as one which can hear cases involving the care of children.

habeas corpus
Literally, "may you have the body". A writ of *habeas corpus* is a claim that can be brought to the High Court demanding that a person who is keeping another person in custody must explain what legal justification exists for such detention.

headnote
A summary at the start of most cases in the printed law reports, prepared by the law reporter and not the court, setting out first the facts of the case and then the decision based on those facts.

hearsay
Something which a person heard someone else say.

indemnity
Compensation for a wrong, or a promise to pay such compensation.

indictable offence
A serious criminal offence, as opposed to a "summary" offence.

injunction
A court order requiring that some particular course of action be taken.

inquest
An inquiry into an unexplained death, conducted by a coroner (sometimes sitting with a jury), to determine who died and in what circumstances, but without attributing criminal or civil liability to anyone who may have been responsible for the death.

interlocutory proceedings
Temporary or provisional proceedings, which precede the final hearing in a case.

judgment in default
A judgment given on a civil claim against someone who has not bothered to defend the claim in any way.

judicial review
Supervision by the High Court of the process used by public bodies when reaching decisions, including decisions to make secondary legislation.

limitation period
The period of time during which the law permits people to bring civil claims against other people (*e.g.* six years for a breach of contract or three months for a claim of discrimination).

locus standi
Literally, "a place of standing". A person has *locus standi*, or simply *locus*, if in the eyes of the law he or she has a sufficient interest in a dispute to justify bringing legal proceedings in relation to it.

mandamus
Literally, "we command". A court order requiring a public body to carry out its legal duty.

obiter dictum
Literally, "something said by the way". It refers to something said incidentally during a judgment which is not crucial to the *ratio decidendi (q.v.)* of the decision in question.

plaintiff
The name given to the claimant in a civil case (called the "pursuer" in Scotland). The other party is called the defendant (or "defender" in Scotland).

plea bargaining
A process by which a defendant or his or her legal representatives seek to negotiate a lesser charge or a lighter sentence in return for the defendant pleading guilty to some lesser charge or co-operating with the police in some other way.

Practice Direction
A statement issued by the head of a court to indicate what procedure he or she wishes lawyers to follow when appearing in those courts.

prima facie
Literally, "on a first look". A prima facie position in a dispute is one which is plausible but for which further evidence is required if it is to be really convincing.

primary legislation
Acts made by the United Kingdom Parliament at Westminster.

pro bono work
Literally, "for the common good". It refers to work done by solicitors or barristers for which they will not get paid.

ratio decidendi
Literally, "the reason for deciding". It refers to the nub of a case, *i.e.* to the principle lying at the heart of the decision.

remand
Sending a person to custody, or releasing him or her on bail, until the court is able to deal with him or her at a future date.

restorative justice
An approach to criminal behaviour which seeks to allow the perpetrator to "restore" to the victim or the victim's community something which has been taken away by what the perpetrator has done.

secondary legislation
Legislation made by a public authority which has been authorised to make it by primary (or "enabling") legislation.

silk
Queen's Counsel (*i.e* a senior barrister).

statutory instrument
The most common type of secondary legislation in Great Britain.

statutory rule
The most common type of secondary legislation in Northern Ireland.

summary judgment
A judgment given against a defendant in a civil case when the court considers that there is no point continuing with the case because the defendant's position is hopeless.

taxation of costs
The calculation by a judicial official - the Taxing Master - of the charges that lawyers can legitimately make for their services.

tort
A wrong (except a breach of contract or a breach of trust) for which the law will provide a remedy under the civil law as opposed to the criminal law. The commonest tort is simply known as the tort of negligence.

trust
A method of holding or managing property whereby a "trustee" looks after the property for the "beneficiaries" of the trust (who may include the person who is the trustee).

ultra vires
Literally, "beyond the powers". It is used to refer, in particular, to secondary legislation which is invalid because it has not been specifically authorised by an enabling Act.

voir(e) dire

Literally, "to speak the truth". It is a stage in criminal court proceedings held in the absence of a jury, sometimes called "a trial within a trial", at which matters of pure law are decided, *e.g.* whether the rules on admissibility of evidence allow some piece of information to be put before the jury or not.

waiver

The abandonment of a legal right. It refers in particular to the Law Society's abandonment of its right to insist that only solicitors working for firms of solicitors can actually do the work of solicitors.

INDEX

Sinn Féin   10-2, 14, 23, 74, 151,
            181, 377
slander   113, 142, 153 (and
  see "defamation")
small claims court   19, 43, 152,
            168-70, 296-7, 299,
            306, Chap. 6.3, 351
small debts   305-6
smoke detectors   60
social care bodies   Chap. 9.8
Social Democratic and
  Labour Party   10-2, 377
Social Fund   121, 386-7, 392
Social Fund Commissioner   392
social security   119, 123-5, 264,
            379, 383, 386,
            Chap. 8.2, 396
Social Security Advisory
  Committee   393, 413
Social Security Agency   150,
            156, 264
Social Security Commissioner 124,
            334, 390-2
social security tribunals   Chap. 8.2
solicitors   128-34
Solicitor General   30
Solicitors Disciplinary Tribunal 132
sources of law   Chap. 2
South Africa   5, 182, 207, 235,
            428, 443
sovereign immunity   38
Speaker   26-7, 79, 180, 337, 377
Special European Union
  Programmes Body   14
Special Immigration Appeals
  Commission   383
special measures direction 267, 343
specified organisation   194
spent conviction   229
Stalker-Sampson Report   206, 217
standard of proof   112, 223-4, 358
Standing Advisory Commission
  on Human Rights   110, 184,
            424,443-4
stare decisis   90
statement of claim   329, 335
statutes   Chap. 2.1
Statutes in Force   67
Statutes Revised   66-7
Statutory Charges Register   50
statutory instruments   71-3, 518
statutory interpretation   Chap. 2.4
statutory officers   43
statutory rules   75-7, 518
stay of proceedings   315
stipendiary magistrate   36, 44, 98
Stormont Parliament   5-6
street-trading   23
strip-searching   70, 231

subordinate legislation   25, 52
subsections, in Acts   62
summary judgment   329, 335, 518
summary offences   Chap. 4.2,
            245-6, 264
summary trial   Chap. 5.4
summons   245-6, 248, 259-60,
            265, 268-9, 284, 295,
            305-6, 310, 315,
            329, 331, 333-5
Sunningdale Agreement   8
supergrass   32
Superintendents' Association   209
supervision order   227, 270,
            355, 362
Supreme Court   5, 17, 36-7,
            40-3, 61, 132, 134,
            164, 170, 282
Supreme Court of Judicature   17,
            37, 39-42
Supreme Court Rules Committee
            34,37
suspended sentence   288, 359, 368

tanistry   2
tape-recording: see "audio-
  recording"
taxation, of costs   518
Taxing Master   43, 156, 164-8, 171
telephone tapping   109
television licence   117, 264
terrorism   178-80
theft   61, 174-6, 191, 228,
            233, 248, 272, 295,
            312, 357, 468
The Times   88, 183
TICs   269
time-barred action   115
  (see also "limitation period")
time limits in criminal
  proceedings   258
tort law   113-4, 469, 471, 518
Trade and Business
  Development Body   14
trade union   52, 118, 134, 142,
            394-5, 398, 438, 440,
            462, 464, 466-7
trading standards   460
traffic warden   50
training school   156, 177, 355, 361
transferred matters   7, 73
treasure   375-6
treaty   9, 97-9, 180-1, 447
Treaty of Amsterdam   99, 103
Treaty of European Union
  (Maastricht)   97
Treaty of Nice   105
Treaty of Rome   99, 103-4
trespass   113